THE
REPORTER'S
HANDBOOK

An Investigator's Guide
to Documents
and Techniques

Second Edition

THE REPORTER'S HANDBOOK

An
Investigator's Guide
to Documents
and Techniques

Second Edition

under the editorship of
JOHN ULLMANN
and
JAN COLBERT
Investigative Reporters & Editors Inc. (IRE)

ST. MARTIN'S PRESS • New York

Senior editor: Cathy Pusateri
Project management: Caliber Design Planning, Inc.
Cover design: Darby Downey

For information, write:
St. Martin's Press, Inc.
175 Fifth Avenue
New York, NY 10010
Cloth ISBN: 0-312-05147-6
Paper ISBN: 0-312-00435-4

Library of Congress Cataloging-in-Publication Data

The Reporter's handbook : an investigator's guide to documents and
  techniques / [edited by] John Ullmann, Jan Colbert & Investigative
  Reporters & Editors Inc.
      p.   cm.
   ISBN 0-312-05147-6 : $24.95
   1. Investigative reporting — Handbooks, manuals, etc.   2. Public
records — United States — Handbooks, manuals, etc.   I. Ullmann, John.
II. Colbert, Jan.   III. Investigative Reporters and Editors Inc.
PN4781.R38   1990
070.4′3 — dc20   90-37266
                                                                    CIP

Acknowledgment

"Military Maneuvers' Basic Training in How to Get Service Records,"
by Mitchell Zuckoff. Reprinted from The IRE Journal, Summer 1989,
pp. 3–6.

 The text of this book has been printed on recycled paper.

In memory of William Farr and Thomas C. Renner

Foreword to the First Edition

The place: Boston. The time: a rainy Friday night in 1976. Some 600 college students have elbowed their way into a small auditorium to hear a panel discussion on investigative reporting. One of the panelists asks how many of the students intend to become investigative reporters.

More than 300 raise their hands.

The catalyst was Watergate. There had to be more Deep Throats out there just waiting to tell all to a bright, young reporter. There were governors, senators, perhaps even another president to be gotten. Not that hard. The only evidence needed was two confidential sources who agreed with each other. Charge!

This, unfortunately, is a view of investigative reporting still held by a substantial portion of the American public. It is increasingly reflected in oppressive judicial decisions and excessive jury awards in matters involving the press. It is an attitude stemming in part from a simplistic and often inaccurate idea of what investigative reporting is, and how, when and why it should be practiced. Bad investigative reporting, and there is still too much of it, feeds the kitty of public distrust.

What is investigative reporting?

It is a question that still provokes argument, even among investigative reporters. Some say investigative reporting is nothing more than a trendy name for good, old-fashioned reporting of the hard-nosed, lots-of-shoe-leather school. They may be right. But many of us believe that investigative reporting can be classified and defined:

> It is the reporting, through one's own work product and initiative, matters of importance which some persons or organizations wish to keep secret. The three basic elements are that the investigation be the work of the reporter, not a report of an investigation made by someone else; that the subject of the story involves something of reasonable importance to the reader or viewer; and that others are attempting to hide these matters from the public.

Watergate is a classic example of investigative reporting. The actions of the president and his associates involved matters of considerable importance to the American people. There was both a need and a right to know. The president and others deliberately attempted to hide the facts. The truth was bared by reporters through their own initiative.

The Pentagon Papers, however, illustrate a popular misunderstanding of when good reporting is investigative and when it isn't. The New York Times, Washington Post and Boston Globe performed a valuable public service in pub-

lishing the Pentagon Papers. The disclosure was a matter of vital public importance. The U.S. government went to court in a vain attempt to keep the Pentagon
Papers secret. Two of the basic elements of investigative reporting were present.
But the Pentagon Papers were the work product of the government, not the press.
They were given to the news media by a former government employee who
believed that the papers should be published. The third element of investigative
reporting was missing. The investigation was not the work product of the
reporter. Lacking this third element, the publication of the Pentagon Papers
clearly was not investigative reporting.

Once defined, investigative reporting loses most of its mystique. It is old-
fashioned, hard-nosed reporting. What delineates it from other forms of reporting is the nature of what is being reported and the amount of original work
involved.

The pervasive question voiced by students that night in Boston was: What
is the best way to become an investigative reporter? The panelists were unani-
mous: Be a good reporter.

It all starts there. A few anonymous sources with trendy code names do not
make an investigative reporter any more than a baseball uniform makes a star
slugger. A good reporter is informed, perceptive, accurate, fair, careful, smart
and widely knowledgeable. He or she is practiced in the craft.

A good reporter sees the forest for the trees, recognizes the lead as it happens and has an experienced eye for quotes, personal traits and events that make
a story live and make its characters emerge from single dimensions. The essential
requisite of a good reporter, like that of any good crafts person, is natural ability,
strongly seasoned with discipline and experience. We are born with natural ability of one sort or another. But discipline and experience take time. Since there are
no instant good reporters, there are no instant investigative reporters, either. The
hallmark of both is consistency. We have all seen reporters and editors basking in
the fame of one good story and then forever sliding from sight. Frequently that
one good story was an accident of time, place and opportunity. Good reporters
consistently do good work. It is an imperative of craft.

Investigative reporters nowadays carry a high profile. Their stories get
strong play; they usually report directly to a top editor; they ordinarily work on
important things; they often get paid more; and the public thinks that their jobs
are glamorous. It all adds up to status.

This status, however, demands high dues. Mistakes cannot be excused with
the ordinary "beg pardon" filler at the bottom of a one-column hole on page 23.
A reporter who mistakenly calls someone a crook had better change his or her
name, move to Anchorage and write poetry.

There is an enormous stress factor and a higher than average rate of burn-
out in investigative reporting. Odd hours and other time demands of the craft
limit social life and wreck marriages. Then there are the nervous publishers,
scared editors, waspish lawyers, envious colleagues and the omnipresent tempta-
tions to cut corners. More than others, it is the investigative reporter who is the
target of the threat, frame, harrassment, slander, loneliness and the libel suit.

The glamour of investigative reporting is far more in the eye of the beholder than the practitioner. On the average, it is nine-tenths drudgery, endless hours sifting through mostly meaningless documents, protracted negotiations with the defensive bureaucrats and lawyers, frequent meetings with dry sources and mentally disturbed crusaders, long nights, cold coffee, busted trails, bottomless pits and, occasionally, heady success.

The best of our investigative reporters—people like the late George Bliss, Clark Mollenhoff, James Polk, Pam Zekman, Jerry O'Neill, Gene Miller, Jack Taylor, Donald Barlett and James Steele—all share certain traits in common. They have desire, drive, judgment, determination, imagination, integrity, logical minds and an innate sense of organization. Most of the traits are self-explanatory. Judgment, because it is so subjective, needs further definition. It is the ability to correctly estimate the nature, scope and importance of a story, and then to report and write it in a professional way. Extremes are avoided; passion is controlled; conduct is guarded.

I stress judgment because it is so vital to the investigative reporter. The nature of the job is such that the reporter or team works for long stretches under very limited supervision. Mistakes in attitudes, ethics, conduct and craft standards can induce slant, error or an appearance of malice that can mar an otherwise good story and return to haunt the reporter on the witness stand. And without judgment, the desirable trait of determination becomes stubbornness, drive becomes obsession, organization becomes rigidity. The line demarking good from bad is sometimes very thin.

Why, then, be an investigative reporter?

For the ambitious, there is a shot at fame; for the caring, there is a chance to right wrong; for the crafts person, there is exciting challenge. When the question is asked of good investigative reporters, though, they usually answer, "It's what I do best."

This is probably true of most people who excel at their jobs. Their natural traits and aptitudes match the demands of a particular craft or profession. It is certainly true of reporters in general. The essential reporter takes to the craft much like a fish takes to water. Given proper training and experience, the reporter will excel. And most of us like to do the things we do best. Ergo, the good investigative reporter.

I like to think that our ancestors had the investigative reporter in mind when they framed the First Amendment of the Bill of Rights. The scene had been set long before by Peter Zenger, one of our first investigative reporters. Inherent in the First Amendment is protection for the press against the oppression of government. Government usually moves against the press when it goes beyond what government is saying and reports what government is really doing. Most such reporters tend to be investigative. If it is the role of the press in our democracy to accurately inform the people, the investigative reporter plays an important part.

This doesn't mean that a newspaper, TV or radio station without an investigative team or at least a full-time investigative reporter isn't doing its job. Most reporters work on investigative stories occasionally. Titles are superfluous. What is important is that an investigative story, when it is done, is done well. And that is what this book is about.

The worst enemy of investigative reporting is not the timid publisher, the oppressive president, the outraged advertiser or even the biased judge. It is bad investigative reporting. When investigative reporting loses its credibility with the people because it is wrong, biased, hyped or otherwise unprofessional, its enemies have both the excuse to destroy it and the public's permission to do so. The current popularity of investigative reporting is making a fad out of the craft. Because so many want to do it, many feel that it can be easily done. The result is ironic: At the same time that we have some of the most professional investigative reporting in the history of American journalism, we also have our greatest volume of bad investigative reporting.

All too often we are seeing traces of the seven cardinal sins of investigative reporting: error, insinuation, distortion, bias, confusion, dullness and superficiality.

Investigative Reporters and Editors Inc. (IRE) was founded in 1975 as a nonprofit education organization to promote good investigative reporting. Starting in Reston, Va., with some 30 reporters and editors, IRE now numbers more than 1,500 working journalists, journalism educators and students.

As IRE developed, it became apparent that the skills and techniques learned on the street by a small number of the nation's best investigative reporters should be shared with all reporters. This information—on sources, interviews and hundreds of other subjects involving hard-news reporting—has never before been made generally available to journalists, educators and students. Through the years, the annual IRE conventions and regional conferences have developed a highly diversified series of panels on subjects ranging from stress to organized-crime reporting.

The panelists are reporters, editors and occasional outside experts who share their knowledge with audiences that grow larger every year. The size of these audiences demonstrates the hunger of working reporters to constantly improve their skills. The IRE education program is both ambitious and unique.

IRE took a quantum leap forward in 1978 when it joined with the prestigious School of Journalism at the University of Missouri, where the organization now has its national office. At the school, IRE maintains a constantly growing resource library for investigative reporters, now totaling 6,000 newspaper and magazine articles, video tapes and transcripts. There is also the annual IRE contest for the best investigative reporting of the year chosen from the nation's newspapers, magazines, radio, TV and books. First-round winners are selected by faculty members at the University of Missouri School of Journalism. The best of the best are judged by a distinguished panel of reporters, editors and educators, all of them with quality experience in investigative reporting. IRE also publishes a quarterly, The IRE Journal, for its members, conducts extensive, in-house training programs for media outlets and prepares educational material for journalism schools.

Now, this book.

It is the nuts and bolts of the hard-news craft. It is the proven work experience of America's top reporters. No pointless war stories here; rather, a blueprint for excellence. It is for all reporters and editors. It is our handbook.

Robert W. Greene
1983

P R E F A C E

I first recognized the need for a book like this in 1976, after arriving to teach at the University of Missouri School of Journalism. Throughout the school year, I was asked by students where to find records related to stories they were pursuing. There must be a book listing the most useful government documents, I thought, so I spent several weeks looking. I didn't find one.

My conclusion was that a comprehensive yet introductory sourcebook was badly needed. That idea was reinforced by the discovery of a number of creditable efforts on a more limited scale by journalists, journalism students and their teachers in such cities as Miami, Seattle, Minneapolis and even Columbia, Missouri, and Ames, Iowa.

In addition, there were several excellent primers on investigative reporting giving tantalizingly brief mentions of records that helped make a stellar investigative report possible.

In an effort to meet the need, the first edition of "The Reporter's Handbook" was undertaken a few years after I became executive director of Investigative Reporters & Editors Inc. in 1978. It took nearly three years and proved to be a difficult task. It involved demanding labor sandwiched between full-time jobs for me and the many journalists and journalism educators across the country who contributed. There was no overall model then, and some chapters had no counterparts whatsoever.

The resulting 504-page book was received by what can be likened to an ovation. It was favorably reviewed in journalism magazines and journals, and even several daily newspapers. Len Downie Jr., a former investigative reporter and now managing editor at The Washington Post, wrote in the Washington Journalism Review, "All reporters and editors . . . —and anyone else seeking help in getting good stories of any kind—should add this immensely valuable how-to handbook to the essential reference books on their desk." David Johnston at The Los Angeles Times wrote in that newspaper, "The public would benefit mightily if news organizations made it standard issue to their reporters."

Reporters, editors and journalism students across the country were drawn to its pages, seeking solutions to reporting problems and ways to get behind or beyond the interview.

This book captures what IRE is all about: The country's top journalists openly and ungrudgingly sharing hard-won reporting secrets with their actual, potential or would-be competitors.

By now, thousands of reporters and editors have attended IRE how-to conferences, many paying their own way. Bosses of bigger newspapers and television stations, understanding the value these give-and-take sessions have for all in journalism, usually underwrite the travel and other costs of their best reporters and editors who speak at IRE conferences, thereby keeping the registration expenses paid by others to a minimum.

Thousands have bought the first edition of this book every year, demonstrating what IRE has always known—working journalists and their soon-to-be colleagues hunger for additional training about where to look to get at the heart of a story.

After scores of IRE conferences and look-a-like sessions by other journalism service organizations, many of the hard-won reporting secrets are no longer secrets. It's a damned good thing, and about time. The purpose of this book is to do away with the hard-won part, too.

There are even competitors to "The Reporter's Handbook" now. IRE and I welcome them. In addition, advanced reporting textbooks that used to be crammed cover to cover with social science methodology tools—but devoid of advice on how to look up a land record, or even why—have now been improved by including a chapter or section on using records and documents.

Most of all, I welcome the new people who have made this revised edition an improvement on the old, and the contribution by some who made the first edition so useful.

First among the new is Jan Colbert, coeditor of this edition. She took the place of Steve Honeyman, now a professional do-gooder in Philadelphia and without whom the records section in every chapter of the first edition would have been but a morsel instead of the banquet the book provided.

Jan is a prototypical hard-worker, even by IRE's incredibly high standards. She's been the organization's associate or acting executive director for six years. It was she who in reality shepherded this book into print, lining up graduate students to produce the records sections and pleading, cajoling or bamboozling professionals into writing the chapter introductions, and later doing it on time, or at least approximating such. All who read this book or attend a successful IRE conference owe her a loud and prolonged thank-you.

She was assisted by a number of people working at IRE headquarters in Columbia, especially Steve Weinberg, who tirelessly read manuscripts, offered support and wrote the bibliography.

My editors in Minneapolis at the Star Tribune, Joel Kramer, Tim McGuire and Mike Finney, have been continual and enthusiastic backers of IRE, allowing their staffers to contribute time and energy, and often picking up their expenses as well as making substantial monetary contributions.

We are all enriched by the work of those authors and contributors whose names appear on the following chapters. It is they who make the IRE experiment of journalist educating journalist the most useful educational experience most of us ever encounter.

John Ullmann
Minneapolis, Minnesota
July 1990

C O N T E N T S

C H A P T E R   4
The Freedom of Information Act
HARRY HAMMITT

PART TWO

INDIVIDUALS

Documenting the Evidence 165

C H A P T E R   9
Tracing Land Holdings   GEORGE KENNEDY   170

Documenting the Evidence 180

C   H   A   P   T   E   R   1   0

Putting It All Together   PATRICK RIORDAN

PART THREE
INSTITUTIONS

C   H   A   P   T   E   R   1   1

Business

For-Profit Corporations   JAMES K. GENTRY

C H A P T E R   1 2

The Work Place   MIKE McGRAW   **261**

C H A P T E R   1 3

Law Enforcement J. HARRY JONES, JR.   **293**

C H A P T E R   1 6

Education   NANCY WEAVER and
REAGAN WALKER

Bibliography   STEVE WEINBERG   433

THE
REPORTER'S
HANDBOOK

An Investigator's Guide
to Documents
and Techniques

Second Edition

Introduction

One of the reasons why daily journalism is criticized for being shallow is that the skills common to most investigative reporters—the ability to locate, understand and ultimately use a vast number of records and documents in order to determine the real story—are unknown to many journalists. Those skills can and should be learned by all reporters. This section describes how this book is organized toward that end.

by **JOHN ULLMANN**

> I keep six honest serving-men
> (They taught me all I knew);
> Their names are What and Why and When
> And How and Where and Who.
> Rudyard Kipling

If the truth will out, we in journalism don't know as much about reporting as we think we do. We like to say among ourselves that "investigative reporting" is redundant, that all good reporters are investigators by definition. But clearly, and at the very least, there is a great difference in the quality of all these "investigative" reports. Most of us don't know as much about investigating as a second-year lawyer, a second-rate insurance investigator or even a rookie cop. The most disreputable shamus knows more about backgrounding an individual through public records than most working journalists; the average stock investment counselor knows more about backgrounding a company than many reporters who cover business as their beat. You need only read the morning newspaper or watch the evening newscast to recognize the truth in this.

Even among ourselves, we tacitly acknowledge the difference by bestowing our highest reporting plaudits on those who do investigations. For example, in the history of the Pulitzer Prizes, most of the awards in the reporting categories have gone to investigative projects.

1

As reporters, we tend to rely on our abilities, learned over time, to ask penetrating questions of sources. However, we often fail to develop the ability to also search out answers in records that, for the most part, are readily available for the asking. The reasons for this lie in the deficiencies of our education in journalism schools, where most of us come from now; in the negative attitude toward midcareer education by our journalism employers; and in a general and pervasive ignorance among ourselves, first as reporters and then as editors, about how much there is still to learn about doing our jobs better.

Journalism School Education

The dour among us have many reasons for maintaining that journalism is not a profession. Journalism has no universally agreed-upon and universally practiced set of ethics or code of conduct related to gathering news; journalism has no built-in mechanism to police its ranks; there is no agreed-upon set of entrance requirements needed, nor is there any basic body of knowledge we all must master before plunging into the field.

But there is another, more fundamental reason why journalism is unlike traditional professions—such as law or engineering.

In such professions, a student learns a great deal of knowledge and comparatively little technique, then sallies forth to practice. In a typical journalism school, the student learns a great deal of technique and very little about how things work—or how to find out how things work.

It is not enough, not nearly enough, that the typical journalism student is required to take three courses outside journalism for every course within.

If you are a typical journalist, like those with whom I come in daily contact, you never have taken a political science course in college or graduate school that explains how power politics works in your community, how influence peddling occurs, how and why political goods and services are delivered—even how to evaluate the performance of a single city department or agency, say, Parks and Recreation.

You never have had an economics course that explains how a local business can affect the outcome of a bidding procedure, influence the growth patterns of a city, or even cheat its stockholders or consumers.

Nor have you ever taken an education course that explains how to evaluate the local school system, how to probe the wisdom of the ways in which it spends its millions of dollars, or even how to evaluate the (now annual) bond issue.

Even if you had been interested while in college, you probably would have been thwarted in your search for these courses—because such nuts-and-bolts courses rarely exist.

Instead, you spent a great deal of time during your journalism education practicing how to ask questions and learning how to arrange the answers in an understandable format. Then, as now, your touchstones were Rudyard Kipling's "six honest serving-men." You need not be a specialist, you were told, you need not be well versed: You need only to ask *who, what, where, when, how* and *why,* and accurately record what you've heard.

Investigative reporters, of course, answer the same questions, but what distinguishes their reporting from that of most of their colleagues is that investigative reporters often know more about how things are supposed to work, and therefore more about how to get the real answers.

Learning on the Job

You can, of course, get by quite nicely without this knowledge. Neither your bosses nor your peers, by and large, have it either. Nor, for the most part, do they believe you need it to perform your job adequately. You are expected to learn what you need to know about the subsystems of society while on the job. In fact, you had better. Unlike most businesses, midcareer training for journalists contains more barriers than gateways if only because these attitudes conspire to work against it.

Fortunately, however, little expertise is expected of us. Provided that we can just get straight what people tell us, what we learn on the job usually will be enough for all but a few of the most experienced of us—and, of course, for the people about whom we are writing. But we try to convince ourselves that, after all, we are telling them all they need to know.

We ask only *whowhatwherewhenhowandwhy,* confident that people will tell us the truth and tell it completely. If there is a conflict, we only get quotes from the "other side," seriously endeavoring all the while to make the story somehow balanced. Let the reader decide which side is truthful, it's not our job; we are recorders, not reporters.

Even divining what questions to ask is no easy task for someone with no real understanding of where to look to find out answers independently. Little wonder that the most commonly used document for most journalists is the telephone book. But when the source at the other end of the receiver is either unable or unwilling to talk, reporters are often stymied, not knowing how or where to uncover the facts themselves.

An Alternative: Learning How Things Work

It needn't always be this way. By listing the most important public records and describing their value, by offering a methodology for a different way to do our job and even a different way to think, this book is intended to train journalists and journalism students to find out how things work.

The underlying principle of this approach is simple: If you want to understand how something works, first find out how it is supposed to work. What are the statutes and what are the implementing regulations? What paperwork is required to document compliance? If professionals are involved, what standards do they use to evaluate themselves? And finally, what are the differences, if any, between what people say they are doing, what they are required to do (or are prohibited from doing) and what they are, in fact, doing?

There are two advantages to this method. By following paper trails, reporters can become educated about how things are supposed to operate. And this very examination often leads to stories.

How This Book Is Organized

The 16 chapters that follow explain how to investigate the most common areas covered by reporters. The introductions to each chapter are written by reporters who are experts in the subject matter, detailing the kinds of stories to look for, sources to develop and pitfalls to avoid. In addition, most introductions go into detail about how to integrate documentary research with legwork and interviews. Following most of these introductions, the sections called "Documenting the Evidence" are lists of key documents at the federal, state and local levels of government, along with non-governmental sources, that every reporter should know about. Explained here is what the document is called, where it is kept, how to get it and how it is useful. Other parts of "Documenting the Evidence" consist of addresses and other information useful to the reporter who needs to get answers fast.

Although each chapter is designed to stand alone, the reader should take the time to read the whole book, as some information isn't repeated throughout. For instance, the documents and techniques offered in the chapter on backgrounding individuals contain excellent advice for those journalists investigating certain aspects of institutions. Reporters investigating the police would find the chapter on courts as valuable as the one on law enforcement.

This book is organized in three parts.

Part I contains four chapters introducing the reader to the use of public documents and offering advice on how to get background information from government publications. "Following the Paper (or Computer) Trail" sets the tone of the book; it offers detailed strategies for gleaning stories out of city and county government along with suggestions about how to organize what you find. "Using Publications" demonstrates how to find and use the myriad published sources available in most libraries, and lists the most useful. "Finding a Government Document: An Overall Strategy" outlines a basic approach for finding a government record or document at the federal, state and local levels; in many ways it is the most important chapter in the book, as it is your key to getting at other documents not described in this book. Finally, the chapter on "The Freedom of Information Act" describes the provisions of the Act and how to make it work for you; it also deals with state and local access statutes.

Part 2 consists of six chapters that deal with different aspects of investigating individuals. "Backgrounding Individuals" explains how to flesh out background information on an individual when you have just a name, and is followed by a listing of where to get birth, death, marriage and divorce certificates. Next, "Using Tax Records" offers avenues for accumulating financial data on an individual. "Finding Out About Licensed Professionals" explains how to obtain information when your target is a member of a licensed profession, craft or trade. "Investigating Politicians" gives advice on investigating both candidates for public office and elected officials. "Tracing Land Holdings" explains in great detail how to decipher land ownership records and uncover land fraud schemes. The last chapter in this section, "Putting It All Together," shows the reporter how to use these various kinds of background information in covering a fast-breaking story.

Part 3 contains six chapters on the institutions most frequently covered by reporters: "Business," "The Work Place," "Law Enforcement," "Courts," "Health Care" and "Education." The business chapter consists of three sections—"For-Profit Corporations", "Not-for-Profit Corporations and Foundations" and "Bankruptcies," whose court proceedings can be mined for business information. The work place has an abundance of publicly available paper trails to follow, most of which are detailed here. Law enforcement and courts, on the other hand, are more source-oriented fields for the reporter, and a number of ways to develop stories are described—in Chapters 13 and 14—along with the few important records. Health care stories can be as important to your readers and viewers as any your news organization will run, and the field's components are analyzed in Chapter 15. Finally, the last chapter, "Education," covers an area often ignored by investigative reporters because of its complexity.

The New Edition

We have been hearing from journalists around the country for years about new public documents that are available and others that went by the wayside. Investigative Reporters and Editors members call us everyday to tell us about new ways to investigate politicians, new ways to analyze government statistics. This made our job easier when it came time to revise "The Reporter's Handbook." This new edition contains many of those ideas, plus 12 completely rewritten chapters and four chapters that have been revised and updated. They all contain scores of new anecdotes and techniques, as well as lists of documents and sources available to all journalists.

Also new to this edition is a selected bibliography containing many of the best books on investigative reporting as well as topical books on everything from organized crime to environmental issues. Steve Weinberg, former executive director of Investigative Reporters and Editors, compiled the list.

All the facts in this edition, and there are thousands, were checked and rechecked by Gerry Everding, a St. Louis journalist who worked with John Ullmann at the Star Tribune in Minneapolis/St. Paul.

Please don't throw your old book away. Combined, the two versions double up on story ideas, tactics and techniques.

How Up-to-Date Is This Book?

We are aware that even now, as you hold this book in your hands, parts of it are incomplete or out of date. To save you time and trouble, we have discussed only the most useful public records; that incompleteness is by design. But other omissions and changes were beyond our control, as the federal government continually reorganizes itself or substantially changes its records system.

Some records we describe as open to the public may in fact be closed by the time you try to get them. Others may no longer be kept by that agency. Still others may no longer be kept at all, or may now be kept on computer and have different access requirements. Therefore, it is wise to have an overall strategy for finding government documents, which we offer in Chapter 3 and help to form in every other chapter.

We designed this book to be a reporter's constant guide. As the repertoire of available records and their locations change, make notes on the new situation in the large margins near the appropriate record entry that have been specifically designed to help you keep this book as up-to-date as possible. If there is not enough space on or near the relevant page for notes, use the blank pages at the end of the book.

And remember, if we tell you a record is public, and the public servants who are custodians tell you it isn't, persist in trying to get hold of it. Our research in preparing this book has shown they often don't know.

Journalism Ethics

Laws governing access to government-held information vary widely from city to city and from state to state, and are even contradictory within the federal government. For instance, while the Freedom of Information Act is a strong and positive disclosure statute, it often conflicts with provisions within the Privacy Act, a statute designed to protect individuals. It is not always clear which law—disclosure or denial—is the governing rule.

It is important to keep in mind, however, that almost every record described in this book is a public record. Nowhere do we suggest that you lie, steal or break any law to gain access to information, although we would be wrong to suggest that there are no reporters who would do one or all of these things for the right story. We do, nonetheless, make a distinction between records that are required to be closed by statute or court order, and those that are merely closed by the practice of the record keepers. When we note that record keepers are not required to divulge information, we often suggest that a source may produce the material for you. This practice is not illegal, nor is it, we think, unethical.

Finally, several of our contributors suggest that it is not always necessary to identify oneself as a reporter; or, that even after proper identification, a reporter be hazy about what he or she is after until it is "convenient" to reveal one's purpose. Other journalists who participated in this project object to this practice, preferring always to identify who they are and what they want at the outset of an inquiry. We leave it to the readers' discretion to decide which position they choose. A more complete discussion of the considerations involved when a reporter uses deception can be found in recent issues of The IRE Journal, IRE's quarterly tabloid magazine, which can be purchased on request from IRE headquarters, University of Missouri, 100 Neff Hall, Columbia, Mo. 65211; (314) 882-2042.

How Readers Can Contribute

When it's time to update this book, again we'll need your help. We are asking for two kinds of material. When you use this book to find a record, but you obtain it in a way other than that described here, please write and tell us about it so that we can share it with other journalists. And if you come across an exceptionally illuminating anecdote from which others might learn, please send us a memo about that, too.

We will ensure that you get full credit in the book, and you will ensure that this book remains what the members of IRE intended it to be: the most useful reference book for journalists ever published.

PART ONE
GETTING STARTED

C H A P T E R   1

Following the Paper
(or Computer) Trail

Learning to follow the trails in the mountains of paperwork all individuals and businesses create each day is one of the skills that separates investigative reporters from their colleagues. This chapter introduces the reader to the techniques of finding and using the many kinds of documentation available, employing as examples those records kept by nearly all city and county governments.

---

by **TOM HAMBURGER, JERRY UHRHAMMER** and
RANDY McCONNELL

For Todd Oppenheimer, formerly of The Independent in Durham, N.C., learning how to find and interpret real estate tax records opened the way to a big story: How Durham County gave hefty tax breaks to wealthy homeowners while middle and lower-class homes were appraised at full value.

The San Jose Mercury News used similar records in courthouses and city halls around the world to put together a Pulitzer Prize–winning story documenting the massive overseas investments of Ferdinand Marcos and a small circle of other prominent Filipinos.

Whether you are tracking a story of corruption in city hall, international deception or housing code violations at your university, the principle "follow the paper trail" applies.

This phrase has been the watchword for investigators in all fields for years. It means figuring out where the documentation to back up your tip or hunch may be found—and how to intercept it legally.

These days following the paper trail requires almost as much time in front of computer terminals as file drawers because many agencies have computerized indexes to their paper documents. But the value of the adage still applies. The computer is simply a tool that helps you follow the paper trail faster and more efficiently.

This chapter provides a simple but basic tool to help investigators. Of course, the execution of a true investigative project requires more than just skill with records. Reporters need organization, persistence, support from management, interviewing skills and, above all, a willingness to ask the deeper questions.

Gene Roberts, executive editor of the Philadelphia Inquirer, defines investigative reporting as "not so much catching the politician with his pants down or focusing on a single outrage, but in digging, digging, digging beneath the surface so we can help our readers understand what's really going on in an increasingly complex world."

Getting Started

The intellectual process that reporters conduct before the investigation begins is often the key to the project.

Successful investigative stories usually begin with a tip or hypothesis that something is wrong. Before you start looking to see that a system isn't working, however, you need to understand how it is supposed to work.

The first step after receiving a tip is to learn how the system functions and where the information you are seeking is most likely to be recorded. If public money is involved, there should be a step-by-step record of how it is spent.

At the early stages of his investigation into tax assessment, Oppenheimer familiarized himself with the details of the property assessment system in Durham County and, for comparison, in other North Carolina counties as well. After talking with assessors, realtors and state agency experts, Oppenheimer developed a methodology for comparing tax assessments among different categories of homeowners.

He chose a nine-month study period, just before and after a countywide reassessment took effect. He then checked sales records for homes in certain price categories to see if the difference in the sale and appraisal figures were roughly the same for low- and high-priced homes. They were not; Oppenheimer knew he had a story.

In 1985 three reporters in San Jose were trying to follow up on tips that Marcos and his close friends and relatives were draining capital out of the Philippines. The first step for the reporters was to learn the way such overseas investments are typically handled. Frequently, they found, foreigners use surrogates, front companies, attorneys or other agents who purchase and manage property on behalf of an overseas client.

Because of this secondhand investment, the reporters realized they could not track property by the usual method of looking up records under the name of the owner. A quick review of California's real estate record system told them that to get their story they needed to find out either the names of the surrogates or the address of the property.

Through a combination of sourcing and paper trail research at courthouses around the globe, the reporters were able to establish that Marcos and others had considerable holdings in the United States and elsewhere. Their research proved the long-denied reality about the behavior of Marcos and his close associates: They had drained millions of dollars out of the Philippines and privately invested the money overseas.

We'll take a look below at the way they—and reporters working on more modest projects—got the material they needed to complete their investigations.

Key Records for Investigative Reporters

The two most important offices for investigative reporters to know in a city or county building are the clerk's office and the finance department. These are the centers of bookkeeping and paperwork for local government, and they function much the same across the country.

The clerk's office is usually the nerve center of city and county government. It's the place to find council minutes, campaign disclosure reports, copies of city codes and general information about how the municipality functions. Finance office records revolve around the collection and spending of the taxpayers' money. In the age of computerization, record systems can vary from department to department, but general bookkeeping and auditing principles will apply to all.

Finance offices typically contain the requisitions, invoices and canceled checks, along with the deeds, contracts, licenses, grants and budgets that tell the story of how public money is spent.

These documents can be the cornerstone for building a story about corruption, misconduct, conflict of interest or just plain mismanagement. For reporters, the preparation that goes into an attempt to obtain information from these offices can mean the differences between success and failure. Some guidelines are:

■ *If it's a question of how the city or county is spending its money, get a copy of the annual budget.* This should give you a basic picture of the money flow. Determine how much money has been budgeted for the specific program you want to examine. Budget preparation documents frequently explain the rationale of a particular program's getting more or less money in the coming fiscal year. Get an idea of that program's relationship to other programs and learn about the working of the branch of the bureaucracy responsible for administering it.

- *Ask the city or county public information officer for a table of organization of the city or county government and information about the specific programs you are investigating.* Asking for these documents at the Minneapolis City Hall led Star Tribune reporters to inquire about a minority contracting program that was said to be bringing in millions of dollars to a relatively tiny minority community. Their inquiry paid off: Within a few months, the newspaper produced a series exposing massive fraud in minority contracting throughout the state, involving tens of millions of dollars. The series led to major reforms as well as federal indictments of company executives and a government official.

- *Review the applicable state laws and regulations and the city and county ordinances or codes.* This step provides you with a baseline by telling you how the system is supposed to operate. If you discover it isn't operating that way, you have a story. Pay special attention to public bidding and purchasing laws, which are often bent, broken or ignored. As you read these laws, take heed of the exceptions, exemptions, emergency provisions and other loopholes through which public bodies can make purchases without competitive bids. Be sure to note also what penalties are invoked for violation of the rules. This kind of review helped reporters at the Seattle Post-Intelligencer in an investigative series on low-income housing. They found that building inspectors were supposed to check residences regularly and issue violation notices and, in the case of repeat offenders, fines. Their check of city building inspection files proved that the city had failed to follow the basic instructions of the law.

- *Ask questions.* Once you have an idea of what you're looking for, go to the city or county finance department and, if necessary, ask for assistance. Try to be general in your request, so as not to reveal your investigative hypothesis. Remember Oppenheimer's approach with the tax assessment records: Shortly after receiving a tip that certain properties were underappraised, Oppenheimer began asking questions of county officials and studying the county's tax records. He also looked for assessment experts, in the courthouse and outside, to help understand the records he would be examining.

- *Cultivate a source within the finance department — someone who can steer you in the right direction when you have questions.* Such sources are fairly easy to acquire. Bookkeepers and accountants, in particular, tend to be protective of the money in their control, and reporters shouldn't be surprised when they get hints like "you ought to look into that revolving fund for so-and-so's office. You wouldn't believe the money they are wasting." Oppenheimer became so well-acquainted with the assessment staff in Durham County that the staff provided tips on record searching and allowed him to use the office computer for his research.

- *Find shortcuts.* Learn whether records are computerized, if not by the municipality then by an independent firm that might be willing to share its resources.

Pete Carey of the San Jose Mercury News found that a private data retrieval service had computerized California's land, title and property indexes. By paying for the computerized list, Carey and his team saved hundreds of hours that would have been spent poring over grantor and grantee indexes in individual county courthouses all over the state. Most important, the computer provided access to cross-indexed information using a name, the address of the property or even the address of the property manager.

When Houston television station KPRC tried to follow a tip that local oil properties were untaxed, the reporters found county records cumbersome and inadequate. Their task was eased when they looked to industry newsletters and other publications that regularly listed the location of oil properties. Newsletters and shipping reports, the reporters found, listed the home counties of ships, oil rigs and other equipment.

The industry reports allowed them to develop their own list of oil property registered in Houston. They then compared their list with the property on the county tax rolls, and discovered $300 million worth of oil property was untaxed. Their story won IRE's top award for 1985.

■ *If your story involves examining a public official's private dealings, or background on an individual, check the city, county and federal court records.* These cases—criminal, civil, divorce, probate, bankruptcy and traffic— can yield nuggets of financial and personal information unavailable in routine public records. Many counties now offer computerized listings and can tell you on the telephone whether any recent suits exist involving the person or business in question. A divorce file or personal injury case can often yield detailed personal and financial information unavailable elsewhere.

■ *Test your thesis.* Early in an investigation, test your investigative hypotheses to see if they are worth investigating further. Near the beginning of his assessment project, Oppenheimer applied two tests. First, he randomly scanned the property record cards and compared the sale and appraisal figures. He noticed a pattern: Owners of expensive homes seem to be getting a tax break because their homes were often appraised well below the sale price, while low or moderately priced homes were usually right on target; he realized "I've probably got something."

Second, Oppenheimer went to experts familiar with assessment procedures and tested his theory. Oppenheimer advises, "Test your hunches as early as you can with experts who can, and want to, pick them apart."

Most experts admire reporters who approach a subject this seriously; you can turn to these people to help you stay on track throughout the investigation.

Many reporters working on investigative projects have recognized the value of outside expert guidance when working on obscure or complex subjects. Newspaper project offices now routinely consult nationally recognized experts to review methodology.

Keeping Tabs on Elected Officials

Thanks to sunshine laws, many key activities of public officials are open to scrutiny.

■ *Campaign contribution reports.* Most jurisdictions require public officials to report political campaign contributions and expenditures. Get a copy of the report so you will know who the politician's financial backers are. Compare votes over a period of years to see whether the politician voted in favor of issues in which his contributors had an interest. Campaign contribution reports for local officeholders should be available at city hall and the county courthouse. Reports on contributions to candidates for national offices are filed with the Federal Election Commission in Washington, D.C., at the state capitol and frequently in city halls and county courthouses.

■ *Financial disclosure.* Many states and municipalities require their top elected and appointed officials to file statements of economic interest, showing their sources of income, ownership of real property and other related information. The statements are usually available in city halls, courthouses or secretary of state's offices. Senators and members of Congress also file financial disclosures at the federal level. (See Chapter 8 "Investigating Politicians.") Their usefulness is limited because they are usually about a year behind. But journalists who keep files of such reports on each politician they are covering can sometimes find interesting nuggets by comparing the statements against a legislative or other public performance record and looking for obvious patterns or conflicts of interest. It's also worth comparing a statement filed during a public official's first years in office with the statement filed for that official's final year in office to see whether he has grown wealthy or made key investments while in public service.

■ *Telephone records.* As with all other expenditures of public funds, those made to cover bills from office and car telephones and telephone credit cards are open to scrutiny. They can be obtained usually from city or county finance offices and can sometimes yield a substantial amount of information. Traditionally, telephone records showed only the telephone numbers of long distance calls initiated by the official or collect calls accepted. With the advent of car phones that has changed.

Most car phone calls are billed individually because there is a charge for any use of the phone, including incoming calls. As a result, car phone records of public officials can provide the only list of local calls made by public officials, both outgoing and incoming. Increasingly, mayors and other top officials in large and mid-size cities are given car telephones. The advantage of checking these telephones was made clear by the St. Paul Pioneer Press when a review of car telephone bills showed that the fire chief had made hundreds of dollars of personal calls from his car, including regular calls to a local tavern. The story resulted in a city investigation. When requesting phone records at the finance office, specify that you wish to see not only the monthly bill for each official's telephone but also telephone credit card records and bills that may have been submitted from car phones or private lines.

■ *Expense account and credit card payments.* Some public officials carry city or county credit cards and bill travel and other expenses directly to the city or county finance office. The finance department files will have the monthly bills which will, in some cases, provide information on the travel and dining habits of key officials. Many hotel bills include a telephone call log detailing charges for each room. In addition to credit card bills, be sure to request copies of expense reports filed by officials.

■ *Time sheets and attendance reports.* If you are building a chronology of events (one of the investigator's most powerful tools), you can find out whether a public official attended work on a given date and whether he or she requested vacation or leave time. In addition to expense vouchers, this is a useful place to check for the travel and attendance record of public officials.

■ *Court cases.* Be sure to run the names of public officials through court records from time to time to see whether they have been picked up on any criminal charges and whether any new information has emerged from civil suits.

While this used to be a time-consuming, cumbersome project, things are starting to change. Many jurisdictions have computerized court records which you can check with the simple push of a button to determine whether an individual has been summoned to court in your county.

■ *Computer data bases.* Every large newsroom now seems to have its tale of good stories resulting from entering someone's name into a data base. When Roy Furmark emerged as a key figure in the Iran/Contra scandal, little was known about him or his background; the wires described him as a mysterious Canadian businessperson. A Los Angeles Times reporter punched Furmark's name into the Nexis data base and learned he was involved in one of the largest bankruptcies in Canadian history, which provided, of course, a voluminous trail of lawsuits and government actions.

The increased use of computers to store government records can be a boon to reporters. The Providence Journal-Bulletin, for example, has compiled a library of computer tapes that includes the record of every criminal defendant who has appeared in Superior Court in recent years, as well as the state's fiscal records.

At the Star Tribune, reporter Eric Black made use of computer tapes maintained by an obscure state agency—the Sentencing Guidelines Commission—to produce a definitive comparison of Minnesota's county prosecutors. A candidate running for prosecutor in the largest county had charged that the incumbent prosecutor was weak on crime and offered an unusual number of plea bargains. Black discovered that the statewide data base allowed him to rank prosecutors on the frequency of their bargaining with criminal defendants. His story settled a hot election dispute.

■ *Computer records tip.* Pete Carey says that his paper wouldn't have been able to complete a project of the scope of the Marcos investigation without the use of computerized real estate listings. But for a brief period during the course of the investigation, he discovered one disadvantage of computer searching. Unless the name you enter is spelled precisely, the computer will not help you. Before you request a computer search—sometimes an expensive proposition —check and double-check the spelling and full name of the person or organization you wish to investigate.

■ *Corporation records.* If a public official lists an interest in one or more corporations or partnerships using an assumed business name, find out who the partners are. Then determine whether they do business with the city or county (for more information on corporate records, see Chapter 11) and whether the public official has been involved in any decisions that could affect his or her partners. Incorporation records are usually maintained by the state; they are useful in a wide range of investigations.

The Denver Post used these records in a project that showed how white-owned corporations were defrauding contracting programs intended to benefit minorities. On several occasions, corporation records revealed the participation of major white contractors in firms that were ostensibly controlled by minorities. Follow-up checks on those firms revealed a high percentage of front companies set up to get contracts reserved for minorities into the hands of white-owned companies.

■ *UCC records.* Most states and counties are repositories of loan disclosures, or Uniform Commercial Code statements (UCC), on all chattel mortgages. The forms are filed with county recorders and sometimes at the statehouse as well. In most states, UCC statements are kept on file for up to five years, even if the debt is paid. The Denver Post reporters investigating minority contract schemes, Bob Kowalski and Lou Kilzer, got tipped to front companies when they examined these records.

They found tips by bracketing their searches, as Kilzer calls it. In checking loan papers for a piece of equipment, Kilzer noted, "you look at other UCC security agreements filed at about that same time."

On several occasions the reporters found that a white-owned company was securing equipment registered to the minority firm. "The only way to find out that there were other parties to the loan was to examine forms from dates on both sides of the minority firm's UCC filing," Kilzer said.

■ *Planning and zoning records.* If you're trying to determine who's who in a real estate transaction, zoning approval files will often provide the information. If a zoning change request comes from a corporation, find out who are the principals of that corporation. Corporation names themselves often don't mean much. Go back to the secretary of state's office to see whether they are public officials, well-known wheeler dealers or even newspaper executives.

■ *Business licenses and applications.* It's illegal to conduct certain types of business unless a license is obtained first. You can use licenses to track the ownership of pornographic theaters and bookstores, dance halls, bars, liquor stores, taxicabs and bingo parlors. Look for patterns in these records and you may find good stories as well. For example, the Star Tribune reviewed liquor licensing regulations in St. Paul and found a pattern of instances where the city council was not informed of violations or repeated police calls even during the regular, required review of a license.

In most states, licenses that individuals obtain—from driver's permits to boat registrations—are public information and can provide valuable details to reporters. Many license records include physical information, photographs and lists of vehicle property. License records are usually available at state offices, not in county courthouses.

■ *Tax court.* State and federal tax courts can yield financial details of individuals that are normally hidden from public scrutiny. These courts decide disputes between the federal and state governments and a taxpayer and the records, including tax returns, are open.

■ *Divorce records.* Another place to find details of an individual's finances are divorce records, which are public. Generally available at county courthouses, these records can guide reporters to a good source of information about someone you are investigating: an angry former spouse.

■ *Health department.* Consumer magazines and entertainment sections have discovered the value of checking county or city health files. They have reported that some of America's favorite restaurants are also the dirtiest. From health records you can learn about the sanitary quality of motels, school cafeterias and other public facilities. You may also find patterns that reveal favoritism or lack of enforcement against certain industries or institutions.

■ *Building inspections.* The city or county building inspector's office can provide a gold mine of detail to investigators. Reporters have used it to iden- a city's worst slumlord or to check whether a building that had a fatal fire had previously been cited for fire-related code violations. Building permits will also tell you whether an individual or company has been expanding or remodeling, as construction permits will be on file here. When checking a tip that a public employee had received a bribe, the Star Tribune checked building records and found that the official had remodeled his kitchen and built an addition to his house about the time the alleged bribe was offered.

■ *Weights and measures.* These quiet regulatory offices, usually ignored by city hall reporters, can yield terrific stories. Weights and measures bureaus are the places that check and regulate such diverse devices as gasoline pumps, scales and taxicab meters. The San Francisco Bay Guardian uncovered a pattern of shortweighing meat at local supermarkets owned by the same chain. The newspaper estimated that systematic shortweighing yielded millions to the chain in the sale of non-existent meat. Although laws against shortweighing are tough (violators are presumed guilty regardless of the reason their scales are off), the Guardian found little enforcement action even against chronic offenders.

Looking Into Government Contracts

The very words *government purchasing* make most reporters' eyes glaze over. However, enterprising reporters have found that reviewing purchasing documents can provide rich investigative material.

Denver's Rocky Mountain News investigated city contracts and produced a steady stream of exposés showing how cronyism between favored contractors and their City Hall benefactors had cost the taxpayers millions.

The stories disclosed that $4.5 million was missing from airport parking funds and that several city concessionaires with close City Hall ties had won lucrative contracts that weren't competitively bid. This series and others disclosed several tricks that can allow apparent low bidders to alter the contract terms after the bid is awarded (see "Checking Low Bidders" in this chapter).

At the start of any investigation into government purchasing, take a look at the laws governing public purchases. This administrative procedure generally provides a step-by-step list of the process for procuring goods and services. Increasingly, the awarding of grants—for providing social services, for example—follows the same broad procedures employed for selecting a building contractor or a supplier of toilet paper.

A crucial question in any discussion of government purchases is whether bids are required on particular items. Do projected costs exceed the limits set forth in the statute? Generally, purchases that take place without the required open bidding are illegal.

A caveat: One mechanism for circumventing bid requirements is dividing up a bulk purchase into small enough purchases to avoid the bid limits. A review of these small purchases during the year may reveal poor planning and management because the government agency didn't seek the discounts available through bulk buying. A city administrator may have deliberately made the small purchases to shift business to a favored supplier or political friend, or to a business in which the administrator has a financial interest.

If you're just starting to look at a suspicious bid, call the losing bidders. They are often willing to help and can give you an insider's look at how the process works.

As you work through the purchasing system, these are the areas specified in the law that you'll want to look at:

- *Informal cost estimates.* Officials are required to seek them even on non-bid items.
- *Notice of bid.* The law likely will prescribe not only when advance notice must be given, but also the medium for the notice. For example, the rules may require that the bid notice be published in a newspaper of general circulation in a specific county or metropolitan area 30 days before bids are due to be opened.
- *Request for proposals (RFPs).* Often used when seeking more flexible, open-ended proposals, especially for services such as consulting.

■ *Preferences for products.* Statutes often mandate that locally produced goods be selected if bids for these goods are equal in price to those of comparable quality produced elsewhere.

■ *Audit requirements.* Statutes may require agency audits of automatic cost increases when these are passed along on products in long-term contracts.

■ *Bid and performance bonds.* The bid bond, posted by the prospective supplier, simply assures the awarding agency that the supplier will accept the contract if its offer is selected. If the contract isn't accepted, the bond is forfeited. The performance bond assures the awarding agency that the supplier will meet the terms of the contract. If cost increases lead the supplier to back out of the contract, the bond is forfeited. The bonds usually are set at a percentage of the contract's estimated value.

■ *Affirmative action compliance statements.* Companies frequently must file these statements to qualify as vendors used by federal and state governments.

■ *Minority contracting requirements.* Municipalities that accept federal Department of Transportation funds are now required to contract a certain percentage of work to woman- or minority-owned businesses. This rule has proved so subject to abuse across the country that it is worth checking regularly.

To test superficially for the presence of minority or women-owned businesses that may be fronts for white, male-controlled companies, Star Tribune and Denver Post reporters checked the following: incorporation records to see whether spouses or white, male contractors were part of the firm; UCC listings to see whether white male contractors had co-signed loans; and the firm's offices to see whether they shared workspace with a white, male-owned company. While these tests won't determine whether the minority or woman-owned company is acting as a front, the close participation of white, male contractors can be seen as a red flag warranting further investigation.

Purchasing Documents

Perhaps more than any other government function, purchasing generates documentation at each step, from a department director's first request to the delivery of the actual goods and services. Among the documents that should be available under access legislation are the following:

■ *Bid specifications.* These documents, available to all prospective bidders, outline in some detail the required goods or services, conditions of delivery, exact bonding requirements, length of contract and procedures for terminating the contract.

Of interest here is whether specifications are written to favor a particular supplier by excluding all but one brand or type of equipment. Justification for a narrowly written specification should be available. Who sought it—the department head or purchasing agent—and why? Did a potential supplier help the agency write the specification and convince officials to favor that supplier's equipment? Check the wording of the specification with the manufacturer's actual product description sheets.

■ *Notice of bid.* A copy of the notice as advertised in the local paper should be routinely filed. Did the bid meet the legal requirements?

■ *The actual bid.* Unless the purchase is of an unusually complicated item, the layperson often can determine whether the bids submitted meet contract specifications.

■ *Bid evaluations.* Often, the lowest-priced bid may be rejected for not meeting specifications or because a potential vendor is regarded as unqualified. These decisions should be documented in written form and routinely kept on file for audit purposes.

■ *The written contract.* This should not vary from the bid specifications unless each variation is supported by documentation.

Checking Low Bidders

In Denver, reporters came up with a series of government stories based on a review of contract performance. They looked, for example, at the city's lease/purchase agreements. The winner usually had the low bid, or close to it. On the surface, nothing appeared wrong.

But the Denver team dug deeper and hit paydirt.

One company, for instance, won a lease/purchase agreement to supply the city's largest computer system. Bid documents showed that firms vying for the contract knew they'd have to pay property taxes on the machines unless the city decided to purchase them. But when reporters checked, they found that the winning company hadn't been making those payments. Further, the city hadn't asked them to. Soon, the paper found other, similar examples. Companies that planned to pay the taxes were losing out to companies that apparently weren't. The Rocky Mountain News showed that those low bids weren't so low after all.

"The lesson here," said reporter Lou Kilzer, "is simple. Don't be fooled by low bids. Look for the end result."

Follow-up Documentation

Purchasing documentation rules can vary widely from jurisdiction to jurisdiction. There are, however, some basic documents reporters should watch for when inquiring into purchasing decisions. The most important documents for following up on the government purchasing process include:

■ *Change orders.* These orders are the root cause of cost overruns. But unlike the Pentagon, American cities must live within their budgets. Change orders can be prime budget busters for your local public works department. Most of these orders are routine. A contractor hired to remove concrete from a city facility might find that the concrete is six inches thicker than the city thought. The city would issue a change order to allow the contractor to remove the extra material. Of course, the contractor's remuneration is altered accordingly.

The potential for dishonesty here is great because those orders don't go through competitive bidding. They often aren't subject to the same research that went into the original request for proposals.

Reporters should pay special attention to any company whose projects routinely get major change orders. Such a company may be unqualified or receiving special favors from the city. Watch carefully for coincidences. For instance, change orders that revise contracts in an amount just under a threshold that would provoke more scrutiny are suspect.

- *Audit reports.* The contract and ordinances may require city officials to audit delivery of services, particularly if these are reimbursed on a per-unit basis. Audits also may be required of certain cost escalations, for example, in energy supply contracts. Were audit reports filed? Did the city monitor the purchasing process as mandated?
- *Tax files.* Check whether vendors who owe back taxes to the city are competing successfully for city contracts.
- *Vendor incorporation and land records.* Government officials are usually prohibited by law from profiting from direct or indirect involvement in their agency's official transactions. Check vendor incorporation and land records to see if there is any corporate involvement between vendors and city employees.
- *Government subcontracts.* Government officials may cloak their private involvement in city business through subcontracts that rarely come under scrutiny in the bid process or by funneling business to a firm owned by friends or relatives, or in which officials have a hidden interest. Check files or visit building sites to determine which companies are obtaining subcontracts.

Auditing the Paper Trails

Auditors follow the paper trail of government financial transactions and represent, in their audit reports, the final step of accountability in public spending. Increasingly, thanks to the lead of the U.S. General Accounting Office, these audits have expanded beyond simple fiscal checks into full-blown reviews of government efficiency and program effectiveness.

Local Audits

Boosts in auditing activity at the local level have come mainly from revenue-sharing authorization legislation and renewed emphasis on stopping government waste that took hold in the 1980s. At the local or state levels, copies of audits should be available from the local or state agency that received the funds or from the federal agency that granted the money.

Federal Audits

At the federal level the main auditing agency is the General Accounting Office (GAO), an independent non-political agency of Congress. This arm of the government conducts legal, accounting, auditing and claims settlement functions and also recommends improvements in government operations. GAO audits are available without charge to the media. To get a list of audits, or to find out if one has been conducted on a subject in which you have an interest, contact the U.S. General Accounting Office, P.O. Box 6015, Gaithersburg, Md. 20877; (202) 275-6241.

Federal agencies now have inspectors general, who regularly conduct audits to identify areas of waste or fraud.

The Department of Health and Human Services (HHS), for example, does regular and comprehensive audits to check expenditures of grant funds. Acting under contract with other agencies, HHS will also audit grants to universities and other institutions that commonly receive federal funding from several federal sources. Copies of reports can usually be obtained from HHS Audit Agency regional offices.

Television station WRC in Washington, D.C., found HHS records helpful in developing a story on sloppy work by medical labs. To qualify for Medicare money, labs are required to submit to HHS inspections. These little-known records were a gold mine for reporter Rick Nelson.

Nelson discovered that up to 40 percent of the medical laboratories in the District of Columbia were cited for not doing important quality control procedures.

Nelson said that the regional offices of HHS's Health Care Financing Administration can provide reporters with computerized printouts showing where deficiencies occur.

Using these reports, Nelson identified health labs that were the worst offenders. The WRC reporter then checked lawsuits and learned of horror stories spawned by faulty lab reports. There was the teenager incorrectly diagnosed with gonorrhea, a man incorrectly told he had AIDs and a woman who was given a hysterectomy because lab reports incorrectly indicated she had cancer. Nelson's series received widespread attention and led to a congressional investigation.

Management Advisory Report and Financial Statement

The more sophisticated audits of governmental agencies generally contain two sections: the management advisory report and the financial statement.

The management advisory report, depending on the audit's scope, may show the agency's compliance with applicable laws and regulations, any deviations from good business practices and the effectiveness of the program being operated.

The keystone of the financial statement, known as the opinion, may take three major forms:

■ *The unqualified or clean opinion.* This means the agency's records were maintained so that the auditors with reasonable confidence could verify the true financial position of the agency, grant or whatever.

■ *The qualified opinion.* This means some record of activities was in such disarray that auditors disclaim responsibility for the accuracy of the opinion. The remaining funds or activities, though, are said to have had sufficient recordkeeping.

■ *No opinion.* The records were in such disarray that the auditors would not vouch for the accuracy of any statements based on the agency's files.

Even with a clean opinion, the agency may have operating problems that will show in the accompanying management advisory report. So don't stop reading after the first page of the financial report.

When dealing with a government agency, also look for these other kinds of financial statements:

■ *The balance sheet.* It lists assets, liabilities and fund balances. Assets typically include the value of investments, property taxes receivable, accounts receivable and supply inventories. Liabilities will include, for example, the agency's outstanding unpaid debts. The fund balance will include unspent but appropriated funds as well as the general surplus.

■ *Statement of revenues, expenditures and encumbrances.* Perhaps the most valuable features of this statement, if fully completed, are indications of whether an agency overspent or underspent its budget, and a comparison of spending for that fiscal year with the previous year.

Often, state laws require special action in advance to authorize budgetary overspending. Check the statements and the statutes to see whether rules were followed in your area.

■ *Statement of changes in financial position.* This statement shows the sources of funds for a fiscal year and how that funding was used.

The most sophisticated audit reports include pages and pages of other statements of financial positions, as well as schedules of supplementary data, all of which may merit analysis. Investments and outstanding indebtedness often are shown in detail.

In general the same principles apply to audits of for-profit corporations. But keep in mind that such audits must be read from a different standpoint; for-profit corporations, unlike government agencies, must be concerned with profit-loss status.

Trying These Techniques

The best tactic for the reporter unfamiliar with following paper trails is to take a well-defined governmental task—say the awarding of office supply contracts by the school system or the hiring of consultants by the city—and examine it using government records.

Follow the supply contract from the enabling statute or ordinance to the actual bid and its performance. Learn the local rules on hiring consultants. Do the same consultants always get the contracts? Why? Do the consultants have any financial ties to public officials? Were they political contributors? How much money does your local government spend on consultants annually?

You may, of course, find nothing wrong. But record searches will familiarize you with the kind of journalism that is more likely to produce stories that really tell readers or viewers how their tax dollars are being used.

Organizing the Material

Getting control of the mountains of data you can glean from public records is the key to a successful reporting project. Veteran investigators know that within a few days the data will overwhelm their memory. As a result, most experienced reporters have developed a variety of systems to keep track of it.

The most common file organizations are alphabetical listings by subject and by name of individuals. In addition, most investigators set up some sort of chronology that allows them to observe patterns or changes in behavior over time.

When the San Jose Mercury News started its probe of overseas Filipino investors, staff members computerized an alphabetical name list containing brief descriptions of each individual and references to the relevant paper property files.

The team also maintained a chronology and charts that showed the relationships among lawyers, dummy corporations, property ownership and the Filipino investors.

Some investigative veterans working on a major project cross-index all their interviews and documents by subject categories. Not only do the indexes enable them to find documents and interview notes quickly, but also serve as a quick reminder of their reporting in each of the many areas of research. These reminders are helpful in a project that goes on for several weeks or months, and are especially useful for major findings.

Computer technology provides a new range of organizing possibilities. In a study of malpractice suits, The Orlando Sentinel used a standard form to enter information from hundreds of lawsuits into the newspaper's computer. Based on a review of every malpractice suit filed in Orange County, Fla., during a five-year period, the computer data allowed the newspaper to challenge popular notions about the malpractice crisis. Despite claims to the contrary, the newspaper found that the doctors sued most often are not those who take the toughest cases or practice on the leading edge of technology. The newspaper showed that the rise in malpractice claims was greatly exaggerated by insurance companies and doctors and that frivolous malpractice suits were rare.

Looking at the System

So far, this chapter has focused largely on using investigative techniques to reveal evidence of shortcomings in the performance of a public official or of a specific program.

These techniques are most useful when they challenge commonly held assumptions and produce a story that tells readers about the way our system of government really functions.

Allen Short experienced this as a reporter for the St. Paul Pioneer Press, when he completed a series showing how powerful political lobbies can affect the cost and fairness of municipal pension plans.

Short's award-winning series began as a routine assignment on the pension benefits available to a retiring federal judge. For the story, Short compared the judge's pension with those offered to other local officials.

Pension records are public, available in each municipality and at the state-house. Short's extra bit of research showed him that there was a much larger issue lurking beyond the spot story of a federal judge's pension.

"What I found was that, while the judge was eligible for a handsome pension, its generosity paled in comparison to that offered to lower-level state and local government pensioners," he said.

Short kept digging. Public information laws gave him access to details of city retirement plans that showed how specific pensioners could retire at an early age, receive seven times the amount they contributed to retirement funds and still hold down high-paying jobs in the private sector.

A review of the state's major plans and comparisons with states that had consolidated pension programs revealed the enormous waste in Minnesota's pension system, a patchwork of 215 independent and costly plans.

To detail the waste, Short went after the expense and voucher records filed by the state's pension officials.

He found that pension board members often flew to exotic destinations to attend investment seminars, ostensibly to learn how to manage their members' funds. Yet, annual pension fund reports showed these presumably well-educated board members were paying professional investment managers tens of thousands of dollars to do the job for which the state officials had been trained.

Consolidation could save money for taxpayers and pensioners. Short looked to see why it wasn't happening.

His inquiry led to the statehouse, where interviews and campaign contribution reports told the story of a powerful pension lobby.

Financial disclosure and lobbying records of state officials showed that the pension crowd had one of the best-financed and most influential political lobbies in the state: a dozen political action committees devoted to the protection and expansion of retirement benefits for about 275,000 state and local government employees.

Using state campaign records, he showed how influential legislators received large contributions each year from the pension lobbies.

His series concluded that though the lobby created by these separate plans produced enviable retirement benefits for some government workers, it had saddled active employees and future generations with the bill for maintaining plans that duplicated administrative services and, in some cases, paid excessive benefits.

Conclusion

Investigative reporting is often like Short's experience: The more you dig, the more you find. Your job doesn't stop with the accumulation of records and proof of improper behavior. The best investigators will devote equal effort to find out *why*.

In his tax assessment piece, Oppenheimer was able to include reasons for the discrepancy in assessments between poor and middle-class homeowners. It didn't occur solely because of favoritism but because the more expensive and intricate the home, the harder it is to assess accurately.

He told his readers that appraisers in his county are often in a rush, so they are lax. Furthermore, they deliberately appraise low to avoid angering prominent citizens.

So his story was not just about unfair assessments. Like Short's pension story or any first-rate investigative piece, it took readers beyond a single outrage and provided broader insight into the way our system really works.

C H A P T E R 2

Using Publications

Before beginning any investigation, you should plumb the material in a nearby library for the valuable background information that it contains on a subject area or the target of your investigation—information that often isn't easily available anywhere else. What exactly is in there, how best to find it and how to use it profitably are detailed in this chapter. Particular attention is paid to those government publications that routinely arrive at the more than 1,300 government depository libraries located throughout the United States.

---

by JOHN ULLMANN and KATHLEEN HANSEN

Once upon a time two patron saints of journalism were sitting around doing what journalists do best because they practice it most—griping about the job. It's not certain where this meeting occurred, but because they are the patron saints of journalism, it can be inferred the temperatures were high, the surroundings sulfurous. (We know what went on only because we located a Miami Herald reporter's interred notes. He observed most of the conversation while hiding behind a wall of flame that only partially and intermittently obscured his vision.)

The fat saint, referred to in a dimly remembered past as Deputy M.E., said, "Wouldn't it be great if they got all the documents and records and put them in one building so reporters wouldn't have to go all over Creation to find them?"

And the thin one, who once was called M.E., said, "Well, not all of them, 'cause then our reporters would get fat and lazy. Just some of the most important ones. And maybe some books, too."

Then the fat one said, "OK, let's use our limited powers and see that it's done. Then all journalists surely will flock to this building, saving time and becoming wiser. Reading things before they write. Not just asking questions. Not just asking dumb questions. Becoming informed themselves before trying to inform others. Maybe they'll honor us with statues outside the entrance. Maybe this magnificent present will be enough to elevate our status and get us out of this damned place. It will be the dawn of a new information age and journalists will be its priests."

The thin one, condemned to this place for once being a jogger, assumed the top guy's reflective pose that had served him so well so long. After a moment's thought, he looked up and said, "N-a-a-w-w-w."

But they exerted their meager influence anyway, for desperate they were, and those things came to pass. All of them.

Many of the most important documents and records (and some books, too) were collected together in one building. The building and all its contents were duplicated across the land. Each building was called a *library* and a new information age was born.

Mostly, however, journalists failed to take advantage of this gift, just as the M.E. foretold, and all the world was a poorer place because of it. And the patron saints of journalism remain to this day in that place.

Why?

There's a lot of great information in a library.

Two-Step Document Searching

Let's focus first on two of the most useful sources to be found in almost any public or university library: congressional hearings and other Senate or House documents, and General Accounting Office (GAO) reports. Then we'll look at statistical sources for context, government and non-government publications useful for ideas, how to plumb some specialized areas such as businesses and legal issues, and other departments in the library.

In nearly every case, the best way to proceed is first find the index, then find the material — a two-step process that saves you and the librarian lots of time.

This method is especially useful for congressional and GAO reports, which are housed in a special enclave within the library, appropriately known as the government documents section. Often, no one in the library knows how to find things there except those librarians who have mastered the government indexing system. So when the government documents librarian is absent, the government documents are not accessible until he or she returns.

Government Hearing Reports

Government hearings and reports published in Washington, D.C., are useful for reporters in Sacramento, Dubuque or anywhere else. Here's a sampling of the nuggets of information that can be found in House or Senate hearings held in March, April and May of 1987:

- During his opening statement at an April 23 hearing of the House Committee on Government Operations, Rep. Ted Weiss, D-N.Y., said, "The committee found (previously) that (Office of Civil Rights in the Department of Education) had circumvented . . . a federal court order requiring the agency to adhere to certain enforcement guidelines, and the OCR had avoided enforcement by referring cases to the Department of Justice, which took no action in the cases.

"OCR now measures desegregation efforts based solely on a so-called good faith standard. As a result, OCR has ignored violations of civil rights laws in states where discrimination continues to exist.

"OCR's regional office staff across the country backdated documents to make them appear in compliance with (the federal court order) and submitted false information to a federal court."

He also said OCR had taken no final action in 10 states whose court-ordered desegregation plans had expired a year earlier.

The cities where the Department of Education acknowledges its offices backdated documents are Atlanta, Boston, Dallas, Kansas City, San Francisco and Seattle. The states referred to by Weiss are Arkansas, Delaware, Florida, Georgia, Missouri, North Carolina, Oklahoma, South Carolina, Virginia and West Virginia.

The committee that day accepted testimony from more than a dozen people on both sides of the issues and the hearing publication itself is nearly 400 pages.

■ An April 9 hearing before the Senate Committee on Governmental Affairs focused on why the Nuclear Regulatory Commission (NRC) needs an inspector general outside the control of the NRC commissioners.

An incident the committee was most interested in occurred a few years earlier: "It appears that in 1983 important NRC documents relating to quality assurance problems at a nuclear power plant were leaked from a commissioner's office to the licensee. In fact, a representative of the licensee distributed the leaked documents to his colleagues with the proviso that further distribution be limited, and I quote, 'to protect the source within the NRC.'

"Incredibly, when the commission was confronted with solid evidence of the possible leak from a commissioner's office, the matter was not referred to (the NRC's existing investigations arm). Instead, commission level officials made a decision that the matter should be handled within the commissioner's office and minimal 'investigation' followed with apparently little effort to make a record of such 'investigation'."

The committee also took testimony from the chief of the existing NRC investigations unit about problems in a number of cities where investigations appear less than adequate.

■ At the opening of a March 18 Senate hearing on problems in the federal war on drugs, Sen. Sam Nunn, D-Ga., cited the disturbing findings of a recent Office of Technology Assessment study.

"Despite a doubling of federal expenditures on interdiction over the last five years, the quantity of drugs smuggled in the United States is greater than ever.

"Only a small percentage of drugs are being seized, and the flow of drugs into this country has not yet been stemmed.

"There is no clear correlation between the level of expenditures or effort devoted to interdiction and the longterm availability of illegally imported drugs in the domestic market.

"Responsibilities of the federal drug interdiction agencies are fragmented and overlapping.

"A lack of an overall direction that would establish a comprehensive approach to planning and operations limits the effectiveness of the interdiction programs."

Testimony from witnesses in and out of government was surprisingly detailed about the way the war on drugs is being lost and what the country's next moves will be.

■ A House subcommittee held hearings March 19 and May 6 that detailed problems in companies across the country where serious underreporting of worker injuries was occurring and, as is usually the case with oversight hearings, produced abundant testimony and expert witnesses.

■ An April 30 House hearing produced extensive data and expert testimony on pesticides in foods, citing specific poisons in specific foods, and why the government has difficulty controlling it.

As these examples illustrate, transcripts of congressional hearings, congressional reports (fact sheets) and congressional committee prints (summaries of actions) can be valuable sources for backgrounding a complicated or controversial topic. They often contain testimony from reliable experts—potential sources for journalists—up-to-date figures, the major charges or points of interest and a useful bibliography for further research, all under one cover.

Remember, step one in the document two-step is to check the correct index. Hearings and reports are listed in the Monthly Catalog of United States Government Publications. This is the basic finding tool for most government documents. Published by the Government Printing Office (GPO), the catalog has indexes by author (since 1976), title, subject and series/report numbers. It also gives the publication's GPO stock number, which you will need, along with the title, if you plan to order your own copy from the government. The catalog designates whether the publication is a depository item, a good initial key that may determine if the publication can be found in your library.

The federal government operates a depository library system that automatically sends out the major items it publishes. There are more than 1,400 libraries participating, including one in each congressional district, so there should be one in your area.

Committee prints include studies on topics of public concern, investigative reports prepared by congressional staff to supplement information developed during the hearing process, confidential staff reports and printed memoranda, analysis of bills and other reference materials. The government has no systematic method for placing these items in depository libraries, but there are several places to look for them.

First, check the Monthly Catalog. All of the examples above are cited in the December 1987 catalog and all were obtained within minutes by the government documents librarian. A few others we wanted, however, hadn't yet arrived. Had we really needed them, we could have called the committees cited in the catalog and requested them.

For committee prints from 1970 to the present, check the Congressional Information Service (CIS) Index, a non-government monthly index that comprehensively includes committee prints along with summaries of congressional hearings, reports, documents and special publications. Earlier committee prints have been indexed in the CIS U.S. Congressional Committee Prints Index, a five-volume work that covers material from the 1830s through 1969. A companion microfiche set provides the full text of all the prints included in the index.

General Accounting Office Hearings

Reporters can benefit from the numerous investigations already done by the General Accounting Office. Created in 1921, the General Accounting Office (GAO) is the investigative arm of Congress. It examines nearly all federal government departments and programs to see how well they are operating. Its 1,000 reports and written comments each year often are as hard-hitting as any investigative series run in the news media.

GAO findings and recommendations often make front-page stories the day they are released, but the value of these studies is long-lived. For example, reporters about to start a project on the construction of a nuclear power plant will find invaluable existing GAO reports investigating cost overruns and the waste that occurs during construction.

There are two major indexes to these reports: GAO Documents, published monthly, and the Annual Report: United States General Accounting Office, which includes a catalog of audit reports issued during the fiscal year.

Here are some examples from the August 1987 GAO Documents.

- A GAO evaluation of performance of Kentucky, Indiana and Colorado in assessing and collecting civil penalties levied against coal mining operators found, among other things, the states were lenient in assessing penalties and hadn't collected $84.8 million of the $89.8 million assessed during the study period. This report had been released June 5.
- A report released July 9 found that various Interior Department agencies were owed scores of millions of dollars in delinquent royalties or fines levied against mining companies, and that much of the money would never be collected.
- A July 17 report said the Food and Drug Administration (FDA) generally had done its job with respect to its safety evaluation of aspartame and found no evidence there had been pressure on a former FDA commissioner to approve aspartame after a board of inquiry revoked an earlier approval because additional research was necessary.
- A July 20 report gave an overall okay to the inspector general operation within the General Services Administration, although it did find need for some improvements.

- A report released the same day said the financial audit of the House of Representative's Beauty Shop Revolving Fund presented the financial picture fairly.
- Another report released on July 20 said the Department of Agriculture (USDA) wasn't stopping farmers' abuse of the $50,000 payment limit in direct agricultural support. The USDA already had overpaid farmers by $15.7 million in the cases reviewed by the GAO.
- A report released on July 21 said the Department of Defense was making progress on its congressionally mandated effort to obtain warranties on weapons systems, but still had room for improvement.

Government Publications

Not even the federal government keeps track of everything it publishes, so how can you know what you want and how to get it? Although the Government Printing Office is the main publisher of federal documents, it prints only an estimated one-third of the total annual volume. The rest is printed commercially. Because so many government documents are not printed by the GPO, federal government information is not easily accessed by the public. But there is a distribution system for the more than 16,000 publications available through the GPO each year. About 3,000 new titles enter the sales inventory annually, and a similar number of titles become outdated or are superseded by revised editions.

In addition to operating 24 of its own bookstores in 21 cities around the country, the GPO maintains one of the largest mail-order services in the world, with nearly 26,000 titles available in 1986. It also administers the depository program.

Begin the two-step search with the following general publications:

- *United States Government Manual.* When trying to figure out which agencies are involved in your topic, start with the United States Government Manual. Organized by agency, it includes names and addresses, phone numbers, regional offices and, most importantly, the responsibilities of each office.
- *Congressional Directory.* Despite its title, this book has a listing of almost all higher-level government employees and agencies, including those in the judiciary and executive branches. It also contains a detailed directory of the congressional apparatus, including committees, subcommittees, boards and commissions, and biographies of all congressional members.
- *Federal Regulatory Directory.* Published by Congressional Quarterly Inc., this book gives in-depth profiles of the major regulatory agencies, including key personnel to contact, organization, information resources and regional offices. It also offers information on other agencies and departments and small units with regulatory powers, many not usually thought of as regulators. It indexes the information by agency/subject and personnel. By using the index, all the offices, agencies and personnel that regulate product safety, for instance, can be identified.

■ *Federal Information Centers.* If you need an answer to a specific question quickly, call the nearest Federal Information Center (see your local telephone directory under "United States Government"). The centers, managed by the General Services Administration, are staffed with people who have a good understanding of the responsibilities of all federal government agencies and departments, and will try to answer your questions.

Government Agency Sources

Now you have some idea of which agencies are active in your subject area. Most agencies issue publications that can be useful in an investigation.

Regulatory Agencies

There are as many as 100 government agencies that exercise some kind of regulatory authority. The forms they require, such as the 10-K for the Securities and Exchange Commission, or the LM-1 for the Department of Labor, have long been primary sources for investigative reporters looking for inside information. (These reports are detailed in the chapters that follow.) These regulatory agencies also produce hundreds of publications that can be found in libraries, including books and magazines useful for background information.

Although there is no one comprehensive list of all agency and department publications, nor are all produced by the GPO itself, three major indexes found in most libraries can help you find them: the Monthly Catalog, the Index to U.S. Government Periodicals (a quarterly index to the contents of 185 government periodicals) and the American Statistics Index. Check all three.

If you are interested in a complete list of what a particular agency publishes, the quickest way to get it is to call the agency's information officer and ask for it. This is recommended because many of the publications are not included in the GPO subscription services, and the only way you can get them is to convince the agency to put you on its mailing list. Libraries may receive some of these lists, even though they may not get most of the publications, so check there as well. Some of the larger or more active agencies, such as the Environmental Protection Agency, publish bibliographies which are often useful places to look.

Federal Advisory Committees and Commissions

More than 4,790 current and historical groups advise, or have advised, the president and various agencies and departments. These range from the eminently forgettable Advisory Committee on the Air Force Historical Program to the potentially helpful Advisory Board on Child Abuse and Neglect and National Crime Information Center Advisory Policy Board. In fact, Federal Advisory committees seem to outnumber the identified problems on the national agenda.

However ineffective this method may be for solving problems, the deliberations and recommendations of these advisory groups, such as the oft-used

Warren Commission report, can provide excellent background for reporters. The hearings held in 1968 by the National Commission on the Causes and Prevention of Violence were published in 1969 as a book, "Mass Media and Violence," that remains one of the most useful references for persons interested in the U.S. news media.

There is no single source for finding these committees and commissions or their reports. The most appropriate government index is the Monthly Catalog, although many committees are not listed. Next, check The Federal Advisory Committees: (Year) Annual Report, prepared by the General Services Administration. It lists all advisory committees initiated, in existence or terminated at the end of the fiscal year, with the responsible agency indicated, and describes activities, status and changes in the composition of advisory committees.

Another good starting point is the Encyclopedia of Advisory Organizations, an index published by Gale Research Co. It lists twice the number of committees that can be found in the government's annual report because it uses a broader definition of "advisory committee." The encyclopedia is updated with interedition supplements titled "New Government Advisory Organizations."

Sometimes you won't have the precise name of the committee or commission, so finding its publications may be difficult. For instance, the Warren Commission report was actually called the "Report of the President's Commission on the Assassination of President John F. Kennedy." Fortunately, there is a publication to help: Popular Names of U.S. Government Reports. Although this is a selective list and is not published annually, it is the place to start when you don't have the full title.

U.S. Bureau of the Census

This agency is the major source of statistics about activities and people in the United States. Its data, which can be helpful for all kinds of background information, fill volumes.

- The major government index is the Bureau of the Census Catalog. It includes product overviews, information about each census publication (agriculture, business, general construction, housing, population, transportation statistics), subscription information and sources of assistance (names and addresses of organizations offering census information and services).
- The U.S. Bureau of the Census's Statistical Abstract of the United States is the major reference for statistics related to economic, political or social conditions in the United States. It covers education, housing, government, health, labor, income, social welfare and dozens of other topics. It also lists sources at the bottom of its tables, giving reporters excellent tips on where to go for further information. Pocket Data Book, U.S.A., is an abridged version of the Statistical Abstract.
- The major non-governmental indexes for statistics from the government and elsewhere are the American Statistics Index (ASI) and the Statistical Refer-

ence Index (SRI). ASI indexes federal government statistics and SRI indexes statistics from private and state government sources, business associations and university research. Both are invaluable for locating the precise figures you need.

■ The other major government offices that publish statistical information are the Bureau of Labor Statistics, the Department of Education Center for Statistics, the National Center for Health Statistics and the Statistical Reporting Service of the Department of Agriculture.

■ Additional statistical reference works include the Congressional District Data Book, which is published by Kraus International and is based on 1980 census data. For sale through the GPO, it summarizes population and housing characteristics. It is updated as congressional districts change. The County and City Data Book has statistical tables covering all 50 states, with information about 3,137 counties and county equivalents, and all cities with 25,000 inhabitants or more. Both books can provide valuable background information, making it possible to compare conditions between your city and others.

■ If one of these conditions is the cost of living, check your library to see if it subscribes to ACCRA Inter-City Cost of Living Index, a quarterly report published by the American Chamber of Commerce Researchers Association that compares the cost of living in several hundred cities. This publication offers a city-by-city comparison of costs for specific food items, such as hamburger and peas, and also includes comparisons using broad categories, such as food, housing and utilities.

■ Another helpful publication for facts and figures related to social issues is the Public Affairs Information Service Bulletin. This index, arranged by hundreds of subjects and authors, culls its data from government documents and about 1,400 periodicals in the social sciences, as well as selected newspapers and magazines.

State Government Documents

More than two-thirds of the states operate some kind of document depository system. Usually the systems are patterned after the federal operation so that copies of major state documents and publications are automatically sent to selected libraries in the state. Depository items usually include copies of all bills and laws, state handbooks and manuals, state telephone directories and most department and agency journals and magazines.

Most states have a legislative reference library, which exists to serve the information needs of legislators. The quality of these libraries varies from state to state. Some are little more than neglected storehouses for forgotten paperwork. Some of the better libraries are open to members of the public, although materials cannot be taken out. The legislative reference library is located close to, if not in, the state capitol, so legislators can have immediate access to the materials. These libraries are major resources for state information.

For instance, the legislative reference library for Minnesota includes copies of documents, tape recordings of legislative debates and speeches, biographical information about appointees and elected officials, newspaper clipping files and position papers from businesses and organizations headquartered in the state.

State agencies produce volumes of statistical and descriptive information filled with data about the area in which you live and that compare your area with those in the rest of the state. Most states maintain a data center that publishes a catalog of documents available to the public. You may also find agency publications by looking in the Monthly Checklist of State Publications, which includes a record of all state publications received by the Library of Congress. Annual publications, series, periodicals, publications of associations of state officials and regional organizations, manuals and statistical reports are arranged by state and issuing agency.

Another good resource is The National Directory of State Agencies (annual). This book gives names and phone numbers of state legislators and office holders, and breaks down each state agency by broad subject matter.

Local Government Documents

Most of the documents published locally, such as budgets and committee reports, probably will find their way into the hands of local city hall reporters automatically. But if you are not the city hall reporter, or if you don't save much of what you receive, you can find some of what you need at the local public library. You might also try the municipal government library, if there is one, which serves a depository function much like the one mentioned for state and federal documents. The municipal government library will have a copy of every document issued by city and county government agencies and departments. Some municipal government libraries also collect information used by city government officials for decision making and management. Clip files, comparative data for cities, periodicals and journals about city management, tape recordings of public committee meetings and similar information is available for use in-house. Again, the quality of these collections and their staff varies, so use your judgment about the need to search further.

In addition to the sources for general background and comparative data about local affairs mentioned above (see Congressional District Data Book, County and City Data Book, and ACCRA Inter-City Cost of Living Index), there are at least three additional sources to check that contain useful information.

1. *The Index to Current Urban Documents* (since 1972) collects such things as budgets, annual reports, audits, environmental impact statements, planning reports and other information from 272 of the largest cities and counties in the United States and Canada. It is issued quarterly, and the information is indexed by subject and geographic area.
2. *The League of Women Voters* in some cities sends members to agency and commission meetings to take notes on the proceedings. Your branch of the

league may be a good source for information in areas that your news organization may not cover on a regular basis.

3. *The Municipal Yearbook*, published by the International City Management Association located in Washington, D.C., gives a variety of information about cities across the country. In addition to profiles of cities (by population, population changes, local government revenue, staffing and other information), the yearbook gives trends, growth, forms of government and other facts. There are succinct chapters that offer analysis and summaries of the data.

Legal References

Because we legislate, then regulate, then litigate everything imaginable in this country, it's good to know the law and why it was passed, the regulations and how they make the law work and what the courts and legal scholars say about how well it is or isn't working.

Law Documents

Before beginning an investigation, reporters should start with the law. The law passes through three phases: Congress creates the legislation; the executive branch issues regulations that interpret it and explain how it will be enforced; and the courts often decide what the law or regulations themselves actually mean.

Checking the history of a piece of legislation gives you a thorough view of what the problems were that the law was trying to address, the alternative legislation that was rejected and the primary sources for information.

The process usually involves 13 steps, each covered by one or more government publications. The steps are listed below in chronological order along with the best sources at each stage, which are usually available in libraries.

1. For background information on possible legislation and the problems Congress seeks to solve, the best sources include the weekly and annual Congressional Quarterly (CQ), the National Journal, the Congressional Record and news magazines and major U.S. newspapers.
2. When a bill has been introduced, assigned a number and referred to a committee, the best sources are the CCH Congressional Index (published by Commerce Clearing House), the Congressional Record, the Digest of Public General Bills and Resolutions, the House or Senate Calendar and the CQ Weekly Report.
3. When the bill is printed, it will be made available through the government documents depository system, and a summary will be included in the Digest of Public General Bills and Resolutions.
4. When the committee holds hearings and/or issues a committee print, the best sources include the Congressional Information Service (CIS) Index and the Monthly Catalog.

5. When the committee issues a report of its findings to the House or Senate, the best sources are the CIS Index, Congressional Serial Set, CQ Weekly Report and the Monthly Catalog.
6. When the proposed legislation actually reaches the House or Senate floor for debate, it is assigned a place on the Calendar; the best sources are the House or Senate Calendar, CIS Index, House or Senate Journal, CQ Weekly Report and the Congressional Record.
7. For records of what action was taken, check the CCH Congressional Index, the journals of the House or Senate, the Digest of Public General Bills and Resolutions, the House or Senate Calendar and CQ Weekly Report.
8. If the bill was amended or no further action was taken, check the Congressional Record for the debate. All original and substitute bills are depository items.
9. If passed, the bill becomes an act of Congress and is sent to the president for his signature. Check the Congressional Record.
10. If signed, the act becomes a law and is assigned a Public Law number. Check the U.S. Statutes at Large. If the act is vetoed and returned to Congress, check the Weekly Compilation of Presidential Documents. Check here also if you want to know whether the president made a statement when signing the legislation.
11. Once the law has been codified, check the U.S. Code Congressional and Administrative News, which gives texts and legislative history of all laws and is organized by session.
12. If you know a bill by subject or name but don't have the public law or bill number, start with the CCH Congressional Index, CQ Weekly Report or Almanac, the Congressional Record, the House or Senate Calendar, U.S. Code, U.S. Code Congressional and Administrative News or the Monthly Catalog.
13. If you have the public law number and seek the bill number, check with the CCH Congressional Index, CIS Index, Digest of Public General Bills and Resolutions or the House or Senate Calendar.
    If you have the bill or public law number and you seek the committee report, check the CCH Congressional Index, Congressional Record, Digest of Public General Bills and Resolutions or the House or Senate Calendar.

The motives and backgrounds of the bill's sponsors and opponents often help a reporter and reader understand how the legislative process really works. There are three major sources to begin backgrounding. Start with the Congressional Directory for general information on members of Congress, then check a CQ Annual for how they have voted on related legislation. Next, look at the current editions of the Almanac of American Politics or its competing book, Politics in America: Members of Congress in Washington for further background, including where your legislators stand on major issues, how they are rated by special interest groups, what their background was before they were elected, chances of getting re-elected and special concerns.

Federal legislation can be tracked by computer, too. These data bases have the advantage of more tailored searching capabilities.

Regulations

Once a law is enacted, it is up to the executive branch to implement it, and that is done through the regulations it issues. Federal regulations are the place to start during an investigation of government performance, including how local government has spent federal funds. One thing to look at is whether agency personnel are complying with the law. Is the agency doing what it is supposed to be doing? Has it refrained from doing the things it is prohibited from doing?

The basic source for these regulations is the Federal Register, a publication that is published five days a week. It contains the new rules and regulations of the executive branch, including those of the independent regulatory agencies; proposed rules and regulations and the dates they go into effect; notices of organizational changes and opinions that are advisory and nonbinding; schedules of open or closed meetings of commissions, boards and other bodies; miscellaneous announcements; and compliance rules for the Freedom of Information Act. It also contains a section on presidential documents, such as executive orders and other rulings that effectively have the force of law. A helpful pamphlet to start with when learning to use the register is The Federal Register: What It Is and How to Use It, a depository item.

Just as all laws are codified in the U.S. Code, so too are federal regulations codified in the Code of Federal Regulations (CFR), the annual compilation of the Federal Register. This is the place to start unless you seek information in the current year, which won't yet have been compiled. For current information, check the Federal Register Index (monthly) or the CIS Federal Register Index (weekly). Aids for finding the regulations are printed at the beginning of each publication.

The Federal Register Finding Aid Guide, published annually, cross-references related material in the U.S. Government Manual, Weekly Compilation of Presidential Documents, Public Papers of the Presidents, Statutes at Large and the U.S. Code.

The basic index is the CFR Index and Finding Aids, published twice a year. Federal regulations may also be tracked by computer. (See the section on data bases in this chapter.)

Court Decisions

Because we are a litigious society, many of our laws and regulations end up being tested, refined, reinterpreted, rewritten or thrown out in court. Tracking these court decisions needn't be left to lawyers or law clerks.

There are three major finding aids: those developed by West Publishing Co., by Shepard's Inc. and by the Lawyers Co-operative Publishing Co., in cooperation with Bancroft-Whitney Co. All have publications designed to guide a researcher through their tracking systems of tens of thousands of opinions issued by courts each year.

In general, first check with the law librarian to find which commercial index is available in the library and how to use it. It doesn't take long to learn what the law is or, at least, gain enough understanding to ask specialists for interpretations.

Remember, we are talking about two legal systems—state and federal. In general, lower court rulings are superseded by higher courts, and federal decisions supersede those made by state or local judges.

Second, check to see if your subject has been treated in the various law reviews and journals. These can help you understand the law, giving opinions on what cases mean, on the weaknesses of existing legislation and on identifying experts to contact. Start with the Index to Legal Periodicals, which is arranged by subject.

Third, find a lawyer specializing in your subject area. There are two places to check: If there is a law school located nearby, start there. If not, check the Martindale-Hubbell Directory, found in most libraries, which lists attorneys, fees, major clients and areas of specialty. It is possible to skip all these procedures and just start by asking lawyers you trust, but this leaves you at the mercy of the lawyers' ignorance and biases, toward either you or the law, with no information with which to evaluate their opinions. Without adequate background, you may never be able to get at what you want, nor will the lawyers always be able to divine what you need.

If you need the information quickly and have a bit of money, or want to save a lot of time on a large research project, two computer indexing services, LEXIS and WESTLAW, are available at many large law or university libraries. (See the section on data bases in this chapter.)

Backgrounding Business

Some common sources to investigate businesses are available in your media organization library or the public library, and you need no Freedom of Information Act to get at them. The most comprehensive business index is the Business Periodicals Index, which covers magazines (and book reviews) dealing with a wide range of business activities. Other indexes include the Business Publications Index and Abstracts, which indexes and summarizes information in 700 periodicals and thousands of books; the Public Affairs Information Service Bulletin, which indexes about 1,400 publications in the social sciences (see "U.S. Bureau of the Census" in this chapter); the Predicasts F & S Index United States, considered the best weekly index for current information on U.S. companies and industries (it also publishes indexes on foreign companies, the annual Predicasts F & S Index International and the monthly Predicasts F & S Index Europe); the Social Sciences Index, which includes economics among the 270 journals it indexes; Current Contents; Social and Behavioral Sciences, a weekly publication that reproduces the tables of contents of more than 1,000 periodicals, including many in business and economics; the New York Times Index; and the Wall Street Journal Index.

For U.S. government publications, check the Commerce Publications Update, the Monthly Catalog and the CCH Congressional Index.

Perhaps the best single book about finding business information is Business Information Sources by Lorna M. Daniells, published by the University of California Press. This book is essential for reporters who will need to research any aspect of business.

There are three basic directories, all published annually with supplements issued throughout the year. All can usually be found in large libraries.

1. *Dun & Bradstreet Million Dollar Directory* lists more than 160,000 companies in five volumes, citing major officers, board of directors, products and services, sales, number of employees and appropriate addresses and telephone numbers. The Directory is indexed alphabetically by company, location and industry classification.
2. *Standard & Poor's Register of Corporations, Directors and Executives* contains three volumes. It lists approximately the same kinds of information for about 38,000 U.S. and Canadian companies, and includes biographies of major figures in business.
3. *The Thomas Register of American Manufacturers* and *Thomas Catalog File* include 21 volumes, which are more comprehensive than either of the above sources. One of their indexes is organized by specific product and includes common trade names.

In addition to these standard references, there are four other sources your library may have purchased:

1. *The Directory of Industry Data Sources*, a five-volume sourcebook published by Ballinger, lists information on market research studies, financial investment reports, special issues of trade journals, statistical reports and studies, economic forecasts, numeric data bases, industry conference reports and government reports. It also includes a listing of monographs, working papers and dissertations.
2. *The European Marketing Data and Statistics* and its companion volume, International Marketing Data and Statistics, both published by Euromonitor Publications Limited, are useful for researching foreign or international firms. The 22nd edition of European Marketing Data and Statistics includes a summary of the latest published statistics on all basic marketing concerns, including the market for consumer goods, along with a full range of market estimates and calculations prepared by Euromonitor. For instance, you can find figures for the butter consumption of France, the likely demand for wool in Germany and similar information.
4. *The Directory of European Business Information*, published by Ballinger, gives information on more than 7,500 businesses.

All of these references are good for data; most are also good for giving you the names of potential sources. In addition, there are several others that should be checked.

- *The Research Centers Directory* annotates more than 6,000 institutions, centers, laboratories and the like by category, including those related to business and labor.
- *The Foundation Directory* lists major U.S. foundations by state and indexes them by category, including those concerning themselves with economics issues.
- *The Directory of Newsletters* lists thousands of newsletters, many related to business and economics. The editors and writers of these publications are also excellent sources because a newsletter makes its money by being ahead of the news.
- *Consumer's Resource Handbook* lists more than 2,000 names and addresses of federal, state and local consumer protection offices, corporate consumer offices, trade associations, consumer-mediation groups and Better Business Bureaus.

(For information of a more specific nature, check the listings of required Securities and Exchange Commission and Federal Trade Commission reports, as well as other sources, detailed in Chapter 11, "Business." That chapter explains how to use these reports and how to investigate a company in the section entitled "Getting Started," and how to use each document specifically is explained after each listing in "Public Documents" and "Other Documents.")

Backgrounding Individuals

If you are researching a specific person, start with Biography and Genealogy Master Index, which compiles the names of people whose biographies have appeared in a biographical directory, dictionary, reference book or magazine. The Biography Index and the Obituary Index to The New York Times also may be useful.

Next, check the Who's Who publications, such as Who's Who in the World, International Who's Who, Who's Who in America, Who's Who in the East and so on. Also check Current Biography, Dictionary of National Biography or the Who Was Who in America with World Notables (for those deceased) and appropriate specialized sources, such as Who's Who in the Arts, Who's Who in Finance and Industry, American Men and Women of Science or Who's Who in Religion.

If your person is an author, check Contemporary Authors, Index to Literary Biography or Authors in the News. Then check Book Review Digest, Book Review Index or Current Book Review Citations to see what the experts thought about the author's work. Also, check the letters to the editor of the magazines that run these reviews to see if someone wrote about the author in subsequent issues, especially if you are reading the author's articles.

If you need experts, and the sources mentioned above weren't sufficient, check the Research Centers Directory, the Foundation Directory, Encyclopedia of Associations and the Directory of Directories, all arranged by broad topic area. For Washington, D.C., sources, check the Washington Information Directory, a list of more than 5,000 sources in and out of government; the Directory of Public Information Contacts, which contains names, addresses and telephone numbers of U.S. government agencies' public affairs officials and information contacts at foreign embassies in Washington; the Researcher's Guide to Washington Experts, a list of more than 13,000 federal data experts, indexed by name and subject area; and The Capital Source, a semi-annual directory of names, titles, addresses and telephone numbers of people and organizations in the federal government, foreign embassies, local Washington, D.C., government, think tanks, major corporations, union and interest groups, trade associations, law firms, advertising agencies, public relations firms and other organizations.

Experts working for specialized publications can be located by using the Standard Rate and Data Service (SRDS) volumes (for "Business Publications" and "Consumer Magazines"), which list thousands of special-interest and trade publications, along with names of major staff members.

Other Sources

Reporters looking for background information will, of course, find a great deal of useful information in other books and periodicals in the library. The basic index to the contents of the library is the catalog, whether in book, card or electronic form. The catalog is indexed by author, title and subject area. An electronic catalog allows reporters to search by keyword along with the more formal methods of searching, so that the phrase "acid rain" can be used as a search term to locate all books and journals in the library that contain those words in the title or subject fields. The most common tool for finding information in about 180 popular periodicals published in this country is the Reader's Guide to Periodical Literature. But there are more than 50,000 magazines published in the United States, most of which are not included in the Reader's Guide.

Nearly every field of endeavor has specialized indexes. For example, scholarly journals are indexed in a variety of subject indexes. Check the library catalog, or the listing of all serials a library receives, and refer to the indexes of the periodicals that look promising. Special subject indexes such as Applied Science and Technology Index, Current Index to Journals in Education or Biological and Agricultural Index may lead you to the information you are seeking.

For example, the company president you are trying to profile won't talk to you. He never talks to local reporters, but it's quite likely he has talked to the trade press and by diligently searching these specialized magazines, you may get his view on things secondhand.

Newspaper indexes are commonly found in large libraries. Separate indexes are available for the New York Times, Wall Street Journal, Christian Science Monitor, Chicago Tribune, Los Angeles Times and Washington Post. Bell & Howell Newspaper Indexes cover a number of important regional newspapers, such as the Denver Post, Detroit News, New Orleans Times-Picayune, San Francisco Chronicle and others. The Canadian Newspaper Index includes a subject and name index for Canada's leading newspapers (Montreal Gazette, Toronto Globe and Mail, Toronto Star, Vancouver Sun, Winnipeg Free Press, Calgary Herald and Halifax Chronicle Herald).

Broadcast news programs are also indexed. The major resource likely to be found in libraries is the Television News Index and Abstracts, which covers the national evening news as broadcast by ABC, CBS and NBC since 1972. It serves as the index to the Vanderbilt University Television News Archives of news videotapes. "The MacNeil Lehrer Report," 1976 to date, is a printed index to microform transcripts of all its programs.

Specialized Libraries

You may need a more specialized library collection than that of the public library. Depending on the city in which you are working, there may be hundreds of specialized library collections that can be tapped. Identifying the library most likely to collect information on your topic is easy, using one of two different directories. The American Library Directory lists 37,148 libraries in the United States and Canada, organized by state and city. All the libraries located in Denver, Colorado, for instance, are listed together, along with information about collection size, special materials the libraries contain, staffing, loan policies and collection development budget. The directory contains information about public, academic, government, law, medical, religious and armed services libraries.

The other major directory that can help identify appropriate libraries for an investigation is the Directory of Special Libraries and Information Centers. This directory lists 18,000 special libraries, information centers, archives and data centers in several volumes. Volume One is organized by library name and includes a description of each library listed. A subject index at the end of Volume One groups together all libraries with an emphasis on health care, for instance. Volume Two includes the "Geographic and Personnel Indexes," and Volume Three contains "New Special Libraries" (a periodic supplement to Volume One). Special libraries often collect materials that general libraries cannot afford or do not need. It, therefore, pays to check whether there is a special library of materials on your investigation topic nearby.

Data Bases

Another way to get information is to ask the librarian to do a data base search for you. The chartered Lockheed Electra exploded and crashed shortly after takeoff from Reno, Nev., killing 70 passengers and crew members returning to Minneapolis from a gambling junket. The date was Jan. 21, 1985. Most of the dead were from Minnesota and the tragedy mobilized scores of reporters, photographers and editors to get information and images on all the angles they could think of for the next day's editions.

A half dozen Star Tribune reporters and photographers flew to Reno, while many more stayed in the Twin Cities to work the phones, find relatives of the deceased and undertake other efforts to round out the coverage.

The next-day story produced by reporter Joe Rigert and research librarian William Rafferty was an exclusive; it started in front of a computer in the newspaper's library.

Rigert set out to examine the accident record of the airplane. Was it unsafe compared to other aircraft? Was it prone to having mechanical problems?

After briefly interviewing Rigert about what he wanted, Rafferty selected NEXIS, a commercial data base containing each day's wire service articles. "Nexis has more local and regional news from around the country than any other single national news source. This is especially useful for news about demonstrations, accidents, murders or news about plane crashes," Rafferty said.

Data bases are electronic libraries. There are thousands available, and they cover nearly all topics. Some specialize in specific topics, such as chemistry or daily actions by the federal government or patents. Some specialize in news publications and wire services.

They can save reporters a lot of time because they can take two concepts, such as organized crime and waste haulers, capture all citations with those two terms and eliminate all the citations where both don't occur.

Instead of being forced to look at every organized crime article to see if it also has information about the mob and its garbage contracts, the computer does it for you and ignores the rest. These data bases earn their reputations by being inclusive on the topic. This means they may have citations not available in the local library, even if you took the time to read through everything. Most data base services will get you the material you seek.

Rafferty started with a broad search, linking Lockheed and Electra with accidents or crashes. The computer found more than 100 articles. Some of these were useful because news accounts gave specific details about other crashes involving the airplane.

Rafferty and Rigert decided to reduce the number of general stories by narrowing the search. They combined the initial concepts with "causes" of the accidents. In this phase, articles citing reports from such agencies as the National Transportation Safety Board (NTSB) and the Federal Aviation Administration were found.

Rigert liked what he was getting: "The NTSB, which investigates airline accidents and recommends corrective action, had found that the Electra had the worst fatal accident rate per hours of flight of any aircraft in common use for a 10-year period. The rate was more than twice that of the Convair propjets and at least five times that of jet airliners.

"The data base search also turned up reports over the years of the plane crashing or being forced to make emergency landings because wings or propellors fell off."

Working by telephone, Rigert supplemented the data base findings with a list of the 17 major crashes of such planes (one of every 10 in the air) and other problems. He obtained this information from federal agencies and an aviation safety watchdog group. The result was a strong, exclusive article produced under stringent daily deadlines.

According to surveys, more and more news organizations are including data base services in their libraries. Electronic searching has enormous power for both finding things you otherwise wouldn't even know existed and for saving hours of tedious research. The actual time it took for Rafferty and Rigert to do the actual computer search is measured in minutes.

So what's the catch?

First, it costs money. Data bases charge from $35 per hour to several hundred dollars per hour. In addition, many charge for each citation you read and for the cost of long-distance phone calls which may be necessary for your computer to talk to theirs.

You can, however, do simpler searches that limit the cost. You can tell a librarian, for instance, not to spend more than $20 or $30. A low-cost search can still save you a great deal of time.

Second, many data bases have only the citation or abstract of the report you need. That means you have to make an additional call and wait to get the actual document. In recent years, however, more and more data bases are inserting the full text into the computer. Why? Because it's more useful for many searchers and the data base can get more money from you for providing the full text as opposed to just an abstract. If you're on deadline, it's worth it.

Finally, data base searching is a sophisticated skill. The articles are filed away by librarians. It takes a trained searcher to be sure you're using the correct terms in the appropriate data bases, or you could waste lots of money on a fruitless search. That means you might have to use an intermediary to find the information.

So, how do you take advantage of the technology?

- *If your news organization does data base searching, get to know the searchers as if they were sources for important stories.* Show them some of the stories you've written over the past year and ask them how, if at all, they might have been improved with a data base search. Ask what data bases they have access to and some examples of how they've already improved stories written by your colleagues.
- *Read some articles on the topic.* There are lots of them available at your local library.
- *Consider getting some training.* Check the local college or university. Ask to be included in the training your researchers may get from the data base vendors.

■ *Learn to check regularly with the researcher on stories you are doing or are thinking of doing.* As Rafferty said about the search he did for Rigert, "I think the success of this particular search, as in most searches, was partly fortuitous. But I stress the importance of the collaborative relationship between reporter and library researcher pooling their knowledge of sources and search skills. Often it is the brainstorming and suggesting before and during the search process that will build a superior strategy and result in better search results."

Conclusion

This chapter should convince you that the information available in a library can be valuable. Take the time to acquaint yourself now with its holdings so you can save time later, when you're on deadline.

Computer Access

by John R. Bender
Editor, FOI Notebook

In 1982, the New York City Police Department started placing many of its records in a computer system that would help it keep track of each person arrested at each stage of the criminal justice process. In Montgomery County, Pa., lawyers with personal computers and modems have 24-hour telephone access to computerized court records. In Florida's Dade County, government workers use their word processors to flash messages to one another, messages that often never exist in paper copy.

State and local governments are finding many ways to handle public business more cheaply and effectively with computers, and reporters who cover government issues are finding that computer records can help them, too.

Elliot Jaspin, formerly of The Providence Journal-Bulletin, used a computer tape with records of 30,000 state mortgages to find that some of them had gone to wealthy persons with political connections instead of the low- and moderate-income persons for whom they were intended. Within five days of getting the tape, Jaspin had learned of a secret mortgage slush fund for politicians and had printed a story.

By contrast, another Journal-Bulletin reporter, Christopher Scanlan, needed two years to prepare a series on arson in Rhode Island that identified landlords with a history of arson and the neighborhoods with the highest arson rates. Although Scanlan used a computer to analyze the data, he had to enter 72,000 pieces of information from paper records on 7,000 punch cards.

The difference between access to paper records and access to computer records is the difference between two years and five days, Jaspin said. In some cases it may determine whether the story is done at all.

The problem is that some officials and judges have been reluctant to grant reporters the same degree of access to computer records that they have to paper records. For example, an Arkansas judge in 1976 refused to declare a computerized voting list a public record. The judge said the tapes were more like office equipment than records.

Because of such attitudes, reporter Thomas J. Moore said, "We need to set the precedent that when you talk about files, these (computer records) are now the government's file cabinets." Moore, who was a national correspondent for the Knight-Ridder Newspapers' Washington bureau at the time, has done several projects using federal computer records.

Some records custodians are equally concerned about the problems computer records may create. These concerns prompted the Public Records Division of the Office of the Massachusetts Secretary of State to call a national conference in January 1987 on public access to computer records.

According to Timothy B. Gassert, legal counsel for the Public Records Division and first assistant legal counsel for the Secretary of State, Massachusetts officials saw three problems emerging from requests for access to electronic records.

"First," he said, "it is difficult for records custodians to transpose existing access principles into computer access principles.

"Another concern is the ready availability of vast quantities of individually identifiable information" and the ability to use it to construct personal profiles of individuals.

A third problem, Gassert said, is that the commercial value of much of the information kept in government computers is greater than what custodians may charge for releasing it under existing laws.

How states address these problems will determine largely whether press and public access to state and local computer records will be generous or grudging.

The open records laws that journalism organizations pushed through state legislatures in the 1960s and 1970s usually assumed that the information was on paper. As soon as governments started keeping records in computer—and reporters started to see how useful such records could be—questions arose about whether the old laws applied to the new electronic records.

Although some early cases like the 1976 Arkansas decision seemed to indicate that computer records would be treated differently, most of the records custodians and others who attended the Massachusetts conference believe existing access laws cover such records.

A 1988 nationwide survey conducted by the Public Records Division found that the laws in 34 states address computer records. Sixteen had definitions of "public record" that specifically included information in computers. Another 14 states had definitions broad enough to encompass such information. In the other four states, the courts or agencies had interpreted the records laws to include computer records.

The survey found no state that exempts from disclosure information stored in computers, but that does not mean persons requesting copies of the documents will receive tapes or disks. Several states let records custodians decide the form in which the information will be released.

According to California's Public Records Act, "Computer data shall be provided in a form determined by the agency." In other states, the statutory language is less blunt. The 1986 revision of the New Hampshire law, for example, says that for records maintained in computer systems, officials "may, in lieu of providing original documents, provide a printout." In South Carolina, the 1987 law says records should be disclosed in the form that is most convenient and practical for the user so long as it is equally convenient for the public agency to provide the records in that form.

State courts usually have held that computer tapes or disks are public records and must be disclosed, even when the information is available in another form. In 1971, for example, the New Mexico Supreme Court held that the public records law applied to computerized voter registration information as well as the written affidavits of registration. Since then, courts in such varied jurisdictions as New York, New Hampshire, South Carolina and Minnesota have reached similar conclusions. The New Hampshire and South Carolina decisions were handed down before the recent changes in the records laws of those states.

Recognition that computer records are public records does not answer all the legal questions. One of the thornier issues is the status of the software used to create and process the information stored in government computers. Public officials, state laws and courts are divided on whether such programs are public records.

Some officials who attended the Massachusetts conference said they had no objections to public access to programs created by government agencies, but private software vendors may not want to do business with governments if their programs will become public records. The issue, many said, is one that will require a statutory solution.

At least eight states—Illinois, Indiana, Kansas, Minnesota, Missouri, Oklahoma, Virginia and Wisconsin—have statutes that specifically say software need not be disclosed, and Oregon exempts software held by the Corporation Division of the state's Department of Commerce. Virginia's law, for example, has one provision that exempts software "developed by or for a state agency" and a separate provision protecting software purchased from private vendors. In many other states, programs sold by private software vendors might be exempt under the trade secret provisions of their laws.

Sometimes, computerized information must be redacted before release to delete exempt information. If this requires the creation of a new program, the cost usually must be borne by the requester.

The Connecticut Supreme Court ruled in a 1984 case that if an agency's computer contains both public information and information exempt from disclosure but the agency's programs cannot delete the exempt information, the agency still may be required to release the public information if the requester pays the cost of programming the computer to retrieve it.

The Massachusetts survey found 13 states that would create such programs at the requester's expense, but 12 said flatly they would not do so no matter who paid. Indiana imposes an additional barrier to access. While Indiana agencies are required to segregate exempt information in records and disclose the rest, this provision does not apply to information on computer tapes or disks where it is available in another form. The survey found only one state, Illinois, where the law would seem to require that agencies create programs to redact records at their own expense.

A related question is whether a new record is created when an existing record is redacted or several records are collapsed into a summary. A truism often repeated in open records cases is that the laws require disclosure only of existing records, not the creation of new ones.

Most courts follow the reasoning of the U.S. Court of Appeals for the District of Columbia in a 1982 case where it held that deleting information—even almost all of it—from a document did not mean a new document had been created, but agencies are not required to collapse information exempt from disclosure into a nonexempt form.

A New York appellate court took a similar position in a 1980 case in which it told a school district to release standardized test scores with the names of the students deleted and the scores scrambled out of alphabetical order. Although the New York court agreed that the state Freedom of Information Law did not require creation of new records, the law defined "record" as "any information" held by a state agency. Scrambling the test scores did not amount to creating new information, the court said.

Regardless of what the laws may say, reporters sometimes find that officials are more wary of releasing computer tapes and disks than they are of disclosing paper files. That reluctance is partly a product of the realization that report-

ers with access to computer data have a more powerful tool for studying the actions of government because they are able to go through entire records systems very quickly.

"That's frightening to government, for now their activities are transparent," said Joel Rawson, executive editor of Lexington's Herald-Leader.

David Ashenfelter, a reporter with the Detroit Free Press, has used computer tapes from the Michigan Department of Corrections for several projects. He said when he first ordered tapes in 1983, officials released a lot of information used to prepare demographic profiles of convicts. The next time he asked for information from the Department of Corrections, he did not get as much data.

"At first they give lots of information, but when they find out what we're doing they invoke privacy exemptions," Ashenfelter said.

Don Gemberling, director of the Data Privacy Division of the Minnesota Department of Administration, said officials sometimes are reluctant to release computer records because the public increasingly is aware of the privacy issues such data systems raise. But the officials do comply with the law, he said.

Those laws may become more restrictive as legislators and the public become more concerned about access to computer records. Gassert said the Massachusetts General Court recently considered a measure that would allow access to government records only in paper form even though they might be available on computers. Although this bill died, the legislature did approve a law that prohibits disclosure of assessors' records maintained in computers.

Most of the assessment records remain available in paper form, Gassert said.

As more records find their way into government computers, more people worry about the use of computers to invade privacy, either by the government or by the press or private business.

For some students of the problem, the simple fact that the records are on computers increases the opportunities for invasions of privacy.

A 1977 report by the Privacy Protection Study Commission of the American Civil Liberties Union Foundation says that among the threats to privacy posed by interconnected computer data systems is the ability of computers to scan large data bases and match information in two or more systems. Persons using computers in this manner could construct a mosaic of information, called a personal data composite, that might invade privacy even if the individual pieces do not.

Robert Brennan, director of data processing for the City of Quincy, Mass., presented to the Massachusetts conference on computerized public records a scenario illustrating this fear.

Enterprising burglars, Brennan suggested, could compile a data base by requesting tapes or disks of municipal records. From these records, they could construct profiles of all the homes in the city, a district or a neighborhood. These profiles—which might include the assessed valuation of the home, occupations of the owners, number of children, pets, and number of automobiles— would show the burglars which homes were potentially the most lucrative and most vulnerable targets.

A Providence Journal-Bulletin project that Jaspin said would have been impossible without computers illus-

trates a more public-spirited use of the power to match records. Using records on 5,000 school bus drivers, 500,000 criminal court cases and 300,000 traffic accidents, the Journal-Bulletin found that many Rhode Island school bus drivers had horrible traffic records. The paper also found that some of them had convictions for drug trafficking.

The fear that public access to computer records might endanger privacy could produce a backlash opposing access to government records, a backlash reporters might be able to avoid by using records responsibly.

Rawson said the legislative climate is one that favors closure of records to the public and the press. If computer records are used in ways that hurt people, then that climate of closure will be encouraged, but if the use is acceptable, the public will support access.

Reporters familiar with computer systems say many of the fears that press or public access threatens privacy are unfounded or greatly exaggerated.

Moore said one reason access to computer records need not lead to invasions of privacy is that truly private records are not available to the press in any form. But even more important is the fact that it is easier for government to "sanitize" computer records than paper records.

Ashenfelter agreed. If particular pieces of information in a computer data system are private but the rest is not, the government can instruct the computer to blank out those fields with the private information. The problem Ashenfelter has encountered is that records custodians sometimes blank out more than they need to because they fear being sued.

Peter G. Gosselin, a reporter for The Boston Globe, used Treasury Department computer tapes to prepare a series on money laundering. He said the fears of invasion of privacy are unfounded if both records custodians and reporters are knowledgeable about computers.

Gosselin used Treasury Department reports of cash transactions in excess of $10,000, records that are potentially sensitive. To get access, the Globe had to write its own program to retrieve the information subject to conditions that were the product of several months of negotiations with Treasury officials.

Among other things, the Globe promised not to look for individual names and to aggregate information in such ways that it would be impossible to identify individuals. Treasury Department programmers checked the Globe's program to make sure it was retrieving only the information agreed to.

Records custodians are more likely than reporters to see a danger in the possibility that bits of electronic data may be assembled in ways that would invade privacy, but they usually agree that computer records should be no less open than the same records in other forms.

Justin Keay, manager of the California Office of Information Practices, oversees that state's privacy laws. He said the possibility of invading privacy by assembling bits of public information "has been a potential threat for a long time." But the fact that information is in a computer should not make a difference in the right of access.

Don Gemberling of Minnesota's Data Privacy Division said, "Philosophically, the ability to profile individuals personally concerns me, but the reality is that if the data are public, then that doesn't change because you put them together."

A greater threat to privacy than the curiosity of reporters is the possibility that government will misuse the vast amounts of information it stores in computers.

"Government is very intrusive into private lives," said Mitchell W. Pearlman, executive director of the Connecticut Freedom of Information Commission. In the process of doing their jobs, government bureaucrats collect lots of information about individuals. Some of it is relevant to the government's job and some is not, but more and more of it is going into computers.

Pearlman recommended independent audits of agency records to decide what needs to be kept and what does not, but he added, "The costs of attacking the problem are monumental."

Jan Goldman, a staff attorney on the American Civil Liberties Union's project on privacy and technology, said what is needed is a national information policy. Such a policy would describe what information the government can have, how it would be used and who would have access to it. At present, the emphasis is on efficiency, not privacy, and these larger questions are being ignored, she said.

While few argue that records in computers should be treated differently from paper records under access laws, there is broad interest in restricting the kinds and quantity of data that governments collect or in making confidential any information that is potentially intrusive. So while the reporter who works with computer records may have the same right of access as one who works with paper records, both may find the supply of available government information diminished in the computer age.

Much of the information in government computers is itself a commercially valuable commodity. Government records custodians are worried that entrepreneurs will take information gathered at great expense to the taxpayers and use it to reap enormous profits. If the people come to see government information as a subsidy to private business, they may become suspicious of government and its efforts to collect information.

Several procedures have been suggested that would make it easier for government to restrict or deny access to commercially valuable information.

One suggestion is to decide whether a record is public by its form, and records in electronic form (and therefore of greater commercial value) would be exempt from disclosure. This proposal would gut state access laws, allowing public officials to avoid scrutiny by placing records in computers.

Another suggestion is to make the requester's intended use of the record the basis for deciding whether to grant access to it. Rhode Island, for example, prohibits the commercial use of information obtained from public records. Violations are punishable by a fine of up to $500 and imprisonment for up to one year. This approach has several defects. One is that requesters might lie about how they intend to use the information, or they could hire a "straw man" to request the records. In any case once a record became public, there would be little government could do to restrict its use.

A third approach, one many states are already using, is to charge higher fees for access to commercially valuable information.

The Massachusetts survey found that states take a variety of factors—printout costs, computer time, costs of program or data base creation, clerical time and others—into consideration when setting fees for access to computer records. Moreover, fees often vary from agency to agency and the laws allow custodians to consider such factors as commercial value in setting the fees.

Minnesota allows agencies to charge persons seeking access to government records a portion of the cost of the development of the program or data base if it has commercial value, Gemberling said.

Justin Keay said the California information practices law generally prohibits the release of information for commercial use unless there is specific statutory approval. In one case where the legislature has granted such approval for motor vehicle records, large-scale commercial users are charged substantial fees.

When commercial value is a factor, the cost of access can go up quickly. In Arizona, a person requested access to a computer tape containing 400,000 Uniform Commercial Code filings. The Secretary of State's office initially refused to produce copies of the tape, but after the requester filed a lawsuit, the Attorney General's office and attorneys for the requester began negotiations over the price for the tapes. Arizona law says that when records are requested for commercial purposes, the custodian of the records may charge a fee based on the cost to the state of obtaining the record, the cost of reproduction and the value of the reproduction on the commercial market. The last figure the state asked was $31,543, according to John Shadegg, special assistant attorney general. The requester neither paid the price nor challenged it in court.

Reporters using computer records that have little commercial value are often able to purchase copies at much lower prices, in part, because it is usually easier and cheaper for the government to duplicate computer tapes than to copy paper documents.

David Ashenfelter said one of his first computer projects, a 1983 story on the disparities in manslaughter sentences handed down by Michigan judges, was based in part on a Department of Corrections tape he obtained for $75. During a more extensive 1985 project on early releases of prisoners, he purchased the entire Department of Corrections' prisoner data base for $400.

Much of this may seem far removed from the worries of a reporter or editor, but any effort to restrict access to commercially valuable public records involves the creation of a "dangerous distinction," as Elliot Jaspin has described it, because almost any record could be commercially valuable.

Although news reporting is not considered a commercial use, newspapers and broadcasting stations are commercial enterprises, and information compiled by reporters might also prove useful to advertising or circulation departments.

The Providence Journal-Bulletin has acquired from state and local governments computer records of various kinds for several years, including information on state finances and state purchasing that could be commercially useful, Jaspin said. To comply with the Rhode Island prohibition on the commercial use of these records, the Journal-Bulletin does not let its circulation and advertising departments use the records, he said.

The danger of the commercially valuable information distinction is that while governments might not use it to deny reporters' requests for information, they may try to charge higher fees (in states where they are allowed) on the basis that the records might be used for commercial purposes.

While most states seem to be moving in the direction of treating access to computer records the same as other records, journalists and news organizations need to be alert to possible wrinkles in laws that could thwart access.

One major concern is laws that give records custodians discretion about whether to release computer information in the form of printouts or copies of tapes or disks. Considering the ease with which computer records can be copied, such discretion seems hard to justify.

Another issue is access to the software necessary to decode and use government data. Those requesting records may have to purchase any commercial software the agency is using, but where government has prepared its own, denial of access to the software may equal denial of the information.

Access may also be restricted by laws that treat redacted or collapsed records as new records. The maxim that agencies need not create new records to fill access requests is a reasonable way of limiting the government's burden to process paper records, but it fails to take into account the ability of computers to edit or summarize records quickly and with little human effort. Access laws in the computer age should afford the public reasonable opportunity to benefit from the power of these machines.

Concerns about invasions of privacy may lead to more exemptions to open records laws, broader definitions of when access jeopardizes privacy and the elimination of some records systems. These changes may be needed to protect legitimate privacy interests, but they may also make it more difficult for citizens to monitor their governments.

Finally, efforts to restrict access to commercially valuable data must be limited to make sure that the definition of "commercial information" is not so broad that it swallows the general principle of access.

The proliferation of computer records systems often conjures up Orwellian visions of government out of control but, according to Jaspin, computers offer the possibility of making government more accountable. With computers to help make sense of government information, he said, 20th-century citizens may be able to follow and influence government's workings just as did the gentlemen farmers of the 18th century.

Federal Computer Records

by John R. Bender
Editor, FOI Notebook

If the status of computer records held by state governments is cloudy because of the diversity of access laws, the status of federal records is not much clearer.

The Freedom of Information Act makes no mention of computers. When the act was amended in 1974, the Senate Report explaining the amendments made only one reference: computer searches for records are analogous to manual searches. From this brief mention, federal courts have generally held that the FOIA applies as fully to computer records as to any others.

In 1979, Judge Anthony M. Kennedy of the 9th U.S. Circuit Court of Appeals reversed a lower court ruling that the FOIA did not apply to computer tapes.

"In view of the common, widespread use of computers by government agencies for information storage and processing, any interpretation of the FOIA which limits its application to conventional written documents contradicts the 'general philosophy of full agency disclosure.'... We conclude that the FOIA applies to computer tapes to the same extent it applies to any other documents," wrote Kennedy, who now is on the U.S. Supreme Court.

A 1982 decision by the District of Columbia U.S. Circuit Court of Appeals agreed that records stored in computers are covered by the FOIA. But where Judge Kennedy's decision seemed to say the act required release in electronic form, the D.C. Circuit's opinion, written by Judge Edward A. Tamm, left that question open. On appeal, the government had argued that the FOIA did not require release of magnetic tapes, but because that issue was not before the district court, the appeals court refused to consider it.

One important case where the courts decided against access to a computer record was SDC Development Corp. v. Matthews in 1976. SDC requested through the FOIA a copy of the computerized version of the medical literature index compiled by the National Library of Medicine (NLM). At that time, NLM was selling the tapes for $50,000 a year. The 9th Circuit upheld the NLM's refusal to release the tapes because Congress had directed it to create the index and sell it to the public.

The FOIA does not allow agencies to charge a premium for access to commercially valuable information, but the 1986 amendments say that when documents are requested for commercial use, agencies may charge reasonable standard fees for search, duplication and review. When documents are sought for noncommercial purposes, agencies may waive the search and review fees and charge only for duplication.

Guidelines from the Office of Management and Budget for implementing the fee waiver provisions of the 1986 FOIA amendments contain a section relating to computer searches. OMB says agencies should charge requesters only for that portion of the operator's salary and central processing unit operating time directly attributable to the records search.

The issue of federal policy regarding access to electronic information is also the subject of an extensive report of the House Committee on Government Operations published in 1986. The report notes that as the government stores more information in electronic form, the possibilities increase for subverting access laws. But electronic storage also carries the potential for making information more easily available to the public.

"Public information maintained by a Federal agency should remain freely accessible and easily reproducible, whether the data is maintained in paper or electronic form," according to the report.

Another of the report's many recommendations is that only the costs of providing the information, not the cost of creating the data base, should be included in charges to information users. "In almost all cases, the basic cost of creating and operating an information system are expenses that would be incurred whether or not the system is shared with the public. . . . As a result, it is appropriate that these basic costs should be borne entirely by the Federal agencies," the report says.

At present, however, access policies may vary from agency to agency, so a reporter interested in using federal computer tapes should start by examining the agency's FOIA rules in the Code of Federal Regulations. Some agencies, like the Treasury Department, have specific provisions covering access to the computerized records, while other agencies' rules may be silent about the issue.

Ethics and Computers

by John R. Bender
Editor, FOI Notebook

Just as the introduction of cameras and tape recorders raised new ethical issues for reporters and editors, so have computer records.

Thomas J. Moore, a national correspondent for Knight-Ridder Newspapers' Washington bureau who has worked with computer records, has identified four ethical issues.

1. *Readers and critics must be satisfied that the data have been used respon-*

sibly. Reporters may base conclusions on their analyses of computer data, but Moore asks, "How is anybody going to know I've done that right? Nobody else has looked at the data that way."

Moore suggests three possible ways to deal with this dilemma. One is to deposit the raw data in a library or research facility where it will be open to examination by anyone who wants to check the reporter's procedures. A second approach would be to provide the data and analysis to experts who would review and discuss them. The third would be to fill any reasonable requests from readers for more data.

2. *The data must be verified.* The fact that the data are on a computer tape does not guarantee their accuracy. Moore said a U.S. Department of Transportation computer tape he used for a story on truck safety contained reports from 137 states—an obvious indication that there were problems with the data.

Peter G. Gosselin of The Boston Globe said he found "weird spikes" in the U.S. Treasury Department data on large cash transactions that he used for a series on money laundering. He discovered that someone had been adding five zeros every now and then to the amounts of the transactions.

The ethical problems posed by inaccurate data may be greater for computer records because quick access to large numbers of files increases the potential for harm, but others argue inaccuracies in computer data pose no special problems.

Gosselin said, "I don't see why anyone should be more fearful of inaccuracy in computer records than any other kind of record." Paper records may give reporters "a warm feeling," but they don't bring them any closer to reality than computer records.

Moreover, except for incredibly gross errors, the mistakes in computer records usually cancel each other out when the data are aggregated, so stories based on computer records may be more accurate, Gosselin argued.

3. *News organizations must make sure the data they collect are kept up to date.* Moore said he was concerned by the extensive data bases a number of newspapers were building on campaign contributions to help them keep track of how donations may affect political decisions. These tapes enable newspapers to keep files on thousands of influential and not-so-influential people. So far, these tapes have been used responsibly, but, Moore said, "We need to think very carefully about accuracy, if we are going to build our own files."

Joel Rawson, executive editor of the Lexington Herald-Leader, said news organizations that maintain large data bases have a responsibility to use the information carefully and update it constantly, which requires a continuing commitment of time, money and dedication to public service.

4. *There must be statistical responsibility.* Reporters who use computer records must be responsible statistically, Moore said. This means drawing the correct inferences from the data.

Statistical responsibility requires the reporter to understand the important measures from the mean to factor analysis. It also calls for an understanding of what such measures do and do not say about the world, such as realizing that a correlation is not proof of a causal connection.

Advantages of Computer-Assisted Reporting

by **John R. Bender**
Editor, FOI Notebook

The power of computers to match files in different data bases or to help analysts detect trends makes them irresistible reporting tools.

Reporters using the traditional tools of the trade might talk to a dozen experts and still not have a good fix on the problem they are writing about, said David Ashenfelter, a reporter for the Detroit Free Press. Those who use a computer to analyze data not only get a better overview of the problem but also can use the computer to select the best examples from the data base to illustrate the issue.

"Another advantage is that once you've run the data, it's hard to attack because no one else has looked at it that way," Ashenfelter said. That's not a license to be reckless or to neglect the duty to verify the data, he added, but it is likely to appeal to libel-conscious editors and publishers.

Ashenfelter, who has used computers for several reporting projects since 1983, most dealing with criminal justice issues, has suggestions for reporters interested in working with computer records.

1. *Be prepared to spend a lot of time and money on the first project.* Reporters have to learn to use computers and figure out what data are on the computer tapes or disks they are using. For his first computer project, a story on disparities in sentences for persons convicted of manslaughter, Ashenfelter used the Michigan Department of Correction's tape containing all state-wide felony sentences. Each sentencing record also included the jurisdiction, judge, race of criminal, prior convictions and other information all in code. Ashenfelter had to find the code for manslaughter cases before he could isolate the 199 cases he was interest in.

2. *Start with a small project that can be accomplished on a personal computer using a program like dBase II.* An analysis of legislator's voting records or the calculation of an area's crime rates (number of crimes per 100,000 population) are fairly simple projects, Ashenfelter said.

3. *Have a good idea of what your story is about before you buy a computer tape.* Computers may make it easier and cheaper to copy large quantities of records, but at $50 to $100 a tape, fishing expeditions can be costly. Without a clear story idea, you can quickly become swamped by data.

4. *The calculations Ashenfelter made for his first computer project required a month to perform on a personal computer.* The calculations for a nearly identical story he prepared later required only three hours on a mainframe. "After that, I swore I'd learn how to use a real computer to do that stuff." He said that reporters contemplating the transition to mainframe computers should remember that some universities sell computer time and that rates are reduced late at night. The Free Press opened a computer account at Wayne State University and hired a consultant, he said, when it began work on a series about an early release program for prisoners.

CHAPTER 3

Finding a Government Document: An Overall Strategy

Every document you may wish to use is not, of course, listed in this book. That would be an impossible task. In addition, some documents that are listed may no longer be where we say they are, or may not even in fact be available, because the government is constantly reorganizing itself and making almost daily decisions as to whether a particular record sought by a member of the public is "public." This chapter gives reporters an overall strategy to follow when seeking any government record, at any level.

---

by **GERRY EVERDING**

You're a reporter in a town with several large defense contractors, and in the last few months there's been a number of stories in the national news about military procurement scandals. You have a couple of days during which there is nothing too pressing, and you decide to find out if there are any local angles to the story that might have been overlooked.

Several national stories have exposed kickback schemes that involved so-called revolving door employees—personnel that move back and forth between jobs with government agencies and the contractors that supply them. You're curious if local contractors rely on a similar revolving door network, but you're fairly certain it wouldn't be too productive to ask the contractors.

You realize you may not find scandal, but with a little luck you should at least be able to produce a profile of a former defense department official now working for a local contractor. As always, you first need to acquire an understanding of how the system works. What you'd like to find is some form of accessible documentation that gives you a better idea—perhaps even a precise picture—of the extent of the revolving door network among locally based federal contractors.

Getting Started

United States Government Manual

It is reasonable to expect that the Pentagon would want to keep track of former employees, especially those who have had access to sensitive defense procurement plans. What agency, branch or office of the federal government is charged with tracking the whereabouts of former employees? You consult the United States Government Manual, published annually by the federal government, one of the basic references for determining what paper trails to follow. This manual gives *short* descriptions of the missions of major government agencies. By reading the section on the Department of Defense, you come across the following paragraph describing one of the duties of the office of the secretary of defense:

> **Production and Logistics.** The Assistant Secretary of Defense for Production and Logistics is the principal staff assistant and advisor to the Under Secretary of Defense for Acquisition for management of DOD production procurement, development of procurement regulations, career management of the workforce, logistics, installations, associated support functions, and related matters.

This seems like a possible source, but you'd like to hone in a bit closer. You scan the Agency/Subject Index and find the citations: "Procurement, see Contracts, Federal" and "Procurement Policy, Office of Federal—90." On page 90, you find this reference:

> **Office of Federal Procurement Policy.** The Office of Federal Procurement Policy Act (88 Stat. 796; 41 U.S.C. 404) established the Office of Federal Procurement Policy (OFPP) within the Office of Management and Budget to improve the economy, efficiency, and effectiveness of the procurement processes by providing overall direction of procurement policies, regulations, procedures and forms.

Your eyes light up when you see the word *forms* and you decide to call the "for further information" phone number given at the end of the office's description. You explain that you're interested in information about any reporting forms that might be required of former Department of Defense personnel. You're transferred to three different offices, and the last tells you the person you need will have to call you back. You decide to look for more specific information.

Zeroing in on the Right Document

Federal Register

One place to start is the Federal Register, which is published five days a week and purchased on a subscription basis by most large libraries. Organized by agency and information type, the Register includes detailed descriptions or the full text of many government documents. Included are agency regulations, executive-branch legal documents, proposed rules, notices and other data the government is required by law to publish. It is here that the nature of many reporting forms required by the government can be discerned because each agency must spell out its regulations in great detail. Rules published in the Federal Register are compiled annually into the Code of Federal Regulations (see the next section). Both publications are found in most large libraries and all depository libraries. They are also in data bases.

Code of Federal Regulations

The Code of Federal Regulations (CFR) is an annual, multivolume compilation of general and permanent rules previously published in the Federal Register. It is organized into 50 titles that represent broad areas subject to federal regulation. Because individual titles are recompiled at various times throughout the calendar year, it's important to check when the title you're interested in was last updated. Check the Federal Register for revisions and other new information that may have been published since the compilation date.

Individual titles are often subdivided into separate volumes for each regulating agency included in a given broad subject area. For example, CFR "Title 21, Food and Drug," contains several volumes of regulations for the Food and Drug Administration and a separate volume for the Drug Enforcement Administration. An alphabetical listing by agency is located in the back of each volume under the heading "Finding Aids." (The Code also includes the regulations regarding agency Freedom of Information Act [FOIA] policies under the heading "Information Availability." To find those agencies that have established FOIA reading rooms for the public inspection of documents, check under the heading "Sources of Information.")

While the 50 titles of the CFR look fairly daunting as you first glance at them on the shelf of your local library, you are fortunate enough to find a useful guide: The CIS [Congressional Information Services] Index to the Code of Federal Regulations. You find the four-volume Subject Index and scan through citations under "Department of Defense." Within minutes you have spotted several likely references, including:

- Conflicts of Interest—officials and employees
  Standards of Conduct [Forms]   32 CFR 40
- Defense Contracts—contractors
  Defense Contracting, Reporting Procedures
  in Defense-Related Employment   32 CFR 40A

You locate the CFR volume Title 32, National Defense, on the shelf, and turn to "Part 40—Standards of Conduct." In a short index immediately below the heading, you find a reference to "40.12 Reporting of DOD and defense-related employment (DD Form 1787)." You turn to section 40.12 and find a detailed but highly legalized description of the reporting form you seek; you will even see a reproduction of the form itself.

In this instance, the CFR provides the full title and form number of the document you seek, but it won't always be as straightforward. Often the CFR will describe disclosure requirements in detail without actually naming the reporting form. Still, the description should supply you with enough information to call the agency and ask on what standard form the information is gathered.

Poring through the CFR can be a dull process, but you're likely to run across information there that otherwise would be missed. For instance, the same section of the CFR that described DOD Form 1787 also described several other forms that might prove equally interesting: "Statement of Employment—Regular Retired Officers (DOD Form 1357)" and "Statement of Affiliations and Financial Interests (DOD Form 1555)"—a form on which current DOD employees and officials are required to report any potential conflicts of interest.

You now make a second call to the Department of Defense armed with plenty of specific information about the documents you seek. A secretary tells you that everyone in the office has left to attend a day-long meeting. You decide to see what else you can dig up while you wait. You can assume that if an agency of the government collects information, some other agency or congressional committee generally wants to study it. The document librarian directs you to a reference book that details such reports.

Congressional Sourcebook Series

It turns out that your search for DOD Form 1787 might have gone more quickly had you known earlier about the Congressional Source Book Series, a three-volume guide to government documents published by the U.S. General Accounting Office (GAO). The volumes are:

- *Requirements for Recurring Reports to Congress*, which describes the requirements of various branches of government for recurring reports to Congress.
- *Federal Evaluations*, which contains an inventory of program and evaluation reports by most departments and agencies in the executive department. Although many evaluations are not for public release, all go to members of Congress, who may cooperate in releasing the data.
- *Federal Information Sources and Systems*, a particularly useful compendium of ongoing executive-branch operations that produce fiscal, budgetary and program-related information.

The Source Book Series seems like a great find, but you soon learn that the GAO ceased publication of the reference guide in 1985. You know that nearly everything in the federal government is revised, renamed or terminated every couple years, but you figure it's worth a try. Much to your surprise, under a section on the Defense Department on page 50 of the 1984 Recurring Reports to Congress, you find the citation:

> R00400–020
> **Report of DOD and Defense Related Employment. (DD-M (A) 1051)**
> **Frequency/Due Date:** Annually/March 31
> **OMB Funding Code/Title:** 97–0100–0–1–051 / Operations and maintenance. Defense agencies.
> **Congressional Relevance:** House Committee on Armed Services; Senate Committee on Armed Services.
> **Authority:** Act of October 12, 1982 (P.L. 97–295, @ 6(b); 96 Stat. 1314; 50 U.S.C. 1436).
> **Availability:** Agency
> **Geographic Relevance:** International/Foreign

Requirement: The Secretary of Defense shall submit an annual report to the Congress containing a list of the names of all employees of the Department of Defense and contractors awarded a negotiated $10 million or more and including part-time employees or consultants, who were previously employed by or served as a consultant to a defense contractor in any fiscal year and whose salary rates in the Department of Defense are equal to or greater than the minimum salary rate for positions in grade GS–13. **Abstract:** This report is a listing of names of persons filing reports for the fiscal year with a salary rate in the Department of Defense equal to or greater than the minimum salary rate for positions in grade GS–13 or employment by a prime contractor at a salary level $15,000. The listings are arranged alphabetically by defense contractor and by military department and defense agency within that alphabetical arrangement. The reporting categories are: 1) retired military officer Maj/Lt. Cmdr or above, 2) former military officer Maj./Lt. Cmdr or above, 3) former civilian employee whose salary was equal to or above minimum GS–13 salary level, and 4) former employee of or consultant to defense contractor awarded a negotiated contract of $10 million or more and who during the last fiscal year was employed by DOD at a salary level equal to or above minimum GS–13 salary. Copies of the report submitted by the present or former officers or employees are also attached, grouped by department or agency affiliation and arranged alphabetically by last name of person filing. Summaries of the number of reports by category submitted by departments and agencies, and corporations, are included. **Agency Contact:** (202) 695–3176.

When you call the agency, the person at the end of the line answers with the name of a DOD office. She knows the report, but her office no longer handles it. Fortunately, she remembers which office is now responsible. One more phone transfer and you're talking to the person who receives all DOD Form 1787s and compiles the Annual Report to Congress. This person points out that the forms are required by law to be made public, but cautions that Privacy Act restrictions cause her to ask that those requesting the forms submit a FOIA request so that personal information can be redacted. But she's willing to consider a phone request if you are looking for a specific document. With a clear path to some of your hard documentation, you set out to find some additional sources to broaden your story.

Locating the Best Sources

Washington Information Directory

Published annually by Congressional Quarterly Inc., the Washington Information Directory is a superb reference book for locating specific government entities—along with their addresses, telephone numbers and key staff members—that might be useful to you. For instance, using the directory's index, we learned about the following non-government and government sources that might be helpful in understanding the scope of the revolving door problem:

Non-government

- *Project on Military Procurement*, 613 Pennsylvania Ave. S.E. 20003; (202) 543–0883. Dina Rasor, project director. Examines specific weapons systems and determines their feasibility and cost effectiveness; promotes reform of the defense procurement system aimed at saving resources without weakening American military capabilities. Sponsored by the Fund for Constitutional Government.
- *Contract Services Assn.* 1350 New York Ave. N.W. 20005; (202) 347–0600. Gary Engerbretson, president. Membership: companies under contract that provide federal, state and local governments and other agencies with various technical services (particularly in defense, space and automatic data processing). Analyzes the process by which the government awards contracts to private firms; monitors legislation and regulations.
- *Defense Budget Project*, 236 Massachusetts Ave. N.E. 20002; (202) 546–9737. Gordon Adams, director. Conducts detailed analyses of defense spending; results available to members of Congress, the media and national organizations.

Agencies

- *Defense Systems Management College* (Defense Department), Fort Belvoir, Va. 22060; (703) 664–6323. Maj. Gen. Lynn H. Stevens (USA), commandant. Academic institution that offers courses to military and civilian personnel who specialize in acquisition and procurement. Conducts research to support and improve management of defense systems acquisitions programs.
- *Defense Department.* Defense Acquisition Regulatory Council, The Pentagon 20301; (703) 697–7267. Charles W. Lloyd Jr., executive secretary. Develops procurement regulations for the Defense Department and advises the secretary on major procurement policies.
- *Defense Department.* Military Manpower and Personnel Policy, The Pentagon, 20301; (703) 697–4166. Maj. Gen. Donald W. Jones, deputy assistant secretary. Military office that coordinates military personnel policies of the Defense Department and reviews military personnel policies of the individual services.

Congress

- *General Accounting Office*, National Security and International Affairs, 441 G St. N.W. 20548; (202) 275–5518. Frank C. Conahan, assistant comptroller general. Independent, non-political agency in the legislative branch. Audits, analyzes and evaluates Defense Department acquisition programs; makes unclassified reports available to the public.
- *House Armed Services Committee*, 2120 RHOB 20515; (202) 225–4151. Les Aspin, D-Wis., chairman; G. Kim Wincup, staff director. Jurisdiction over military weapons procurement.

■ *Senate Armed Services Committee*, SR–222 20510; (202) 224–3871. Sam Nunn, D-Ga., chairman; Arnold L. Punaro, staff director. Jurisdiction over military weapons procurement legislation; military procurement (excluding construction) for all the armed services including the navy; naval petroleum reserves; and military contract services.

Congressional Directory

Published annually, the Official Congressional Directory has all of the government entries that Congressional Quarterly's Washington Information Directory does, plus additional names of key staffers. It does not list non-government sources, making it less inclusive and, therefore less useful.

Data Base Searching

Your story is starting to shape up. You have a fairly firm idea of your key areas of interest. Now's a fine opportunity to try an on-line search of a commercial data base to broaden your perspective. You decide to access NEXIS, a business-oriented data base maintained by Mead Data Central Inc., of Dayton, Ohio. It contains the full-texts of stories from a large, national selection of newspapers, journals and magazines.

You search initially using the key words *defense department* and *revolving door*, but your search locates more than 500 stories that contain this combination of key words. You further limit the search by adding two more key words: *employment* and *regulation*. The search yields 74 stories that contain all four words and lists them chronologically in a browse menu.

The first relevant article is a 1,005-word story published just a week earlier in the national law newspaper Legal Times. It provides a detailed overview of a recent move by Congress to repeal the "procurement integrity amendments to the Office of Federal Procurement Policy Act." It goes on to give a lengthy background on scandals that prompted the amendments and the controversy that led to their repeal.

Several more stories located in the search provide the names of a half dozen members of Congress who have fought for passage or repeal of the amendment. Another potential source is the author of a story on the difficulties of mandating integrity in the procurement industry; he's described in the tagline as a 10-year veteran of the Office of Management and Budget, director of the Federal Acquisition Institute and founder of a "management consulting firm specializing in federal procurement policy."

An entry from the Bureau of National Affairs Inc., Daily Report for Executives, provides a 455-word description of a General Accounting Office report that found "A Majority of Former DOD Workers Did Not Comply with 'Revolving Door' Law." The account even provides you with the GAO accession number (GAO/NSIAD–89–221; 9/89), which leads you directly to the report on the shelf of your depository library. The GAO investigation is packed with background on inadequacies in the revolving door reporting disclosure system. An introductory page to the GAO report tips you to several congressional oversight committees that had instructed GAO to carry out the investigation. It also makes reference to a section of U.S. law (10 U.S.C. 2397), which describes the DOD's "revolving door disclosure system." An appendix also includes a copy of DOD Form 1787. In retrospect, you realize that you might have located this report by consulting one of the monthly or annual indexes to GAO reports, which are available by free subscription through the agency's public affairs office.

Familiar Ground: Using the Telephone

On-line data bases and printed reference guides can be invaluable tools for tracking down unknown documents, but often persistence on the telephone can be just as effective. After locating what appears to be the right agency, simply call the agency and ask what, if any, reporting system exists and what the forms are that contain the information you seek. It may be helpful to scan the blue pages contained in many local phone directories for the numbers of local, state or federal agencies with branch offices in your area. Remember to ask what other government agencies may have similar or related programs. Always be sure to get the full name, job title and department of everyone you talk to; sooner or later someone will try to direct you back to an office your inquiry was transferred from previously; you can expect to talk to two or three people in a department before finding someone who is familiar with the document you seek.

Super Sleuthing: Federal Government Internal Record-Keeping Agencies

The federal government has two internal record-keeping agencies generally not known to reporters: the Office of Management and Budget and the National Archives Records Administration. Both usually require a visit to Washington, D.C., but for projects requiring extensive research, it may be well worth the trip.

The Office of Management and Budget

The federal government makes a sustained effort at keeping track of all reporting, record-keeping, disclosure and labeling procedures required of its various agencies. The Federal Report Act of 1942, as amended by the Paperwork Reduction Act of 1980, requires most executive departments, commissions, independent agencies and government-owned or -controlled corporations to submit proposed information-gathering procedures together with Standard Form (SF) 83 (see the next section) for approval by the Office of Management and Budget (OMB). Its Office of Information and Regulatory Affairs prints them out from its central computer in an 800-odd page monthly inventory. Arranged in alphabetical order by agency name, and broken down further by agency departments, the printout lists the information collection procedures imposed on the public by nearly every government unit that collects information from 10 or more people. Listed are the titles of every current form or other procedure for collecting information, frequency of use, expiration date and OMB clearance number (the internal tracking number used by the OMB). Although obsolete procedures are dropped from the inventory, previous inventories will have them.

The OMB allows visitors to view the printout and it answers telephone inquiries, but refers mail requests to the specific agency. Each agency headquarters receives a copy of its section of the monthly inventory. Write to Public Records Room, Office of Information and Regulatory Affairs, Office of Management and Budget, New Executive Office Building, Washington, D.C. 20503.

The printout is easy to use. For example, under the Department of Health and Human Services, there might be a program listing titled: "A Study of the Effectiveness of Drug Abuse Treatment." To find out more about the information forms used in this study (and a great deal about the program that uses them), match the OMB clearance number with the original SF83.

SF83   All agencies submit forms for clearance with SF83. Information contained in the forms is extracted and entered in OMB's central computer system. Files derived from this data base are available for public inspection and reproduction in the OMB's Public Records Room in the New Executive Office Building, next to the White House.

The SF83 lists the agency name, officer in charge of the study, exact title, form expiration date, whether it is new or revised, frequency of use, collection method, collector of the information (the agency may have hired a firm for the study), type of respondents (businesses or individuals), a brief description of the respondents (demographic), estimated number of respondents, whether the information sought is received voluntarily or if it is mandatory and whether it is confidential. SF83s are accompanied by supporting statements that explain the project in greater detail and state the arrangement with the contractors about who will be the custodian of the study. The General Accounting Office and any federal bank supervisory agency are exempt from filing SF83s. In addition, some grant arrangements, interagency information forms and all judicial-proceeding forms are excluded.

The OMB maintains public docket files containing background documents and other correspondence related to the form approval process and to the draft regulation approval process. For information, call the Docket Library at the number above.

The National Archives

Federal departments and agencies don't keep all of their records forever, but they can't just throw them away. Most of the more important records end up in the National Archives, which, in most cases, is very cooperative in according access.

Until April 1985, the National Archives were maintained by a branch of the General Services Administration (GSA) known as the National Archives and Records Services (NARS). The agency has since attained independent status and is now known as the National Archives and Records Administration (NARA).

NARA is in charge of federal records disposition, and publishes guidelines for the disposal or destruction of government documents. Each federal government component is required to maintain a records disposition schedule based on these guidelines.

According to provisions of the Records Disposition Act, files cannot be transferred from an agency without NARA permission. Files that are not used often but not yet scheduled for disposal are routinely transferred from the originating agency to one of 14 regional Federal Records Centers.

When seeking any government record it is important to keep in mind the distinction between records stored in the National Archives and those held in Federal Records Centers.

The National Archives contain only those records that have been selected for permanent retention. Access to the Archives is liberal because most of the material is dated and kept primarily for public use.

Federal Records Centers, although maintained by NARA, have much stricter access policies because records stored there remain in the legal custody of the creating agency. In most cases, no access is allowed without written permission from that agency.

Records stored at the Federal Records Centers can be recalled and used by the creating agency and later returned for storage. Sensitive classified materials may be stored at a record center indefinitely. Non-sensitive materials no longer of use to an agency may be disposed of or sent to the National Archives for permanent public use.

Agencies wishing to send materials to a Federal Records Center must fill out Standard Form 135 describing the record and identifying the NARA approved retention period. The record centers will accept no record unless it is properly scheduled for disposal or retention. NARA reviews the SF135s and may accept or reject the transfer.

The form contains the title of the file and the name of the officer responsible for it. The level of classification is usually indicated on the form, but the description may not always reveal the specific information contained there. In some cases, the description may be as vague as "Boxes 1 thru 10, classified material."

However, when government officials tell you that a record never existed, has been thrown away or is simply too hard to find, it is the Form 135 that may help you prove them wrong.

These storage centers for Federal Records Centers and the National Archives are, as you might imagine, simply warehouses filled with boxes of folders and records. Form 135s are compiled to form a contents list for each box. These lists can be the keys to gaining access to the boxes and folders you need.

Begin the process by contacting the agency that you suspect may have maintained the records you seek. Ask them if records on a specific program or operation exist, and if so, where the files are now maintained.

If the records are held at a Federal Records Center, you'll need written permission from that agency to gain access to the files. If the agency refuses access, request the Form 135s on the records—these are normally public records and should be provided by the agency. The SF135s may provide a better idea of what types of records are maintained and allow you to narrow the scope of your Freedom of Information Act request to specific documents, files or boxes of records. (See Chapter 4 for more information on using FOIA.)

If the records have been transferred to the National Archives, you may request information on accessing the files by contacting the National Archives Record Administration, Washington, D.C. 20408. National Archives' records generally are open to the public, however, records of certain sensitive operations, such as the early atomic warfare planning and policy records, may require a FOIA request and are screened before release.

NARA should be able to direct you to the national or regional archives branch where the records of a particular agency or operation are maintained. The archives branch also will have a copy of the SF115s for all records maintained there. Gaining access to the forms may require a trip to the branch where the records are stored, but if a request is specific, some archivists may be willing to send copies of the relevant Form 115s.

Unlike most public documents, which are printed by the U.S. Superintendent of Documents and identified by a standard filing system known as SuDoc Numbers, documents maintained in Federal Records Centers are filed according to the same identification system used by the originating agency. These systems vary widely from agency to agency, so it is a good idea to contact the agency and familiarize yourself with possible filing procedures before you visit a record center.

If you're looking for material that was once classified or that you suspect someone may have once tried to conceal, be on the lookout for codes and other tactics used to obscure the true contents of the files you seek. Bring along a list of any project code names, government contract numbers, agency abbreviations, supervisory officers, project locations, dates and other clues that may lead you to files of interest. Obviously an agency is unlikely to entitle a file as "Plans to Terminate Soviet Spies," but it may describe it as "Anti-Espionage Activities."

Before visiting a record center it is a good idea to call ahead and discuss the search with an archivist, most of whom are more than willing to help. They can warn you about any obstacles to access and offer suggestions on how best to prepare for the visit. Some may be willing to have files pulled and waiting when you arrive.

NARA computers can track what records were transferred from what agency on what date. NARA compiles a Comprehensive Records Control Schedule that is supposed to contain a listing of each agency's file system. Theoretically, every file system—including those for sensitive and classified material—is reported to NARA.

NARA keeps a Records Control Schedule for each agency in its files and sends a copy to the agency itself. NARA also conducts periodic audits to determine if an agency is complying with terms of its Records Control Schedule. Audit results are not published, but are available to the public on request.

"SUSPENSE" OR TICKLER FILES   "Suspense" or tickler files are derived from the Comprehensive Records Control Schedule to remind records managers when specific files are to be transferred. They are arranged by date and often include a sample of the documents or files to be transferred.

RECORDS MANAGERS   Records officers should be familiar with an agency's holdings, even when, as often is the case due to budget cuts, the position is filled by a secretary, rather than a trained office manager. In any case, records managers are potentially valuable sources for reporters.

NARA ANNUAL REPORT   Not all records are catalogued, either on purpose or because they were overlooked in the inventory. Other records are not scheduled for any particular date of disposition, which means they are now considered permanent records and may be kept indefinitely. For example, corporate tax returns are retained indefinitely; the IRS keeps them in case they are needed in future antitrust or bankruptcy litigation. The NARA Annual Report shows that most agencies sometimes do not dispose of records exactly as planned, so don't hesitate to request records that supposedly have been destroyed.

Getting Hold of Recently Declassified Material

Information about recently declassified records can be found in several published sources often available at major public libraries.

"Prologue," a quarterly publication of the National Archives, contains a list of documents declassified since the last issue.

The Declassified Documents Reference System, a collection of more than 25,000 documents declassified under executive order and the Freedom of Information Act, is produced by Research Publications of Woodbridge, Conn.

The Retrospective Collection to Declassified Documents includes information on 8,000 documents originally released by government agencies after Congress revised the Freedom of Information Act in 1974. The two-volume retrospective collection presents material on documents from the Korean War through 1974.

Declassified Document Catalog, issued six times a year, offers updates on documents declassified during the previous quarter have been available on an annual subscription basis since 1975. Each declassified record, report or paper is abstracted and arranged according to issuing agency. An index at the end of each catalog includes headings in areas such as persons, countries, conflicts and technical subjects. Cumulative indexes are issued annually. The full text of documents is available on microfiche.

Gaining Access to State and Local Documents

States and municipalities operate under a myriad of disclosure statutes, regulations and conventions. The general procedure, however, is the same as that for getting federal documents. Start by learning what the government unit is required to do. Check the state statutes and the regulations. Learn the record-keeping procedures of the custodians as well as possible. The importance of this, if not obvious from the above discussion, is shown repeatedly throughout the chapters of this book where successful investigations are analyzed.

Finessing Restrictive State and Local Disclosure Attitudes

At the federal level, reporters are aided by a strong disclosure statute, the Freedom of Information Act, when faced with bureaucrats who refuse to divulge documents. How to use it is described in the next chapter (see Chapter 4, "The Freedom of Information Act"). Sometimes you can save yourself a great deal of grief and time at the local level by trying to figure out where the same or similar information is kept at the federal level. The federal government is often more willing to let citizens in on its operations, and when it isn't, you may be able to force disclosure through the use of the Act. In general, however, at the state and local levels, access can be a formidable problem for reporters, often requiring exceptional persuasive powers, or a willingness to sue for access.

Obtain copies of your state and local open-records laws and know them thoroughly so that you can quote them to public officials reluctant to produce the records you seek. Many state press associations have printed them on cards easily carried in wallets. Remind recalcitrant bureaucrats that their provisions are the law, and ask them to cite specifically which state law or local ordinance they think allows them to close the record to the public. Then write down their answer and get their name and title, just as if you were going to do a story about the denial (which you might). Ask who their supervisor is. Be polite but firm, explaining that you intend to follow up any denial all the way to court, if necessary.

A useful strategy adopted by many reporters when denied access to documents or records that should be open is to persuade the city's attorney to call the reluctant city official (that is, once having convinced the lawyer that there is no legal basis for the denial). If this tactic fails, it may be useful to ask your managing editor or station manager to call the mayor or city manager and ask him or her bluntly what it is that the documents contain that causes the city to want to keep them secret from its citizens. It is an unusual politician that doesn't get the drift of a conversation like this and decide that a policy of disclosure is better than one of denial, where there is no clear justification for denial in the law. And perhaps even more important, your managing editor or station manager often will know the city's mayor or manager socially, as most reporters won't (and won't want to).

In addition, news organizations should be prepared to file motions in local courts forcing compliance with state and local access laws when the news organization is substantially sure of winning and making good case law. News organizations that convince city officials of their seriousness about informing the public can go a long way toward creating a climate of openness just by periodically demonstrating a willingness to seek judicial relief.

Conclusion

Creativity in following paper trails and in figuring out where you can legally intercept them can pay great dividends. A team of reporters once spent many months examining a proposed multimillion dollar coal gasification plant to be located in the Columbia, Mo., area. The more experts they talked to and the longer they researched, the worse the proposal looked. After a few months of what the proponents considered to be negative reporting, they formed a nonprofit corporation which exempted them from state disclosure laws, even though many members were government employees officially representing their community's interests in the project. They attracted a grant from an organization called the Ozark Regional Commission (ORC), enabling them to hire a consulting firm to study an aspect of the proposal that had been hammered away at in numerous stories.

Reporters asked the proponents for a copy of the preliminary progress report, having marked on our calendars the date they were to receive it.

No dice, they said.

Reporters asked the consultants for a copy.

No dice, they said.

Reporters asked the director of the Ozark Regional Commission for a copy.

No dice, he said.

Then reporters decided to find out where the ORC gets its money. By using the United States Government Manual, they learned that the ORC is an agency of the U.S. Department of Commerce. They called the department to see if those in charge had gotten the report and if they'd release a copy, fully prepared to file an FOIA request if they denied access.

Sure, they said, it's our policy to give our information when we can.

The newspaper received a copy within a few days.

In short, it almost always pays to take the time to do the extra homework of learning the law, the regulations and the agency's compliance procedures instead of blindly stumbling about searching for the information. It won't be very easy if you are on a daily deadline, but investigative reporting on a daily deadline is a nonsequitur. What may look like a short, easy story today may come back to haunt you as an ongoing, amazingly complex project that demands a greater understanding than is likely to be produced by either hit-or-miss document requests or routine telephone interviews.

C H A P T E R 4

The Freedom of Information Act

Judging by the infrequent use they make of it, most journalists are unfamiliar with the Freedom of Information Act. But it is to their advantage to become familiar with this muscular disclosure law, which helps reporters gain access to federal records and documents that are often unavailable by any other means. This chapter describes how to use the Freedom of Information Act and includes a copy along with model letters for requests and appeals.

by HARRY HAMMITT

In 1986 the Pulitzer Prize for national reporting went to the Dallas Morning News for an investigative series by reporters Craig Flournoy and George Rodrigue on the state of federal fair housing. Much of the information that made the series possible was obtained by Flournoy and Rodrigue under the Freedom of Information Act (FOIA).

The Pulitzer Prize for biography in 1987 was awarded to David Garrow for his book "Bearing the Cross: Martin Luther King and the Southern Christian Leadership Conference." And in 1989, Bill Dodman, then of the Atlanta Journal-Constitution, won the Pulitzer Prize for investigative reporting for a series on racial discrimination in mortgage lending by banks and savings and loans in Atlanta.

As imperfect as it may be, the Freedom of Information Act continues to be an important tool for reporters, scholars and public interest groups in their attempts to monitor the behavior of government—to discover the extent of government action or inaction and the how and why of government decision making.

Many reporters believe the Freedom of Information Act is of little value—it takes too much time and there are too many exemptions under which agencies can withhold information. As a group, journalists do not use the statute frequently. Businesses and prisoners account for a majority of each year's requests. But even though reporters do not use the Act themselves, they are frequently the prime beneficiaries of information released to public interest groups who analyze the information and, in turn, provide reporters with stories. The handful of reporters who have trained themselves to use this valuable tool have produced a number of exclusive stories that otherwise might never have seen their way into print or onto the airwaves.

FOIA History

Congress approved the Freedom of Information Act in 1966 in large part to codify a philosophy of open government. The Act created a sweeping change in public access to federal records in the executive branch by allowing any person, regardless of nationality or need, to obtain documents not falling under one of nine exemptions. (For more information, see section "Exemptions" at the end of this introduction as well as "Text of the Freedom of Information Act" at the end of this chapter.) For the first time, the burden of proof was placed on the government to show why information could be withheld from the public.

The statute required agencies to publish in the Federal Register the procedures for filing FOIA requests and to make available policies and policy interpretation adopted by agencies but not published in the Register. It instructed agencies to maintain public reading rooms containing copies of final agency opinions, administrative staff manuals and instructions affecting the public, and current indexes of administrative matters that could be used in locating the agency's publicly available information.

In the wake of the Watergate investigations, Congress revisited the FOIA in 1974, amending the statute to ensure easier and speedier access to documents. The amendments required agencies to establish uniform and reasonable fees for locating and duplicating records (fees which would be waived if the information was in the public interest) and to set time limits for responding to requests, appeals and lawsuits. Agencies were instructed to release all nonexempt portions of records. The courts' authority to review agency decisions was broadened and recovery of legal fees by a prevailing requester was allowed.

Except for a correction to one of the exemptions made in 1976, the FOIA remained unchanged until the fall of 1986. Then, as a rider to anti-drug abuse legislation, the statute was amended once more, changing the law enforcement exemption slightly and providing a new set of provisions regarding fees. For the first time, categories of requesters were established. The range of assessible fees depended on the category in which a requester belonged. The press and scientific and educational institutions received preferred status, while commercial users had to pay a higher percentage of the actual costs of processing requests. The standard for granting a waiver of fees changed from one of "primarily benefiting the general public" to "significantly contributing to public understanding of the operations or activities of the government." By changing the standard, Congress intended to liberalize the waiver of fees and repudiate a tight-fisted interpretation of the old public interest standard by the Department of Justice.

The FOIA applies to all administrative agencies of the executive branch, including the armed forces, but not to Congress, the courts or the president's immediate staff. The executive branch includes executive offices (Office of

Management and Budget, for example), departments (Department of Defense), bureaus (Federal Bureau of Investigation), councils (National Security Council), commissions (Commission on Civil Rights), government corporations (Overseas Private Investment Corporation), government-controlled corporations (Amtrak) and regulatory agencies (Food and Drug Administration).

Getting Started

The first step in any successful hunt is to figure out what information is needed and which government agency has it. How to do that is covered extensively in the previous chapters and those that follow, but several points are worth emphasizing.

- *Don't make an FOIA request unless absolutely necessary.* Try to get the information another way, if possible. It is much quicker to get the documents following alternate pathways. Before making a request, check the agency's public reading room for the information, or consult its public affairs office. If you have a source inside the agency willing to provide you with a copy of a document, get the source to release it to you outside the FOIA. However, a great deal of government information is available only through the FOIA.
- *Plan ahead.* Using the FOIA takes time and may be impractical if you have a short deadline. But if you are working on a project with an extended deadline the FOIA may be useful. Allow at least several months for a response and make your request far enough in advance to accommodate that constraint. Even if you have no specific story in mind, you may want to make an FOIA request on some interesting subject; you may find the information will provide the basis for a story. For instance, many reporters have found national stories based on information the government has on famous persons.
- *Make your request as precise as possible.* The government can refuse requests that are overly broad. (See "Filing the Request" in this chapter.)
- *Determine which government office has the information you seek.* Before making a request, determine exactly what type of records you are looking for and what agency (or agencies) is likely to have the information. Descriptions of the functions of various agencies may be found in the United States Government Manual. You may wish to call an agency you think may have the information you seek and sound them out or request further information on the agency's programs from the public affairs office.

  The better job you do pinpointing the agency with the information you need, the higher your chances of getting a response that suits your needs. If you guess wrong and send a request to an agency that does not have the information, the agency, in theory, should refer your request to the correct agency. However, the agency is just as likely to respond to you that it has no records and force you to keep looking for the right agency. So do some old-fashioned reporting to find the right agency before you make the request.

■ *Become familiar with an agency's regulations so you know what its functions are and how it is supposed to carry them out.* Copies of an agency's regulations should be available directly from the agency. They are also contained in the Code of Federal Regulations. Under the FOIA heading, it explains procedures for dealing with FOIA requests and gives each agency's definitions of related terms, such as records and receipt of requests. It outlines procedures for processing requests and rules that help or limit the release of information. These rules will give you criteria to evaluate the handling of FOIA requests, and they supply arguments to bolster appeals, if needed.

Notice, in particular, that agencies start the FOIA's time limits running only after a request has reached the proper office. It is important to address your request according to the agency's regulations to ensure it arrives at the proper destination. Also, some agencies allow you to file requests with field offices that may be more receptive or helpful in locating specific information. Other agencies require all requests to be addressed to a central office from where they are then routed internally or to the appropriate field office. In this case, you may waste time by sending a request to a field office which will then be sent back to a central office before returning to the field.

■ *Before filing an FOIA request, check the agency's FOIA reading rooms to find out whether someone has already made the same request previously.* If so, you can save time and avoid costly search fees. For example, the Nuclear Regulatory Commission is known for its comprehensive list of fulfilled FOIA requests. The NRC publishes weekly and monthly announcements of released material and can locate processed FOIA requests by number, requester and subject. Other agencies, particularly the FBI, keep copies of the most popular documents in their reading rooms. Agencies like the FDA list all requests received, giving each a chronological file number and a description of the subject, thus a requester may be able to ascertain if the subject matter of a previous file has been released and then request that file.

Filing the Request

Begin your letter by citing the FOIA statute, then requesting the information. Agencies will generally process a request for information under the FOIA, regardless of whether the statute is cited, but it is best to cite it explicitly.

You are not required to explain why you want the material or for what purpose it will be used. However, under the 1986 FOIA amendments, you should establish your credentials as a member of the press. If you are working as a free-lancer, you are required to provide evidence of a "solid basis" for believing your work will be published. Also, include information concerning how release of the records will significantly contribute to public understanding of government operations or activities if you are requesting a waiver of any duplication fees.

Even though the law states that you need only "reasonably describe" the records sought, try to be as specific as possible, quoting the title, number or date of the document; who wrote it; which division published it; a code name for the project; and published accounts of the material sought, if known.

If the topic is broad, break it down into categories and file separate requests for each area. Agency personnel are usually daunted by massive requests that appear likely to evolve into major problems for them; such requests may well go on the back burner because of the perceived difficulty in responding. Indicate your willingness to work with the agency to narrow or focus your request. The agency may be able to help you locate the specific records you need without the burden of processing volumes of peripheral materials. Avoid asking for "All records pertaining to..." This may unnecessarily delay fulfillment of the request, as the agency may send it to all of its various divisions and offices. Word the letter in a positive manner. Avoid qualifiers such as "Records you may have..." The agency is more likely to divulge potentially embarrassing information if perceived that you know it exists.

You may qualify for a waiver of copying fees if the material sought would significantly contribute to public understanding of government operations and activities. According to Justice Department guidance issued in the spring of 1987, agencies should consider six factors in granting a fee waiver:

1. Does the subject matter pertain to the activities of government?
2. Will disclosure likely contribute to public understanding?
3. Will the information increase public understanding?
4. Will release result in a "significant" contribution to public understanding?
5. Does the commercial interest in release outweigh the public interest?
6. Will release primarily satisfy a public or commercial interest?

Although the long-term validity of these guidelines is questionable, it is best to provide general answers to these questions in your initial request for a fee waiver. If you are denied a fee waiver, agencies will, as a rule, allow you to appeal the denial. The 1986 amendments also allow you to contest a final agency denial in court, but the court's review is limited to the record created at the administrative level, so make sure your arguments to the agency are as complete as possible.

Write the request on the letterhead of your news organization. (A sample request letter appears at the end of this chapter.) All FOIA requests should be in writing, although some agencies will occasionally accept requests over the phone. The Department of Justice has advised agencies that they should accept requests sent by FAX machine. Regardless, always maintain a paper record of your request and related correspondence. Date and file a copy of each request. If you call an agency directly, keep notes concerning the name and title of the employee, the date and gist of the conversation. File these notes, too. It will be important to have a copy of all correspondence if you appeal. If you need to phone the agency frequently to move along your request, it is best to develop a working relationship with one or two persons who may be more likely to aid you once

once you have won their trust. Government employees, like reporters, can get exasperated at the idiosyncrasies of the bureaucracy. Often they would like to see the same result that you are seeking in requesting the information. Or, they may feel sorry for you if you are constantly butting your head against a stone wall.

It is good practice to call the agency every so often to check on the status of your request. Let them know that you are still interested in the information and that you are willing to help in any way you can.

Mark your letter on the front of the envelope to the attention of the FOIA office. You may wish to pay extra postage for a return receipt to prove that it was mailed and received. The 10-day reply time, which can be extended another 10 days under unusual circumstances, such as the need to review large amounts of records or to consult with other agencies having an interest in the records, will not begin until the request reaches the proper person within the agency. If you send the request to the wrong agency, it will sometimes be forwarded or, often, just returned.

After your letter has been received, you may be given an identifying number and told your request will be processed in turn. Make note of this number; it will speed tracing efforts if you have questions or receive no reply.

Because of the tremendous overlap of responsibility in the federal government, you may save time in the long run by requesting the information you desire from all custodians whom you suspect may have the documents you seek. Former Washington Post reporter Scott Armstrong has frequently requested the same information from several different agencies, often finding that one agency will release information that was withheld by another. Where the responsibilities of the federal government overlap with those of the states, consider making requests to various pertinent state agencies. Each state is governed by its own open record laws, not the FOIA, but you may find interesting information generated on the state level, or obtain federal information forwarded to the state which was not released to you by any federal agency.

It is a good idea to ask the agency if any other government entity has requested information on your subject. For instance, the Equal Employment Opportunity Commission may be investigating allegations of discrimination on the part of a corporation you are investigating and, therefore, may have requested a report from the Department of Labor on the relationship between the union and the corporation. This request could include records not normally a part of the file, and it also may be a good tip that the company is being looked at from angles you didn't think of.

Request information from field offices if the agency's regulations provide for direct response by that office. The Defense Department, Department of Health and Human Services and the Veterans Administration all allow requests to be granted at various levels in field offices. This is particularly true of the Defense Department, where military bases and specialized components all have authority to release information directly. Denial authority, however, rests with a high-level field officer or headquarters.

Agency Responses to the Request

The law requires agencies to reply to FOIA requests within 10 days. Under extenuating circumstances, the law allows another 10 days for the reply; however, the agency must inform you if it is taking an extension. The length of time for replies usually is determined by the backlog of FOIA requests. Many agencies will respond within a reasonable time that may be longer than the law allows. Agencies with the greatest number of files, such as the FBI and the Department of Justice, may take months to reply. As a rule of thumb, you should expect a response from most agencies within one to three months.

Agency FOIA offices suffer from a combination of too few staffers and too many requests, a situation that has made it virtually impossible for agencies to comply with the statutory time limits. Backlogged agencies may assign your request a number and then keep you waiting your turn. While this may be a convenient practice from a bureaucrat's point of view, it is a violation of the literal language of the FOIA. However, the "first in, first out" method of processing requests has been judicially sanctioned. If you have a pressing need for the documents, call the agency and explain the urgency of the request. Keep a written record of any conversations you have with agency personnel; you may want to send a memo describing your understanding of the conversation to the agency for the file.

If you do not hear from the agency within two weeks, phone and ask about the status of your request. Remind the agency employee of the time limits. Again, be assertive but not belligerent. Try to get a definite date for release or, at a minimum, a generalized timetable for completion of your request.

If this does not produce results, write the agency another letter. State that if the agency does not comply by a certain date, you will interpret the excessive delay as a "denial in effect." This means you could follow the appeal procedure as if the agency had informed you of a formal denial. Keep copies of all correspondence, in case you go to court.

The FOIA allows you to go to court if the agency does not comply with your request within a reasonable amount of time. But most courts would consider this an unnecessary burden; at best, you may end up with a court decision allowing the agency to continue to process your request in good faith with the knowledge that the court may follow up on its progress. It is better to file an appeal of a "denial in effect" with the agency and await an administrative decision. This device does more to get your request noticed than to get it fulfilled. A higher-level authority within the agency is unlikely to reach any substantive decision except to admit that your request has not been processed. However, getting your request noticed will result in more attention being paid to it, culminating in a somewhat faster response.

Denials

There are several reasons an agency may cite for not complying with a request, some of which already have been mentioned. An agency may contend that your request is not specific enough, or it may refuse to release records until you agree to pay for them. But there are other reasons for denying access to records. These are embodied in the statute's nine exemptions, which are discussed in greater detail later in this chapter.

The nine exemptions cover specific areas—national security, confidential business information and law enforcement records. There is an exemption for records that cannot be released because release is prohibited by another statute, one which covers internal government memoranda that are predecisional in nature or covered by a recognized discovery privilege and one that sanctions withholding information that would constitute a clearly unwarranted invasion of privacy. One of the more peculiar exemptions allows the government to withhold records pertaining to internal personnel matters, not because the information is sensitive in any way or would harm government operations, but because it is too trivial to be of any interest to the public.

An agency may also respond that it has no records. Although such a response is not a formal denial, most agencies allow requesters to appeal a "no records" response. In sensitive situations, usually involving classified information or law enforcement files, the government can refuse to either confirm or deny the existence of records.

Some agencies may be unwilling to release information that originated in another agency, claiming they are only "custodians" of the materials. Many of these agencies feel they are not qualified to assess the releasability of these files. Nor do they want to harm their working relationship with the originating agency. Usually they will confirm the existence of the files and direct you to the proper agency.

Appeals

If your FOIA request is denied, file an appeal. The appeal will be decided by someone higher up in the agency; by statute, the agency has 20 working days in which to respond to an appeal, but, as is the case with requests, appeals invariably take much longer than the statutory limit, often requiring a year or more before a final determination is made. An appeal is also required in most instances to preserve your right to eventually go to court.

Follow the administrative guidelines for appeals cited in the denial letter. If none are cited, check the agency's regulations in the CFR or contact the FOIA office for specifics on its appeal procedures. As a last resort, appeal to the head of the agency.

Although agencies generally do not require you to include justification for appeals, it is a good idea to include as much supporting evidence as possible in your letter. The agency's final decision will inevitably be based on a weighing of the arguments provided by the requester and the denying office. If you provide no arguments in your appeal, it is more likely that the official reviewing the material will side with the initial agency determination. If the reason for the original denial is not clear, ask the agency for clarification. Cite FOIA provisions that you think are applicable to show the agency that it may have made a mistake in the law. Cite relevant cases. Remember that you can also challenge the adequacy of the search. If you believe the agency has more records than it admits to having, argue that the search was inadequate. If you have obtained agency records through another source, send the agency sample copies to support your argument that the search was not thorough.

Even if you did not request a fee waiver in your original letter, most agencies will review a request for a waiver on appeal. Provide the same types of information and arguments discussed previously under "Filing the Request."

Although it is not necessary, consider having a lawyer sign the appeal letter so the agency can see you are serious about pursuit of disclosure. If you are the requester of record, you will also have to sign the letter. Threaten to sue if the information is not released. (A sample appeal letter can be found at the end of this chapter.) As always, show the agency you are familiar with its regulations, operations and the law and that you won't be swayed in your efforts to win release.

Subtle and not-so-subtle pressure tactics may be helpful. During the process of gathering information for one of the hundreds of FOIA requests, Jack Taylor of the Dallas Times-Herald filed with the Bureau of Indian Affairs; he learned that a high-ranking BIA official had supposedly circulated a memo telling BIA employees not to attend the confirmation hearings of the new department head. Taylor filed an FOIA request for the memo and was told that the agency could find no record of it. A source told Taylor that bureau employees had scurried around looking for copies of the memo to destroy after receiving his request. Taylor filed an appeal, reminding the bureau that it is illegal to destroy government property without proper authority. The BIA sent him the memo.

Later in his investigation, Taylor learned that the BIA had assigned an employee to think of ways to thwart his FOIA requests. Taylor sent the BIA an FOIA request asking for secret memos discussing how to block FOIA requests. "I expected them to deny it," Taylor said [which they did] "otherwise they would be admitting guilt. But I wanted them to know I knew what they were doing."

Going to Court

If all administrative appeals have failed, or you have been denied total or partial access to documents, consider filing a lawsuit. You do not necessarily need a lawyer to file a lawsuit; faced with legal action, many agencies, depending on the information in dispute, will negotiate settlement for partial or full disclosure. Assess your case before committing yourself to filing suit. If it appears clear to you on the basis of the case law that the agency's position is strong, you may conclude that going to court will not accomplish anything. Filing suit will not necessarily result in further disclosure, but it may cost you and your organization valuable time, resources and money. However, don't be discouraged from proceeding in court if you believe you have reasonable grounds for doing so.

Should you decide to go ahead with a lawsuit, it may be wise to hire a lawyer to help prepare the case and to represent you in court. However, you can represent yourself, and because FOIA litigation is mostly a matter of filing motions rather than appearing in court, you may wish to consider that alternative. Be aware that because of the backlog in cases it may be months before yours is considered and may take a year or more before the court decides the case.

Although statistics compiled by the U.S. Administrative Conference in 1986 indicated that in the FOIA suits resulting in a final court judgment the government won more than 80 percent of the time, these statistics do not reflect the partial disclosures or negotiated compromises that are common in FOIA litigation. Assuming you have a reasonable case to begin with, your chances of getting more information through litigation are fairly good.

Considering all this, carefully assess your case and decide if the documents are worth the time and trouble. Try to obtain the financial and moral support of your news organization. Your editor might want to fight the case on principle.

If you cannot get financial backing from your news organization and your bosses do not see a conflict of interest, ask public interests groups, law schools and lawyers for help. If your case involves a significant FOIA dispute or might set an important precedent, it is likely that someone or some organization would be willing to represent you for a nominal fee or even without charge. Three starting points for this help are:

1. Your local American Civil Liberties Union chapter
2. The Freedom of Information Clearinghouse, P.O. Box 19367, Washington, D.C. 20036
3. The Reporters Committee for Freedom of the Press, Suite 504, 1735 I St. N.W., Washington, D.C. 20006

The Reporters Committee also operates a hotline to give advice on FOIA problems. The hotline is in operation seven days a week, 24 hours a day. The number is (800) FFOI-AID or (202) 466-6312.

The Justice Department produces two publications that provide guidance to agencies and may be of use in filing suits to the extent that they indicate the positions taken by the government on various FOIA issues. The quarterly FOIA Update is a newsletter designed to educate government FOIA personnel about the law and provides advice on legal FOIA issues as well as a short discussion of recent significant court decisions. The Freedom of Information Case List is an annual compilation of court cases relating to the FOIA, Privacy Act, Sunshine Act and Federal Advisory Committee Act. It also contains an extended guide to the legal interpretations of the provisions of the FOIA. Copies of these publications are available from the GPO.

How to File an FOIA Suit

FOIA suits can be filed in any of three different locations: (1) where you reside; (2) where the documents are located; or (3) the District of Columbia. Many requesters prefer to file in the District of Columbia because the court there has the most experience with FOIA suits and is less likely to misinterpret the law. The Justice Department handles the government's side in almost all litigation arising from denials of FOIA requests.

Filing procedures and fees ($120 in D.C.) vary by district court, so phone the court to obtain the proper instructions. The following filing procedure is required by the District Court for the District of Columbia.

- *Submit the proper forms.* Write to the clerk of the court, U.S. District Court, District of Columbia, Third and Constitution N.W., Room 1825, Washington, D.C. 20001, and request the one-page instruction sheet; one copy of the Civil Cover Sheet and one copy of the Summons in a Civil Action for each agency being sued, one for the Attorney General and one for the U.S. Attorney. You will also want to have copies for yourself.
- *Complete these forms and prepare your lawsuit.* State the facts of the case, that the government has either improperly withheld records or has failed to respond within the statutory time list, and the relief sought (usually the release of records).
- *Mail these forms along with the original and five copies of the lawsuit to the clerk of the court.* Include a check for $120. The court will cash your check and send you a receipt. The original and one copy are for the court. The court will stamp and return the summons and the four copies of the lawsuit to you. By registered or certified mail, send one copy to the agency and one copy to the Attorney General at the Department of Justice. The third copy is for the U.S. Attorney in the district where you are suing and must be served by hand from a special processor or server who is over 18 and not a party to the suit. Where service is local, delivery can be made by a friend, but it is important to get a receipt from the government to prove it received the summons. The fourth copy is for your files.
- *Photocopy the registered or certified mail receipts and the affidavit of delivery from the summons server for your records.* Mail the originals to the clerk of the court to prove the summons were served.

The government must respond to the suit within 30 days. Invariably, the response will not be very enlightening. At this time, you may file a motion for a Vaughn index. If a Vaughn index will not provide all the answers you will need to pursue your case, you may also request limited discovery on such issues as records maintenance, how the search was conducted, and what kinds of records the agency has in its possession.

If the court grants your Vaughn motion, the agency is required to submit an affidavit itemizing and indexing each document withheld from you. This affidavit will give a general description of the content of the withheld document, and, perhaps, the author and the date. It must also include justification for nondisclosure on an item-by-item basis; however, in some cases courts have allowed agencies to supply justifications for nondisclosure on a category-of-record by category-of-record basis.

Exemptions

There are nine areas of exemptions to the FOIA specified in the law. FOIA annual reports show that some agencies use certain exemptions more than others, but generally the ones invoked most often are those pertaining to law enforcement records, inter- or intra-agency memos, invasion of privacy and confidential business information.

Exemption (b) (1)

Exemption (b) (1) concerns documents that are properly classified and, if disclosed, would harm the national defense or foreign policy. Just because the document has been classified does not mean it cannot be released. Upon receipt of an FOIA request the agency must review the records to make sure they were properly classified; records are also subject to a mandatory declassification review to determine if any information that is currently classified can be declassified and released. If the requested records contain a mixture of classified and non-classified information, the non-classified information must be released if not protected by another exemption.

The classification of national security information has been governed by various executive orders since 1940. Periodic reviews by government agencies and nongovernmental organizations have found widespread abuse, including overclassification and inadequate review of procedures. However, the Reagan administration's Executive Order No. 12356 on classification, still in effect, encourages broad classification of documents if disclosure could reasonably be expected to harm national security. Information can remain classified for as long as its release could be expected to harm national security. The Executive Order also permits the reclassification of documents after they have been declassified, including reclassification after an FOIA request has been made for them.

Although Congress in 1974 clearly intended to instruct courts to review withholdings under Exemption (b) (1), as a compromise with the administration it told courts to give great deference to agency expertise when it came to national security issues. As a result, courts have consistently declined to second-guess the need for classifying certain information and have restricted their review to procedural matters concerning whether the information was correctly classified.

One area the requester can challenge in court is the classification procedure, but if the procedure is found to be adequate a court will not release national security information. Even if a judge finds improprieties in the classification procedures, it is still likely he or she will accept the agency's national security claims and uphold the use of the exemption. However, there is some indication that courts are beginning to question the need to retain classifications for old documents. Several courts, although declining to order release, have suggested that information 30 to 40 years old need no longer be protected.

A listing of documents recently declassified by the National Archives can be found in Prologue, a quarterly Archives publication. Most major libraries receive this periodical.

The National Security Archive

The National Security Archive, housed in the Brookings Institution in Washington, D.C., was formed by reporters Scott Armstrong and Ray Bonner in the fall of 1985. Armstrong, who until recently served as the Archive's executive director, says the goal of the organization is to collect, catalog and analyze government records pertaining to foreign policy, defense and national security, and to make "document sets" available to reporters, scholars and research libraries.

The Archive intends to organize the information topically, on such subjects as Iran and Central America, providing the public with a more detailed picture of foreign policy and defense decision making. Much of the information will come from the donation of records by reporters and scholars, but the Archive is prepared to make extensive use of the FOIA.

As the Archive, which opened to the public in January 1987, continues to collect and analyze records, its importance to reporters, particularly those on deadline, will increase dramatically. Information that once had to be pried out bit-by-bit by individual requesters will have been collected in one place and annotated by experts, providing an excellent source of information for the press.

Many national security-oriented agencies, and the Justice Department in particular, have been alarmed at the possibility of such a clearinghouse, and the Justice Department has taken whatever steps it can to block the Archive's access to government information through the FOIA. However, the concept of the Archive has won wide support in Congress and in press and public interest groups, and its role in preparing a chronology of events on the Iran-Contra affair, used by the House and Senate Select Committees, has bolstered its public stock further.

Exemption (b) (2)

Exemption (b) (2) covers matters "related solely to the internal personnel rules and practices of an agency." Generally this exemption has been limited by the courts to include matters concerning agency rules not deemed to have a legitimate public interest. These include employee parking regulations, sick leave and vacation time, for example. The Supreme Court has ruled that the exemption does not cover internal personnel practices where there is a "substantial potential for public interest outside the government."

The exemption has been used to withhold file markings and internal numbering systems and has also been found to govern internal agency instructions to investigators, inspectors and auditors when release would reveal confidential investigatory techniques and procedures that would seriously hamper the detection of violators. However, the 1986 amendments have moved most if not all of this protection to Exemption (b) (7) and at this point it is unclear whether agency manuals will fall under Exemption (b) (2) in the future. Since Exemption (b) (7) covers law enforcement materials, it is possible that release of an agency manual used for regulatory monitoring might fall short of enforcement purposes but would still compromise the agency's monitoring program. In such an instance, the manual may still be covered by Exemption (2).

Exemption (b) (3)

Exemption (b) (3) applies to information that is "specifically exempted from disclosure by statute" (other than the FOIA) when the statute leaves no discretion in the matter on the part of the agency or establishes particular criteria for withholding. In effect, the exemption allows the government to withhold information when other laws require it to be withheld. Examples are income tax returns, some types of census and patent information, and grand jury materials.

No exhaustive list of (b) (3) statutes exists, although the American Society of Access Professionals has put together the most comprehensive list of such statutes. There is no real way to challenge an agency's use of a statute except through a court challenge; however, at the administrative appeal level you can argue that the cited statute does not meet the criteria set out in Exemption (b) (3): Occasionally one of the congressional subcommittees complains to an agency about a (b) (3) statute and such criticism often results in discontinuance of the statute's use to justify nondisclosure. Many (b) (3) statutes are buried in agencies' authorization bills and thus are difficult for press and public interest groups to scrutinize adequately during the legislative process. The Defense Department in 1984 was awarded its own (b) (3) statute concerning technical data and NASA has also asked Congress for the same authority in its enabling statute.

Such statutes can be extremely broad. In 1985 the Supreme Court ruled that the National Security Act was a (b) (3) statute because it made the director of the CIA "responsible for protecting intelligence sources and methods from unauthorized disclosure." By ruling that courts cannot second-guess the director's designation, the CIA can withhold any information on intelligence sources and methods, even if it consists of public information such as newspaper clippings.

Exemption (b) (4)

Exemption (b) (4) protects "trade secrets and commercial or financial information obtained from a person and privileged or confidential." *Person* is defined as a corporation, partnership or individual.

There is a two-pronged harm test used by courts in deciding the applicability of Exemption (b) (4). Release of information must either harm the ability of the government to receive such information in the future, or cause substantial competitive harm to the person furnishing the information. A third test that is sometimes used involves a decision as to whether release would harm a government interest. In order to meet the first harm test, the information must be provided voluntarily. Courts have ruled that information provided under statutory requirements cannot be considered under the first test.

There are numerous categories of business records held by federal agencies. Some general categories likely to be protected are technical designs or data of value to a company and its competitors, internal cost information for current or recent periods, information on financial conditions which, if released, might harm the furnishing company, resumes and salaries of key company personnel and information on customers and sources of supplies.

Congress has considered legislation providing businesses with an opportunity to challenge an agency determination to release confidential information and a right to court review if the agency decided to go ahead with such a release. The legislation passed the House in 1986 but died in the Senate. However, a 1987 executive order requires agencies to notify businesses that an FOIA has been submitted for their information and allows the companies to comment on release of their information. Some companies mark information confidential when submitted. The company is given a chance to give its views, although the final determination is to be made by an agency. If the agency decides to release the information, a 10-day grace period is usually provided to allow the company to go to court if it chooses to do so.

Because the confidentiality of information may lessen with the passage of time, it is possible an agency will release information that at one time would have been protected if it determines that it is no longer confidential.

Exemption (b) (5)

Exemption (b) (5) applies to "inter-agency or intra-agency memoranda or letters which would not be available by law to a party other than an agency in litigation with the agency." The exemption protects such records as advice, recommendations and proposals before the fact. It does not protect essentially factual information, except when it is inextricably intertwined with deliberative matter or with the deliberative process.

This exemption was enacted to protect the deliberative policy-making process of government and to ensure the free exchange of ideas. While courts have ruled that predecisional memoranda, rules and letters regarding policy alternatives are not required to be disclosed, records reflecting an agency's final decision, or predecisional records referenced in a final decision, must be released once the agency adopts the decision.

As interpreted by the courts, the exemption also applies to common civil discovery privileges, allowing the government to withhold records that reflect attorney work-product or attorney-client communications. The Supreme Court has also ruled it protects recognized privileges, such as one allowing the government to withhold statements pertaining to air crashes.

Carl Stern of NBC said that Exemption (b) (5) is one of the most abused. "It's a blanket thing they throw at you. About 97 percent of government documents are internal or intra-agency, but that doesn't automatically exempt [them],"

Stern said. "They have to find something in [the document] that if released would prevent the free flow of ideas. They won't release a document if it has subjectivity intertwined with objective material—even if the only subjective thing in it is the salutation. They forget about the severability/segregability requirement. There has to be something in the document that is not subjective." An agency need not show that release of information would hinder the flow of advice and ideas, only that it falls within one of the privileges recognized under Exemption (b) (5) case law.

Exemption (b) (6)

Exemption (b) (6) covers "personnel and medical files and similar files, the disclosure of which would constitute a clearly unwarranted invasion of personal privacy." The term "clearly unwarranted" has been interpreted as meaning that a balancing rest must be applied when an agency determines the applicability of Exemption (b) (6) to personal information. The degree of invasion of the individual's privacy must be weighed against the public interest in disclosure. However, following a 1989 Supreme Court ruling, courts were forced to reassess the balancing test, and it is currently weighted in favor of privacy. The exemption does not apply when an individual requests information about himself or herself or furnishes the agency with an affidavit from the individual whose file is requested granting permission to the requester to see his or her file.

The government has increasingly expanded its concept of privacy relative to Exemption (b) (6) and the companion exemption (b) (7) (C), which applies to invasion of privacy in the context of law enforcement records. Contesting a line of cases coming out of the Court of Appeals for the District of Columbia Circuit that held Exemption (b) (6) applied only to "intimate" personal details similar to those to be found in medical and personnel files, the government convinced the Supreme Court to significantly broaden the scope of the exemption, allowing agencies, in practice, to withhold any personal information. Such an interpretation has led agencies to release the body of a letter, but withhold the names of the sender and receiver of the letter.

Exemption (b) (7)

Exemption (b) (7) was the only exemption to be amended in 1986. The amended language covers "records or information compiled for law enforcement purposes," but only to the extent they are included in one or more of six specific categories outlined below. The exemption applies only to documents, not the entire file. Each file document must be reviewed, and portions that do not fit into one of the six categories must be released.

The exemption was previously amended in 1974, providing that as a threshold matter the records had to have been created for "investigatory" purposes. Although the importance of this distinction was eroded by the courts, its intention was to prohibit law enforcement agencies such as the FBI from withholding all their files merely on the basis that they pertained to law enforcement matters. The agency had to show the files were actually investigatory in nature before the six categories could be applied. The term "investigatory" was dropped in 1986, so agencies need no longer prove an investigative purpose in the collection of the records.

Law enforcement materials can be withheld if one of the following categories applies:

- *Exemption (b) (7) (A)* covers records that could reasonably be expected to interfere with enforcement proceedings. The rationale here is that the government should not be forced to reveal details of an ongoing law enforcement investigation, particularly to the suspect or his associates. This category, as do the others in Exemption (b) (7), applies to civil as well as criminal law enforcement records.
- *Exemption (b) (7) (B)* prevents release if it would deprive a person of a right to a fair trial or an impartial adjudication. This exemption is aimed at pretrial publicity and is rarely invoked.
- *Exemption (b) (7) (C)* covers information whose release could reasonably be expected to constitute an unwarranted invasion of privacy. Because personal information in law enforcement files has a greater potential for embarrassment than in other contexts, the burden of proof required for this category, which largely parallels Exemption (b) (6), is less stringent. The exemption is used quite frequently; the FBI uses it routinely as a basis for its refusal to "neither confirm nor deny" the existence of a file on any named individual, unless there has been previous agency acknowledgment that such a file exists. It is also used to withhold the names of government employees, such as FBI agents, appearing in the file. This can lead to anomalous results; the Warren Commission that studied the assassination of President Kennedy released the names of all FBI agents who participated in the investigation, but some of those names are no longer available under the FOIA.
- *Exemption (b) (7) (D)* covers information that could reasonably be expected to reveal the identity of a confidential source or, in the case of a criminal law or national security investigation, could reveal information supplied by the confidential source. This category was amended in 1986 to include state, local and foreign agencies or authorities, or private institutions providing information on a confidential basis. Courts have held that confidentiality does not have to be explicit, but can be implied. Before the 1986 amendments, this category was limited in that confidential source information was protected if it came *only* from a confidential source. Now, any information supplied by a confidenial source can be withheld, even if the information has already been made public.
- *Exemption (b) (7) (E)* applies to information that would disclose techniques and procedures for law enforcement investigations or prosecutions, or would disclose guidelines for law enforcement investigations or prosecutions if such disclosure could reasonably be expected to risk circumvention of the law. This category was expanded in 1986 to encompass law enforcement manuals that had previously been withheld under Exemption (b) (2).

- *Exemption (b) (7) (F)* covers information that could reasonably be expected to endanger the life or physical safety of any individual. This category was originally meant to protect undercover agents and law enforcement officials. It was changed in 1986 to cover the physical safety of any individual.

    Congress also provided three categories of exclusion in the 1986 amendments, all pertaining to law enforcement investigations. Information that falls into any of these specific categories is to be treated as being outside the provisions of the FOIA. Although these provisions have not yet been used, they allow agencies to refuse to either confirm or deny the existence of such records. At this point it is a matter of debate as to whether an agency has a responsibility to search for such records before issuing a neither confirm nor deny response.

    The three categories encompass:

- *Records pertaining to a criminal law violation* where there is reason to believe the subject of the investigation is unaware of it and release of records could reasonably be expected to interfere with enforcement proceedings. Such records can be excluded only during the time these circumstances continue to exist. If the suspect becomes aware of the investigation, through indictment or arrest for example, then the exclusion is no longer applicable. However, even if the investigation becomes a matter of public knowledge, the material may still be exempt under one of the six categories of Exemption (b) (7).
- *Informant records maintained by a criminal law enforcement agency* that are maintained under the informant's name or personal identifier. If these records are requested by a third party under the informant's name or identifier, their existence need not be acknowledged.
- *Records maintained by the FBI* pertaining to foreign intelligence or counterintelligence, or international terrorism. The existence of records must be classified information, and as long as their existence remains classified the Bureau may refuse to acknowledge their existence.

Exemption (b) (8)

Exemption (b) (8) covers information "contained in or related to examination, operating, or condition reports prepared by, on behalf of, for the use of an agency responsible for the regulation or supervision of financial institutions." This exemption, passed at the behest of the banking industry, is used by a handful of agencies that regulate or monitor financial institutions or markets. Courts have ruled it applicable to stock and commodity exchanges. Its coverage is extremely broad and can be used to withhold vast amounts of information. It has been rarely litigated, but has become of greater interest to the press as a result of the collapse of a number of banks and savings and loan institutions. Legislation has been offered that would amend the exemption to include a harm test, thus narrowing its applicability to those situations where release could be shown to be harmful in some respect. It is possible that Congress will accept such a change, but certainly not any time in the near future.

Exemption (b) (9)

The least used of all exemptions, this exemption covers "geological and geophysical information and data, including maps, concerning wells." Included at the urging of the oil industry, the exemption is rarely cited and has been litigated in only three cases. Although historically it was thought to be limited to oil and gas wells, the Interior Department has used it occasionally to withhold information on water wells. It has also been used, unsuccessfully, to apply to exploratory drilling for uranium.

Conclusion

Studies continue to show that journalists do not make much use of the Freedom of Information Act. But the Act can be a very useful tool to save legwork and get information that bureaucrats would otherwise be reluctant to provide. Reporters should find it a valuable tool in tapping into the reams of federal information. They should become familiar with its provisions and use it whenever necessary.

SUGGESTED READINGS

FOIA Issues

There are a number of government and commercial publications specializing in Freedom of Information Act issues, the best of which are listed below:

FOIA Update is published quarterly by the Justice Department's Office of Information and Privacy. This small publication keeps government employees up to date on how the Justice Department interprets the Act and what judicial interpretations mean to those who put the decisions into action. It is, therefore, extremely useful to requesters as well. Copies are available from the Government Printing Office.

How to Use the Federal FOI Act, a short but comprehensive booklet on how to make the FOIA work, published by the Reporters Committee for Freedom of the Press, 1735 I St. N.W., Suite 504, Washington, D.C. 20006. Another good short guide is "Using the Freedom of Information Act: A Step by Step Guide," written by Allan Adler, formerly of the ACLU, and available from its Washington office at 122 Maryland Ave. N.E., Washington, D.C. 20002. A more extended treatment of this subject is given in "A Citizen's Guide to How to Use the Freedom of Information Act and the Privacy Act in Requesting Government Documents." Issued originally in November 1977 by the House Government Operations Committee, the report has been revised and updated. It is available from the Government Operations Committee and, frequently, from the FOIA offices of the larger departments.

Access Reports is a biweekly newsletter reporting on FOIA and information access issues. The publication offers comprehensive coverage of FOIA cases and also covers cases and policies pertaining to the Privacy Act, Sunshine Act and Federal Advisory Committee Act. Published by Access Reports Inc., 417 Elmwood Ave., Lynchburg, Va. 24503; a year's subscription costs $300.

Privacy Times is a biweekly newsletter covering privacy issues. The newsletter also provides a great deal of coverage of FOIA issues. Published by Privacy Times Inc., P.O. Box 21501, Washington, D.C. 20009; a year's subscription costs $225.

Federal Information Disclosure is a legal treatise on FOIA by Jim O'Reilly, an attorney and longtime observer of the way in which the statute works. This was the first treatise published and, as a result, is the one most frequently relied on by courts. Its detail may be more than is needed in most cases, but could be useful as a reference work. Published by Shepard's/McGraw-Hill, Colorado Springs, Co.

Information Law: Freedom of Information, Privacy, Open Meetings, and Other Access Laws is a two-volume legal treatise by Washington attorneys Burt Braverman and Frances Chetwyn. The book offers a thorough examination of the FOIA and is perhaps too detailed to be much use on a day-to-day basis for the working journalist. However, it may be a good reference book to have on hand. Published by Practicing Law Institute, New York, N.Y.

The News Media and the Law is published quarterly by the Reporters Committee for Freedom of the Press and contains summaries of major legal actions related to press law.

Other Sources of Information About FOIA Litigation

The Center for National Security Studies in Washington, D.C., annually publishes "The (year) Edition of Litigation Under the Federal Freedom of Information and Privacy Act." The best manual for litigation, it is available from the ACLU at 122 Maryland Ave. N.E., Washington, D.C. 20002.

The Office of Information and Privacy at the Justice Department annually publishes the "Freedom of Information Case List," an updated listing of all cases decided under the FOIA. It also includes an interpretative guide to the FOIA and a listing of cases decided under the Privacy Act, the Sunshine Act and the Federal Advisory Committee Act.

DOCUMENTING THE EVIDENCE

REQUEST LETTER

Date

Name of Agency Official
Title
Name of Agency
Address
City, State, Zip

Dear＿＿＿＿＿＿ :

      Under the provisions of the Freedom of Information Act, 5 U.S.C. 552, I am requesting access to ... (identify the records as clearly and specifically as possible).
      (Optional: I am requesting this information because ... state the reason for your request if you think it will assist you in obtaining the information.)
      If there are any fees for searching for, or copying, the records I have requested, please inform me before you fill the request. (Or: ... please supply the records without informing me if the fees do not exceed $＿＿＿ .)
      As you know, the Act permits you to reduce or waive the fees when the release of the information is considered as ''primarily benefiting the public.'' I believe that this request fits that category and I therefore ask that you waive any fees.
      If all or any part of this request is denied, please cite the specific exemption(s) which you think justifies your refusal to release the information and inform me of your agency's administrative appeal procedures available to me under the law.
      I would appreciate your handling this request as quickly as possible, and I look forward to hearing from you within 10 working days, as the law stipulates.

                  Sincerely,

                  (Signature)
                  Name
                  Address
                  City, State, Zip

APPEAL LETTER

Date

Name of Agency Official
Title
Name of Agency
Address
City, State, Zip

Dear_____ :

    This is to appeal the denial of my request for information pursuant to the Freedom of Information Act, 5 U.S.C. 552.

    On (date), I received a letter from (individual's name) of your agency denying my request for access to (description of the information sought). I am enclosing a copy of this denial along with a copy of my original request. I trust that upon examination of these communications you will conclude that the information I am seeking should be disclosed.

    As provided for in the Act, I will expect to receive a reply within 20 working days.

    (Optional: If you decide not to release the requested information, I plan to take this matter to court.)

    (Optional: It is sometimes helpful to set out some of your legal arguments in your administrative appeal. Otherwise, all that the appeal authority has is the denial authority as argument.)

Sincerely,

(Signature)
Name
Address
City, State, Zip

TEXT OF THE FREEDOM OF INFORMATION ACT

552. Public information; agency rules, opinions, orders, records and proceedings.

(a) Each agency shall make available to the public information as follows:

    (1) Each agency shall separately state and currently publish in the Federal Register for the guidance of the public—

        (A) descriptions of its central and field organization and the established places at which, the employees (and in the case of a uniformed service, the members) from whom, and the methods whereby, the public may obtain information, make submittals or requests, or obtain decisions;

        (B) statements of the general course and method by which its functions are channeled and determined, including the nature and requirements of all formal and informal procedures available;

        (C) rules of procedure, descriptions of forms available or the places at which forms may be obtained, and instructions as to the scope and contents of all papers, reports, or examinations;

        (D) substantive rules of general applicability adopted as authorized by law, and statements of general policy or interpretations of general applicability formulated and adopted by the agency; and

        (E) each amendment, revision, or repeal of the foregoing.

Except to the extent that a person has actual and timely notice of the terms thereof, a person may not in any manner be required to resort to, or be adversely affected by, a matter required to be published in the Federal Register and not so published. For the purpose of this paragraph, matter reasonably available to the class of persons affected thereby is deemed published in the Federal Register when incorporated by reference therein with the approval of the Director of the Federal Register.

    (2) Each agency, in accordance with published rules, shall make available for public inspection and copying—

        (A) final opinions, including concurring and dissenting opinions, as well as orders, made in the adjudication of cases;

        (B) those statements of policy and interpretations which have been adopted by the agency and are not published in the Federal Register; and

        (C) administrative staff manuals and instruction to staff that affect a member of the public; unless the materials are promptly published and copies offered for sale. To the extent required to prevent a clearly unwarranted invasion of personal privacy, an agency may delete identifying details when it makes available or publishes an opinion, statement of policy, interpretation, or staff manual or instruction. However, in each case the justification for the deletion shall be explained fully in writing. Each agency shall also maintain and make available for public inspection and copying current indexes providing identifying information for the public as to any matter issued, adopted, or promulgated after July 4, 1967, and required by this paragraph to be made available or published. Each agency shall promptly publish, quarterly or more frequently, and distribute (by sale or otherwise) copies of each index or supplements thereto unless it determines by order published in the Federal Register that the publication would be unnecessary and impracticable, in which case the agency shall nonetheless provide copies of such index on request at a cost not to exceed the direct cost of duplication. A final order, opinion, statement of policy, interpretation, or staff manual or instruction that affects a member of the public may be relied on, used, or cited as precedent by an agency against a party other than an agency only if—

    (i) it has been indexed and either made available or published as provided by this paragraph; or

    (ii) the party has actual and timely notice of the terms thereof.

(3) Except with respect to the records made available under paragraphs (1) and (2) of this subsection, each agency, upon any request for records which (A) reasonably describes such records and (B) is made in accordance with published rules stating the time, place, fees (if any), and procedures to be followed, shall make the records promptly available to any person.

(4) (A) In order to carry out the provisions of this section, each agency shall promulgate regulations, pursuant to notice and receipt of public comment, specifying a uniform schedule of fees applicable to all constituent units of such agency. Such fees shall be limited to reasonable standard charges for document search and duplication and provide for recovery of only the direct costs of such search and duplication. Documents shall be furnished without charge or at a reduced charge where the agency determines that waiver or reduction of the fee is in the public interest because furnishing the information can be considered as primarily benefiting the general public.

(B) On complaint, the district court of the United States in the district in which the complainant resides, or has his principal place of business, or in which the agency records are situated, or in the District of Columbia, has jurisdiction to enjoin the agency from withholding agency records and to order the production of any agency records improperly withheld from the complainant. In such a case the court shall determine the matter de novo, and may examine the contents of such agency records in camera to determine whether such records or any part thereof shall be withheld under any of the exemptions set forth in subsection (b) of this section, and the burden is on the agency to sustain its action.

(C) Notwithstanding any other provisions of law, the defendant shall serve an answer or otherwise plead to any complaint made under this subsection within thirty days after service upon the defendant of the pleading in which such complaint is made, unless the court otherwise directs for good cause shown.

(D) Except as to cases the court considers of greater importance, proceedings before the district court, as authorized by this subsection, and appeals therefrom, take precedence on the docket over all cases and shall be assigned for hearing and trial or for argument at the earliest practicable date and expedited in every way. [Note: Section D deleted July 1989.]

(E) The court may assess against the United States reasonable attorney fees and other litigation costs reasonably incurred in any case under this section in which the complainant has substantially prevailed.

(F) Whenever the court orders the production of any agency records improperly withheld from the complainant and assesses against the United States reasonable attorney fees and other litigation costs, and the court additionally issues a written finding that the circumstances surrounding the withholding raise questions whether agency personnel acted arbitrarily or capriciously with respect to the withholding, the Civil Service Commission shall promptly initiate a proceeding to determine whether disciplinary action is warranted against the officer or employee who was primarily responsible for the withholding. The Commission, after investigation and consideration of the evidence submitted, shall submit its findings and recommendations to the administrative authority of the agency concerned and shall send copies of the findings and recommendations to the officer or employee or his representative. The administrative authority shall take the corrective action that the Commission recommends.

(G) In the event of noncompliance with the order of the court, the district court may punish for contempt the responsible employee, and in the case of a uniformed service, the responsible member.

(5) Each agency having more than one member shall maintain and make available for public inspection a record of the final votes of each member in every agency proceeding.

(6) (A) Each agency, upon any request for records made under paragraph (1), (2), or (3) of this subsection, shall—

(i) determine within ten days (excepting Saturdays, Sundays, and legal public holidays) after the receipt of any such request whether to comply with such request and shall immediately notify the person making such request of such determination and the reasons therefor, and of the right of such person to appeal to the head of the agency any adverse determination; and

(ii) make a determination with respect to any appeal within twenty days (excepting Saturdays, Sundays, and legal public holidays) after the receipt of such appeal. If on appeal the denial of the request for records is in whole or in part upheld, the agency shall notify the person making such request of the provisions for judicial review of that determination under paragraph (4) of this subsection.

(B) In unusual circumstances as specified in this subparagraph, the time limits prescribed in either clause (i) or clause (ii) of subparagraph (A) may be extended by written notice to the person making such request setting forth the reasons for such extension and the date on which a determination is expected to be dispatched. No such notice shall specify a date that would result in an extension for more than ten working days. As used in this subparagraph, "unusual circumstances" means, but only to the extent reasonably necessary to the proper processing of the particular request—

(i) the need to search for and collect the requested records from field facilities or other establishments that are separate from the office processing the request;

(ii) the need to search for, collect, and appropriately examine a voluminous amount of separate and distinct records which are demanded in a single request; or

(iii) the need for consultation, which shall be conducted with all practicable speed, with another agency having a substantial interest in the determination of the request or among two or more components of the agency having substantial subject-matter interest therein.

(C) Any person making a request to any agency for records under paragraph (1), (2), or (3) of this subsection shall be deemed to have exhausted his administrative remedies with respect to such request if the agency fails to comply with the application time limit provisions of this paragraph. If the Government can show exceptional circumstances exist and that the agency is exercising due diligence in responding to the request, the court may retain jurisdiction and allow the agency additional time to complete its review of the records. Upon any determination by an agency to comply with a request for records, the records shall be made promptly available to such person making such request. Any notification of denial of any request under this subsection shall set forth the names and titles or positions of each person responsible for the denial of such request.

(b) This section does not apply to matters that are—

(1) (A) specifically authorized under criteria established by an Executive order to be kept secret in the interest of national defense or foreign policy, and (B) are in fact properly classified pursuant to such Executive order;

(2) related solely to the internal personnel rules and practices of an agency;

(3) specifically exempted from disclosure by statute (other than section 552b of this title), provided that such statute (A) requires that the matters be withheld from the public in such a manner as to leave no discretion on the issue, or (B) establishes particular criteria for withholding or refers to particular types of matters to be withheld;

(4) trade secrets and commercial or financial information obtained from a person and privileged or confidential;

(5) inter-agency or intra-agency memorandums or letters which would not be available by law to a party other than an agency in litigation with the agency;

(6) personnel and medical files and similar files, the disclosure of which would constitute a clearly unwarranted invasion of personal privacy;

(7) investigatory records compiled for law enforcement purposes, but only to the extent that the production of such records would (A) interfere with enforcement proceedings, (B) deprive a person of a right to a fair trial or an impartial adjudication, (C) constitute an unwarranted invasion of personal privacy, (D) disclose the identity of a confidential source and, in the case of a record compiled by a criminal law enforcement authority in the course of a criminal investigation, or by an agency conducting a lawful national security intelligence investigation, confidential information furnished only by the confidential source, (E) disclose investigative techniques and procedures, or (F) endanger the life or physical safety of law enforcement personnel;

(8) contained in or related to examination, operating, or condition reports prepared by, on behalf of, or for the use of an agency responsible for the regulation or supervision of financial institutions; or

(9) geological and geophysical information and data, including maps, concerning wells.

Any reasonably segregable portion of a record shall be provided to any person requesting such record after deletion of the portions which are exempt under this subsection.

(c) This section does not authorize withholding of information or limit the availability of records to the public, except as specifically stated in this section. This section is not authority to withhold information from Congress.

(d) On or before March 1 of each calendar year, each agency shall submit a report covering the preceding calendar year to the Speaker of the House of Representatives and President of the Senate for referral to the appropriate committees of the Congress. The report shall include—

(1) the number of determinations made by such agency not to comply with request for records made to such agency under subsection (a) and the reasons for each such determination;

(2) the number of appeals made by persons under subsection (a) (6), the result of such appeals, and the reason for the action upon each appeal that results in a denial of information;

(3) the names and titles or positions of each person responsible for the denial of records requested under this section, and the number of instances of participation for each;

(4) the results of each proceeding conducted pursuant to subsection (a) (4) (F), including a report of the disciplinary action taken against the officer or employee who was primarily responsible for improperly withholding records or an explanation of why disciplinary action was not taken;

(5) a copy of every rule made by such agency regarding this section;

(6) a copy of the fee schedule and the total amount of fees collected by the agency for making records available under this section; and

(7) such other information as indicates efforts to administer fully this section.

The Attorney General shall submit an annual report on or before March 1 of each calendar year which shall include for the prior calendar year a listing of the number of cases arising under this section, the exemption involved in each case, the disposition of such case, and the cost, fees, and penalties assessed under subsection (a) (4) (E), (F), and (G). Such report shall also include a description of the efforts undertaken by the Department of Justice to encourage agency compliance with this section.

(e) For purposes of this section, the term 'agency' as defined in section 551(1) of the title includes any executive department, military department, Government corporation, Government controlled corporation, or other establishment in the executive branch of the Government (including the Executive Office of the President), or any independent regulatory agency.

PART TWO
INDIVIDUALS

C H A P T E R　　　　5

Backgrounding Individuals

Throughout our lives we all generate a cornucopia of information on which the savvy investigator can feast. This chapter highlights a basic checklist of the most common documents, with examples of how to find them and how to make use of them.

At the end of the chapter are listings of where to find birth and death, marriage and divorce records in each state.

by JACK TOBIN

The call for help came from a lawyer-friend. He was trying to untangle a dispute over a will written in 1940. The signer, of course, was dead. So were the lawyers who had drafted it and the secretary who had typed it. The only person who might still be alive to testify about the signer's soundness of mind was another secretary, who had witnessed a codicil to the will. Her name was Jane Smith. That's all we knew, and it was one of the most common names among the more than 10 million people in the Los Angeles area.

I found her in three months. Here's how.

To begin with, I made the assumption that Jane had been employed in the office of the long-dead lawyer who had drafted the will. Using an employee to witness a will is a common practice in law offices. My first stop was the archives of the Los Angeles central library, where I asked for the 1940 edition of the Polk's

City Directory. Four Jane Smiths were listed as secretaries. I started a separate notebook page for each. Then I tracked each Jane, going forward in the directory year by year. R.L. Polk and Company gave up trying to keep track of L.A.'s exploding and transient population not long after World War II—a great loss to reporters. But I had addresses from the last edition, so I could use the telephone book. That led me forward a few more years before each trail disappeared.

One of the last city directories had listed an employer of one Jane Smith. It, too, was a law firm, now defunct. From the Yellow Pages of that year's phone book, I got the names of the firm's member-lawyers. The bar association was able to supply the home address of a retired partner.

Yes, he remembered Jane. No, he had no idea what had become of her. But he did remember that she had gotten married and he recalled her married name.

The county recorder's office keeps the marriage license file. Jane Smith's husband had come from another state. A call to the motor vehicle department there turned up his driver's license, with his current home address. I made another call. A man answered. I made my inquiry. After a pause, I was talking to the right Jane Smith.

It's easy to trace people's footsteps, once you learn how.

You may not have a lawyer-friend in need as I did, but knowing how to track down the Jane Smiths of this world and how to find out the details of their lives is a valuable skill for any reporter. Let me remind you of some sources you might otherwise overlook and suggest a few that may be new to you.

Getting Started

Newspaper Libraries

Whether you are trying to find a person or find out about that person, always start with the sources closest to you. Go to the newspaper library and check the clip file. Some homework may have been done for you. The spelling of the name and the correct middle initial will be essential in using public records. Look for age, address, occupation and names of acquaintances.

Telephone Books

Next, pick up the phone book. The White Pages may give you an address and provide a check on spellings. If your target has an unusual name, look for others like it. You may find a relative or you may have been misled in other records by a look-alike name. The Yellow Pages may help you, as they helped me to find Jane Smith's former employer. You may be able to learn something about your target's business or competitors. They could be sources, too.

City Directories

The City Directory may be more helpful. Although directories are no longer published for some large cities, they are found in most towns, big and small. Not only are you likely to find the name and address of the target of your investigation, but you may find the occupation and name of spouse listed, too. In the criss-cross directory you can learn the names of the neighbors by looking up the street address.

Neighbors

A nosy neighbor can be a great source. I once was trying to find someone who had moved out of an apartment building 20 years before. The manager was no help, and tenant records went back only five years. Instead of a record, I found a tenant, an elderly woman, who for years had had little to do but keep track of her fellow occupants. She knew my target and where he had gone. She also knew—as I learned over two painfully slow hours—the whereabouts and personal habits of nearly everyone else who had lived in that building during her 31 years there.

Most of the time, most people are happy to tell what they know to a willing listener.

Driver's License and Motor Vehicle Registration Records

Driver's license and motor vehicle registration records are available for the asking in some states. In other states, you will have to go through a friendly cop or prosecutor. Full name, correct address, date of birth and social security number are recorded here. The make and model of car may also be useful.

Voter Registration Records

Voter registration records aren't used as often as they could be. From these records, you can learn subject's full name, current address, city, often a home telephone number, usually a social security number, party affiliation, registration date and whether the registration was a new or changed address. In many registrar's offices, you can check back files as well. If you are able to trace someone to a specific address, but he or she has since moved, the post office will provide a forwarding address for about $1, provided, of course, that the person left a change of address card.

I found one woman through voter registration records when all other public records failed. She had been married twice. The name I knew her by was her first married name, under which she continued to vote despite having adopted the new name (which I didn't know) on her driver's license, car registration and other records.

A tip: As is true of many other records, voter registration records are often on microfilm or microfiche and not easy to read. A small enlarging glass may save eyestrain.

Birth Records

If you know or can guess the state in which your target was born, birth records can provide useful information. You will find names and addresses of parents at the time of your subject's birth, the place of birth, parents' occupations and the names of the attending physician and the hospital. Birth records can lead you, as they have led me, to those few people who have left no other paper trail. A person may not drive, vote or own property, but if he or she was born in the United States, somebody has a record of it. All you have to do is find it.

Listed at the end of this chapter are the offices in each state that keep birth, death and marriage certificates. These are not always public records, however. Check state laws.

Uniform Commercial Code Filings

Easily found but seldom used are Uniform Commercial Code filings. They're kept in the secretary of state's office in most states, and sometimes in the county recorder's office as well. Uniform Commercial Code filings are the listings of debts filed by lenders to protect themselves. For example, you can find out here if your target has taken out a big loan and put up for security assets you didn't know he or she had—such as, real estate, stocks and bonds or a diamond necklace. You'll need a name, and sometimes an address, to tap this lode.

Court Records

Perhaps the richest lode of all for the investigative reporter is property records. See Chapter 9, "Tracing Land Holdings," which is devoted to them.

Not far behind in general usefulness are the records of court proceedings, both civil and criminal. Criminal records, leaked from a friendly law enforcement agent or disclosed in a congressional hearing or other public forum, are old stuff to most investigators. Civil court records are not as commonly used, but you shouldn't overlook them.

Take the case of Howard Hughes. He didn't have a driver's license. He never voted. He owned little in his own name. But he was sued. The suit was filed by a former aide, Robert Maheu, after Hughes said in a rare television interview that Maheu had "stolen me blind." Maheu sued for slander, won, saw an appeals court reverse the decision and finally settled out of court. The real winners were all those who hungered for details of the life of the world's most famous recluse. The exhibits in the case filled a room. They amounted to millions of pages of testimony, depositions, accounting reports and tape-recorded conversations. Donald Barlett and James Steele of the Philadelphia Inquirer mined those riches for their definitive biography of Hughes, titled "Empire."

Most of the records of current court cases, criminal or civil, are public. You can look up the file in the court clerk's office where the case was tried if you know the name of either the plaintiff or the defendant. The alphabetical listing will give you a case number, which you can use to ask for the file. You'll find many of the most interesting documents in the exhibit file, where both sides enter anything they can find to bolster their cases or denigrate their opponent. Check the U.S. District Court as well as local courts. The filing systems are similar.

Bankruptcy Court

While you're in the federal building, drop by the bankruptcy court. When an individual goes broke or a business seeks legal protection from its creditors, financial secrets are laid bare in the bankruptcy court files. Names of creditors, amount of debt and statements of assets are all there for the taking. Check both individual and company names. If the case is old, the file may be in a government archive, and you will have to wait several days to get it. (For more details on how to use bankruptcy court records, see Chapter 11, "Business.")

U.S. Tax Court

An even more specialized and less-known court is the U.S. Tax Court, located in Washington, D.C. This is the ultimate arbiter of disputes between the Internal Revenue Service and the taxpayer. The cases that go there usually are big, invariably complicated and sometimes fascinating. By the time the IRS gets through with an opponent, it knows most of what there is to know about him or her. Much of that information is on the tax record. The problem with the tax court as a source is that you almost have to be a certified public accountant to understand much of what you find there. U.S. Tax Court case files are maintained solely at the court's Washington, D.C., headquarters, but copies of these files may be requested by phone. (For more details on how to use the U.S. Tax Court, see Chapter 6, "Using Tax Records.")

Probate Court

Probate Court can be a good place to learn not just about the dead but about their heirs and living associates. A perusal of any prominent person's estate will yield interesting stories. Examination of the estate of a business wheeler-dealer or a criminal boss can turn up material of real substance. Probate will show what that person owned and to whom it was left. Sometimes it is just as interesting to see what was not owned or who was written out of the will. The owner of a major Las Vegas casino, who had lived like a millionaire, left an estate of less than $10,000.

One reason probate court isn't covered as thoroughly as it might be is the time lag between the death and the determination of probate: It can be months, even years. The probate of Howard Hughes' estate produced some good stories. The government, with huge tax revenues at stake, challenged the accuracy of the estate inventory prepared by a major public accounting firm. That's not a bad story in itself.

Divorce Court

While you are checking your target's civil and criminal case file, finding out what the IRS has on him or her and plowing through his or her godfather's probate, don't forget to find out whether he or she was ever divorced. If he or she was, you may really strike gold.

Consider the case of Herman Talmadge, a former senator from Georgia who, at one time, was a power to be reckoned with both in his party and in the upper reaches of the U.S. government. Then he divorced his wife. Out of the bitter proceedings emerged tales of kickbacks, hidden cash and campaign contributions converted to personal use. In the end, he was rebuked by his no-longer-so-respectful colleagues.

The advent of the no-fault divorce may be a boon to society, but it is a loss to investigative reporting.

Listed at the end of this chapter are the offices in each state that keep divorce records, and how far back they go.

Immigration and Other Court Records

In some special cases, other kinds of government records will be of use. Immigration court records don't fall into the hands of reporters very often, with one exception: When a deportation effort winds up in court, these federal records become part of the file, open along with the rest of it. Among those whose deportation cases get that far are various upper-level operatives in organized crime. The intelligence reports included in some of their cases are a veritable history of the mob in this country. The files, which can be located in the clerk's office of the U.S. District Courts where the trials were held, are largely untouched by reportorial hands.

One caveat to remember. Everything in a court case file is not true. The file is made up of charges and, while reporters covering the case may report the accusations that are made, you may need to verify the truthfulness of the information yourself.

Unusual Printed Sources

If the individual you are trailing happens to be or to have been a president of the United States, documents of the General Services Administration (GSA) can help. I used GSA records, along with building permits from the city of San Clemente, to expose the vast sums of taxpayer money that were used to perfect Richard Nixon's coastal estate there.

The Nixon case also produced a classic example of editor-induced frustration. I had a tip from a subcontractor whose name I found in GSA files that

Nixon's personal servants were being paid with National Park Service funds. I advised Time's editors to check that tip, not with an agency head who would certainly deny it, but with a payroll clerk who probably would show us the records. A member of Time's Washington, D.C., bureau went instead to the head of the Park Service, who denied it. The Washington Post later broke my story.

University Theses and Dissertations

A final source—one I'll bet few of you have used—is university theses and dissertations. These obscurely titled, minutiae-filled research papers that students write to earn their master's and doctoral degrees can be very useful. It isn't always easy to figure out what the tome is about from reading its title in the library. It isn't always easy to figure it out after you've read the whole thing, either. But I recently used two for major stories.

A piece for Sports Illustrated on the progress of athletes toward degrees was aided immeasurably when I discovered that a former UCLA fullback had written a doctoral dissertation at another school on that precise topic. It was, so far as I know, the only documented study of its kind then in existence.

The second case arose during the backgrounding of a Sports Illustrated story on the Arizona State football scandal in the fall of 1979. I remembered that the athletic conference that predated the Pac-10 conference, of which Arizona State is a member, had been destroyed in the mid-1950s by scandal. The story of the earlier conference had been detailed in a master's thesis done at UCLA. That thesis was easy to find. I wrote it.

Military Maneuvers: Basic Training in How to Get Service Records

by Mitchell Zuckoff
Boston Globe

For Darrow "Duke" Tully, the masquerade was up.

Tully had made a splash, not only as publisher of The Arizona Republic and The Arizona Gazette, but also through his reputation as a retired Air Force colonel who was shot down over Korea, flew 100 missions in Vietnam and possessed enough medals and ribbons to make Michael Jackson envious.

Then in late 1985, an aggressive local prosecutor, Tom Collins, began looking into Tully's background in the course of preparing a libel suit against the newspapers. (As a law-enforcement agent, Collins had access to records and information that are unavailable to journalists and the public.) With Collins ready to disclose that Tully's military career was complete fiction, the Duke came clean.

But that is only part of the story. The bad news is that, if not for an angry prosecutor and Tully's almost unceasing escalation and public display of his fantasy, he might have remained a "hero."

Specific factors working in favor of Tully and other Walter Mitty characters will be discussed below, but the bottom line is this: The government system that provides public information on former military personnel is fraught with land mines (a fire at the main repository destroyed 18 million records in 1973), ambushes ("sensitive" requests can become caught in a fine-tuned bureaucracy) and snipers (extremely specific information is often needed for successful searches and crucial information is off-limits without veterans' consent).

For journalists questioning the claims of public figures—from candidates to criminals—the only solution is to understand the system's strengths and weaknesses and to find ways to work within and around them.

In most cases, the search for military personnel information begins and ends at a hulking, five-story glass and steel building in Overland, Mo., on the outskirts of downtown St. Louis. The building is home to the military section of the National Personnel Records Center, a division of the National Archives and Records Administration. Across town is the center's other half, a building filled with files on the federal government's former civilian employees.

The military center is the physical custodian of roughly 80 million 20th century U.S. military records, about 50 million of which are the personnel files of one-time soldiers, sailors, pilots, etc. The remainder range from routine reports to hospital records, reflecting the military's love affair with forms in triplicate.

The records are kept in 1.8 million cardboard boxes, each 1 cubic foot in size, on 11-foot-tall metal shelves painted military green. Each storage floor is double the width of a football field and twice its length ("including end zones," said management analyst Norman R. Eisenberg). Clerks scurry up and down ladders to get at the boxes, making it look like a giant shoe warehouse catering to people with size 24 feet.

About 8,000 of the records are kept away from the millions of grunts and swabbies in what is known as the "VIP Vault." Here Elvis Aaron Presley and Jimi Hendrix rub shoulders with the likes of President Bush, Gen. Douglas MacArthur (who takes up almost an entire shelf), Jimmy Carter, Audie Murphy, Joe Louis, Glenn Miller and Clark Gable, whose discharge papers are signed by Ronald Reagan, the head of the wartime film unit.

All records at the center are technically governed by the same rules, but access to the VIP records is especially guarded: "What we have here is the government's business, nobody else's," Eisenberg said. In other words, requests for information on well-known veterans are likely to come under closer scrutiny, increasing the chances that the material requested will be unavailable.

The center receives roughly 1.8 million information requests yearly. Two-thirds come from veterans, their families or the Veterans Administration. The bulk of the inquiries received by the center are from individuals or agencies seeking a Separation From Service form and/or benefits eligibility data.

Another frequent user is the Defense Department, which examines the records for security investigations, reenlistment approval and medical studies, such as the most recent Pentagon review of Agent Orange and radiation. Requests also come from various federal, state and local authorities for court proceedings, law enforcement and benefits eligibility decisions.

"A very, very small number of requests come from the media, maybe 1,000 to 2,000 yearly," said Paul D. Gray, assistant director for military personnel records, who oversees nearly 500 employees as the center's top on-site official.

Gray is an affable, bearded 44-year-old Air Force veteran of Vietnam who has held his job since 1980. All media requests cross his desk, so Gray is perhaps the key player in this process, a man who wields great power over reporters on the trail of would-be Omar Bradleys.

Gray is well-schooled in the details and the language of the Freedom of Information Act and the Privacy Act; reporters dealing with him should know the basic rules governing the release of military personnel records.

1. All requests must be written and must specifically cite the FOIA as the basis under which the information is sought. Telephone inquiries won't do because a signature is required; however, telefaxed requests with a signature are accepted. Gray will return information via overnight mail if the requesting party pays for it. There is no cost for media requests.

2. Requests should ideally be made on a copy of Standard Form 180. However, a simple letter will do if the inquiry includes:

- The correct spelling of the veteran's name.
- His or her military service or Social Security number.
- Approximate dates and branch of service, if known.
- What information is needed and why.

- The address to which the reply should be sent and a telephone number.
- The requesting party's signature.
- This is optional, but it helps if the letter is on some type of official stationery.

If all this information is provided and the system works the way it is supposed to, a response might be on its way within a day or so. If not, it could take weeks to track down a file, or it could simply be impossible to do so, Gray said.

3. Working to accommodate both Privacy Act and FOIA requirements, the military allows the center to release the following information (ask for each item specifically):

- Veteran's date of birth and correct name.
- Dates of service.
- Marital status.
- Dependents, including name, sex and age.
- Date of any change in rank/grade.
- Salary, although not likely to be available because most of the center's files do not contain pay records.
- Duty assignments, including geographical locations.
- Military and civilian education level but not schools attended or dates of attendance.
- Decorations and awards.
- Duty status (active, reserve, discharged, retired or deceased).
- Photograph (if available).
- Records of courts-martial unless classified.

If a veteran is dead, the center also may provide place of birth, date and geographical location of death, place of burial and service number.

Journalists should be warned that a note on Form 180 firmly states that only the veteran, his or her next-of-kin and federal officers are authorized to receive records from the center. The form says others must receive permission from the veteran or, if deceased, his or her family. Don't let that warning end a search before it begins.

Gray said the military allows public release of all the above materials to anyone—not just journalists—who cites the FOIA as the law under which the information is being sought. When told that IRE was aware of at least one journalist whose request had been turned down for lack of an authorizing signature, Gray said that was a mistake that would not happen again as long as he is in charge.

Note: Because these rules are made not by the center but by the Defense Department, the same information—as well as confirmed future assignments and office phone numbers—can generally be obtained for current military personnel. However, the request has to be made directly to the branch in which the person is serving.

4. That's the good news. Now here's the good stuff the military does not release without the veteran's written approval:

- Disciplinary records, except public courts-martial.
- Discharge status (honorable, dishonorable, general, etc.).
- Facts and circumstances surrounding discharge.
- Medical records.
- Other information contained in service jackets protected by privacy regulations.

"It's a whole different ballgame if you can get a release from the subject," Gray said. "If you do, anything is fair game."

In other words, don't expect information provided by the center to form a compelling narrative unless the veteran is cooperating fully.

That might seem fairly straightforward, but reporters should be forewarned that it is far more complicated in practice.

First, before even making the request, journalists should try to determine whether the records are stored at or destined for the center. The best way to do this is by using the back page of Form 180, which gives an unusually detailed, easy-to-follow explanation of where different records are supposed to be, plus the addresses of the record custodians to whom inquiries should be made.

For example, records of active duty Air Force personnel are kept at the Air Force Manpower and Personnel Center at Randolph Air Force Base in Texas. When airmen and women go on reserve status, their records are sent to the Air Reserve Personnel Center in Denver. After discharge, retirement or death, the records go to St. Louis, most often to gather dust indefinitely.

While the center is the final repository for most military records, Vice President Dan Quayle's file will never make it there. National Guard records remain with the adjutant general in each state, District of Columbia and Puerto Rico. Another quirk is that the Army keeps the files of retired living veterans at the U.S. Army Reserve Personnel Center, located adjacent to the records center but under separate jurisdiction.

The problem with all this, of course, is that a military file is harder to track down if a reporter does not know in which branch a person served. A comprehensive quick-search database does not exist, and we have no easy way to determine in all cases whether someone was in the military without information from the veteran, the family or the employer.

That is one reason Tully's exposure was largely his own fault. When Republic City Editor Richard Robertson got wind of Tully's lie, he wrote to the center asking for information on his boss's military record. The story broke (Tully confessed) before Robertson received a response, but even if it had arrived in time, the reply would have said that no file could be found.

"I cannot verify that a person has never been in the military," Gray said. "Just because we don't have a record doesn't mean a person didn't serve." (In cases such as Tully's, where a reporter knows the supposed service branch, the next step would be contacting the Air Force directly.)

When the center is supposed to have a file but none is found, it could mean the person is lying. On the other hand, it might mean a veteran's separation was too recent for the file to reach the center; the branch that created it repossessed it for some reason; or the file was somehow misplaced or destroyed, Gray said.

That leads to a second problem with the system: the fire. Shortly after midnight, July 12, 1973, an intense fire broke out on what was the sixth floor of the center. No cause has ever been established, and no one was hurt. But fueled by tons of paper in a building that lacked smoke alarms, sprinklers and fire walls, it burned for four days.

In the end, the blaze destroyed the entire top floor and affected the 23 million records kept there. Of those, 18 million were destroyed, while the rest sustained varying degrees of smoke, water and fire damage.

The real problem, continuing even today, is that no one knows exactly whose records were lost. The records do not have an index; they merely were filed in alphabetical order in blocks that corresponded to major military periods.

What is known is that the fire destroyed about 80 percent of the records for Army personnel discharged between Nov. 1, 1912 and Jan. 1, 1960, and about 75 percent of the records for Air Force personnel with surnames from Hubbard through "Z" discharged between Sept. 25, 1947, and Jan. 1, 1964. A number of others also were destroyed.

No effort was made to reconstruct or index all 18 million missing files, Gray said, because of the time and cost needed for such a task. However, about 1.6 million of those records have been reassembled to one degree or another using information available through other sources and copies of documents sent by veterans themselves.

Although a master index and far better fire protection are in place today, the fire continues to haunt the center in terms of time and resources spent rebuilding charred, moldy and destroyed records. Fire-related costs of about $1 million a year are expected to continue well into the next century, Gray said, a hefty sum compared with the center's annual budget of about $10 million.

A third major hurdle in the process is the heavy reliance on service and Social Security numbers, which most reporters are unlikely to obtain without help from a cooperative source.

The center's master index is not very sophisticated and is based on information reminiscent of interrogation scenes in old war movies: name, branch and Social Security or service number. The Army and the Air Force changed from service to Social Security numbers on July 1, 1969; the Navy and Marine Corps did so Jan. 1, 1972; and the Coast Guard followed Oct. 1, 1974.

Gray and Eisenberg both stressed that the need for the identifying numbers is "almost absolute."

"There is that rare case where a name is so unique that I can obtain just one record" by checking the index, Gray said, "but don't count on it."

He said that if a search turns up only a couple of possible files, he might pull and check them against other information provided by the reporter. But if 30 people have the same name—not unusual when millions of records are involved—"no way," Gray said.

"It's a judgment call on my part," he said. "We control the resources. But for the most part, we work with the media."

But that cooperation has limits, it seems. First, Gray made it clear that he prefers inquiries that closely follow the FOIA format, are sent by overnight mail and request overnight return.

"That tells us that they have gone the extra mile, and that demonstrates a sense of urgency, to which we respond," he said. In those cases, the response could be in the mail the same day.

But then again, Gray can use a heavy dose of discretion when dealing with requests he considers "sensitive."

This became clear when Gray was asked to run two searches for IRE, both without service or Social Security numbers, to test the system. The plan was to run one search on a well-known politician and the other on an unknown whose file was possibly affected by the fire.

The politician originally was to be U.S. Sen. John F. Kerry, D-Mass., a decorated Navy veteran of Vietnam.

"Choose someone else," Gray said.

"Why?"

"Just choose someone else. It would be better."

Upon further discussion, it became clear that Kerry would be considered a "sensitive" subject because of an antiwar protest in which he tossed service medals over a fence. After some further haggling, during which Gray suggested that an entertainer be chosen rather than a politician, he agreed to a search of U.S. Sen. John McCain, an Arizona Republican who was a POW and a Vietnam war hero.

Moreover, Gray said he would classify as sensitive an inquiry that he knew would turn up information that could be embarrassing to a veteran. As an example, he said that might be the case if a politician claimed he won the Silver Star but a check of his file turned up no such decoration.

In cases like that, which might attract what he called "adverse attention," Gray said, "we would much prefer the legal custodian of the record handle the release."

The process of red-flagging and referring the request to one of the military branches, Gray acknowledged, increases the chances of an additional delay, and that the reporter will ultimately be frustrated in the search.

Gray also noted that, unlike many journalists, he considers the 10-day requirement of FOIA as merely a time frame in which the center must acknowledge receipt of a journalist's request, effectively giving himself free rein on how long before the information is provided.

For the sake of contrast, consider the approach taken at the National Archives Building.

Largely because privacy considerations no longer are applied as strictly (almost all its military personnel records are from the 18th and 19th centuries), the archives makes complete military service records freely available to the public for genealogical and other research.

"There are virtually no restriction on the files we have here," said archives spokeswoman Jill Brett.

Ironically, the result is that a reporter might have better luck proving or disproving a claim about a politician's ancestor being a Civil War hero than about the politician's service in Vietnam.

With all that in mind, here are a few additional hints to help reporters locate military records:

1. Gather all available information in advance from the subject's statements (some legislators are quick to cite their military pasts during floor debates), public documents (Social Security numbers might appear on candidacy papers, in lawsuits, etc.) and sources willing to provide specifics without going back to the subject.

2. Consider the information provided by the military as fodder for additional questions, rather than as final answers themselves. A "no file" response or the absence of detailed information does not necessarily signify a dead end.

3. Contact current and former employers, who might remember an old resume that listed military information differently or in greater detail.

4. Don't overlook the town or city hall in a person's birthplace or current residence; some keep lists and detailed histories of local residents who went off to war. Also, the military sends copies of discharge and retirement papers to adjutant generals in each state. Policies vary, but most keep them in a central repository, Gray said.

Rhode Island, for example, made a list of everyone from the Ocean State who served in the military in World War II.

5. Contact veterans' groups, both locally and nationally, to see if they can provide information or strategies to check a claim. For the most part, they will be helpful in making sure no one is wrongly taking credit for their sacrifices. For example, if a politician claims he fought in a certain unit, a veterans' group might find others from that unit to test the target's recollections.

6. Don't neglect military historians at universities and the Pentagon itself. Facts about geographical and chronological postings—provided by the personnel center—can be used by experts to create partial narrative histories of military service.

7. Perhaps most importantly, carefully follow all the instructions (cite FOIA, ask for specific information, use service/Social Security numbers if available, etc.) when dealing with the center or any other military records repository. Adhering to the military's rules will save time and increase a reporter's chances of determining whether a person's past includes feats of heroics or feet of clay.

Conclusion

Follow the two pieces of advice on using all of the records mentioned so far. First, make a point of making friends with the people who work in the offices where you regularly search records—not the department heads, but the people who know how the place really works. A sympathetic chief clerk can ease your work load greatly and sometimes can even lead you out of a dead end.

Second, whenever possible, get certified copies of every record you think will be important. They are handy to have when your own and others' lawyers come asking to see proof. I learned that the hard way during an investigation of Jimmy Hoffa. I failed to buy a certified copy of a key record in the recorder's office in a small Alabama county seat. A lawsuit was threatened. I went back to the office and discovered that the document had been neatly sliced from the book. The registrar refused to contact the lawyers involved to try to reconstruct it. I breathed a sigh of relief when no suit was filed. I haven't failed to get a certified copy since.

There are other records useful in exploring the lives of individuals. Most of them are detailed in the following chapters.

DOCUMENTING THE EVIDENCE

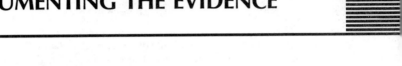

WHERE TO WRITE FOR VITAL RECORDS:
BIRTH, DEATH, DIVORCE AND MARRIAGE

Birth and Death Records

An official certificate of every birth and death should be on file in the locality where the event occurred. These certificates are prepared by physicians, funeral directors and other professional attendants or hospital authorities.

The federal government does not maintain files or indexes of these records. They are permanently filed in the central vital statistics office of the state, independent city or outlying area where the event occurred.

To obtain a certified copy of a certificate, write or go to the vital statistics office in the state or area where the birth or death occurred. The offices are listed below.

Send a money order or certified check when writing for a certified copy because the office cannot refund cash lost in transit. Type or print all names and addresses in the letter.

Births occurring before birth registration was required or births not registered when they occurred may have been filed as "delayed birth registrations." Keep this in mind when seeking a copy of the record.

If possible, give the following facts when writing for birth or death records.

1. Full name of person whose record is being requested.
2. Sex and race.
3. Parent's names, including maiden name of mother.
4. Month, day and year of birth or death.
5. Place of death (city, town, county or state; and name of hospital, if any).
6. Purpose for which copy is needed.
7. Relationship to person whose record is being requested.

Marriage Records

An official record of every marriage should be available in the locality where the marriage occurred. These records are filed permanently either in a state vital statistics office or in a city, county or other local office.

If possible, give the following facts when writing for marriage records.

1. Full names of bride and groom.
2. Month, day and year of marriage.
3. Place of marriage (city or town, county and state).
4. Purpose for which copy is needed.
5. Relationship to person whose record is being requested.

Divorce Records

An official record of every divorce or annulment or marriage should be available in the locality where the event occurred. These records are filed permanently either in a state vital statistics office or in a city, county or other local office.

If possible, give the following facts when writing for divorce records.

1. Full name of husband and wife.
2. Date of divorce or annulment.
3. Place of divorce or annulment.
4. Type of final decree.
5. Purpose for which copy is needed.
6. Relationship to persons whose record is being requested.

The following list was taken from data published by the U.S. GPO.

ALABAMA
Bureau of Vital Statistics
Department of Public Health
Montgomery, Ala. 36130
(205) 261-5033
Birth and Death. State has records since January 1908.
Marriage. State has records since 1936. For earlier records, write Probate Judge in county where license issued.
Divorce. State office above has records since January 1950. For earlier records, write Clerk or Registrar of Court of Equity in county where divorce was granted.

ALASKA
Alaska Department of Health
Bureau of Vital Statistics
Pouch H-02G
Juneau, Alaska 99811
(907) 465-3391
Birth, Death and Marriage. State office has records since 1913.
Divorce. State office has records since January 1950. For certified copies, write Superior Court in judicial district where divorce was granted. Juneau and Ketchikan (1st District), Nome (2nd District), Anchorage (3rd) and Fairbanks (4th).

ARIZONA
Division of Vital Records
State Department of Health
P.O. Box 3887
Phoenix, Ariz. 85030
(602) 255-1080
Birth and Death. State office has records since July 1909 and abstracts of earlier records filed in counties.
Marriage and Divorce. Write to Clerk of Superior Court in county where license was issued or divorce was granted.

ARKANSAS
Division of Vital Records
Arkansas Department of Health
4815 W. Markham St.
Little Rock, Ark. 72201
(501) 661-2336
Birth and Death. State has records since February 1914 and some Little Rock and Fort Smith records from 1881.
Marriage. State has records since 1917. Full certified copy may be obtained from County Clerk in county where license was issued.
Divorce. State office has coupons since 1923. Full certified copy available from Circuit or Chancery Clerk in county where divorce granted.

CALIFORNIA
Vital Statistics Branch
Department of Health Services
410 N St.
Sacramento, Calif. 95814
(916) 445-2684
Birth, Death and Marriage. State records since July 1905. For earlier records, write County Recorder in county where event occurred.
Divorce. Records available only from Clerk of Superior Court in county where divorce granted. State office can search records to identify county where record is held.

COLORADO
Vital Records Section
Colorado Department of Health
4210 E. 11th Ave.
Denver, Colo. 80220
(303) 320-8333
Birth and Death. State has death records since 1900 and birth records since 1910; also earlier births for some areas.
Marriage. State has index of records for 1900–39 and 1975 to present. Inquiries will be forwarded. For years not indexed or certified copies, write to County Clerk in county where license issued.
Divorce. State has index for 1900–39 and 1968 to present. Inquiries forwarded. For years not indexed or certified copies, write Clerk of District Court in county where divorce granted.

CONNECTICUT
Department of Health Services
Vital Records Section
Division of Health Statistics
State Department of Health
150 Washington St.
Hartford, Conn. 06106
(203) 566-1124
Birth and Death. State has records since July 1897. For earlier records, write Registrar of Vital Statistics in town where event occurred.
Marriage. State has records since July 1897. For certified copy, write Registrar of Vital Statistics in town where license issued.
Divorce. State index of records since 1947. Inquiries forwarded. For certified copies, write Clerk of Superior Court in county where divorce granted.

DELAWARE
Office of Vital Statistics
Division of Public Health
P.O. Box 637
Dover, Del. 19903
(302) 736-4721
Birth and Death. State office has records for 1861 to 1863 and since 1881, but no records for 1864 to 1880.
Marriage. State office has records since 1847.
Divorce. State has records since 1935. State does not issue certified copies, but will forward inquiries or search and verify essential facts. For full certified copies, write Prothonotary (records before 1975) or Family Court (records since 1975) in county where divorce was granted.

DISTRICT OF COLUMBIA
Vital Records Section
425 I St. N.W. Rm. 3009
Washington, D.C. 20001
(202) 727-5316
Birth and Death. State has death records since 1855 and birth records since 1871, but no death records filed during Civil War.
Marriage. State has records since January 1982. For certified copy, write Marriage Bureau, 515 Fifth St. N.W., Washington, D.C. 20001.
Divorce. For records since September 16, 1956, write to Clerk, Superior Court

for the District of Columbia, Family Division, 500 Indiana Ave. N.W., Washington, D.C. 20001. For earlier records, write Clerk, U.S. District Court for D.C., Washington, D.C. 20001.

FLORIDA
Department of Health and Rehabilitative Services
Office of Vital Statistics
P.O. Box 210
Jacksonville, Fla. 32231
(904) 359-6900
Birth and Death. State has some birth records since April 1865 and some death records since August 1877; majority of records date from 1917.
Marriage and Divorce. State has records since June 1927. If exact date unknown, office will do year-by-year search and certify results.

GEORGIA
Department of Human Resources
Vital Records Unit, Room 217-H
47 Trinity Ave. S.W.
Atlanta, Ga. 30334
(404) 656-4900
Birth and Death. State has records since January 1919. For earlier records in Atlanta or Savannah, write to the county Health Department.
Marriage. State has centralized records since June 1952; will issue certified copies for central records and forward inquiries on earlier dates to Probate Judge in county where license issued.
Divorce. State has records since June 1952; it will not issue certified copies, but will forward inquiries to Clerk of Superior Court in county where divorce granted.

HAWAII
Research and Statistics Office
State Department of Health
P.O. Box 3378

Honolulu, Hawaii 96801
(808) 548-5819
Birth and Death. State office has records since 1853.
Marriage. State office has records since July 1951.
Divorce. State has records since July 1951. For certified copy, write Circuit Court in County where divorce granted.

IDAHO
Bureau of Vital Statistics
State Department of Health
Statehouse
Boise, Idaho 83720
(208) 334-5988
Birth and Death. State has records since 1911. Write to County Recorder in county where event occurred for earlier records.
Marriage and Divorce. State has records since 1947. Earlier records with County Recorder in county where license issued or divorce granted.

ILLINOIS
Division of Vital Records
State Department of Health
605 West Jefferson St.
Springfield, Ill. 62702
(217) 782-6553
Birth and Death. State has records since January 1916. For earlier records or certified copies, write County Clerk in county where event occurred.
Marriage and Divorce. State has records since January 1962. For earlier records write County Clerk in county where license issued or Circuit Court where divorce granted.

INDIANA
Division of Vital Records
State Board of Health
1330 West Michigan St.
P.O. Box 1964
Indianapolis, Ind. 46206
(317) 633-0274

Birth and Death. State has birth records since October 1907 and death records since 1900. For earlier records, write to Health Officer in city or county where event occurred.

Marriage. State has marriage index since 1958. For earlier records or certified copies, write to Clerk of Circuit Court or Clerk of Superior Court in county where license was issued.

Divorce. Write County Clerk in county where divorce was granted.

IOWA

Department of Public Health
Vital Records Section
Lucas Office Building
Des Moines, Iowa 50319
(515) 281-5871

Birth, Death and Marriage. State has records since July 1880.

Divorce. State office has only brief statistical record since 1906. For certified copies or more detailed information, write Clerk of District Court in county where divorce was granted.

KANSAS

Office of Vital Statistics
Kansas State Department of Health and Environment
900 Jackson St.
Topeka, Kan. 66612
(913) 296-1400

Birth and Death. State office has records since July 1911. For earlier records, write to County Clerk in county where event occurred.

Marriage and Divorce. State office has marriage records since May 1913 and divorce records since July 1951. For earlier records or full certified copies, write to District Judge in county where marriage license issued or divorce granted.

KENTUCKY

Office of Vital Statistics
Department of Health Statistics

275 E. Main St.
Frankfort, Ky. 40621
(502) 564-4212

Birth and Death. State has records since January 1911 and some earlier records for cities of Louisville, Newport, Lexington and Covington.

Marriage and Divorce. State office has records since June 1958. For earlier records or full certified copy, write to Clerk of County Court where license or decree was issued.

LOUISIANA

Division of Vital Records
Office of Health Services and Environmental Quality
P.O. Box 60630
New Orleans, La. 70160
(504) 568-5175

Birth and Death. State has most records since July 1914; also has birth records from 1790 and death records from 1803 for city of New Orleans.

Marriages and Divorce. Full certified copies of records for Orleans parish issued by state. For other parishes, write Clerk of Court in parish where license was issued.

MAINE

Office of Vital Records
Human Services Building
State House, Station 11
Augusta, Maine 04333
(207) 289-3181

Birth and Death. State records since 1892. For earlier dates, write to the municipality where event occurred.

Marriage and Divorce. State records since 1892. For full certified copies, write Town Clerk in town where license issued or District Court in division granting divorce.

MARYLAND

Division of Vital Records
State Department of Health

State Office Building
P.O. Box 13146
201 W. Preston St.
Baltimore, Md. 21203
(301) 225-5988
Birth and Death. State office has records since 1898; some Baltimore records from 1875.
Marriage. Records since June 1951. For earlier records or certified copies, write Clerk of Circuit Court in county where license issued or Clerk of Common Pleas in Baltimore.
Divorce. Records since January 1961. State office will verify some items and forward inquiries, but will not issue certified copies. For full certified copies, write to Clerk of Circuit Court in county where divorce was granted.

MASSACHUSETTS
Registry of Vital Statistics
150 Tremont St., Room B-3
Boston, Mass. 02111
(617) 727-0110
Birth and Death. Records since 1896. For earlier records, write State Archives, State House, Boston, Mass.
Marriage. State office has records since 1891.
Divorce. State office has index only since 1952. Inquirer is directed where to send request. For certified copies, write to Registrar of Probate Court in county where divorce was granted.

MICHIGAN
Office of State Registrar
Center for Health Statistics
Michigan Department of Public Health
3500 N. Logan St.
Lansing, Mich. 48909
(517) 335-8655
Birth and Death. State office has records since 1867. Records also available from County Clerk in county where event occurred. Detroit records on births since 1893 and on deaths since

1897 can be obtained from the City Health Department.
Marriage and Divorce. State has marriage records since 1867 and death records since 1897. For full certified copies, write to County Clerk in county where license issued or divorce granted.

MINNESOTA
Minnesota Department of Health
Section of Vital Statistics
717 Delaware St. S.E.
Minneapolis, Minn. 55440
(612) 623-5121
Birth and Death. State office has records since January 1908. For earlier records, write Court Administrator in county where event occurred or the St. Paul City Health Department, if the event occurred in St. Paul.
Marriage and Divorce. State has index of marriages since January 1958 and divorces since January 1970. Inquiries will be forwarded. For full certified copies, write to Court Administrator in county where license issued or divorce granted.

MISSISSIPPI
Vital Records
State Board of Health
P.O. Box 1700
Jackson, Miss. 39215
(601) 354-6606
Births and Deaths. State office has records since 1912.
Marriage. Statistical records only from January 1926 to July 1, 1938, and since January 1942. For full certified copy, write to Circuit Clerk in county where license issued.
Divorce. State has records since 1926, but does not issue certified copies. Inquiries will be forwarded. For earlier records or certified copies, write Chancery Clerk in county where divorce granted.

MISSOURI
State Department of Health
Bureau of Vital Records
P.O. Box 570
Jefferson City, Mo. 65102
(314) 751-6376
Birth and Death. State office has records since January 1910. For St. Louis, St. Louis County or Kansas City records before 1910, write city or county health department.
Marriage and Divorce. State has index of marriage and divorce since July 1948. Inquiries forwarded. For certified copies, write Recorder of Deeds in county where license issued or Circuit Court in county where divorce granted.

MONTANA
Bureau of Records & Statistics
State Department of Health
Helena, Mont. 59620
(406) 444-2614
Birth and Death. State office has records since late 1907.
Marriage and Divorce. State has records since July 1943; will verify items and forward inquiries. For earlier records or certified copies, write District Court in county where license issued or divorce granted.

NEBRASKA
Bureau of Vital Statistics
State Department of Health
301 Centennial Mall South
P.O. Box 95007
Lincoln, Neb. 68509
(402) 471-2871
Birth and Death. State office has records since late 1904 and can provide information about earlier birth records.
Marriage and Divorce. State has records since 1909. For certified copies, write County Court in county where license issued or District Court in county where divorce granted.

NEVADA
Division of Health
Vital Statistics
Capitol Complex
Carson City, Nev. 89710
(702) 885-4480
Birth and Death. State has records since July 1911. For earlier records, write to County Recorder in county where event occurred.
Marriage and Divorce. State has indexes since January 1968 and will forward inquiries. For earlier records or certified copies, write County Recorder in county where license issued or County Clerk in county where divorce granted.

NEW HAMPSHIRE
Bureau of Vital Records
Human Services Building
6 Hazen Drive
Concord, N.H. 03301
(603) 271-4654
Birth and Death. State has some records since 1640. For copies, write State or City Clerk in place where event occurred.
Marriage and Divorce. State has marriage records since 1640 and divorce records since 1808. For full certified copies, write Town Clerk in town where license issued or to Clerk of Superior Court in county where divorce granted.

NEW JERSEY
State Department of Health
Bureau of Vital Statistics
CN 360
Trenton, N.J. 08625
(609) 292-4087
Birth, Death and Marriage. State office has records since May 1878. For records from May 1848 to May 1878, write to Archives and History Bureau, State Library Division, State Department of Education, Trenton, N.J. 08625.

Divorce. Write to the Superior Court, Chancery Division, State House Annex, Room 320, CN 971, Trenton, N.J. 08625.

NEW MEXICO
Vital Statistics Bureau
New Mexico Health Services Division
P.O. Box 968
Santa Fe, N.M. 87504
(505) 827-2338
Birth and Death. State office has records since 1920 and delayed records since 1880.
Marriage and Divorce. Write to the County Clerk in county where marriage license was issued or to the Clerk of the Superior Court in county where divorce was granted.

NEW YORK (EXCEPT NEW YORK CITY)
Bureau of Vital Records
State Department of Health
Empire State Plaza
Tower Building
Albany, N.Y. 12237
(518) 474-3075
Birth and Death. State office has records since 1880. For records before 1914 in Albany, Buffalo and Yonkers or before 1880 in any other city, write to Registrar of Vital Statistics in city where event occurred. For the rest of the state, except New York City, write to state office.
Marriage. State has records since 1880. Write to City Clerk in Albany or Buffalo or Registrar of Vital Statistics in Yonkers if marriage occurred in one of these cities between 1880 and 1907.
Divorce. State has records since 1963. For earlier records or certified copy, write to County Clerk in county where divorce granted.

NEW YORK CITY (ALL BOROUGHS)
Bureau of Vital Records
Department of Health of New York City

125 Worth St.
New York, N.Y. 10013
(212) 619-4530
Birth and Death. City office has birth records since 1898 and death records since 1920. For Old City of New York (Manhattan and part of the Bronx) birth records for 1865–1897 and death records for 1865–1919, write to Archives Division, Department of Records and Information Services, 31 Chambers St., New York, N.Y. 10007.
Marriage. City Archives Division (see above) has records from 1847 to 1865, except Brooklyn records for this period, which are filed with County Clerk's Office, Kings County, Supreme Court Building, Brooklyn, N.Y. 11201.
Records from 1866 to 1907 available from City Clerk's office in borough where marriage performed.
For records of 1908 to May 1943, New York City residents write to City Clerk in borough of bride's residence; and non-residents write to City Clerk in borough where license was obtained. For records since May 1943, write to City Clerk's Office in borough where license was issued. License includes names, ages, birthdates and date and place of marriage. Any additional information—matrimonial history, parents' names and countries of origin—must be requested. Mail requests must include return postage.

Bronx:
City Clerk's Office
1780 Grand Concourse
Bronx, N.Y. 10457

Brooklyn:
City Clerk's Office
Municipal Building
Brooklyn, N.Y. 11201

Manhattan:
City Clerk's Office
Municipal Building
New York, N.Y. 10007

Queens:
City Clerk's Office
120-55 Queens Blvd.
Kew Gardens, N.Y. 11424
Staten Island:
City Clerk's Office
Staten Island Borough Hall
Staten Island, N.Y. 10301
Divorce. State has city records since 1963. Earlier records with County Clerk.

NORTH CAROLINA
Department of Human Resources
Division of Health Services
Vital Records Branch
P.O. Box 2091
Raleigh, N.C. 27602
(919) 733-3526
Birth and Death. State office has birth records since October 1913 and death records since January 1930. Death records from 1913 through 1929 available from Archives and Records Section, State Records Center, 215 North Blount St., Raleigh, N.C. 27602.
Marriage and Divorce. State has marriage records since January 1962 and divorce records since January 1958. For earlier records or certified copies, write Registrar of Deeds in county where marriage performed or Clerk of Superior Court where divorce granted.

NORTH DAKOTA
Division of Vital Records
State Department of Health
Office of Statistical Services
Bismarck, N.D. 58505
(701) 224-2360
Birth and Death. State office has some records since July 1983; years from 1894 to 1920 are incomplete.
Marriage. State office has records since July 1925. State does not issue certified copies, but will verify some items and forward inquiries. Full certified copies

available from County Judge in county where license issued.
Divorce. State has index of records since July 1949; some items verified; inquiries forwarded. Full certified copies available from Clerk of District Court in county where divorce was granted.

OHIO
Division of Vital Statistics
Ohio Department of Health
G-20 Ohio Department Building
65 S. Front St.
Columbus, Ohio 43266
(614) 466-2531
Birth and Death. State office has records since December 1908. For earlier records, write Probate Court in county where event occurred.
Marriage and Divorce. State records since September 1949. State office will not issue certified copies, but will verify all items and forward inquiries. For full certified copies, write Probate Judge where license issued or Clerk of Court of Common Pleas in county where divorce granted.

OKLAHOMA
Vital Records Section
State Department of Health
N.E. 10th St. and Stonewall
P.O. Box 53551
Oklahoma City, OK 73152
(405) 271-4040
Birth and Death. State office has records since 1908.
Marriage and Divorce. Write Clerk of Court in county where license issued or divorce granted.

OREGON
Oregon State Health Division
Vital Statistics Section
P.O. Box 116
Portland, Ore. 97207
(503) 229-5710

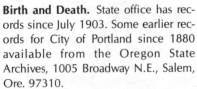

Birth and Death. State office has records since July 1903. Some earlier records for City of Portland since 1880 available from the Oregon State Archives, 1005 Broadway N.E., Salem, Ore. 97310.
Marriage and Divorce. State has marriage records since 1906 and divorce records since 1925. For earlier records or certified copies, write County Clerk in county where license issued or divorce granted.

PENNSYLVANIA
Division of Vital Records
State Department of Health
Central Building
101 S. Mercer St.
P.O. Box 1528
New Castle, Pa. 16103
(412) 656-3100
Birth and Death. State office has records since 1906. For earlier records, write to Registrar of Wills, Orphans Court, in county seat where event occurred.
For events in Pittsburgh from 1870 to 1905 or in Allegheny City, now part of Pittsburgh, from 1882 to 1905, write to Office of Biostatistics, Pittsburgh Health Department, City-County Building, Pittsburgh, Pa. 15219. For events in Philadelphia from 1860 to 1915, write Vital Statistics, Philadelphia Department of Public Health, City Hall Annex, Philadelphia, Pa. 19107.
Marriage and Divorce. State has marriage records since January 1906 and divorce records since January 1946. State office does not issue certified copies, but will forward inquiries. For full certified copies, write Marriage License Clerks, County Court House, in county where license issued or Prothonotary, Court House, in county where divorce granted.

PUERTO RICO
Division of Demographic Registry and Vital Statistics

Department of Health
San Juan, Puerto Rico 00908
(809) 728-4300
Birth and Death. Central office has records since July 22, 1931. For earlier records, write to local Registrar (Registrador Demografico) in town where event occurred.
Marriage and Divorce. Central records since July 1931. For earlier records, write local Registrar where marriage license issued or Superior Court where divorce granted.

RHODE ISLAND
Division of Vital Statistics
State Department of Health
Cannon Building, Room 101
75 Davis St.
Providence, R.I. 02908
(401) 277-2811
Birth and Death. State office has records since 1853. For earlier records, write Town Clerk in town event occurred.
Marriage and Divorce. State office has marriage records since 1853. For divorce records, write to Clerk of Family Court, 1 Dorrance Plaza, Providence, R.I. 02908.

SOUTH CAROLINA
Office of Vital Records and Public Health Statistics
State Department of Health
2600 Bull St.
Columbia, S.C. 29201
(803) 734-4830
Birth and Death. State office has records since January 1915. City of Charleston births from 1877 and deaths from 1821 are on file at Charleston County Health Department. Ledger of Florence City births and deaths from 1895 to 1914 on file at Florence County Health Department. Ledger of Newberry City births and deaths from late 1800s filed at Newberry County Health Department.

Marriage. State has records since July 1950. For certified copies or records since July 1911, write Probate Judge in county where license issued.
Divorce. State has records since July 1962. For certified copies or records since April 1949, write Clerk of county where divorce petition filed.

SOUTH DAKOTA
State Department of Health
Center for Health Policy and Statistics
523 E. Capitol
Pierre, S.D. 57501
(605) 773-3355
Birth and Death. State has records since 1905 and access to some earlier records.
Marriage and Divorce. State has records since 1905. For certified copies, write County Treasurer in county where license issued or Clerk of Court in county where divorce granted.

TENNESSEE
Tennessee Vital Records
Department of Health Cordell
Hull Building
Nashville, Tenn. 37219
(615) 741-1763
Birth and Death. State has birth records for entire state since 1914; Nashville since 1881; Knoxville since 1881; and Chattanooga since 1882. Death records for entire state since 1914; Chattanooga since 1872; Knoxville since 1887; and Nashville since 1874. Birth and death records by school district are available for July 1908–June 1912. For Memphis births from April 1874 to December 1887 and November 1898 to January 1914, write to Memphis-Shelby County Health Department, Division of Vital Records, Memphis, Tenn. 38105.
Marriage and Divorce. State has records since July 1945. For certified copies, write County Clerk in county

where license issued or Clerk of Court in county where divorce granted.

TEXAS
Bureau of Vital Statistics
Texas Department of Health
1100 West 49th St.
Austin, Tx. 78756
(512) 458-7380
Birth and Death. State office has records since 1903.
Marriage and Divorce. State has records since 1968; it issues no certified copies, but will search and verify essential facts. For earlier records or certified copies, write County Clerk in county where license issued or District Court in county where divorce granted.

UTAH
Bureau of Vital Records
Utah Department of Health
288 North 1460 West
P.O. Box 16700
Salt Lake City, Utah 84116
(801) 538-6105
Birth and Death. State office has records since 1905. If event occurred from 1890 to 1904 in Salt Lake City or Ogden, write to City Board of Health. For records elsewhere in state from 1898 to 1904, write to County Clerk in county where event occurred.
Marriage and Divorce. State office has records since 1978; will provide short form certified copy. For full certified copy, write County Clerk in county where license issued or divorce granted.

VERMONT
Vermont Department of Health
Vital Records Section
Box 70
60 Main St.
Burlington, Vt. 05402
(802) 863-7275
Birth, Death and Marriage. State office has records since 1955. For records

prior to 1955, write to Division of Public Records, 6 Baldwin St., Montpelier, Vt. 05602. Full certified copy available from City Clerk in town of birth, death or license issuance.

Divorce. State has records since 1968. For full certified copy, write to City Clerk in town where divorce granted.

VIRGINIA
Division of Vital Records
State Department of Health
James Madison Building
P.O. Box 1000
Richmond, Va. 23208
(804) 786-6228

Birth and Death. State has records from January 1853 to December 1896 and since June 14, 1912. For records between those dates, write to Health Department in city where event occurred.

Marriage and Divorce. State has marriage records since January 1853 and divorce records since January 1918. For full certified copies, write to Clerk of Court in county or city where license issued or divorce granted.

WASHINGTON
Vital Records
P.O. Box 9790, ET-11
Olympia, Wash. 98504
(206) 753-5396

Birth and Death. State has records since July 1907. Records for Seattle, Spokane and Tacoma also available from City Health Department. For records before 1907, write to the County Auditor in county where event occurred.

Marriage and Divorce. State has records since January 1968. For earlier records or full certified copies, write to County Auditor in county where license was issued or County Clerk in county where divorce was granted.

WEST VIRGINIA
Division of Vital Statistics
State Department of Health
State Office Bldg. No. 3
Charleston, W.Va. 25305
(304) 348-2931

Birth and Death. State office has records since January 1917. For earlier records, write to Clerk of County Court in county where event occurred.

Marriage. State has records since 1921; certified copies from 1964. For earlier records, write County Clerk in county where license issued.

Divorce. State has index since 1968. Certified copies not available, but some items verified. For earlier records or certified copies, write Circuit Court, Chancery Side, in county divorce granted.

WISCONSIN
Bureau of Health Statistics
Wisconsin Division of Health
P.O. Box 309
Madison, Wis. 53701
(608) 266-1371

Birth and Death. State has scattered records earlier than 1857. Records before October 1907 are very incomplete.

Marriage. State has records since April 1836. Records before 1907 are incomplete.

Divorce. State has records since October 1907.

WYOMING
Vital Records Services
Division of Health and Medical Services
Hathaway Building
Cheyenne, Wyo. 82002
(307) 777-7591

Birth and Death. State office has records since July 1909.

Marriage and Divorce. State has records since May 1941. For earlier records or full certified copies, write to County Clerk in county where license issued or Clerk of District Court where divorce granted.

CHAPTER 6

Using Tax Records

Although the tax records of individuals are not available to reporters under most circumstances, there are times when access is allowed, such as when a dispute between a taxpayer and the Internal Revenue Service (IRS) reaches the U.S. Tax Court or when the IRS seeks a tax lien. In addition, records of sales, business, property and other taxes may divulge a great deal about individuals and the companies for which they work. "Follow the dollar" is a useful maxim for investigative reporters, and tax dollars are part of that trail.

This chapter introduces the legal methods available for the search and concludes with a detailed listing of the tax forms that exist on the record.

by DAVID B. OFFER

Let others curse the tax collector. Investigative reporters know that to tax is to create stacks of documents that often yield important information to journalists who know where to look.

Although it is true that most tax information is legally protected and, therefore, usually impossible to obtain, it still is important to think of tax records as potential sources of information. Even some federal income tax returns are available, if you know where to look.

Let's say you are investigating Sam Shady, owner of a sleazy bookstore and massage parlor. You begin by checking the ownership of the building in which the store is located, tracking all property and business records, such as articles of incorporation, examining zoning records and building inspection reports, and thumbing through litigation files at the county courthouse.

But what might you find in tax records?

- You can learn if the state or federal government has filed tax liens seeking to collect unpaid back taxes from Shady or his business.
- If Shady has been fighting the feds over taxes, you may get lucky and find the case has gone to U.S. Tax Court. That's a gold mine for reporters who know where to dig.
- You can look at hidden taxes—the licenses and permits issued by city and village officials and regulatory agencies to keep track of business.
- You can see how government agents handle the tax dollars they collect.

Let's look at these possibilities.

Tax Liens

A good way to start is to check for state or federal tax liens.

A tax lien is a legal claim filed in court by the government against a person or business owing taxes. Liens are not criminal matters; they are civil claims. Normally they seek to attach money and/or property to pay the taxes before it has reached the individual or company. The public list of liens is kept in the county, state or federal courthouse or the local recorder of deeds office. Liens show whom the government is pursuing and how much is sought.

Even when not investigating a specific individual, it is a good policy for investigative reporters to check these lists regularly. They are often the first signs that a business or individual is in financial trouble, and that can be important news. Lists of people who have owed taxes for a long time can themselves become the basis for interesting stories.

Perhaps the most spectacular use of tax lien files was made by Donald L. Barlett and James B. Steele, the Pulitzer Prize–winning investigative team of the Philadelphia Inquirer. As part of a major investigation into the operation of the Internal Revenue Service, Barlett and Steele reviewed 20,000 tax liens, and from these discovered fascinating examples of government ineptitude and questionable practices. Among them:

- *A physician who owed more than $900,000 in federal income taxes.* He held no property in his own name and said the IRS was being "very nice" by not "trying to push" him during negotiations over the huge tax bill. The doctor had once admitted delivering a bribe to a judge in a tax-evasion case involving a Mafia figure.
- *An insurance executive who owed more than $2 million in back taxes.* He was sentenced to six months in jail for a tax violation but never served a day because no one bothered to find him.
- *A man who sold his $190,000 home and placed other assets in trust to avoid payment of a tax bill of more than $740,000.* The man shipped many of his belonging to England and left the country himself before the IRS started trying to collect the money due.

Not every reporter will uncover such flagrant abuses of the law, but there may be some of equal importance in unchecked files around the country.

In addition to showing who owes money to the government, lien files also show when the money has been paid. Liens are withdrawn when a taxpayer pays back taxes, plus any required interest or penalties.

Withdrawal of liens is another story because often the amount owed is greatly reduced after a conference between the government and the taxpayer. Details of a lien reduction become public only when both parties agree the full amount of the lien is owed, but the payment is reduced because the taxpayer is old, sick or otherwise unable to pay. In such cases involving federal tax liens, an IRS Form 7249-M (Offer in Compromise) must be filed detailing the reason for lien reduction. Form 7249-M is public information and should be available through your local IRS office. (See Documenting the Evidence section at the end of this chapter for more information on obtaining Form 7249-M.) If the government reduces a lien amount because it is uncertain the full amount is owed or because it wishes to avoid a costly court battle, details of the reduction are considered confidential taxpayer information and are not made available to the public.

Court Records

Everyone knows one thing about state and federal income tax returns: They are secret, unavailable to snoopy reporters or anyone else. Occasionally reporters with excellent sources can obtain a copy of someone's tax returns—Jack White won a Pulitzer Prize for reporting Richard Nixon's attempts at federal tax avoidance—but most officials won't even leak tax information.

There are, however, places where alert reporters may find tax information and returns. The most fruitful and accessible sources are court records. These should always be checked in investigative work, as they can reveal important tax information:

- In some states, people seeking property settlements in divorce matters must submit copies of their income tax returns to the divorce court. These may be available under the state open-records laws.
- Tax records and returns also may be introduced in evidence in state and federal lawsuits dealing with financial matters.
- Tax returns are part of the record in many kinds of criminal cases.
- Sometimes old tax records can be found in probate court when wills are filed and property distributed among a dead person's heirs and friends.

U.S. Tax Court

When tax payment claims by the government are disputed, they often end up in U.S. Tax Court. It is located in Washington, D.C., but judges travel throughout the country holding hearings on tax cases. The court is public and so are its records, including tax returns. Additional financial information is submitted in evidence and testimony under oath by those involved in a dispute.

The court does not deal with criminal matters. Rather, it interprets technical points of tax law. Tax court cases can involve deficiencies or overpayments of estate, gift, personal, excise, corporate and holding company taxes; penalties imposed on not-for-profit corporations and foundations; disputes over tax-exempt status; and qualifications of retirement plans. The Taxpayer's Bill of Rights, passed in 1988, gave the U.S. Tax Court new authority to review and restrain IRS actions, including the assessment and collection of taxes and interest, as well as the use of property seizures and tax penalties. Although the issues may be complex, the cases can make news, particularly when they involve people whose financial backgrounds are of interest to investigative reporters.

Often millions of dollars are at stake in hearings ignored by both the press and the public.

Sometimes tax court cases stem from the reluctance of a person to part with tax dollars. For example, Xavier Hollander, the "Happy Hooker," went to tax court to challenge IRS claims that she owed taxes on $130,000 of unreported income from her profitable business as a prostitute and madam in New York.

Hidden Taxes

Most governments, at every level, obtain the majority of their revenue through income, sales or property taxes. But these certainly are not the only taxes that government collects and reporters should consider this when seeking stories. Hidden taxes – permits, licenses, utility fees and similar charges required by various state and city agencies – can provide important information for reporters. Because their collection is less sophisticated and less carefully monitored than that of property or sales taxes, there is a greater possibility of wrongdoing.

Consider hunting and fishing licenses. In most states, these are sold by sporting goods stores or municipal government offices, which are required to turn the proceeds over to the state. Sometimes the store or municipality is allowed to keep a small fee for going to the trouble of taking care of the license sales for the state.

But in many states, there is little supervision of these license sales. In rural Wisconsin, where lots of people like to hunt and fish, the Milwaukee Journal discovered a county clerk selling licenses but putting the money in his own private savings account to earn interest. Eventually he turned the money over to the state Department of Natural Resources, but he kept the interest. If you multiply his interest earnings by the hundreds of license dealers in any state, the amount of income lost to the state might be significant.

How Tax Money Is Handled

Reporters should be aware that state and local governments don't immediately spend all the money they collect. If they are efficient – and honest – they invest those funds to earn interest.

Their investment policies can make interesting stories. Has the mayor decided to place unneeded city funds in the bank where he or she happens to have a large personal loan at an exceptionally low rate of interest? Are funds left in no-interest checking accounts at the bank run by the comptroller's uncle instead of being put into interest-bearing savings accounts, money-market funds or bonds? In short, what are the state's investment policies and who established them? These and similar questions can generate stories.

Many states have investment boards or agencies which operate in secrecy, not because they seek to hide things but because no one has ever asked what they do. A reporter who asked might learn, for example, that even before the state decides where to open its account, certain banks are favored. Millions of dollars are involved, but the public seldom knows about the decisions.

The figures involved may not be as large, but counties, cities, villages, rural fire districts and other government agencies, too numerous to mention, all collect taxes. Where they keep them — in the pocket of the tax collector, in the local bank or in risky stocks and bonds — is seldom reported, but often important.

Don't forget to see that the taxes are actually collected. Are out-of-state firms paying the requisite state corporate income taxes? How about visiting athletes? One newspaper discovered that golfers who were winning thousands of dollars in local tournaments were not paying state taxes on them.

Conclusion

People who don't pay taxes or who fight the government over the amount of money they should pay are often the kind of people journalists should investigate.

John Marshall said, "The power to tax involves the power to destroy." For journalists, however, the government's power to tax is a source of news.

DOCUMENTING THE EVIDENCE

FEDERAL TAXES

Internal Revenue Service Records

The U.S. Internal Revenue Service (IRS) opens little of its information to the public. Usually available for public inspection are records of liens, real estate and other property sales, returns of tax-exempt organizations and applications filed by such organizations for tax-exempt status (see Chapter 11, "Business," under "Not-for-Profit Corporations and Foundations") and records of compromises resulting from negotiations between taxpayers and the IRS relating to income, profits, estate or gift taxes.

The IRS maintains a public affairs office at each of its seven regional and 53 district offices, as well as at its 10 national service centers. Often the best first step is to call the nearest IRS public affairs office and simply ask how to obtain the documents.

Abstract and Statement (Of an Offer in Compromise)/IRS Form 7249-M. If an individual owes back taxes to the federal government and the IRS settles its claim for less than what is owed, Form 7249-M must be filed. You should check this routinely.

The form contains a detailed financial summary of the individual, including where he or she works and take-home pay, liabilities and assets and so on.

The forms are located in the regional IRS public reference room and then sent to the IRS Washington, D.C., office on an annual basis. If you can't get to a reading room to see if anything exists on the individual you are backgrounding, write or phone the regional office or the Washington, D.C., office listed following. If a Form 7249-M has been filed on the individual, copies should be available on request.

IRS Publications. The IRS has a number of publications of value to reporters seeking background information on taxes. The following publications can be obtained by writing to Headquarters, Internal Revenue Service, 1111 Constitution Ave. N.W., Washington, D.C. 20224.

- *Internal Revenue Collection of Excise Taxes* is a quarterly press release providing excise tax revenues for the quarter just concluded, the same quarter for the previous year and the completed portions of the current and previous fiscal years. Revenue sources are divided into several broad areas: alcohol, tobacco and stamp taxes; manufacturers' excise taxes; retailers' taxes; and miscellaneous taxes, including telephone and teletype, domestic and international air transportation, narcotics, betting, truck highway use, private foundation and employee pension fund taxes.
- *Statistics of Income, Individual Income Tax Returns* consists of two publications offering data about nationwide trends on individual income based on tax returns. The first is a preliminary annual report, based on a probability sampling of filed individual returns, that provides statistical information about selected income and tax items, income by exemption, use of tax credits,

source of income by marital status and general sources of income by state. The second is a final annual report on individual income taxes providing much more detail about this information as well as statistics on the number of returns, deductions and exemptions, the method of tax computation and rates, age exemptions and retirement income credit. The data in both publications are divided by state and region, marital status and selected financial items.

■ *Statistics of Income, Corporations Income Tax Returns* consists of two annual publications that provide data obtained from corporate income tax returns. A preliminary report contains estimates of income statements and tax items of U.S. corporations, with breakdowns for major industry groups. A final report goes into greater detail and includes income and financial data organized by industry or size of corporation; income subject to tax; preference items (such as investment credits); and special corporations returns, such as those from small businesses.

■ *Statistics of Income, Business Income Tax Returns* is broken down into a preliminary and a final annual report providing income statistics of partnerships and sole proprietorships. Together, they cover such areas as revenue, assets, dividends, depreciation, income taxes and tax payments. Preliminary SOI reports are published in the SOI Bulletin as released. Data in final SOI reports may be several years old before actual publication.

■ *Annual Report of the Chief Counsel and Commissioner for the Internal Revenue Service* covers such activities as criminal prosecution; general litigation, including tax underpayments and requests for refunds; interpretations of present law; and proposed tax legislation and regulations. The Commissioner's section of the report covers the general workings of the IRS, summarizing the events of the year, including the collection of revenue, assistance to taxpayers and enforcement of tax laws.

■ *Internal Revenue Service Tax Guides,* covering many areas, are available to help people understand the workings of the IRS and its tax-collecting procedures. IRS publication 910, "Guide to Free Tax Services," provides a list of all tax guides.

■ *Internal Revenue Service Operations Manual* covers such areas as administration, audits and investigations, delinquent accounts and returns, employee plans and exempt organizations and appellate, technical and training materials. The Manual can be obtained by written request through the Freedom of Information Act to the Internal Revenue Service at the address at the beginning of this section.

All of the above IRS publications and forms are free and can be obtained by calling 1–800–TAX–FORM.

U.S. Tax Court Case Files

Case files can be obtained at U.S. Tax Court, 400 Second St. N.W., Washington, D.C. 20217, or copies may be ordered by phone. If you know only the name of the case, first call the Tax Court's petitions section, (202) 376–2764, and ask for the docket number of the case. You'll need the docket number to order copies of the case file from the Tax Court's public files office, (202) 376–2727. Court clerks usually don't have time to describe the file's contents in detail, but they will provide a page count. If the file is extensive, you may be able to narrow your request by first buying a copy of the docket sheet, which in a page or two provides a complete record of the case, including dates on which new documents were added to the file. Copies are 50 cents per page. Requests totaling more than $100 may require advance payment.

A caveat: Stories about locals with federal tax problems are a great deal harder to come by since mid-1982. Thanks to a change in the way U.S. Tax Court clerks segregate cases, they no longer are organized by state. Persons seeking to protest this change can write to the clerk of the U.S. Tax Court at the address listed above.

STATE TAXES

Statistical Report of Tax Revenue

Most states will provide a detailed breakdown of the revenue generated through taxes, including corporate, business, income, use, gasoline, fuel, cigarette and alcoholic-beverage taxes. To obtain these reports, start with the state Department of Revenue.

Corporate Tax Records

The amount of information available to reporters in corporate tax records varies from state to state, but you may be able to find the following: exact corporate title, address, date opened for business, officers and directors, corporation identification number, filing date of return, name and title of persons signing return and amount of delinquent taxes. These initial records may be obtained from the state Franchise Board or Department of Revenue. Appeals to the state Board of Equalization or records of court action will reveal detailed information on the tax status of a corporation that might otherwise be closed to public scrutiny.

Personal Income Tax Records

Most information regarding state personal income taxes is confidential. However, in some states you may be able to find out if a person has paid or is delinquent in paying taxes by appealing to a state Franchise Board or Department of Revenue.

Tax Liens

A state tax lien is filed by the state attorney general's office in the district court located in the county where the taxpayer lives. The information in tax liens may provide the reporter with a detailed look at a person's income and expenses not available elsewhere. The case file may include allegations of unpaid taxes, the taxpayer's state and federal returns and other supporting documents for the contested period and the final court ruling.

LOCAL TAXES

Property Tax Records

The property tax system begins with the local assessor, who assesses all parcels of real and personal property subject to taxation in his jurisdiction by establishing the value of the property and levying the tax. The county's assessor records—usually arranged both alphabetically and geographically and kept in the local assessor's office—will describe improvements, last date of assessment, name of legal owner and mailing address for the property.

The assessment rate can be used to calculate the market value of a specific piece of property. First, the formula being used to calculate the assessment rate must be determined by inquiry at the local assessor's office. (Usually the assessment formula will be a fraction, such as one-third or one-half, of the property's real value.) Multiply the property's assessed value by the assessment rate to determine its market value.

The tax rate applied to that market valuation is determined by the appropriate elected body, such as the county commissioners, city council, school board or special district governing body. All tax rates generally are compiled on a single form when the county collector mails the tax bills to property owners.

Appeals

Most states have set up an administrative system for deciding appeals of the assessor's decisions, rather than immediately taking complaints to court. Typically, a county or city board of equalization will hear appeals of disgruntled property owners. The board's files will contain a number of records, including, in some jurisdictions, transcripts of hearings and written presentations of appellants. Further appeal can be made to state tax commissions or boards of equalization, which file similar information. The records of local and state boards provide useful information about the varying levels of valuation for properties within the same area and for similar properties in an area.

State laws often restrict increases in property taxes that a community might seek to assess when market valuations increase substantially. Although taxpayers cannot simply refuse to pay what they think is an unlawfully high tax, they can pay taxes in protest. These amounts then are deposited in escrow accounts until a court rules on the property tax rate. Records on the protested taxes generally will be found in the collector's office and in the applicable trial court.

(See Chapter 9, "Tracing Land Holdings," for more detailed information about property taxes.)

Other Tax Revenue

Most cities and counties usually are willing to provide a detailed breakdown of revenues acquired from property, sales and cigarette taxes, as well as income from city auto stickers and other taxes. Often they will allow you to look up records of payments by individuals or companies. Reporters should check these sources routinely when backgrounding individuals or companies, as this gives a good, quick glimpse at gross income and other business information often unavailable elsewhere. To get this breakdown, check with your finance department, auditor or other comparable city or county agency.

HIDDEN TAXES

Business Licenses

City, county and state governments usually require licenses of all businesses operating within their jurisdictions. Information includes at least the name and address of the business and its owners and the fee or tax paid for the license. Often there is other interesting information, too. Check with the city or county clerk and your secretary of state's or treasurer's office.

ADDITIONAL SOURCES FOR INFORMATION ON TAXES

- *American Bar Association* has a permanent group that studies the overall tax apparatus and issues reports, evaluations and recommendations. Write to Taxation Section, American Bar Association, 1800 M St. N.W., Washington, D.C. 20036.
- *Public Citizen Inc.* is an umbrella organization for several public interest groups. Its tax reform research group makes recommendations about the overall tax system, including tax policy and administration, from the citizen's viewpoint. Write to Public Citizen Inc., Tax Reform Research Group, 215 Pennsylvania Ave. S.E., Washington, D.C. 20003.
- *Tax Foundation Inc.* is a private organization that researches federal fiscal matters and prepares reports for public officials, the media and its members, mostly individuals and businesses. Write to Tax Foundation Inc., One Thomas Circle N.W., Suite 500, Washington, D.C. 20005.
- *National Taxpayers Union* is a public interest group whose members primarily are individuals. Write to National Taxpayers Union, 325 Pennsylvania Ave. S.E., Washington, D.C. 20003.
- *Daily Tax Report*, published every business day by the nongovernmental Bureau of National Affairs, covers nearly all levels of government taxation, including administrative tax actions, federal tax court decisions (full or partial texts), legislative activity, laws, rulings and regulations. This is an expensive publication, so first check a library, law school or local tax specialist. If you can't find a copy, write to Daily Tax Report, Bureau of National Affairs, 1231 25th St. N.W., Washington, D.C. 20037.

CHAPTER 7

Finding Out About Licensed Professionals

When the individual you are backgrounding belongs to one of the many licensed or certified crafts, trades or professions, additional information is usually available from state boards, which are responsible for licensing and regulating, and from national and local trade associations that your target may belong to. This chapter explains how to tap into the flood of applications, licenses and publications that surrounds every licensed profession—even some that you may not know are licensed—using insurance as an extended example and concluding with guidelines on looking at the performance of the licensing boards themselves.

The chapter ends with a sampler of fifteen of the most common professions, and the names and addresses of more than four dozen related associations.

by MYRTA PULLIAM

There are phonies everywhere—doctors, lawyers, psychiatrists, teachers, contractors—and they make good stories. The following are a few examples.

- In Harlem, a man impersonated a nurse for three months. When caught, his case set off a review by New York City's Health and Hospitals Corporation of the credentials of 3,500 nurses registered with a referral agency.
- Seventeen transit employees were performing engineering work without proper state licenses—a felony in New York.
- Stories of bogus lawyers and doctors abound. There are pharmacists who are not licensed or qualified dispensing drugs. Other people claim to be counselors, psychologists and psychiatrists and are not.
- Outside Buffalo, a "doctor" treated thousands of people but had never attended medical school. He had been a general practitioner for six months after reading medical textbooks.

The potential is even greater than what those stories describe. Because certain professions are licensed and regulated, there are records, standards, associations—a potentially massive paper trail that can tell you a lot about a person, profession, organization or trade.

The obvious professions that require licensing are the three original ones—theology, law and medicine. (See Chapter 14, "Courts," Chapter 15, "Health Care," and Chapter 16, "Education.") But there are also many other professionals who are regulated and licensed, at least in some states. Among them are teachers, funeral directors, real estate salespersons, accountants, cosmetologists, opticians, veterinarians, building contractors, securities dealers, architects, parimutuel workers, engineers, armed guards, bail bondspersons, bar owners, car salespersons, day care operators and private investigators.

In Florida, the Hollywood Sun did a series on phony professionals. Among other things, the paper found that some licensed professionals had backgrounds that might have prevented them from practicing their profession in Florida. To get the information for the series, the paper used disciplinary reports and investigative files at the state Department of Professional Regulation and the county Consumer Affairs Division.

Here are some places to look for information about licensed professionals:

- *Licenses and license applications.* Usually open to public inspection, they can yield a wealth of information about an individual. But remember, often people fill out applications themselves. Beware of such things as credentials based on fake diplomas and people who lie to hide criminal misconduct.
- *Performance standards.* Required by law or custom, they can help reporters evaluate a member's conduct.
- *Complaint and investigation files.* Some states have departments to handle complaints for licensed trade or regulated professions; some professions have associations which investigate charges of misconduct. Not all records in all states are open to the public.
- *Trade associations (and their publications).* These can provide reporters with information about the members, often using research not readily available anywhere else.

Another story to look into is what the regulatory agencies are doing. How do impostors get away with this?

Licenses and License Applications

To be licensed, a professional must meet certain standards. These may cover such areas as age, citizenship, residency in the state, education, examinations, experience and moral character. In addition, often applicants must demonstrate competence, either through testing or prior on-the-job experience, before a license will be issued. For instance, to obtain a real estate broker's license in Arizona, the applicant must demonstrate an understanding of the following: the principles of real estate conveyances; the general purposes and legal effects of agency contracts, deposit receipts, deeds, mortgages, deeds of trust, security agreements, bills of sale and land contracts of sales and leases; the principles of business and land economics; and appraisals.

Professionals can be licensed and regulated at the state or local level. Sometimes, in large cities, licenses are required at the local level even though none is required by the state. For instance, New York City requires hundreds more occupational licenses than does New York State.

The first place to check for license requirements is within state statutes and local ordinances. Information spelled out in regulations commonly includes the following: definition of the occupation; professional standards; persons the article does and does not cover; operation and makeup of the regulatory board (including its purpose, duties, powers, membership and records); description of the license application; requirements to obtain a license and when requirements may be waived; license renewal; fees; the complaint process; grounds and procedures for suspension and revocation; and the appeal process.

Next look at the license application form for more specific information, such as full name, age, address, place and date of birth, education, present and former employment, membership in professional organizations, character references, physical description and photo and arrest record. Keep in mind that how much of this information is publicly available varies greatly from state to state, city to city and even profession to profession within the state or city.

Some states have established reciprocity agreements, allowing those professionals to practice in their state if they are licensed to practice in another state with similar requirements and standards. In such cases, look for information in the original licensor-state's files as well. Professionals licensed in some states are not licensed in others. For instance, social workers are licensed in California, but not in Missouri. Hawaii, unlike most states, requires that tattoo artists be licensed, and California regulates its yacht and ship salespersons.

Performance Standards

Having received a license, professionals must adhere to certain performance standards or face losing it through suspension or revocation. Again, reporters should first turn to the statutes. These laws establish the minimum standards professionals are legally required to meet; to reporters they represent the basis for evaluating complaints about performance.

Most often, grounds for license revocation or suspension fall into the following areas: felony conviction, obtaining fees by fraud or misrepresentation, drug or alcohol abuse, mental incompetence (as judged by a court), fee splitting, dishonorable or unethical conduct that deceives or harms the public and loss or suspension of a license in another state.

For example, embalmers in Missouri can have their licenses denied, suspended or revoked if found guilty of unprofessional conduct such as "use of any advertisement or solicitation which is false, misleading or deceptive to the general public." Arizona real estate brokers can lose their licenses through suspension or revocation for employing unlicensed salespeople, issuing an appraisal report on real property or cemetery property in which they have an interest without disclosing that interest, or violating federal fair housing laws, Arizona civil rights laws or any local ordinances of a similar nature.

Letters of Complaint and Investigation Reports

A complaint, either by a fellow professional or a member of the public, usually initiates an investigation. In some states, however, regulating boards have the power to start an investigation, and sometimes the investigation can be triggered by a complaint from a non-governmental professional association. For instance, the state association of engineers may investigate one of its members and submit its findings to the appropriate licensing authority, state attorney general's office or local district attorney's office for action.

Most states do not release complaint files against a professional until the process has reached an advanced stage, such as the determination of probable cause that there was misconduct or after disciplinary action has been taken. If the charges are not substantiated, the matter is dropped and access to the files becomes almost impossible without the aid of a source.

The amount and kind of information available to the public in complaint files varies from state to state. For example, in Florida the case files of disciplined doctors are available for public inspection, but not in Missouri. There is variation even within a state. For instance, Missouri protects the case files of disciplined doctors, but case files on lawyers can become public if the state Supreme Court is asked to take disciplinary action against them.

Sometimes a grievance goes directly to court. An accountant makes a mistake on a client's tax return, causing an IRS investigation. Faulty wiring by an electrician starts a fire in a home. An insurance agent promises a certain type of coverage which the company refuses to honor when presented with a claim. These involve damages that only a court can remedy. If a professional is disciplined by a state or non-governmental association, he or she may appeal the action in court. In all of these situations, important information may be discovered in records previously closed, such as complaints, depositions, motions and responses. Check the index of your local circuit court or court of common pleas.

Professional and Trade Associations and Their Publications

Professional and trade associations, and their publications, can be tremendously useful for reporters to obtain information about members and professional standards, identify potential sources and be informed about current research.

There is nothing to compel an association to release information about its members, of course, but many will at least confirm whether a particular person is a member and, if so, will release standard biographical data about that person. Large associations, such as those of lawyers, doctors and engineers, have national, state and sometimes even local chapters. It is wise to check all levels.

Some associations produce membership directories, available from their headquarters (or from a friendly local member). Investigative Reporters and Editors Inc., for instance, publishes a membership directory that is available only to its members. It lists each member by state, news outlet, job and topics in which the member has some expertise, such as "organized crime, environment and kickbacks." Remember, however, that information in directories usually is supplied by the member, and it can be self-serving or even fictitious.

It is common to find that these associations work closely with state governments to develop the official state standards and act as the primary policing body for the profession, either quasi-officially or simply from tradition, turning over to enforcement agencies findings of flagrant abuses.

Start by checking the Encyclopedia of Associations to see if and where a professional association exists. Names of specialists in the subject area that you can contact directly can also be found in the Encyclopedia.

Detailed instructions about where to start, along with a sampler of 15 regulated crafts and professions and about four dozen related professional organizations, are listed in the section "Documenting the Evidence" at the end of this chapter.

Plugging Into the Professional Network: An Extended Example

Suppose you get a reliable tip that an elaborate insurance ripoff scheme, involving claims for arson and car theft, is operating in your city. It is likely to include thugs in and outside the insurance industry. A check with the various sources described above — among them local insurance agents, insurance associations and law enforcement agencies — would produce the following potential resources:

■ *American Insurance Service Group.* Headquartered in New York City, this national insurance trade group services the property/casualty insurance industry. It has conducted hundreds of seminars on arson control and investigation, and has worked with federal agencies and other insurance trade associations to coordinate arson-prevention measures. The Property Insurance Loss Register (headquartered in Rahway, N.J.), specializing in fire and theft insurance claims, has developed a computerized registry of fire and theft insurance claims in excess of $1,000 from reports furnished by about 900 insurance companies. Known as PILR, the registry includes the names of the insured, names of property owners, partners or corporate officers; names of spouses and tenants, and any aliases; type of occupancy, mortgages and other financial data; cause of loss, if known; time and date of loss; insurer(s); and the amount of coverage. The information is not for general use, so reporters need a local claims adjuster associated with a member company as a source.

■ *Insurance Crime Prevention Institute.* This national, not-for-profit organization consists of 300 companies. Headquartered in Westport, Conn., its primary purpose is to investigate fraudulent property and casualty insurance claims, and refer its findings to law enforcement agencies. It initiates its own fraud investigations and provides speakers for training sessions. It also publishes a 38-page handbook, "Insurance Fraud: ICPI Handbook for Insurance Personnel," designed primarily for law enforcement personnel but containing useful information for investigative reporters.

- *National Association of Insurance Commissioners.* Headquartered in Kansas City, it consists of all the state insurance commissioners. Its primary role is to produce background papers on the insurance field. The reports generally are available upon request.

- *National Automobile Theft Bureau.* Headquartered in Palos Hills, Ill., it provides a not-for-profit service paid for by member insurance companies that offers free investigative assistance to law enforcement agencies in the areas of motor vehicle thefts, auto fires and related fraud schemes. The bureau operates a central data bank, the North American Theft Information System—with retrieval computer links in Atlanta, Boston, Chicago, Dallas, Detroit, Cerritos, Calif., and New York—containing information on auto theft cases. The information is for clients only; you will need a source to gain access to it. Bureau specialists have developed audiovisual training programs which aid police investigating auto fires. The bureau also has published a pocket manual, "The Investigation of Automobile Fires."

- *Society of Chartered Property and Casualty Underwriters.* This national association of underwriters and other insurance industry professionals, focuses on continuing education for its members. Headquartered in Malvern, Pa., it has a nationwide network of chapters and conducts extensive workshops and clinics. It produces a newsletter, The CPCU Journal, nine times a year and publishes monographs on research results.

Investigating the Protectors

When reporters conduct an investigation of harmful doctors or atrociously run nursing homes, both of which are licensed by the state, only part of the story should be about the abuses uncovered. What about the state and local boards and agencies that license these individuals and are charged with enforcing the laws and standards of their profession? In other words, where were the protectors?

The place to start is with the state law that created the board in the first place. What are the boards supposed to be doing, specifically, what are the regulations that have been promulgated to achieve the legislative mandates? What have they actually done?

By checking the boards' budgets, invoices, vouchers and number of inspections they have performed or cases they have heard; by examining the inspection and investigation reports; by talking with the regulated as well as the regulators and consumers, you may find distinct patterns buttressed by figures that show how well the boards perform their policing duties.

If they are doing poorly, why? Who are the board members and what are their backgrounds? Were they once members of the regulated body and do they have vested interests in its lackadaisical enforcement? How are the staff investigators trained, and on what are they told to focus? How do their counterparts within a state and around the country go about their jobs? Is the funding of board activities sufficient, or is it tied to fees that haven't been raised in 20 years? How do the cases fare that they take to court? These are but a few of the questions that you will need to explore.

Conclusion

The techniques used to investigate the background and performance of licensed professionals are usually the same, whatever the field. First find out whether these professionals do in fact have a license; then learn the basic procedures they follow as well as how the professionals evaluate themselves; check the law to see what conduct is required of them and what is prohibited. Then try to find out whether the professionals' conduct measures up to the law's requirements and, if not, what, if anything, is being done about it.

DOCUMENTING THE EVIDENCE

PROFESSIONAL ORGANIZATION SAMPLER

There are numerous professional associations that may be useful to reporters seeking information about individual members or about a profession itself, more than could possibly be listed here. What we have done is to list below, in alphabetical order, 15 of the more common professions, trades or crafts for which states and cities commonly require licenses, along with nearly four dozen related associations. The first entry after the name of the profession, in boldface, is the largest organization to which a licensed practitioner in that field is likely to belong. The additional organizations may prove helpful for gleaning further information about that topic.

A more detailed listing of professional organizations can be found in such resources as The Help Book and the Encyclopedia of Associations, both of which can be found in libraries. Another source of information about a profession's practices and problems is its special-interest and trade publications, some of which are published by the organizations listed below. Start with the subject index of Standard Rate and Data Service, available in libraries.

Many of the professions listed below have been organized by labor unions. In some fields, such as those of electricians and plumbers, workers are more likely to belong to a labor union than to a trade association. No labor unions are listed here, but it is a good idea to check locally to see if the craft has a union, or to check the Department of Labor annual listing, The Register of Reporting Labor Organizations. Labor unions are a good source for information about the craft in general and its specific problems as well.

Remember, most organizations are set up to help their members or to promote a cause. Information from them should be judged accordingly. In addition, those organizations that produce rosters of members usually just reprint information supplied by the member and make no effort to verify it.

ACCOUNTANTS
American Institute of Certified Public Accountants
1211 Ave. of the Americas
New York, N.Y. 10036

Financial Accounting Foundation
401 Merritt Seven
P.O. Box 3821 High Ridge Park
Stamford, Conn. 06905

Institute of Internal Auditors
249 Maitland Ave.
Altamonte Springs, Fla. 32701

AMBULANCE DRIVERS
National Registry of Emergency Medical Technicians
P.O. Box 29233
6610 Busch Blvd.
Columbus, Ohio 43229

American Ambulance Association
3814 Auburn Blvd.
Suite 70
Sacramento, Calif. 95821

AUCTIONEERS
National Auctioneers Association
8880 Ballentine
Overland Park, Kan. 66214

COSMETOLOGISTS
National Cosmetology Association
3510 Olive St.
St. Louis, Mo. 63103

National Accrediting Commission of Cosmetology Arts and Sciences
1333 H St. N.W., Suite 710
Washington, D.C. 20005

National Association of Accredited Cosmetology Schools
5201 Leesburg Pike
Suite 205
Falls Church, Va. 22041

National Interstate Council of State Boards of Cosmetology
P.O. Box 11390
Capitol Station
Columbia, S.C. 29211

DAIRY PRODUCTS HANDLERS
American Dairy Association
6300 N. River Rd.
Rosemont, Ill. 60018

International Association of Milk, Food and Environmental Sanitarians
P.O. Box 701
Ames, Iowa 50010

DOCTORS
American Medical Association
535 N. Dearborn St.
Chicago, Ill. 60610
(Note: In addition to statewide and even citywide medical associations, there are scores of other medical associations usually organized by medical specialty. For more detailed information, see Chapter 15, "Health Care.")

ELECTRICIANS
International Association of Electrical Inspectors
930 Busse Hwy.
Park Ridge, Ill. 60068

Electricity Consumers Resource Council
1707 H. St. N.W., 10th Floor
Washington, D.C. 20006

National Rural Electric Cooperative Association
1800 Massachusetts Ave. N.W.
Washington, D.C. 20036

FUNERAL DIRECTORS
Continental Association of Funeral and Memorial Societies
2001 S St. N.W., Suite 630
Washington, D.C. 20009

Federated Funeral Directors of America
1622 S. MacArthur Blvd.
Springfield, Ill. 62794

National Foundation of Funeral Service
1614 Central St.
Evanston, Ill. 60201

National Funeral Directors and Morticians Association
5723 S. Indiana Ave.
Chicago, Ill. 60637

HAZARDOUS-WASTE MANAGERS
National Solid Wastes Management Association
1730 Rhode Island Ave. N.W., Suite 1000
Washington, D.C. 20036

Hazardous Materials Control Research Institute
9300 Columbia Blvd.
Silver Spring, Md., 20910
(Note: Institute publishes a directory of about 2,000 organizations involved in hazardous waste control.)

U.S. Council for Energy Awareness
1776 I St. N.W.
Washington, D.C. 20006

American Nuclear Energy Council
410 First St. S.E.
Washington, D.C. 20003

Government Refuse Collection and
Disposal Association
8750 Georgia Ave., Suite 123E
Silver Spring, Md. 20910

Southwest Research and Information
Center
(National Campaign for Radioactive
Waste Safety)
P.O. Box 4524
Albuquerque, N.M. 87106

Environmental Research Foundation
P.O. Box 3541
Princeton, N.J. 08543

Radioactive Waste Campaign
625 Broadway, Second Floor
New York, N.Y. 10012

Union of Concerned Scientists
26 Church St.
Cambridge, Mass. 02238

Waste Watch
Box 39185
Washington, D.C. 20016

LAWYERS
American Bar Association
750 N. Lakeshore Dr.
Chicago, Ill. 60611
(Note: As with doctors, there are state
and city organizations for lawyers as
well as scores of legal associations
organized around specialties. For more
detailed information, see Chapter 14,
"Courts.")

PESTICIDE HANDLERS
Association of American Pesticide
Control Officials
2004 Lasuer Rd
Richmond, Va. 23229

Professional Lawn Care Assoc. of
America
1225 Johnson Ferry Road N.E., Suite
B-220
Marrietta, Ga. 30067

National Pest Control Association
8100 Oak St.
Dunn Loring, Va. 22027

PSYCHOLOGISTS
American Psychological Association
1200 17th St. N.W.
Washington, D.C. 20036

National Association of School Psychologists
1511 K St. N.W., Suite 716
Washington, D.C. 20005

REAL ESTATE AGENTS
National Association of Realtors
430 N. Michigan Ave.
Chicago, Ill. 60611

International College of Real Estate
Consulting Professionals
120 Sixth St., Suite 808
Minneapolis, Minn. 55402

American Institute of Real Estate
Appraisers
430 N. Michigan Ave.
Chicago, Ill. 60611

Realtors Land Institute
430 N. Michigan Ave.
Chicago, Ill. 60611

Institute of Real Estate Management
430 N. Michigan Ave.
Chicago, Ill. 60611

National Association of Industrial and Office Parks
1215 Jefferson Davis Hwy., Suite 100
Arlington, Va. 22202

National Association of Real Estate Editors
Box 324
North Olmstead, Ohio 44070

American Resort and Residential Development Association
1220 L St. N.W., Suite 510
Washington, D.C. 20005

Society of Real Estate Appraisers
225 N. Michigan Ave., Suite 724
Chicago, Ill. 60601

TEACHERS
National Education Association
1201 16th St. N.W.
Washington, D.C. 20036

American Federation of Teachers
555 New Jersey Ave. N.W.
Washington D.C. 20001
(Note: As with doctors and lawyers, there are scores of organizations for teachers, primarily organized around specialized topics. For more detailed information, see Chapter 16, "Education.")

CHAPTER 8

Investigating Politicians

When election time rolls around, politicians make grandiose promises and kiss babies. What reporters need to do is look behind those facades presented by the candidates.

Investigating a campaign runs the gamut from finding out who contributes to the campaign and why, to checking candidates' resumes and examining their marital and mental stability. The digging could find unholy alliances and weaknesses that could hinder candidates in their elected jobs. This chapter will show you how to probe these issues.

by PENNY LOEB

Money greases the political machine. Campaign contributions, loans, speaking fees, even a legislator's investment in a business owned by someone affected by a law up for vote are some of the ways money is used to buy influence.

Many of these financial arrangements can be found in public records, such as Federal Election Commission (FEC) campaign contribution records. But it's not enough just to list who gives what to which candidate or what investments a candidate has.

The real story is why a person or a business gives something to a candidate—and what they get in return. Many stories like the following two are waiting to be told.

Late one night in June 1984 as Rep. Dan Rostenkowski, an Illinois Democrat, and Republican Sen. Robert Dole of Kansas were trying to iron out differences in their tax bills, the question of a tax break for commodity traders arose.

Everyone knew Rostenkowski had close ties to the traders, a small but wealthy group mostly from his home state. But Dole was a different story, or so it seemed. In 1981, he had been instrumental in closing a tax loophole favored by the industry.

However, something had changed in three years. In a matter of moments, Dole quickly agreed to Rostenkowski's proposal that gave 333 commodity traders a special tax amnesty worth at least $300 million, not available to others.

What caused Dole's change of heart was the question asked by Florence Graves and Lee Norrgard in their 1985 Common Cause article. A check of his campaign contributions showed Dole's Campaign America political action committee (PAC) received $70,500 from the commodity traders in 1983–84, six times more than the traders gave his PAC in 1981–82.

A favorite anecdote of Brooks Jackson, Wall Street Journal reporter and author of "Honest Graft: Big Money and the American Political Process," is the following about New York Republican Sen. Alfonse D'Amato.

In the mid-1980s, D'Amato chaired the Securities Subcommittee in the Senate, which oversees legislation relating to Wall Street. When he ran for re-election in 1986, D'Amato was heavily supported by PACs from the financial industry. He even sent an aide to Drexel Burnham's California office—the heart of Drexel's junk bond operation—and asked the firm to put on a fund-raiser for the 1986 campaign. The event was held at a fancy restaurant and raised $33,000.

A week later, D'Amato chaired a hearing in which Drexel Burnham asked that the sale of junk bonds to federally insured savings institutions not be restricted.

Drexel Burnham got its way. The junk bonds sales weren't restricted, even though many banks in weakened financial condition had invested in Drexel's junk bonds.

You can begin tracking the dollars flowing to a candidate by getting his or her contribution records. These are probably easiest to get for congressional and presidential candidates. Contribution reports are kept by the Federal Election Commission, with originals for congressional candidates filed with the House of Representatives and Senate. (For complete details on what is available, see "Candidate's Financial Disclosures" later in this chapter.)

Federal candidates are required to report all contributions of $200 or more from individuals and all size contributions from political action committees and political party committees, as well as any size bank loan.

Individuals can give $1,000 to a candidate in a primary and an additional $1,000 in the general election. An individual can give $25,000 total to all candidates in one calendar year. Candidates are required to identify contributors by address, occupation and place of work. Some contributions lack the occupation information, however.

Businesses can't give directly to candidates. Instead, they form PACs, which in most cases can give up to $5,000 to a candidate. Sometimes businesses exceed the PAC limit by putting contributions in employees' names. Checking occupations of individual contributors can sometimes reveal patterns of giving from industries impacted by decisions of the committees on which a member of Congress sits.

Contributors find legal ways around the limits. Sometimes a number of individuals from the same firm will contribute to a candidate, thus exceeding the limit for a business' PAC. Or several members of a family will contribute, surpassing the limit for one person.

Brooks Jackson found that a fund-raiser for Sen. Terry Sanford, a Democrat from North Carolina, inserted a small card in a mailing. The card explained that a husband and wife could each make a $1,000 contribution to both the primary and the general elections. Then, they could give $5,000 each to a statewide committee for Democratic candidates and $15,000 or $20,000 to the Democratic Senatorial committee, which would spend it to support Sanford's campaign.

Individuals can give up to $20,000 to a national party committee each year. The committee must report these contributions to the Federal Election Commission (FEC).

Sometimes you will find outright violations. Brooks Jackson found an executive at the brokerage house of E.F. Hutton who totally denied making the contributions listed in his name to D'Amato. Moreover, he said he didn't like D'Amato. This was a violation of the federal election law that was never investigated by the enforcement arm of the FEC.

Though the FEC does an excellent job of keeping and releasing contribution records, it does a lousy job of enforcing campaign finance laws. The lack of enforcement of these laws can make good stories.

Contributions channeled through state party organizations go unreported to the FEC. Often they are in amounts expressly prohibited in federal elections. The Bush and Dukakis campaigns raised more than $20 million in these "soft money" contributions in the 1988 campaign. The Republican Party released the identities of 249 contributors who each gave $100,000 or more of this soft—sometimes called sewer—money to the Bush campaign. The Democrats released a list of approximately the same number of large contributors.

The FEC has refused to take action against these soft money contributions that exceed federal limits.

Another area to explore are PAC contributions to candidates. In the 1988 federal elections, 3,683 PACs gave more than $172 million to 873 House candidates, 101 Senate candidates and 25 presidential candidates, according to a report by the Washington Post.

Though PACs are limited to contributions of $5,000 per candidate for each primary and election, a big loophole exists for "independent expenditures" by a PAC in support of a candidate. No limits are set for these expenditures, which include payment for television ads. The Washington Post found that $1 out of every $10 PACs spent in the 1988 federal elections was for independent expenditures. Some outlays totaled more than $300,000 each. Records of these expenditures are kept by the FEC.

The FEC provides two types of computer services to newspapers. The FEC has a data base that can be searched using a personal computer for $25 an hour. Some newspaper libraries have access to the FEC data base. The FEC will also sell newspapers computer tapes. Computer experts at a newspaper can extract specialized information from the tapes. The Washington Post has made extensive use of the tapes, including using them for the analysis of PAC contributions in the 1988 election.

The Washington Post used computers to search tapes of Dukakis contributions and found that he did take money from special interests, though he said he didn't. By searching by occupation, the Post found that 35 members of the law firm that served as bond counsel to Massachusetts gave a total of $25,740, most on the same day.

Another way that corporations and others seek to influence public officials is through speaking fees, known as *honoraria fees*. As of 1989, senators can keep $35,800; house members can keep $26,850. Sometimes they give excess amounts to charities. In 1987, members of Congress collected nearly $10 million in honorariums.

Members of Congress are required to report honoraria fees on their financial disclosure reports (see "Records," later in this chapter for details).

An official with the GTE Corp., a leading defense contractor, makes it clear what's involved in honoraria payments, according to a January-February 1989 Common Cause article. He is quoted as saying that by giving honoraria to members of Congress, "We have their full time and attention—a captive audience. It would take three or four (campaign) fund-raisers over a couple of years to get the same kind of relationship."

An attempt was made in Congress early in 1989 to raise pay for members and eliminate honoraria fees. It failed.

Even examining the reasons that the excess fees are donated to charity can be revealing. When he was a representative from Wyoming, Defense Secretary Richard Cheney donated his $2,000 honoraria fee from the Tobacco Institute to Needs Inc. in Cheyenne, Wyo. The money helped some needy people—and earned the appreciation of the influential directors of the group. "They (members of Congress) can do themselves a lot of electioneering good. (Donating excess honoraria) gives them a lot of zonk," former Internal Revenue Service Commissioner Sheldon Cohen told Common Cause.

Legislators don't have to reveal to whom they give, although some do.

Another aspect of legislators' and candidates' finances to be explored is their investments. Records of investments can be found in disclosures most officeholders are required to file as well as in more obscure records, such as wills. (See "Candidates' Financial Disclosures" later in this chapter for details on obtaining financial disclosures.) Be suspicious if legislators are living beyond their means. It could indicate they are taking bribes.

Rep. Fernand St. Germain of Rhode Island grew wealthy partly through investments in an old friend's housing projects, according to Brooks Jackson's book, "Honest Graft." That friend, Roland Ferland, became one of the biggest developers and managers of federally subsidized housing in the Northeast. Meanwhile, St. Germain's place on the Banking Committee helped him wield increasing influence over the Department of Housing and Urban Development, which falls under the Banking Committee's jurisdiction. St. Germain was able to get more than the average share of subsidized apartments for Rhode Island.

St. Germain didn't invest in any of Ferland's federally subsidized apartments. However, he profited through other projects owned by Ferland.

As you check a legislator's investments, look at the committees on which he or she sits. At one point, one-third of the House Agricultural Committee members owned farms. Can they be objective on farm policy? Can a legislator who owns stock in a defense manufacturer be objective on defense spending?

Also check whether the incumbent has income from a second job. The time taken up by the job could affect his performance in office. The job, too, could pose a potential conflict of interest. Find out whether a politician's relatives have been benefiting from his or her legislative decisions. For example, is the politician's brother a lawyer whose clients get government contracts?

Campaign contributions and other financial disclosures are probably easier to track on the federal level, thanks in part to the sophistication of the FEC record keeping. However, much work can be done on the state and local level.

Find where campaign contributions are filed for your locality, and read the campaign finance laws. Don't forget to check the contribution limits. Check for contributions that exceed the limits. (A list of state offices that oversee contributions appears in the "Documenting the Evidence" section of this chapter.)

All these contribution and financial records can seem impressive by themselves. But don't forget that what you are really looking for is why those contributions were made and what the givers received in return.

This is not always easy to find, since there may not be a clear quid pro quo, as can be seen in the previous examples. Brooks Jackson recommends asking some of the big donors. You might be surprised at what they say.

With members of Congress, begin by checking what legislation they have pushed and what agencies fall under the jurisdiction of their committees. Then see if those who benefit from the legislation or agencies also gave to the senator or representative.

Sometimes even the legislator who received the contributions will tell you what he or she did for that money. D'Amato was asked what he did in a way that challenged him to respond, which he did—effusively.

On the local level, look at appointments and contracts, especially unbid ones. Look at who designs the new jail, who does the survey work. Who does a city hire to lobby the federal government? Who gets the zoning variances? Which investment firms do the bond underwriting?

The Florida Times Union input into a computer all the contributions for the Jacksonville city council members and mayor. The paper found that 95 percent of the city's professional service contracts went to campaign contributors and the bulk went to the biggest givers. The paper tried to find out who all the contributors were by checking city directories, clips and corporation records. Unless you know who the contributors are, you won't know what the contributions mean. The president of a company may not contribute, but 10 employees may. This project was useful not just for one series, but as a resource for future daily stories. The data base can be checked when other contracts are awarded. It may show that the business winning the contract may have given to all legislators who voted in its favor.

In smaller cities and towns, politicians often don't make the bulk of their income from public office, and campaign contributions are fairly small. Look, though, at whether a politician's business has been a subcontractor on a government contract. If the politician is a lawyer, look at who his or her clients are.

While looking at contributions, don't forget to examine how the money is spent. Some expenditures can be surprising.

The Tennessean found that Rep. William Boner, a Democrat from Tennessee, used some of his contributions to pay rent on a building he owns. Boner also created two computer companies, which leased computer equipment to the campaign. Boner's campaign also bought him a luxury Pontiac, pickup truck, mobile phone and $5,000 worth of furniture for his home. The campaign also employed Boner's sister and paid her more than $25,000 over three years.

Some members of Congress keep a large share of their contributions instead and build up big war chests. If they were elected before 1980, they can take their money with them when they retire. One congressperson from New York had stockpiled more than $800,000 by the middle of 1988.

Numerous senators and representatives have hundreds of thousands of dollars more than they need for a reelection campaign. If they aren't stockpiling, sometimes they give it to fellow legislators' campaigns. As Washington Monthly reported, the recipients feel somewhat obligated to return the favor, perhaps as support for a bill in the future. "What develops is an 'I was there when you needed me' sort of relationship," one congressperson said.

Finally, these huge stockpiles of money are a deterrent to anyone considering a run against the incumbent. In 1986, 98 percent of members of the House were reelected.

Campaign money and other financial ties are just one aspect to look at when examining a candidate's suitability for public office.

Look, too, at who candidates really are, not who they say they are. Check their resumes. It's surprising how many people in high political offices lie about their backgrounds.

The elder affairs secretary in Massachusetts in the Gov. Edward King Administration said he had an undergraduate degree from the University of Heidelberg and a graduate degree from Cambridge University. He actually was a high school dropout from Lynn, Mass. The misspelling of Heidelberg on his resume was a sure clue.

What should and what shouldn't be revealed about a candidate's personal life can be debated endlessly. Should investigative reporters spend their time in hiding in bushes, checking on a candidate's extramarital affairs? Should the press report on a candidate's history of psychiatric illness?

The determining factor should be: Could what the candidate is doing affect his or her ability to carry out a public role?

The fact that a candidate is having extramarital affairs is not as important as the lies the candidate tells about the affairs. Psychiatric treatment may not hinder a member of Congress, but some believe it would be a detriment for a president, who must decide whether to fire the missiles.

The Miami Herald reporters and editors who worked on the Gary Hart-Donna Rice story said at an IRE panel in 1987 that the issue was not Gary Hart's sex life. It was whether he was telling the truth about being a faithful husband.

A candidate's mental stability or truthfulness aren't the only parameters for checking his or her capability for an elected post. Examine the candidate's performance in that post if the candidate is running for re-election. If he or she is running for the job for the first time, examine the candidate's performance in past jobs. If the job was in the public sector, audits may be available. Talk to past and present employees who worked for or with the candidate.

Personal qualities, such as tenaciousness, can have a bearing on how a person performs in office. Has the candidate been able to overcome obstacles in the past? Does he or she try to succeed at whatever task attempted?

Don't overlook a candidate's religion. It could influence his or her vote on abortion and other controversial issues.

Has a candidate's family ever interfered with his or her ability to perform a job or elected position? A spouse may try to get involved in running the legislator's office or campaign and hurt rather than help.

Check the people close to candidates. Who are their rainmakers, the ones who bring in the campaign contributions and the endorsements? Are any of those people convicted criminals, under investigation or members of organized crime?

Finally, in some municipalities that have adopted campaign finance reform laws reducing contribution limits, new ways to influence candidates are being found. This was first seen in New York City in the 1989 mayoral campaign. One candidate received the support of many unions and several Democratic party leaders early on. All the papers duly reported the endorsements. Some noted that these endorsements could provide workers to coax voters on primary day. But only a few reporters bothered to ask what the unions and party leaders expected in return for their endorsements. Jobs in their candidate's administration was the answer.

Federal Candidates*

The Federal Election Commission has a small group of people in the press office who are very helpful to reporters. They can provide many kinds of records within a day or so, many of which are free. The FEC also has a public records office,

*Scott Moxley, a public information specialist at the FEC, assisted in compiling the remaining sections of this chapter.

which charges for records and takes several weeks to fill an order. To contact the office write or call: Federal Election Commission, Press Office, 999 E St. N.W., Washington, D.C. 20463; (800) 424-9530.

The FEC provides a number of publications about campaign finance and about using its records, including: "Using FEC Campaign Finance Information"; its annual report; informational brochures on advisory opinions, corporate/labor activities and other frequently asked questions; and campaign guides that explain how the law affects candidates, parties, corporations/unions and nonconnected PACs. Ask the FEC for a complete list of its publications.

All presidential and congressional candidates' reports are filed with the FEC. Individual contributors are identified by name, town, state, zip code, amount given, date given, which election given for (primary or regular) and, in many cases, by occupation and place of employment. Computer indexes provide detailed information beginning with the 1977–78 election cycle. Microfilm records go back to the 1972 elections.

Who Is Running?

The fastest way to find out who's running is to call the FEC, which can tell you who filed a statement of candidacy in your district or who registered a committee. Computer Index A (arranged by type of office sought) lists all candidates within a state and congressional district. It also gives their party affiliations and addresses.

Computer Index 93 gives the name and address of a candidate's principal campaign committee, as well as any other committees authorized by a candidate. FEC Form 1 (Statement of Organization) and FEC Form 2 (Statement of Candidacy) provide the same information.

Who Gave Campaign Contributions?

There are two ways to find who gave or loaned money to a candidate and his or her committee(s). FEC Form 3, Schedule A (campaign finance reports) itemizes any contributions from an individual totaling more than $200 a year. It also gives the contributor's address and usually the occupation and place of work. Contributions from PACs, political party committees and any bank loans are itemized, regardless of amount. Schedule C of a campaign's reports itemizes outstanding loans.

Senate candidates file the originals of their financial reports with the Secretary of the U.S. Senate, Office of Public Records, Hart Building, Suite 232, Washington, D.C. 20510; (202) 224-0322. House of Representatives candidates file their originals with the Clerk of the U.S. House of Representatives, Office of Records and Registrations, Room 1036, Longworth House Office Building, Washington, D.C. 20515; (202) 225-1300. Within 48 hours of filing their originals, congressional candidates file copies with the FEC. Most are filed the same day.

Presidential candidates and political action committees file the originals of their reports with the FEC.

In election years, candidate committees must file within two weeks after the end of each quarter. They also must file 12 days before the primary and 12 days before the general election as well as 30 days after each. Any contributions over $1,000 must be reported up to 48 hours before an election. In non-election years, candidate committees report twice a year, Jan. 31 and July 31. PACs have the option of reporting monthly or quarterly in an election year. In off years, they file semiannually.

The second way to check contributions to candidates is by using the FEC computer indexes.

Computer Index G lists all contributors of $500 or more at one time to a candidate committee and usually gives contributors' addresses and occupations and the date of the contribution. Another listing of the G index gives, alphabetically, all contributors of $500 or more to any federal candidate, identified by candidate, date and amount.

Computer Index E gives a summary of all money a candidate has raised and spent. It also lists:

- All PAC and political party contributions.
- Independent expenditures made by individuals, groups and political committees to advocate a candidate's election or defeat. In addition, three Independent Expenditure Indexes, published periodically, provide summary and detailed information on all independent expenditures made for and against candidates.
- Special "coordinated" expenditures made by political party committees on behalf of a candidate.
- Partisan communications made by unions and corporations on behalf of, or in opposition to, a candidate.

Computer Index L lists summary figures for each authorized candidate committee selected on the basis of criteria the researcher specifies. The index prints total figures for receipts, disbursements, transfers, contributions, loans, loan repayments and debts. The resulting report is like a bank statement with a lot of summary numbers. You can use Index L to find how much a candidate got from PACs and how much cash on hand and debts a campaign has.

You can compare money raised and spent by all candidates for one office by finding their names on Index A and ordering Indexes E or L for all the candidates. For more detailed information, examine reports filed by each candidate's campaign committee.

How Are Candidates Spending Contributions?

For itemized lists of expenditures over $200 by a candidate's campaign committee, ask for FEC Form 3, Schedule B.

Computer Index E lists summary figures on expenditures. Computer Index L lists total figures for receipts selected on the basis of criteria the researcher chooses.

How Much Was Raised and Spent in a Previous Campaign?

The FEC's "Reports on Financial Activity" contain information on receipts and disbursements for all candidates running for federal office since 1977. (Receipt and disbursement figures in these reports, unlike figures in the computer indexes and campaign finance reports, have been adjusted for transfers between committees.) These reports are arranged by state, so you can easily compare all the campaigns within a congressional district or state during each election cycle.

Computer Index E contains information on total receipts and disbursements for federal candidates during specific election cycles to the present.

Computer Index L includes summary totals of receipts and disbursements for each candidate selected on the basis of criteria the user designates. The information is available for election cycles beginning in 1985.

The FEC's "Disclosure Series Nos. 6 and 9" contain information on total adjusted receipts and disbursements for the general election campaigns of all House and Senate candidates during the 1975–76 election cycle.

The first and second pages of a campaign's year-end report include totals for financial activity during that year.

Other Candidate Records

Statements of independent expenditures list unaffiliated groups that spent money on a candidate's campaign. They're rare and often of interest. The statements cover money spent either to help elect or help defeat a candidate without the "cooperation, consent or consultation" of the campaign. These may be found on the FEC E Index.

Debt settlements show how much a candidate owed at the end of a campaign, how much was repaid and who forgave debts to the candidate.

Using Computers to Investigate Campaign Spending

FEC records are now available through a computer data base, the Direct Access Program, that some newspapers have on-line. This data base can be searched for all contributions to a certain candidate. The FEC also offers on-line computer information to owners of personal computers. They cost $25 an hour.

The FEC also sells computer tapes for about $600 that contain all contributions of $500 or more to all federal candidates for a two-year election period.

The Campaign Research Center, 1010 Vermont Ave., N.W., Suite 710, Washington, D.C. 20005; (202) 347–5400, is a non-partisan group established to help reporters access computerized information, including campaign funds, voting records and committee assignments. For a reasonable fee, the center provides comparisons of contributions and voting patterns; comparisons of contributions and sponsorship of special interest legislation; identification of obscure individual contributors; and a breakdown of PACs by industry and legislative interest.

Candidates' Financial Disclosures

Members of Congress, presidents, vice presidents, often their spouses, candidates and higher level congressional employees must file financial disclosures.

Presidential and vice presidential candidates file with the FEC 30 days after becoming candidates or May 15, whichever is later, at the Office of Government Ethics, 1201 New York Ave., N.W., Suite 500, Washington, D.C. 20005; (202) 523-5757.

Senate Public Financial Disclosure Reports are filed with the Senate Office of Public Records, 232 Hart Building, Washington, D.C. 20510; (202) 224-0322. The reports must be filed by senators, senatorial candidates, officers and employees of the legislative branch, principal assistants to members of the Senate, employees designated to handle political funds and other highly paid employees. Reports include: name; job status; income from honoraria, dividends, interest, rent, capital gains, trusts, estates and other sources; gifts of transportation, lodging, food or entertainment; reimbursements; property; liabilities; transactions in securities, commodities, futures and real property; non-governmental positions; agreements for future employment or continuation of payments or benefits; and "blind-trust" financial arrangements. Various minimum or maximum amounts govern what must be reported. Most categories require disclosure of financial dealings affecting spouses or dependents. The filing deadline is May 15 or within 30 days of becoming a candidate or employee.

House of Representatives financial disclosure statements must be filed by members, candidates, officers or employees making more than the GS-16 salary, and any employee designated as a principal assistant to a representative. Reports are filed by May 15 each year with the Clerk, U.S. House of Representatives, Office of Records and Registration, Room 1036, Longworth House Office Building, Washington, D.C. 20515; (202) 225-7103.

House members, candidates and employees report much the same financial information as senators. They are also usually required to report financial information on spouses and children.

Other Disclosures Required From Members of Congress

For complete lists of required disclosures and filing dates, check with the Senate Office of Public Records, Office of the Secretary; the Clerk of the House of Representatives, Office of Records and Registration; and Committee on Standards of Official Conduct, U.S. House of Representatives, Room HT-2, Capitol Building, Washington, D.C. 20515; (202) 225-7103.

Disclosures required by senators, and Senate employees, often include:

- *Registration of Mass Mailings.* Contains name of senator, year of mass mailing, description of groups receiving mailing and copy of what was mailed. Filed with Senate Office of Public Records. Contact Senate Select Committee on Ethics, 220 Hart Building, Washington, D.C. 20510; (202) 224-2981.

- *Foreign Gifts.* Required by senators, officers and employees who accept a tangible gift with a retail value in the United States of more than $165 from a foreign government or agent thereof. Filed with Select Committee on Ethics.
- *Foreign Travel.* Filed by senators, officers or employees who accept travel or travel expenses from a foreign government or agent for travel outside the United States. Filed with Select Committee on Ethics.
- *Foreign Educational Travel Report.* Filed by Senate and House members who accept an invitation to participate in educational programs sponsored by a foreign government or foreign educational or charitable organization that involve travel to a foreign country and are paid for by that foreign government or organization. Filed with the Select Committee on Ethics.
- *Conflict of Interest Report/Statement of Outside Business Professional Activity or Employment.* Filed by Senate officers and employees with any outside business or professional activity or employment for compensation. Filed with employee's supervisor.

Don't overlook more traditional sources of documents, such as divorce suits, that disclose information about a candidate's finances. Former Sen. Herman Talmadge, D-G, and former Illinois Attorney General William Scott both found themselves in campaign finance trouble because their estranged wives reported more financial information to the divorce court than Talmadge and Scott had disclosed as candidates.

If you are looking for evidence that a candidate has pocketed campaign money, look for the records that show he or she is living beyond his or her means: boat and airplane registrations, lavish vacations, summer homes and other real estate. Compare what a candidate spent to what he or she reported as income.

Individual Contributors

Names of individual contributors are one of the biggest sources of information for reporters. The FEC can check its computer records for current years and has microfilm records that can be searched to find to which candidates the person in which you are interested gave money. If you purchase the computer tapes from the FEC, they can be programmed so that all contributions made by one person can be found.

When searching for contributions by one person or group of people, try to think of all the ways that could be used to get around contribution limits. Find as many of a contributor's relatives and business affiliations. Does the person's company(s) have a PAC? Did company officers and employees give? Check by the person's ZIP code (the FEC can't check a street address). Did the person use initials instead of a first name? Think about misspellings.

New York Newsday checked families, companies and business affiliates for the largest contributor to New York Gov. Mario Cuomo. The aggregate contributions were nearly three times that shown for just the person.

Political Action Committees (PACs)

Reports of the more than 4,200 political action committees (PACs) that contribute to federal candidates are also filed with the FEC. PACs are all political committees that have not been authorized by candidates or political parties. They include separate segregated funds sponsored by corporations and labor organizations.

Computer Index B lists all PACs in alphabetical order and indicates for each committee:

- Address of the PAC.
- Name of the PAC's treasurer.
- Connected organization (if any).
- Whether the PAC has qualified as a multicandidate committee.
- PACs identification number.

FEC Form 1 (Statement of Organization) gives the name of the sponsoring organization and identifies any affiliated PACs.

A computerized Sponsor-Committee Index lists the parent organizations and identifies their separate segregated funds. A computerized Committee-Sponsor Index lists the PACs and then identifies their sponsors.

The different types of PACs include: non-connected, trade membership (such as the American Medical Association), cooperative (such as dairy farmers), corporations without stock (such as law firms), corporate, and labor. Ideological PACs are among the most active.

The Almanac of Federal PACs gives thumbnail sketches of major PACs, including their major legislative goals.

How Much Money Has a PAC Raised and Spent?

FEC Form 3X, pages 1 and 2, summarizes a PAC's receipts and disbursements for the reporting period covered and gives year-to-date totals. This information is also found on Computer Index C, which also gives totals for the election cycle to date.

Computer Index K lists summary figures for each PAC selected on the basis of criteria the researcher identifies.

The FEC's "Reports on Financial Activity" contain information on receipts and disbursements for all PACs supporting federal candidates from 1977 to the present. FEC press releases also give summary information on PAC receipts and disbursements.

Which Candidates Has a PAC Supported?

Schedule B of FEC Form 3X lists candidates to whom the PAC contributed. Schedule E shows independent expenditures the PAC has made for or against a given candidate.

Computer Index D (arranged by PAC name) lists candidates who have received contributions and contributions of services and goods other than money from a PAC.

Who Has Contributed to a PAC?

Schedule A of FEC Form 3X lists each individual whose combined contributions have totaled more than $200 a year. Computer Index G lists any person giving $500 or more to a PAC. You can ask for a specially programmed Index G with a list of contributions from other political committees to a PAC, regardless of amount.

Do Several PACs Support the Same Candidate(s)?

Computer Index E identifies all the political committees that have contributed to, or spent money on behalf of or against a particular candidate.

Computer Index Combined D can be used to identify all the candidates to whom a group of PACs (that you select) have contributed. This index also shows total independent expenditures the PACs have made on behalf of, or against, the candidates.

Other Reports

Partisan communications made by unions and corporations are reported on FEC Form 7 when their total communication costs exceed $2,000 per election.

Political Party Committees

Computer Index B arranges all registered political committees by state and includes listings of registered political party committees within each state.

For major contributors to a party committee, check the committee's reports (FEC Form 3X, Schedule A). These list each individual whose combined contributions total more than $200 to the committee during the year. Contributions from other political party committees and PACs are also itemized on Schedule A, regardless of amount.

Computer Index G lists any individual who has made a contribution of $500 or more to a committee. It also lists contributions from other political party committees and PACs, regardless of amount.

To find which candidates a party committee has supported, check Computer Index D. It lists contributions, including in-kind contributions, and any special coordinated expenditures they have made on behalf of candidates.

Contributions to candidates are also found on the political party committee reports: FEC Form 3X, Schedule B shows contributions, contributions in-kind or loans a committee has made to candidates. Schedule F shows any special coordinated expenditures a committee has made on behalf of candidates.

CONTRIBUTION LIMITS

	To each candidate or candidate committee per election*	To national party committee per calendar year	To any other political committee per calendar year	Total per calendar year
Individual	$1,000	$20,000	$5,000	$25,000
Multicandidate Committee†	$5,000	$15,000	$5,000	No limit
Other Political Committee	$1,000	$20,000	$5,000	No limit

*Primaries, runoffs and general elections are considered separate elections with separate contribution limits.
†A multicandidate committee gives to at least five registered federal candidates and has at least 50 contributors.

Prohibited Contributions

The following contributions are prohibited:

- *Contributions made from the treasuries of corporations, labor organizations and national banks.* Additionally, national banks and federally chartered corporations may not make contributions in connection with any election, including state and local elections. Contributions may, however, be made from separate segregated funds (PACs) established by corporations, labor organizations, national banks and incorporated membership organizations.
- *Contributions from federal government contractors.* The prohibition applies to contributions from the personal or business funds of individuals or sole proprietors who have entered into a contract with the federal government. It does not apply, however, to personal contributions by employees, partners, shareholders or officers of businesses with government contracts, nor does it apply to PACs established by corporations or labor organizations with government contracts.
- *Contributions from foreign nationals who do not have permanent residence in the United States (those without green cards).* Additionally, foreign nationals may not make contributions or any other expenditure in connection with any election, including state and local elections.
- *Contributions of cash that in aggregate exceed $100 from one person.* If a committee receives a cash contribution exceeding $100, it must return it.
- *Contributions made by one person in the name of another.*

Other Information Available From the FEC

■ Advisory opinions from the FEC are available, as is the index of the opinion.
■ Audits (GAO 1972–74, FEC 1975–present).
■ Court cases.
■ MURs (closed enforcement actions and index). MURs have useful information but are not used by reporters as frequently as they could be. If an audit has been conducted by the FEC of a candidate committee or a PAC, the audit may include a lot of records not normally available. Complaints under investigation aren't public, but the FEC will confirm whether a certain committee or PAC is being investigated.

FEC press people can often answer questions about election laws and regulations.

Lobbyists and Lobbies

You can also track the influence of lobbies, watching where their contributions go and why. If a lobby is seeking to influence an elected official, it can give a campaign contribution. However, a lobby trying to influence an agency regulating its industry must take a different approach. Here the money comes in such forms as a free trip to an industry convention or free lunches.

At the federal level, lobbyists are defined as people who seek to influence the outcome of legislation before Congress or receive any contribution or expend any money to influence the vote on legislation.

Lobbyists, as well as lawyers, are listed in the Washington Representatives Book, published annually.

Lobbyists must register with the Secretary of the Senate or Clerk of the House of Representatives (see "Federal Candidates" in this chapter for addresses).

The registration report contains name, business address, name and address of employer in whose interest the lobbyist is working, duration of employment, salary paid and by whom, and types of expenses allowed by employer. Reports must be filed before beginning lobbying activities.

To find who contributed to the lobbyist, check the quarterly lobbyist reports. These contain the name and address of each person contributing $500 or more since the last report; the total contributions made to or for the lobbyist during the calendar year and for what purpose expenditures were made; the names of any papers, periodicals, magazines or other publications in which the lobbyist has published any articles or editorials; and the proposed legislation he or she is employed to support. Reports must be filed between the first and 10th day of the month in January, April, July and October.

State Elections

Laws on campaign contributions for state and local candidates vary. You will have to contact the board of elections or other office that has jurisdiction over the campaign in which you are interested. Ask what the regulations are for contributions, disclosures, PACs, political parties, lobbyists and other issues related to elections.

DOCUMENTING THE EVIDENCE

WHERE TO WRITE FOR REPORTS ON CANDIDATES' FINANCES

The following are the addresses of state offices, which keep copies of federal campaign finance reports.

ALABAMA
Elections Division, Office of the
Secretary of State
Room 21, State House
11 Union St.
Montgomery, Ala. 36130
(205) 261-7210

ALASKA
Office of the Lt. Governor
State Capitol, Room 311
Juneau, Alaska 99801
(907) 465-3520
    Mailing address
    State of Alaska, P.O. Box AA
    Juneau, AK 99811-0111

ARIZONA
Office of the Secretary of State
State Capitol, West Wing, 7th Floor
1700 W. Washington Ave.
Phoenix, Ariz. 85007
(602) 542-6167

ARKANSAS
Elections Division
Office of the Secretary of State
State Capitol Building, Room 026
Little Rock, Ark. 72201
(501) 882-5070

CALIFORNIA
Political Reform Division
Office of the Secretary of State
1230 J St., Room 219
Sacramento, Calif. 95814
(916) 322-4880

Mailing address
P.O. Box 1467
Sacramento, CA 95807

COLORADO
Elections Division
Office of the Secretary of State
1560 Broadway Suite 200
Denver, Colo. 80202
(303) 894-2211

CONNECTICUT
Elections Division
Campaign Finance Unit
Office of the Secretary of State
30 Trinity St., Room 114
Hartford, Conn. 06106
(203) 566-3059

DELAWARE
Office of the Secretary of State
Townsend Building
Dover, Del. 19901
(302) 736-4111
    Mailing address
    P.O. Box 1401
    Dover, DE 19901

DISTRICT OF COLUMBIA
Office of Campaign Finance
Reeves Municipal Center, Room 440
2000 14th St. N.W.
Washington, D.C. 20009
(202) 939-8710

165

FLORIDA
Division of Elections
Office of the Secretary of State
The Capitol, Room 1801
Tallahassee, Fla. 32399-0250
(904) 488-7690

GEORGIA
Elections Division
Office of the Secretary of State
State Capitol, Room 110
Atlanta, Ga. 30334
(404) 656-2871

HAWAII
Campaign Spending Commission
335 Merchant St., Room 215
Honolulu, Hawaii 96813
(808) 548-5411
    Mailing address
    P.O. Box 501
    Honolulu, HI 96809

IDAHO
Elections Division
Office of the Secretary of State
205 State House
Boise, Idaho 83720
(208) 334-2852

ILLINOIS
State Board of Elections
1020 South Spring St.
Springfield, Ill. 62704
(217) 782-4141
    Mailing address
    P.O. Box 4187
    Springfield, IL 62708
Also: State Board of Elections
Suit 14-100
100 West Randolph St.
Chicago, Ill. 60601
(312) 917-6440

INDIANA
Office of the Secretary of State
State House, Room 201
Indianapolis, Ind. 46204
(317) 232-6531

IOWA
Campaign Finance Disclosure
Commission
507 10th St., 7th Floor
Des Moines, Iowa 50309
(615) 281-4411

KANSAS
Office of the Secretary of State
State House, Room 234 North
Topeka, Kan. 66612-1584
(913) 296-2236

KENTUCKY
Registry of Election Finance
1604 Louisville Rd.
Frankfort, Ky. 40601
(502) 564-2226

LOUISIANA
Elections Division
Office of the Secretary of State
State Capitol, 19th Floor
Baton Rouge, La. 70804
(504) 342-4976
    Mailing address
    P.O. Box 94125
    Baton Rouge, LA 70804-9125

MAINE
Commission on Governmental Ethics
and Election Practices
State Office Building, Station 101
Augusta, Maine 04333
(207) 289-4178

MARYLAND
State Administrative Board of Election Laws
11 Bladen St.
Annapolis, Md. 21401
(301) 974-3711
    Mailing address
    P.O. Box 231
    Annapolis, MD 21404-0231

MASSACHUSETTS
Division of Public Records
Office of the Secretary of State
1719 McCormack Building
One Ashburton Pl.
Boston, Mass. 02108
(617) 727-2832

MICHIGAN
Elections Division
Office of the Secretary of State
Mutual Building, Fourth Floor
208 N. Capitol Ave.
Lansing, Mich. 48918
(517) 373-2540
    Mailing address
    P.O. Box 20126
    Lansing, MI 48901

MINNESOTA
Elections Division
Office of the Secretary of State
180 State Office Building
St. Paul, Minn. 55155
(612) 296-2805

MISSISSIPPI
Office of the Secretary of State
401 Mississippi St., Room 223
Jackson, Miss. 39201
(601) 359-1350
    Mailing address
    P.O. Box 136
    Jackson, MS 39205

MISSOURI
Division of Campaign Reporting
Office of the Secretary of State
Truman Office Building, Eighth Floor
Jefferson City, Mo. 65101
(314) 751-3077
    Mailing address
    P.O. Box 1370
    Jefferson City, MO 65101

MONTANA
Office of Political Practices
1205 Eighth Ave.
Helena, Mont. 59620
(406) 444-2942

NEBRASKA
Office of the Secretary of State
State Capitol, Suite 2300
Lincoln, Neb. 68509
(402) 471-2554

NEVADA
Office of the Secretary of State
Capitol Complex
Carson City, Nev. 89710
(702) 885-3178

NEW HAMPSHIRE
Office of the Secretary of State
State House, Room 204
Concord, N.H. 03301
(603) 271-3242

NEW JERSEY
Elections Division
Department of State
C.N. 304 107 W. State St.
Trenton, N.J. 08625-0304
(609) 292-3760

NEW MEXICO
Office of the Secretary of State
Executive-Legislative Building,
Room 400
Sante Fe, N.M. 87503
(505) 827-3620

NEW YORK
State Board of Elections
One Commerce Plaza, 18th Floor
Albany, N.Y. 12260
(518) 474-8200
    Mailing address
    P.O. Box 4
    Albany, NY 12260

NORTH CAROLINA
Campaign Reporting Office
State Board of Elections
Raleigh Building, Room 809
5 West Hargett St.
Raleigh, N.C. 27601
(919) 733-2186
    Mailing address
    P.O. Box 1934
    Raleigh, NC 27602

NORTH DAKOTA
Office of the Secretary of State
State Capitol, First Floor
Bismarck, N.D. 58505
(701) 224-2900

OHIO
Office of the Secretary of State
30 E. Broad St., 14th Floor
Columbus, Ohio 43266-0418
(614) 466-2585

OKLAHOMA
Council on Campaign Compliance and
Ethical Standards
B-2A
118 State Capitol
Oklahoma City, Okla. 73105–4802
(405) 521-3451

OREGON
Elections Division
Office of the Secretary of State
141 State Capitol
Salem, Ore. 97310
(503) 378-4144

PENNSYLVANIA
Bureau of Commissions, Elections &
Legislation
305 North Office Building
Harrisburg, Pa. 17120
(717) 787-5280

RHODE ISLAND
Elections Division
Office of the Secretary of State
100 N. Main St.
Providence, R.I. 02903
(401) 277-2340

SOUTH CAROLINA
State Election Commission
2221 Devine St., Room 105
Columbia, S.C. 29205
(803) 734-9060
    Mailing address
    P.O. Box 5987
    Columbia, SC 29250

SOUTH DAKOTA
Office of the Secretary of State
State Capitol Building, Second Floor
500 E. Capitol
Pierre, S.D. 57501-5077
(605) 773-3537

TENNESSEE
Elections Division
Office of the Secretary of State
James K. Polk Building, Suite 500
Nashville, Tenn. 37219-5040
(615) 741-7956

TEXAS
Disclosure Filing Division
Office of the Secretary of State
State Capitol, Room 127
Austin, Texas 78711
(512) 463-5704
    Mailing address
    P.O. Box 12070
    Austin, TX 78711

UTAH
Office of the Lieutenant Governor
State Capitol Building, Room 203
Salt Lake City, Utah 84114
(801) 538-1040

VERMONT
Office of the Secretary of State
Redstone Building
26 Terrace St.
Montpelier, Vt. 05602-2198
(802) 828-2363
    Mailing address
    Pavillion Office Building
    Montpelier, VT 05602-2198

VIRGINIA
State Board of Elections
101 Ninth Street Office Building

Richmond, Va. 23219
(804) 786-6551

WASHINGTON
Public Disclosure Commission
403 Evergreen Plaza FJ 42
Olympia, Wash. 98504-3342
(206) 753-1111

WEST VIRGINIA
Office of the Secretary of State
State Capitol, Room 157-K
Charleston, W.Va. 25305
(304) 345-4000

WISCONSIN
State Elections Board
132 E. Wilson St., Third Floor
Madison, Wis. 53702
(608) 266-8005

WYOMING
Elections Division
Office of the Secretary of State
106 State Capitol
Cheyenne, Wyo. 82002-0020
(307) 777-7378

CHAPTER 9

Tracing Land Holdings

"Land endures," is a favorite slogan of real estate developers. True. But how land is used changes. Ownership changes. So does value. Those changes, like the land itself, shape the lives and fortunes of individuals, neighborhoods, even cities and regions. Good reporters traditionally have searched out the corruption and favoritism that often accompany big developments, zoning changes and land purchases by public agencies. Such investigations still yield important stories. Stories that may be even more important, however, are now written by reporters willing and able to examine the broader issues and the broader impact of land use policies and patterns.

This chapter shows you both kinds of stories and describes the sources you can use. You will see that the sources are much the same. The differences arise more from the amount of time and energy you have to invest—and from the imagination you bring to the task.

by GEORGE KENNEDY

Sometimes a story is so big nobody sees it. That was the case with the blight that had rotted the heart of Saginaw, Michigan. The Saginaw News undertook a computer analysis of city records, followed up with days of legwork and told the story of "Saginaw's Vanishing Neighborhoods" in a six-day, 17-story series that opened the city's eyes. Sometimes the story is that all previous stories were wrong. That's what the Atlantic Monthly's Gregg Easterbrook discovered when he looked into the much-publicized crisis of America's vanishing farmland. A rereading of the documents and interviews with experts disclosed that earlier calculations—and stories and policy decisions based on those calculations—were plain wrong.

Sometimes the story is about how public land is being used. In Alaska, where most of the state is publicly owned, The Anchorage Times revealed that many people and companies were using public land as if they owned it. The governor, for example, was a partner in an illegal hunting lodge.

Sometimes the story is about the person who is buying and selling. The San Jose Mercury News won a Pulitzer Prize for reporting the investments of the Philippines' Marcos regime in American land and buildings. The Village Voice disclosed how a little-known New York tax lawyer was helping Ferdinand and Imelda Marcos transfer millions of dollars from the Philippines into New York real estate.

170

These stories differ in scope and subject matter, but they have at least one thing in common: Each is based on information from public records. For reporters, that's the beauty of looking at land. More than most areas of investigation, land uses and abuses are recorded and available for inspection. The documents used in these and other stories include ownership records, zoning records, building and other permit records, inspection records and court records. Most of the stories these records tell, of course, are routine. But you just might find a disappearing neighborhood, reappearing farmland, a trespassing governor or an investment-minded dictator.

Bringing the Picture Into Focus

The Saginaw News conducted some record checks for what was intended to be a story on landlords. The records were, in the words of Metro Editor Paul Chaffee, "a mess." A little more interested, reporter Ken Kolker used a portable computer to enter data into a Lotus 1,2,3 spreadsheet. Chaffee explains what happened next: "The figures on housing demolitions were staggering. Whole sectors of the city had disappeared, leaving vast tracts of weeds and concrete slabs." The newspaper set out to answer the question: Why?

The answers emerged only after two months of organizing the city's records and putting them into The News' computer, followed by extensive interviewing and the legwork of going to the abandoned neighborhoods and examining condemned homes. The answers included, according to Chaffee, "an inept housing inspection department, an out-of-control welfare system, destructive tenants and a mixture of inexperienced and exploitive landlords."

The reporting was based on analysis of inspection records, census reports, circuit court files on landlord-tenant disputes, fire department logs and inspection records, old city directories and city histories, city ordinances and city council minutes. Human sources included national experts on housing decay, tenants, landlords, inspectors, city and state officials, neighborhood leaders and former residents.

After the series went to print, two housing inspectors resigned. The News had caught them licensing apartments without inspecting them. But far more important results were the beginnings of a reexamination of the policies and ordinances that had permitted, even encouraged, the blight. The newspaper initiated development of the organization that helped the poor buy homes.

Instead of just exposing a lazy inspector or a sleazy landlord, The News reporters coupled computer analysis with old-fashioned street reporting—and had the imagination to see that the facts added up to a pattern of municipal self-destruction. This is one of a growing number of investigative projects that employs technology to pursue the kind of analysis that Ida Tarbell, Upton Sinclair and other ancestors of today's investigative reporting sought. Tarbell and Sinclair didn't have computers, but they had the same kind of vision and many of the same kinds of records.

Like the Saginaw News, The Independent of Durham, N.C., won an IRE award for a real estate investigation. The Independent took a hard look at the system of property tax reassessments in Durham County and found that not all reassessments were created equally. The stories alleged no wrongdoing, but documented that the homes of the wealthy tended to be assessed at a much lower percentage of the market value than did the homes of the poor and the middle class. This means that the wealthy were paying less than their fair share of the costs of public schools, local government and all other services that depend on property tax.

Perhaps as much courage as imagination is required to challenge the conventional wisdom. Gregg Easterbrook has made a career of doing that. For the Atlantic Monthly in 1986, he took on the collective wisdom of the nation's leading conservationist organizations, newspapers and the federal government. All had endorsed and acted on the belief that urban sprawl was eating up valuable farmland at a dangerous and increasing rate. Easterbrook thought this belief was a myth. So he went back to the original studies that formed the basis of the myth and sought independent experts, who described flawed methodology, mistaken assumptions and political pressure.

Easterbrook's own methodology was nothing fancy, simply reading and interviewing. He needed no computer, just the public record and a good idea.

Tracking the Bad Guys

The increasing emphasis on stories that analyze systems or re-examine accepted truths does not mean that exposures of malfeasance or corruption are old-fashioned or unimportant. As Bob Greene of Newsday told the 1987 national conference of IRE, "Like the hustlers say on TV, dealing in real estate is still one of the quickest ways to make a buck. And you can make money even faster if you're willing to bend the rules a bit."

Greene outlined three of the most popular types of fraud.

The Swindle

The swindle involves selling land that doesn't exist, land owned by someone else, land without clear title or misrepresenting the value or utility of the land that is sold.

The outright swindle is obvious. Misrepresentation can be more subtle. Are we talking about desert land without water? Forest land 50 miles from the nearest road or electric wires? Are prospective customers shown artists' renderings of never-to-be-built swimming pools, golf courses and clubhouses promised as part of the dream community they are being hustled to buy?

Is the salesperson pitching phony figures about how fast the land is increasing in value? The clincher usually sounds something like this: "The land has doubled in value over the past two years, and we expect it to double again over the next two years. If you buy now, you'll wind up owning the land for nothing because when it doubles again in value, you'll be even." This argument carries a built-in urgency. Since the value of the land is going up almost every day, the quicker you buy, the cheaper the price. And, the cheaper you buy, the greater your eventual profit. Unfortunately, people in a hurry to buy often don't take enough time to find out what they're getting. This is precisely the type of selling climate in which real estate swindlers do their best work.

The color slides are beautiful. The land is billed as the ideal spot for a retirement home. The price is going up every day. The downpayment is usually not much more than the cost of a trip to Florida or Arizona to look at the offered real estate. As a result, too many real estate buyers save on travel expense and make a down payment on the land without making the inspection trip.

The Zoning Hustle

Another way to make money on real estate is through rezonings. This is most easily accomplished with the aid of a politician or a member of the planning and zoning board who secretly gets something of value for approving an unpopular application.

Applying for rezoning means you are seeking to use your land for a purpose different than the rest of the people in the neighborhood. For example, if you want to put up an oil-refinery in a neighborhood of residential homes built on two-acre plots, your zoning application is sure to produce opposition. If you are dealing with crooked officeholders, the heat of the opposition determines the size of the bribe that must be paid.

The fact that officials vote for a rezoning, variance or building plan despite bitter public opposition doesn't automatically mean they are taking bribes or doing something dishonest. They may be voting for something that will benefit the whole community in the face of opposition from folks who think only in terms of their own property. But a pattern of such rezoning is suspect.

Another good rule to keep in mind is: Where land is in short supply, the more people you can put on a given piece of property, the more profit you can make and the higher the value of the land. Depending on locality, some of the most desirable zonings in descending order are:

1. *Cemeteries.* Highest price per square-foot. Most people on the smallest plots needing the least amount of roads, parking spaces, sewer mains, street lights, and so forth.
2. *Trailer parks.* Many people on tiny plots are captive customers for extra services provided by the landlord such as water, electricity, heating, sewage facilities and even convenience groceries.
3. *High-rise apartments and office buildings.* Again, a heavy concentration of people on a minimum-sized plot of land.
4. *Garden apartments.* More land to house the same amount of people, but still less than required for single-family developments.
5. *Shopping centers.* Commercial applications.

6. *Gas stations and convenience stores.* These are usually rationed in residential areas.
7. *Single-family homes.* The bigger the plot, the more costly to build. Builders are also usually required to construct roads and sewers, provide lamp posts, sidewalks and so on.

People who live in luxurious, single-family residences don't want trailer camps in their neighborhoods. Anyone who lives in a house or a garden apartment doesn't want a high-rise built next-door or down the block. Among other things, it blocks the view, requires more parking and overpopulates the neighborhood. People also frequently oppose rezonings for industrial use, gas stations and, sometimes, shopping centers. Most prefer that these be built in someone else's neighborhood.

The following methods illustrate some of the ways in which unscrupulous politicians and/or officeholders have been bribed in the past for favorable votes on building or development plans, rezonings and variances.

1. *Straight cash.* Most effective.
2. *Collateral Deal.* You are a member of the zoning board in Minneapolis. At my suggestion, you buy a piece of Florida land for $10,000. You vote on my Minneapolis rezoning. Two months later, through one of my other corporations, I buy your Florida land for $110,000. You received a $100,000 bribe that you can report as a capital gain on your income tax return. Who will ever know the difference?
3. *Ownership.* I either give you stock in the corporation that owns the land you have just voted to rezone or stock of equal value in one of my other corporations.
4. *Favorable Business Dealings.* As a builder or developer, I get my insurance, construction bonds, building supplies, engineering, architectural, drafting or design services, etc., from a firm which is owned by you or one of your relatives or which quietly pays you commissions for bringing in business.
5. *Fringe Benefits.* I provide you with gifts, or the vacation use of my Florida or San Diego condo, etc.

Inside Knowledge

Fortunes can be made by those who have specific advance knowledge of public actions affecting the value of land, such as community master plans or the exact locations of exits to a superhighway planned by the state or federal government.

Suppose, for example, I am tipped that a new community master plan will allow high-rise apartments in what was previously a low-density residential area. I can buy the best land in the area now and sell it at four or five times the price to prospective apartment builders when the master plan is made public. This advance knowledge is as good as owning my own mint.

Or, suppose, the state plans to build a limited access, superhighway through what is now largely farmland. The exits will be 15 miles apart. I am tipped as to the exact locations of the exits. I buy all the land around the planned exits. The farmers who sell me the land don't know about the planned exits, so they sell at a low price. When the highway is completed, I make a bundle selling or leasing the land around the exits for gas stations, motels and fast-food restaurants.

All that's needed is someone inside government who can tip me the information. Bribes often help.

More than once, we have found that government officials with this type of inside knowledge have gone into the land business for themselves, using front persons to do the actual buying and selling.

These are just a few of the ways to make illegitimate money at real estate.

Getting Started

Now, how do you go about getting these and other stories? Where are the records? What can they tell you? And how do you know where to start?

The guide at the end of this chapter (see "Documenting the Evidence") shows where the records generally are kept and what they contain. Before you get specifics, you may need a few suggestions about where to pick up the paper trail and where to find some help in following it.

A good place to start is with the most basic question about land: Who owns it? Who owns downtown? Who owns the worst slum housing? Who owns the tract the city plans to buy for a landfill? Who owns the vacant land being opened to development by a new taxpayer-financed road? Who owns the land being condemned for an airport or a dam, and who owns the adjacent land that will increase in value 10 times once the new facility is constructed?

In seeking the answers to questions of ownership, don't forget that persons manipulating the system seldom do business under their own names. Dummy corporations and trusteeships are devices commonly used to shield the true identities of owners. Sometimes those shields can be penetrated by using records in the secretary of state's corporation division or by using Uniform Commercial Code filings. Florida and Illinois, alone among the states, allow ownership to be concealed in blind trusts. But even those occasionally can be penetrated by checking the address to which the tax bills are mailed. Sometimes these dummy corporations end up in civil lawsuits and thus have their secrecy shorn away. (For detailed advice on how to use these records, see Chapter 11, "Business," and Chapter 14, "Courts.")

Good stories also lie in the records of how land is used. Zoning is a great source of corruption. Since every step of the zoning process is supposed to be documented and open to public inspection, a missing record or a secret decision is in itself a story. But governmental controls and potential corruption extend far beyond zoning.

Permits

In cities and towns of any size, permits are required for everything from construction of a building to operation of a restaurant on the 14th floor. The issuance of nearly every permit is supposed to be preceded by an inspection. You won't often encounter corruption of this process as blatant as that found by the Chicago Sun-Times reporters when they bought and operated their now-famous "Mirage Bar," but you may well find anything from slipshod inspections of new construction to the fact that limits on occupancy have been ignored.

Inspection Records

Check the inspection records of your city's bars and restaurants. Are deficiencies noted? Have they been corrected? Look at the fire inspections of hotels and apartment houses. For example, the Columbia Missourian found disabled people quartered on the upper floors of housing for the elderly, above the reach of the fire department's tallest ladder. Public facilities have legal limits on the number of people allowed inside at any time. Check the most popular nightspots. Are they complying with their occupancy limits? Does anybody enforce the law?

Housing Standards

Like Saginaw, nearly every city has minimum housing standards. In nearly every city, they are widely ignored. Find out why. Have there been inspections? Has there been prosecution of violators? One common excuse for failure to enforce codes is that the old and poor who own substandard housing cannot afford to fix it. But what about churches, corporations or newspaper publishers who also do business as slumlords? Maybe the inspectors will tell you that the law is unenforceable. That's a story, too.

The Monroe (La.) Morning World assigned two reporters and a photographer for more than three months to produce a 12-page special section on the 40 percent of the city's housing that was substandard. Starting with the parish (county) tax rolls and deed books, they identified the slumlords. City records showed that the housing code was unenforced. The stories identified the slumlords and described their property and the tenants who occupied it. The city's building inspector was fired after one story revealed that he himself was a slumlord. Substandard housing became a public issue in Monroe for the first time.

Assessments and Taxation

Delving into assessments and taxation can be equally rewarding. The assessed amount—that fraction of its market value—is set by law and varies from state to state. The trick is in the determination of value and in the time between reassessments.

Any real estate agent will tell you that the three most important factors determining the value of a house are location, location, location. For other kinds of property, it isn't quite so simple. Zoning is a major determinant. Future use as envisioned in a master plan is another. Access, improvement and tax rates all help determine what undeveloped or commercial property may be worth. Most of the decisions involve subjective judgments and are therefore susceptible to influence and graft. Even professional, honest appraisers develop reputations as either buyers' appraisers, who usually set low values, or sellers' appraisers, who consistently arrive at high values.

So a good story lead can be found by checking the assessments of the homes of public officials and of large downtown businesses and industries. If nothing else, you will get an education in an arcane craft as the assessor tries to explain why prime downtown property is worth less per square foot than is the neighborhood store of an African-American, a Chicano or anyone with little political clout.

An even more important story or series could be about these inequities themselves, which are built into most assessment systems—deliberately or otherwise—and favor the wealthy, the influential and the well-established over the poor, the unimportant and the newcomers. For example, in some states property generally is reassessed only when it changes hands. This operates to the advantage of longtime residents and those holding land for development; it also tilts the advantage to established merchants over would-be competitors. Any general time lag in reassessment best serves the interests of those with the most valuable or most rapidly appreciating property. The losers, in addition to those already mentioned, include local public schools, city and county governments and fire protection districts. The nature and degree of inequity is a worthy subject for investigative reporters.

Following the Dollar

There are many stories that can be based on records detailing the way land is owned, used and taxed. The best overall advice to find these stories is Clark Mollenhoff's dictum, "Follow the dollar." In the context of land use, that dictum can be applied by asking yourself two deceptively simple questions about any suspect situation: (1) who stands to benefit from this and (2) who stands to be hurt?

The tentative answers to the first question will give you clues to who may be corrupt, and will also guide you toward the records you should check. For example, suppose the city council approves, over strong neighborhood opposition, the rezoning of a vacant tract for a shopping center. Who stands to benefit? The owner of the land, of course; the shopping center developer; the merchants who will move into the center; and the people who will lend the money, sell the materials and do the construction. After checking through deed and mortgage records, you should examine the documents submitted with the rezoning application. Also, cross-check property ownership, corporate ties and outstanding debts of the council members.

Who stands to be hurt? In this example, as in many real-life cases, the identities of those who will be hurt probably are easier to ascertain. The neighbors will be upset and vocal. Equally upset, if less noisy, will be the small neighborhood merchants facing new competition. The losers are potential sources of information. They may know or can find out details, names and connections that the records don't reveal. They may have done some of the digging for you, and they may help you do the rest.

Using Human Sources

Other human sources can be important in the use of land records, sometimes even more so than documents. For almost any story, you can find people willing and able to guide, interpret and explain.

On the Scene

Start with the people on the scene. The time spent befriending a junior planner, a deputy tax assessor or a clerk at the recorder's office will pay off over and over. These are the people whose jobs it is to know what is in the records and how to get at it. A little attention to them on your part often can transform these experts into instructors for your crash course in using their resources. You are more likely to learn about a special file of properties seized for back taxes, or how to retrieve the records stored in the subbasement, from a clerk who likes you.

Outside Experts

There are outside experts, too—people who make their living researching for lawyers, real estate companies and others. Dozens of Miami Herald stories about land deals, for example, have drawn on the expertise of Charlie Kimball, a professional real estate consultant whose knowledge of property values and land use in South Florida is unsurpassed. Out of friendship, shared goals or for money, such experts can be put to work explaining and amplifying the numbers and abbreviations you find in the files. Don't overlook, for this purpose, professional real estate appraisers, realtors and land developers. It's their business to know.

Special Interest Groups

Finally, when you can, draw upon the special-interest group whose interest you share at the moment. Neighborhood associations may have banded together against blockbusting. They probably will have at least some of the information on land sales and ownership that you need for a story on the subject. Sources like Ralph Nader may be working the same territory you are.

They'll try to use you, but you can use them, too. An urban league chapter or other group may be fighting discriminatory assessments or unequal enforcement of city codes. They usually will share what they have gathered, but remember to verify the claims and records they cite.

Movers and Shakers

All of this is only half the game. The other half is the basic tool of any reporter's trade—knowing the community. If you have worked at getting to know the mayor, the tax assessor and the head of the planning and zoning board—the movers and shakers—you will be in a better position to determine whether that innocent-looking zoning variance or assessment reduction is really what it appears to be. Using the tips described and the record guide that follows, you should be able to track down those situations that aren't so clean.

DOCUMENTING THE EVIDENCE

PRIVATE PROPERTY OWNERSHIP AND TAXATION

Before undertaking the time-consuming and laborious steps described below, check with the local assessor's office. Often, with just an address, the cross-indexed files will yield the owner's name and other particulars, such as the zoning and the value of the property. Or, if your organization is willing to foot the bill, hiring a title-search company can save you vast amounts of time and can find information you might overlook. If those hints can't be followed, then you can find most of what you need by using the following records.

Note: If you think you know the name of the owner (say, from looking at a city directory that lists addresses and identifies occupants), start by looking that person's name up in the grantor-grantee index (see following).

Plat Records

In determining who owns a parcel of property, the first step is locating the legal description of the land. To find this, except in more sophisticated city and county filing systems, street addresses are not sufficient. Turn, instead, to documents called plat records, which are generally available for inspection in any city planning or public works department. The city's plat maps indicate how land has been divided for future or completed developments; for example, a parcel of land shown on the plat map may have the legal description "Goodrich Subdivision, Block 6, Lot 10."

Master Plans. If the property lies in an unincorporated area, consult the county's master plan. This can be located in such offices as the county planning department, county clerk, assessor or recorder of deeds. The master plan consists of maps dividing property parcels throughout the county into ranges, then townships and finally sections. A common legal description might be "the northwest quarter of the southwest quarter of Section 9, Township 45, Range 13." A section has 640 acres: one-fourth of 640 is 160; one-fourth of that is 40. So, in this example, the reporter knows he or she is dealing with 40 acres.

Tract Indexes

With the legal description of the land in hand, go to the local assessor's office. Using a tract index, which lists parcels of property according to location, the assessor should be able to identify the taxpayer or owner-of-record, who in most cases is the true owner of the property.

Sometimes, though, the owner may be an obscure, even dummy, corporation. Among the records to use in finding the owner's true identity are mortgages and Uniform Commercial Code filings.

Mortgages

The owner probably didn't pay the full cost of the property when the deed changed hands. The recorder of deeds will have a separate index for mortgages, usually called the deed book. The index will tell you who has the mortgage, the length of the mortgage and how much the monthly payment is. Usually, the index does not reveal the sale price. The federal real estate transfer tax—which indicated a property's sale price within $1,000—was eliminated in 1965. Some states, however, have reinstated similar taxes of their own. In Iowa, for example, a $69.30 tax payment indicates that the property sold for an amount between $63,001 and $63,500. The mortgage index also will direct you to the file of deeds. You seldom will need to examine the deed itself.

Uniform Commercial Code Filings

Even if the mortgage has been paid, the owner may not have unhampered control over the property. If he or she pledges it to a lender as security for another loan, the lender may file a statement showing such collateral under the Uniform Commercial Code (UCC) with the secretary of state's office and, sometimes, with the county recorder's office. The land described in the filing, Form UCC1, is easily recognizable by its legal description. UCC filings usually are filed by the name of the lender and the borrower. If you are interested in more information about a borrowing or lending corporation, keep the following in mind:

- Secretary of state offices or state corporation commissions require varying degrees of disclosure by corporations operating within their boundaries; almost all require annual filings that show at least the date of incorporation, the names of current directors and officers and the authorized business agent.
- All states maintain "fictitious names" or "doing business as" (DBA) directories to identify the real owners of such businesses as "Ajax Cleaners Inc.," where, obviously, the owners are not named Ajax or Cleaners. Check with the secretary of state's office.
- The address in the county tax collector's office for mailing the corporation's tax bills may be the home or business address of the true owner.

(Additional ways to trace corporation owners are detailed in Chapter 11, "Business.")

Grantor or Grantee Indexes (Inverted Indexes)

With the owner identified, reporters can outline the history of the tract's ownership through public records. The recorder of deeds usually maintains documents on property transactions in two indexes, each arranged alphabetically, one according to the grantor (seller) and the other according to grantee (buyer). (In some jurisdictions, the grantor/grantee index is called the inverted index.) Each index gives the names of both parties, the date the official transaction was recorded, the legal description of the property and the type of deed or other legal instrument conveying ownership. By tracing backward in time from buyer to seller, the ownership history can be established.

Many municipalities have computerized their land records on one index, allowing reporters to get all the information at one time by knowing either the name, address or legal description. Even where this is not the case, a professional title or abstracting company may have the information on its computer, available for a fee.

Liens

Outstanding claims may be carried by the property as it travels from owner to owner. For example, if a developer obtains work or materials from a contractor, the contractor probably will file a mechanic's lien on the property, usually in the state circuit or district court. That lien remains on the property until someone—the contractor or the owner—pays the developer. Final liability for paying the liens lies with the owner of the property.

Assessment Records

The officials in charge of assessments typically work from two indexes: the tract index, described above, and an owner's index, which indicates in one group of records how much property an individual or corporation owns within a particular jurisdiction.

Recorded on a card, the assessment on an individual property will give the assessed value, owner's mailing address, last date of assessment, assessment of both land and buildings, amount of acreage and date of building construction. These cards are also likely to give the best indication of improvements, such as those to buildings, floor area and bedrooms, the overall condition and any special landscaping. (For another place to look at paperwork related to building or improving property, see "Building" below.)

In states with personal property taxes, separate cards indicate such information as how many boats, cars, mobile homes, recreational vehicles, television sets, livestock or tractors an individual owns. Statements of farm income, needed for preferential assessment in some states, also will be filed there.

Property Tax Collection Records

The official in charge of tax collection may provide notations of discrepancies in the form of records of tax payment, incorrect addresses and incorrect taxpayers-of-record. The most valuable records, though, can be lists of those properties whose taxes are delinquent and eventually would be subject to sale for back taxes. It is always good to check, for instance, that would-be office holders are not delinquent in paying their share of taxes to the community in which they seek office. If the city sells the land, it will keep a separate record on who bought it. Be sure to check state statutes or local ordinances governing property sold for back taxes. Often the evicted owner has a one- or two-year grace period during which he or she can buy back the property.

INTERSTATE LAND SALES

Housing and Urban Development Office of Interstate Land Sales Registration

The Interstate Land Sales Full Disclosure Act of 1969, as amended, requires most developers to submit a registration (there are no forms) with the U.S. Department of Housing and Urban Development (HUD) if they plan to sell lots using any form of interstate commerce. Interstate use of the mails or advertising in news media with interstate circulation was usually enough to establish jurisdiction. But the Act also sets up numerous exemptions.

The Act was revised in 1978–79 to include developers of 25 or more lots under a common plan. However, only developments of 100 or more lots are required to file reports with HUD. Developments in the 25–100 lot range are subject to the anti-fraud provisions of the Act, but are not required to submit a filing.

The Act, as revised, exempts developments in the following categories from all provisions of the Act:

- If subdivisions have more than 25 lots, but fewer than 25 are offered for sale or lease under a common promotional plan—for example, if a subdivision contains 33 lots, but nine are set aside for a public park.
- If all lots in the subdivision are 20 acres or more.
- If the sale of lots is to builders.
- If the real estate is zoned for industrial or commercial development; if street access is approved; if the buyer is a corporate entity; and if title insurance accompanies the sale.

Developers in the following categories are exempt from the filing requirements of the Act, but are subject to the Act's anti-fraud provisions:

- If the property is free of all liens, encumbrances and adverse claims; if the purchaser makes an on-site property inspection; and if all sales are limited to residents of the state. Even if landowners are in this category, they must apply for a statement of exemption and provide it to the buyer. The seller also must make available to HUD potentially valuable information about the development, including a plat of the offering, evidence of title and a statement of reservations, restrictions, taxes and assessments. This information may be obtained from HUD under the Freedom of Information Act. (For more information about how to make this request, see Chapter 4, "The Freedom of Information Act.") Also check with known buyers, who should have received any statement of reservations prior to purchase.
- If the subdivision is made up of single-family homes only; is located where a local government sets minimum standards for lot size, roads, drainage, water supply and sewer systems; is constructed to meet all local codes and standards; has utilities extended to the lots; provides each buyer an on-site inspection; is not sold through direct mail or phone campaigns; and if title insurance accompanies the transaction. HUD considers mobile homes, townhouses and one- to four-family residences as single-family homes.

Sales pursuant to court order had been exempt from the Act, but this exemption is no longer allowed.

There may still be other special exemptions from some reporting requirements, but usually the reason for exemption is recorded. For a $500 fee, a developer may seek a HUD advisory opinion on whether the subdivision qualifies for an exemption from registration. The opinion request must be accompanied by a "comprehensive statement" of the characteristics and operation of the subdivision. The department also may ask for such further information as a plat of the property in question; the number of lots planned on those properties; the acreage of each lot; the real estate agents involved; the marketing plan and advertising material; and the sales contract, complete with any restrictive clauses.

The two main documents submitted by developers that can't find an exemption are:

- *Sample Property Report*. This often-thick report includes the official title of the developer, the "risks of buying land"; the method of sale and type of deed; the names of persons who hold liens against the property; and much additional information. It must be updated if conditions change.
- *Statement of Record*. Incorporates all information in the sample report, but also includes the names of additional states in which the developer has registered the subdivision; any states that suspended registration or prohibited sales there, with the reasons for suspension or prohibition; any Securities and Exchange Commission (SEC) filings that relate to the subdivision, and any disciplinary action the SEC may have taken against the developer; the name, address and IRS identification number assigned to the developer; the telephone number of the landowner; and, most importantly, financial statements of the developer and a current "title opinion," which details ownership of the property being developed.

After the documents are submitted, HUD reviews the data and issues a disclosure document, which essentially is a "purified" Sample Property Report and a synopsis of the Statement of Record. Unless a copy of the disclosure document is provided to the buyer before a contract is signed, the buyer has two years to rescind the contract. Even when the disclosure document is provided, the buyer has a seven-day "cooling off" period in which to cancel the contract.

Some states, such as California, Arizona, Florida, Georgia and Minnesota, have their own requirements for disclosure and registration, and HUD accepts those state filings as meeting all or most federal requirements. Reporters may wish to contact the state office of land sales registration and save time. A spokesman for the HUD Office of Interstate Land Sales Registration has said that all records discussed here are open to protect the buying public.

FEDERAL REAL PROPERTY

The General Services Administration (GSA) generally governs the use and disposal of federal real property, except for that which is in the public domain, national park or forest land, and minerals or rights designated by the Secretary of Interior for disposition under public land mining and mineral leasing laws. The federal government not only buys new property; it also routinely disposes of property it owns that is surplus to its needs.

The GSA annually submits inventories of real property owned, rented, sold or otherwise disposed of by the United States to the Senate Appropriations Committee and the House Committee on Government Operations. It collects that information from government agencies using these forms:

- *Annual Report of Real Property Owned or Leased by the United States/GSA Form 1166* is submitted by each government agency to the GSA Office of Finance and Administration by September of each year. Information includes name of reporting agency; name of installation; address; use; method, date and cost of acquisition or rental; number, date acquired, floor area and cost of buildings; type of buildings, such as hospitals or prisons; and other improvements such as harbors, reclamation projects, airfields, railroads and monuments.

  OMB Circular A–11 requires federal agencies requesting funds for real property acquisition to justify the acquisition in their budget submissions. The agency must show that the property acquisition is allowed under GSA regulations and that the agency has worked with GSA to ensure no existing facilities owned by the government would fulfill the agency's needs. OMB reviews the budget submissions and usually contacts GSA to verify information submitted by an agency. These OMB internal certification procedures were once detailed in standardized forms, but it appears these forms are no longer required. An OMB official said the forms were dropped to cut bureaucratic red tape and help speed the budget process. The OMB budget review process may be detailed in internal memoranda and other correspondence, but locating and requesting the information may now be much more difficult.

- *Summary of Number of Installations Owned or Leased by the United States/GSA Form 1209* includes cumulative information on the number of installations an agency owned at the end of the prior year, the number added since and the number disposed of. It also contains similar information on leased properties, including the annual rent, floor space and acreage of installations.

- *Report of Excess Real Properties of the United States/GSA Form 118* lists real property and related personal property under agency control that is excess to its needs. The data include name and address of the agency; custodian of the property; property's name and address; number of buildings on the property; floor area, number of floors and load capacity; government investment in the property; annual rent, if any; lease requirements; other federal agencies interested in taking over the property; and general description of the neighborhood.

- *Requests for Transfer of Excess Real and Related Personal Property/GSA Form 1334* indicates activity between two government agencies. The document shows the use of property and buildings; the government's interest (owned or leased); area; and acquisition cost.

The GSA's annual reports to Congress can be found in most government depository libraries. The reports also can be obtained from your local member of congress, from the GSA itself (18th and F Streets N.W., Washington, D.C. 20405) or probably from the agency reporting to the GSA, if the reporter explains that they are public records available from the GSA's central office anyway.

PLANNING

Master Plan

When population density increases and citizens impose planning and zoning to guide growth, the first major document to emerge is the master plan, which outlines how the area is to be developed. Green pastures are tabbed as future industrial parks; cornfields are envisioned as moderately dense single-family homes; a deteriorated single-family neighborhood is slotted for apartment houses.

In effect, the community sets out the patterns of future growth it wants, based on utility hookups, schools, transportation facilities, shopping patterns and the location of flood-prone areas, among other considerations. The plan often includes general locations and sizes of streets, bridges, parks, waterways, public buildings, public utilities and public housing, along with zones for different types of residential, commercial, industrial and institutional development. If zoning variances are granted with regularity, compare the master plan with current zoning maps to see if the master plan is followed or ignored. The maps, along with the master plan itself, are located in city or county planning offices.

Subdivision Records

Large changes in a master plan may occur when developers propose new residential, commercial or industrial subdivisions and developments. Most cities and counties spell out the procedures developers must follow, from proposal through final approval or denial. The usual route is for the developer to work up comprehensive plans for informal review by the city planning staff. These plans and any modifications to them go to a planning and zoning board, which will hold public hearings and then vote on granting zoning changes. In most areas, the city council or other overall governing body has final approval.

The creation of a new subdivision actually involves replatting, creating new legal descriptions for each land parcel in the subdivision. The steps and information available are as follows:

- The process begins with a preliminary plat that identifies the general efforts of the development. If there is no broad opposition, a detailed rezoning application will be filed with the city, including a map showing how the developer plans to lay out the property for sale. Documentation in the planning staff files should address issues of access to the property, including the impact of the property's new use on nearby roads and, for large changes, the city's major thoroughfares; the feasibility of additional utility hookups on the property; the potential for drainage; and whether the tract lies in flood-prone areas. A *caveat*: The planning staff may have referred the developer's application to other city departments, such as public works or utilities, so look for their written responses to questions of feasibility as well.

■ The final plat and rezoning request, with all final documentation, is submitted to the planning and zoning board and/or city council. The map accompanying the application should indicate all streets, utilities and easement rights (agreements of neighbors, if needed, that sewer lines and utilities can be dug or strung across their property). If approved, the plat will be filed with the county recorder and the developer may next seek building permits.

If the property is outside the jurisdiction of a municipality, look to state laws to see which agency has jurisdiction. When the subdivision is large enough to require filing with the HUD Office of Interstate Land Sales Registration, get copies of all HUD documents (see Interstate Land Sales above).

A–95 Reviews/Executive Order 12372

The A–95 Review Process was a program established by the federal government to ensure that the funds it provides for federal programs at the state and local levels do not conflict with local long-range planning and zoning goals or duplicate existing efforts. Under the A–95 Review Process, local review bodies, called clearinghouses, were set up to review applications for federal grants and make recommendations to the granting agencies. The recommendations might include comments from state and local environmental agencies, civil rights leaders or other citizens' groups with opposing viewpoints.

In October 1983, the A–95 Review Process was replaced by Executive Order 12372. The order reaffirmed the goals of the A–95 program, but provided state and local governments with greater flexibility in deciding how to set up their review processes. The order also gave increased emphasis to accommodate state and local recommendations and concerns. Although state participation remains voluntary, only Alaska, Idaho, Kansas, Nebraska and Minnesota have chosen not to take part in the program.

The order applies automatically to about 265 assistance programs carried out by the 23 grant-making agencies. The order permits each state, in consultation with local elected officials, to establish and design its own intergovernmental consultation process and select which programs covered by the order will be subject to state review. After a state selects a program or activity for review, federal agencies covered by the order are required to use the state process in obtaining the views of state officials. The agencies also must continue to follow any other consultation procedures contained in state statutes and regulations.

States participating in the program are required to establish "single points of contact" (SPOCs) where those considering application for federal funds can be informed of the process. These contact points are designated by the state governor and are usually located in the state's office of planning, budget or community affairs, often

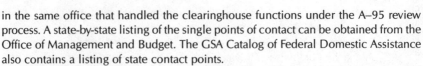

in the same office that handled the clearinghouse functions under the A–95 review process. A state-by-state listing of the single points of contact can be obtained from the Office of Management and Budget. The GSA Catalog of Federal Domestic Assistance also contains a listing of state contact points.

Federal grant-seekers may be required to apply to the state, which then generally has about 60 days to review the proposal. State comments, generally known as "State Process Recommendations," are sent along with the application to the appropriate federal agency.

The granting agency must accept the state's concerns or notify the state in writing why not. The agency must then wait 15 days after notification before awarding funds for the project. During this time the state may take further action to prevent funding. State recommendations accepted by the federal agency generally become a part of the agency's funding guidelines and are written into grant requirements.

Most federal agencies are reluctant to talk about the status of applications once the funding selection process has begun. Those seeking information about grant applications or state recommendations may wish to call the single point of contact or the applicant, but access to review process paper work may vary from state to state.

A listing of state single points of contact and federal agency E.O. 12372 contacts is included at the end of this chapter.

Zoning

Typically, zones within a city are classified as agricultural, residential, commercial, office or industrial. Each of these ways of using land is more intensive than the one named before it—that is, it has a greater impact on the environment and requires more support from city services and local utilities. A type of zone may be classified even more specifically; for example, a residential zone may be restricted to single-family, multifamily or some other type of housing.

Two general types of zoning exist: pyramidal and horizontal. *Pyramidal zoning* allows all or most less-intensive land uses within a district than the type prescribed by the zoning law. Single-family homes, for example, may be built on land zoned for apartments and stores. *Horizontal zoning* requires that property within a district be used for the specifically prescribed purpose and none other. The nature of a city or county's zoning ordinances usually is determined by state enabling legislation, so start with the state statutes. The type of information required will be spelled out there, as well as in local ordinances.

Rezoning Applications

An owner submits a rezoning application, usually to the local planning and zoning commission, when seeking to change his or her property's zoning. The application ordinarily will include street address, size of the tract, location of the deed, location of the original survey plat or survey, current zoning statutes, current use of the property, proposed use under the city or county master plan, reason for requesting the rezoning change, future development plans and timetable for development. Owners of record are listed, as well as any resident business agents. The application may also include an accurate legal description of each zone district on the property, a map of the property and any special requests. Ordinarily, a filing fee is charged to defray the city's or county's costs when rezoning requests are required to be advertised in local newspapers.

Notification

Under some state laws, owners of abutting or nearby property must be advised of the rezoning application so they may comment on the change at a public hearing or in written comments to the local zoning commission. The planning staff should keep a record of those notices and who received them.

Recommendations

In more sophisticated planning and zoning operations, the zoning commission's staff or the city's planning staff will review the request in the context of the master plan and recommend action in a formal report to the commission. Usually, if the change is congruent with the master plan for development, the staff will recommend approval.

Hearings

Generally, the application goes through a public hearing before the zoning commission, a commission vote and then perhaps another hearing and vote by the local governing body. Each step is documented, including minutes of the hearings and tabulation of the votes. Look for changes negotiated with staff members after public hearings by comparing the original request and amended requests. Look for any special interests held by the commission members in the changes they vote on.

Zoning Variances

Depending on state statutes and local ordinances, variances from existing zoning may be obtained from boards of adjustment or other panels because of hardship. Applications to these boards should contain the same kind of information as in rezoning requests, along with a statement of the hardship that the applicant believes justifies the variance. The procedures for acceptance or denial are the same as rezoning requests.

BUILDING

Building Permit Applications

In most cities and counties of substantial populations, a building permit is required before construction of new buildings or major modification of existing structures can begin. The application, filed with the city clerk or public works office, may list the address of the site, the owner, the contractor, a copy of the plat, dimensions of the building being modified, value of the building before and after improvements, a statement of how the building will be used and, occasionally, identification of the personnel working on the project. (Some communities require the builders to hire workers who have passed special competency examinations. Boards of electricians, plumbers and other specialists will have lists of licensed workers. Shoddy contractors, of course, can cut costs by hiring unqualified personnel.)

Building Inspections of Ongoing Construction

Ordinances may require that a city or county inspector visit the site during actual construction to check whether the foundations, wiring and other features comply with standards and whether the building code in general is being followed. The public workers office conducts these inspections and should have files including reports of when visits occurred and checklists that indicate what violations, if any, were found. Copies of building electrical, energy and other mandatory codes for construction should also be available from the department.

Appeals of inspectors' decisions are often heard by a special board or review panel. That panel may approve a variance from the building-code provisions for reasons of hardship, or it may rule against the inspectors' interpretation of code provisions. These files should contain the names of the complainants, their written petitions for appeal and the commission's staff decision.

Certificates of Occupancy

In communities that require building inspections, no new or structurally-altered building may be occupied or used until a certificate of occupancy has been issued by city or county officials. The certificate file should include checklists showing that the structure complies with building and sanitation codes. The file should also include documentation of special requirements, such as the state inspections needed before nursing homes, child care centers or hospitals may open.

Some communities certify residential structures for a maximum number of occupants. That device, according to theory, helps prevent overcrowding that may lead to deterioration and flight from the neighborhood. The certificate of occupancy may cite a city or county review of the maximum occupancy requirement that resulted in a variance for this project.

Building Inspections for Existing Structures

Some cities and states require regular inspection of commercial, residential, retail and industrial properties for compliance with building, fire, electric, safety, sanitary and other codes. Check appropriate state statutes and ordinances for the scope and timing of the inspections and to identify where the inspection files are kept.

Inspection files should contain the building's address, owner, dates of all inspections, any follow-up inspections, checklists of violations, notices of violations, statements from owners on what improvements have been made, complaints and the like. Special instructions are often run in conjunction with licensing programs. For example, barber shops are checked for certification of personnel and health conditions; restaurants, hotels and motels will have sanitary and fire inspections.

Cities and states may set up boards to consider appeals of administrative actions such as condemnations of structures, revocation of licenses because of unsanitary conditions or other disputes. Information in these files can reveal a great deal about how the owners operate.

STATE SINGLE POINTS OF CONTACT

ALABAMA
Mrs. Moncell Thornell
State Single Point of Contact
Alabama State Clearinghouse
Department of Economic &
Community Affairs
P.O. Box 250347
3465 Norman Bridge Rd.
Montgomery, Ala. 36205-0347
(205) 284-8905

ARIZONA
Ms. Janice Dunn
Arizona State Clearinghouse
3800 N. Central Ave., 14th Floor
Phoenix, Ariz. 85007
(602) 255-5004

ARKANSAS
Mr. Joseph Gillesbie
Manager, State Clearinghouse
Office of Intergovernmental Service
Department of Finance and Administration
P.O. Box 3278
Little Rock, Ark. 72203
(501) 371-1074

CALIFORNIA
Glen Stober
Grants Coordinator
Office of Planning and Research
1400 10th St.
Sacramento, Calif. 95814
(916) 323-7480

COLORADO
State Single Point of Contact
State Clearinghouse
Division of Local Government
1313 Sherman St., Room 520
Denver, Colo. 80203
(303) 866-2156

CONNECTICUT
Under Secretary
Attn: Intergovernmental Review
Secretary
Comprehensive Planning Division
Office of Policy and Management
80 Washington St.
Hartford, Conn. 06106-4459
(203) 566-3410

DELAWARE
Francine Booth
State Single Point of Contact
Executive Department
Thomas Collins Building
Dover, Del. 19903
(302) 736-3326

DISTRICT OF COLUMBIA
Lovetta Davis
State Single Point of Contact
Executive Office of the Mayor
Office of Intergovernmental Relations
District Building, Room 416
1350 Pennsylvania Ave. N.W.
Washington, D.C. 20004
(202) 727-9111

FLORIDA
Karen McFarland
Director of Intergovernmental
Coordination
Single Point of Contact
Executive Office of the Governor
Office of Planning and Budgeting
The Capitol
Tallahassee, Fla. 32399-0001
(904) 488–8114

GEORGIA
Charles H. Badger
Administrator
Georgia State Clearinghouse
270 Washington St. S.W.
Atlanta, Ga. 30334
(404) 656–3855

HAWAII
Mr. Harold S. Masumoto
Acting Director
Office of State Planning
Department of Planning and Economic
Development
Office of the Governor
State Capitol
Honolulu, Hawaii 96813
(808) 548–3016

ILLINOIS
Tom Berkshire
State Single Point of Contact
Office of the Governor
State of Illinois
Springfield, Ill. 62706
(217) 782–8639

INDIANA
Frank Sullivan
Budget Director
State Budget Agency
212 State House
Indianapolis, Ind. 46204
(317) 232–5610

IOWA
Steven R. McCann
Division for Community Progress
Iowa Department of Economic
Development
200 East Grand Ave.
Des Moines, Iowa 50309
(515) 281–3725

KENTUCKY
Robert Leonard
State Single Point of Contact
Kentucky State Clearinghouse
2nd Floor, Capital Plaza Tower
Frankfort, Ky. 40601
(502) 564–2382

LOUISIANA
Colby S. LaPlace
Assistant Secretary
Department of Urban & Community
Affairs
Office of State Clearinghouse
P.O. Box 94455, Capitol Station
Baton Rouge, La. 70804
(504) 342–9790

MAINE
State Single Point of Contact
Attn: Joyce Benson
State Planning Office
State House Station #38
Augusta, Maine 04333
(207) 289–3261

MARYLAND
Mary Abrams, Director
Maryland State Clearinghouse
Department of State Planning
301 W. Preston St.
Baltimore, Md. 21201-2365
(301) 225–4490

MASSACHUSETTS
State Single Point of Contact
Attn: Beverly Boyle

Executive Office of Communities &
Development
100 Cambridge St., Room 1803
Boston, Mass. 02202
(617) 727-7001

MICHIGAN
Manager
Federal Project Review System
P.O. Box 30242
Lansing, Mich. 48901
(517) 373-6223

MISSISSIPPI
Cathy Mallette
Clearinghouse Officer
Department of Finance and
Administration
421 W. Pascagoula St.
Jackson, Miss. 39203
(601) 960-4280

MISSOURI
Lois Pohl
Federal Assistance Clearinghouse
Office of Administration
Division of General Services
P.O. Box 809
Truman Building, Room 430
Jefferson City, Mo. 65102
(314) 751-4834

MONTANA
Deborah Stanton
State Single Point of Contact
Intergovernmental Review Clearing-
house
c/o Office of Lieutenant Governor
Capitol Station
State Capitol, Room 202
Helena, Mont. 59620
(406) 444-5522

NEVADA
John Walker
Clearinghouse Coordinator

Nevada Office of Community Services
Capitol Complex
Carson City, Nev. 89710
(702) 885-4420

NEW HAMPSHIRE
Jeffery Taylor, Director
New Hampshire Office of State
Planning
Attn: Intergovernmental Review
Process/James E. Bieber
2 1/2 Beacon St.
Concord, N.H. 03301
(603) 271-2155

NEW JERSEY
Nelson S. Silver
State Review Process
Division of Local Government Services,
CN 803
Trenton, N.J. 08625-0803
(609) 292-9025

NEW MEXICO
Dorothy Rodriquez
Department of Finance and
Administration
Room 190, Bataan Memorial Building
Santa Fe, N.M. 87503
(505) 827-3885

NEW YORK
New York State Clearinghouse
Division of the Budget
State Capitol
Albany, N.Y. 12224
(518) 474-1605

NORTH CAROLINA
Mrs. Chrys Baggett, Director
Intergovernmental Relations
N.C. Department of Administration
116 W. Jones St.
Raleigh, N.C. 27611
(919) 733-0499

NORTH DAKOTA
William Robinson
State Single Point of Contact
Office of Intergovernmental Affairs
Office of Management and Budget
State Capitol, 14th Floor
Bismarck, N.D. 58505
(701) 224–2094

OHIO
Larry Weaver
State Single Point of Contact
State/Federal Funds Coordinator
State Clearinghouse
Office of Budget and Management
30 East Broad St., 34th Floor
Columbus, Ohio 43266-0411
(614) 466–0698

OKLAHOMA
Don Strain
State Single Point of Contact
Oklahoma Department of Commerce
Office of Federal Assistance Management
6601 Broadway Extension
Oklahoma City, Okla. 73116
(405) 843–9770

OREGON
Attn: Delores Streeter
State Single Point of Contact
Intergovernmental Relations Division
State Clearinghouse
155 Cottage St. N.E.
Salem, Ore. 97310
(503) 373–1998

PENNSYLVANIA
Sandra Kline
Pennsylvania Intergovernmental
Council
P.O. Box 11880
Harrisburg, Pa. 17108
(717) 783–3700

RHODE ISLAND
Review Coordinator
Office of Strategic Planning
Department of Administration
Division of Planning
265 Melrose St.
Providence, R.I. 02907
(401) 277–2656

SOUTH CAROLINA
Danny L. Cromer
State Single Point of Contact
Grant Services
Office of the Governor
1205 Pendleton St., Room 477
Columbia, S.C. 29201
(803) 734–0435

SOUTH DAKOTA
Susan Comer
State Clearinghouse Coordinator
Office of the Governor
500 East Capitol
Pierre, S.D. 57501
(605) 773–3212

TENNESSEE
Charles Brown
State Single Point of Contact
State Planning Office
309 John Sevier Building
500 Charlotte Ave.
Nashville, Tenn. 37219
(615) 741–1676

TEXAS
Thomas C. Adams
Office of Budget and Planning
Office of the Governor
P.O. Box 12428
Austin, Texas 78711
(512) 463–1778

UTAH
Dale Hatch, Director
Office of Planning and Budget

State of Utah
116 State Capitol Building
Salt Lake City, Utah 84114
(801) 533–5245

VERMONT
Bernard D. Johnson
Assistant Director
Office of Policy Research &
Coordination
Pavilion Office Building
109 State St.
Montpelier, Vt. 05602
(802) 828–3326

VIRGINIA
Nancy Miller
Intergovernmental Affairs Review
Officer
Department of Housing & Community
Development
205 N. Fourth St.
Richmond, Va. 23219
(804) 786–4474

WASHINGTON
Marilyn Dawsen, Coordinator
Intergovernmental Review Process
Department of Community
Development
9th and Columbia Building
Olympia, Wash. 98504-4151
(206) 753–4978

WEST VIRGINIA
Fred Cutlip, Director
Community Development Division
Governor's Office of Community and
Industrial Development

Building #6, Room 553
Charleston, W. Va. 25305
(304) 348–4010

WISCONSIN
William Carey
Federal-State Relations Coordinator
Wisconsin Department of
Administration
101 South Webster St., GEF 2
P.O. Box 7864
Madison, Wis. 53707-7864
(608) 266–0267

WYOMING
Ann Redman
State Single Point of Contact
Wyoming State Clearinghouse
State Planning Coordinator's Office
Capitol Building
Cheyenne, Wyo. 82002
(307) 777–7574

PUERTO RICO
Patria Custodio/Israel Soto Marrero
Chairman/Director
Puerto Rico Planning Board
Minillas Government Center
P.O. Box 41119
San Juan, Puerto Rico 00940-9985
(809) 727–4444

VIRGIN ISLANDS
Jose L. George, Director
Office of Management and Budget
No. 32 & 33 Kongens Gade
Charlotte Amalie, Virgin Islands 00802
(809) 774–0750

This list was compiled from information available from the Executive Office of the President, Office of Management and Budget; updated September 2, 1988.

FEDERAL AGENCY EXECUTIVE ORDER 12372 CONTACT LIST

ACTION
Mr. Willard L. Hoing
Ms. Maxine Polsky
1100 Connecticut Ave. N.W.,
Room 5201
Washington, D.C. 20525
(202) 634–9212

U.S. DEPARTMENT OF AGRICULTURE
Mr. Gerald Miske
Supervisory Program Analyst
USDA/South Building, Room 1369
14th and Independence Ave. S.W.
Washington, D.C. 20250
(202) 382–1553

U.S. DEPARTMENT OF COMMERCE
Alison Kaufman
Director, Intergovernmental Affairs
Main Commerce Building, Room 5413
14th and Constitution Ave. N.W.
Washington, D.C. 20230
(202) 377–3281

CORPS OF ENGINEERS
James Schooler
U.S. Army Corps of Engineers
DAEN-CWP-A
20 Massachusetts Ave. N.W.
Washington, D.C. 20314-1000
(202) 272–1978

U.S. DEPARTMENT OF DEFENSE
Ken Matzkin, Staff Contact
Office of Economic Adjustment
Department of Defense
400 Army Navy Dr.
Arlington, Va. 22202
(703) 697–0041

U.S. DEPARTMENT OF EDUCATION
Leroy Walser, Staff Contact
EO 12372-CFDA #84
Department of Education, MS 6401
400 Maryland Ave. S.W.

Washington, D.C. 20202
(202) 732–3679

U.S. DEPARTMENT OF ENERGY
Steve Lerner
Office of Intergovernmental Affairs
Department of Energy CP-60
1000 Independence Ave. S.W.
Washington, D.C. 20585
(202) 586–5466

**U.S. ENVIRONMENTAL PROTEC-
TION AGENCY**
Corrine Allison, Staff Contact
Grants Specialist (PM-216)
Grants Policy & Procedures Branch
Grants Management Division
Fairchild Building, 8th Floor
499 South Capitol St. S.W.
Washington, D.C. 20460
(202) 382–5294

**FEDERAL EMERGENCY
MANAGEMENT AGENCY**
William Coe
Office of Program Analysis & Evalua-
tion
500 C St. S.W., Room 406
Washington, D.C. 20472
(202) 646–2667

**U.S. GENERAL SERVICES
ADMINISTRATION**
John Butler
Committee Management
General Services Administration
18th & F Sts. N.W., Room 7030
Washington, D.C. 20405
(202) 501–0188

**U.S. DEPARTMENT OF HEALTH AND
HUMAN RESOURCES**
Bob Maslyn, Staff Contact
Division of Assistant Policy
200 Independence Ave. S.W.
Washington, D.C. 20201
(202) 245–0931

U.S. DEPARTMENT OF HOUSING AND URBAN DEVELOPMENT
Mildred Weber
HUD Office of Intergovernmental Affairs
451 17th St. S.W., Room 10140
Washington, D.C. 20410
(202) 755–6480

U.S. DEPARTMENT OF INTERIOR
Ceceil Coleman
Division of Acquisition & Grants
Department of Interior
18th & C Sts. N.W., Room 5524
Washington, D.C. 20240
(202) 343–3474

U.S. DEPARTMENT OF JUSTICE
Bill Lucas
Director of Liaison Services
Department of Justice
10th & Constitution Ave. N.W., Room 4213
Washington, D.C. 20530
(202) 633–3465

U.S. DEPARTMENT OF LABOR
Sue Ironfield
Intergovernmental Affairs
Department of Labor, Room S1.506
200 Constitution Ave. N.W.
Washington, D.C. 20210
(202) 523–7086

NATIONAL AERONAUTICS AND SPACE ADMINISTRATION
Curtis Graves, Chief
Deputy Director for Civil Affairs
NASA
Washington, D.C. 20546
(202) 453–8351

NATIONAL ENDOWMENT FOR THE ARTS
Rene F. Hill
National Endowment for the Arts

1100 Pennsylvania Ave. N.W., Room 602
Washington, D.C. 20506
(202) 682–5429

NATIONAL SCIENCE FOUNDATION
Maryanne Moulton
Division of Grants & Contracts
National Science Foundation
1800 G St. N.W., Room 1140-D
Washington, D.C. 20550
(202) 357–9496

OFFICE OF MANAGEMENT AND BUDGET
Kimberly Armstrong Newman
Government Operations/ Intergovernmental Affairs
725 17th St. N.W., Room 10202
Washington, D.C. 20503
(202) 395–6911

U.S. POSTAL SERVICE
Bill Mathews
U.S. Postal Service
475 L'Enfant Plaza S.W., Room 4141
Washington, D.C. 20260-6431
(202) 268–3120

U.S. SMALL BUSINESS ADMINISTRATION
Martin Teckler
Associate General Counsel for Legislation
Small Business Administration
1441 L St. N.W., Room 706
Washington, D.C. 20416
(202) 653–6644

TENNESSEE VALLEY AUTHORITY
Jon Loney
Tennessee Valley Authority
1D53 Old City Hall Complex
Knoxville, Tenn. 37902
(615) 632–8111

U.S. DEPARTMENT OF TRANSPORTATION
Don Bard
Program Analyst
Department of Transportation
400 7th St. S.W., Room 9401
Washington, D.C. 20590
(202) 366–4268

U.S. VETERANS ADMINISTRATION
John Forster
Office of Intergovernmental Affairs
Veterans Administration
Mail Stop 61B, Room 1017
810 Vermont Ave. N.W.
Washington, D.C. 20420
(202) 233–3116

C H A P T E R   1 0

Putting It All Together

The real test for reporters, of course, is putting all of the preceding information to use. Since most of us are not full-time investigative reporters and work on fierce deadlines and minuscule budgets, we've chosen a fast-breaking story as an example of how to use much of the information in the preceding chapters.

---

by PATRICK RIORDAN

You're methodically researching your project on the ridiculously expensive monorail the county wants to build at the new zoo when your editor starts flailing his or her arms and shouting at you. The police desk has an update on a bust at a disco last night. They found in the back room 10 bales of marijuana, 20 kilos of cocaine and 100,000 Quaaludes. A Colombian citizen was among those arrested.

The police are cooperating with the Drug Enforcement Administration, but not with you. They're giving out nothing beyond the arrest sheets.

There are a hundred unanswered questions: Who owns the disco? What else does this person own—land, buildings, cars, boats, airplanes? What's the disco owner's economic background? Has the owner ever been accused of a crime? Does the owner use corporations to hide behind? Is there a limited partnership involved? Who are its investors? How much did they invest? Who's in business with this person?

Public records will answer every one of those questions for you in a few hours.

Let's suppose the police are really playing hard-to-get and won't even tell you the name of the disco owner. You can still find it.

You have the address of the disco from the arrest sheet or the phone book. Go to the office of the tax collector, or the office where deeds are kept on file, and ask a clerk to help you convert the street address into a legal description of the property. In an urban area, that'll be a block number and one or more lot numbers in a particular subdivision.

For example, suppose the disco is located at 3000 Coral Blvd. in Miami. Either by asking a clerk or by using the county real estate plat map yourself, you find that 3000 Coral Blvd. is in Miami's Urban Estates subdivision and that your particular address is Lots 5,6 and 7 of Block 5.

With that information you can find the owner in one of two ways.

The easy way: If your county keeps abstract books, tract indexes or a property index, look up the book or microfilm reel for your subdivision. In that book, flip through pages or unreel film until you come to Block 5. Then go to the very last entry under Block 5 and work backward. The first entry you come to for Lots 5, 6 and 7 is the most recent. It reflects the current owner.

The harder way: If you don't have abstract books for each subdivision, work through the tax roll. You may need to convert the legal description of the land into a folio number, composed of the block and lot numbers, a code number for the subdivision and municipality, and other code numbers for section, range and township—terms you'll encounter more often when you're researching rural acreage. Each piece of property in your county has a unique folio number. Once someone has shown you how to determine it, go to the tax roll and look it up. The folio number shows who's paying the taxes. About 99 percent of the time, it's the owner. (In Florida and Illinois, you may have a hidden land trust with a trustee paying the taxes. Good luck.)

No matter how you get the name of the apparent owner, it's a good idea to double check. Go to the office where the deeds are kept. It's the recorder's office in some states, the register of deeds, clerk's office or official records office in others.

In this case, the current owner appears to be something called Taca Corp. Now ask for the grantor and grantee indexes (also known as the official records index, the deed index or the index to real estate transfers). To find the owner's deed to the disco property, look up Taca Corp. in the grantee index. There you'll find a reference to Book 289, Page 34. Find Deed Book 289 on the shelf or in a microfilm drawer. Turn to page 34, and you've got the deed.

Taca Corp., it appears, acquired title to the property from Charles Candyman, a name that's vaguely familiar. The corporation owes $50,000 on the property to First Smugglers' Bank and Trust Co. That's its first mortgage. It also owes another $375,000 to Candyman, payable in quarterly installments over 10 years. That's the purchase-money second mortgage.

Find out how much it owes by checking in the deed book a few pages before and after the deed for a mortgage. Mortgages are usually filed with the deed, but not always. Look in the index to mortgages under Taca Corp. to be sure.

From the legal description, the deed and the mortgages, you now know precisely what property was bought and sold, who bought it, who sold it and who's financing it.

You can also figure out how much it cost. The amount isn't spelled out directly, but it's indicated clearly by the amount of documentary tax paid to record the deed. Sometimes called the recordation fee, this tax corresponds mathematically to the value of the transaction. In Florida, for example, $3 worth of stamps must be attached to the deed for every $1,000 of value. On a $100,000 transaction, there would be $300 worth of stamps. In the District of Columbia, where the tax is 1 percent of the value of the transaction, the amount is shown by an imprint, not by actual stamps. A $100,000 transaction costs $1,000 to record. In other jurisdictions the tax rate varies. Find out what yours is from the county office that records deeds and charges the tax, or look up your state law.

After computing the indicated value of the transaction, you note in the grantor and grantee indexes that Taca Corp. seems to have several other deeds on file. But before proceeding, you decide to learn a little more about Taca.

The courthouse office where occupational licenses are kept sheds little light on the subject. Taca holds the local business license in its corporate name.

You could check the utilities office to see who pays the water and electricity bills, but you are too busy and decide to pass for the moment.

You call the secretary of state's office to ask for the corporate information office. It will give you a lot of information on the phone and send you more by mail. Always ask for current officers and directors, including their addresses; the corporate address (also called the registered address); the name of the registered agent; the nature of the business in which the corporation engages; and whether the corporation is up-to-date on its franchise tax.

Also ask for the date of incorporation. If you're persuasive enough, you can sometimes get someone to find the original articles of incorporation. From those you can get the names of the incorporators (the people who formed the corporation), the name of the attorney who handled the paperwork, the name of the notary public who notarized the corporate charter and, sometimes, a more detailed statement about the business in which the corporation engages.

In this case, one name jumps out at you: It's Charles Candyman, the guy who sold the disco to Taca.

He turns out to be the president of Taca, its registered agent and one of its original incorporators three years ago. His lawyer, a well-known criminal defense attorney, is Taca's corporate secretary—a little out of his line.

Before you get off the phone, call another agency in the capital, the Uniform Commercial Code Office. That's where people file evidence of secured debts, such as car or boat loans, or of business loans backed by accounts receivable, inventory or fixtures.

Taca, you discover, owes a restaurant supply company for its kitchen and bar equipment at the disco, but that's all.

Now you call the nearest office of the Alcoholic Beverage Commission or the Division of Beverage, or whichever agency licenses bars in your state. The agency will have in its files a complete list of all owners of the disco if it has a liquor license.

Since you know the owner is Taca, you can get a list of stockholders. It turns out that there's only one: Candyman.

A picture is emerging.

The disco where the police found the drugs has a complicated corporate structure, but only one man behind it all. That man receives large sums of money in the form of mortgage payments. This could be a clever scheme to steal from the business and declare bankruptcy. Or it might be Candyman's way of establishing a large, on-the-record taxable income for IRS consumption, in order to conceal his real income from drug smuggling.

Back to the deed books.

Those other transactions involving Taca now become much more interesting than they were before. You get copies of all deeds involving the company, and your paper reimburses you. (If it doesn't, deduct them on your income tax return and look for another job.)

With each deed the pattern grows stronger. In your county alone, Taca owns 50 acres near the new free trade zone, a key parcel next to the seaport and two old downtown hotels in the path of a new convention center, along with three condominium apartments and the disco where the drugs were found.

You extend your research. The Uniform Commercial Code office didn't have any record of loans on cars, airplanes or boats. Maybe that's because Candyman paid cash for his smuggling vehicles. You call the motor vehicle records office in the state capital and explain the general nature of the inquiry. A state employee looks up Candyman and Taca. Candyman owns a new Seville in his own name with no lien on it. He paid cash. Taca owns three large, straight-body trucks and a jeep, all free and clear.

The Department of Natural Resources (or the agency that licenses boats in your state) looks in its files for Candyman and Taca and discovers three Donzi speedboats, each capable of outrunning anything owned by the U.S. Customs Service.

Finally, the state motor vehicle office or the state Department of Transportation, depending on where you live, looks up Candyman and Taca. The corporation, it seems, owns two aircraft: a plush, radar-equipped Piper Aztec, suitable for spotting ships at sea and hauling cocaine, and a Convair 220, capable of hauling 10,000-pound payloads.

Taca begins to look like a smuggling conglomerate.

En route to the office, you check the court clerk's office. You look up Taca in the index to see if anyone has ever sued it. There's only one case—a slip-and-fall on the dance floor, settled out of court. You look up Candyman and find a divorce file. Not much you don't already know, except that in the property settlement there's a reference to Taca Investors Ltd.

You double back to the deeds office and look up Taca Investors Ltd., kicking yourself for missing it the first time. You find three deeds and a limited-partnership declaration.

According to the deeds, the partnership owns an apartment building, rural acreage that includes a landing strip and some oceanfront land with a canal leading to a privately maintained channel where smugglers have been arrested before. Best of all, the declaration of partnership lists Candyman, his lawyer and a city councilman as limited partners. The general partner is our old friend Taca. According to the declaration, each investor put up one-third of the investment.

But only the general partner, the corporation, can be held financially account-able, and its liability is limited by the state corporation laws.

One last stop—at the criminal-court building—confirms what you thought you remembered: Nine years ago Candyman was convicted of selling 600 pounds of marijuana and a kilo of cocaine to an undercover cop.

He's got a record as a dealer; he's tied to a public official; he owns boats, planes, trucks, a landing strip and a secluded harbor, all of which he paid cash for; and his criminal defense attorney is his business partner.

You put it all together and call a friendly cop. You tell him or her what you have. The cop trades you a little information in return: Candyman is about to be arrested, along with five of his lieutenants. He or she asks you to hold the story out of the first edition until Candyman is arrested. You spend the time polishing the writing.

Everything you have is tied to a public record. Everything is demonstrably true, documented and libel-proof.

This illustration is not entirely fictitious. A similar story—minus the limited partnership—was written by a Miami Herald reporter. It was not done on deadline, but it could have been: All the information was gathered in a single day. Any good reporter with a solid knowledge of public records could have done it.

Of course, records are no substitute for shoeleather or sources. To make your story come alive, you ultimately have to talk to people on the record. But knowing how to run the records comprehensively can help you to ask better questions.

PART THREE

INSTITUTIONS

C H A P T E R   1 1

Business
For-Profit Corporations

Among the most difficult stories to tell are those involving businesses. Penetrating the secrecy is difficult for most reporters. Understanding what you manage to ferret out is often as hard as the sleuthing itself. Learning your way around, however, is not impossible, and the many sources available, both printed and human, as well as the kinds of stories you can explore, are fully described here.

    Our discussion begins with for-profit corporations.

---

by JAMES K. GENTRY

When business editor Doug Oplinger checked the Dow Jones wire for activity in Goodyear Tire & Rubber Co. on the afternoon of Oct. 7, 1986, he was surprised to see that trading exceeded 1.5 million shares for the day, more than twice the normal activity. The reason: takeover rumors.

    "Obviously something was going on and we knew we had to find out what," said Rick Reiff, then a reporter with the Akron Beacon Journal.

    The effort to identify the acquirer started a quest that tested the Beacon Journal staff's ability to think creatively, to identify key human sources and to decipher crucial Securities and Exchange Commission documents. The efforts of Oplinger, Reiff and several other reporters resulted in a 10-week series of articles that won the Beacon Journal the Pulitzer Prize for general news reporting in 1987.

For Reiff, the first key to the puzzle was to determine who was buying Goodyear stock. "Through some sources on Wall Street, I learned that Merrill Lynch was rumored to be the buyer," Reiff said. "But I couldn't confirm it so we didn't use the information right away."

Goodyear activity subsided for two weeks but when it resumed, Reiff knew the source he needed: the Goodyear specialist, the New York Stock Exchange (NYSE) floor trader who makes a market in the company's stock by matching buyers and sellers. Goodyear was asked to help arrange a contact with the specialist, but to no avail. So Reiff called the NYSE and obtained the name of the firm making the market. He asked the NYSE to ask the specialist if he would talk with a reporter. The specialist's answer was a surprising yes.

The next morning Reiff was in New York on the exchange's floor, talking with Christopher Bates, the Goodyear specialist. "Chris thought it was great to be interviewed," Reiff recalled. "He had a connection with Canton, Ohio, and that made it better. The other brokers got a kick out of the interview, too."

Reiff spent about an hour talking and observing. Bates pointed out traders for the various brokerage firms, and then gave Reiff the information for which he had traveled 400 miles. "Chris identified the Merrill Lynch guy and said he'd been the one buying heavily," Reiff said. "So I approached the broker, who told me a single customer was buying all the shares." Although Reiff was unable to identify the individual buyer, the information led to the first media report the next day stating that Merrill Lynch was acquiring shares on behalf of an unknown "investor."

The next break came a day later. "A source inside Goodyear called one of our people to say that Sir James Goldsmith was the buyer," Reiff said. "The company had hired the Carter Organization to find out who it was, and Carter had done its job." The tip led to another first report for the Beacon Journal. The paper followed that report with an extensive profile of Goldsmith.

Soon, Goldsmith's Goodyear holdings moved above 5 percent so the British raider was required by Securities and Exchange Commission regulations to file a 13–D, which identifies the acquirer of the stock and the target, and contains a wealth of information for business reporters.

"We ran a weekend story based on Goldsmith's Friday filing of the 13–D, but three days later we came back with a much more thorough story based on the document," Reiff said. "It was the definitive story on the financing and for the first time reported that Merrill Lynch had taken the unusual step of taking an equity position in the deal. This made it much more ominous for Goodyear."

Before the Goldsmith-Goodyear fray was over, the Akron paper had given it some 100 stories and had illustrated that the best business reporting, like any good reporting, requires determination, creative thinking and a solid mix of human and documentary sources.

Getting Started

What separates a business story from a sports story, lifestyle story or any other story is the knowledge required to ask the right questions, to recognize the newsworthy answers and to write the story in a way that readers without specialized knowledge will understand. Reporters who understand the subject can explain what the jargon means.

The starting point in writing a business story is similar to the first step in reporting any story—understanding the subject you're writing about. For business reporters, this almost always means some basic research. That means library work—in your newspaper's morgue, in a university or public library, or through a data base search.

When the Beacon Journal reporter Reiff wanted to write his Goldsmith profile, he went to the Akron library and looked at the Reader's Guide to Periodical Literature and the Business Periodicals Index. Through these sources he located several stories on Goldsmith in Forbes, Fortune and Business Week, and had them copied. The paper ran a data base search that yielded more citations and a few documents. "In a matter of hours, I had an extensive amount of information about Goldsmith," Reiff said. "Another editor recalled a book called 'Takeover' that featured Goldsmith, and I called the author for some insights. So we were able to run the first profile of Goldsmith."

Hanson Trust also had been identified as a part of the takeover group so the Beacon Journal used a similar strategy to develop a profile of the British conglomerate.

The second step in backgrounding is to obtain key public documents, including the annual report, the 10–K, the proxy statement and any other relevant filings. (For detailed information about these forms, see "Documenting the Evidence" at the end of this chapter.) When Business Week senior writer Chris Welles was working on a story about Kennecott Corp. several years ago, he followed this strategy. After obtaining the basic documents listed above, he also obtained several other valuable documents, as he explains below:

- *A prospectus* from a recent debt offering—a Securities and Exchange Commission (SEC) mandated disclosure statement of material financial information that must be given to all investors in a company's new issues of securities—contained data on Kennecott's copper-mine production that was not in the 10–K.
- *An offering circular* distributed to shareholders of Carborundum, a concern acquired by Kennecott in a controversial deal that became a major part of the story, contained several other important facts. Shareholders of Kennecott were so angry about the $568 million Kennecott paid to acquire Carborundum that they had sued—unsuccessfully—to block the deal.
- *Court documents* connected with this litigation figured significantly in the story. Briefs by the plaintiffs contended, for instance, that First Boston Corp., a prestigious investment bank involved in the deal, had a serious conflict of interest.
- *Minutes* of a Kennecott board of directors meeting revealed the haste and cursoriness with which the directors had considered the acquisition. Also in the court files were letters written to the court protesting the deal by several large investors in Kennecott stock. I was able to obtain interviews with several of

them. Most would only talk on a background basis. But one man, the chairman of a mining company owning 134,000 shares who was also a director of a mutual fund that owned 265,000 shares, was willing to be quoted by name, saying that the Carborundum deal "was a very stupid move" and that "if I had recommended a deal like that to my shareholders, I would have felt like a real idiot."

Public Documents

For years the Securities and Exchange Commission has operated under the principle that companies should make available a maximum amount of information so that stockholders can make the most informed decision regarding management's performance. Much of that information is made public through SEC filings. In recent years the SEC has required less information, but corporate filings remain valuable sources for reporters. Since these documents are public, companies should send them to you at your request. If they don't, private organizations such as Disclosure Inc. will provide the documents for a fee.

Many reporters mistakenly ignore the most basic of corporate documents, the annual report. "I always read the annual report after the 10-K, proxy and prospectus, so I can get the party line," said Gretchen Morgenson, an associate editor at Forbes. Occasionally, the report will reflect the financial health of the company. The 1980 Chrysler Corp. annual report was a classic; the company reported a net loss of $1.7 billion in a 32-page, black and white, pictureless book. By contrast, in 1982 Chrysler boasted a profit of $170 million in a splashy, multicolored report that included a color portrait of Chairman Lee Iacocca. Most annual reports' letters from the chairman are noteworthy for the amount of obfuscation, but a few CEOs, like Berkshire Hathaway's Warren Buffet, are refreshing exceptions.

Business reporters frequently find the annual report's most interesting information in the footnotes. For example, in recent years one way companies have improved their bottom line without earning a cent has been to change upward the assumed rate of return on their pension funds, which means they need to use less cash to fund pensions and therefore can claim more money as profit.

In 1985, Time revised its pension figures to reflect the assumption that the interest rate on all monies invested for pension use would rise from 8 percent to 10 percent and that its pension funds would therefore grow at the higher rate. The change in assumption had two effects. First, since Time believed the pension fund would grow faster because of the increased rate of return, the company would not have to put as much money into the pension pot. Its earnings for 1985 increased, therefore, not because of an increase in profits from operations but simply because of a changed accounting assumption.

The second effect, and one with longer-range implications, has to do with interest rate trends. Interest rates were much lower than they were in the early 1980s. So was the assumption that Time's pension funds would continue to draw 10 percent interest realistic?

Footnotes also may explain big one-time gains from accounting rule changes that began showing up in 1987's fourth-quarter results. A new Financial Accounting Standards Board rule on handling of deferred taxes resulted in higher profits.

The annual report also can gives clues to story ideas that may be more fully explained elsewhere. A Texas Commerce Bancshares Inc. report, in a footnote on page 40, refers to "certain related parties," that is, directors and officers of the bank who had received millions of dollars in loans that the company was writing off. A look at Texas Commerce's proxy statement that year filled in the missing information with two and one-half pages of explanation, names of the relevant officers and the amounts of their loans.

In recent years, the proxy most frequently has been used to learn the salaries of top executives for magazines' and newspapers' annual "highest paid executives" lists. But the document can yield other information. In a proxy, CBS Inc. detailed the costs of dealing with advances by Fairness in Media. The CBS proxy for an earlier year noted that former anchorman Walter Cronkite had a contract paying him $1 million annually for seven years for acting as special correspondent and consultant, and for various "special assignments." Interesting nuggets of information are found under mundane headlines like "other matters," "additional information" or "legal proceedings."

Another key document is the prospectus. Forbes' Morgenson likes the prospectus "because it tells what the risks are," she said. "Those risks could be from competition, shareholder dilution in the offering, conflicts of interest in the offering, lawsuits pending that could have material effects, and insider shares eligible for sale in the future. It also tells what the company will do with the proceeds and gives good financial data." By using the prospectus and other documents, Morgenson developed a scathing story on Pattern Corp.'s questionable financial condition after Fortune and Business Week had praised the company.

In a preliminary prospectus for an offering of three million shares of Texas Air common stock, Texas Air warned that if financial results at its People Express continued to deteriorate, then "People Express could determine to seek protection from its creditors and reorganization of its obligations."

Drexel Burnham Lambert Inc. disclosed in a preliminary prospectus for a new bond fund that the SEC staff had recommended civil charges against the firm and several key employees, and that the firm was under investigation by a federal grand jury. Inclusion of the information underscored the investigation's potential impact on investors.

With the plethora of takeovers in recent years, business reporters have found themselves wading through 13-D, 14-D1 and 14-D9 forms. Reiff, for example, used Goldsmith's 13-D to determine the raider's amount of ownership, his bankers and other interesting information. "That's where we learned where the funds were coming from, Goldsmith's buying pattern, how the Merrill Lynch financing was being handled," he said.

When Ted Turner set his sights on taking over CBS Inc., his Turner Broadcasting System Inc. filed a 14-D1 that outlined, among other things, the "high-yield securities" that would be used in the acquisition. CBS responded with a 14–D9 that argued that the "junk bonds" presented "grossly inadequate" consideration for CBS stockholders and that the recapitalization proposal was "financially imprudent."

Other Printed Documents

The paper trail doesn't stop with the SEC. Business Week's Welles likes to cite "Empire," a 687-page examination of Howard Hughes and his business empire, written by Donald L. Barlett and James B. Steele, the award-winning reporters for the Philadelphia Inquirer. The duo looked through some 250,000 pages, and copied some 50,000 pages of documents, nearly all of them public. In their preface, the authors refer to:

> thousands of Hughes's handwritten and dictated memoranda, family letters, CIA memoranda, FBI reports, contracts with nearly a dozen departments and agencies of the federal government, loan agreements, corporate charters, census reports, college records, federal income-tax returns, Oral History transcripts, partnership agreements, autopsy reports, birth and death records, marriage license applications, divorce records, naturalization petitions, bankruptcy records, corporation annual reports, stock offering circulars, real estate assessment records, notary public commissions, applications for pilot certificates, powers of attorney, minutes of board meetings of Hughes's companies, police records, transcripts of Securities and Exchange Commission proceedings, annual assessment work affidavits, transcripts of Civil Aeronautics Board proceedings, the daily logs of Hughes's activities, hearing and reports of committees of the House of Representatives and Senate, transcripts of Federal Communications Commission proceedings, wills, estates records, grand jury testimony, trial transcripts, civil and criminal court records.

"The good news," said Steele, "is that there is an incredible amount of information in the public record. The bad news is that it's not all in one place." For Empire, they gathered material from:

> sources in more than fifty cities in twenty-three states and five foreign countries, from Bayonne, New Jersey, to Santa Ana, California, from Nassau to Tokyo. The papers were drawn from nearly fifty different offices, agencies and departments, from the Los Angeles Police Department to the Department of Defense, from the Nevada Gaming Commission to the Quebec Securities Commission.

Welles said his own most varied use of public documents was during the three-month investigation for New York magazine into the financial activities of the Rev. Sun Myung Moon's Unification Church.

I gathered relevant documents and other information from numerous government agencies including the Internal Revenue Service (IRS), the Securities and Exchange Commission (SEC), the Department of Commerce, the Department of Defense, the Immigration and Naturalization Service and the Comptroller of the Currency. I consulted local real estate records and information on file with attorneys general in a half dozen states. And I went through nearly a dozen lawsuits filed in several states against the church.

Perhaps the most useful single set of documents was obtained from the Department of Commerce of Moon-controlled corporations in South Korea. Previous articles on the Unification Church had speculated on Moon's corporate connections in Korea, but none had any hard information. During an interview with a Commerce official, I learned that for a modest fee it was possible for anyone to obtain reports from the American Embassy in Seoul on most major Korean companies engaged in international trade. (Similar reports are available on other foreign concerns.) I got copies of the reports on Moon's companies and was surprised at the detail they contained: sales, earnings, major products, number of employees, capitalization and major shareholders.

Most companies would prefer to disclose only the information required by the SEC, but when a corporation sues or is sued, an extensive amount of material becomes available. In preparing her story on Jim Walter Corp. for the Jackson (Miss.) Clarion-Ledger, Maria Halkias found court records of great value. "A complicated lawsuit filed by consumers, subcontractors or former employees can tell a lot about a company's personality that doesn't always come out in the interviews," she said. "The discovery period often makes public exhibits that would be difficult for a reporter to get his hands on, such as contracts, memos, correspondence, working papers, etc. Also, depositions can reveal company practices or intentions that would probably be denied in an interview."

The company's 10–K report will disclose significant litigation involving the corporation. Welles notes that these suits are usually reported on when they are filed but are seldom followed up. Therefore, a year-old suit could generate extensive files through discovery. He cites the 38 cartons of court records that Barlett and Steele examined while researching Empire. The documents, which had accumulated during Hughes' 10-year struggle to control Trans World Airlines, were tucked away in a federal warehouse in Bayonne, N.J.

If the business under investigation is privately owned—its stock is not sold to the public—court records can be particularly vital. Reporters Edward M. Eveld and Mark Davis used a variety of court actions and exhibits to develop a fascinating profile of Oklahoma tycoon Charles Joseph Bazarian for the Tulsa Tribune.

Bankruptcy records have become particularly valuable for business reporters. Fortune associate editor Peter Nulty put together a short profile of the woes of former U.S. Secretary of the Treasury John Connally through bankruptcy records. Also worth noting are tax proceedings, SEC actions and, on a local level, divorce cases.

Companies not only disclose information through SEC filings and the court system, but also file with other government agencies, such as the Federal Communications Commission, the Interstate Commerce Commission, the Food and Drug Administration, the Labor Department and many state agencies.

Welles relied on FCC filings by the then-private Chicago Tribune to learn the identity of major stockholders. Mike McGraw, then a reporter with the Hartford Courant, wrote interesting stories based on a variety of documents from the Labor Department. Bob Sherefkin, a business reporter with the Flint (Mich.) Journal, developed a hard-hitting series on local mismanagement and corruption, based on U.S. Department of Housing and Urban Development audits and documents.

Company documents and other valuable data may surface in congressional hearings and reports. Welles drew much of the best material for his book on the New York Stock Exchange and the brokerage industry, "The Last Days of the Club," from the 29 volumes of hearings and reports from several years of investigations by two congressional subcommittees.

Other information can be obtained from a number of additional printed sources. They include:

- *Trade press.* In these magazines and newspapers you will find grocers talking with grocers, undertakers talking with undertakers, and bankers talking with bankers. Although many of these publications are less than hard hitting in their reporting, you still can learn important issues in a field, how an industry markets its products and services, and what legislation it fears and favors.

    Interested in health care and physicians? Try Medical Economics, where investigative reporter Jessica Mitford said you will find "many a crass and wonderfully quotable appeal to the avarice of the practitioners of the healing arts." When Welles wrote a piece on the health hazards of modern cosmetics, some of his best information came from trade magazines. He found specific periodicals by looking in the Business Periodicals Index and the F & S Index of Corporations and Industries.

    To find relevant trade publications, consult the Standard Periodical Directory, Ulrich's International Periodicals Directory, Gale Directory of Publications and Broadcast Media and the F & S Index.
- *Newsletters.* Such publications, usually printed without advertising, have become an important source of inside information in recent years. Some are ideological, but others can be valuable. To find newsletters, consult the Newsletter Yearbook Directory.
- *Trade and professional associations.* Although lobbying groups clearly represent the interests of their members, they can provide commentary on current issues or give explanations from the perspective of the industry. When The New York Times reported on the revival of the moving industry, the Household Goods Carriers Bureau, a major trade group, was an important source. To find trade associations, look in the Encyclopedia of Associations or the National Trade and Professional Associations of the United States.

■ *Investment publications.* The best sources of basic corporate data are regularly updated reports from Standard & Poor's, Moody's and Dun & Bradstreet, all of which may be found in university and public libraries. Regular reports from Value Line Investment Survey and Standard & Poor's also are available. S&P's Compustat Services Inc. provides a variety of statistics, including data in the annual Business Week 1000.

Regular analyses of companies and industries are issued by securities analysts with large brokerage houses such as Merrill Lynch, PaineWebber and Salomon Brothers. Since brokerages are reluctant to criticize corporations publicly, these reports tend to be bullish or neutral. But they frequently contain industry data that you might not find elsewhere.

Basic corporate data are available from publications such as Dun & Bradstreet's Million Dollar Directory and Middle Market Directory, and from Standard & Poor's three-volume Register of Corporations, Directors and Executives. The 11-volume Thomas Register of American Manufacturers and Thomas Register Catalog File are more comprehensive than the other two.

For guidance through the maze of documents, directories and source books, several books are particularly valuable. They are "Business Information Sources," Revised Edition, by Lorna M. Daniells (University of California Press); "Where to Find Business Information," by David M. Brownstone and Gorton Carruth (John Wiley & Sons); Encyclopedia of Business Information Sources (Gale Research Co.), and "Building Corporate Profiles: Sources & Strategies for Investigative Reporters," by Alan Gugenheim, (Salem Press).

Human Sources

Written records can lay the foundation for a business story, but human sources are essential to providing the richness and detail that make stories come alive. In many cases human sources are essential when records don't exist. The Beacon Journal's Reiff got his first big break when the floor specialist agreed to talk with him and identified the buyer of Goodyear stock. The paper got another break when a Goodyear insider provided the name of the raider.

By casting his net wider and wider, Reiff eventually was able to put together a profile of Jeffrey Berenson, a lead partner in Merrill Lynch's merger and acquisition group who was architect of the deal. "Only two pieces had been written about him," Reiff said. "But those gave us some leads."

Reiff knew Berenson was a Princeton University graduate, so he called the alumni office. "They gave me his bio and even had clips on him, including his marriage to the daughter of the chairman of Morgan Guaranty Trust," Reiff said. "The alumni office was glad to help with a story on an alum."

Reiff then called Princeton's romance languages department from which Berenson graduated and got quotes from two former professors who said they remembered only that Berenson had written one of the most brilliant undergraduate theses ever. So Reiff called the Princeton archives and convinced a librarian to pull Berenson's thesis on Goya and to read the concluding eight or nine paragraphs. "It was truly incredible writing," Reiff recalled.

Reiff called Berenson's father in California. The senior Berenson gladly provided details on the son's childhood and how he got into investment banking.

Reiff, meanwhile, had been trying to reach Berenson at Merrill Lynch. Reiff sent the banker clips of his stories to show that the Beacon Journal was covering events responsibly. Finally, Berenson returned Reiff's call, talking only long enough to apologize for being so elusive and to say, "Among the many things I'm doing, Goodyear is but one." Reiff combined that quote with his other research and had the first extensive profile of Berenson.

Morgenson, the Forbes editor, urges reporters to be cautious about all human sources. She said, "Cultivate a nice variety but try to know their biases. What are they trying to gain through giving information to you? Be skeptical of fancy titles and fancy degrees. Be skeptical of everyone and everything. Your name is going to be on that story," she said.

"Be skeptical of the accepted thought at the moment. The consensus may be wrong. If you refuse to accept the consensus, you'll do better reporting and it will be a stronger case." Here are some important human sources:

- *Company officials.* The most knowledgeable, and frequently most reluctant, sources are the executives and other employees of the company you're investigating. Reporters always should attempt to talk with key corporate officials. Although officials often are interesting and well-informed, not all will be glad to talk with you. In recent years, however, companies and top executives have started to realize the importance of communicating their point of view to the public. In fact, many companies are putting executives through training sessions to prepare them to talk with print and broadcast journalists.
- *Former employees.* The best business reporters say that frequently their most valuable sources are former employees at the company under investigation. According to Welles, "Nobody knows more about a corporation than someone who has actually worked there." But, he warned, "Many, probably most, have axes to grind, especially if they were fired; indeed, the more willing they are to talk, the more biased they are likely to be." Good reporters will show care in using this material.
- *Analysts.* Many reporters seem to think no story is complete without a quote from a securities analyst. Analysts can be valuable if they are not overused and if you obtain a variety of expert opinions. Don't, however, assume analysts are infallible. "With analysts, optimism seems to be king," Morgenson said.
- *Academics and other experts.* Most universities have faculty members with varied areas of business and economics expertise. Often they are good sources for local reaction to national developments or analysis of economic trends. A number of private firms specialize in collecting and analyzing economic data, such as the Wharton Economic Forecasting Associates or Data Resources Inc.
- *Additional sources.* It is always wise to contact a company's customers, suppliers and competitors. Customers provide insight into how services are perceived.

Suppliers and competitors provide insights into how a company is marketing its products, its cash flow situation and so on. Although suppliers and competitors are usually reluctant to be quoted by name, you may occasionally unearth a gem.

In a Wall Street Journal story about Bijan Pakzad's high-priced clothing store on Rodeo Drive, the owner of Giorgio's, a competitor, said that Bijan was "the most damaging thing to ever come to Rodeo." Welles also suggests contacting trade organization officials, consultants, advertising agency executives, bankers, institutional investors, lobbyists, legislators and their staffs, and law enforcers and their staffs.

Financial Institutions

One of the biggest ongoing stories of the last few years is the savings and loan debacle. Through a combination of relaxed federal rules, incompetent regulators and unethical operators, the savings and loan industry chalked up as much as $250 billion in losses over the past 10 years. Because those losses were federally insured and because the cleanup of the industry will be with us for some time, business reporters should become familiar with the rudiments of financial institutions.

With savings and loans, the key players are the Resolution Trust Corp. (RTC), the new agency charged with taking over insolvent savings and loans and selling or liquidating them, and the Office of Thrift Supervision, the successor agency to the Federal Home Loan Bank Board. The vast majority of RTC-held property is in Texas, Arizona and Colorado, but most states have some RTC involvement.

To keep up with the financial condition of savings and loans in your area, obtain savings and loan call reports, known as thrift financial reports, from the Office of Thrift Supervision in Washington or your region. To put your local institutions in context, contact your regional OTS office and ask for regional peer-group numbers. For expert analysis or commentary, reporters can contact a number of nationally known consulting firms, including Sheshunoff and Co. in Austin, Texas; Ferguson and Co. in Washington; IDC Financial Publishing in Heartland, Wisc.; and Ely and Co. in Alexandria, Va.; or K.H. Thomas Associates in Miami.

While the savings and loans have dominated the headlines, some experts have been warning that the nation's banks might be in line for a similar disaster. For example, if all the ailing banks were closed down, the Federal Deposit Insurance Corp.'s $14 billion insurance fund could be exhausted. To stay on top of local bank performance, obtain bank call reports from the FDIC's regional or national disclosure offices, or state bank regulators. For a fee, reporters can obtain more detailed information through the Uniform Bank Performance Report, the Peer Group Report and the User's Manual by making a written request to: FDIC Uniform Bank Performance Report, Department 4320, Chicago, Ill. 60673.

Still other financial institutions worthy of examination are your local credit unions, which some experts say also are in dangerous condition. To obtain semiannual call reports on federally chartered credit unions, contact the National Credit Union Administration; for state chartered institutions, contact state regulators. For expert commentary, contact Callahan and Associates in Washington.

Honing Your Skills

There's nothing easy about becoming a good business reporter. It requires hard work and a commitment to learning skills many reporters ignore.

For example, good business reporters should try to develop the ability to understand numbers. Businesses' success is measured in numbers; reporters should be able to explain the winners, the losers and abusers. Unfortunately, most reporters find accounting and finance as inherently appealing as quantum physics or microbiology. But good business reporters must develop those skills by taking college courses, attending short courses or reading books.

Two simple booklets are Understanding Wall Street, published by the New York Stock Exchange, and How to Read a Financial Report, published by Merrill Lynch. More extensive books are "How to Read a Financial Report," Second Edition, by John A. Tracey (John Wiley & Sons) and "Quality of Earnings," by Thornton L. O'Glove (Free Press).

Likewise, the ability to decipher documents doesn't come easily. It comes from hours of practice. For example, the more prospectuses you read, the more readily you will be able to find their hidden gems. Practice by regularly looking through corporate and related documents. A 5-inch thick 10–K might not be your idea of light reading, but the document can provide fascinating insights.

All the number crunching and document searching can be meaningless if you don't contact the proper sources. That requires tireless interviewing. Welles said, "There have been many people who've told me a great deal, but I've always felt the need to check their impressions and anecdotes with other people to make sure I was getting the story right. Invariably, those impressions and anecdotes had to be modified or discarded."

Using a wide variety of sources should reduce the chances of being fooled. Welles cautioned, "I never feel comfortable in accepting what the person (source) tells me unless I've been able to confirm it with at least two other sources with different interests to protect."

Not-for-Profit Corporations and Foundations

Organizations cleared by the Internal Revenue Service (IRS) to operate on a not-for-profit status must file forms detailing income and outgo with the IRS each year. Many of these forms, as well as those submitted by private foundations, charities, universities and not-for-profit hospitals, are available for inspection and should be routinely checked each year. How to do that is detailed in this section.

---

by **GERRY EVERDING**

The souvenir program for the Bahia Shrine Temple circus held in Orlando, Florida, in 1983 tugged forcefully at the local heartstrings. It was packed with testimonials and photographs of patients treated in the Shrine's 19 orthopedic and three burn centers for children. There was a photo of a bandaged, smiling two-year-old recovering from severe burns and another showing a clown cheering up a wheelchair-bound child. Local businessmen who were told the circus would benefit such children filled the program's pages with paid ads and purchased blocks of tickets.

The circus was a tremendous success. It made an $81,000 profit, more than any circus in the Orlando chapter's 22-year history. Unfortunately, not a penny went to provide medical care to disabled and burned children. Instead, the Orlando Shriners placed the money in the bank and drew on it for temple-related travel and entertainment, the upkeep of the fraternity's private bar and restaurant, and the payment of utilities and other expenses.

The Shrine fraternity, which operates the nation's largest charity, has been misleading the public for years. And not just in Orlando. Fewer than ten of the 175 Shrine circuses held each year donate any money to the hospitals. In 1984, the circuses reaped an estimated profit of $17.5 million. The charity's own records show the hospitals received only one percent of that, a total of $182,000. When you add the revenue from the fraternity's other fund-raising activities—football games and the sale of Shrine newspapers, for example—less than one-third of all receipts actually went to pay for the treatment of Shrine hospital patients.

So begins an investigation of charity funds by reporters Gary Marx and John Wark that appeared in the January 1987 issue of Washington Monthly under the headline: "Faith, Hope and Chicanery: Want to do some Good? Ask your favorite charity how it spends its money."

Marx and Wark first broke the story of the Shriners in a four-part series in the Orlando Sentinel. Like many investigative projects, the story began with a tip from a disgruntled insider. But, according to Marx, the story never could have been written without information gleaned from hundreds of IRS records.

"Someone had leaked us a few internal documents, but we didn't have enough to write the story and the Shrine wasn't giving us anything," Marx said. "It was the IRS Form 990's from individual temples that really helped us put it all together."

The IRS Form 990, a tax return for not-for-profit organizations, contains detailed information on how an organization raises and spends money. Marx and Wark used the 990s to help them decipher Shriner finances. Among their findings:

- IRS records showed the Shriners spent more money in 1984 and earlier years on conventions and parties than on the hospital charity.
- Records showed the fraternity spent roughly $86.3 million in 1984, with about $42 million going to pay general operating expenses of the Shriner's members-only clubhouses, bars, restaurants and golf courses and another $21 million for conventions, parties, picnics, dinners, dances, ceremonies and gem-studded jewelry for Shrine leaders.
- A fund containing money contributed by the public for hospital endowment was used to provide almost $1 million in low-interest or no-interest loans to 13 top Shrine officials.
- The fraternity's board of directors—who can spend as much as $180,000 of their own money to get elected to the board—receive free trips to exotic places and an expense account that sometimes reaches near the six-figure range.

Charity regulators in six states began investigations of Shrine finances and fund-raising activities and the Shrine board of directors reportedly adopted a number of fund-raising reforms.

Most would agree the vast majority of the nation's charities are legitimate, well-intentioned concerns, but as Marx and Wark pointed out, operations such as the Shrine fraternity are not unique. Marx and Wark's Washington Monthly article described a variety of questionable charity actions gleaned from a 1986 meeting of state regulators and assistant attorneys general in San Antonio:

- The Rainbow Foundation, an organization that had been raising funds in Texas and California to buy dying children their last wish, was forced into receivership by the state following complaints that contributions were not being spent as advertised. State investigators found foundation records so incomplete "we'll never know how much money they had." The records did show that the foundation administrator used the funds to rent a home in Houston and to pay for personal trips to Switzerland and the Cayman Islands.
- A charity dedicated to multiple sclerosis research and supported through rock concerts was shut down after investigators found that $1 million had been spent on administration and only $67,000 on medical research. A state-appointed receiver filed suit charging that most of the money went to exorbitant salaries and administrative expenses paid to a charity administrator and her lover.

- An organization sold commemmorative coins nationwide for the Christa McAuliffe scholarship set up at the New Hampshire high school where the space shuttle crew member had taught. Salespeople told those buying the coins for $19.95 each that all proceeds went to provide college scholarships, but the legitimate fund never received any money.
- A charity called Missing Children USA Inc. led contributors to believe it was a not-for-profit organization that published a monthly magazine with pictures of missing children. Investigators forced it to close after discovering it was a for-profit company that had published only one issue.

These charities eventually gained the attention of state regulators, but many more manage to operate for years without detection. Reporters seeking to do some good in their communities may be well advised to find out how local charities raise and spend money. Most will find that charity in many ways has become a big business—often one with little regulation.

Americans' contributions to charity and other volunteer organizations exceeded $100 billion for the first time in 1988, according to figures compiled by Independent Sector, a coalition of 660 of the biggest national charities and foundations. And charity is not the exclusive domain of the rich and famous.

Another Independent Sector study found that 75 percent of American families contribute to charities, giving an average of $790 per year. About half of all adult Americans are active in volunteer work, dedicating on average five hours a week. In 1988, Americans pitched in for a total of nearly 15 billion voluntary hours.

When President Bush speaks of his "thousand points of light," it is groups such as the Salvation Army, United Way and Red Cross that most likely come to mind. But about one million other organizations also have been granted exempt status to work for the public welfare.

In 1987, the U.S. Treasury Department estimated that the nation had approximately 1.2 million exempt organizations, including 340,000 churches; 390,000 religious, educational, charitable and scientific organizations; 130,000 civic leagues and social welfare organizations; and 355,000 mutual benefit organizations, such as labor unions, chambers of commerce, veterans groups, mutual insurance funds and cemetery companies.

Reporters will find it worthwhile to shed a few "points of light" on the financial operations of community hospitals, trade associations, universities and other exempt groups. The first step in investigating any not-for-profit group is to find out under what status it has gained exemption.

Most not-for-profit organizations qualifying as tax-exempt do so under Section 501 of the Internal Revenue Code. Congress saw fit to grant exempt status to these groups, but it also passed myriad rules and regulations governing their operations. The Revenue Code includes more than 20 categories of not-for-profits, each with its own unique set of provisions.

Churches, for example, are not required to file for tax-exemption, and few do. Most other groups must seek exempt status by filing an application with the

IRS. Those that have annual gross receipts in excess of $25,000 also must file annual financial reports. Most of these records are open to the public.

Most not-for-profits are at least partially exempt from income tax, but keep in mind that gifts to only a few categories of not-for-profits can be claimed as deductions by the donor. Chief among "tax-deductible" groups is the 501(c)(3) category, broadly termed "charitable" organizations.

Section 501(c)(3) organizations must be organized and operated exclusively for one of the following purposes: charitable, religious, educational, scientific, literary, testing for public safety, fostering national or international amateur sports or the prevention of cruelty to animals or children.

Private foundations are a special subset of Section 501(c)(3) organizations that operate under slightly different regulations. To qualify as a private foundation, a charitable organization must distribute at least 3 percent of its gross assets annually toward the fulfillment of its tax-exempt purpose.

Foundation managers must operate their own charitable programs or make grants to other groups that serve the common welfare. Most foundations receive large contributions from a few donors and many small contributions from the general public.

The IRS keeps track of these groups by requiring annual filings of information returns: IRS Form 990–PF for private foundations, and IRS Form 990 for most other not-for-profits. New for 1989 is a shorter, two-page IRS Form 990EZ for use by some small charities.

What the 990–PFs Show

Form 990–PF has 19 parts that are potentially useful to reporters.

- Part 1 separates income and spending. Interest, dividends, rents and profits from the sale of real estate and published matter are considered taxable income and are itemized. Tax-exempt income includes contributions, gifts, grants, dues and assessments. Some foundation managers try to conceal taxable income.

    Who gets a foundation's money is broken down by recipient. Expenditures are listed separately as contributions, gifts and grants. Reporters can use this part to document any foundation ties to politicians. Remember that gifts to individuals generally are not allowed, but there are exceptions, such as scholarships.
- Part 2 states assets, liabilities and net worth at the beginning and end of the fiscal year. A foundation must list each debt it owes and the stocks and bonds it owns. Sometimes, foundations state the value of assets differently for tax purposes than they do for public consumption.
- Part 3 shows how the foundation's appraised net value has changed in the past year. The change may be real or merely the result of bookkeeping tricks.
- Part 4 lists sales of stocks and bonds during the year and current real estate

holdings. Reporters may find clues here about a foundation plan to expand facilities. Also find out if the foundation has requested building permits or zoning changes by checking records at city hall.

■ Parts 5 and 6 are the calculation of tax on taxable income.

■ Part 7 contains a listing of political activity, unspent income and changes in control of the foundation.

■ Part 8 lists contributors, officers, directors, and gives salaries of the five highest-paid employees. Foundations are required to spend a percentage of their annual income, but some try to avoid this by shuffling funds between related foundations. Check for interlocking trusteeships that may signal questionable transfers.

■ Parts 9 through 15 disclose how the foundation spent most of that year's income. Foundations that support individuals or organizations through grants must pay a tax on excess undistributed income. Those that run their own charitable programs must spend on average 85 percent of their income over four years or lose exempt status. A lot is at stake, and the IRS rules on violations. Expenditures near year's end might bear scrutiny if a foundation is near its limit.

■ Part 16 requests information on financial ties between the foundation and its managers. Foundations must list managers who have made substantial contributions to the foundation during the tax year and those who own more than 10 percent of the stock in any business entity in which the foundation also owns more than a 10 percent stock share. Under federal tax law, these individuals are prohibited from engaging in certain transactions with the foundation.

This section also requests information on the availability of assistance from the foundations, a listing of grants and donations paid out during the year or approved for future payment and the purpose of each grant or gift. If the recipient is an individual, the foundation must disclose any relationship to foundation managers or substantial contributors.

■ Part 17 summarizes the foundation's grants and other programs, and includes information on investments, such as low-interest loans that are allegedly related to the foundation's charitable mission.

■ Part 18 requests an itemized list of the foundation's income-producing activities, including any business ventures that are unrelated to its tax-exempt purpose. (See the "Unrelated Business Income Tax" section in this chapter.)

■ Part 19 requests information on financial ties between the foundation and other not-for-profit groups, such as affiliated charities.

The Foundation Center

Despite laws requiring private foundations to make their 990–PFs available to the public, journalists continue to report cases in which a group has refused access. One resource to keep in mind for such situations is the Foundation Center, a group that obtains IRS records on foundations and opens its files to the public.

The Center is an independent national service organization established by foundations to provide information on private philanthropic giving. It publishes a number of well-indexed directories on foundations and grants, and maintains a national network of foundation information centers.

Remember: the Center only has information on foundations. It does not maintain files on colleges, churches, public charities or other tax exempt organizations, such as the United Way, that receive money from too many donors to qualify as private foundations.

The information centers are free and open to public use. However, there is an associates program that gives you access to a toll-free number where you can obtain telephone references, customized computer searches and other information for an annual fee of $475. The Center maintains four extensive reference collections at its offices in New York City, Washington, D.C., Cleveland and San Francisco. About 175 affiliates operating out of locations such as major public libraries offer access to the 990–PFs for most foundations that operate in their region. Call (800) 424–9836 for information on nearby cooperating collections.

- The Foundation Center
  8th Floor
  79 Fifth Avenue
  New York, N.Y. 10003
  (212) 620–4230
- The Foundation Center
  Room 312
  312 Sutter Street
  San Francisco, Calif. 94108
  (415) 397–0902

- The Foundation Center
  1001 Connecticut Avenue, N.W.
  Washington, D.C. 20036
  (202) 331–1400
- The Foundation Center
  Kent H. Smith Library
  1442 Hanna Building
  1422 Euclid Avenue
  Cleveland, Ohio 44115
  (216) 861–1933

Getting Started

The Center annually publishes the Foundation Directory, which can be found in most libraries. The 12th edition, published in 1989, describes 6,600 corporate, independent and community foundations that have assets of at least $1 million, or have given at least $100,000 in annual grants. The listings include the names of donors, officers, directors and contact persons, as well as assets and expenditure totals.

Reporters researching the influence of foundations in their area will find the directory's indexes by state and by city helpful. The directory also includes specialized indexes, for example, by subject and by type of support. The directory costs $125 for paperbound copies, and $150 for hardbound copies.

The starting point for reporters trying to determine who gets foundation money may be the Foundation Grants Index. Many grants approved in the past year are indexed by key word and recipient. The cost of the index is $65.

Other publications include the National Data Book, which gives brief descriptions of about 30,000 U.S. foundations, and the Source Book Profiles, which gives detailed information on the top 1,000 foundations. All of the

Center's publications, or a catalog of publications, can be obtained by writing its New York office at the address listed earlier.

Other Not-for-Profit Organizations

There are thousands of philanthropic organizations operating around the country that are not foundations but pay no taxes. These include colleges and universities, churches, medical clinics, hospitals and charitable organizations, such as the United Way. Other non-charitable, tax-exempt organizations such as social clubs, lodges, business groups, police organizations, labor unions, and trade associations also must make their tax forms available to the public. Of interest to reporters is how these organizations collect their money and how much of it actually goes into operating the programs they tout when seeking their funds.

The major form required of these organizations is Form 990. Like Form 990–PF, it describes in detail income and outgo, lists major officers and salaries and states the purposes of the organization. Form 990 is very useful for seeing how much money collected by the group is used for administration.

The classic case in this area was done by the late Paul Williams, an editor for the Sun Newspapers, a weekly chain of seven newspapers with a circulation of about 50,000 in suburban Omaha, Neb. Williams also was a founding member of Investigative Reporters and Editors Inc.

In 1971, Williams and his staff decided to inform their readers about Boys Town, a local home and community for homeless boys founded by Father J. Flanagan. Boys Town already had an impressive national reputation, generated in part by a 1938 MGM movie starring Spencer Tracy and Mickey Rooney. Millions more had heard about it through a letter-writing campaign.

Williams' team began by learning everything it could from public records. They studied the articles of incorporation on file with the Nebraska secretary of state, state educational records required of the school at Boys Town and other property and tax records. They also found that the home's post office handled a "staggering" 36 million pieces of mail each year.

Williams checked with charity experts and got estimates that mailing of this volume of fund-raising letters might generate as much as $15 million a year. Shortly thereafter he and his team learned about and obtained the home's Form 990s. Within minutes, the 990s allowed the home's net worth to be estimated at $191,401,421. Williams had his story.

Standards, Creative Bookkeeping and How Charities Spend Funds

What percentage of the funds raised by a charity end up paying for administrative costs? How much money should a charity spend on projects intended to bring in more donations? How much of a donation actually goes to charitable programs?

Mismanaged charities can be as big a problem as scam charities, and the line between the two is often blurry. One of the most common problems in the charity industry continues to be excessive fund-raising costs. Another common abuse is the use of creative bookkeeping to disguise high administrative expenses.

Charities, regulators and industry groups have long battled over the issue of accountability, but no universal solution has emerged. A number of organizations have voluntary standards for charities, but attempts to make these guidelines legal and binding generally lose out in court. State efforts to regulate charities have been equally ineffective.

The National Charities Information Bureau, a charity watchdog group, recommends that charities spend at least 60 percent of their total income on program services. Many charities surpass this goal, but some generally respectable national groups often fall short of the 60 percent guideline.

Charities have a wide range of missions and equally diverse styles of fund-raising. It may be impossible for one uniform code of conduct to apply to all charities, but voluntary standards can be useful to reporters seeking a bench mark for abuse.

The Philanthropic Advisory Service of the Council of Better Business Bureaus has developed standards of ethical conduct for charities, and it also offers tips to donors on giving wisely. A reporter examining a charity's spending habits may wish to follow the Council's formula for comparing expenses in three categories: program services, management and general fund raising.

- *Program Service Costs* are those that are directly related to the charitable mission. Examples might include research grants made to scientists, salaries of doctors and nurses working in overseas missions, food supplies sent to starving children or pamphlets explaining a disease to the public.
- *Management and General Costs* are expenses associated with day-to-day administration of the charity, including such items as office supplies, rent, salaries of administrative personnel and fees paid to accountants and lawyers.
- *Fundraising costs* might include the printing and mailing of appeals, advertising in magazines and newspapers and fees paid to professional fundraisers.

Standards published by the Council generally call for at least half of a charity's total income to be spent on programs, for no more than half of the charity's total income to be spent on administrative and fund-raising costs, for at least half of public contributions to be spent on programs and for no more than 35 percent of contributions to be spent on fund raising.

Not-for-Profit Activities and State and Federal Regulation

Although most not-for-profit organizations must answer to the federal government concerning IRS-controlled tax issues, the enforcement of most consumer fraud, false advertising and other legal issues falls primarily on the shoulders of state regulators.

In some states, oversight of charities and other not-for-profits is handled almost entirely by the state attorney general. Other states have set up special offices, usually within the secretary of state's office, to register and monitor charitable activities.

Some states are doing an excellent job of reporting on charitable activities and many of them now require organizations filing the IRS Form 990 to submit a copy to the state as well. New York, California, New Jersey and Minnesota have entered all information from the completed 990s into a computer data base. And at least some data are computerized in Connecticut, Illinois, Indiana, Maryland, Massachusetts, Nevada, New Hampshire, Pennsylvania, Tennessee and Virginia.

About 35 states have adopted charitable solicitation laws, but they generally lack strong enforcement provisions. Some states have charitable reporting forms that are more detailed than the 990s. Many require professional fundraisers to file extensive reports, including copies of any contracts with charities.

Reporters seeking information on state regulation of charities may wish to contact the National Association of Attorneys General. The attorneys general have been pushing for stronger state laws on fund raising and other charitable activities, but most of their efforts have been struck down in court.

The attorney general's office can be a great source. Reporters at the Star Tribune in Minneapolis, for example, obtained valuable information for a series on charitable gambling abuses by perusing 990s required to be filed with the Minnesota attorney general's charities review division.

New Legislation Regarding Not-for-Profits

In recent years Congress has begun to focus increased attention on tax-exempt organizations, passing legislation in the areas of lobbying, political campaign activity, fund raising, partnership involvements and sales-leasebacks. Allegations that exempt groups are competing unfairly with for-profit entities are expected to spur a new wave of legislation in the early 1990s.

Reporters should be aware that the Revenue Act of 1987 contains a number of provisions affecting tax-exempt organizations. The most significant change is a new law requiring tax-exempt groups filing form 990 to make their completed returns available for public inspection at their main offices. This is a welcome change since obtaining the forms from the IRS can be a grueling process. (See "Documenting the Evidence" at the end of this chapter for more information.)

For a thorough update on federal laws governing not-for-profits, check "The Law of Tax-Exempt Organizations" by Bruce R. Hopkins. The fifth edition was published by John Wiley & Sons in 1987, and annual updates are issued as supplements. Hopkins, a Washington, D.C., lawyer, is considered one of the nation's top experts on not-for-profit tax laws.

Disclosure of Non-Tax-Deductible Donations

As of February 1988 any fundraising solicitation made by or on behalf of a not-for-profit organization must include a warning statement if the requested donation is not tax-deductible. The change is part of an IRS effort to educate taxpayers about what contributions are in fact deductible.

One purpose of the statements is to reduce the likelihood that taxpayers will deduct contributions made to non-charitable, tax-exempt groups, such as labor unions, trade associations, social clubs, political organizations and political action committees. The law allows these groups to solicit funds, but donations are not considered charitable and are not deductible unless they can be justified as business expenses. The required disclosure statement is intended to clarify the law and prevent misleading solicitations.

Disclosure of Relations With Other Exempt Organizations

New provisions in the 1987 Tax Act require charitable groups to make detailed disclosures of any relationships or transactions with other charitable and political organizations. The new rules are designed to spotlight charities diverting tax-deductible funds for non-exempt uses, such as political activity. The new provisions require charities to disclose any sharing with other exempt organizations of salaried employees, office space, mailing lists and other expenses; and any transfer of funds, including any sale, lease, loan, contribution, grant or other transaction.

Disclosure of Availability From Federal Government

As of 1989 any Section 501(c)(3) organization that offers to sell or solicits donations for information or routine services that are readily available free or at a nominal charge from the federal government must disclose that fact in a conspicuous manner when making the offer.

Lobbying Restrictions

Some types of not-for-profit organizations face loss of tax-exempt status if the IRS finds that they are excessively engaged in activities designed to influence legislation or the election of a candidate to public office. The Revenue Act of 1987 includes provisions for a penalty in the form of a 5 percent excise tax on an organization that makes excessive legislative expenditures, and a like tax on the organization's directors and officers, who, without reasonable cause, willfully cause the organization to lose tax-exempt status because of political activities.

However, tax-exempt groups frequently push the limit on lobbying and political activities, and with only 2.5 percent of exempt groups being audited annually by the IRS, there is little risk involved in stretching legal bounds.

In 1989, for example, the Washington-based National Journal discovered that the Republican National Committee (RNC) had helped set up a group called Lawyers for the Republic to compile election data for redistricting efforts after the 1990 census. Originally the RNC had planned to spend at least a million dollars on this politically vital task, but now it will get the information free from Lawyers for the Republic, which unlike the RNC, runs on tax-deductible donations.

Links between politicians and tax-exempt groups are fertile ground for investigative reporting. For example, Sen. Alan Cranston, D-Calif., established several tax-exempt voter registration groups in the months before the 1988 election. The groups were ostensibly non-partisan, but workers said it was understood they were to register Democrats. What's more, a major contributor to the group was savings and loan executive Charles Keating, on whose behalf Cranston later interceded with federal savings and loan regulators.

Another National Journal study found that half of all senators and about one-third of all House members were either founders, officers or directors of tax-exempt groups. Five presidential candidates in 1988 set up tax-exempt groups, and while these organizations were supposed to be doing research and education, at least one became involved in flagrant political activities, such as sponsoring fundraisers.

Unrelated Business Income Tax (UBIT)

Charges that not-for-profits use tax breaks to compete unfairly with for-profit businesses have caused a bitter debate among special interest lobbyists on Capitol Hill. The House Ways and Means Committee has held seven hearings on the issue since 1987, but politicians have been unable to agree on legislation.

The issue of unfair competition by tax-exempt groups pits a wide range of pro-business groups against some of the nation's largest and most respected not-for-profit and charitable organizations. YMCAs draw complaints from health and racquet clubs. The National Geographic Society is under attack for garnering a 40 percent share of the world atlas market. Underwriters Laboratories—the not-for-profit group responsible for all those UL stickers on your appliances—faces allegations that it is attempting to force commercial labs out of business and establish a monopoly over the testing of electronic equipment manufactured as far away as West Germany.

At the heart of this dispute is "unrelated business income tax (UBIT)," which not-for-profit organizations must pay on income from activities "not substantially related" to their exempt purpose. Tax-exempt organizations are required to report their liability for the UBIT on an annual tax return, *IRS Form 990–T*, and pay tax on such activities at the applicable corporate or trust rate. (Note: Form 990-T is not public. It is considered the same as a confidential "for-profit" tax return.)

For-profit business concerns argue that the tax on unrelated income is simply not working as a deterrent to competition from not-for-profit groups. Many small, for-profit businesses say they are feeling the pinch of competition as not-for-profits utilize their tax advantages to push into new commercial ventures. Not-for-profits say they are simply finding new ways to carry out their missions.

A common theme of recent Ways and Means Committee testimony was that the IRS lacks the information Congress needs to determine if not-for-profits have strayed too far into competition with business. Thus, in 1989, many tax-exempt groups for the first time will be required to disclose a detailed analysis of taxable and exempt incomes.

Those with receipts over $100,000 or assets above $250,000 must file an expanded five-page Form 990 that lists taxable and exempt income by fund-raising activity, including a detailed explanation of each exempt activity.

Charities owning interests in taxable concerns must describe the interest in detail—an information request some attribute directly to a rash of "unfair competition" charges levied against tax-exempt community hospitals. If you're wondering how community hospitals compete, consider this bit of congressional testimony:

> The diverse, non-traditional businesses which community hospitals have engaged in through affiliates include commercial cleaning, interior decorating, computerized billing for doctors, catering, health and fitness clubs, travel agencies, marketing of frozen foods for the elderly, data processing, day-care centers, and medical hotels . . .

Present laws fully exempt research by universities, colleges and hospitals from the unrelated business income tax, regardless of whether the research is related to any educational or scientific purpose. Pro-business lobbies argue that abuse of the academic exemption is widespread. In Nevada, for example, a state university underbid a small business and won several marketing and opinion-polling contracts. At the University of Pittsburgh, a professor was found to be grossing $60,000 a month testing households for radon.

Current law provides for the taxation of income derived by tax-exempt organizations from any trade or business that is regularly carried on by the organization and that is not substantially related to the performance by the organization of its exempt purpose. Income derived from debt-financed property also is subject to tax.

But there are also many exemptions from unrelated business income tax, including dividends and interest, royalties, certain rents, gains on the disposition of capital assets and income derived from certain research activities, conventions, fairs, trade shows and bingo games. Proposed reforms could limit some of these exemptions.

A common complaint from for-profit businesses is that not-for-profits figure out ways to avoid paying taxes by hiding income from unrelated business activities. A charity might, for instance, charge large amounts of overhead costs against its business income in order to avoid showing profits. Government studies seem to support the notion that not-for-profits are underreporting incomes.

As of the end of 1985, the IRS Exempt Organization Master Files listed approximately 850,000 tax-exempt organizations with total revenues exceeding $300 billion a year. Yet an IRS study found that only 27,000 tax-exempt organizations, or 3 percent, reported having any unrelated business income in 1986.

A must read for anyone considering a story on the commercial ventures of not-for-profits are the three volumes of hearings on this issue entitled: "Unrelated Business Income Tax, Hearings Before the Subcommittee on Oversight of the Committee on Ways and Means, House of Representatives, One Hundredth Congress, First Session, June 22, 25, 26, 29, and 30, 1987." The book should be available at most federal document depository libraries.

DOCUMENTING THE EVIDENCE

HOW TO OBTAIN RECORDS ON NOT-FOR-PROFIT ORGANIZATIONS

IRS records can be a gold mine of information on not-for-profit organizations, but before you go off in search of this panacea, a word or two of caution. Despite new laws requiring disclosure on request, many organizations may make access difficult and don't expect the world on a platter from the IRS.

Reporters who have tried to get Form 990 and Form 990–PF from the IRS during the last decade generally have no shortage of horror stories about lost requests, incomplete returns and delays of months and years.

The Orlando Sentinel's efforts to get 990s on local Shrine temples provide a good illustration. The IRS was able to provide the newspaper with only 343 of the 685 forms requested, and two-thirds of the forms provided were missing important information.

In 1983, the U.S. General Accounting Office studied 10,930 1981 returns of tax-exempt private foundations and found that 94 percent "did not completely respond to certain public information reporting requirements." Organizations were found to have omitted information about gifts, grants, donations, expenses, assets, liabilities and net worth, as well as names of administrators. A 1988 GAO study found one-half of all Form 990s were incomplete.

A good lesson to be learned from the problems described above is that any request for records from the IRS should be as specific and detailed as possible. Every exempt organization is required to have an Employee Identification Number—use it on all requests, to speed processing. Other valuable information to include when possible is the group's precise name, exact address, zip code, location of home offices and dates of any returns you wish to examine.

Some IRS disclosure officers say that reporters can unnecessarily lengthen response time by mistakenly requesting the forms under the Freedom of Information Act. The forms should be requested under the provisions of Internal Revenue Code section 6104—not under FOIA.

Both exempt organization returns and approved exemption applications will continue to be available for public inspection through the IRS. The IRS has frequently changed its policies on how to order tax records by mail, but current publications suggest sending a written request to the director of the IRS district office in which you desire to view the records. Often the best first step is to call the IRS public affairs office in Washington, D.C., and get advice on how to get the forms you want.

Now that the law requires not-for-profits to make many of their IRS records public, journalists should consider it their job to make sure local not-for-profits abide by IRS reporting requirements. File suit when necessary to obtain documents, and better yet, consider instituting a policy that requires a not-for-profit seeking news coverage to submit its IRS records along with its press releases.

IRS Form 990–PF/Return of Private Foundation

Reporters should note that section 6104(b) of the Internal Revenue Code requires foundations to make their most current annual Form 990–PFs available to the public for a 180-day period each year. Foundation managers must provide a copy of the return free of charge upon request or make it available for inspection during regular business hours at the organization's principal office.

These disclosure requirements apply only to information reported on or with the Form 990–PF and its attachments, not to the list of contributors. Information that is not required, but which is provided to the IRS on a voluntary basis, must also be made available for inspection.

Foundations filing Form 990–PF also must publish a notice stating that the forms are available for inspection for the next 180 days. The notice must appear in a newspaper of general circulation in the county in which the foundation has its principal offices, and must be published by the due date for filing the annual return. A copy of the notice should be attached to the form filed with the IRS.

IRS Form 990/Return of Organization Exempt From Income Tax

The IRS now requires all organizations filing the Form 990 to make their three most recent annual returns available for public inspection during regular business hours at the group's principal office, and in some cases at regional offices. The new public disclosure requirements do not apply to forms filed before 1986, and there is no obligation to provide returns filed more than three years ago. Nor do the new disclosure standards apply to private foundations

Groups filing the 990 are required to make available all parts of the return and all required schedules and attachments, with one notable exception: they do not have to give out a list of contributors. Failure to make the 990s available is subject to a $10 a day fine, with a maximum fine of $5,000 per return.

IRS Form 1023 or 1024/Application for Recognition of Exemption

Any organization that submitted an application for recognition of exemption (including Forms 1023 and 1024) to the IRS after July 15, 1987, must make available to the public a copy of its application, any papers submitted in support of the application and any letter or other document issued by the IRS in response to the request. As in the case of annual returns, the application and related documents must be made available for inspection during regular business hours at the organization's principal office and at each of its regional or district offices having at least three employees. Groups can be fined $10 for each day they fail to make the application available to the public.

ADDITIONAL SOURCES OF INFORMATION
ON NOT-FOR-PROFIT ORGANIZATIONS

Philanthropic Advisory Service
Better Business Bureau
4200 Wilson Blvd., Suite 800
Arlington, Va. 22203
(703) 276–0100

A national watchdog group that publishes standards for and makes investigations of groups that solicit funds from the public. It has files on about 7,000 organizations and publishes evaluations on about 400 groups that are nationally active. The evaluations include information about a group's background, governing body, fund-raising practices, tax-exempt status and finances. It also publishes Insight, a quarterly newsletter on philanthropy.

Independent Sector
1828 L Street, N.W.
Washington, D.C. 20036
(202) 233–8100

A membership organization that represents about 650 national tax-exempt organizations, foundations and corporations, coordinates national efforts to encourage giving and volunteering and often testifies before Congress on issues related to tax-exempt groups.

National Charities Information Bureau
19 Union Square
New York, NY 10003
(212) 929–6300

A watchdog group that issues standards for not-for-profit performance. It provides evaluations of about 400 national charities, including data on boards of directors, conflicts of interest, accountability, budgets and "ethical audits" of fund-raising tactics.

National Federation of Independent Business
600 Maryland Ave., S.W., Suite 700
Washington, D.C. 20024
(202) 544–9000

A membership organization representing the interests of more than a half-million small-business owners. The group is active in efforts to halt "unfair competition" from not-for-profit entities.

Business Coalition for Fair Competition
1725 K Street, N.W., Suite 412
Washington, D.C. 20006
(202) 887–5872

A coalition of 29 national trade associations whose members are affected by the commercial activities of not-for-profit entities. It lobbies against "unfair competition" from not-for-profits and seeks reform of laws on unrelated business income of tax-exempt groups.

National Association of State Charity Officials
c/o J. Michael Wright
Office of Consumer Affairs
P.O. Box 1163
Richmond, Va. 23209
(804) 786–2042

Professional organization of state officials who regulate charities under the federal state statutes; organized to facilitate administration of state laws regarding charitable solicitations and regulation by recommending uniform formats for the reporting of charitable solicitations.

Bankruptcies

There aren't many places reporters can go to get a detailed, candid picture of the finances of a business concern or corporation, but court documents, and especially bankruptcy-court proceedings, are one such place. The kind of information available and how to understand it are explained in this section.

---

by **ELLIOT JASPIN**

James V. Macalush was a man with a problem.

When he tried to declare bankruptcy, the court began investigating his tangled finances. And although he needed to get out from under a mountain of debts, Macalush, a former township supervisor in Carbon County, Pa., apparently believed too much light shed on the wrong areas could be a problem to him.

For example, who had given him $16,000 in what he called a "friendly gesture"? At first, Macalush said the donors "were very close friends" who had given the gift because they knew he was in financial trouble. When pressed further he would only identify those philanthropic friends as "five families in Pennsylvania."

Later in the bankruptcy testimony, Macalush was asked to break down his personal finances. He said he was working at night in a restaurant without salary to pay back a favor to the two owners of the restaurant. They were identified as a son and a close relative of a man believed to be one of the leading organized crime members in northeastern Pennsylvania.

A year later, Macalush's testimony embarrassed him further when Bill Ecenbarger, a Philadelphia Inquirer reporter, learned that Macalush had been appointed to a patronage job in the state revenue department. Using Macalush's bankruptcy-court testimony, Ecenbarger wrote a story that led to Macalush losing his job as a tax examiner and pleading guilty to welfare-fraud charges.

For business reporters, an examination of bankruptcy-court records almost always will result in a story. The death of a major industry in a community may involve some of its most powerful people and institutions and will surely have a significant impact on the community's economy. And if fraud can be found, so much the better for the story.

Bankruptcy-court records usually are located in U.S. district courts, found in at least one location in each state. The petitioner's "statement of affairs," which is part of the court records, lists the name, address, occupation, income from trade or profession, income from other sources, bank accounts, safe-deposit boxes, property held in trust, loans repaid, property transferred to others, suits, executions and judgments, a schedule of liabilities and assets, name of attorney and names of trustees.

Drew's Law

Fraudulent financial failures are built upon Drew's Law: "If you don't pay your overhead, your gross is net." Thus, if you run a plant that assembles widgets and don't pay the supplier for parts, your profit is 100 percent.

In one scheme of this sort, a man bought two factories that produced the same item. The factories supposedly operated independently of one another except when it came to ordering supplies. Then, the owner would use the credit of Factory A to buy his equipment and have it trucked to Factory B, where the product would actually be made. Because Factory A rarely paid its bills, it went bankrupt while Factory B turned a marvelous profit.

Another technique is to buy an old, established firm, use its credit to buy merchandise that can be easily disposed of, such as jewelry, and declare bankruptcy when the time comes to pay suppliers.

Yet another variation is to buy a company using a bank loan and convert all of its assets to cash, which you either spend on yourself as company expenses or funnel to a confederate. When the money runs out, you declare bankruptcy.

All of these schemes ultimately lead to bankruptcy court and, if a newspaper is alert, fall into the arms of a waiting reporter. The problem reporters will have is not where to get the information for such a story, but rather how to organize and understand the enormous mass of sometimes arcane material that reporters will surely find.

When wading through a case file, it will help if you keep in mind that no matter how complex the financial or legal transactions may become, a fraudulent bankruptcy still boils down to the following analogy: The fox is stealing chickens out of the henhouse. The fox may pose as a chicken while passing the contents of the coop to a confederate on the outside. He may order more chickens and not pay the supplier, burn down the henhouse and all its records and then declare bankruptcy. But any way you cut it, he is stealing chickens. Therefore, a reporter's paramount objective is to find out who the foxes are and how they are getting the chickens out.

Bankruptcy-Court Records

Finding out who the foxes are may seem to be a simple job, but in fact those who actually own a corporation may be well-hidden. The company president could be a front for one of the creditors who is actually running the show. Or the company may have secret stockholders.

Because bankruptcy records normally identify the operating officers of a company, they are reporters' first concern. The backgrounds of corporate officials must be rigorously checked. How have they operated other businesses? Who are their friends and former business associates? What loans have they received and from whom? What are their real names?

This preliminary investigation by reporters may lead to some fairly remarkable results. In one case, the head of a brewery passed himself off as A. Bart Starr. But his real name was Gordon Andrews, and when reporters caught up with him he had just been indicted for heroin possession.

Once you think you know who the nominal owners are, analyze bankruptcy records to determine who the actual owners may be. An invaluable tool is the list of the company's creditors and its accounts receivable. The list of creditors is one of the first things filed in a bankruptcy proceeding, and an accounts receivable, if there is one, can usually be obtained after a little poking around. On both lists, look for either unusual entries or entries that represent major creditors.

For example, an airport in Opa Locka, Fla., was on the list of creditors in the bankruptcy proceedings of the Blue Coal mining company in Pottsville, Pa. Since it was unlikely that Blue Coal had ever sold a ton of coal below the Mason-Dixon line, how could it run up a bill with a Florida airport? After some checking it was clear that the owners of Blue Coal had used company money to rent a plane they used to fly all over the country for their personal pleasure. A passenger on one of those jaunts was a supposed creditor of the company, but he was later identified as one of the persons really running Blue Coal.

When a bankrupt company owes or is owed a substantial amount of money, it's wise to check out the debt. How was it incurred? Who owns the company that is doing business with the bankrupt company? How long has the debt been carried? What the reporter is looking for here is evidence the deal was not an arm's-length transaction.

A classic example of this kind of scam was uncovered by Jonathan Kwitny of the Wall Street Journal. He found a dairy in New Hampshire buying milk on credit from local farmers, making it into mozzarella cheese and then selling it to a distributor in New York. The dairy failed to pay the farmers and it was declared bankrupt. When the investigators looked at the dairy's records, they found that the dairy also owed money to the New York distributor because the mozzarella was going rancid as soon as it was shipped out of the plant. Sometimes, according to the records, the cheese went rancid even faster than the dairy could make it. Some legwork showed that the cheese manufacturer was actually controlled by the distributor and the bankruptcy was a device to avoid paying the farmers.

Using the Creditors

In addition to the records that the bankrupt company must file with the court, reporters may also have a powerful ally in the creditors. Under the bankruptcy laws, the creditors form a committee that works with the bankruptcy judge to dispose of the company's assets. If the creditors believe they are being swindled by the bankrupt company, they have a vested interest in helping reporters uncover the suspected fraud. (Conversely, a cool reception by the creditors may indicate that some or all of them are actually in league with the bankrupt company.) In addition, the creditors may start their own investigation—an investigation that energetic reporters can monitor and use to advantage.

205A Examination

One of the main tools of the creditors' investigation is the 205A examination, named after the section of the bankruptcy code that governs the procedure. In the 205A examination, the debtor is questioned by a lawyer for the creditors in an attempt to determine if the bankruptcy is fraudulent. Even though the transcripts of such an examination may be entered in the court record, it is worthwhile for reporters to personally observe these interviews. If the creditors are cooperative, gaining access may not be a problem. However, if there is resistance, there is case law to support access by the public: *Winton Shirt Corp. v. Elizabeth Trust Co.*, 104 Fed Reporter, 2nd series, 777.

Court Dockets and Other Records

Finally, reporters should cull through the various pleadings and petitions in the court docket for interesting revelations. In this area, anything can turn up—and often does.

Once the bankruptcy-court docket has been analyzed, a process that may take months, the next step is to check these records against documents that the company may have filed elsewhere. The discussion of business documents will show you what they are (see "Documenting the Evidence" at the end of this chapter).

Trade publications and newspaper morgues are useful for finding out what company officers were saying prior to the bankruptcy. Other courthouse records can be valuable in an attempt to flesh out the history of the company. If the industry is regulated, check with the regulatory agency.

By the time the documents search is complete reporters usually begin to see a pattern emerging. The key may be a passing reference in the bankruptcy docket to a relationship between the bankrupt company and another company. At the secretary of state's office, incorporation papers may show that the relationship is more than just a casual encounter. And in state regulatory records there may be a document showing that the two companies were investigated by the agency because they appeared to be acting as one concern.

Former Employees

Now it is time to talk to former employees of the company. In these interviews reporters enjoy an advantage that they often do not have when investigating a healthy business. Not only are former employees more willing to talk, since they have nothing to lose, but some may be eager to impose their own interpretation of events on the story. The junior vice-president in charge of paper clips may claim that if the company president had only followed his advice on fasteners, the company would have held together. Listening despite the fellow's self-serving purposes, reporters also may learn that the company president was musically inclined—he kept meeting with men who carried violin cases.

You also may find disgruntled employees who were swindled. In one particularly vicious scheme, the company president sold bonds to his employees to help finance the company. For those people who couldn't afford the bonds, the president arranged with a local bank for the employees to get personal loans to cover the cost. The employees never knew the bonds were unregistered (and hence, did not have to meet Securities and Exchange Commission standards). The bank was worried because it had loaned huge amounts to the business and saw the bonds as a way to stave off disaster. The company's finance plan was a sham, and when the company folded, the employees were left to pay off personal loans for worthless bonds.

Although a bankruptcy investigation has distinct advantages for investigative reporters, writing the story has certain drawbacks. Tortuous financial manipulations, arcane legal and business jargon, and the lack of drama in many business dealings may scare off readers.

One solution is to lead with or play prominently what the bankruptcy will cost the average reader. When businesses go bankrupt, people are sometimes hurt without knowing it. Higher taxes, unemployment, loss of public confidence and higher prices, caused by a manipulation of the free market, all hurt the public. If these results can be explained, the reader may take a deeper interest in a story.

Even in investigations where no financial chicanery can be found, a story on a bankruptcy is a worthwhile public service.

DOCUMENTING THE EVIDENCE

SECURITIES AND EXCHANGE COMMISSION

The primary source of publicly available information about the more than 11,000 companies selling public stock in the United States, as well as the 75,000 brokers and 10,000 institutional investors, is the Securities and Exchange Commission (SEC), headquartered in Washington, D.C.

About 180 different forms are used by the commission, all of them described in Title 17 (Commodities and Securities Exchange section) of the Code of Federal Regulations. All forms can be obtained by writing to the Securities and Exchange Commission, 450 Fifth St., Washington, D.C. 20549. Information about records can be found in the Manual of General Record Information, available from the SEC by writing to the Securities and Exchange Commission, Public Reference Branch, Room 1024, at the address above.

Another useful source of information on the SEC is the Federal Securities Law Reporter, a six-volume compilation of securities laws, bulletins, forms and reporting requirements published by Commerce Clearing House Inc. The set is held in three-ring binders and kept up-to-date with inserts.

Form 10 and Form 8–A/Registration Statements

The law requires companies offering securities for public sale to register those offerings with the SEC if the securities are to be listed on a national stock exchange, or if the company has assets of $5 million or more and 500 or more shareholders.

Most companies register initial offerings of public stock with the SEC on standard Form 10. Form 10 is used by companies that have not previously reported to the SEC, usually because they have never offered stock for public sale. Form 8-A is a short version of Form 10 filed by companies that have reported to the SEC, but never had to file Form 10. Form 8-A allows companies to meet the requirements of Form 10 without resubmitting information in previous SEC reports.

The SEC also has a wide range of specialized registration forms that it requires of public offerings made by companies in certain industries. These usually request much of the same information as Form 10, as well other data specific to an industry or situation.

Form 10–K/Annual Report

Form 10-K, the annual report, is the most comprehensive document filed by companies selling stock to the public. It includes such information as the types of business of the parent firm and subsidiaries, competitive aspects of the field, descriptions of property owned, any oil or gas production, corporate organizational structure, major

238

lawsuits pending, volume of foreign sales, recent decisions voted or announced at stockholders' meetings, and names and backgrounds of major officers and directors.

Also listed are patents, trademarks, franchises and concessions held by the company, as well as the firm's sources of raw materials. Any major changes during the past year in the company's financial standing are recorded, and sales, revenues and dividends are itemized. The form includes audited balance sheets for the two most recent years and audited statements of income and changes in financial position for each of the most recent fiscal years. This provides information on the company's growth.

The annual report is the place to start when seeking details beyond those available in city hall or your secretary of state's office.

Form 10–Q/Quarterly Update

Form 10–Q is an update of Form 10–K and is required to be filed within 45 days after the close of each of the corporation's first three fiscal quarters. Unlike the 10–K, this form is not audited before filing, which means there is no guarantee the company followed generally accepted accounting practices in preparing the figures. The 10–Q contains quarterly financial statements, but you should be wary when using unaudited figures.

The most important information disclosed in this report are legal proceedings involving the company and material changes in corporate operations, such as long-term contracts, new financial arrangements and business combinations.

Questions voted on at annual meetings can be found in the proxy statement; the results of these votes must be reported in the next 10–Q.

Form 8K/Current Update

Form 8K must be filed within 15 days after any significant changes in the company's ownership and finances. Such changes include altered control of the company, the nature of the transfer of control, major purchases of other companies, the hiring of new auditors and bankruptcy or receivership proceedings. The financial statements of companies bought or sold are included here.

A change of auditors may be a tip-off for reporters to probe further, as the outgoing auditors may have resigned because they questioned the accounting practices used by the company.

Prospectus

A prospectus is a detailed description of a company filed when the company is about to put new securities up for sale. It contains information about the company's operations and finances, its properties, other companies under its control, and how it intends to use the money gained through the stock sale. Reporters can learn a great deal about a company from its prospectus, and later gauge the company's progress by comparing its goals as stated in the prospectus against its actual performance.

You can almost always get this form from the company's public relations office or from a stockbroker.

A prospectus is required only when securities are being offered to the public. Companies seeking to make private sales of non-stock securities, such as bonds and notes, may not be required to file a prospectus, but they often circulate similar reports known as Private Placement Memorandums. While these reports are not public, reporters may be able to learn of their contents by checking with money managers at large pension and mutual funds, which may have been solicited for investment.

Williams Act Filings/Mergers and Acquisitions

The Williams Act requires the filing of various documents with SEC by corporations, partnerships and individuals involved in the purchase or sale of securities, especially activities such as mergers, leveraged buyouts and hostile takeovers.

Disclosure requirements of the Act generally apply only to activities that involve the sale, purchase or ownership of more than 5 percent of the securities of a publicly held company that is either listed on the stock exchange, or is worth more than $1 million and has 500 or more stockholders.

The Williams Act is designed to protect stockholders through the full and rapid disclosure of actions that could prompt changes in stock price. The SEC requires many of these filings to be made "as soon as practical" after a covered action takes place. Amended reports must be filed if any information in the initial report changes. A description of the reports follows.

Schedule 13–D/Report of Securities Purchase   These reports must be filed by investors within 10 days of the purchase of more than 5 percent of a company's securities. It includes a description of the securities, sources of funds for the purchase and background on the buyer. If the buyer is a company, background must be filed on officers, directors or partners of the company and any parent or subsidiary companies. The report must describe the purpose of the purchase and be updated if motives change.

Schedule 13E–3/Transaction Statement   Schedule 13E–3 is filed when a public company or affiliate goes private, often by leveraged buyout.

Schedule 13G/Annual Report   Schedule 13G is a short-form of 13-D filed by entities that own 5 percent or more of a public company, but are exempt from filing 13-D. This includes insurance companies, banks, pension funds, broker-dealers and other institutional investors who are not seeking control of a company.

Schedule 14–D1/Tender Offer Statement   This statement must be filed by anyone bidding to acquire more than 5 percent of a company covered by the Act. It identifies the principals, past dealings between the two companies or their directors, the amount and source of funds for the purchase, names of any persons or firms retained to help with the sale, financial data concerning the offer and the actual tender offer.

Schedule 14–D9/Solicitation Recommendation   Schedule 14–D9 is a company's official notice to the SEC as to how management is responding to a tender offer for acquisition of its stock. If the company plans to fight the acquisition or enter into negotiations with other buyers, these plans must be detailed.

Proxy Statements

The proxy statement, a detailed notice to a company's stockholders of its upcoming annual meeting, contains an outline of matters to be voted on at the meeting, such as the election of new directors or the sale by the company of large quantities of securities. It also discloses the salaries of top officers making more than $40,000 yearly. The results of the election can be found in the next 10–Q.

Proxy statements can be gotten from the company's public relations office.

Forms 3, 4, 5 and 144/Identifying "Insiders" and Other Stockholders

Forms 3, 4 and 5 are used by the SEC to track "insider trading." Form 3, filed when a company is formed, is required of officers, directors and any person or institution who then owned more than 10 percent of the company's original stock. Those who file Form 3 must also file Form 4 every time they dispose of any of their original stock, showing whether the change resulted from a sale or gift. Form 5 is an annual report filed by insiders and major stockholders.

Holders of small amounts of stock can also sometimes be identified. For instance, investors may own shares of a company that does not offer its stock for sale to the public. If those investors wish to sell small amounts of that stock outside the company, they must file Form 144, which describes the extent of their holdings, their relationship with the company issuing the stock and the name of the person they got the stock from in the first place. If the stock was a gift, they must say so.

The question of gifts, addressed in Forms 4 and 144, is an important one. Gifts can signal ties between persons previously thought to be unconnected. An analysis of the purpose and timing of gifts may reveal important events occurring out of public view.

Investment Adviser and Broker-Dealer Records

When New York City nearly went bankrupt—and when Cleveland actually did—an outraged press and public asked: How could this have happened? Clues, if not direct answers, lie in the SEC files.

Form MSD All banks or bank divisions that handle the sale of municipal securities must register with the SEC on Form MSD. The bank must name employees involved in city finances and state whether any have participated in fraud or faced disciplinary action. The bank must also provide background information on those employees, from the high school they attended to their last 10 years of business experience. The idea behind Form MSD is to flush out salespeople unqualified to manage a city's investment.

Forms BD and ADV Similar information to that on Form MSD is available on Form BD for stock salespeople, called broker-dealers, who are members of registered associations, and on Form ADV for investment advisers. Broker-dealers sell securities, while investment advisers stick mainly to giving advice on which securities to buy and sell. Form ADV requires these advisers to disclose the identities of directors, officers, partners and principal shareholders of their companies.

With passage of the Government Securities Act in 1986, the filing of Form BD is now required for broker-dealers who deal solely in securities issued by a governmental body or its direct agent. Such broker-dealers had been exempt from filing Form BD.

Form X–17A–5/Annual Report   Broker-dealers who handle large numbers of investments must file detailed reports of their operations and finances not only each year but each quarter and month as well. Part III of the X–17A–5 annual report filed by these broker-dealers is a one-page summary known as a "Focus Three." Part III is generally the only section of the report available for public inspection, but in some cases, the entire audited annual report will be disclosed on request.

How sound are the finances of the broker-dealers who do business with the major institutions in a community? Do conflicts of interest exist? This massive report can provide many answers, although a financial expert may be needed to unravel the skein of figures found there.

Make your request for all the above forms to the Freedom of Information Officer, Securities and Exchange Commission, 450 Fifth St., Washington, D.C. 20549.

Investment Company Records

Investment companies, such as mutual funds, are a large force in the business world. More and more investors are entrusting their money to these companies, which in turn pour that accumulated money into their own investments. The investment companies have two theoretical advantages over individuals: professional research and enough money to diversify broadly as a hedge against poor investments. Their critics, however, point out that these companies often do no better than individual investors. Because of the uncertainties under which these companies exist, the SEC requires them to file extensive reports on their operations.

First identify the company's major shareholders. Forms 3, 4 and 5 and Schedules 13–D and 13–G will help you do that (see above).

Form N–1R/Annual Report and Form N–1Q/Quarterly Update   If one of those major shareholders is an investment company, look for Form N–1R, the company's annual report. Companies that file Form N–1R must also file its quarterly version, Form N–1Q. This form brings up-to-date major changes occurring in the company's property and in who controls the company. The company also must explain any change in accountants. This report will identify directors, officers, advisory board members and investment advisers, and show the family relationships among them. Perhaps there is a link there.

If not, go back to Forms 3, 4 and 5 and Schedules 13–D and 13–G filed by the investment company's major stockholders, or go to Form ADV filed by its investment adviser (see above). Continue until the missing connection is uncovered or it is clear no connection exists.

EDP Attachment to Form N–1R   Other forms offer various pieces of information about investment companies. Some investment companies, called open-end companies, continually buy back their own stock and offer it for sale again. They must file an EDP attachment to Form N–1R. The attachment names the banks in which deposits are kept and the average monthly balance of these deposits. The names of those banks can provide more leads to the people who control the company's money.

Form N–5/Registration Statement and Form N–5R/Annual Update   Form N–5 is the registration statement required of small business investment companies (SBICs) approved as such by the Small Business Administration. Most SBICs purchase a variety of securities, then sell their own shares to other investors. The N–5 is the initial document filed; the N–5R is the annual update.

Information available includes the company's prospectus, the types of business it conducts, any pending lawsuits against it, tax status, corporate organization structure, directors' and officers' names, addresses and salaries, identities of investment counselors, statements of investment policy, financial data such as balance sheets and long-term debt statements, and a summary of earnings for the past five years including net sales and dividends.

The information provided by SBICs on Form N–5R is substantially the same as other investment companies provide on Form N–1R annual reports. But there's more. Form N–5R requires the identification of anyone who owns at least 5 percent of the kinds of stock that allow him or her to vote at the annual stockholders' meetings.

Make your request for the above forms to the Freedom of Information Officer, Securities and Exchange Commission, 450 Fifth St., Washington, D.C. 20549.

Form N–SAR/Semiannual Report   The SEC is implementing an automatic data processing system known as the EDGAR (Electronic Data Gathering, Analysis and Retrieval) System. Many companies are submitting information required by forms N–1R, N–1Q, N–5R and the EDP attachment to Form N–1R on a form introduced in January 1985, known as Form N–SAR. As a result, many "N" forms described above may be obsolete. However, the SEC keeps back filings available for about six years.

The form is designed for completely electronic submission. Most questions are stated so they can be answered with a yes or no reply or by filling in a dollar amount. The thrust of the new program is to avoid duplicate submission of information previously reported to the SEC.

Updated information from the N–SARs is entered into a computer data base on the investment company industry. Information previously required by the N–1Q is an item on the N–SAR. Most N–1R data is on the N–SAR, except for information on directors, which can be found in other reports. The N–SARs are accessible under the Freedom of Information Act. Information cleared under FOIA will be released in computer printouts that contain only the company's answers. This information can be compared to a blank N–SAR form to determine how the company responded to a specific question.

In addition to the use of the EDGAR System in the investment company reporting section of the SEC, approximately 250 companies have volunteered for electronic submission of a wide range of other SEC reports.

Utility Records

Public utilities—such as electric, gas, gas pipeline, water, sewer, telephone, telegraph, mobile telephone, airlines, buses, railroads, trucking and freight companies, inland water carriers and others—usually are regulated within the states where they do business, in addition to the major federal regulatory agencies. Be sure to check state statutes and regulations in addition to the federal commissions mentioned below.

The nation's 15 or so public utility holding companies file certain records with the SEC. These holding companies have only one purpose—to hold stock in companies that actually provide the services. Privately-owned utilities outnumber the public holding companies 5-to-1 but the latter still control 20 percent of the nation's electricity production.

Form U–13–1/Mutual Service Companies   Holding companies seeking to form another kind of company, called a mutual service company, must file an application with the SEC on Form U–13–1. A mutual service company is owned by the parent holding company. It looks after financing, engineering and accounting for the system's captive companies. This three-level arrangement of companies is supposed to hold down operating costs. Information requested on the form should show whether the mutual service company can do its job "at a reasonable saving" over a similar company outside the system.

In general, someone not numbed by column after column of figures may be able to spot unusual costs in the contract agreements, or compare them to costs for similar services by other utilities not required to file these forms.

Make your request for utility records to the Freedom of Information Officer, Securities and Exchange Commission, 450 Fifth St., Washington, D.C. 20549.

Form U–13–60/Mutual Service Company's Annual Report   A major document for investigating utilities is Form U–13–60, the mutual service company's annual report. It is similar to the corporate 10–K in that it seeks a comprehensive description of the company's operation and finances. But there is much more here.

Information available should include annual and quarterly reports on finances, operations, investments, affiliates and subsidiaries, officers and directors with their addresses, changes in ownership and control, political or campaign contributions and advertising expenditures.

Say, for example, that an electric power company has been drawing criticism for expensive "image" commercials on television, which consumers think they ultimately will be billed for. How much does the company generally spend on advertising? The answer is, to some extent, available on Form U–13–60—if the company is part of a holding company system. This form categorizes the mutual service company's public relations efforts, listing who was paid for advertising and how much. The form is explicit and detailed: who received how much in political contributions, who are the company's creditors, who paid dues for memberships in professional associations, a department-by-department analysis of salaries and how much the company paid to lawyers, auditors and engineers.

Form U5S/Annual Report   Form U5S is the annual report of a holding company system. It includes information on the parent company and any subsidiary holding companies and mutual service companies in the system. It provides much of the same data as the U–13–60, but also describes pending litigation, relationships among the parent's captive companies and the principal shareholders.

Real Estate Investment Company Records

Combining information from local land records with SEC documents filed by certain real estate firms may yield significant results. A reporter covering the local zoning commission, for example, may find that land just approved for lucrative commercial development had been bought for a low price several months before by a firm that specializes in real estate investments. The reporter is suspicious. But where does he or she turn for more information? Two basically similar forms may provide the needed details.

Form S–11/Registration Statement   Companies that invest in real estate generally file Form S–11 when seeking SEC approval to offer stock to the public. This form describes the location and financing of the company's real estate holdings, identities of tenants renting the most space in certain buildings, and any risks connected with the properties the investors should be aware of. The S–11 gives the names and salaries of directors and top officers.

Each company that files an S–11 must later file a prospectus (see above). Real estate firms with prior experience in this area must detail their last five years' experience in real estate investment.

Thanks to these forms, reporters may discover that one of the company's directors is the brother of the zoning commission chairman, or that several commission members are major stockholders in the company.

Forms N–8B–1 Through N–8B–4   Forms N–8B–1 through N–8B–4, filed whenever companies want to offer more than $1.5 million of stock within a year, require disclosures concerning any real estate investments they intend to make.

Form 2A   Companies offering smaller amounts of stock than $1.5 million within a year do not have to file the forms listed above. But after they sell the stock and spend the money they must file Form 2–A, which describes how the money was spent, including any real estate purchases.

Make your request for all the real estate forms to the Freedom of Information Officer, Securities and Exchange Commission, 450 Fifth St., Washington, D.C. 20549.

Additional SEC Material for Backgrounding

- *SEC Today* is a daily summary of major filings and actions taken against companies by the commission. Each issue lists the companies preparing to offer their stock for sale to the public, as well as individuals who have just bought large amounts of a company's stock. It also reports on companies that have violated commission regulations. SEC Today is published by a commercial publisher, the Washington Service Bureau, 655 15th St. N.W., Washington, D.C. 20005. At $205 per year, you may want to use it at your local library.
- *Official Summary* is a monthly publication giving brief descriptions of the buying and selling of securities by insiders: directors, officers and major shareholders. It is expensive, so you may wish to consult it in your government depository library or at a local stockbroker's office.

- *SEC Monthly Statistical Review* provided monthly data in tabular form about new batches of stock for sale, the volume and value of trading on the stock exchanges and filings of Forms 8–K and 144 (see above). The last issue was published in February 1989, but back issues should be available at your government documents depository library.
- *SEC Docket* is a weekly compilation of new rules, changes to old rules and reports of action taken against companies in violation of SEC regulations. It is published by a commercial publisher, Commerce Clearing House, 425 W. Peterson Ave., Chicago, Ill. 60646. The Docket is expensive, so you may wish to read it at your local library or at a local stockbroker's office.

SEC Investigation Files

If you want to know whether your target has been the subject of an SEC investigation, the place to start is the Securities Violations Bulletin, published quarterly and consolidated into annual volumes. Look in the index for the name of the company and its chief officers. Listed will be the date and place of the SEC filing, the alleged violations and the outcome of the investigation. Check your local library for a copy or contact the SEC Public Reference Branch, Room 1024, using the address listed at the beginning of this section.

If your target is listed in the Bulletin, write the SEC for the "Opening" and "Closing" reports of the investigation. The opening report summarizes why an investigation was started, giving the allegations and the names of the players. The closing report describes what action, if any, was taken. If these reports look useful, then write for the entire file.

If at first you ask only for the opening and closing reports, you will get a quicker response from the SEC—and if, from the reports you can tell there's no story in the case, you will save yourself copying fees and possibly also a time-consuming Freedom of Information Act fight over access to specific documents in the case file.

FEDERAL TRADE COMMISSION

The Federal Trade Commission (FTC) was created to protect the public from anti-competitive behavior and unfair or deceptive business practices. Of all the federal agencies, it has the broadest authority over domestic business practices.

The Department of Justice and the FTC share jurisdiction over U.S. antitrust laws. The commission's Bureau of Competition investigates and prosecutes companies using unfair business methods that reduce competition, and has the authority to block mergers that it believes violate antitrust laws. The commission gathers detailed financial information from the companies it investigates to aid in its examination of proposed corporate mergers and consolidations. For example, the commission might investigate whether the takeover of a small company by a larger business would increase the chance that the small company would later be shut down.

The FTC uses two primary methods to enforce compliance: cooperative agreements and mandatory orders, which have the force of law. The commission compiles enormous amounts of information about U.S. companies, both large and small, most of which is of value to reporters investigating a company.

Amendments related to the FTC and its Freedom of Information Act disclosure requirements that went into effect in 1980 allow the FTC to withhold information it collects from businesses and leaves to its discretion whether other categories will be open.

As always, when trying to determine what records are open, start with the Code of Federal Regulations. For instance, under the FTC listing, turn to the index under "Freedom of Information" and "Privacy Act."

Documents listed below can be requested by writing the FTC, Sixth Street and Pennsylvania Avenue N.W., Washington, D.C. 20580.

Public Reference Branch Records

The public reference branch of the FTC houses the records of its law enforcement activity. Among the records maintained there are bound volumes of commission decisions; motions to limit or quash investigation-related subpoenas; petitions requesting action by the commission; records of contracts between commission members and persons involved in actions before the commission (called the sunshine calendar); advertising substantiation material; compliance reports filed by companies under commission order to stop or change certain practices, to divest themselves of certain holdings or to carry out remedial actions; and all public comments on cases pending before the commission.

Information considered nonpublic by the commission includes data from commission personnel and medical files, trade secrets (such as customer names) submitted by business, portions of correspondence related to deliberations and any records relating to a pending investigation that would interfere with the investigation if disclosed.

As with all agencies at all levels, it is helpful to have precise information to identify records you are seeking: case number and document number, or at least the names of the companies involved in the case. All cases are given docket numbers in one of three categories. "D-number" dockets refer to cases under litigation, "C-number" dockets identify consent matters and 7-digit number dockets refer to nonpublic investigations.

The FTC public reference branch is located in Room 130 at the address listed previously. All FOIA requests must be marked as such on the envelope for a speedier response.

Hart-Scott-Rodino Notification Report/Antitrust Information

The Antitrust Improvement Act of 1978 requires large companies considering certain mergers and acquisitions to file notification reports with the FTC. These reports, commonly known as Hart-Scott-Rodino Notification Reports, are generally required of all mergers or acquisitions in which one company has assets or sales of $100 million or more; the second company has assets or sales of $10 million or more; and the value of the acquisition is $15 million or more. However, there are numerous exceptions regarding who must file.

The reports include a detailed description of the proposed acquisition or merger, including the date of the proposed transaction, financial statements, copies of reports filed with the SEC, assets and voting securities to be acquired and detailed information on lines of commerce and revenue broken down by Standard Industrial Codes (SICs). The FTC reviews the information to determine if the acquisition or merger poses a threat to free commerce. It has the power to block a merger or acquisition and can assess stiff penalties if a transaction covered by the act is completed without FTC approval. Although these reports contain a wealth of information about potentially newsworthy mergers, they are nearly impossible to obtain. One FTC official said the agency often requires a court order before releasing notification report information to other government agencies. However, someone with a source inside a company may be able to request a copy of the report. Regulations concerning the Antitrust Improvement Act are contained in 16 CFR Parts 801 through 803. A detailed explanation of requirements under the Act can be found in "Acquisitions Under the Hart-Scott-Rodino Antitrust Improvement Act," a legal reference book published by the Law Journals Seminars Press of New York.

The FTC generally has 30 days to review the notification report before issuing a decision on the merger or acquisition. However, companies may request early termination of the waiting period, which allows the FTC to notify the companies of its decision prior to the close of the 30-day period. Most companies request early terminations and the FTC generally grants them unless there are perceived problems that require lengthy investigation. If an early termination is granted, the FTC is required to print the names of the companies involved in the transaction in the Federal Register. Early terminations also are listed in the "Antitrust Trade Regulations Reporter," published by the Bureau of National Affairs. An early termination notice may tip reporters that a major merger or acquisition is about to become final.

Form 44/Initial Phase Investigation Action Request And Form 62/Full Investigation Closing Form

Hundreds of investigations may be going on at any one time, and many open and close with little fanfare. The initial information is collected on two forms. Form 44, the Initial Phase Investigation Action Request, identifies the companies targeted for investigation and offers brief comments on why the investigation has been requested. Form 62, Full Investigation Closing Form, is a request by a commission division to close an ongoing investigation with an explanation of why. Neither of these forms is now available through the FOIA. Query the division having jurisdiction over the particular business practice.

Additional FTC Material for Backgrounding

The Federal Trade Commission regularly conducts studies to determine major characteristics of a broad cross section of American businesses. The following are the primary studies.

Quarterly Financial Report   The Quarterly Financial Report is based on confidential forms QFR 101 and QFR 102, which are filed quarterly by companies selected by the U.S. Census Bureau to provide a broad cross-section of American business. This report gives up-to-date aggregate statistics on the financial results and positions of U.S. corpo-

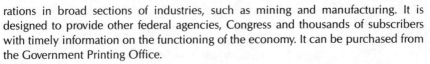

rations in broad sections of industries, such as mining and manufacturing. It is designed to provide other federal agencies, Congress and thousands of subscribers with timely information on the functioning of the economy. It can be purchased from the Government Printing Office.

Advertising Claims Investigations and Actions   The Federal Trade Commission conducts advertising claims investigations and can take actions to prevent false advertising practices. Case files, some of which are public record following an investigation, can be requested under the Freedom of Information Act from the FTC's Bureau of Consumer Protection.

CONSUMER PRODUCT SAFETY COMMISSION

A major function of the Consumer Product Safety Commission (CPSC) is conducting research into product safety and publishing information about it. The Commission maintains an Injury Information Clearinghouse to collect, investigate, analyze and disseminate injury information relating to the causes and prevention of death, injury and illness associated with consumer products, whether or not related to actual product defects.

The CPSC regulates all consumer products with the following exceptions: tobacco and tobacco products, motor vehicles and motor vehicle equipment, pesticides, aircraft and related equipment, boats, drugs and devices, cosmetics and food. These products are regulated by other federal agencies. Consult the U.S. Government Manual or the Washington Information Directory for more information.

The CPSC generally will not disclose any information it gathers during investigations of a possibly hazardous product, but the commission's enabling legislation does require some information to be disclosed on request, even during an investigation. Check the Code of Federal Regulations, Title 16, Part 10.15 for details. It also holds hearings on product safety that are open to the public, and its decisions, defect notices and related orders are published.

District offices of the CPSC sometimes may tell you if any complaints have been made against a certain product. Do not neglect to use the resources of the state and local consumer protection agencies. The Better Business Bureau may also provide limited information on complaints. To request information relating to a specific CPSC case, make an FOIA request to the Office of the Secretary, U.S. Consumer Product Safety Commission, Washington, D.C. 20207.

INTERSTATE COMMERCE COMMISSION

The Interstate Commerce Commission (ICC) is responsible for the regulation of interstate surface transportation throughout the United States. Regulated companies include certain classes of railroads, bus lines, trucking companies, freight forwarders, water carriers and also coal slurry pipelines. The ICC regulates rates, mergers, monopoly pricing and destructive competition, and other areas set by law. It also decides disputes between carriers.

ICC records are abundant. The most valuable are its quarterly and annual financial reports, which provide a complete financial history of the carrier. Expenses, income, property ownership and other areas are covered. Almost every corporation has some dealing with interstate commerce and a carrier. These reports can be obtained from the Washington headquarters of the ICC.

ICC records related to settling disputes between carriers are available for public inspection. Permits and certification can provide valuable information on the carrier's rates and the type of freight they transport. To obtain information on a specific company, make your request to the Office of the Secretary, Interstate Commerce Commission, 12th Street and Constitution Avenue N.W., Washington, D.C. 20423.

OTHER REGULATORY AGENCIES

There are many state and federal agencies barely covered in this book that a reporter might approach for certain kinds of information related to business practices. For example, the Federal Communications Commission regulates the licensing of radio and television stations, the U.S. Department of Agriculture conducts inspections of food-processing plants, and the Civil Aeronautics Board has an abundance of information on airlines. Other agencies might include the Environmental Protection Agency and the Equal Employment Opportunity Commission. To determine which agencies or departments might have information related to the particular business you are investigating, start with the U.S. Government Manual and follow the suggestions for using it found at the beginning of Chapter 3, "Finding a Government Document: An Overall Strategy."

BANKS

Bank regulators are almost as tight-fisted with their records as the bankers they regulate, and the secrecy is protected by many statutes. The Freedom of Information Act exempts the banks' trade secrets and confidential commercial information from public release; even the accessible records are tightly controlled. For example, Federal Deposit Insurance Corporation regulations permit the release to affected banks' directors and authorized personnel of all examination reports except the supervisory section, but only with the written consent of the agency's director or the director's designee.

Three prime bank regulators operate at the federal level. The Comptroller of Currency in the Treasury Department charters national banks; the Federal Reserve Board of Governors, in addition to overseeing all national banks, admits state-chartered banks into that system; and the Federal Deposit Insurance Corp. (FDIC) regulates state-chartered, federally insured banks not in the reserve system. Other banks come under state regulation. The triad of regulators generally have worked to eliminate overlapping and to standardize procedures and records.

The following records are among those available.

B–8s/Cease and Desist Orders

Cease and Desist Orders are aimed at unsound practices by a bank that threaten to jeopardize financial stability. These generally provide a comprehensive view of bank

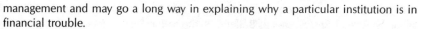

management and may go a long way in explaining why a particular institution is in financial trouble.

The Comptroller of the Currency issued 31 cease and desist orders in 1987, most of which had to do with insider abuses in banks with serious financial problems. Less serious forms of formal enforcement action taken by the Comptroller in 1987 include 87 binding agreements, 23 memorandums of understanding and 22 removals of officers.

The policies of some bank regulatory agencies make it difficult, if not impossible, to gain access to cease and desist orders. Even those you are able to obtain may have large sections expurgated to protect allegedly sensitive information.

The Comptroller and the Federal Reserve Board generally do not release information that would allow a cease and desist order to be traced to a specific bank. The Comptroller maintains the orders are exempt from the Freedom of Information Act, while the Reserve Board cautions that any order obtained under FOIA will be edited to remove information identifying a specific bank or employee.

The FDIC, however, will provide copies of any cease and desist orders that have been issued against a bank if a Freedom of Information Act request is made. You may use the FOIA to request a particular order or all orders issued against a bank during a specified period. Make your request for specific B–8s to the Federal Deposit Insurance Corp., 550 17th St. N.W., Washington, D.C. 20429. When requesting the release, you may seek a waiver of processing fees by stating the information would be in the "public interest." (For more specific information, see Chapter 4, "The Freedom of Information Act.") Otherwise the FIC will levy search and copying fees, and sometimes expensive computer charges as well.

The F Series of Reports

The F series of reports must be filed with the FDIC, the Comptroller of the Currency and the Federal Reserve Board by banks with more than 500 stockholders. The reports essentially cover the same ground as the Form 10–K and other reports that publicly held corporations must file with the Securities and Exchange Commission (See "Securities and Exchange Commission" at the beginning of this section.) The 435 bank holding companies file Form 10–Ks and related reports rather than the F series.

Make your request to the Comptroller of the Currency, 490 L'Enfant Plaza East S.W., Washington, D.C. 20219, or to the Federal Reserve Board, 20th Street and Constitution Avenue, Room B1122, Washington, D.C. 20551 or to the FDIC Disclosure Unit at the address listed previously.

Bank Charter Applications and Challenges

Important information is contained in bank charter applications and challenges, including transcripts and exhibits from the hearings before the Comptroller and the Federal Reserve Board, plus the text of the decision. Make your FOIA request to the Comptroller of the Currency or the Federal Reserve Board at the addresses listed previously.

Bank Applications and Federal Reserve Board Opinions

Bank applications and Federal Reserve Board decisions on branch openings and bank-related purchases of subsidiaries may reveal management problems. The opinions are available from the Secretary of the Board and are published in the monthly Federal Reserve Board Bulletin. Write to the Federal Reserve Board at the address listed previously.

Public Portions of Annual Reports

Annual reports from state-member banks of the Federal Reserve can be very useful. Write to the Federal Reserve Board at the address above.

Regulation O/Loans to Executive Officers, Directors and Principal Shareholders of the Member Bank

The Federal Reserve Act was amended in 1983 to change reporting and disclosure requirements concerning loans made to executive officers, directors and principal shareholders of member banks. Under Regulation O of the Act, member banks are required to make available to the public on written request the names of each of its executive officers and each of its principal shareholders to whom, or to whose related interests, the member bank has outstanding extensions of credit that equal or exceed 5 percent of the bank's capital or unimpaired surplus of $500,000, whichever is less. No disclosure is required if the aggregate amount of outstanding credit to the individual and related interests does not exceed $25,000. The bank is not required to disclose specific amounts of individual extensions of credit. Principal shareholders are defined as anyone who directly or indirectly owns, controls or has voting power over more than 10 percent of any class of voting securities.

Prior to 1983, disclosure of "insider indebtedness" information was required on forms FFIEC 003 and FFIEC 004, commonly known as the "Bert Lance Law" reports.

FFIEC 003/Report on Ownership of the Reporting Bank and Indebtedness of its Executive Officers and Principal Shareholders to the Reporting Bank and to Correspondent Banks is no longer required, but some information from Part II of FFIEC 003 is now included on quarterly Call Reports filed with the FDIC. The "Insider Indebtedness to the Reporting Bank" section of the Call Report includes much of the same information on executive and principal shareholder indebtedness as that required to be disclosed under Regulation O described above. Call Reports can be obtained by writing the FDIC Disclosure Unit, Room F–518, 550 17th St. N.W., Washington, D.C. 20429.

Form FFIEC 004/Report on Indebtedness of Executive Officers and Principal Shareholders and Related Interests to Correspondent Banks contains information similar to that on the FFIEC 003, but it is filed by the individual bank executive or principal shareholder who has outstanding debt with a correspondent bank.

The FFIEC 004 contains information on the maximum amount of indebtedness of the executive officer or principal shareholder and each of that person's related interests to each of the member bank's correspondent banks during the previous calendar year, including a description of terms and conditions, maturity date, payment terms, security, if any, range of interest rates and extension of credit.

The FFIEC 004s must be submitted to the board of directors of the member bank by January 31 of the year following incursion of the debt. The bank is required to maintain records of the filings for three years, but is not required to file copies with any regulatory agency or to divulge contents of the reports to the public.

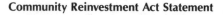

Community Reinvestment Act Statement

The Community Reinvestment Act (CRA) encourages every financial institution, whether it is a commercial bank, a savings bank or a savings and loan association, to develop an affirmative obligation to make loans in every neighborhood of its service area. This law stipulates that the bank make public certain records relating to its credit policy, such as a map defining its entire lending area; low- and moderate-income neighborhoods may not be redlined, or excluded. The bank must make available a list of the kinds of loans available, specific enough to include residential loans for one-to four-dwelling units, small business loans, housing rehabilitation loans, farm loans, commercial loans and others. It must also make public an official CRA Public Notice to be reviewed annually by the institution's board of directors that sets out the requirements of the Community Reinvestment Act and names the body that regulates the bank's activities. The banking institution must post this notice at each of its offices other than off-premise, electronic-deposit facilities. The bank's CRA statement is available to anyone, on request.

A file must be kept of any signed comments received from the public within the past two years that specifically relate to the CRA statement or to the bank's performance in helping meet the credit needs of the community, together with any responses the bank wishes to make. The file must be made available on request. The CRA encourages banks to include a description of their efforts to evaluate and help meet community credit needs, including efforts to offer and publicize special credit-related programs. Although these specific activities are encouraged rather than required, the CRA does take the lender's efforts into consideration when deciding whether to grant approval on applications for facility expansion or new services.

The information contained in the file is an excellent starting point for investigating redlining by financial institutions. These reports also are useful in evaluating the bank's community reinvestment policies and practices.

Financial institutions are rated on how well they meet CRA guidelines, and new laws require ratings issued after June 1990 to be disclosed on the institution's premises. The ratings are: 1) outstanding, 2) satisfactory, 3) need to improve and 4) substantial non-compliance. Documents detailing the rating process need not be disclosed, but the ratings themselves can help pinpoint problem institutions.

Mortgage Loan Disclosure Statement

The Home Mortgage Disclosure Act requires depository institutions with assets of more than $10 million and at least one branch in an urban area to disclose the number and total dollar amount of mortgage loans made by the institution. The Mortgage Loan Disclosure Statement is required of all commercial banks, savings banks, saving and loan associations, building and loan associations, homestead associations (including cooperative banks) or credit unions that make federally related mortgage loans.

Regulations approved in 1988 require mortgage disclosure statements to be filed by the mortgage banking subsidiaries of bank holding companies and savings and loan holding companies. Although sunset clauses have allowed the Act to expire for short periods in the past, the legislation was made permanent in 1988.

Part A of the statement reports the loans written by that institution, organized by census tract and listed by type of loan, number of loans and total dollar amount. Types of loans include Farmers Home Administration and Department of Veterans Affairs, home improvement, nonoccupant, multifamily dwelling and conventional loans. If the bank has redlined any neighborhoods, this will show up in Part A as blocks of census tracts in which the bank has made few or no loans. Part B reports on mortgages bought from other institutions. It will tell how much business a particular financial institution is doing in the secondary market.

The Mortgage Loan Disclosure Statement, together with the Community Reinvestment Act Statement (see above) and census information (describing income, housing and racial makeup of the community), can provide reporters with a detailed look at how the bank is meeting the credit needs of the community.

Financial institutions have 90 days after the close of the calendar year to prepare this data. Parts A and B are on hand at the home office or branch in a census tract of the particular bank and must be kept and made available for five years. Comparing several years' records enables a reporter to determine the lending patterns of the financial institution.

Statements of Financial Condition

For state-chartered banks that don't participate in the FDIC or Federal Reserve programs, the public must rely on state bank examiners for oversight. What should be available from those sources are statements of financial condition, as well as lists of officers and directors.

SAVINGS AND LOAN INSTITUTIONS

The Financial Institutions Reform, Recovery and Enforcement Act of 1989 (FIRREA), commonly known as the "S & L Bailout Bill," transferred regulation of savings and loans from the Federal Home Loan Bank Board to the Treasury's Office of Thrift Supervision (OTS), and to the Federal Deposit Insurance Corp. The Act also established the Resolution Trust Corp. (RTC) to handle the liquidation or merger of hundreds of insolvent savings and loans.

Information available from the Office of Thrift Supervision is almost the same as that which can be obtained from the regulators of commercial banks: summaries of cease and desist orders, quarterly reports and applications, challenges, exhibits and so on. The increase in recent years of savings associations converting from mutual to stock form has resulted in more savings and loans being subject to SEC filing requirements. Since OTS acts as a regulatory agency under the Securities and Exchange Act of 1934, many SEC reports, such as the 10–Ks and 8–Ks, may be on file with OTS. Make your request to the Office of Thrift Supervision, 1700 G St. N.W., Washington, D.C. 20552, or contact the nearest OTS district office.

Savings and loans also are now required to file a number of reports with the Federal Deposit Insurance Corp., including applications for deposit insurance, mergers with non-insured institutions and insurance fund conversions. Make your request to the Federal Deposit Insurance Corp., 550 17th St. N.W., Washington, D.C. 20429.

The Resolution Trust Corp. is headquartered in Washington, D.C., but it has regional offices in Atlanta, Kansas City, Dallas and Denver. For information on disposition of RTC-held property, contact the office in your region.

CREDIT BUREAUS

The Fair Credit Reporting Act of 1971 restricts the availability of information that credit bureaus gather on individuals. Credit reports may be furnished only in response to a court order, upon written request of the individual named in the report, or to a person with a substantial business need for the information, such as for the purpose of extending credit, writing insurance policies or providing employment. Even the federal government is authorized to receive only a consumer's name, address, former addresses, place of employment and former places of employment.

However, these provisions do not apply to commercial credit reports on corporations and similar business entities. Most large newspapers and television stations already have standing relationships with credit bureaus because they extend credit to advertisers and are therefore likely to have access to a bureau's information about a business, including major loans and mortgages outstanding, past defaults, bankruptcies, liens against property, pending litigation and general credit-worthiness among retailers and suppliers.

Rules governing credit bureaus may be on file in your state capital, depending on state statutes.

CREDIT UNIONS

Credit unions are likely to be regulated at one or both of two levels: the National Credit Union Administration, with main offices in Washington, D.C., and six regional branches (see the U.S. Government Manual for specifics); or a state credit union regulatory agency.

The National Credit Union Administration oversees 13,500 federally chartered or federally insured credit unions, or most of the roughly 15,000 credit unions operating in the United States. State agencies regulate the state-chartered credit unions.

The following documents are among those available from the National Credit Union Administration.

The Credit Union Directory

The Credit Union Directory lists all federally insured credit unions under the Administration's jurisdiction by state, including the credit union's name, identification number and address.

Financial and Statistical Report/NCUA Form 5300 Call Report

The Financial and Statistical Report, commonly known as a "call report," must be submitted to either the NCUA or state regulators by mid-January and by mid-July on operations for the past six months. These reports typically don't become available to the public until at least six weeks after submission. Federally insured state credit unions report their financial statement; income and expense statement; statistical loan information; statistical share information; line of credit information and miscellaneous data. Federally chartered credit unions supply essentially the same information, but in a different format.

Financial Statement The financial statement includes loans to members; loans purchased from liquidating credit unions; allowances for loan losses; net loans outstanding;

cash and petty cash; investments broken down by passbook accounts, certificates of deposit and government obligations; loans to other credit unions; land, buildings and other fixed assets; accounts payable; statutory reserve; special reserve for losses; and reserves for contingencies.

Income and Expenses Statement   The income and expenses statement includes interest on loans, income from loans, interest on real estate loans, income from investments, employee compensation, employee benefits, travel and conference expenses, association dues, office rent and supply expenses, educational and promotional expenses, professional and outside services' costs, insurance costs, annual meeting expenses and the allocation of net gains or losses that year to dividends, statutory reserves and undivided earnings.

Statistical Loan Information   The statistical loan information details the age of delinquent loans, total loans to members, rate and amount of interest refunds paid by quarter, loans made in the last month of the current year, loans made since the credit union was organized, loans charged off since the union was organized and recoveries on loans charged off since the union was organized.

Statistical Share Information   The statistical share information includes a classification of savings accounts showing the number and aggregate amount of deposits in each category; the number and aggregate amount of miscellaneous share accounts, such as the shares held by non-members, and their total value; and an indication of when the credit union posts dividends and interest (daily, monthly, quarterly, or whatever). The section also provides information about dividends paid or declared by quarter according to interest rate and aggregate dollar amount, interest on deposits by quarter, dividends paid or declared on share certificates by quarter and total savings by shares and deposits.

Other statistical information includes number of accounts at year's end; number of members; whether a payroll deduction or military allotment plan is provided by the sponsor; amount of state and local government obligations, stocks and bonds held; insurance reserve; investment valuation reserve; and maximum unsecured loan limit.

Line of Credit Information   The credit union must indicate whether it has a self-replenishing line of credit program and, if so, must report the active accounts and outstanding balances, approved accounts and total maximum credit lines approved and total funds advanced under the line of credit agreement in that year.

Miscellaneous Data   Regulators often add requirements for additional disclosure to obtain information that they deem necessary to address emerging problems in the industry.

NCUA Examinations

Make your request to the National Credit Union Administration main office or appropriate regional branch to obtain the latest financial report from a particular credit union.

The administration conducts regular examinations of the management and solvency of credit unions, but their reports are rarely, if ever, made public even under the Freedom of Information Act. The same secrecy holds true for such administrative actions as cease and desist orders, a preliminary warning letter on management practices and the removal of credit union officers. A suspension order may be released, however, particularly if the news media have already reported the suspension. The order prohibits the credit unions from all activities except loan collection and therefore prevents a run on the accounts.

State credit union regulatory agencies generally will follow the same policies and reporting requirements of the National Credit Union Administration—and concentrate their work on state chartered credit unions that do not seek federal insurance. Check your state regulations.

Credit Union National Association

The Credit Union National Association (CUNA), the principal trade group representing credit union officers, offers a wide variety of data and background material about the field. Similar information is available from state credit union leagues in all 50 states. For more information, contact Jerry Karbon, Media Relations Manager at CUNA, 5710 Mineral Point Rd., Madison, Wisc. 53701; (608) 231–4043.

FOREIGN CORPORATIONS

Form 6–K/Annual Report

Many foreign companies sell their stock in the American markets. These companies, like American companies regulated by the SEC, must file an annual report. This report, Form 6–K, describes any changes in the company's ownership or in its own captive companies, and it identifies directors and officers.

Make your request to the Freedom of Information Officer, Securities and Exchange Commission, 450 Fifth St., Washington, D.C. 20549.

Profiles of Foreign-Based Companies

The International Trade Administration (ITA), a branch of the Department of Commerce, is responsible for assisting American firms in developing their export potential. ITA monitors and controls exports for reasons of national security, foreign policy or short supply. It also issues export licenses and answers questions about U.S. trade regulations.

One of the ITA's most useful services for reporters is providing profiles of foreign-based companies. Information includes officers, date of establishment, work force, reputation, nature of business, countries where sales are made, financial and trade references, summary evaluation and background, including financial standing.

Profiles can be obtained by written request to any district office of the International Trade Administration. Check with the Department of Commerce to determine the nearest office.

Banks often provide business profiles of overseas firms through their own foreign offices or correspondent banks. Write, for instance, to Chase World Information Center, Chase Manhattan Bank, 1 World Trade Center, New York, N.Y. 10048.

If you, or your newspaper, have some money to spend, purchase the services of a credit bureau providing overseas business profiles.

Finally, foreign involvement in U.S. business has captured the interest of Congress, so check the U.S. Monthly Catalog for useful hearings.

INSURANCE COMPANIES

Perhaps unique among major business concerns, insurance companies and their regulation have remained the preserve of state governments, except for those companies coming under the jurisdiction of the Securities and Exchange Commission.

At least, you should be able to get the annual reports from each company doing business in your state. These reports detail the capital stock issued, dividends declared, value of real estate owned, cash balance, secured loans, receivables, other securities, probable bad debts, outstanding indebtedness, losses due, losses pending, reserve required by the state to cover risk, number of agents employed, total outstanding risk, receipts from other sources and expenditures for all purposes.

The state's files on insurance companies doing business in the state should include inspection or audit reports, complaint records, standard rates, copies of policies offered for sale or in effect, statement of registration of securities, regulatory fees collected by the state and licensing records of agents.

To get these records, start with your state insurance superintendent or division, and the state statutes.

Insurance Handbook for Reporters

The Insurance Handbook for Reporters provides a general explanation of different types of insurance. It also includes information on the leading insurance companies, a glossary of terms and a reference guide to periodicals about the industry. Some of the general areas discussed include auto, residential and health insurance, and the different kinds of insurance firms. Terms and concepts explained in the last area include: capital stock insurer, mutual insurer, reciprocal exchange, property/casualty life insurer, government insurers, internal organization of insurance firms and various departments within companies.

The insurance handbook can be obtained for free by writing to the Media Relations Department, Allstate Insurance Co., Allstate Plaza F–3, Northbrook, Ill. 60062.

The Insurance Information Institute offers a similar publication entitled Insurance Facts. This annual report provides financial data on industry performance in the previous year and examines insurance trends relating to the civil justice system, disasters, automobile accidents and world affairs.

Insurance Facts can be obtained by writing the Insurance Information Institute, Publications Service Center, 110 Williams St., New York, N.Y. 10038.

STATE REGULATION

States require varying degrees of corporate disclosure from businesses that operate within their boundaries. Usually on file are the company name and address, officers and directors, profit or not-for-profit status, date of inception or registration. Check first with the office of your secretary of state.

In addition, some states may divulge the amount of sales taxes a corporation has paid. This information can be interpreted to determine the corporation's approximate volume of business. Check with your state department of revenue.

Issues of securities within a state generally call for still more corporate disclosure. State laws often require companies to file such information as the type, number and value of securities; a list of adverse orders, judgments and decrees related to securities the company has previously offered; business history; options to purchase securities; principal security holders in the company; and the remuneration for directors and officers.

Other businesses likely to come under state regulation include, among others, alcoholic-beverage manufacturers and their retail and wholesale outlets, savings and loan associations, restaurants and even barber shops. These firms also are likely to come under state regulation for a variety of purposes ranging from the content and value of liquor shipments to sanitation to loan rates to financial stability. Always check state statutes and regulations for special state requirements when investigating a company.

Franchise brokers in California, for example, must register with the state, providing their names and addresses, adverse court orders and judgments affecting them, the franchise contract and other details of the agreement, number of franchises existing in the state and a financial statement. California also requires disclosure from real estate syndicates that issue securities, including general partnerships, limited partnerships, joint ventures and unincorporated associations. The data on file include type, number and value of securities; financial standards for investors; description of property purchases; compensation of general partner or controlling party; profile of general partner; title report; and operating statement.

Write to the California Department of Corporations at one of four offices: 1025 P St., Room 205, Sacramento, Calif. 95814; 600 S. Commonwealth, Los Angeles, Calif. 90005; 1390 Market St., San Francisco, Calif. 94108; or 1350 Front St., San Diego, Calif. 92010.

Some companies provide more information than usual if they apply to become state government vendors and must have their corporate strength evaluated. For example, Minnesota asks companies to supply the sites of plants or warehouses, size of operation, normal value of inventory, length of corporate operation, customer references, bank references and names of officers. You may obtain this information from the state purchasing or procurement authorities.

LOCAL LICENSES AND TAXES

Municipal business tax forms, if they are required and open for inspection, offer a wealth of information about a company, including the name of the firm, address, affiliation with any national corporate headquarters, local franchise holder, franchise agreement and date of last renewal.

If state sales tax records are closed to the public, the business may have to report the amount of the business tax or the actual sales volume to city officials anyway to calculate the business tax. If so, the amount of the business tax also can be interpreted to disclose further information. Check with the municipal license tax office or its counterpart.

Additional business license taxes may be imposed on special business activities, including cigarette taxes, liquor license taxes, food market licenses, recreational business licenses, solicitation licenses, excavating licenses or permits, hotel and motel licenses and others. The license application files may contain pertinent vital statistics on the firm and its owners, depending on local requirements.

PROBATE COURTS

If the owner or a principal in a privately held corporation dies, the probate court files on the decedent should reveal how his or her interest in the firm was liquidated. Among the documents is the will, which indicates how the property was to be disposed of—as a trust fund, as a legacy to an heir or in some other form. Also included are the names of the decedent's attorney and an executor, if one is named. Otherwise, the court will appoint an administrator.

The estate appraisal, if one is conducted, provides an inventory of real estate, personal property, business holdings, stocks, bonds and other tangible assets, along with their values. In calculating the worth of a share in a privately held corporation, the appraisal may disclose operating statistics such as sales volume, annual net profits and other information otherwise not available. Comparable market prices and values often are used to prepare such appraisals.

Inheritance taxes owed to state and federal governments will diminish the value of property passed on to heirs. Periodic settlements of the estate filed by the executor or administrator show how the payments are being made. For instance, if the payments are being made by liquidation, the probate file will show the amounts received for all assets disposed of. On the other hand, the estate for some time could continue to receive income from various holdings, such as a wholly owned or partially owned corporation that had been privately held.

The records can be extremely detailed. In one case, the settlement indicated the estate paid an off-duty policewoman $30 to watch the decedent's apartment during the funeral.

The records are likely to show family relationships in some detail. Contested wills, in addition, will indicate rivalries within those families for control of the estate. The estate will reveal a number of vital statistics about the decedent as well as his or her standard of living.

In addition to the handling of estates, probate courts may handle cases involving guardianship, mental illness and competency that ordinarily would be closed to the public.

C H A P T E R 12

The Work Place

In an era when the size and expertise of the business desk is improving markedly, the amount and quality of work-place reporting is dwindling. Some news organizations no longer staff the labor beat, noting the precipitous erosion of union power and membership. But as union power has been declining, the work place overall has seen massive structural changes. Now more than ever, work affects most Americans more than any other single activity. Consequently, it is time to start reexamining the work place—both union and non-union—and to begin seeing workers and work-place documents as valuable alternative routes to all kinds of other investigative stories.

by MIKE McGRAW

The police lead a disheveled, unemployed father of three to a patrol car and shuttle him off for questioning. Left in the aftermath of what appears to be stress-induced temporary insanity are the bodies of his wife and young children.

The police aren't talking; the neighbors say they don't know anything; the editor is screaming for details; and you've got nothing but blind alleys.

But only a few miles away, tucked in a file drawer in the state office building, there's a pubic record that includes a tape recording in which the father pleads for unemployment benefits during a hearing with a state referee.

It begins with an admission that he's seeing a psychiatrist for depression after being laid off from his job and ends with his screaming at the referee that if something doesn't go his way soon, he can't be held responsible for his actions.

Admittedly, the records in question aren't available in some states; in many others they have never been requested.

The workplace and its records contain a wealth of story ideas and resources for enterprising reporters. But as organized labor has lost much of its clout and membership over recent decades, many editors have wrongly assumed that covering the labor beat is no longer necessary. But, because major changes are under way in the work place, now is the time to increase labor coverage, not decrease it.

Covering union-management relations has often been the limit of traditional labor reporting. Unions are important. They still represent millions of workers, and strikes can impact heavily on the rest of us. Union leaders' political ambitions and their access to power and money open the door for abuses of the members who pay their salaries.

But limiting work-place coverage to unions and unionized companies disenfranchises fully 75 to 85 percent of the nation's work force from scrutiny by the media, and closes the door to great stories.

Waiting for the picking are work-place records that show how a union leader might have a relationship with the company that could conflict with his or her duties to union members; how the space shuttle program was a disaster waiting to happen; how undocumented workers are developing potentially fatal liver diseases from using chemicals whose labels they can't read.

This all takes place against a backdrop of dramatic changes in the American work place—changes occurring at an alarming pace.

Beleaguered union leaders and hard-nosed managers are challenging one another with new strategies in an environment in which the traditional strike may no longer be the ultimate weapon. Non-union workers are learning through recent court decisions that they may have the power to challenge the centuries-old legal principle that bosses can fire any worker for good reason, bad reason or no reason at all.

A new generation of younger workers is breaking into a world of work fundamentally different and potentially much more frustrating than that which their parents experienced. Some work-place experts have argued, for example, that the huge expansion in jobs in recent years has been concentrated in low-paying, service-industry and less-stable, high-tech jobs—a development that could ultimately result in a disappearing American middle class.

We've already reached the point where workers' lives and those of their families can be thrown into chaos by such diverse occurrences as a leveraged buyout of a corporate parent, changes in the value of the American dollar overseas, a drop in the consumer price index, the current price of labor in a Mexican border town or the introduction of a new chemical process on the manufacturing floor.

If you don't see much drama in those stories, consider that some economists claim to have proven a direct correlation between each percentage point increase in the unemployment rate and the rates of suicide, homicide, divorce and child abuse.

In addition, employers, employees and unions are being forced to deal with prickly new work-place challenges, such as how best to deal with the expanding need for quality child care; how to manage the AIDS epidemic's effect on the work place; how best to handle the drug testing demands of employers; and how to cope with invisible health threats.

Clearly, knowledge of the work place and an understanding of some of these profound changes isn't just required for the thinning ranks of reporters stalking the labor beat. It is an important source of news for any enterprising journalist looking for new ideas or an alternative route to the timeless themes that drive investigative reporting.

The following examples illustrate possible stories.

■ A building under construction by union crews collapses, killing 10 workers. Using some of the sources listed later in this chapter, you might find that the construction companies involved had a horrible safety record, including numerous previous accidents, and that past practices were never corrected; that safety and health inspectors had been to the site before and failed to catch obvious problems that may have contributed to the collapse; and that one of the union officials responsible for safety on the job had a conflict of interest because his son was the top officer of one of the contracting companies.

■ A military plane crashes halfway around the world, killing the entire crew aboard. The Air Force blames the plane's avionics system, made in your hometown. By looking in the right places, you might find that the company fired all its quality control inspectors the previous year to save money, that other employees had been complaining about poor quality parts and that Pentagon auditors had given the company poor marks in previous inspections.

■ A school bus accident injures 20 children. You might find records showing that the driver of the bus and co-workers had complained long and hard about mechanical problems, including faulty brakes, and one of the company's two mechanics was fired last month for carping about having to take short cuts in repairs.

The potential of work-place sources is enormous, but here's one important rule: Disgruntled former employees can be great sources to get you started, but be careful. Triple check everything they tell you until you can establish a record of reliability; make them show you previous employment evaluations and anything else you can get your hands on describing their previous work record. Always use them only as a starting point and always rely primarily on current employees in good standing.

The following are some of the most important agencies and sources with which to get acquainted in your area, whether you cover the work place as a regular beat or just want to tap into work-place records for a particular project.

The National Labor Relations Board

The National Labor Relations Board (NLRB), made up of more than 30 regional offices around the country, is an independent federal agency that settles disputes between unions and management, between unions and aggrieved members and between management and small groups of non-union workers.

The board enforces a comprehensive federal labor law passed to maintain an equitable balance of power between labor and management, to protect the rights of union members or non-union workers acting as a group from illegal acts by management and from their own union, and to protect workers involved in union-organizing drives from retaliation by bosses.

The board also conducts and insures the integrity of elections in which workers can choose to unionize. Under certain circumstances, the board also conducts elections in which workers can choose to vote out a union that has been representing them.

Board offices usually consist of a regional director, a regional attorney and a number of investigators, some of whom are lawyers. All board offices make available to the public a docket of recently filed and pending charges.

The process works like this: An aggrieved party, let's say a union member who feels the union is refusing to represent him or her in a grievance with management, files a "charge" with the local office. He or she can do this on his or her own, without the aid of a lawyer.

The charge, which is a public record listing the union member's name, home phone number, employer, union and a description of his or her gripe, is assigned to a board investigator, who interviews all the parties involved. The investigator recommends to the regional attorney or regional director whether the charge has "merit."

If the board investigator finds no merit in the claim and the regional director agrees, the charge is dropped. However, the union member can appeal to a higher level of the board. If the investigator does find merit in the claim, he or she makes a recommendation to the regional director who issues a "complaint," which is a public record much like an indictment.

The regional director then gives the other party, in this case the union, a chance to settle the matter informally. If a settlement can't be reached, a hearing before an independent administrative law judge is scheduled. These hearings are public, and transcripts of them are available at board offices.

The law judge issues a decision, also public, and either party can appeal the findings to the five-member, presidentially-appointed National Labor Relations Board in Washington, D.C. The NLRB's findings can be appealed to the courts and, eventually, to the U.S. Supreme Court.

Many unions have denounced the agency, claiming that the Reagan administration had packed it with pro-management officials—usually former management lawyers—and, therefore, have refused to seek the board's sanction of union elections.

Unions can and sometimes do organize employers without a NLRB-conducted election by pressuring them to recognize there is sufficient interest among employees to join.

The best sources on the board are the regional director and regional attorney. Individual investigators also might be excellent sources who can say, for example, whether internal board decisions about whether to pursue specific cases represent pro-union or pro-management biases.

One method of contacting potentially helpful investigators is through local officials of the union that represents them—the independent National Labor Relations Board Professional Association.

Board clerical workers can also be helpful, and one way to get to know them is to make regular visits to board offices to check docket sheets for pending cases that might lead to good stories.

The Federal Labor Relations Authority, and various state labor relations boards or public-employee relations boards, provide the same services for federal, state and local workers, respectively.

The U.S. Department of Labor

A myriad of divisions of the U.S. Department of Labor (DOL) are charged with enforcing hundreds of federal labor laws, including those guaranteeing safe and healthful work places, payment of minimum and overtime wages, and protection for whistle-blowers. The department also helps states fund and administer programs providing unemployment benefits, workers' compensation and job training programs. It audits and requires annual financial reports from unions and various employee pension, health and welfare funds.

Start with the information officer in the Department's regional office nearest you. They are located in Boston, New York, Philadelphia, Atlanta, Chicago, Kansas City, Dallas, Denver, San Francisco and Seattle. Field offices of various DOL divisions are spread throughout those districts.

The following is a breakdown of some important DOL divisions by function.

Union/Management Financial Information

Private industry's labor union annual financial reports and some company filings can be obtained from the Office of Labor Management Standards (OLMS), based in Washington but with field offices in more than 30 cities. The office enforces the Labor-Management Reporting and Disclosure Act, which includes requirements that unions file annual financial reports and undergo audits. The office also conducts civil and criminal investigations of unions and educates union members about their rights under federal law.

Union Reports

LM–1 or LM1–A   A union's initial filing, which should include its constitution and bylaws, composition of members, name of parent body or bodies, expected annual receipts, names and titles of officers, date of the next union election, any fees or dues required and whether work permits are required.

LM–2   This is the standard four-page annual union financial report commonly filed by calendar year, and usually available for the previous year by early spring. It must be filed by all unions with receipts of $100,000 or more. It contains names and salaries of officers and most employees, receipts and disbursements, including those to charities, real estate purchases, trust funds and whether losses of funds or property were discovered. These reports can also be used to notify the government of the termination of a union through a merger, consolidation or dissolution. One-page LM–3 reports are required from unions with less than $100,000 in gross annual receipts.

Don't overlook LM–2s of parent, or international unions. You may find your local union leader is making a good salary at home, yet holds two or three other positions with the parent union—a plan that can double or triple his or her salary.

LM–15   This report must be filed by a parent union 30 days after it suspends autonomy of a union local by putting it under "trusteeship" or "supervision," a move often resulting from election irregularities, an attempt to control dissident members and officers or financial irregularities. The report requires a reason for the trusteeship and an accounting of union finances at the time it took effect. Follow-up reports are required every six months explaining why the trusteeship was continued, and an LM–16 is required when trusteeship is lifted, including the method of selecting officers left in charge. Watch these closely. Trusteeships can be abused by officials of parent unions who don't like leaders chosen by the local union or who want to bring members of a certain local in line with other locals.

LM–30   These reports aren't filed often because they are potentially incriminating and could be used to convict a union official of violating federal laws. They require union officers or employees to disclose whether they, their spouses or children have financial interests or dealings with an employer whose employees are represented by the union.

Management Reports

LM–10   These reports aren't filed often either, because they can be incriminating. They are basically used to report illegal payoffs made to convince union officials to take actions that could benefit the boss at the members' expense. They require employers to disclose whether they have made payments to a union—its officials or employees—whether any payments were made to try to persuade the union or its members one way or the other about bargaining rights, or to obtain information about union activities. Employers also must disclose arrangements with consultants aimed at accomplishing the same ends.

LM–20 and 21   Requires consultants themselves to disclose the same information required above from employers, whether they work for a union or management. The LM–21 is a report on any fees received. You won't find many of these either, but it is worth a quick check.

S–1   These forms, ordered from the OLMS Washington office, can contain a gold mine of information about internal union corruption. They are required from all surety companies that bond union officials or union trusts, pension plans or health and welfare plans. Information includes the date of the company's loss, name of the (union) insured, the kind of a bond in force, the gross loss claimed and the amount paid.

The OLMS also publishes guides that can save you time and money in ordering forms. The registers, which include filing numbers that can speed your document request, include The Register of Reporting Labor Organizations, Register of Reporting Surety Companies, Register of Reporting Employers and Register of Reporting Labor Relations Consultants.

Wage Enforcement and Whistle-Blower Protection

Information on enforcement of minimum, subminimum and overtime wage provisions and protections for whistle-blowers, migrants and children comes from DOL's wage and hour division, part of the department's Employment Standards Administration. Information can include reports about closed investigations of employers fined for failing to pay federally required minimum wages or premium pay (time-and-a-half) after 40 hours in any one week. These reports can often show a clear pattern of illegal procedures, such as companies that deduct from workers' paychecks to make up for cash drawer shortages.

The division investigates complaints of violations of child labor laws and migrant and seasonal worker legal protection. Regulations require, among other things, that youths not be employed in hazardous occupations. Such violations are becoming more common with the labor force shrinking.

The division reviews requests from employers who want to pay less than the minimum wage (no less than half) to workers deemed incapable of producing at the same rate as a "normal" worker. These usually include mentally retarded workers, whose work can be considered therapeutic. But abuses abound, and the division has granted permission to state agencies to pay less than the minimum wage to clients, such as veterans, who were not producing below normal. The arrangements allow some state agencies to keep their payrolls down by having clients perform routine tasks such as lawn work at hourly wages as low as $1.50.

The division also enforces numerous federal whistle-blower statutes passed to protect workers who are threatened, fired or demoted for reporting illegal or improper activities, including unsafe working conditions. Private-industry whistle-blower cases are heard by Labor Department administrative law judges in open hearings.

Federal government whistle-blowers can often get their cases before the federal Merit Systems Protection Board, which holds hearings and collects evidence in cases involving the firing or discipline of federal employees.

The Government Accountability Project, a private, non-profit organization in Washington, D.C., offers legal assistance to all kinds of whistle-blowers and lobbys for protective legislation.

Pension Plans and Other Trusts

This information can be obtained from the Pension and Welfare Benefits Administration (PWBA), or the division's Public Disclosure Room. The form to request is the 5500 and its Schedule B attachment, the annual financial report that all union trust funds must make to the IRS and DOL's PWBA. If a union or management official wants to dip into the deepest pocket around, these funds are it.

Form 5500, required under the Employee Retirement Income Security Act (ERISA), details assets of the pension or health and welfare plan, the number of participants, names of trustees, employees and outside consultants and institutions that handle the assets, administrative costs and a breakdown of investments and other financial transactions.

ERISA, approved in the early 1970s as a result of the bankruptcy of several major pension funds, assigns fiduciary responsibilities to plan trustees and limits the kinds and quality of investments they can make.

The reports first are sent to the IRS, which evaluates them for continuing tax-exempt status, then forwards them to DOL. The forms can be ordered from DOL, but by the time they get there, they are fairly old. If you need a current one, go to the IRS service center nearest you, but expect a four-to-six-week delay.

Besides giving you clues about how union and management can steal dollars from such funds (hiring a brother-in-law to administer funds at inflated costs or investing in a friend's venture), the forms are valuable for other stories.

Some companies in recent years have been declaring pension funds "overfunded" under federal regulations, allowing them in some cases to cash the fund out, purchase annuities for remaining and future recipients, and take the excess assets as operating capital. Workers' future retirement funds are then dependent on the financial health of the insurance company providing the annuities.

Some funds have also played a part in reducing the sales price of a dying company. For example, Company A owes millions to its underfunded pension plan, but agrees to a sale to Company B for cash and agreement that Company B make good on the debt to the pension fund.

Company B gets a bargain-basement price, fails to make good on the pension fund debt, then files bankruptcy and attempts to dump the ailing plan on the government's Pension Benefit Guaranty Corporation (PBGC), an agency that underwrites pension plans.

The Supreme Court and Congress in recent years have made rulings and passed legislation that may stem such abuses by requiring financial tests of pension plans and their sponsoring companies, but the area bears continued scrutiny.

Records and officials of the PBGC, based in Washington, can be valuable sources in such cases. The agency is charged with protecting the retirement income of some 40 million workers in 100,000 private sector "defined benefit" pension plans. When plans fail, the PBGC, which is financed with "insurance premiums" charged to all private pension plans, takes over the plans and guarantees that a basic level of retirement benefits will continue to be paid. As a result, the quasi-governmental agency is a billion dollars in debt and going deeper.

Racketeering

The Labor Department's Office of Inspector General, besides being the "junkyard dog" that watches out for waste, fraud and abuse in the agency, conducts investigations into alleged cases of labor/management racketeering, often working with the Department of Justice's Organized Crime Strike Force, and conducts and supervises audits relating to other department operations.

Local agents may investigate a union car leasing scam, where inflated prices of automobiles for union officials are partially kicked back to the union leader, or shakedowns in which construction companies are required to pay off a union official before certain operations are performed.

The office may also investigate allegations that a federally funded job training program is double-dipping—getting money from two different government agencies, such as the Veterans Administration and the Labor Department, for training the same worker.

There are not many records here unless an investigation is closed, and the investigators are often closed-mouthed. But the local IG investigator may be able to help you come up with the names of certain unions that bear scrutiny or may steer talkative dissident union members your way.

Safety and Health

One of the most important Labor Department agencies—and one that seems always to be at the center of controversy—is the Occupational Safety and Health Administration (OSHA).

OSHA has historically been the recipient of more harsh congressional criticism—for either being nit-picking or not tough enough on multiple violators—than any federal agency except the Pentagon and the Environmental Protection Agency. That's not surprising; besides the fact that safety costs time and money, the issue has ardent constituents on all sides. Unions find OSHA a good vehicle for pounding Republican administrations, and besides, safety and health is one of the most emotional and politically hot issues Congress can get involved in.

In addition, the agency has been notoriously slow in adopting new standards, particularly for newly-introduced industrial chemicals and processes.

It is a fascinating agency to cover, but one on which you have to keep a close watch. Its leaders are politically keen and adept, after years of criticism, at putting on a pretty face. But OSHA records can lead you to some great stories.

Like many other federal enforcement agencies, OSHA is divided into regional administrative offices around the country, with area offices serving under them. Each area office is divided between safety inspectors (often former union construction workers or management safety experts) who investigate physical hazards and injuries, and health inspectors (often recently graduated industrial hygienists) who investigate health matters such as injuries from toxic chemicals.

OSHA covers only private industry employees, but some states have set up mirror agencies to cover municipal and state workers. Federal workers are covered under agency-by-agency plans.

States also have the option of enforcing private industry safety and health themselves, as long as their rules are at least as stringent as federal rules. If your state enforces OSHA rules, be sure to order OSHA audits of how well the state has performed.

The agency is understaffed, given its congressional mandate to guarantee safe and healthful work places for all Americans. Until recently, it had taken a soft approach to enforcement, with top officials saying they can do more to improve safety and health through an attitude of cooperation with employers than tough enforcement.

OSHA basically conducts three types of inspections: programmed inspections (companies in especially dangerous industries randomly picked by computers for "wall-to-wall" scrutiny); inspections usually resulting from a signed complaint by a worker or union official; and accident inspections, usually triggered when one or more workers is killed or five or more are hospitalized.

Workers can also request an "Imminent Danger" inspection, which usually means the worker believes lives are at stake. That often forces the agency to assign a high priority to the complaint.

Inspections can result in no citations, "other-than-serious" citations, "serious" citations or "willful" citations, the latter meaning that OSHA believes the company knew it was violating a safety rule that could kill or seriously injure a worker, but violated it anyway. Proposed fines—based on the company's size, past history and other factors—are usually issued for serious or willful citations.

The company has 15 days to contest the citations, request an "informal conference" about them, or pay the fines.

An informal conference, usually held with the OSHA area director, often results in reductions in fines by as much as 80 percent in return for a promise by the company to "abate" the safety hazards. (Companies can ask for "variances" from OSHA regulations under special circumstances, but the agency has been criticized for allowing the variances under questionable circumstances and letting them go on too long.)

If no settlement is reached there, the company can appeal to the independent Occupational Safety and Health Review Commission, which assigns administrative law judges who hear arguments from OSHA and the company, then make a decision that can be appealed to the courts.

For a time during the Reagan administration, OSHA inspectors did not visit companies whose OSHA-required logs of accidents and injuries showed rates below the average for their industry. But then OSHA began to inspect record-keeping practices and found many companies understating injury rates in apparent attempts to avoid inspections or higher insurance premiums.

Huge fines resulted. What also resulted, eventually, was the agency finally abandoning its practice of foregoing inspections of companies with low accident figures.

OSHA depends on civil enforcement of its regulations, but can request that the United States Department of Justice conduct criminal investigations under the Occupational Safety and Health Act. But few referrals are made to the Department of Justice and very few of those are chosen for investigation. The ones that are have seldom resulted in indictments or convictions.

Part of the problem is that OSHA's proof in civil investigations won't pass the more stringent legal tests required in criminal cases. As a result, in some areas—most notably Los Angeles, Dallas and Chicago—local prosecutors have had some success in indicting and convicting company officials in particularly egregious cases under state law charges of negligent homicide or other theories. Some courts, however, have ruled that OSHA jurisdiction is a pre-emption in such cases.

Once an OSHA case is closed, you should have no trouble getting an inspection report, which usually lists the hazards found and proposed fines. Also ask for the inspector's handwritten notes. You may have to file a Freedom of Information request for those, and you may get refused or they might be heavily censored, but the agency has released them in the past, and they can be worth the trouble.

Don't wait for that, however. If a work place accident occurs locally, whether OSHA investigates or not, immediately ask the agency for a computer printout on the enforcement history of the company. It's something the agency runs anyway if it is investigating. It can be difficult to read; have a local official walk you through it.

The report will tell you when and where the company was cited and for what, how much in fines was proposed and paid, how many workers were involved, whether it was a unionized company and whether the hazard was abated. If a case is appealed to the review commission, most records and all hearings should be open to you.

Get the agency's rulebooks so you can interpret citations on inspection reports. Title 29 of the Code of Federal Regulations (Parts 1901 to 1999) contains most OSHA standards and rules. Don't let a local OSHA official tell you there is no standard for a particular hazard. The agency has a general duty or catchall standard that has been applied liberally.

If you have trouble dealing with your local area director, appeal to the regional director. You may get a more understanding point of view there. Most regional offices have a labor liaison (usually a former union official) whose job is to stay in contact with local union leaders. Become acquainted with him or her.

Try getting into the agency with a story on staffing levels—comparing the number of inspectors to the number of businesses and the number of accidents they are expected to investigate each year. Talk to local agency leaders, inspectors and union leaders. Many states also have pro-worker watchdog Committees on Occupational Safety and Health (COSH).

If you are concentrating on one company, you can get access to company medical records, a list of toxic substances and exposure records under an OSHA rule that requires the company provide the information within 15 days to any employee or an employee representative (this can be you, or a union official). OSHA 200 forms, listing a summary of all injuries and illnesses, must be posted annually in work places. Visit the plant yourself or ask a worker to read it to you.

Other possible sources on the agency and safety and health include:

- The Annual Survey of Occupational Injuries and Illnesses, published by the Bureau of Labor Statistics, will help you determine the most hazardous work places in your area.
- First injury reports, collected by your State Worker's Compensation division, list details for each serious injury or death in the work place.
- Various OSHA advisory committees (members of management, labor and the public that advise in different areas), meet regularly at OSHA headquarters in Washington, D.C.
- Labor unions are great safety and health sources, particularly the AFL-CIO safety and health department, Oil, Chemical and Atomic Workers, the United Rubber Workers and the United Auto Workers.
- Many schools and universities have safety or health programs, or occupational medicine clinics.
- OSHA grants money to committees and groups around the country to fund safety and health awareness programs. Ask OSHA for the New Directions grant recipients in your area.
- Other good sources include congressional committees (order testimony from previous oversight hearings); Washington-based OSHA newsletters, including the Occupational Safety and Health Reporter; and the Chicago-based watchdog group, the National Safe Workplace Institute.

State Labor Departments or Departments of Industrial Relations

These agencies often provide federally-mandated benefits, such as unemployment compensation. Activities and available information vary from state to state, but can include enforcement of state minimum wage, child labor, migrant worker and overtime laws, which can be more stringent than federal rules; enforcement of state laws governing the activities of private employment agencies; and enforcement of state whistle-blower laws, which vary widely from state to state.

State labor departments sometimes provide labor mediators or free arbitration services to public and private employee unions. In addition, some state labor departments provide applications for and enforcement of alien employment certification rules. The federal-state program allows employers to bring in alien workers for certain jobs if they can prove no U.S. worker is available with the same skills.

Ask for a printout of recent certifications. You may find some surprises. In one case, a military base hired a Polish barber despite the fact than an injured Vietnam veteran holding a state master barber's license had applied for the job.

Some state labor departments require abbreviated financial statements from public employee unions, information that is not required on the federal level. Check your state labor statutes for more sources of information on programs administered by this agency.

Federal Mediation and Conciliation Service and State Counterparts

The Federal Mediation and Conciliation Service (FMCS) is an independent federal agency with local offices and commissioners in most large cities. The agency is supposed to be notified by unions at least 30 days ahead of the expiration of labor contracts, and often assigns local commissioners to help resolve disputes before or after strike deadlines.

These commissioners, usually former management or union negotiators or officials, vary widely in background and abilities. In many cases, their job is to find ways for one side or the other to back off from earlier public negotiating stands and still save face.

They can be great background sources about where strikes stand and what the most difficult issues are, but if you compromise this background information just once, the commissioner will lose all credibility with both sides and you will lose a potentially excellent source. In highly visible disputes, expect him or her to try using you to get messages across to one side or the other.

Many states also have mediation services to work with public employee unions and management or to team up with federal mediators.

State and federal mediators, union and management officials, and members of the union negotiating committee (who are often politically active or power hungry) should provide plenty of sources about what's going on in the negotiations.

Arbitration Services

Many arbitration services are available to settle disputes, including the American Arbitration Association and the FMCS's Division of Arbitration Services. Although hearings held by arbitrators are not normally open to the public, reporters can attend by permission. Accounts of past arbitration hearings can often be found in published volumes.

Many states offer free or low-cost arbitration services to public and private employee unions; these decisions are often public and can be great sources for story ideas. For example, an arbitration award may be the only document available detailing the disciplinary action of a town patrolman alleged to have stopped young women, whom he then sexually harassed.

You may find decisions upholding disciplinary actions against guards at the state prison for sleeping while on duty, or find a pattern in decisions holding as too harsh the firing of cab drivers for overcharging trips from the local airport.

In some states you can get information on specific agencies, or even private companies, by checking a number of arbitration cases filed under the name of the agency or company.

There are generally two types of arbitration. Grievance arbitration takes place when an individual employee challenges an action of management through the union contract, and the matter can't be settled by local union and management officials. It then is appealed to a neutral, third-party arbitrator who hears evidence from both sides and issues a decision. These hearings sometimes are public, but few reporters have asked to attend.

Interest arbitration takes place when labor and management can't agree on the terms of a new contract, and usually occurs in the public sector. If strikes are prohibited (usually the case with public employees) or both sides want to avoid a strike, they can turn the matter over to an arbitrator who will hold hearings and issue a decision.

The agency's general counsel is often the best source with which to start.

State Employment Security Divisions

A valuable and often overlooked source on companies, government agencies, unions and individuals is the state unemployment office. It is also one of the most valuable resources for information on non-union companies and employees.

You can use records of these agencies and the human sources they suggest to put together a list of former employees of a company you're investigating, to look for trends in local employment patterns or to find out why workers often get fired. You can use them to plumb the depths of local alcohol or drug abuse problems among certain employers or gather the names of current workers at a certain firm.

The stories told in the forms available from these offices range from an employee being fired for sitting on the copying machine and selling the results to co-workers to the firing of a slightly retarded dishwasher by a new restaurant manager for dropping and breaking a small stack of dishes.

The system works this way: Whenever workers are fired or quit for what they feel are valid reasons, they can claim unemployment benefits, which are paid out of the state's unemployment trust fund, financed by employer taxes. The more successful claimants an employer has, the more taxes the firm pays. Hence, many employers will try to keep costs down by challenging all or most of the claims by former employees.

The benefits are provided under a federal-state system, but eligibility criteria, benefit levels, procedures and available records vary from state to state.

The former employee makes an initial claim at the local unemployment compensation office. The employer is notified of the claim and given a chance to contest it. A hearing is held before an impartial referee.

That decision can then be appealed to the state's employment security board of review, and from there to the state courts.

It is not until the first hearing is held, in many states, that the names of claimants or companies become available.

Copies of claims and referees' decisions can be filed either in employment security offices closest to an employee's residence or in the office closest to the employer, so you may have to check several offices.

Start with the manager of the office where the company is based, checking logbooks for cases involving that company. A two-to-three-page synopsis of a decision in each individual case should be made available, except in some states where local laws keep them private.

If you want more detail, you should be given access to a one- or two-hour tape recording of the entire hearing, during which both sides usually open up because they don't think the information will go public.

You can get the name, address and often the Social Security number of the claimant, who usually represents him or herself, and the name of the company representative. This can be used to widen your circle of sources among other current and former employees.

Studies have shown that workers who file unemployment claims are also likely to file other kinds of complaints with state human resources departments, the Equal Employment Opportunity Commission or other agencies. The best agency sources are referees and local office managers.

Appeals of referees' decisions often end up with the statewide employment security appeals division, which sets precedents in unemployment insurance claims. Most states require that those precedent-setting decisions be made available to the public.

Appeals of those decisions go to the state court system.

State and Municipal Occupational and Professional Licensing Boards

These state and local agencies, often set up because of pressure from groups trying to control the number and quality of practitioners, test and license a number of different kinds of workers. Many states require that such diverse groups as engineers, architects, accountants, television repair people, welders, plumbers and electricians be tested and certified.

The tests are often prepared or approved by groups of practitioners themselves, but some states have gone to professional, standardized-testing firms to insure integrity in the testing procedures.

Check the boards closely. You may find, for example, that all the members of the electricians' proficiency board are members of different locals of the International Brotherhood of Electrical Workers, and few, if any, non-union electricians make it over the hurdles.

You may also find a situation like the following: A nuclear power plant is under construction in your area, requiring that hundreds of out-of-state plumbers and pipe fitters be brought in to complete the job. Because all are required to pass the local proficiency exam, copies of the tests start showing up on the job site, or are sold through the operator of the local lunch wagon.

Also check the penalties levied against unlicensed workers; the boards are notorious for going light on their colleagues.

Some of these agencies publish annual directories of licensed engineers and architects, providing a quick reference guide to individuals or companies you may be looking into.

Labor Lawyers and the Courts

Labor law has undergone so many fundamental changes in recent years—changes that are still occurring—that the courts and labor lawyers have become potentially excellent sources.

So many labor cases are making it into the courtroom now that firms specializing in labor law are expanding rapidly, and labor law specialists are now developing courtroom techniques they seldom needed in the past, when most of their cases were held before unemployment or workers compensation hearing officers.

Try to get a copy of your state bar association's listing of its labor law section, and get to know the chairperson. Get acquainted with labor law specialists at firms in your area. Get on mailing lists of employment law newsletters published by those firms for their big corporate clients. They can be an excellent source for keeping up with important local decisions.

Ask your paper's court reporter to look for employment-related lawsuits involving individual workers, companies or unions.

One rapidly expanding area in many states involves civil suits taking the position that a job loss constitutes a breach of an oral, written or implied contract. That's part of an expanding legal theory called the erosion of the "employment at will doctrine." The doctrine, from English common law, long held that the boss could fire workers for "good reason, bad reason or no reason at all."

The suits, usually filed by fired or demoted non-union workers, often seek millions of dollars in damages. Records from these suits can give you insight on how a company or industry operates and a chance to use the disgruntled former employee to widen your circle of sources inside a company.

Many states also have whistle blower protection laws allowing workers to file civil suits if they are fired, demoted or harassed for reporting or refusing to perform illegal or improper activities.

More and more, workers are filing suits against their own unions, alleging, for example, that the union failed to represent them adequately in return for union dues, or that it failed to live up to its stated or contractual duty to help provide a safe work place.

The way work-place law has been expanding, you're likely to find almost any kind of claim in the courts these days.

Defense and Labor

The defense budget has been called the biggest public works project since Roosevelt, and for good reason. It employs millions of workers all over the country.

Big contractors have become so politically astute that they are spreading subcontracts for weapons systems—and jobs—all over the country, particularly in districts where they need the local congressman's support.

Check congressional directories to see if any of your members of Congress are members of defense appropriations committees. Check to see which companies in your area produce weapons systems or components. Then see if the company is unionized—most of them are—and spend time with the local union leader.

Particularly around the time the union's contract expires, you might pick up potential story ideas about how the company recently laid off a number of quality control inspectors, about how supervisors force through non-conforming parts because the contractor is behind schedule or about how they force workers to illegally charge time on one government contract to the budget of a separate contract.

Check with the nearest office of the Defense Contract Administration Service, one of the Pentagon agencies charged with keeping an eye on contractors. Ask for the local chief of quality assurance; ask him or her about quality problems in local defense plants. Ask if the office has recently completed any Quality System Review audits, which grade a contractor on assuring quality.

Don't let them refuse to give it to you based on claims that it contains proprietary information. They have been released under FOI in the past, after being cleansed of supposedly proprietary items.

Other Helpful Reference Books and Sources

- *Corruption and Racketeering in the New York City Construction Industry, the Interim Report of the New York State Organized Crime Task Force.* This may sound too localized, but it lists construction scams typical of what goes on all over the country. It's a good backgrounder.
- *Directory of U.S. Labor Organizations*, published by the Bureau of National Affairs. It lists most major unions and state central bodies, their addresses, phone numbers and top officials.
- *Dictionary of Occupational Titles*, published by the U.S. Department of Labor, is a listing of almost every job you can imagine, including salary ranges, job descriptions and future prospects.
- *Union Democracy and Landrum Griffin, Union Democracy in the Construction Trades* and other pamphlets published by the Association for Union Democracy, based in Brooklyn, N.Y. It also publishes regular newsletters. Officials there can be helpful on backgrounds of certain unions and rights of dissident union members.
- *The Unemployment Benefits Handbook* by Peter Jan Honigsberg.
- *The Law of the Workplace, Rights of Employers and Employees,* by James W. Hunt.
- *Weekly Summary of NLRB Decisions,* available from the Washington, D.C., office of the National Labor Relations Board.
- *Reports on work place and labor issues* published by the U.S. General Accounting Office. Get on the mailing list and you'll receive an order form each month of recently published studies, organized by subject area.

- *The National Right to Work Committee*, in Washington, D.C., decidedly anti-union organization, but a potentially good source on union excesses.
- *The free labor news clipping service* provided by most regional Labor Department information offices.
- *Free union newsletters*. Get on the mailing lists for as many as you can. They are great sources for story ideas and help you keep up with the hot topics. "Solidarity" by the United Auto Workers, the United Mine Workers Journal and publications by the Service Employees International Union and the American Federation of State, County and Municipal Employees are among the best.

DOCUMENTING THE EVIDENCE

U.S. DEPARTMENT OF LABOR LABOR-MANAGEMENT SERIES

To obtain any of the following forms, write to the Office of Labor-Management Standards, Department of Labor, Washington, D.C. 20210, or the closest Department of Labor (DOL) regional office. If you can, cite the file number of the labor organization, which can be gotten from the Register of Reporting Labor Organizations (see below).

Form LM–1/Labor Organization Information Report

Form LM–1 provides general information about the operation of the union, including the union's principal mailing address, the name and title of each officer, qualifications for or restrictions on membership, the election process of officers, procedures for the discipline or removal of officers or agents for breach of trust, suspensions and expulsions of members (including the reasons and process, notice, hearing, judgment and appeal procedures) and the issuance of work permits. It also explains the union's bargaining procedures, such as authorization for bargaining demands, ratification of contract terms and authorization for strikes.

The report provides limited financial background information but includes fees for initiation and membership, fees for work permits, levying of assessments, authorization for disbursements of funds, audit of financial transactions and the imposition of fines. It also gives the dates of the union's fiscal year and expected annual receipts and tells which annual report the union is required to file.

Much of this same information can be found in the constitution and bylaws of the organization, which also must be filed with DOL.

A supplement to Form LM–1, Form LM–1A, is filed for any later additions. Other changes must be provided in the annual report (LM–2 or LM–3), described below.

Forms LM–2 and LM–3/Labor Organization Annual Information Report

Generally, forms LM–2 and LM–3 are the most useful up-to-date forms about a union's finances. The LM–2 must be filed by all labor unions with total annual receipts of $100,000 or more. The LM–3 is a shorter version required of unions with receipts of less than $100,000. Both are filed annually.

Local state and central labor councils, as well as public employee labor organizations, are exempt from filing these and other reports required under the Labor-Management Reporting Disclosure Act. Many file them anyway, just to cover all bases, apparently confident no one is likely to read them.

Information in the LM–2 and LM–3 reports include all assets and liabilities, sources of income and services, all allowances and other direct or indirect disbursements to each officer regardless of amounts and to each employee who received more than $10,000 during the year from any reporting union or its affiliated union, total disbursements and the purposes for which they were made, and whether the union acquired any goods or property in any manner other than by purchase or disposed of any goods or property in any manner other than by sale.

These reports include all direct and indirect loans totaling more than $250 made to any officer; employer or member, loans made to any other person or business enterprise; and a statement giving the purpose of each loan, the security furnished (if any) and the arrangements for repaying the loan. It is often good to check, for instance, if the collateral furnished is of equal value to the loan.

They also state whether the union participated in the administration of a trust or other fund or organization for the purpose of providing benefits for members or their beneficiaries. (However, Form 5500, described below, is the best source for information concerning pension funds.)

Other information includes whether the union has discovered any loss or shortage of funds or other property, whether it was insured, the amount recoverable, the date of its next regular election of officers and rates for dues and fees.

Don't overlook the LM–2 filed by the international union or governing body. Often loans are made by the international to the local for special organizing drives or strikes, or to pay judgments against the local as a result of court actions or arbitration awards. Sometimes an international union may hire additional personnel, such as union organizers or special business agents, and assign them to a local union. It is often fruitful to check on the kinds of support that a local is getting from its international parent. Another thing to look for on these reports is whether any union officer holds a number of highly paid posts at the same time.

Forms LM–2 and LM–3/Union Termination Reports

The financial portion of Forms LM–2 and LM–3 must be submitted by the labor union, along with a detailed statement of the circumstances and the effective date of the union's termination or loss of reporting identity, within 30 days of the action. A union absorbed by another labor organization must report the name, address and file number of that organization.

The circumstances surrounding a union's termination may reveal financial information about the union that takes it over, as well as leads about problems the local had with the international.

Form LM–10/Management Employer Report

Form LM–10, an annual report filed by employers, is used to state payments to or other financial arrangements with any union, its officers or employees other than those allowed under the Labor-Management Reporting Disclosure Act. For example, payments to individuals for help in persuading others to comply with the company's bargaining position would come under this category.

The financial information in this report is usually of little value, as no employers are going to file a report showing they may have broken the law. Names of union lawyers or management consultants are also included in LM–10, however, and can prove useful.

Form LM–15/Trusteeship Report and
Form LM–15A/Schedule of Selection of Officers and Delegates

The parent union assuming control or trusteeship of another must file Form LM–15 to disclose the reasons for taking control and when it happened. The report must provide a complete account of the financial situation at the time of the takeover.

A related form, LM–15A, must be filed along with LM–15 whenever there is a convention or meeting of the policy-determining body to which the subordinate union has sent delegates. This report is useful in determining the influence one particular union has over another.

Form LM–16/Termination of Trusteeship Information Report

Form LM–16 must be filed when the parent union relinquishes control of a union held in trusteeship. It includes the date and method of termination and the names, titles and method of selection of the subordinate union's officers.

Form LM–20/Agreement and Activities Report

Form LM–20 is required to be filed by persons, including labor relations consultants and other individuals and organizations, who make an agreement or other arrangements with an employer to undertake certain activities related to the collective bargaining rights of persons working for the employer. Examples of such agreements are a labor consulting firm that agrees to help an employer persuade employees not to exercise the right to organize and bargain collectively, or to supply the employer with information concerning the activities of employees of a labor organization in connection with a labor dispute. The form calls for the name, mailing address and description of the party filing; nature of agreement or arrangement; name and address of employer; date entered into agreement; object and description of activities; and names of employees to which the efforts are being directed.

Form LM–21/Receipts and Disbursement Report

Form LM–21 details the receipt and disbursement of funds involved in carrying out the type of arrangements described in LM–20. Individuals, consulting companies and organizations that receive funds from an employer for the purpose of influencing labor relations are required to outline where the payments came from and the amount; disbursements to employees and officers; related expenses for administration, publicity and professional fees; and any disbursements to outside parties made for the purpose of influencing employees for or against collective bargaining or to supply an employer with information concerning labor activities.

Form LM–30/Union Officer and Employee Report

Form LM–30 details some of the personal holdings of union officials and employees and can give valuable insight into their financial backgrounds. It consists of three parts, in which officials must disclose whether they:

- "Held an interest in, engaged in transactions (including loans) with, or derived income or other economic benefit of monetary value from an employer whose employees (the union) is actively seeking to represent." (Part 1)
- "Held an interest in or derived some economic benefit with monetary value from a business (1) a substantial part of which consists of buying from, selling or leasing out, otherwise dealing with the business of an employer whose employees (the labor union) represents or is actively seeking to represent, or (2) any part of which consists of buying from or selling or leasing directly or indirectly to, or otherwise dealing with your labor organization or a trust in which your labor organization is interested." (Part 2)
- "Received from an employer (other than 1 or 2 above) or from any labor relations consultant to an employer any payment of money or other thing of value." (Part 3)

The requirement of Part 3 is seldom met because it amounts to confessing that the law may have been broken. The value of the section is seen after a reporter discovers something, such as an executive director of a local chapter of the National Electrical Contractors Association giving the local business manager of the International Brotherhood of Electrical Workers (IBEW) a shotgun for Christmas, representing a conflict of interest.

Part 2 is important because many labor officials will disclose the required information. An example of the kinds of things to look for is a local union business manager who is both a trustee of a pension fund and a director of a bank which does business with the union and the pension fund. The union officer would have to disclose whether the bank purchased any mortgages from the pension fund or sold any to it, if it has bank accounts for the pension fund or local and what the union official was paid in director fees. The union official would also have to disclose if he or she owned any stock, when it was purchased and, sometimes, even the purchase price.

LMSA S–1/Surety Company Annual Report

Firms involved in administering a union's benefit fund must file the LMSA S–1 financial report. The amount of the premium and detailed information related to losses are included in this report.

In some cases, one company administers benefits for several different unions, or administers several different funds for one union. Fees often are based on hourly wages and the number of workers under the plan. You may find that the same company charges widely differing rates for the same kind of work.

Write to the Office of Labor-Management Services, Department of Labor, Washington, D.C. 20210, or the closest DOL regional office.

Register of Reporting Labor Organizations

The Register of Reporting Labor Organizations provides a listing of labor organizations required to file reports with the Department of Labor under the Labor-Management Reporting Disclosure Act. The publication is arranged by state in alphabetical order with listings under the following headings: AFL-CIO Trade Councils, Directly Affiliated Labor Unions, Affiliated Labor Organizations and Unaffiliated Labor Organizations. Subordinate local units of labor organizations also are listed. Each listing is assigned a file number that may speed answers to reporters' queries.

Write to the Secretary, Department of Labor, Washington, D.C. 20210, or the closest DOL region office.

LABOR ORGANIZATIONS AND CONTRACTS

Union Constitutions and Bylaws

Union constitutions and bylaws provide the basic structure and internal mechanisms of the labor organization. Areas covered include: qualifications for or restrictions to membership, levying assessments, participation in insurance or other benefit plans, authorization for disbursement of funds, audit requirements and procedures for the calling of regular and special meetings.

These dictums include procedures for selecting union officials and representatives to other labor organizations; disciplining and notice requirements such as fines, suspensions and expulsion; authorization for bargaining demands; ratification of contracts; authorization for strikes; and issuance of work permits.

Pay close attention to the internal mechanisms laid out in the union's constitution and bylaws for leads into how the leadership may circumvent reporting to the membership.

Write to the Secretary, Department of Labor, Washington, D.C. 20210, or the closest DOL office, or get a copy of the constitution and bylaws from the local union hall.

Union Contracts

Many states keep on file major collective bargaining agreements in the public and private sector. These agreements include contract obligations of both the employer and the labor union. Benefits such as vacation and sick leave, job descriptions, pay scales and working conditions are covered in these contracts.

Some states have on file memoranda of understanding—agreements between the employer and union that do not appear in the contract. You need to request these records specifically.

Union contracts are useful for any investigation of a labor organization. For example, by comparing union contracts within an industry, you may be able to determine if a union is so dominated by a certain company—receiving substantially lower wages and benefits than other companies in the industry offer—that it has become almost part of that firm. Some contracts are kept confidential by the employer at the union's request. If this is the case, you should ask to see in writing the stipulation closing the file. If public employees or public dollars are involved, the contract should be open.

Some states have a "union agreements index" usually arranged by international union name and usually including the local covered by the agreement, employer's name and effective dates of the contract.

These records can be obtained from the state DOL or other comparable state agency.

About 8,000 collective bargaining agreements of private industries and the public sector are available from the Bureau of Labor Statistics. These include virtually all pacts covering 1,000 or more employees, exclusive of railroads and airlines, which are the responsibility of the National Mediation Board (see below, "National Mediation Board Case Files").

Write to the Division of Development and Labor-Management Relations, Bureau of Labor Statistics, Washington, D.C. 20210.

National Labor Relations Board Files

The National Labor Relations Board (NLRB) is an independent federal agency that administers laws relating to collective bargaining, unfair labor practices and other labor relations issues. The agency issues about 1,000 decisions each year that apply government regulations and rulings to individual labor disputes. Most decisions relate to two broad areas of labor relations:

- *Unfair Labor Practices.* Labor management disputes covered in unfair labor practices records include bad-faith bargaining, questions of representation, contract violations, arbitration, collective bargaining rights, organization tactics, election challenges (union officers or collective bargaining) and internal union problems.

   The initial form filed is called a "charge." The parties involved are listed on the charge as well as the nature of the charge. As investigation of the charge progresses, other information may include investigation findings, transcripts of hearings, decisions and appropriate affirmative actions.

   Some of the more common unfair labor practices include interference with the formation of a union, work slowdowns or stoppages and certain types of boycotts.
- *Certification and Decertification.* When a labor union becomes the official bargaining unit for employees, the NLRB certifies the election results. It is a regular occurrence for the employers or unions to challenge the results if they lose. Other investigated issues included in this file may be questions related to representation, such as disagreements arising over whether certain employees are considered members of management or labor.

   The initial form filed by an employer or labor organization in a union election case is called a petition. Investigations, hearings and elections also are included in the files.

Reporters interested in a particular dispute should try to get the full name of the case, if possible, and call the regional office, which should be able to provide the charges filed in the case and the disposition.

The NLRB keeps files containing hearing records on all cases for which there was a trial. The files contain records of all charges, complaints and decisions relating

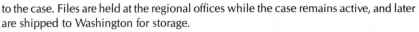

to the case. Files are held at the regional offices while the case remains active, and later are shipped to Washington for storage.

Remember, the NLRB can act only when it is requested to do so. Individuals, employers or unions may initiate cases by filing charges of unfair labor practices or "petitions" for employee representation elections.

Charges and petitions are filed in the NLRB field offices. The NLRB regional director then conducts hearings to determine if a charge or petition warrants further action. Two-thirds of all unfair labor charges are either withdrawn or dismissed at the hearing level.

If the NLRB determines the charge has merit, it will issue a "complaint" and take further action to see the unfair labor practice is halted. It may seek an injunction in district court to prevent or remedy an unfair labor practice.

Regional NLRB decisions on certification petitions or charges of unfair labor practices may be appealed to the national level. When the NLRB settles a dispute at the national level, these findings and recommendations are known as "decisions."

Unfair labor practices are filed by number and letter, classified as "C" cases, and the agency publishes a daily register of decisions. The NLRB classifies certification and decertification files as "R" cases.

NLRB files can be obtained from the National Labor Relations Board, 1717 Pennsylvania Ave. N.W., Washington, D.C. 20570, but officials generally recommend that reporters check first with the regional office where the case arose. The regional offices can order copies of inactive files stored at the national office, but the process can take several weeks.

Grievances

Under union contracts, employees may file grievances against the employer that deal with a wide range of topics, including working conditions, promotions and alleged discrimination. The record includes the name and address of the complainant, nature and basis of the complaint, name and address of respondent, labor organization and employer. If the employee feels that the union has failed to handle properly his or her grievance, he or she can appeal to the NLRB, charging that the union has failed to provide adequate representation.

Complaints filed by federal employees against their union can be obtained from the Federal Labor Relations Authority (FLRA) in Washington, D.C. If public employees are involved at the state or local level, check the appropriate government agency (such as the state division of labor or city personnel office). Some jurisdictions close the records until the grievance procedure is completed.

National Mediation Board Case Files

Information in National Mediation Board case files deals with labor-management disputes in the railroad and airline industries, including the collective bargaining procedures, arbitration and questions of representation. Copies of collective bargaining agreements, awards and interpretations are generally available for public inspection. In addition, to their value in providing information related to the unions involved, they also are useful for stories on the business side, as they provide vital information related to costs.

Copies of case files can be obtained through a Freedom of Information Act request to the National Mediation Board, 1425 K St. N.W., Washington, D.C. 20572. Information related to railroads can be obtained from the National Railroad Adjustment Board, 175 W. Jackson St., Suite A935, Chicago, Ill. 60604. A Freedom of Information request may be necessary to obtain individual case files.

Federal Mediation and Conciliation Case Files

If the employer and labor organization reach an impasse in contract negotiations, the Federal Mediation and Conciliation Service (FMCS) may be called in to work out a compromise, if both sides agree.

The initial form, a dispute notice, must be filed at least 30 days in advance of a contract termination or reopening date. This record provides the names of the company and union involved in the dispute, contract expiration date and, occasionally, the names and addresses of contacts.

Local commissioners working the case are the best sources. Dispute notices can be obtained from the Federal Mediation and Conciliation Service, 2100 K St. N.W., Washington, D.C. 20427, but all other information obtained by the FMCS is generally considered confidential.

The Bureau of National Affairs (BNA), a private corporation, publishes Labor Arbitration Reports, a complete record of labor arbitration settlements; it is available at most large libraries or by writing the Bureau of National Affairs, 1231 25th St. N.W., Washington, D.C. 20037.

Arbitration Case Files

Another option in labor-management disputes is to call in an independent arbitrator. The American Arbitration Association, a non-governmental organization, provides a listing of individuals who act as neutral parties. You may wish to background the individual chosen for possible leanings either toward management or labor.

Although the association is non-governmental, it sometimes is willing to be open with reporters. Write the American Arbitration Association, 140 W. 51st St., New York, N.Y. 10020.

Case files of arbitrations handled by FMCS are available from its Division of Arbitration Services. Case files can be obtained by written request under FOIA from the Division of Arbitration Services, Federal Mediation and Conciliation Service, U.S. Government, Washington, D.C. 20427.

PENSIONS

Form 5500 Pension Plan Description, Summary

Form 5500, the annual report, provides the most complete information available about union pension funds. Areas covered include financial statements and schedules, assets and liabilities, receipts and disbursements, changes in fund balance and schedules of assets held for investment purposes, detailed information on transactions with parties of interest and those exceeding 3 percent of the value of the plan's assets, opinions of an independent accountant and insurance data for some plans.

This is the basic document for investigating a corrupt union or union and management hierarchy suspected of stealing from a pension fund. For example, examine all loans made from the pension fund. Do the parties have any direct relationship with union officials? Does the security for the loan equal its value? Look at the potential conflicts of interest. What is the relationship between the accountant and the union? With whom does the union invest its money? Be sure to order Schedule B also, which provides information on the number of participants, cost and whether annual contributions have been made.

Write to the Pension and Welfare Benefits Administration, Department of Labor, Washington, D.C. 20210, or the closest DOL regional office. It may now take up to two months to get copies of this form as it first must go to the IRS, which deletes from the report all personal income statements. Some DOL officials estimate it may be two or three years before a Form 5500 submitted to the IRS is processed and made available to the DOL for disclosure. Be persistent and try to obtain the form directly from the IRS.

UNION POLITICAL ACTIVITIES

FEC Form 1/Statement of Organization, Political Action Committees

Many unions operate political action committees (PACs) to support candidates for federal office. Any union that decides to form a PAC must file a Statement of Organization within 10 days of that decision. FEC Form 1 includes the names and addresses of the committee and the labor union, the custodian of record, the principal officers and a list of all banks, safety deposit boxes and any other fund repositories. Upon dissolution, all committees must notify the Federal Election Commission, 999 E St. N.W., Washington, D.C. 20463. (For more detailed information, see Chapter 8, "Investigating Politicians.")

State and Local Levels   At the state and local level, labor unions are required to document their PACs in a Statement of Organization similar to FEC Form 1. Areas include addresses of committee, name of the candidate and union, committee officers and other information.

These reports may be useful in establishing the local union's sphere of influence by analyzing the activities of those receiving the money from labor.

Check your state law, the state elections commission, the secretary of state's office and the local city or county clerk.

FEC Form 3/Disclosure Report of Receipts and Expenditures, Political Action Committees

Labor unions operating PACs also must submit the Disclosure Report of Receipts and Expenditures at preset intervals based on the election year.

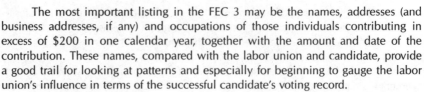

The most important listing in the FEC 3 may be the names, addresses (and business addresses, if any) and occupations of those individuals contributing in excess of $200 in one calendar year, together with the amount and date of the contribution. These names, compared with the labor union and candidate, provide a good trail for looking at patterns and especially for beginning to gauge the labor union's influence in terms of the successful candidate's voting record.

Write to the Federal Election Commission, 999 E St. N.W., Washington, D.C. 20463.

State and Local Levels   Labor union PACs supporting candidates or ballot measures at the state or local level must usually disclose their finances in a disclosure report which is like FEC Form 3. Information filed includes officers and their addresses, the amount of money on hand at different reporting times, receipts and fund-raising events, the total dollar value of in-kind contributions, the name and address of each contributor and the candidate supported.

As with other union financial reports, the contributions to a political campaign can provide information useful for investigating a union, such as loans showing possible connections between the union and the official.

Check with your secretary of state, state election commission or city or county clerk about the availability of state or local campaign contribution disclosure reports.

WORKERS' COMPENSATION RECORDS

The administration of workers' compensation varies from state to state, but generally employers must file injury claims with a board, commission or some administrative body that keeps records. If an employer contests a worker's claim, the case goes before that body. It is in those case files you can find a collection of valuable information, although you might have to get around privacy issues.

To get a broader view of injury claims in your state, look for the annual reports by the workers' compensation board or commission, state Labor Department, the U.S. Chamber of Commerce and the National Safety Council. OSHA and the Bureau of Labor Statistics, both part of the U.S. Labor Department, also collect injury statistics, but methods of collection vary widely and result in a wide range of estimates.

Also, contact your state and private universities, where the best studies are usually done (often by economics professors). There also is a series of studies of state workers' compensation systems published by the Workers' Compensation Research Institute in Cambridge, Mass. Other organizations that put out reports or have more up-to-date knowledge (although each has its own viewpoint) are insurance company associations and state trial lawyer associations.

OCCUPATIONAL SAFETY AND HEALTH ADMINISTRATION

OSHA Form 200/Employer's Log and Summary of Occupational Injuries and Illnesses

OSHA Form 200, an annual summary of work-related injuries and illnesses, is supposed to be posted each January in a conspicuous place in the work place. Visit the plant yourself or ask an employee to read it for you.

Occupational Injuries and Illnesses of the United States (Year)

A helpful tool in determining which work places are the most hazardous in your area is this annual survey, published by the Bureau of Labor Statistics, Washington, D.C. 20212. Employers are chosen randomly to participate in the survey and are not named.

Different industries are given percentage ratings according to hazards, such as injuries, illnesses and fatalities. Several states compile similar statewide lists through their labor bureaus. The list indexes industries by Standard Industrial Classification (SIC) codes, which are deciphered in the Thomas Register, available in any library.

OSHA's Access to Records Rule

Under this helpful OSHA regulation, workers or their representatives (this can be a reporter, union official or anyone with written permission) must be granted access on 15 days notice to certain company health records. Company records available under the rule include employee medical records and any analysis of them; a list of toxic substances in the work place; and any exposure records, including any monitoring of the work place, biological monitoring and material safety data sheets. A formal complaint can be lodged with OSHA by the worker or a representative if access is denied.

OSHA Hazard Communication Standard/The Right-to-Know Law

Under OSHA standards passed in 1983 and phased into effect during 1985 and 1986, employers are required to let workers know which chemicals in the work place are hazardous and how to protect themselves against those hazards. OSHA estimated at the time of the standards' adoption that there were more than 575,000 chemical products in American work places. The standards were designed to provide an estimated 14 million workers in 300,000 manufacturing establishments with greater access to information on chemical hazards in the work place.

Under the so-called right-to-know law, containers of hazardous chemicals must provide an immediate warning to workers; more detailed information on the chemical and its hazards must be made available on material safety data sheets; and the employer must offer training to ensure that workers understand the labels and know how to handle hazardous substances safely.

Many states had their own versions of right-to-know laws prior to passage of the federal standards. OSHA's standards pre-empt state laws covering hazardous communication in states without state OSHA programs; states with their own OSHA programs must have state right-to-know laws approved by OSHA.

The OSHA standards place the burden of assessing hazards and developing labels on the companies that manufacture or import chemicals. Companies using the materials are required to retain labels and provide information and training to employees.

OSHA regulations called for employers to be in compliance with all provisions of the standards by May 1986, but many companies had difficulty meeting the deadline.

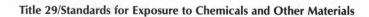

Title 29/Standards for Exposure to Chemicals and Other Materials

Title 29 of the Code of Federal Regulations (Parts 1901–1999) contains OSHA's standards for exposure to specific chemicals, mists, fumes, dusts, etc., as well as the government's rules for state occupational safety plans, inspections and employers' reporting requirements. Most of the standards are "consensus" standards developed by the affected industries years ago and adopted wholesale by the government. As more information becomes public on substances, the standards are often challenged in court as being too generous or restrictive. Standards for specific work-place hazards can be obtained from the Occupational Safety and Health Administration, Third Street and Constitution Avenue N.W., Washington, D.C. 20210. "A Pocket Guide to Chemical Hazards," published by the National Institute for Occupational Safety and Health (NIOSH), is available for purchase from the U.S. Government Printing Office. NIOSH'S Washington-area office is at the Hubert Humphrey Building, 200 Independence Ave. S.W., Washington, D.C. 20201. It has a large research facility in Cincinnati, Ohio.

NIOSH also conducts health hazard evaluations (HHEs) at work sites upon request. Check with one of NIOSH's three regional offices for HHEs that have been done in your area, or write to National Institute for Occupational Safety and Health, Hazard Evaluation Service Branch, U.S. Department of Health and Human Services, Cincinnati, Ohio 45226.

The National Institutes of Health (NIH) can provide access to computerized information on the most recent research on harmful effects of various chemicals. Contact the NIH National Library of Medicine, 8600 Rockville Pike, Bethesda, Md. 20894.

OSHA Inspector's Reports on General Plant Conditions

Information on general plant conditions can be obtained through a firm's latest inspection by either the state OSHA agency or the federal OSHA office in your state. OSHA Inspector's Reports are public information, but they are subject to the Privacy Act and can be screened for confidential information.

OSHA Form 7/Complaint and Imminent Danger Inspection Request

You also can file a Freedom of Information Act request for a copy of the complaint, OSHA Form 7, or the "Imminent Danger Inspection Request," which may have sparked the inspection. Both are usually filed by workers or their union representatives, but the name of the person filing may be deleted if anonymity has been requested.

OSHA Citations

OSHA citations are supposed to be posted conspicuously in the work place. If the company or the government appealed the citation, the Occupational Safety and Health Review Commission will have the files. OSHA citations are public information and in most cases a Freedom of Information Act request should not be necessary.

OSHA Printouts

Until recently, the Office of Information at OSHA's headquarters would provide a computerized printout of a company's reporting history under a Freedom of Information Act request. However, because of recent budget cuts and regulation changes, OSHA is considering whether such computer searches fall under the category of "special statistical studies." One OSHA official has said the agency may discontinue computer search services or begin requesting payment for the full cost of any search.

Publications

The Occupational Safety and Health Reporter, a non-governmental publication, lists all appeals to the State Occupational and Health Review Commission by name of employer, address and some information about the case. It is published weekly by the Bureau of National Affairs, 1231 25th St. N.W., Washington, D.C. 20037.

The Occupational Health and Safety Letter, published bimonthly, is a timely source of information on worker safety and health. Many law offices, especially workers' compensation firms, subscribe. Try business libraries or medical libraries, too. For your own copy, write to Environews Inc., 952 National Press Building, Washington, D.C. 20045; (202) 662–7299.

Reporters can get the industry side of worker health through the American Industrial Health Council, 1330 Connecticut Ave. N.W., Suite 300, Washington, D.C. 20036.

HEALTH AND SAFETY EXPERTS

Labor Unions

Union health and safety committees historically have been lax in alerting workers and management to work-place hazards. But this is changing and some unions are good sources of the causes behind members' deaths and injuries. National labor unions with good health and safety expert include:

- AFL-CIO, Department of Occupational Safety and Health, 815 16th St. N.W., Washington, D.C. 20006.
- Oil, Chemical and Atomic Workers' Union, Health and Safety Division, P.O. Box 2812, Denver, Colo. 80201.
- United Rubber Workers Union, 87 S. High St., Akron, Ohio 44308.
- United Auto Workers, Health and Safety Department, 8000 E. Jefferson, Detroit, Mich. 48214.

Schools and Universities

Another useful source is the Women's Occupational Health Resource Center, 117 St. John's Place, Brooklyn, N.Y. 11217.

Many universities also fund "Worker Extension Schools," or "Labor Schools." Some offer occupational safety and health programs and use experts who know conditions in local plants. The University and College Labor Education Association (UCLEA) publishes an annual directory of member institutions and professional council members. It can be obtained by writing Gene Daniels, Labor Education and Research Service, Ohio State University, 35 East Seventh St., Suite 200, Cincinnati, Ohio 45202.

Schools of public health are good sources, especially those at Harvard University, the University of Illinois and the University of Pittsburgh. Also try the University of Cincinnati's Department of Environmental Health and the Mt. Sinai School of Medicine's Environmental Science Laboratories in New York City.

For more information on worker health and safety, see Chapter 15, "Health Care."

CHAPTER 13

Law Enforcement

Law enforcement should always be a prime source of curiosity to the news media. Are your police honest? Are they efficient? Do any of them abuse their power? Can they solve crimes? Are they doing all they can to prevent crimes? Do they respect the rights of others, or have they become arrogant, above the law? The news reporter's most important question is: Are there any sources inside the department on whom I can rely for the truth?

by J. HARRY JONES, JR.

To most police officers reporters are welcome only as long as they are not only anti-crime, but pro-police. If reporters turn a critical eye on the department or any of its knights in blue, immediately they become an enemy to be shunned, misled, sometimes even harassed.

No matter how noble some police officers might be, they know that out there among the public are lots of people who fail to appreciate them, who misunderstand them, who may even dislike them. Second from the top on their list of enemies — just below the criminals — are journalists.

Police officers and journalists, as a matter of fact, are two of the most cliquish tribes in modern civilization. And they are often instinctively hostile to one another.

This does not make investigating law enforcement easy.

The task has become more difficult in recent years as the educational background of police officers improves and entire departments become more computerized and sophisticated in the way they handle the news media.

Police departments are leaning more and more heavily on the image makers of public relations to help them deal with the press. (They call it "public information," but don't be fooled by that euphemism.)

Another very real problem every newspaper faces is the fact that a large segment of its readers will side with the police in most disputes.

A law-and-order mentality is pervasive in our country. Attack the police, no matter how legitimately, and you are going to find a lot of people out there who will be madder at you than they are at the police miscreants.

"So what?" they will demand. "It's the killers and muggers and rapists out there you ought to be after, not the men and women who go out and risk their lives every day to keep our city safe."

It is not always as easy as one might think to determine just how good or bad a police department is by looking at it. There are some investigative approaches and techniques that can work for you, however.

First, as a point of reference, let's consider the question of what a good police department is really like.

The Ideal Police Department

Who appoints the chief of police—the mayor, the city council, a city manager or (as in St. Louis and Kansas City) a board of police commissioners appointed by the governor? Did the appointer have the guts and good sense to choose an honest, strong-willed professional with no political connections? Or did he or she select some politically savvy law-keeper who will acquiesce when asked to give special treatment to the politically or financially powerful in the city?

In a perfect police department, everyone from the chief down to the newest recruit at the Police Academy abhors police corruption. No one would dream of doing anything dishonest. Police officers would even turn in their best friends in the department if they caught them so much as fixing a traffic ticket.

The perfect department's internal affairs division is choice duty because it doesn't have much to do. When handed a case, however, it investigates the accused officers with the same vigor that it would use for the head of organized crime in the city. If the accused are found guilty, the discipline against them is harsh, and the rest of the department welcomes the severity of punishment instead of complaining of unfairness or lack of understanding.

This ideal department wouldn't have to be pressured into establishing an independent citizens' review panel to look into complaints about officers from the public—in fact, it has already asked for one to be set up and staffed by independent citizens not connected with the department. When asked, the department cooperates fully with the panel.

Citizen complaints are rare in the ideal department. All the racists and sadists and trigger-happy cowboys have been weeded out of the force early in their careers. Race relations, in fact, aren't much of a problem. Bigotry is viewed as synonymous with stupidity within the police ranks. A real effort began long ago at minority hiring. Minority representation on the department is at least equal to the percentage of each minority group in the city's population.

Police Academy training is tough and thorough, with a strong emphasis on civil liberties and respect for one's fellow human beings. Entry into the academy isn't easy either. Weak or incompetent candidates wash out early. A lot of officers are studying off-hours to earn A.A. or B.A. degrees; a few are even working toward master's degrees.

The chief of our ideal department has set up a system of promotions that is fair and wise. The chief's top commanders have earned their jobs; so have his or her captains, lieutenants, detectives, sergeants and the rest. Every department will have its political game-playing by the ambitious, but the members of this one rise in rank for what they do and how they do it, not who they are or who they know.

The pay in this department is good. The department is not short-handed. Still, everyone finds enough work to fill each eight-hour day. No police officer's union or "fraternal order" has formed because no one has really felt the need for one.

Amazingly, the detectives in this department get along splendidly with the county and city prosecutor's office. (Since this is Utopia, the prosecutor's office is just as honest and efficient as the police department.) Rarely does a police officer take a case to the prosecutor if it isn't strong. Rarely does the prosecutor find a reason not to file a charge brought by the police. Nor are arrests made frivolously and without sound cause.

No one in this department has shot anyone in a long, long time except in clear-cut cases of protecting the public, another officer or him or herself from imminent danger. There are two reasons for this: The police are taught a profound respect for human life, and the chief has imposed a tight firearms policy—one much more restrictive than that which the state laws dictate.

The department's intelligence division keeps track of organized crime almost as well as the FBI does, although it lacks some of the federal agency's Congress-approved tools. The federal investigative agencies have learned they can trust this city's police, and they swap information much more freely than in most cities.

The department's juvenile bureau is staffed carefully by men and women with compassion, tact and firmness. Its arson squad has actually solved some cases without the help of finding the arsonist's own charred remains on the scene.

No, not all of the crimes in this town are solved, not by a long shot. Even in this hypothetical situation, it wouldn't be fair to suggest even a 75 percent rate of success. But the detectives are bright, hard-working, thorough. They don't muddy crime scenes or overlook important details, and they aren't afraid to admit what mistakes they make.

Their testimony in court is straight, accurate and honest—no embellishments just to help "keep the bad guys off the streets."

Crime in this city continues, but the criminal element knows this isn't a good city in which to do business, and many crooks have moved elsewhere to avoid this city-with-good-cops. For one thing, the law-abiding citizenry has so much confidence in their department that they cooperate with it practically all the time. They call the police when they see something suspicious. They usually testify willingly in court when necessary to help identify the right wrong-doer. Try to intimidate a potential witness and these police officers come down on you hard. A witness can feel protected in this city.

The public information officer for this department understands the media and its needs. With little to hide, this officer almost always tells the truth. Within the confines of state disclosure laws, the public information officer even volun-teers information at times, and if the officer doesn't have an answer to a question, he or she usually knows whom to have the reporters call to find the answer.

The biggest problem the media have with this perfect police department is the absence of leaks within it. Respectful of civil rights and liberties, the police officers know their state's disclosure laws and abide by them. The nosy newsper-son who would rush into print with undocumented police suspicions has a rough time covering crime in this city.

Of course, your police department doesn't measure up to this ideal. In fact, it may fall short in several or even all of these areas. Uncovering these shortcom-ings won't always be easy—especially if you're going to be looking for records and documents to bolster or prove your case. Such records often exist, as you will see, but privacy laws being what they are today, you may have to start with a source.

Developing Human Sources

Sources inside a police department are usually essential to a successful investiga-tion of police misconduct. They can alert you to a problem, point you in the right direction or even smuggle out of the department the documents that back up their claims. (Praise be for the duplicating machine.) Police officers, like a lot of other people, write lots of revealing memos to each other, as well as official reports stamped "Confidential."

Policing the Police: Two Success Stories

In 1987, David Freed, a law enforcement reporter for The Los Angeles Times, was surprised to hear a deputy district attorney boast about how strong a case he had against two accused armed robbers. The defendants, he said, actually had been observed in the act by Los Angeles police detectives as they robbed a video rental shop and savagely beat two employees.

But why, Freed asked, didn't the police intervene to prevent the bloodshed? The prosecutor said he didn't know.

Freed went elsewhere for an answer. The headline over the story that resulted read: "Citizens Terrorized as Police Look On." It was an amazing story of official police ineptitude and heartless insensitivity to the police's traditional role of protecting the public from crime.

Freed's story speaks for itself:

> On a November morning in 1986, two robbers entered a videotape rental shop near Koreatown, slammed clerk Eunsook Oh to the floor and tore off her jewelry.
> One of the robbers clubbed manager Brian Ahn with a revolver and kicked him in the face, then put the gun to Ahn's head and demanded that he lead them to the shop's safe.

Ahn's terrified clerk reached for an alarm. She didn't need to. Already outside, watching, were 10 undercover police detectives. They had been following the suspects for two days and watched them go into the shop. They already had ample reason to make an arrest that would have prevented the attack. Now they let it run its course—and readied their shotguns.

For the Special Investigations Section of the Los Angeles Police Department, the tactics were standard procedure.

The secretive, 19-man unit watches armed robbers and burglars but rarely tries to arrest them until after the thieves have victimized shopkeepers, homeowners and others, an investigation by The Times found.

According to The Times editors who submitted Freed's work to the IRE for an award, Freed's "nine-month investigation documented a long-standing pattern in which detectives of the Los Angeles Police Department's Special Investigations Section ignored legitimate opportunities to arrest dozens of dangerous felons, waiting instead to watch them commit potentially violent acts of armed robbery or burglary and arrest them afterwards."

In effect, the LAPD's SIS detectives were using unsuspecting citizens as live bait, The Times observed.

Freed also discovered that this same SIS unit was killing suspects at a rate far higher than was explainable.

"Its detectives have killed 23 suspects and wounded 23 others since 1965, when the SIS was formed," he wrote. "In addition the surveillance detectives have been involved in more than 20 other incidents in which they shot at suspects and missed."

A majority of those shot, he found, had been shot in the back. The SIS was killng far more people than the LAPD's SWAT team, in fact.

How did Freed do it? "By studying criminal court records and copies of arrest warrants buried in the archives of more than a dozen courthouses," The Times editors said. He also reviewed hundreds of police reports and press releases dating back to 1977 involving more than 600 incidents in which suspects were wounded or killed by LA police.

The Times had to threaten a lawsuit before reporters could get many of the files.

Countless interviews, of course, were also necessary, including those with officials from other departments who were willing to express their opinion of the LAPD's human bait operation. Commented one: "I've never seen anything like this. The fundamental standard of police work is to protect life. That's not consistent with a strategy in which you let a guy rob a place and hope he doesn't kill someone."

If Freed had some confidential sources within the department for the story, he did not blow their cover. That he probably did is suggested in the advice to journalists he provided in the application for the IRE award. This advice was: "Work hard at developing police sources before embarking on a subject which the department may have spent years trying to cover up."

What did Freed and The Times accomplish?

The public became aware of a problem. It seems safe to assume that SIS officers functioned more discreetly as a result of the publicity.

Freed also prompted issuance of a new police policy. The LAPD put out a new order, titled "Reverence for Human Life." It instructs the LAPD's finest not to put innocent people's lives in jeopardy in the course of their police work.

Far more common than the indiscretions of the Los Angeles SIS unit is the simple phenomenon of routine, run-of-the-mill police brutality. Give a young man or woman a .38, a slapper, a night stick, all the other armaments of modern police work and a license to use them almost with impunity, and at least some are going to abuse their privilege. It's up to the press to see that such abuses occur as infrequently as possible.

The "use of excessive force by an officer" was the deserved target of a team of three reporters from the Orange County Register in 1987.

Their problems were magnified by the fact that they were examining police activity in 26 cities and one county, Orange, with a total population of 2 million people. They zeroed in on 645 claims that had been filed against police officers between 1983 and 1986. They not only examined records, but interviewed claimants, attorneys, police officers, their supervisors and university researchers.

Nearly every government unit tried to keep records from the newspaper. They went to court three times to obtain what they wanted. The six-month effort by reporters Michael A. Lednovich, Donna Wares and Barry Klein enabled them to conclude, among other things:

- That at least 467 of the 2,332 cops in Orange County—one in five—had been accused of excessive force; that less than 2 percent of them had been named in 17 percent of the cases examined.
- That officers were almost never prosecuted for using excessive force (only one of the 467 was) and state law enabled police departments to keep secret whatever, if any, internal disciplining is carried out.
- That 93 percent of those filing complaints had no felony convictions.
- That three of the county's 24 police department were hit with almost half the complaints—those in Santa Ana, Huntington Beach and Newport Beach.
- That taxpayers paid at least $3.2 million to settle excessive force claims in the four years. The highest was for $395,000 to the mother of a 5-year-old who was mistakenly shot and killed by a police officer in Stanton.

Off-the-Record Informants

Another thought on developing sources within the police ranks was suggested by James Dygert, a former reporter and city editor at the Dayton Daily News: In addition to developing low-level and clerical sources, Dygert said it often pays off to cultivate a top-level source "who likes to think he can control a reporter by giving him off-the-record information, thus preventing him from using it until the source gives the go-ahead.

"Some journalists argue against off-the-record arrangements," Dygert said, "but I suspect that's because they don't understand how to use them to their advantage. I always found I was in a much better position when I had possession of the information under that restraint rather than not have the information. Once I had the information I usually could figure out a way to get it out and use it without violating any understanding with the source, such as going back to the source and persuading him to let me use it on a non-attributable basis because I was getting it from other sources anyway but preferred to work with him."

Although it usually is hard to prove something is amiss inside a law enforcement agency, it usually is pretty easy to sense a bad situation. Sometimes you can feel it in the atmosphere at police headquarters. A department riddled with political intrigue, ineptness or corruption simply has a different feel to it than an honest, well-run organization. Maybe it's the way police employees interact, the way certain officers whisper in corners, watch each other or talk about each other behind their backs. Or it might be their nervousness when you, the reporter, visit the department.

Insiders

If either your prosecutor's office or police are in need of reform, there's always the chance one will blow the whistle on the other.

Police often don't like prosecutors because they won't file charges as often as police would like. Prosecutors often become angry at the police for bringing them poorly prepared cases.

Each possesses documents—files on specific cases—that you probably shouldn't be allowed to see but can, with the help of a friendly source. (Frequently that part of the "secret" report that will be of value to you is *not* that part of the report that has justified its labeling as secret. It is good to remember this so that in the process of exposing either the police or the prosecutor you don't wrong some innocent—or presumed innocent—person in the process. Both agencies, of course, love the privacy laws because they not only protect the innocent, they keep some of the law enforcement agency's mistakes out of public view.)

If you have good sources inside any of the federal investigative agencies or the U.S. attorney's office, query them about local law enforcement. They usually have good insight on just how good or bad, honest or dishonest, the locals are. They also have access to records that are hard to get.

If you *don't* have good sources within federal law enforcement, develop some. Excellent, generic sources on crime and corruption are federal agents who are frustrated by the fact that they know so much but can't do anything because their agency lacks jurisdiction. They may be whistle-blowers and will risk censure from bureaucrats to leak the pertinent data to a trustworthy newsperson.

Note that I used the word *trustworthy*, not *friendly*. If you play up to law enforcement agents, be they local, state or federal, you may win friends, but you won't always win respect. The newsperson whom an officer respects—and thus will leak sensitive information to—has sights set for the jugular vein and won't be anyone's patsy.

Private detectives also are sometimes good sources about what's going on inside police departments. It's not that all private eyes are trustworthy. It's not that most private eyes, if they do feed you some good information, aren't doing it to settle some private grudge. But you take your sources where you can get them, evaluating their information carefully.

Yet another good source can be the professional informants. Some informants perform their function to stay out of jail. Others do so just for the thrill of it. If they are good police informants, they can just as easily be made good sources for you.

Using the Records

Crime Statistics

If you do sense a less-than-perfect situation, among the many places to start looking are the department's own crime statistics, produced monthly for the local city council or other governing body. Don't just look at the totals. Examine the details. Compare them with statistics in each category—such as rape or other felonies,— from past years (especially if the department appears to have slipped from a good to a poor status recently). Look for trends. Play with the statistics. Approach the raw facts (assuming that what is published is factual) from different angles. Look for conclusions the police appear to have ignored. Inquire if the police have in some drawer somewhere other compilations that they did not bother to publish. You may come up with some pertinent questions with such efforts—maybe even some surprising answers.

When David Burnham of The New York Times was covering the criminal justice system, he used to warn his readers not to take raw crime statistics too literally: "A number of surveys conducted by the President's Crime Commission, the Justice Department and the Census Bureau have shown that many people do not tell the police when they have been the victim of a crime. Because of this, it is not known whether changes in the number and rate of crimes reported to the police parallel changes in the total number of crimes that are committed."

Burnham offers more guidance in a 1977 IRE pamphlet: "Crime Statistics: How Not to be Abused." Reporters and editors should show great caution about suggesting that increases or decreases in the number of arrests for any given crime reflect changes in criminal activity. Almost always, changes in the number of arrests are the result of changes in police department policy, such as the number of men assigned to a special unit—gambling, for example—or the imposition of a secret arrest quota."

Police chiefs have been known even to fake sudden increases in crimes to influence the upcoming police budget.

Subpoenas

One fertile source of documented, on-the-record information about crime (or at least about what crimes a grand jury may be investigating) are the returns on grand jury subpoenas—particularly those demanding certain specific records to be brought by a witness under subpoena. Affidavits filed in support of search warrants or permission to eavesdrop electronically sometimes also become matters of public record in the U.S. District Clerk's office and can provide good leads, if not thoroughly developed news stories.

An informant approached two Los Angeles Times reporters to report that an investigation was underway into the dealings of a Burbank accountant who supposedly had bilked investors out of $10 million in a phony plan involving bicycle imports from Hong Kong. He also maintained the investigation was being kept quiet because some police officers were investors in the scheme and had even induced others to invest. The informant said he knew that the district attorney's office had seized the accountant's records as part of the investigation.

No one at the district attorney's office wanted to talk to the reporters. They quickly headed for the Burbank municipal court to look up recent search warrants, which become public record in California 10 days after they are filed. They found the warrant for the accountant's records, and also the documents attached to the search warrant and to the affidavit filed to support its issuance. These documents enabled them to publish a story the next day with the following details: The accountant had a record of embezzlement; his record was known to at least two of the detectives who had invested and sought out other investors; and about half of the members of the Burbank Lions Club were among the victims. One of the documents included a complete list of the complaining victims with their addresses and telephone numbers. Another revealed that the accountant had sent an envelope filled with cash almost every day for four months to a racing form publisher suspected of being a major bookmaker.

The supporting documents are so complete because they are what law enforcement agents use to persuade a judge to issue the search warrant. The tougher the judge's reputation for demanding sufficient evidence, the more complete will be the report.

Coroner's Report

A frequently neglected arm of law enforcement well-deserving of close scrutiny by reporters is the coroner's or medical examiner's office.

Remember the old television series "Quincy" starring Jack Klugman? He played a cross between a doctor and a detective on the staff of the Los Angeles County Coroner's Office. Real coroners and medical examiners seldom get that involved, but they play an important role in the justice system and should be cultivated as sources of information.

In one case, a woman appeared to have died from a flaming car crash. The story first hit the newspaper as a traffic collision account. But after the autopsy, it became a murder investigation: The coroner's pathologist found she had a bullet hole behind her ear.

Autopsies rarely provide that kind of surprise, but they can supply information about the victim that will add interest to even routine crime reports. By reading the autopsy report, you can learn quite a bit about the dead person. Instead of the imprecise estimates of friends or police, the report will tell you exactly how much the victim weighed and exactly how tall the victim was. It will give details of the victim's physical condition prior to dying. There will be notations about scars and any abnormalities. It will also show if there were any signs of alcohol or drug use.

Medical examiners and coroners are in a peculiar position, balancing on the tightrope between the two professions of law and medicine. Not only responsible for determining the identity of the dead and the time and cause of death, which are medical questions, these officials also have the task of determining the legal issue of the manner of death.

The cause of death refers to the actual medical reason for death, such as heart failure or a knife wound. Manner refers to the circumstances—natural, accidental, homicidal or suicidal—under which the person died. Close attention should be paid to the coroner's findings at the early stages of an investigation because they sometimes disagree with the preliminary findings detectives have announced to the news media.

Coroners can provide crucial clues to detectives. For example, a medical examiner for New York City was called to help in a case in which a young woman was raped and strangled in an upstate community. He discovered a contact lens in one eye of the dead woman and directed the police to search the car of the suspect for the other lens. It was found and became a key factor in gaining a conviction.

Medical examiners and coroners deal with traumatic deaths, and their findings can influence insurance settlements, prosecutions and product safety. A ruling of suicide can cost a family of the deceased the double indemnity life insurance payments. Successful prosecution of a murder case many times can turn on the findings of the coroner. Although they usually deal with death after the fact, their work also can lead to the prevention of death through the reporting of unsafe products.

One warning: Don't hold your local coroner or medical examiner to the standards of Quincy, who, for instance, always seems able to pin down the time of death as being between 2:30 and 2:45 in the morning. Dr. Henry Ryan, Maine's chief medical examiner, said he has suffered from comparison with the intrepid Quincy. "When testifying in a case, I always feel extremely proud when I can narrow the time of death down to a six-hour period.

"We can be pretty accurate within 24 hours of death, but the further away from the time of death, the more leeway you have to give us," he said. "Of course, the only way to know exactly when a person died is if he swallowed a watch and then was shot right through it—the shot killing him and stopping the watch simultaneously."

A NOTE ABOUT CORONER INCOMPETENCE   [The following is based on Louisville Courier-Journal reporter Joel Brinkley's article in the Fall 1982 issue of IRE Journal.]

Each of Kentucky's 120 counties elects a coroner every four years, and I spent most of 1980 studying them for the Courier-Journal because in many counties they didn't seem to have the faintest idea what they were doing.

In McCreary County, Ky., the coroner was a junk dealer who said he completed the eighth grade. In Wayne County, he was a fundamentalist minister who preached divine healing, curing the sick with anointment and prayer. Clinton County's coroner was a country-and-western disc jockey who freely admitted that he would fail a coroner competency test, if one existed. And in Garrard County, the coroner was a grocery warehouse clerk who said he had no need for formal training. He learned how to do the coroner's job from his friend Moose Moss, manager of the local loan company.

If yours is one of the 32 states that still employs lay coroners in some or all counties, you'll probably find that your state is much like Kentucky: Many of the coroners are inept; others are corrupt; some are both.

Coroners have a great deal of power and responsibility, as explained above, but even so, most states require no training of them. Few states even give their coroners handbooks that tell them how to do their jobs.

Some coroners attend training courses, study on their own and do a fine job. But many others don't. And when those coroners rule on a cause of death, too often they are dead wrong.

Oklahoma's chief medical examiner, Dr. A. Jay Chapman, said, "When you get into it, you see just how terribly the public is served by some of these untrained coroners. It's just incredible."

"It's like using a plumber when you need a urologist," said Dr. William G. Eckert Jr., president of the National Association of Medical Examiners.

And in Chicago, Cook County's medical examiner, Dr. Robert J. Stein, asked, "What the hell do these people know as far as death investigation is concerned? I'll tell you what they know. They don't know a damned thing."

There's a simple explanation for this. Just read the state statutes that specify who is allowed to run for the elective office of county coroner. In most of California, candidates must be 18 years old and residents of the county they want to serve. That's all.

In Mississippi, candidates must be registered voters who've never denied the existence of a supreme being. In Kentucky, they must be 24-year-old county residents who have never fought a duel. And in Pennsylvania, the statutes specify no qualifications at all.

There are exceptions. In Ohio and Kansas, for example, all coroners must be physicians. In Connecticut and Nebraska, they must be attorneys. But in most states, coroners must meet only age and residency requirements, so voters are lucky if their coroner is simply unqualified. They're lucky because in the next county over, the coroner may even be illiterate.

Coroner's errors aren't always the product of ignorance. Sometimes the explanation is greed. In most states, a curious thing happens when the filing deadline for coroner elections draws near. In county after county, funeral directors begin crowding into the courthouse clerks' offices. Every one of them files to run for coroner, and in most counties funeral directors win. In Kentucky, 80 percent of the coroners are funeral directors. In Illinois, it's 50 percent. And at first glance, that might seem reasonable. After all, who's more qualified to deal with dead bodies than a funeral director?

Almost anyone. Coroner's offices present funeral directors with so blatant a conflict of interest that most often they can't possibly do their jobs correctly. Some funeral directors/coroners use their authority to muscle their way onto death scenes. They grab the body before other funeral directors can get near it and then rush the corpse back to the funeral home, hoping the family won't want to move it and will buy an expensive funeral.

Most aren't so direct. But even a well-intentioned funeral director is repeatedly tempted to slough off the coroner's job. Imagine a typical call. A funeral director/coroner is summoned to a home where a middle-aged man has apparently died in his sleep. There the person has two roles: As the coroner, he or she must investigate and assign the official cause of death. And as a funeral director, he or she will want to sell the family a funeral.

Suppose some bit of evidence, such as an empty pill bottle beside the bed or an open jar of rat poison, catches his or her eye and suggests that the death might not be natural. Will the funeral director/coroner investigate and call the police, upsetting the family and risk losing a several-thousand-dollar funeral? Maybe. Maybe not.

Most often, the coroner/funeral director problem leads to less dramatic problems. No family wants to admit to a suicide, so coroners often face pressure, subtle or direct, to say that a suicide was an accident. If coroners are trying to ingratiate themselves with the family so they'll get the funeral, they may agree that a man with a bullet wound in his temple shot himself by accident while cleaning his gun.

When North Carolina replaced its elected coroners, most of them funeral directors, with physician/medical examiners during the early 1970s, the number of deaths attributed to accidental shootings suddenly plummeted. At the same time, the state's suicide rate rose. Poisoning deaths tripled.

That's the way death investigation works in much of America—not exactly as it's depicted on the TV show "Quincy." Should you decide to write about the coroners in your state, jut how difficult will it be? Obviously, it's not impossible, but chances are you will have tackled easier projects.

There are some problems you'll certainly face. First, hardly anyone knows or cares about the problem. You'll find few advocates. No citizens' groups. No reports from legislative commissions declaring a crisis in death investigation. No national interest groups lobbying for change because, as one medical examiner put it, "Dead people don't vote." It's hard to find an aggrieved victim because most victims of coroner incompetence are six feet underground. And in many states, you won't even find a central office that can tell you who all the county coroners are.

The most sympathetic voices you'll hear will be those of hospital pathologists who perform autopsies for coroners on occasion. The pathologists, particularly those in small towns, will be able to tell you about the people who died under suspicious circumstances but still received no autopsy.

In counties with funeral director/coroners, talk to the embalmers in competing funeral homes for stories of bodies spirited away in the night. Sometimes the state medical association will be interested in the problem, as will the state prosecuting attorney's group. And if your state has a resident forensic dentist or forensic anthropologist (bone specialist), often one or the other will have stories to tell.

In terms of paper trails, about the only government records you're likely to find are death certificates, and at first I didn't think Kentucky's would be of much use. After all, even in a state as small as mine, 65,000 people die each year and the certificates are filed by date.

You may find, however, that most of the facts on those certificates are recorded in the state vital statistics computer, as they are in Kentucky. And if you can convince your vital statistics department to order a computer run for you, you're in business.

Additional Story Ideas

Police scandals can pop up in unexpected places.

For instance, The Boston Globe's investigative Spotlight Team found dirt under the fingernails of those who were taking advantage of a statewide program to encourage police officers to get better educations.

Massachusetts police had been receiving sizeable salary increases for 15 years for completing college-level courses during off-duty hours. Reporters Stephan Kurkjian, Daniel Golden and M.E. Malone reported in January, 1985: "The noble idea of encouraging police to seek higher education had turned into a much-abused, $12 million-a-year program in Massachusetts, providing hefty pay increases to many officers for securing quick and easy college degrees."

One small school west of Boston issuing more graduate degrees in criminal justice than any other college in the country, required little or no reading or writing in its courses. At another, police officers were routinely falsifying attendance records for absent police officers.

On the day the report hit the streets, one target, Northeastern University in Boston, suspended four instructors and cut the size of its criminal justice program by two-thirds. Two other colleges announced radical changes in their programs to toughen degree requirements and strengthen instruction.

If you smell political influence in the department, don't overlook records of police purchases such as cars, tires and all the other items police take bids on from the general marketplace. Who do the contracts go to, and are the bids written in such a way that only the favored can get them?

Don't overlook the identities of whom the police have hired to do their lobbying for them in the state capitol. (And what they're lobbying for—laws that would enhance the efforts of law enforcement, or just higher pay for police?) Kansas City's police department was mightily embarrassed (or at least should have been) in 1980 when its lobbyist was caught conning a respected state senator out of two tickets to a World Series game in Kansas City and giving them to Nick Civella, then head of organized crime in Kansas City, and his bodyguard. The lobbyist subsequently resigned his prestigious job with the police.

An excellent test to determine the quality of a police department is the manner in which the police investigate and discipline themselves. If the investigations are haphazard and the punishments light, your police department is almost certainly abusing its power on the streets.

Another test is how secretly or openly the police force deals with internal scandals.

The National Crime Information Commission

The National Crime Information Commission (NCIC) is a nationwide computer network run by the FBI. It contains felony arrests and convictions of many Americans.

Bruce Selcraig, a freelance investigative reporter, notes that when police officers arrest someone they first run a license check to learn if any local warrants are outstanding. This is done at the scene of the arrest. Next, an NCIC check may be made to find out about any outstanding warrants elsewhere, plus any record of a prior felony arrest.

Reporters who have friends inside law enforcement may make use of this, but the practice is not without risks to cooperating officers. NCIC information is not supposed to be available to the news media. In fact, if you file a Freedom of Information Act request with the NCIC, one reporter learned, authorities will contact your target before responding. If you can talk police officers into using their access to NCIC to help you, bear in mind that they must register their names in the NCIC log and list the reason for the request.

Cooperating With the Police

Practically every newsperson has cooperated with the police at one time or another. There is nothing necessarily wrong with that. Not if real crime was the target.

Members of the media also are members of the public. They have just as much of an obligation to help law enforcement agencies prevent or solve crimes as anyone else—as long as this duty doesn't jeopardize their effectiveness at gathering news.

This naturally creates a dilemma. How can a newsperson cooperate with the law against crime and at the same time serve as a watchdog against abuses of policing authority?

The answer is, not easily, and many news organizations have solved the problem by having one set of reporters who constantly cooperates with the police while another set of reporters keeps its eyes on those who enforce the law.

Cooperation between police and reporters can prove a real public service, or it can turn the reporter into nothing more than an arm of law enforcement. The latter is, naturally, to be avoided.

Law enforcement has certain tools with which to investigate crimes that are forbidden the reporter, such as the use of most kinds of electronic surveillance, the power to convene a grand jury, the power to grant witness immunity and the power to subpoena witnesses or evidence. Most reporters have sources within law enforcement that can feed them information obtained from these tools. But, obviously, this can be abused. Be sure to know your news organization's policy on cooperation, and be sure you are willing to protect your police sources from their own departments.

Conclusion

Various privacy laws in recent years have dried up the availability of many records that police reporters used to be able to pick up and quote from routinely. Sometimes a reticent police officer will misuse the privacy law to hide more than he or she has to. It's good to know the rules before you start asking. Some reporters even carry copies of the appropriate state statutes in their billfolds for purposes of reference and/or intimidation.

When the reporter and policeman enter a gray area on the release of information, it sometimes helps to threaten to sue for the information. It also helps if your newspaper, television station or radio station already has demonstrated a willingness to get involved in such access suits.

But the best way is to establish a rapport with local law enforcement personnel based on mutual trust and respect. Police officers are important to reporters as sources. And police department activities should be high on any news organization's list of possible targets for close scrutiny.

DOCUMENTING THE EVIDENCE

LOCAL LAW ENFORCEMENT AGENCIES

Police Arrest Reports

Local police keep arrest records on individuals who have been arrested and charged with various criminal offenses. These records normally are filed under the individual's name. The contents of arrest reports vary from city to city, but there are some common denominators. The information contained in them usually includes the suspect's name and address, date and place of birth, sex, race, occupation, general physical characteristics and special marks, name of complainant or victim, time and place of arrest, arresting officer, type of crime, facts relating to arrest, whether the suspect has been fingerprinted and/or photographed, evidence, witnesses and other related information.

The availability of arrest records to reporters also varies from city to city. Check the local ordinances. Essentially, if the police department is required by ordinance to keep arrest information in the form of a log or blotter (usually kept at the desk of the duty sergeant), it is a public record unless specifically exempted. This does not mean that police custom in your locale allows you access. However, you may find after consulting an attorney that a suit will successfully open these records.

These records can be very useful in tracking the activities of an individual. A friendly police source may be necessary to get them. Keep in mind that these are arrest, not conviction, records, and often the disposition portion of the file will be incomplete. Check the court records for the final disposition.

If the suspect gets to court, most of the information in the arrest records becomes part of the court record, which is open. (For more information, see Chapter 14, "Courts.")

Police and Sheriff Jail Books

The jail book lists who has been incarcerated and contains such information as the person's name, date of birth, address, sex, race and physical description; the name of the arresting agency; date of commitment to the county jail; who makes bond and how; discharge date; and suspected offense. It usually is indexed chronologically.

Access varies widely, but usually the jail book is open. It is kept at the county jail or the sheriff's office.

The information is supposed to be expunged if the suspect is not charged, if charges are dropped or if the suspect is acquitted, but often it is not. The jail book can therefore be an exceptionally valuable record when reporters cannot gain access to the arrest record.

Other Police Reports

Complaint Reports Complaint reports are kept in numerical sequence and contain the details of the complaint, name of the person who made it, date and time of the complaint, name of the person who received it and name of the officer who was assigned to the complaint. The dispatcher's log also gives much of the same information.

Uniform Accident Reports Uniform accident reports are submitted to the state whenever the police respond to an auto accident. They contain the names of those involved, traffic and weather conditions, arrest or citation information, facts about the accident and other information.

Arrest or Accident Cards Arrest or accident cards are made for each person arrested and each vehicle involved in an accident. The cards usually are kept alphabetically and may contain information on more than one accident or arrest. Information includes name, description of person, date of arrest or accident, file number (record of arrest report number), charge, name of arresting or investigating officer and case disposition.

Monthly Reports Monthly reports usually are made to city government about the number of offenses reported, total arrests (broken down by crime) and amount of revenue from traffic tickets, parking meters, court fines and other sources.

Sheriff's Office Records

Log A log of all writs served by the department can provide a large amount of important information.

Preliminary Reports Preliminary reports contain all complaints or requests for assistance, including the type of complaint and details, responding officer, time and other information. The reports usually indicate how the complaint was disposed of and may show if a report was made.

Monthly Financial Reports Monthly financial reports list the money collected and are itemized by case number and name of the defendant. This report usually is sent on a regular schedule to the county auditor or treasurer.

Monthly Summaries Monthly summaries provide information on the number of miles patrolled and subpoenas served by sheriffs, training hours for deputies, number of complaints received, number of arrests for felonies and misdemeanors, and number of inmates in custody and jail days served.

Sales Records Sales records include the court order for the sale, such as confiscated property or foreclosed land, description of the property, copies of the public notices and other documents pertinent to the sale, including amount received.

Police and Sheriff's Annual Budget

Local law enforcement budgets are part of the city or county budgets. An exact break-down of salaries, equipment and other costs usually is available, with the exception of funds used for undercover agents. These can be useful in evaluating the overall effectiveness of police operations by showing which areas receive priority. Once you know this, you can try to find out why.

Budgets can be obtained from the city or county finance office, city clerk, city manager or mayor.

STATE AND FEDERAL LAW ENFORCEMENT AGENCIES

State Crime Bureau Statistics

Many states have a central coordinating office, such as a state crime bureau, that collects statistics from throughout the state in order to compile an overview of crime in the state. These offices can be useful for background information.

Office of Justice Programs Grant Program File

The Office of Justice Programs is the principal federal agency coordinating U.S. Department of Justice funding of criminal justice programs operated by local law enforcement agencies, courts and corrections systems throughout the country. The office can access computerized files containing descriptions of federal criminal justice program grants, subgrants, contracts and interagency agreements, as well as the year of the award, fiscal year funding project summary and assessment summary.

From here, go to the state department of public safety or other office designated to receive and administer federal funds (often called a criminal justice planning agency), and from there to the local police department receiving the grant.

Write the Office of Congressional and Public Affairs, Office of Justice Programs, U.S. Department of Justice, Washington, D.C. 20531.

Office of Justice Programs Annual Report

The Office of Justice Programs publishes an annual report summarizing the agencies' activities during the previous year. The report gives general overviews of key criminal justice programs carried out on national and state levels.

Write the Office of Congressional and Public Affairs, Office of Justice Programs, U.S. Department of Justice, Washington, D.C. 20531.

Application for Licenses to Engage in the Firearms and Explosives Businesses

Under the Gun Control Act of 1968, the federal government requires those engaging in the sale of firearms to be licensed. Information on the application includes name and address, type of license—manufacturer, importer, collector, dealer, pawnbroker—

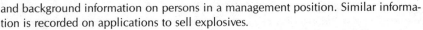

and background information on persons in a management position. Similar information is recorded on applications to sell explosives.

Make your Freedom of Information Act request to the Disclosure Office, Bureau of Alcohol, Tobacco and Firearms, Washington, D.C. 20226.

Federal Inspection Reports of Firearms and Explosives Licensees

The Bureau of Alcohol, Tobacco and Firearms of the Department of the Treasury conducts annual inspections of federal firearms and explosives licensees to assure compliance with federal laws and regulations. These reports include information on the possible illegal trafficking of firearms and explosives. Inspectors look at the type of explosives and weapons sold by the licensee, and a major portion of the report deals with any stolen items.

Make your Freedom of Information Act request to the Disclosure Office, Bureau of Alcohol, Tobacco and Firearms, Washington, D.C. 20226.

In addition, federal law requires licenses for certain types of firearms, such as automatic submachine guns. Applications for these licenses contain some potentially valuable information about the buyers and sellers of the weapons. However, this data is not a matter of public record unless it should come out in a court proceeding. This doesn't happen often because frequently the matter has come before the court only because the owner of such a weapon has failed to obtain a license.

Friendly sources inside the government enforcement agency might be of help, but this involves considerable risk. The agency enforcing the firearms laws is the Treasury Department's Bureau of Alcohol, Tobacco and Firearms, Washington, D.C. 20226.

Applications for Alcohol Importers' and Wholesalers' Basic Permits

Under the Federal Alcohol Administration Act, an importer or wholesaler of distilled spirits, wine or malt beverages must register with the Bureau of Alcohol, Tobacco and Firearms. The application includes the names of the individuals with a financial interest in the business—including amount, officers and directors, loans and stock—the business history of those individuals, their credit rating with details, their other business interests and the names of manufacturers or distributors for whom the wholesaler has been designated as the agent. Some of this information may be deleted before the application is released.

The bureau may also provide reporters with inspection reports and listings of authorized businesses.

Make your Freedom of Information Act request to the Disclosure Office, Bureau of Alcohol, Tobacco and Firearms, Washington, D.C. 20226. Many states obtain similar information and will make it available for inspection.

BACKGROUND SOURCES ON LAW ENFORCEMENT AGENCIES

- *Annual Report of the Attorney General of the United States* is an annual publication giving an overview of the activities of law enforcement groups under the jurisdiction of the Justice Department. Information includes the annual costs of judicial districts, such as expenses for witnesses and salaries of U.S. attorneys and marshalls; number of warrants served and cases filed; and financial summaries of fines, forfeitures, penalties, foreclosures and bonds forfeited. Write to the Attorney General of the United States, Department of Justice, Constitution Ave. and 10th St. N.W., Washington, D.C. 20530.

■ *Crime in the United States* is an annual compilation of Uniform Crime Report data submitted to the Federal Bureau of Investigation by about 16,000 police agencies across the country.

A large portion of the report deals with major crimes as defined by the bureau: murder, forcible rape, robbery, arson, aggravated assault, burglary, larceny theft and motor vehicle theft. The report also contains aggregate statistics on crimes such as common assault, vandalism, possession of weapons, various sex offenses, narcotics, driving while intoxicated, disorderly conduct and many others.

Statistics are broken down by state, city, suburb, race, sex, age, number of law enforcement officials in the geographical area and number of arrests in rural and urban areas.

There are, of course, many pitfalls in using these and other aggregate crime statistics. In the first place, of course, many crimes go unreported to the police. The FBI does not list white-collar crimes or a company's policy about forcing employees to work in unsafe places, resulting in injuries. And many crimes do not fit easily in one or even two categories.

Crime in the United States can be obtained from the U.S. Government Printing Office. For semiannual press releases updating recent trends in crime statistics, write the Federal Bureau of Investigation, Ninth Street and Pennsylvania Avenue N.W., Washington, D.C. 20535.

■ *National Crime Survey,* compiled by the Bureau of Justice Statistics for the Office of Justice Programs, is an analysis of surveys in which citizens are asked if they have been victims of a crime, what kind of crime and whether it was reported to the police.

These reports offer an opportunity to check the accuracy of other crime statistics. And because the surveys are conducted by one agency, they eliminate potential errors caused by police departments using different record-keeping procedures.

Write to the National Criminal Justice Reference Service, Box 6000, Rockville, Md. 20850.

■ *Crime Statistics: How Not to be Abused,* by New York Times reporter David Burnham is a useful primer on how to evaluate crime statistics, including the kinds of questions reporters need to ask, and where soft spots are likely to be found.

Send $1.25 to Investigative Reporters & Editors, Inc., P.O. Box 838, Columbia, Mo. 65205.

■ *Police Department Organization Manuals* are good source books for reporters because they spell out the paper trails laid out in local police departments

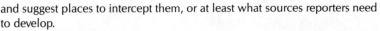

and suggest places to intercept them, or at least what sources reporters need to develop.

To get one, ask your community relations or public relations officer at the police station, or acquire one from a police source.

- *Agency Issues* is a monthly publication dealing with problems and issues in police department personnel areas. This can be useful background information to evaluate the local police department and to help understand police union demands at the end of a contract period.

    Agency Issues is distributed to members only, but it may be possible to obtain copies by writing the International Personnel Management Association, 1617 Duke St., Alexandria, Va. 22314.

- *Scientific Sleuthing Newsletter* is a quarterly publication dealing with trends and technological advances in the field of forensic sciences. Write to Scientific Sleuthing Newsletter, c/o James E. Starrs, National Law Center, George Washington University, Washington, D.C. 20052.

- *American Institute for Research* publishes project reports based on research examining facets of the criminal justice system, including the personnel training and selection, manpower, delinquency, employment equity and feasibility studies.

    Write to the American Institute for Research, 3333 K Street N.W., Washington, D.C. 20007.

- *Universities* are excellent places to find experts and studies related to law enforcement. Many community colleges, colleges and universities have departments or schools of police science devoted to law enforcement training and employ teachers who conduct research into various aspects of law enforcement.

    Contact the schools' information offices for material about their programs and faculty, usually published annually in the college catalogs.

- *Inslaw, Inc.* is a for-profit corporation that develops procedures and information software systems for criminal justice agencies, such as the prosecutor's management information system (PROMIS), which is in operation at about 50 locations in the country. INSLAW also has many publications useful to the reporter backgrounding police systems.

    Write to INSLAW, Inc., 1125 15th St. N.W., Washington, D.C. 20005.

- *Directory of Automated Criminal Justice Information Systems* is an annual publication describing computer data retrieval systems used by criminal justice agencies. Information includes the type of computer systems, population kept by the system, type of document, others sharing the data and how the system functions. The Directory also lists the name, address and phone number of the person to contact concerning the system.

    Write the National Criminal Justice Reference Service, Box 6000, Rockville, Md. 20850.

- *Drug Enforcement Administration* publishes a magazine, Drugs of Abuse, and publishes fact sheets with information about drug abuse, enforcement efforts, diversion efforts, technology identification and prevention.

Write to the Drug Enforcement Administration, 1405 I Street N.W., Washington, D.C. 20537.

- *Citizen's Crime Commissions* endeavor to monitor the local criminal justice system and to educate the public about crime problems in their area. They conduct their own investigations, especially in the areas of organized crime and public official corruption, and have extensive files.

Write to the individual crime commission directly, using the following addresses.

ARIZONA
Tucson Urban Area Crime
  Commission
c/o Charles W. King
6245 E. Broadway, Suite 510
Tucson, Ariz. 85701

CALIFORNIA
Burbank Citizens Crime Prevention
Committee c/o S.G. Pearson
224 E. Olive Ave.
Burbank, Calif. 91502

FLORIDA
Dade-Miami Criminal Justice Council
1500 N.W. 12th Ave., Ninth Floor
Jackson Medical Tower Miami, Fla.
33136

GEORGIA
Metropolitan Atlanta Crime
  Commission
100 Edgewood Ave. S.E., Room 128
Atlanta, Ga. 30303

HAWAII
Hawaii Criminal Justice Commission
222 S. Vineyard St., Suite 703
Honolulu, Hawaii 96813

ILLINOIS
Chicago Crime Commission
79 W. Monroe St.
Chicago, Ill. 60603

KANSAS
Wichita Crime Commission
460 Broadway Plaza
Wichita, Kan. 67202

LOUISIANA
Metropolitan Crime Commission of
New Orleans Inc.
1107 First NBC Bldg.
New Orleans, La. 70112

MISSISSIPPI
Mississippi Coast Crime Commission
1401 20th Ave.
P.O. Box 1962
Gulfport, Miss. 39501

MISSOURI
Kansas City Crime Commission
906 Grand Ave., Suite 840
Kansas City, Mo. 64106

NEW YORK
Citizens Crime Commission
  of New York
355 Lexington Ave.
New York, N.Y. 10017

PENNSYLVANIA
Citizens Crime Commission
  of Philadelphia
1518 Walnut St., Suite 307
Philadelphia, Pa. 19102

TEXAS
Greater Dallas Crime Commission
1310 Annex, Suite 201
Dallas, Texas 75204

VIRGINIA
Craig Baughan
6009 Old Orchard Dr.
Richmond, Va. 23227

CHAPTER 14

Courts

Experienced reporters have long been drawn to the court house, seeking the key records that will undergird their investigative projects. The other chapters in this book are replete with outstanding reporting efforts in which court records proved to be the foundation.

This chapter, however, is about investigating the court system itself, including the judges, lawyers, prosecutors, court clerks, bail bondspeople and others charged with making the system work.

It covers the political campaign contribution through the judge's decision, from arrest to probation, traffic court through criminal court, showing how the system works and where to probe when things have gone awry.

It examines the creative efforts of reporters in Chicago, Cleveland, Dallas, Detroit, Indianapolis, Miami, Milwaukee, Minneapolis, New Orleans, Philadelphia, Richmond, Seattle and St. Louis, sharing tips and insights drawn from a wide range of experience with the legal system.

But this isn't just a chapter about big-city court problems. It is about understanding how justice is dispensed and where to look to see if it's failed, in big towns or little towns, large systems and small.

---

by FREDRIC N. TULSKY

The Court as a Political System

Just like city hall or presidential politics, the courts are a political system.

To begin investigating the courts, you must first know how your judges are chosen. In the federal system, judges are appointed by the president and confirmed by the Senate, often with the backing of the state's U.S. senators and other party officials. In the state system, judges either are appointed (usually by the governor, with legislative approval) or elected by the voters.

Either system is in some ways political. Supporters of the elective system contend that it is less elitist (and more likely to have minorities and women in office) and more democratic. Supporters of the appointive system contend that studies disprove such a system is elitist, and also maintain that it helps minimize the politicization of the courts. At the least, they say, such a system will limit the number of attorneys who lack ability but are well-connected.

What effect does the political process have on the court system?

In the elective system, few voters in major cities know anything about the judicial candidates. To win office, a judicial candidate needs money and political support, requirements that can raise troublesome ethical issues.

Running for judge requires money, and this money largely comes from lawyers. The judges' campaign reports are a matter of public record, but are often overlooked.

Consider, for example, the work of Sheila Kaplan for Common Cause magazine. While judicial elections were "once the K-Mart of political elections," she wrote, lawyers and other special interest groups with a stake in court decisions are now footing the bill in many of the 38 states that elect judges, as campaign spending has skyrocketed.

She described a prominent Florida lawyer who was asked for a contribution on behalf of a judge, days before he was to try a non-jury case before that candidate. She reported that while Texaco and Pennzoil were battling out their $11 million lawsuit in Texas courts, the two firms representing the oil giants combined to contribute almost $400,000 to Texas judges, including some to state Supreme Court justices who were not even up for re-election.

Consider, as well, Philadelphia, where the voters put in office more than 100 trial court judges. With so many faceless candidates for so many seats, the voters rely largely on sample ballots distributed by ward leaders and political candidates to decide how to vote. A Pulitzer Prize for investigative reporting was awarded to Philadelphia Inquirer reporters for a series that demonstrated many of the failings of such a system. The series told of one judge, seeking election to a higher trial court, telling party officials at a ward meeting, "They say you're not supposed to do favors in the courtroom, and that's not the rule in my courtroom. Just don't get caught."

Inquirer reporters H.G. Bissinger and Daniel R. Biddle studied the campaign reports of successful judicial candidates over a five-year period, noting lawyers who were campaign officials and those who were contributors. They also obtained from court administrators computer printouts for the same years, listing the cases assigned to each judge and identifying the attorneys.

Using a computer, Bissinger and Biddle compared the outcome of cases where supporters appeared before the judge to the normal outcome in the court system. Lawyers who were active in campaigns for Municipal Court judges won 71 percent of their cases before those judges, while only 35 percent of all Municipal Court defendants won their cases.

Sometimes, too, unexpected outcomes occur when a politician has an interest in a case. Cleveland Plain Dealer reporters Ted Wendling and Rosemary Armao wrote about Medina County, Ohio, "a community in which justice is tainted by political manipulation and incompetence, and where the powerful and well-connected are frequently not held to account for their actions."

The reporters found case after case in which the politically influential had received what appeared to be special treatment over the past decade. The story developed as a grand jury began hearing evidence surrounding alleged criminal conduct by a court employee, who boasted in conversation secretly tape-recorded by a police informant that he was being protected by judges.

The reporters went back and showed a long history of political favoritism in the county. In case after case, they found the normal handling of a criminal investigation was altered because of concerns for the impact on political figures who were implicated in the crimes.

Even as isolated cases, such stories tell a great deal about the judicial system. The Inquirer has reported on one case where a defendant was given unusually high bail after being arrested and charged with burglary. The victim, who was the mother of a local politician, contacted top court officials and got them to intervene with the bail commissioner, who reduced the amount.

In another case, a Republican party official who held a court job faced charges that he had violated state income tax laws. Uncontradicted testimony showed the official had earned substantial income over several years, yet never filed a state income tax form. The official's defense was the character testimony of more than 30 people, many of them politicians. The judge, saying he was impressed with the strength of the character witnesses, found the defendant not guilty.

The court system is also used to provide political rewards. Constitutionally separated from other branches of government, the court system may not fall under civil service regulations that cover the rest of local government. Thus, the court system can become a leading avenue for patronage positions used by political parties. In Philadelphia, for example, there are more than 2,000 court posts, none of which are civil service.

Find out how people get these jobs. Find out what testing is required, what qualifications are set, whether the court administrators accept and consider letters of support from politicians. Then look at how many of those with jobs are politically connected, and how many of those jobs are filled through nepotism.

The Inquirer court series showed the $55 million annual court payroll included relatives of at least 30 of the city's 120 judges as well as of other court administrators. The deputy court administrator, who had four relatives on the payroll, was quoted as saying he was "just sorry I can't get more of my family members on the court." The series also described a judge's intervention when a court administrator tried to discipline a habitually tardy court employee who happened to be the judge's son.

Ask, too, who gets special appointments in the court system.

Which attorneys get court appointments, and how much money do they collect? Which attorneys are appointed as trustees and guardians, positions that can be incredibly lucrative? Many court systems, overloaded with cases, are turning to masters and arbitrators to resolve disputes without wasting a judge's time. Who gets these appointments? What connections to the judges and politicians do all these people have?

A major finding of an Indianapolis Star Study of bankruptcy court was cronyism in appointments. The court had awarded more than $14 million in professional fees over a four-year period. Much of that money went to attorneys with political ties to, or even financial relationships with, the judges who appointed them.

One judge awarded more than $112,000 in legal fees to political allies who rented office space in a building he co-owned. Former U.S. Senator Birch E. Bayh was paid more than $100,000 as the receiver in one case. Bayh had been appointed receiver by a judge who owed his seat, in part, to Bayh's support.

Look, too, at what people who receive such appointments do for their money. Detroit News reporters Fred Girard, Norman Sinclair and Nat Abbate studied abuses by attorneys appointed to represent defendants on their appeals. Not only did they find that judges in many cases gave the appointments to cronies, they also studied the vouchers submitted by those attorneys. The vouchers showed, for example, lawyers charging for visits to defendants in prison. Comparing the bills to the visitor cards on file in the basement of the state prison, they found the public had been charged for dozens of visits that never took place.

They found that some lawyers were charging the public for full appeals, when in some cases no appeals were even filed. They found court-appointed lawyers who kept their clients waiting for months or years.

The Court as a Dispenser of Justice

Do not expect to step into the court beat and break major stories overnight. But by developing sources, using public records and understanding the process, enterprising reporters can play a critical role as watchdog of the system.

Keep in mind that criminal justice officials, especially in big cities, cope with competing pressures. Between the prosecutors' anti-crime push and the explosion of civil litigation, more cases will constantly come into the system. It will be impossible for each case to go to trial without the system, in any major city, breaking down.

The public may think all criminals should be locked up. But that same public has no interest in providing the money it would cost to build enough prisons so everyone convicted of a crime carrying a jail sentence is incarcerated in prisons that meet constitutional standards. The move by many states to mandatory prison sentences for certain crimes exacerbates this shortage. Often, county jails are filled predominantly with persons who have been arrested but not yet tried, putting more pressure on the system to dispose of its cases quickly.

A warning: Do not expect to prove that judges and prosecutors are taking payoffs, until the day that reporters have legal authority to subpoena witnesses and conduct electronic surveillance. Reporters are not, at any rate, prosecutors; it is valuable enough to tell readers what their officials are doing, so that they can make informed choices. In doing so, reporters can creatively use sources and records to question judicial conduct, whether money changed hands or not.

In the Inquirer's court series, reporters Biddle and Bissinger did exactly that. They exposed a series of cases in which judges had made crucial decisions after private conversations with attorneys for only one side present.

In one case, for example, a man was arrested by police, who saw him on the ground with his pants down, on top of a woman he was hitting in the face. The man was tried without a jury by a judge, who found him not guilty of attempted rape and aggravated assault, but guilty of only simple assault.

The defendant was sentenced to spend three to 23 months in jail, but was released after 30 days. Why? The judge had granted a petition, filed by the attorney, asking the judge to reconsider and reduce the sentence. Both the defense attorney and the judge later conceded to reporters that the judge had privately suggested the attorney file a petition.

Take the hypothetical case of a judge giving probation to someone convicted of a serious crime, an incident that is routine in many court systems. There may be good reasons for such a sentence: It may be the defendant had no record, was unlikely to repeat his or her crime and the crowded prisons did not justify incarceration.

On the other hand, a check of the defendant's background may reveal he or she had been involved in a series of violent crimes and the resulting convictions call into question the judge's sentence. Such records are always worth checking. Maybe the judge has a history of inappropriate sentences, which further checking in court records could prove.

Reporters do not have to show that the judge got "paid off." The judge's actions alone are worthy of coverage. The story would not only help inform the public, but also may make the judge think more carefully the next time.

Consider the hypothetical case of an attorney who repeatedly does well before a certain judge. Of 10 cases before the judge last year, six ended in the charges being dismissed without a trial.

Checking the records may show a pattern, for example, of the cases being dismissed because the prosecution witnesses never appeared. Perhaps all were routine cases that amount to nothing. On the other hand, an enterprising reporter could pull the files in each of those cases. From the documents inside—perhaps an arrest warrant, a complaint, the preliminary hearing transcript—the reporter could find the names of those prosecution witnesses. By tracking them down, the reporter may find that in each case, the witnesses never received subpoenas and had no idea the cases were scheduled. Even without showing that money was paid, the reporter could have shown that justice was subverted.

There may be times, however, when reporters do actually learn of payoffs. When that happens, enterprising reporters will know how to use the records and resources of the beat to develop the story.

Consider, again, the City of Philadelphia. Reporter William K. Marimow learned from his sources that the FBI had evidence of judicial wrongdoing. The FBI had been investigating a local union it believed was engaged in extortion to promote its ends, and had received court authority to plant wiretaps within the union hall. The FBI not only found the union officials strong-arming contractors to use union members, but also found that around Christmas the union members had filled envelopes with cash to give to judges.

At least 14 judges, according to Marimow's sources, had been scheduled to receive the cash, which ranged from $300 to $500. Marimow wrote an initial story, based on his sources, reporting on the investigation and what had been found.

He turned to the Code of Judicial Conduct, the standards adopted by the state Supreme Court to spell out appropriate judicial behavior. Those standards, as in most states, are based on model rules created by the American Bar Association. In Pennsylvania, the code prohibits the "appearance of impropriety" by a judge, and local bar association leaders contended such gifts appeared to violate that canon. But in adopting the code, Marimow further pointed out, Pennsylvania had been one of the very few states to delete a provision of the model code that sharply limits the gifts a judge may accept.

Next, Inquirer reporters waited for May 1, the deadline in Pennsylvania for every judge to file financial disclosure forms which list his or her financial dealings during the previous year. On those forms, every judge must list any gifts of $200 or more, or face misconduct charges.

On that date, two Inquirer reporters went to the state court administrative office, expecting to see a large crowd of competitors who, knowing that judges had taken cash, would be scrutinizing those reports.

Instead, the reporters found themselves alone in the administrative office that day, and reported the following morning that nine judges had reported on their disclosure forms that they received cash gifts the previous December from Roofers Union officials. Two other judges, including the presiding judge of Municipal Court, invoked the Fifth Amendment on the forms, refusing to answer the question. One judge had filed his form in early January—before Marimow had made public the FBI probe—and listed no gifts. In late April, he filed an amended form listing the union gift.

A later story began with Marimow's sources, who said union officials had decided whom should receive cash by reviewing their list of judges who received gifts in 1984. But going back to the financial-disclosure reports for that year—a year when the judges had no reason to think they would be scrutinized—no judge reported receiving such a gift.

When the stories broke, state court officials allowed the judges who admitted taking such gifts to remain on the bench, noting that they lacked authority to suspend a judge from office until the Judicial Inquiry and Review Board, the agency responsible for judicial conduct investigations, recommended action. One story in The Inquirer developed because the reporter knew one of the judges implicated in the probe was on "senior" status, meaning he was no longer subject to election, but had taken semiretirement in which he served at the "pleasure" of the state Supreme Court Chief Justice. Within hours of a call to the justice, asking if he was still "pleased" by the service of the senior judge, the chief justice announced the judge's suspension.

Finally, Inquirer reporter Biddle detailed in other stories the outcomes of cases in which union members had been arrested and charged with crimes, and had their cases assigned to judges who had received the union gifts.

Such stories demonstrate what enterprising reporters can do to use sources and judicial standards to develop stories. But it is not necessary to rely on cash gifts to evaluate how well the judicial system administers justice.

Reporters can do so by understanding each step of the process. Look at, for example, the steps in the criminal process. (These may vary slightly from state to state, but there should be similar constitutional safeguards):

- The suspect's treatment upon arrest.
- The preliminary hearing.
- The assignment of cases.
- The pretrial hearing.
- The trial, from jury selection through verdict.
- The post-trial proceedings, at which the defense attorneys in losing cases will ask the judge to overturn the verdict, based upon errors they contend occurred, followed by sentencing.
- Direct appeals, at which defense attorneys will renew their contentions before appellate courts that the verdict was the result of an improper proceeding.
- Collateral appeals, following exhaustion of the direct appeal, at which the defendant can seek to win a new trial by showing an error of constitutional dimension took place.
- Probation and parole.

Each step of the process may lead to stories raising questions about the criminal justice system.

Post-Arrest Processing

After arrests for most crimes, suspects are taken to the police station where they are processed, including fingerprinting and photographing; where a check of their criminal records are conducted; and where, in many cases, the police will seek to conduct interviews. The suspects will spend considerable time in holding cells, until they can finally come before a judge or magistrate who will set bail after reviewing the charges and the defendants' background.

The local public defender, prison society officials and private attorneys should be able to help you answer the following questions:

- What are the conditions like in those cells? What kind of food and medical care is available to prisoners at those stages? Are the police trained to identify epileptics and diabetics, and not treat them like drunks?
- How long does it take suspects to come before the magistrate? Do not look just at the average time. How long are the delays on Saturday nights? How does this compare to comparable cities? What do the state high court decisions say about such delays?

Preliminary Hearing Delays

Depending upon state law, defendants may be charged with a felony either through an indictment or presentment, handed up by a grand jury that has evaluated the case, or by the police or prosecutors, in which instance a judge or magistrate must independently review the charges within days of arrest and determine if enough evidence exists to hold the defendant for trial.

What happens when the complaining witness fails to appear for such hearings, as commonly occurs? If a suspect is held in custody, must he remain there while the case is being delayed? For how long? Is this process abused?

Case Assignment

Court systems are likely to use one of two methods to decide which judge gets which case. The federal courts, and some local court systems that emulate this system, use a random-assignment system, in which cases are assigned by a "wheel" or "lottery" to judges in equal number. The judge then keeps the case from start to finish and is responsible for scheduling his cases. This system is favored by some because it discourages "judge-shopping," in which attorneys may be able to use influence to get their cases before a favored judge.

On the other hand, such a system can be inefficient, and therefore cause problems in court systems burdened by backlogs. Some judges will be sitting idly, if the case they have scheduled breaks down unexpectedly. Some judges are better administrators than others. For such reasons, some courts use a system in which a master room, or calendar room, feeds cases out one-by-one for trial as judges become available.

Such a system gains efficiency at the expense of some cases being assigned to certain judges through improper means. Study the assignments; see if some lawyers seem to appear before some judges more often than others. See if some lawyers do particularly well before some judges; then see if there are particular connections between that judge and lawyer.

Many major court systems have special programs, in which some categories of cases are assigned to specially selected judges. Rob Warden, editor of the Chicago Lawyer, studied a group of 10 Chicago judges specially assigned to complex cases because of their "special skills or temperament."

His story showed the group included one judge rated unqualified by the bar association and the Chicago Council of Lawyers, which cited in particular his "inappropriate" temperament; another judge with the least experience of any in the division; a judge charged with bias against women litigants and attorneys; and another charged with poor judicial temperament. A check of appellate cases showed two of the judges being frequently reversed.

Pretrial Hearings

Before a case goes to trial, a defendant might file motions seeking to prevent evidence from being introduced, contending that the state improperly obtained the evidence.

Such motions will be heard by the judge in a pretrial hearing; at this stage allegations of police misconduct, in particular, are commonplace. A defendant who has given the police an incriminating statement, for example, will contend at this stage that the statement was in some way not voluntary and, therefore, should be suppressed from the jury.

The Philadelphia Inquirer won the Pulitzer public service medal after reporters Jonathan Neumann and Marimow spent months studying transcripts of pretrial suppression hearings from dozens of homicide trials and, ultimately, documented a pattern in which homicide officers had repeatedly been accused of beating confessions out of suspects.

Over a three-year period, the Inquirer found 80 cases in which judges had refused to allow the confession into evidence after finding the police had committed misconduct. In many cases, after the police interrogation the suspects required hospital treatment.

Keep in mind that the issue of how a defendant was treated by police often comes down to the word of the defendant against that of several police. Some judges will routinely accept the police version of what occurred, no matter how suspect the story or how many times the same police officers have offered the same account in other cases. Other judges may be overly suspicious of the story given by a police officer, and refuse to admit critical evidence. Know which judges are which.

Jury Selection

In 1986, The Dallas Morning News examined jury selection practices in Dallas County and found that prosecutors routinely excluded 90 percent of eligible blacks from jury service in felony and capital murder cases.

On the other hand, Miami Herald reporters Sydney Fuerdberg and Ann Macari used a computer study to discover what surprised them as much as court officials: The Circuit Court jury system was racially integrated, they found.

Their systemic look at the court system grew from criticisms that it was discriminatory after an all-white jury acquitted a Miami police officer in the shooting death of a black man.

The reporters checked the races of 9,000 people from voter registration cards. Then, using a computer analysis, backed up with interviews, they found that the court system had racially balanced juries, though not intentionally: Prosecutors tended to exclude blacks while defense attorneys excluded whites.

The Trial and Appeal

How quickly do cases get to trial?

Justice delayed is justice denied, said British Prime Minister William Ewart Gladstone. Presumably, the case he had in mind has been resolved, but his theory remains true.

Criminal suspects have some constitutional protection on this issue: Every defendant has the right to a "speedy" trial, though that term may be elusive. Each state is likely to have its own rules governing such rights, either through state appellate court decisions or state rules adopted by the appellate courts. Court realities, however, may make a sham of such rules.

In Pennsylvania, for example, state Supreme Court decisions dating back to the mid-1970s guaranteed that defendants should expect to be tried within 180 days of arrest, absent delays for which the defendant is responsible, or the charges should be dropped. But due to the flood of cases coming into the system, combined with prosecutors who oppose plea bargaining, it has become increasingly impossible to meet that deadline in big cities.

Thus, more recent court cases modified the rule: If the delay in getting to trial is the fault of the prosecutor, the defendant could expect to be released. But if the problem was that the courts were overcrowded, delays could occur beyond 180 days.

Such rulings may not mean much in the abstract. But keep in mind that many people remain in jail until their trials only because they are poor and cannot afford bail. Often, they have not been convicted of anything. The local public defender, if there is one, or private attorneys who take court appointments should have the names of persons who suffer from such delays.

On the other hand, in any system suffering from jail overcrowding, there are going to be suspects released from jail, pending trial, who commit new crimes. Local prosecutors are likely to be able to identify such cases.

The priority to try criminal cases creates pressures that affect other aspects of the system, including Family Court, where Charles Dickens' notion of cases dragging on forever may become reality.

One caveat: Speed is not everything. Court administrators may be overly concerned with the raw numbers: Their job is to see that the backlog diminishes. But achieving justice and disposing of cases are not synonymous. In big cities with crowded dockets, one way to avoid a serious backlog is to overload the judges' dockets, especially in such less-visible areas as Family Court. In Philadelphia, for example, for a time judges assigned to Juvenile Court came in each morning finding as many as 50 cases listed before them for hearings each day. Attorneys and interested parties who go into such rooms have plenty to say about the quality of justice in such situations.

Do not be afraid to examine guilty verdicts that may be miscarriages of justice. Every so often, reporters learn from defense attorneys, advocates for prisoners or other defense-related sources of cases in which someone may be wrongly convicted.

It is not easy to second-guess a jury, and such a story must be carefully and thoroughly reported. Some defendants do get railroaded through the system, and by identifying such an incident and re-examining the facts, reporters can protect people from governmental abuse.

In studying such incidents, look closely at what evidence the jury heard. What was the prosecution case, and what makes it suspect? Is it built on the word of people who may be unreliable, for reasons the jury never learned? Is it based on police testimony that can be disproven?

Look, too, at what evidence may have been withheld, either because it was not available at the time of trial or because of the judge's rulings. Examine this evidence closely, and do not assume the new evidence is true just because you want it to be. If a prosecution witness now is recanting his or her testimony, that does not mean the new version is true. Is the witness being pressured to change the story? Has the witness been given a lie detector test? (Such a test may not prove anything; but if someone refuses to take one, or takes one and fails, it may give a reporter pause.)

Inquirer reporter John Woestendiek, whose beat was penal and mental institutions, once received a telephone call from a staff member at an organization that Woestendiek had cultivated—the Pennsylvania Prison Society— to say she had passed his name along to the family of Terence McCracken Jr., a suburban man whom, his family contended, was wrongly convicted of murder.

Woestendiek met with the suspect's father, a man who had once been a member of Pennsylvania's notorious motorcycle gang, the Warlocks. When Terence McCracken Sr. told Woestendiek that his son had been home the day of the crime, he was hardly persuasive. But Woestendiek was intrigued by other details the father offered: His son signed for a registered letter at about the time of the crime, and two other men had originally been charged with the crime but later got off, and since had come close to admitting to the father that they had committed the murder.

Woestendiek went to the jail, where McCracken, who had been in jail for two years at this point, agreed to write down and send the reporter an account of how he spent his day March 18, 1983, the day that someone had robbed a local delicatessen and killed a 71-year old customer.

Woestendiek read the trial transcript, and also interviewed in jail one of the other two men initially charged with the crime—William Verdekal, who had been arrested (and later convicted) for another armed robbery, at which time the police seized a gun that tests showed had been used in the delicatessen killing. (Murder charges were brought against Verdekal and his associate, but dismissed after the conviction of McCracken.)

At first, Verdekal was uncooperative, telling Woestendiek he wanted to help but also wanted protection—a request the reporter could not honor. But Verdekal agreed to meet Woestendiek again, and ultimately said that his partner committed the robbery and killing while he waited outside. Neither man knew McCracken at the time of the incident, he said.

Both Verdekal and McCracken separately took and passed lie-detector tests administered by a recognized expert hired by The Inquirer.

Jurors, meanwhile, told Woestendiek that the testimony concerning a gunshot residue test had been critical evidence to them during the trial; Woestendiek tracked down a scientist who had helped devise the test, and who concluded, after reviewing the case, that the test of McCracken had been improperly interpreted.

The evidence that Woestendiek uncovered, through the experts and through more than 100 interviews, led to stories that ultimately won him a Pulitzer Prize for investigative reporting.

Plea Bargains

Another matter to investigate is whether cases are generally coming to trial or not. Many criminal justice systems depend on plea bargaining, in which defendants agree to plead guilty, generally to lesser charges, with some understanding of what sentences they will face.

Often people react negatively to such deals, and many would-be prosecutors campaign against them. But they are a fact of life in court systems across the country; without them, defendants would lose incentives to plead guilty, the criminal courts would be clogged, and money would be wasted on unnecessary trials. Such bargaining is not inherently evil. But inevitably, the more a system can be bent, the more likely cases will occur in which someone with connections can get special benefits.

Do certain lawyers seem able to negotiate successful plea bargains more than anyone else? Know what standards exist for plea bargaining. Stay on guard for cases where those standards appear to be ignored.

Look, too, at how prosecutors handle specific types of cases. The prosecutor has wide discretion in what charges are brought. Some prosecutors may respond to a court system overcrowded with criminal cases by not even seeking convictions for the most serious crimes; additionally, if prosecutors minimize the importance of a crime, they may not properly prepare their cases.

The investigative team of WCCO-TV, in Minneapolis heard that city prosecutors were failing to handle assault cases effectively, both by failing to charge suspects with serious crimes and by failing to contact victims in many cases.

The reporters examined Municipal Court records, police reports, attorney files and court transcripts. They interviewed judges, police officers, clerks and court officials. In some cases, suspects were charged with misdemeanors based on accusations they had slashed victims with knives, threatened them with guns or beaten them unconscious. Three out of four victims of such attacks had not ever been contacted by prosecutors.

The stories led to city officials adopting a crime-fighting plan that included hiring new attorneys and planning for a victims' advocate. Many cities already have such advocates, or at least have private groups devoted to victims' rights. Such organizations are natural watchdogs against undercharging.

On the other hand, look as well at the number of cases that go to trial and end in convictions on something less than the major charge. If, in case after case, the prosecutor brings an aggravated assault charge that ends up in a misdemeanor assault conviction, this may suggest he is overcharging.

Some prosecutors may routinely prosecute on the stiffest possible charges, without evaluating the facts of an individual case, merely to protect their "law and order" image. Defense attorneys are natural sources for this phenomenon.

There may, too, be other explanations for cases that end in a compromise verdict. In states that have approved mandatory sentencing laws, some judges who dislike the law and want to avoid its harsh application may do so by finding the defendant guilty of something less than the crime that was committed. See if prosecutors detect such a pattern.

Sentencing

Judges have traditionally enjoyed wide latitude in imposing sentences, based on a defendant's past history, the nature of the crime, any peculiar circumstances and a range of other factors. But a judge's own philosophy can play a critical part, leaving defendants' fates tied to the luck-of-the-draw in the judge who hears the case.

Detroit Free Press reporters David Ashenfelter and John Castine found that sentences varied widely for similar manslaughter convictions across Michigan. Two similar killings would earn one defendant probation and another six years in prison.

The articles developed because the reporters recognized the larger picture that needed answering, based on the controversy over the lenient sentencing of two men convicted of manslaughter for killing a man with a baseball bat. Using state Department of Corrections computer tapes containing information on 30,000 sentences, the reporters fed data into their own computers, looking for manslaughter convictions.

They found 199 such cases, and through court records, police reports, newspaper clippings and interviews, the two reporters found gross disparities in sentencing.

Richmond Times-Dispatch reporters Ray McAllister and Mike Grim completed their own computer study of sentencing practices in the Virginia court system. Their stories were developed not because of any knowledge that things were wrong, but simply because such a comprehensive study had never been done there.

The reporters picked 28 localities, dissecting robbery sentences by such variables as race of defendants, their ages and education, where the trial occurred as well as whether the trial had been jury or non-jury and whether the defense attorney was court-appointed or privately retained.

Appellate and Collateral Attacks

Which judges are overturned most? Which assistant prosecutors repeatedly engage in misconduct that wins them convictions but lead to reversals later? (Some prosecutors may even cause mistrials to be declared based upon their misconduct). How do you know?

First, get to know the lawyers in the appellate divisions of the prosecutor's and public defender's offices; if there is one, and the leading criminal appellate attorneys. Talk to the trial lawyers about whom they consider to be the worst prosecutors and judges, and find out why.

Remember that unlike the defense attorney, the ethical obligation for a prosecutor is not to be purely an advocate. Prosecutors, in representing the people, are supposed to seek justice, not convictions.

You can do your own research. Get to know your local law library. Learn how to look up what your state appellate courts have ruled on specific issues. Look up their cases on judicial and prosecutorial misconduct.

Additionally, watch for the bizarre, even at the post-trial stages of the proceedings. Keep in mind that for the prisoner who has been convicted and sentenced, there are not many options. Both the direct appeals and collateral attacks on the conviction represent the last hopes of relief for prisoners sitting in jail. It has become routine for prisoners, facing years in jail unless they can prove a constitutional violation, to contend that their own attorneys failed to provide effective representation.

While such claims had become commonplace, The Inquirer, in its court series, found a new twist. A reporter was in a courtroom one day when he watched an experienced defense attorney, one of the busiest in town, come into court, take the witness stand at such a hearing, and describe a series of errors he had made at trial—such as having a list of witnesses who would have provided an alibi for the defendant, but whom the attorney never bothered to call as witnesses or even interview before trial.

The testimony was startling, and the reporter set out to determine if this was an isolated case, or part of a pattern. Interviewing dozens of attorneys, and going through court records, it became clear that a small group that included several active, prominent local attorneys had admitted to errors that would have been shocking to first-year law students in case after case. No one seemed to realize this pattern was going on; but ultimately, the paper identified more than 30 cases in which egregious errors had been admitted. One former prosecutor had so testified in four different cases.

One attorney "forgot" to call to the witness stand, during a first-degree murder trial, the defendant himself, though, according to the attorney's later testimony, the defendant wanted to testify, had been prepared by the attorney and the attorney thought he would help his defense. A defendant has an absolute right to testify on his own behalf.

Another attorney testified he had counseled his client to lie during pretrial questioning by the judge when he said he wanted to waive his right to a jury trial—another right every defendant has.

None of the attorneys ever had been publicly disciplined for such errors.

While such testimony would, at first blush, appear to ruin an attorney's reputation, several defense attorneys said that, to the contrary, some attorneys engaged in such testimony as a way of getting business: It gave them the reputation among prisoners as attorneys who would do what they had to for their clients.

Furthermore, research into the state court decisions showed that, ironically, in trying to prevent new trials from being awarded, the state Supreme Court had indirectly helped create such testimony by setting a tough standard for granting a new trial. It was not enough to show that the trial may have come out differently had the attorney chosen a different strategy; the defendant would have to show that the attorney had no tactical basis for the course he or she chose at trial, and that the attorney's failure likely affected the outcome of the case. What the court had not counted on, clearly, was attorneys taking the stand to say they had no good reason for what they did.

Pardons and Early Release

Once a prisoner has lost all hope of overturning a conviction, there still remains the chance that a sentence will be commuted or conviction reversed by the governor. When such special treatment occurs, and how, is a matter worth studying.

New Orleans Times-Picayune reporters Peter Degrusy and J. Douglas Murphy spent two months checking the Louisiana court system after the release of a convicted pimp who once operated a well-patronized French Quarter brothel. The man had been sentenced to five years for possessing stolen property, but was freed after sixteen months because of a presidential pardon.

The reporters learned that the governor had been begged by a state legislator to commute the sentence. The legislator, the reporters also learned, had been paid $2,000 by the convict, who had failed to report the payment to the state ethics commission.

Based on that incident, the reporters probed the records concerning pardons generally. They went through the files of each hearing before the pardon board, noting from the record any political figures involved in the case and attorneys involved in the hearing.

Those hearings, and extensive interviews, showed that the law firm of the governor's executive counsel had the busiest pardon-board business in the state.

Over three years, that firm handled more than 100 cases before the board, and had successfully won at two out of three hearings.

The governor reacted favorably when public officials recommended his intervention, which occurred in more than 100 cases. Some officials maintained they made those recommendations—even for murderers, rapists and armed robbers—as a service for constituents; others said they were paid a fee for their service. The reporters studied the state ethics commission report, to examine which officials had reported being paid and how much.

Beyond Criminal Court

The point is simple: A good reporter, covering the legal system like any other beat, knows the process of government. Such knowledge can yield good stories at any level of the court system. Beyond criminal court, there are other courts to investigate: civil court, divorce court, juvenile court, municipal court and federal bankruptcy court.

As with the criminal justice system, such courts should be scrutinized for how effectively they operate. For example, St. Louis Globe-Democrat reporters Richard Krantz suspected something was awry at Traffic Court. After months of research, Krantz was able to show that an estimated $1 million yearly was going not to the city, but being pocketed by court officials who were able to cover up their scheme on the official records.

The key to their story was understanding the process, and closely watching the court. Krantz would sit in court and write the name of every defendant who was called, which ones appeared and which ones did not, and the disposition of each case.

He then went to the records, and compared what he had seen with what the records showed. The record of each case showed nothing particularly unusual, without first-hand knowledge of what had occurred in court. He discovered case after case in which defendants had failed to appear in court, but the official file showed the case marked "bench probation," meaning the defendant had appeared and been given a sentence in which no money was paid.

Krantz called the defendants at home and heard the same illegal scheme being repeatedly described:

A defendant gets a traffic ticket. On the day he or she goes to court, the defendant is approached in a hallway before court begins by a bail bondsman or court clerk who offers to help the defendant pay his ticket early and avoid waiting for hours. The defendant would be brought inside the courtroom, pay a clerk a fine—for example, $20 for running a red light—and go home. But that money never reached the city treasury.

The Milwaukee Journal ran a series reporting that many poor people ended up in jail—often without hearings—because they were unable to pay fines for summary citations such as jaywalking and disorderly conduct.

Reporter Nina Bernstein found the city's Municipal Court had established a conveyer-belt justice system that carried people from the streets to the prisons without any representation.

When people received summary citations, she found, the fines were almost automatic. When those fines went unpaid, she found, the defendants often were sent to jail without any representation, because such representation is not guaranteed for municipal violations.

Bernstein documented the story by sitting in Municipal Court and watching what took place. She interviewed defense attorneys, prosecutors, social workers, clerks, judges, police officers and the victims. She used computer records and files in the clerks office to track individual cases.

A month after Bernstein's story appeared, the court's chief judge announced that such imprisonment would no longer be automatic for unpaid fines.

There has recently been an enhanced awareness of the court division—in many areas, called Family Court—that oversees cases of child neglect and spousal abuse. State laws, in many cases, limit rights to access. But even with such limits, reporters can find a wealth of other sources for such stories: Juvenile divisions of the police department; domestic-abuse divisions of prosecutors; local and state social service departments; officials of juvenile institutions. There are likely attorneys, either private or part of a defender office, who are local experts and receive frequent court appointments on behalf of victims in such cases. And there are child advocacy groups in many cities.

Reporters often use civil court records to develop stories. But in 1988, Washington Post reporters Elsa Walsh and Ben Weiser went beyond that coverage: They studied the growing number of cases in which judges across the country would routinely grant confidentiality requests. Such orders turned the public courts into private justice, limiting public awareness of dangers ranging from unsafe fuel tanks to incompetent doctors. They did the story by hard work. They talked to trial lawyers, asking if they knew about any big cases that had been sealed. They looked for patterns of corporations using such requests as a strategy. They scrutinized court dockets for cases that had been turned confidential. They talked to courthouse employees.

And in its study of bankruptcy court, The Indianapolis Star found cronyism in appointments; private contacts between lawyers and judges; perquisites being given to officials by firms benefiting from appointments; and lax oversight of the finances of bankrupt firms. Again, the series required hard work: 150 interviews and examination of thousands of pages of record.

Policing Legal Wrongdoing

Often, stories on the judicial system raise issues about judicial and attorney misconduct.

Each state's high court adopts rules that define misconduct. But how are these rules enforced?

Each state has two organizations, responsible either through the state constitution or through court rules with enforcing the conduct of judges and lawyers. For lawyers, it may be either a separate state agency or the bar association; for judges, it will likely be a separate state agency. Generally, such agencies have the power to take action themselves, or recommend that the court take action ranging from private reprimand to disbarment or removal from office.

The proceedings are often tightly guarded by law, and may only become public if and when some form of public discipline is recommended. Such privacy protects judges and lawyers from being tarnished by unfounded complaints, but it can lead to situations in which inappropriate behavior is whitewashed.

Who sits on these groups, and how good is the job they do? Is the judicial review board dominated by judges unwilling to challenge their colleagues? Does the attorney review board similarly protect lawyers?

Get whatever information is public about the number of cases in which discipline has taken place over the years. Look at the specific cases. Find out how many complaints the agency has, and how many staff members exist to investigate those complaints. Compare that percentage to that of beauticians, doctors, real estate agents and other state-licensed groups.

Talk to lawyers you trust about the job the agency is doing, and look particularly at how the agency handled cases in which a judge's or lawyer's actions have been publicly challenged. If a lawyer testifies for the prosecution in a court case that he paid bribes, for example, find out why he is still practicing.

Obviously, in developing these types of stories, reporters must thoroughly understand the process. But that is only a starting point.

Reporters must have good sources on the beat. It is too easy to rely only on the prosecutors, who have more power to intimidate judges by public condemnation than do defense attorneys. Develop sources on both sides. Know the various outside lobbying groups on behalf of victims' rights, prisoners' rights, citizens' crime commissions, court reform efforts and so on. Get to know the people within the system: the court officers, administrative staff and employees who keep the system working.

As on any beat, it takes time and effort to develop sources. The best method for doing so is: Prove yourself to be someone worthy of trust, by being honest, accurate, thorough and fair in dealing with people and in writing your stories.

In questioning the quality of justice, reporters must know how to evaluate what has taken place. A good starting point is the law library, where appellate decisions lay out standards binding on trial courts.

Each court system will have a set of rules, adopted by the top appellate court and the local court, to govern many procedures.

Each state will have two codes of conduct, defining unacceptable behavior by attorneys and judges. Get copies of these codes. Get copies of the model codes from the American Bar Association, headquartered in Chicago. Know the standards, and know in what ways your state may have watered down the model rules.

On questions involving judicial discipline, another critical organization is the American Judicature Society, which can answer questions concerning the judicial canons in each state and also has studied specific cases of judicial discipline nationwide.

Look, too, for independent experts. The American Bar Association officials, as well as the leaders of the bar association in any local area, can often speak out on the administration of justice. Both the national and local organizations have committees with members that specialize in particular areas of the law, and provide expertise in everything from criminal law to divorce to professional responsibility. So, too, can such legal experts as law school professors and respected retired judges.

On questions involving the courts as an institution, the National Center for State Courts, headquartered in Williamsburg, Va., is devoted to such areas as court administration, management and personnel issues.

Using Courts for Other Stories

One final reminder about the courts: They provide a mountain of records that should be used in many stories well beyond the court system.

Any reporter doing a serious study of an individual or corporation should, early on, check both state and federal court records. Such records can provide a wealth of information, leads and sources. They also have the advantage of being privileged—so that reporters who correctly quote from court records need not fear the threat of libel.

The federal system is retained on a microfiche index, so reporters can look up names and quickly gather a list of cases. State court systems vary—many now employ computers that can conduct such searches, but others still retain such records only in a jungle of docket books.

Civil cases will provide a wealth of information that can be at the heart of any story. Much of the detail in civil lawsuits can be found in the pretrial discovery that occurs as attorneys prepare their case. The parties will be required to respond to written interrogatories, giving details about their backgrounds and about the incident in dispute. Further, the parties and other witnesses will submit to sworn depositions that will include far more information than generally is admissible in court.

Inquirer reporter Marimow, for example, won his second Pulitzer Prize after he detailed a pattern of the city's police dogs attacking citizens accused of doing nothing to provoke such attacks. As Marimow wrote, "A three-month Inquirer investigation has found that a hard core of errant K-9 police officers, and their dogs, is out of control."

In addition to many interviews, Marimow documented his story in part by looking up lawsuits filed against the police department and the officers assigned to K-9 duty, and carefully reviewing those files. The lawsuits often detailed the injuries suffered, and the events that led up to the attacks.

In one case, Marimow found that the police department had prepared, in response to a pretrial request by the defense attorney, a list of 46 dog bites that had occurred the previous year. That list, Marimow found from his own research, was not complete.

Such suits can be helpful in doing stories on virtually anyone. An Inquirer series on the local transit system, showing the system was unsafe because of years of neglect and inadequate funding for maintenance, was built largely on lawsuits against the transit agency.

By looking up such records, in addition, a reporter often will discover excellent sources. Ex-spouses and people who take their grievances to court often have stories to tell about their antagonists that may go far beyond the case.

Additionally, in the case of private individuals and corporations, reporters are advised to also check federal bankruptcy court and tax court records, where overlooked files hold a wealth of information.

DOCUMENTING THE EVIDENCE

CASE FILE PRIMER

Although each court jurisdiction may have different kinds of forms found in case files, generally the forms fall into the following categories.

- A *complaint* or *petition* is usually the first document filed in civil cases. It gives the names of the plaintiff and the defendant and spells out the alleged facts and what the plaintiff wants.

  A complaint is also usually the first document filed in criminal cases. In some states, such as Minnesota, a complaint form is used as an arrest warrant. This document alleges that an offense has occurred and that there is probable cause to believe that the defendant, who is named in the complaint, committed the offense. If the defendant asks for a preliminary hearing and probable cause is then established, he or she is bound over to the court. A separate statement of probable cause may be filed in this situation and will include the defendant's name, the alleged facts, the offense, the recommended bail and the name of the complainant—usually a police officer.

- An *information* in many states follows a complaint and is the first document filed in district court. In some places an information is used only for misdemeanors. An information is similar to the complaint alleging that a crime took place and that an individual committed it. It includes the date and location of the offense, in some cases the name of the victim and some facts about the case. It provides the specific charge(s) on which the defendant will be tried.

- An *indictment* is issued by a grand jury in a criminal case involving a felony, and in certain instances a misdemeanor, and takes the place of the complaint-information process. As with the complaint or information, the indictment states that a crime took place and alleges that the individual named committed the crime. With an indictment, the case is brought directly to district court and the preliminary hearing is bypassed.

- A *motion* is used in both civil and criminal proceedings. Motions common in civil cases include those seeking dismissal or summary judgment because of factual deficiencies or those asking the court not to accept certain evidence or legal arguments. In criminal cases, there may be motions to strike prior convictions charged in the information or complaint, motions to dismiss because of the lack of a speedy trial, motions to dismiss because of denial of due process, motions to suppress evidence and motions to request an insanity hearing. Sometimes motions are filed orally, but a written record exists in the transcript or may be recorded on the docket.

- An *answer* is filed in response to a motion or a complaint made by the other party. Answers may be presented orally.

- A *subpoena* is a document ordering the presence of a person in court or the production of evidence. The evidence asked for can provide important leads about individuals who have knowledge about the case.
- A *docket* is one of the more useful documents as it includes all actions of the court, such as decisions on motions, bail reduction, orders for discovery, change of venue, change of attorney and final disposition. It lists these actions chronologically.
- A *demurrer* is filed in a civil action by the defendant when it is believed that a particular defect in the complaint exists or that the complaint itself does not show liability.
- A *deposition* is the sworn written testimony of witnesses, sometimes in the form of answers to written questions or interrogatories.
- An *interrogatorie* is a question submitted to both sides by the attorneys.
- An *application for a search warrant* and a *supporting affidavit* show who conducted the search, statements of probable cause that are used to justify the issuance of the warrants and the specific items or individuals sought.
- A *trial brief* may be filed by either side in both civil and criminal cases. It states what facts are to be proved and what law applies to those facts.
- A *writ* is an order judges grant instructing a party to do or not to do certain things. For example, a write of habeas corpus is granted to determine if a prisoner has been held legally.
- A *jury instruction* is usually submitted by each attorney to the judge, who has the discretion to accept, modify or reject it. In general, jury instructions deal with points of law and set the boundaries within which the jury must make its decision. Sometimes these instructions form the basis for the appeal by the losing party.
- A *judgment* is the official disposition of the court. It usually includes the name of the defendant, the specific charge, the date and nature of the plea, the names of the attorneys who represented each side, the name of the judge who presided and the disposition itself.
- A *transcript of the final disposition* contains the decision of the court, including the sentence when a criminal defendant has been found guilty.

Civil Case Files

Civil case files offer a wealth of information related to specific cases as well as investigations of individuals, businesses and corporations or courtroom operations.

Civil actions, also called *torts*, usually are brought against individuals or organizations by other individuals or organizations, and sometimes by or against the government. The actions may be brought to win money damages, to compel someone to act or to stop someone from performing an act. Civil actions include such areas as business transactions, property rights, accidents, libel, divorces, child custody, mental competency and the legality of ordinances, statutes and laws.

Civil case files are obtained from the court clerk. You may need the case number, which you can find through the chronological index of actions or the alphabetical (or vertical) index filed by the defendant's name.

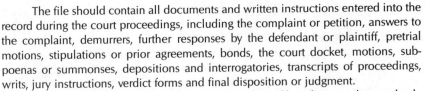

The file should contain all documents and written instructions entered into the record during the court proceedings, including the complaint or petition, answers to the complaint, demurrers, further responses by the defendant or plaintiff, pretrial motions, stipulations or prior agreements, bonds, the court docket, motions, subpoenas or summonses, depositions and interrogatories, transcripts of proceedings, writs, jury instructions, verdict forms and final disposition or judgment.

Reporters should form the habit of checking these files whenever they are backgrounding an individual or company. It may save time, and it may be the only source open to the reporters for certain kinds of information, especially financial and general business facts and allegations. The files can produce new angles and new sources, and the information usually is privileged as far as libel is concerned. Remember, however, everything in the files is not true, and shouldn't be reported as such. Check the allegations out as best you can.

Criminal Case Files

Access to criminal case files may vary from jurisdiction to jurisdiction, but they are almost always open to reporters when the cases are current. As with all areas of investigative reporting, but especially in this area, reporters need to become completely familiar with the procedures of the court.

The case file is obtained from the court clerk. To receive the file, usually you must know the case number. This is obtained by looking at the chronological index or the alphabetical index (vertical index) under the defendant's name. If the defendant is acquitted or charges have been dropped, the case file is closed. In many jurisdictions, however, the jail record book often has information of value and is rarely pursued (see "Jail Book," below).

In the file you may find an information sheet, complaint, indictment, affidavits, warrants, bail affidavit and receipt, subpoenas, application for warrant, the court docket, and (sometimes) transcripts, list of exhibits, motions and answers, jury instructions and verdict forms and final disposition or judgment.

Criminal case files are essential for covering a specific case and for backgrounding defendants. They can also help establish important patterns, such as whether defendants receive fair and speedy trials. The files can be useful to see what the interests at the start of the trial were and how well they were served by checking all correspondence between the defense and prosecuting attorneys with respect to plea bargaining.

Prosecutor's Case Files

The prosecutor's case file is the most complete file on a case available, but because it is not a public document, you will need the aid of a friendly prosecutor to see it.

Chronological Indexes of Civil and Criminal Case Files

Usually there are separate abstract indexes for civil and criminal cases, both kept by the court clerk but in separate files. The indexes give the most complete information except, of course, for the case files themselves. Included in each index entry is the complaint (in a civil case) or the charge (in a criminal case), names of defendants and plaintiffs (in a civil case), the date of filing, the case number and the disposition, if one has been reached yet.

Court reporters normally check the indexes daily for spot news stories.

Remember that in criminal cases, the information usually is expunged after a certain time period if the defendant has been acquitted or if the charges have been dropped.

ADDITIONAL INFORMATION

Jail Book

The jail book is kept at the jail and usually includes the names of persons arrested and the arresting agency, date of commitment to jail, suspected offense, address of prisoner, terms (such as whether the person is being held for another law enforcement agency and the amount of bond), discharge date, why the prisoner was discharged and the number of days spent in jail. This information is usually organized by date rather than by prisoners' names. Jail books are open and they often contain information closed off in other court or police records.

Bail Investigation Reports

Although the background check on a defendant prior to setting bail may be very thorough, only the most general information is available to the reporter unless a friendly judge or court clerk allows an examination.

Available are the names of the defendant and judge, defendant's address, offense and very general evaluative comments. The file is kept with the court clerk.

Pre-sentence Investigation Reports

Before passing sentence in a criminal case, the judge may order a pre-sentence investigation report to be conducted by a probation officer. The investigation may include extensive interviews with the defendant and his or her relatives, friends, employers and attorneys. The report includes the defendant's previous criminal record, nature of the current offense, education, vocational training, marital status, religion, family background and psychiatric and medical history.

These reports are closed to reporters without the aid of a source. Sometimes the person convicted may open them to you if dissatisfied with his or her sentence.

PRISONS

The most information about a prisoner that you can get from a prison is that he or she is in confinement. Although prisons keep extensive records on inmates, a source is necessary for access to the information.

Records relating to the operation of the prison, including how it spends its money, are public and can be obtained either at the prison or at the state division of corrections or similar agency.

GRAND JURIES

Laws governing grand jury activity vary widely from state to state. Federal grand juries operate under yet another set of rules.

A grand jury is a panel of citizens convened to inquire into alleged violations of the law and determine whether there is sufficient evidence to formally accuse a person or persons with crimes. A grand jury may consist of anywhere from 12 to 33 members. How they are selected varies in different jurisdictions.

Grand jury proceedings are always held behind closed doors, and for good reason. They are technically under the control of a judge, but they are almost always manipulated by the prosecutor.

Many reporters have spent long hours outside grand jury rooms waiting to see which witnesses go in and out and how long they spend inside and—when the law permits—to ask them what was asked and what they said before the grand jury.

In many states witnesses are forbidden by law from revealing anything that went on inside the grand jury room. Grand jurors, of course, are also legally restrained from talking about their work in the grand jury room. But some grand juries leak like sieves, thanks to a friendly prosecutor, a talkative juror, maybe even an injudicious judge.

The prosecutor or court clerk will usually have the names of the grand jurors available for public inspection. The office that pays them their per diem expenses also will have their names. Subpoenas issued for witnesses sometimes are public record, and other times are not. Bear in mind that witnesses are also paid expenses.

Not all indictments become public immediately after they are handed down. Some remain secret for a time—usually while authorities look for the person who has been indicted.

Some grand juries also draw up final reports that may prove of widespread interest. These reports can deal with just about anything the grand juries wish—barring interference by the presiding judge. For example, the report could contain the extent of organized crime's influence in a city all the way to conditions found while investigating the county jail or city dog pound. They normally are written for public consumption.

JUVENILE CRIMES

Police and court records related to crimes or "delinquency" by juveniles are closed to the news media on the theory that youngsters in trouble with the law have enough problems already without adding public exposure. State juvenile codes vary in a lot of ways, but all demand secrecy. Juvenile court hearings usually are held secretly too.

The exceptions to this rule occur in one of two ways:

- When the judge agrees to allow a reporter access to some files and entry into the courtroom if the reporter agrees to withhold identification of the youth in trouble. This is not uncommon. Many judges believe such coverage will add to the public understanding of juvenile delinquency.

■ When the judge binds the youth over to a court of adult jurisdiction because of the gravity of the crime.

Most secrecy laws in juvenile codes prohibit *release* of information about the offender, not *publication* of such facts.

LOCAL AND STATE COURT CASES

Court Finance Reports

In many states, the court clerk must report monthly to the appropriate state judicial overview agency an accounting of all money received and spent, including who received the money, when, why, the amount and check number, the date and case number, and the name of the defendant.

Check with the court clerk or appropriate state agency. (Sometimes this may be the state Supreme Court clerk if the state operates a unified bar system.)

Annual Reports to State Judicial Commissions

Each state court submits a report to its state judicial commission detailing the number of civil, criminal and juvenile cases disposed of, the number of cases with and without juries and other information, depending on state requirements.

Check with the court clerk or the state judicial agency.

Complaints Against Attorneys

The bar advisory committee of the state bar association or other comparable state judicial commission investigates complaints received about the conduct of judges and attorneys, including prosecutors.

Information available varies greatly from state to state, but often open are the case files of those actually disciplined, or, in some cases, the initial complaint. After the investigation, a report usually is made to the state Supreme Court for possible action.

Start with your state bar association.

Financial Background Reports on Judges

Many states require candidates for state judgeships to file reports detailing their personal finances. Check with your state elections commission or other appropriate state agency.

BACKGROUND INFORMATION

On the Courts

All federal courts, except for the U.S. Supreme Court, come under the jurisdiction of the Administrative Office of the U.S. Courts, 811 Vermont Ave. N.W., Washington, D.C. 20544. For U.S. Supreme Court data, write the U.S. Supreme Court Building, 1 First St. N.E., Washington, D.C. 20543.

- *The Federal Judicial Workload Statistics,* a quarterly compilation, gives information about civil and criminal workloads in U.S. Courts of Appeals, District Courts and the federal probation system. The information includes the number of cases filed and terminated and the number appealed, the number of civil and criminal cases filed, including a listing by the nature of the suit or type of offense, the number of bankruptcy cases, figures for the number of persons received for or removed from supervision in the federal probation system, trials by number and length, number of grand and petit juries, special court hearings, dispositions by magistrates and other cases opened and pending, including how many hours in court.

  Although the statistics themselves rarely make worthwhile stories, they can be used to evaluate case loads and final dispositions in your jurisdiction and offer insight into such areas as the quality of the local public defender system.

  Write to the Administrative Office of the U.S. Courts.
- *Federal Offenders in the U.S. District Courts* is a statistical annual giving information on the disposition, sentence, type of counsel, age, sex and prior records of federal criminal defendants in U.S. District Courts.

  This publication can be especially useful for measuring the consistency and quality of the justice dispensed in your area. For instance, are there major differences in the sentences handed down by sex or any other demographic category?

  Write to the Administrative Office of the U.S. Courts.
- *Annual Report of the Director, Administrative Office of the U.S. Courts,* primarily gives statistical information related to civil and criminal cases, trials, juror use, probation, bankruptcy cases, special courts, naturalizations, dispositions by magistrates, number of judges and administrative personnel, appropriations and operating costs.

  Useful are the statistics related to the different types of civil cases, such as antitrust, land condemnation, environment and other areas.

  Write to the Government Printing Office.
- *Federal Court Management Statistics* gives a very specific and detailed annual breakdown of court workloads and management data for the 11 federal Courts of Appeals and the 94 District Courts. Profiles for each U.S. Court of Appeals include civil and criminal appeals filed, terminated and pending, actions for each judgeship or panel, number of opinions, reversals,

denials and time elapsed. Profiles for each District Court include much of this same information.

Write to the Administrative Office of the U.S. Courts.

- *Grand and Petit Juror Service in U.S. District Courts* gives an annual statistical look at jury use (grand and petit) for federal District Courts, including the number of grand juries, proceedings by indictment, percentage of jurors selected, not selected and challenged and profiles of juries.

Write to the Administrative Office of the U.S. Courts.

- *Report on Applications for Orders Authorizing or Approving the Interception of Wire or Oral Communications* is an annual report breaking down the requests from county, state and federal officials related to wire tapping and surreptitious tapings of conversations. Data on applications are from reports required of state and federal judges and prosecuting attorneys.

Listed are jurisdictions with statutes authorizing the interception of wire or oral communications, intercept orders issued by judges and the offenses involved, types of surveillance used, arrests and convictions as a result of intercept orders installed and motions to suppress the information gained from the intercepts.

Write to the Administrative Office of the U.S. Courts.

- *Tables of Bankruptcy Statistics with Reference to Bankruptcy Cases Commenced and Terminated in the U.S. District Courts* is published every 10 years giving detailed information on the number and type of bankruptcy cases by district and circuit. The description of cases includes a breakdown by occupation, special relief cases, amount of liabilities and payments to creditors, administrative expenses and total assets. A similar 10-year report is issued for civil and criminal courts.

Write to the Administrative Office of the U.S. Courts.

- *The Federal Judicial Center* is the research agency for the federal courts in such areas as systems and technological development, continuing education, litigation process, jury management, sentencing and probation and federal court administration and management. Research is conducted at the request of the courts.

A list of project reports, a newsletter and other information are available from the Federal Judicial Center, 1520 H St. N.W., Washington, D.C. 20005; (202) 633–6011.

- *The Fund for Modern Courts* organizes and coordinates citizen court-watcher projects throughout New York State and is in contact with less formal organizations in 10 other states. It conducts research into court issues, holds citizens forums and monitors such areas as judge demeanor, time spent on the bench, physical condition of courtrooms and the general administration of justice in state and local courts.

Write to the Fund for Modern Courts, 36 West 44th St., Suite 310, New York, N.Y. 10036–8181; (212) 575–1577.

- *National Center for State Courts* is an organization established to assist state courts in the areas of organization, administration, personnel statistics, information management, technology, press and government relations.

Write to the National Center for State Courts, 300 Newport Ave., Williamsburg, Va. 23187; (804) 253–2000.

■ *American Judicature Society* is the nation's oldest and most broad-based court reform organization, that keeps a file of case histories about judges who have been disciplined or investigated and not disciplined. It publishes a monthly magazine, *Judicature,* which deals with problems in local, state and federal courts. It also publishes a number of specialized reports dealing with court issues.

Contact the American Judicature Society, 25 E. Washington St., 16th Floor, Chicago, Ill. 60602; (312) 558–6900.

■ *U.S. Parole Commission Annual Report* includes information on sentencing, supervision of parolees, parole decisions and reviews, biographical information on commissioners and statistics on parole hearings.

Write to the Department of Justice, U.S. Parole Commission, 5550 Friendship Blvd., Chevy Chase, Md. 20815; (301) 492–5990.

■ *Children in Custody: A Report on the Juvenile Detention and Correction Facility Census* is an annual publication with information on the number of juvenile facilities, number of juveniles held and types of offenses, description of public facilities that hold children awaiting court action and those already adjudicated.

Write to Public Affairs, Office of Justice Programs, 633 Indiana Ave. N.W., Washington, D.C. 20531; (202) 307–0703.

On the Prisons

The following reports and publications are issued by the Bureau of Prisons, which has jurisdiction over all federal penal and correctional institutions. To obtain a copy, write the Bureau of Prisons, 320 First St. N.W., Washington, D.C. 20534; (202) 307–3198.

■ *Commitments and Discharges for the Month* gives a breakdown by region and facility of transfers, civil courts, military courts, parole, mandatory releases, mandatory release violations and expirations of sentence. An annual publication gives the same information for the year.

■ *Federal Prisoners Confined* is a weekly publication giving the total inmate population for each region and facility and a comparison with the previous year.

■ *The Federal Prison System* is an annual publication describing the overall prison system, including organization, new institutions, inmate education, vocational training programs, health and other services and staffing.

■ *Federal Prison System Facilities* is a directory of central and regional offices, correctional facilities and staff training centers. Each profile covers location, population capacity, security class, staffing, education and training opportunities, drug abuse programs, experimental programs and other services.

■ *Indexes for Final Opinions and Orders, Statements of Policy and Interpretations and Administrative Staff Manuals and Instructions* for federal prisons gives the numerical and alphabetical listing of policy statements for the following areas: general management and administration, laws and legal matters, personnel management, budget management, research and development statistics, accounting management, procurement and warehouse management, commissary management, miscellaneous business and fiscal management, custodial management, safety standards and procedures, jail administration, facilities and equipment, industrial management, medical services management, parole board and information systems.

These policy statements from the Bureau of Prisons should be useful to reporters beginning investigation of a penal institution.

Write to the Bureau of Prisons.

- *Operations memoranda* are usually interpretations of policy statements and can be requested for areas relating to specific problems with prisons. These may be helpful to reporters trying to probe conditions and operations within a prison.

Other Sources of Information on Prisons

- *National Prison Project* is a private organization interested in prisoners' rights and overall conditions in prisons. The organization is also involved in class action suits on behalf of prisoners.

Contact the National Prison Project, 1616 P St. N.W., Washington, D.C. 20036.

On Law Enforcement in General

- *Office of Justice Program* can provide information on federal grants to law enforcement agencies through a computerized data retrieval system. Department of Justice grants involve millions of dollars awarded to local jurisdictions, and reporters can begin here to assess how this money is being used. Areas covered include police, courts, corrections, juvenile justice, evaluation, community crime prevention, advanced technology and any criminal justice-related programs.

Information may include a description of the grant, subgrants, contracts and interagency agreements, as well as the year of the grant award, a fiscal year funding project summary and an assessment summary.

Contact Public Affairs, Office of Justice Programs, U.S. Department of Justice, Washington, D.C. 20531; (202) 307–0703.

- *National District Attorneys Association* is a private organization composed mostly of prosecutors, that conducts such projects as technical assistance, victim-witness assistance, economic crime prevention, juvenile justice standards and evidence tracking. It operates a child-support enforcement clearinghouse and provides information on that topic.

Contact the National District Attorneys Association, 1033 N. Fairfax St., Suite 200, Alexandria, Va. 22314.

- *National Legal Aid and Defender Association* acts as a clearinghouse for information about civil legal aid and defense services for indigents accused of crimes. The civil division advocates for legal representation for the poor and a variety of civil matters. The defender division has as its members most of the public defenders in the country and represents their interests at the state and local level. The association conducts research in areas of standards and goals, technical assistance and evaluation.

Contact the National Legal Aid and Defender Association, 1625 K St. N.W., Suite 800, Washington, D.C. 20006; (202) 452–0620.

■ *SEARCH Group Inc.* is a private organization that often works with state and federal governments as a consultant in the application of new technology to the justice system. It can be useful to reporters trying to understand the newer types of computer record systems being introduced in criminal justice systems throughout the country.

Contact SEARCH Group Inc., 7311 Greenhaven Dr., Suite 145, Sacramento, Calif. 95813; (916) 392–2550.

■ *Midwest Research Institute* performs contract research of criminal justice agencies in such areas as standards and goals, training, crime laboratory planning, crimes against the elderly and other areas.

Its studies and experts can be good sources for reporters evaluating the justice system in their own areas. The organization's specialties include police, courts, corrections, juvenile justice, evaluation, community crime prevention, advanced technology and information systems training.

Contact the Midwest Research Institute, 425 Volker Blvd., Kansas City, Mo. 64110.

■ INSLAW Inc. is the leading software vendor of legal case tracking and workflow management systems. It serves criminal justice agencies including courts, prosecutors, corrections, probation and parole.

There are many INSLAW publications of value as background information available to reporters.

Contact INSLAW Inc., 1125 15th St. N.W., Suite 300, Washington, D.C. 20005; (202) 828–8600.

■ *Center for Women Policy Studies* maintains a comprehensive library on issues affecting women and makes available research packages, called the Domestic Violence Research Collections, on family violence and women offenders.

Contact the Center for Women Policy Studies, 2000 P St. N.W., Washington, D.C. 20036; (202) 872–1770.

■ *Directory of Correctional Services Agencies* contains a list and description of service agencies, which can be obtained by writing the Wisconsin Correctional Service c/o Rick Tannen, 436 West Wisconsin Ave., Milwaukee, Wis. 53203.

■ *Directory of Institutions and Agencies* and *Directory of Jail and Detention Centers* are annual publications listing all correctional institutions and related agencies.

Write to the American Correctional Association, 8025 Laurel Lakes Ct., Laurel, Md. 20707; (301) 206–5100.

■ *American Bar Foundation* is the research affiliate of the American Bar Association, and does basic empirical research on legal institutions. The foundation looks at the theory and functioning of legal institutions and professions.

C H A P T E R   15

Health Care

Americans spend more than a billion dollars a day on a health care system they don't understand and that frequently works against them. Reporters who know where to look will find doctors whose incompetence kills their patients, health insurance plans that withhold benefits, federal payment systems that encourage inadequate care and hospitals that generate unnecessary care to fill unneeded beds.

This is a good time to report about health care because intensified concern over quality and cost are generating new public documents.

This chapter profiles the major issues and institutions in the health care field, suggests the kinds of stories that can be done about them and details what documents to use and where to find them.

---

by PENNY LOEB and DOLLY KATZ

Reporting about health care is difficult because reporters don't come to the subject with the common knowledge that serves as a guide through many other kinds of stories. We have some general knowledge about how courts work, what unions do, what schools are supposed to do, what a contract is and how a law is made.

But the field of medicine has an aura of mystery and omnipotence, and a body of arcane knowledge that can be daunting to reporters, patients and the public alike.

How does a health maintenance organization work? How can unnecessary hospitals exist without going bankrupt and why is it bad for a community's health to have six open heart surgery facilities instead of one? If a researcher has proved that eating cockroaches cures cancer, how can it not be true?

The answers to those questions are vitally important to the public. Many areas of investigative reporting expose corruption, save money, improve institutions and put people into and out of jobs and jails. Medical reporting does that, too. But it can also regularly save lives by warning people about questionable treatments, doctors and hospitals, and by educating people about the true relationship between medicine and health.

The role of medical reporters has expanded as the field of medicine has expanded, and now involves everything from "pure" medical reporting (should estrogen routinely be given to post-menopausal women to prevent osteoporosis?) to questions of ethics (how do we distribute scarce organs for transplants?) and economics (do for-profit hospitals provide care more economically than not-for-profits?), to sophisticated computer analysis (how much do surgical death rates vary from hospital to hospital?).

Fortunately, as the subject has grown, so have the records that illuminate it. Almost every procedure in medicine and health care generates a record. Virtually every individual and institutional health care provider and insurer—doctors, hospitals, health maintenance organizations—is licensed by the state or federal government, or both. As the payer of a third of all medical bills, federal and state governments require extensive documentation from hospitals and health care professionals of how, when, where and for whom they provided medical care. Local, state and federal agencies collect masses of data. Every health professional has a national organization that studies its members and itself.

Furthermore, much of the record is public. Of course, much of it is also difficult to understand. But doctors, researchers, hospital administrators and health care experts at all levels are available to explain it.

It has been said that doctors and scientists don't like to talk to reporters. If that was once true, it isn't anymore. The medical and health care establishments now cater to reporters. Part of the reason is that an oversupply of doctors and hospitals have made health care a buyer's market. Also, researchers have come to recognize the importance of public understanding to research funding. Scientists, like anyone else, like to see their names in print.

Most are happy to talk with and even lend their expertise to reporters conducting investigations. John Fried of the Long Beach Press Telegram assembled a panel of doctors to evaluate autopsy records of patients who died in emergency rooms. They determined that as many as half of the patients could have been saved if they'd been taken to hospitals with the proper facilities and specialists.

But beware: the complexity of medicine makes it possible to find someone or some research that will support almost any assertion. Keep the following suggestions in mind when investigating the health care field:

- Be cautious about reporting research that has not been published in a refereed journal—one with panels of experts who judge the soundness and importance of the work.

  The Dec. 24, 1985, New England Journal of Medicine, one of the nation's most prestigious medical journals, contains two conflicting studies on estrogen, a hormone commonly proscribed for post-menopausal women. One, by the eminent researchers of the Framingham Heart Study, concluded that estrogen greatly increases the incidence of heart disease. The other, by equally distinguished Harvard researchers, said that giving estrogen to post-menopausal women reduces their risk of heart disease.

  You will seldom be so lucky to find conflicting scientific evidence conveniently available in the same journal. But keep in mind that it almost certainly exists, or is being readied in some other laboratory. But even the finest research by the most eminent scientists is seldom the definitive word on a subject. And most always, a discovery illuminates only a small piece of a medical puzzle. Most findings are not accepted until they have been duplicated by at least one other researcher.

- If you're looking for trends in diseases, operations, infant mortality, license revocations or spending, compare changes over several years, ideally five or more. A single year's increase or decrease is too often due to chance.

  Statistics can fool you in other ways, too. A massive increase in reported cases of a particular disease could signal an epidemic—or it could mean that doctors have become more alert to its symptoms and are reporting it more accurately.
- Learn how to use the Index Medicus, the medical field's equivalent to the Reader's Guide to Periodical Literature. You will find studies and articles on almost any subject you're investigating: physician incompetence, unnecessary surgery, dumping of poor patients on public hospitals or variations in death rates among hospitals. Moreover, you'll find excellent commentaries on the articles in the often-pithy letters to the editors, which the Index Medicus also chronicles. You'll find doctors calling each other names and attacking each others' studies in remarkably frank language. Even if the articles don't answer your questions, they'll tell you who the experts are, and you can ask them yourself. You can find the Index Medicus in medical school libraries, hospitals and large public libraries.

  While you're there, become acquainted with Medline and the other enormously useful computer indexes, which—for a fee—will search the Index Medicus for you.
- Learn something about medical statistics and the techniques researchers use to evaluate controversial data. A number of books explain these techniques to the layperson: one is "Nutrition, Stress and Toxic Chemicals," by Dr. Arthur Vander (University of Michigan Press). They'll teach you what questions to ask and how to tell when you're being sold a bill of goods.

Medicare

Medicare is the single greatest source of fuel for the nation's health care engine. Because it pays 40 percent of all hospital bills, Medicare helps determine the quality, amount and kind of care given to all Americans, not just the elderly whose bills it pays.

Medicare is changing, and so, consequently, is health care. Reporters need to follow these changes to document who gets the money, who gets helped and who gets hurt.

Created in 1965, Medicare expanded the elderly's access to health care. But it also stimulated massive—and excessive—hospital construction and lit an inflationary fire under health costs.

The reason for this rise in health costs was the method of payment the hospital industry extracted from Congress in exchange for its support of Medicare. The method was called cost-plus: hospitals were paid their costs, plus an extra 2 percent. Since the more a hospital spent the more it was reimbursed, hospitals were encouraged to spend as much as possible.

The result was a 900 percent increase in the nation's medical bills, which rose from $41.9 billion in 1965 to $425 billion in 1985.

In 1982, the government decided enough was enough. Late the following year, it introduced a system intended to control costs. Instead of paying hospitals after the fact, Medicare now sets payments in advance for 478 illnesses, called diagnosis-related groups (DRGs). A hospital gets a certain amount per illness, regardless of how long the patient stays or how much care is delivered. State Medicaid programs, which insure poor people, have begun to institute their own DRG payment plans.

The DRG System

As health economists have known for decades, every attempt to control costs stimulates doctors and institutions to find new ways to make money. The old cost-plus system was easy to abuse, but the new one can be abused, too. Old people are the first to pay the price.

Under the DRG system, hospitals make money by providing treatment that costs less than the DRG payment. In many cases, less is better for the patient: the cost-plus system rewarded unnecessary care and overlong hospital stays. But the DRG system creates an incentive for undertreatment.

One way hospitals can save money now is by discharging patients a day or two sooner. Some old people have died because they had no one to care for them when they went home.

Reporters trying to ferret out the new system's problems can get help from universities, consumer health groups and government agencies that have begun their own investigations. Check for studies in medical journals. Contact the Health Care Financing Administration, which administers Medicare and has contracted studies on DRGs and their effect on health care.

In your community, look for hotlines that take complaints about early discharges. Talk to not-for-profit home health agencies and advocacy groups for the elderly, like Detroit's Citizens for Better Care, which monitors the area nursing home industry. Every state is required by federal law to have an ombudsman program for long-term care. They may know Medicare recipients with stories to tell.

Your area Peer Review Organization (see "Hospitals" later in this chapter) will have evidence of problems with specific hospitals. A hospital discharging patients too soon will have a high readmission rate. Another hospital may be increasing its revenues by assigning patients to more expensive DRGs than the ones appropriate to their illnesses. The Rand Corporation of Santa Monica, Calif., has done studies on this.

Look at the DRG system itself. Is it saving the government as much as it should? The General Accounting Office estimated the DRG system would overpay hospitals by more than $8 billion by 1991.

Is DRG even a good system? It was rushed through Congress in 1982 with little study. Some experts believe the real fuel for cost inflation is a surplus of doctors and hospitals. Until the oversupply is eliminated, they say, we can't have both cheap and high-quality health care. Two think tanks exploring this issue are the Center for Policy Studies in Minneapolis and the Center for Hospital Finance and Management at the Johns Hopkins Medical Institution in Baltimore.

Impact on Other Health Care

Some of the problems the government is shedding with DRGs are landing on the nursing homes and home health care agencies. They seem ill-prepared to deal with the influx of sicker people. Problems to look for are discussed in the applicable sections.

Health Insurance

With the new Medicare system in full operation, watch for changes in the treatment of patients who have other kinds of insurance. Somebody has to pay for those often overbedded and overequipped hospitals. You may find non-Medicare patients staying longer and getting more tests as hospitals try to recoup income they used to get from Medicare patients. Major employers in your area who pay for their employees' health insurance may have evidence of such trends.

Watch the balance sheets that health insurance companies submit to the insurance commission in your state. Are profits falling? Are rates increasing? Why? Is it because of the Medicare changes? Are the insurance companies doing anything to compensate?

A 1983 law gives some employed Medicare beneficiaries the option of designating a private company as their primary insurer. More than 75 percent of the 2.2 million employed beneficiaries choose private insurance companies because deductibles are lower than Medicare's. However, the insurance companies often treated Medicare as the primary insurer instead. The government has filed suit against several companies, charging they improperly passed tens of billions of dollars in bills on to Medicare.

The Medicare changes are giving the elderly another kind of insurance problem as well. Because they can't go in or stay in the hospital, more elderly people are going to nursing homes and home health care agencies. They don't realize until they get there that neither Medicare nor other insurance pays much of the costs of alternative services.

Hospitals

Something is wrong in your community's hospitals. Patients are being admitted unnecessarily for treatment they don't need or could be performed on an outpatient basis. Patients are suffering avoidable complications and dying needlessly.

Hospitals are building more beds and buying more machines than the community can use efficiently. Some hospitals are so desperate that they are giving kickbacks to doctors that send them patients.

In the past, revelations about such hospitals occurred almost randomly and were heavily dependent on information from insiders.

Since 1985, however, reporters have had a tool—although imperfect and difficult to use—that allows them to conduct systematic investigations of all the hospitals in a community, state or even the nation.

This tool is the Peer Review Organization (PRO) that Congress required be set up in each state to scrutinize the quality and cost of care provided to Medicare patients.

With computer data on every Medicare patient, each PRO searches for trouble spots: hospitals with inappropriate admissions, high rates of complications or a high mortality rate. In April 1985, the Health Care Financing Administration (HCFA) declared that much of the information the PROs collect about hospitals is public.

Here's how to use the PRO data and other information to find out how well your local hospitals serve the public.

Patient Care

Among the first reporters to make extensive use of the PRO data were Thomas J. Moore and Michael York of Knight-Ridder newspapers, who did a computer analysis of deaths after coronary artery bypass surgery at almost 500 hospitals nationwide. They found 44 hospitals with 1984 death rates at least double the national average, and one hospital—Memorial of South Bend, Ind.—where nearly one of every four Medicare patients who had the surgery died before they could leave the hospital. They concluded that more than 1,000 Medicare patients died needlessly in 1984.

Their story began where another newspaper story ended.

In early 1986, newspapers across the country filed Freedom of Information Act requests for a HCFA study based on data from the nation's PROs. The study, originally reported in The New York Times, was an attempt to help PROs identify hospitals with unusually high death rates.

Although the list of hospitals with higher overall death rates was widely reprinted, few reporters understood how to use the data, and hospital administrators nationwide—and the study's author—claimed it was meaningless. The story quickly died.

Moore, Knight-Ridder's specialist in statistical analysis, read the study and realized it had to be based on an elaborate computer tape. He requested a copy of the tape from HCFA, put it on a computer, and extracted the data about bypass operations. He and York analyzed the data, discussed it with some of the nation's most respected heart surgeons and published their findings.

Data on deaths at individual hospitals for any of the 478 DRGs reimbursed by Medicare are available from your state PRO. Some two dozen state Medicaid programs compile their findings.

Procedures of particular interest include the nine "tracer conditions" picked by a panel of PRO doctors because of their frequency, potential for abuse, high risk or high-tech requirements. They include: congestive heart failure; acute myocardial infarction, or heart attack; pneumonia; gastrointestinal hemorrhage; cholecystectomy, or gall bladder removal; coronary artery bypass surgery; and pacemaker implants.

This information will not be easy to get or interpret. Read the documents section for all the ways HCFA and the PROs can stonewall you.

You also need to know the limits of your data, so you can defend your findings with confidence. Hospitals were able to bury the initial HCFA mortality study by claiming those with higher death rates had "sicker" patients. Moore and York consulted the medical literature, the experts and their own analysis, and concluded that—at least for bypass operations—severity of illness cannot explain the great differences in death rates among hospitals. While it's obvious that some bypass patients in any particular hospital are sicker than others in that same hospital, these differences tend to balance out when hospitals are compared with each other.

But other limitations are real. For example, hospitals that keep patients longer tend to have higher death rates, simply because their patients have a greater opportunity to die before discharge. If two patients at different hospitals both die 10 days after their operations, but one was discharged to a nursing home on the seventh day, that death won't be assigned to the hospital. Death rates based on time, not place—say, 30 days after admission—are a fairer measure of a hospital's performance. But neither HCFA nor most PROs currently provides death rates that way. While this doesn't mean you should avoid mortality studies, you and your readers should be aware that every study has its limitations. PROs are an evolving tool, and it will take time for us to learn how to use it.

PRO Objective

Michigan doctors needlessly hospitalized some 25,000 Medicare patients a year in 1982 and 1983. More than 3,400 elderly Alabama residents received permanent heart pacemakers they didn't need. Over 500 New Yorkers who died of pneumonia could have been saved. In North Carolina, more than 400 people died while undergoing cataract surgery, a procedure that should produce almost no fatalities.

These are the conclusions of state PROs. They are contained in documents called objective summaries, which outline each PRO's two-year plan to improve quality of care and reduce unnecessary admissions as part of the agency's contract with HCFA. These documents are public, and they make revealing stories in themselves. An enterprising reporter who collected all 50 could write an impressive account of unnecessary admissions, deaths and disability in the nation's hospitals.

Of even more interest would be the names of problem hospitals the PROs identify in their reviews. Michigan, for example, targeted eight hospitals with unusually high rates of unnecessary admissions. HCFA regulations don't specify that PROs must reveal this information, but they don't prohibit disclosure. California sometimes conveniently identifies errant hospitals by the provider numbers on their Medicare cost reports, which are public records.

Private Studies

The Ford Motor Co. spends almost a billion dollars a year on health insurance premiums, which adds close to $300 to the cost of every car sold in America. A natural interest in controlling health care costs prompted Ford officials to study employees' hospital admissions in southeastern Michigan.

The company discovered it was spending $20 million a year on unnecessary care in the Detroit area alone. When it compared prices and practices of the 70 area hospitals, Ford found the charge for treating an uncomplicated heart attack ranged from $3,400 to $6,300, and the length of stay from five to 11 days. Unhappy Ford executives called a meeting of hospital representatives, gave each a confidential file with its individual ranking and threatened to publicize the data if the hospitals didn't improve.

Ford has not made good on its threat. But you may be luckier with another company. Find a major employer in your area and ask its employee health benefits representative if the company has done a similar study.

Licensing Agencies

A more traditional source of information is the state agency that licenses hospitals. They are usually located in the state health department. While they rarely revoke licenses, they may try to do so, and records of those attempts should be public. Periodic reports filed after routine inspections can give you a detailed picture of an individual hospital's problems. The nurse investigator who inspected one Michigan hospital found poorly maintained rooms, severe staff shortages and dissatisfied patients. Recordkeeping was so poor that, in three different sections of a patient's record, her bedsore was described as being in three different places on her body.

Edifice Complexes

In Kalamazoo, two major hospitals fewer than two miles apart compete for patients with helicopters. One helicopter carries patients to 452-bed Burgess Medical Center, where in 1986 the occupancy rate stood at 72 percent, down from 84 percent three years earlier. The rival chopper flies to a 178-bed Bronson Methodist Hospital, where in 1986 a third of the beds were empty on any given day.

Although the state health planners originally vetoed Bronson's bid for a helicopter, the hospital finessed the state by setting up an independent corporation to run the helicopter.

That set other hospitals thinking, and now the skies above Michigan have become crowded. When The Detroit Free Press checked, cardiologists at Catherine McAuley Health Center in Ann Arbor, five miles from the University of

Michigan Hospitals, were complaining they weren't getting their fair share of heart attack victims because the University of Michigan helicopter took most of them to University Hospitals. Now McAuley doctors want their own helicopters.

The situation offers rich opportunities for satire: Kalamazoo television station WKZO aired a spoof in which the two helicopter teams fought for the patronage of a homemaker who had cut her finger on a tomato can.

But it is a serious problem. The seemingly insatiable appetite of hospitals and doctors for more machines, more buildings and more services—what health planners have dubbed their edifice complex—is expensive and dangerous.

Too many machines and beds waste money which comes out of the public's pocket, in the form of health insurance premiums and Medicaid and Medicare payments.

Even worse, they waste lives. Doctors, nurses and technicians need to be busy to retain their skills. Too many machines at too many hospitals divide the patient population into segments too small to maintain expertise. Moore and York found in their bypass study that mortality rates went up as the number of operations performed at a hospital went down.

The number of machines or operations can provide good focal points for a story. Find out how many hospitals in your community have cardiac catherization laboratories, how many procedures each lab performs and what experts recommend as the minimum number of procedures per lab.

The place to begin is your local health planning agency or health systems agency, if you still have one. The federal government used to require them to review and comment on hospital proposals for new construction. Congress cut off their money in 1986, but a number survive on local funds, and will have the data you need. Most of them will welcome you with open arms and shower you with studies they've done on the need for—or lack of—various machines.

If you don't have a local planning agency, your state health department probably does. If your state has a certificate of need law, the health department must approve any new hospital construction or service that will cost more than a certain dollar limit. You should be able to see each hospital's application for a particular machine, the state planner's comments and rationale for acceptance or rejection, and the state's final decision.

Names, addresses and telephone numbers of your local and state health planning agencies can be found in that gem of a hospital reference work, the American Hospital Association Guide to the Health Care Field, which also will indicate the local hospitals with cardiac catherization labs, CAT scanners, open heart surgery facilities and other services. If you can't find an AHA Guide, call your state or local hospital association.

If your state has abandoned health planning, find out what's happened to hospital construction since then. In Arizona, four new open heart surgery programs opened in Phoenix within a year after the certificate of need law was repealed. The rate of open heart surgery in the city increased almost 20 percent, and the number of procedures per unit dropped to fewer than half the minimum number previously required by health planners.

Other Sources

Don't overlook the tipsters and professionals who can provide leads, access and insight. If you are investigating a particular hospital, talk to employee union leaders who can put you in touch with nurses and technicians at the hospital. Find recently retired doctors who no longer feel threatened by loss of referrals or hospital privileges. Talk to administrators at other hospitals; they are usually knowledgeable about hospitals in their communities and can give you valuable direction and tips, even if they may not be willing to talk on the record.

Veterans Hospitals

The nation's largest medical system—the Department of Veterans Affairs (DVA)—is the least covered.

While the press hasn't been looking, veterans died needlessly at more than a dozen hospitals with poor heart surgery programs, DVA patients have been guinea pigs for interns sent over from nearby medical schools; federal spending cuts have reduced services and DVA patients have won malpractice suits that cost taxpayers $18.3 million in 1983.

The stories can be developed by digging into DVA records, as Fred Schulte of the Fort Lauderdale News and Sun-Sentinel found. After two court cases and a trail that began four years earlier, Schulte's story exposed excessive heart surgery deaths at more than a dozen DVA hospitals. Schulte says any reporter can use the Freedom of Information Act to investigate conditions at DVA hospitals.

For patient care, look at reports from the DVA on injuries and patient satisfaction surveys, DVA Inspector General audits, audits of hospitals by the General Accounting Office and transcripts of Congressional Veterans Affairs Committee hearings.

Look, too, at malpractice cases filed under the Federal Tort Claims Act. Talk to the American Legion, which inspects DVA hospitals and local veterans groups. Ask the National Academy of Sciences in Washington if there are problems with medical trainees working at DVA hospitals.

Finally, there's a record that Schulte's newspaper went to court to get—DVA medical quality assurance documents. A secrecy provision buried in a $2 billion veterans' bill made these documents confidential in 1980. The Sun-Sentinel won them in a court battle through a legal technicality. But now the law has been changed so reporters can get at least part of these records. Statute 38 USC Sec. 3305 allows release of mortality statistics. However, statistics will be kept secret if they are for a procedure done by one doctor because release would identify the doctor.

Doctors

Some of the most hair-raising stories reporters can write are about incompetent doctors and the failure of our regulatory system to protect the public from them.

One of the authors (Dolly Katz) came across her first phony doctor during an investigation of Detroit's abortion clinics. At one substandard clinic, the patients talked about a "Dr. Mike" who operated on them although the only licensed physician at the clinic was Joseph Rucker. "Dr. Mike" turned out to be an ex-convict with no medical training whom Rucker allowed to perform second-trimester abortions. As for his own skills, Rucker left two women sterile after botched abortions and attempted an abortion on a 14-year-old whose daughter was later born with a piece of her scalp missing.

After the first story appeared, the state of Michigan took off in hot pursuit of Rucker's license. The state got it—nine years later. During that time, Rucker used money he continued to earn from Medicaid—over $1 million in a four-year period—to hire some of the state's best legal talent for his defense.

Rucker's case is not unusual, as a subsequent series by the Detroit Free Press showed. State boards revoke, suspend or limit about 1,200 doctors' licenses a year. But even by the conservative estimates of organized medicine, 15,000 to 25,000 of the nation's 550,000 doctors are unfit to practice.

With so many out there, an incompetent doctor is likely to cross a reporter's path once in a while. You can use the occasion to spotlight an individual doctor or as a springboard for a more extensive look at the profession and how well your state regulates it.

A story about an incompetent doctor often begins with a phone call from a victim. Occasionally, one victim's documented experience is dramatic enough to form the basis for the whole story. More often, you'll need to establish a pattern of incompetence or criminal activity.

An easy place to start is your circuit court, where you can find out how many times the doctor has been sued and the details of the cases. Aside from the obvious spectacular cases, look for patterns. One Michigan hand surgeon, for example, made a practice of performing extensive surgery on patients with relatively minor injuries, often making the patient worse in the process.

Plaintiffs' attorneys, if they specialize in malpractice, can be good sources. Ask the attorney who filed suit against the doctor whether it was an honest mistake or rank incompetence. Particularly if the case is already settled, the attorney probably will be glad to give you an honest appraisal, and also may steer you to doctors with even worse records.

Next check with the state licensing board for past disciplinary actions and any charges pending against the doctor. In some states, including Michigan, records of cases that were investigated and closed with no action also are public.

Your state board or the American Medical Association can tell you if the doctor holds licenses in other states. Check the doctor's record with those boards. (The language to use is that you want to "verify a license.") You may find the doctor has come to your state to escape another board's sanctions.

Ask your state Medicaid division how much money the doctor earned in the previous year and where the doctor ranks among the state's top Medicaid earners. Then find out if the Medicaid fraud unit is curious about how the doctor earned that much. One Michigan doctor did it by billing for 96,000 home visits in two years.

Medicare officials will tell you whether they've suspended the doctor and payments.

If you suspect the doctor is involved in illegal drug sales, call the state police. They may have a drug diversion unit that cooperated with the licensing board. Also contact the regional or national office of the Drug Enforcement Administration (DEA). At a minimum, the DEA must tell you whether the doctor's federally controlled substances license—a license to prescribe narcotics and other addictive drugs—has ever been revoked, and whether the DEA has an open case against the doctor.

It's always good to alert the public to an incompetent doctor. But collecting scalps has its limits. The real problem, after all, is not that bad doctors exist—any profession is bound to have a few bad apples—but that they're allowed to continue practicing.

Regardless of what state you're in, your board of medicine almost certainly is not doing its job. The reasons may vary from state to state, but generally include lack of money, lack of commitment by the medical profession and public ignorance of how the system works. People are being maimed and killed as a result.

The Detroit Free Press evaluated the Michigan Board of Medicine in 1984 by examining six years' worth of cases. In Michigan, as in many other states, most of the board's records are public. Access to a lot of the rest came by cultivating board attorneys, investigators, administrators and clerks, many of whom really want to see the system work better. Based on the Free Press series, here are some avenues to follow to document your state's poor performance.

- Determine what percent of the cases result in disciplinary actions and the nature of those actions—did they include a high proportion of suspensions and revocations, or were most of them wrist-slapping reprimands? With 20,000 doctors licensed to practice in Michigan, the state revokes only three licenses a year.
- Calculate how long it takes from the time a complaint is filed with the board of medicine to the time the board's final action takes effect. In Michigan, the average case took 2½ years to wind its tortuous way through long investigations, extended hearings and attorneys' delaying tactics. During that time, the doctor continues to practice. A month before her license was suspended on incompetency charges filed four years earlier, Dr. Carol Varner misdiagnosed a woman's diabetes as a case of nerves. The woman died the next day.
- Evaluate the role of the courts in blocking the medical board's disciplinary actions. In Michigan, judges routinely stayed board actions—for an average of two years per case—while the doctors' appeals inched through the courts. The judges consistently ignored a state Supreme Court directive that stays be issued only in cases where the appellant is likely to be successful.
- Find out where the initial accusations come from—a patient, pharmacist, doctor or medical society. Although the profession's code of ethics requires doctors to report their incompetent colleagues, you'll probably find that individual doctors and local medical societies almost never report a doctor to the state licensing board, even though they're aware of the problem. Medical

societies alerted Michigan's board to only four of the 193 incompetent doctors the board dealt with in six years.

■ Find out what happens to doctors who lose their licenses. The Free Press found that many simply go to other states and set up practice. Dr. Lois Dunegan joined the surgical staff of a Pennsylvania hospital after Michigan suspended her license for surgical errors that resulted in the death of a 19-year-old woman. After five states and a Canadian province revoked his license, Dr. Jesse Ketchum managed to get a job as an anesthesiology resident in Florida, where errors caused brain damage in a healthy 63-year-old woman.

Many other doctors who lose their licenses get them back after a year or so. Doctors who sell or abuse drugs typically are allowed to continue practicing medicine, but are temporarily prohibited from prescribing narcotics—a curious penalty, since it means that while the profession doesn't trust the doctor with dangerous drugs, it trusts the doctors to perform surgery.

The Free Press series stimulated some changes, but no fundamental ones. Those will come only when doctors assume their proper responsibility to police their profession and when the public gains an awareness of how the state licensing systems can work for them.

Journalists can play a role in making the public more aware in the following ways:

■ In addition to large projects, make the medical board part of a regular beat. Tell the public when a doctor is formally charged. The case may take years to be decided. In the meantime, the public should know that the state attorney general has probable cause to believe that a particular doctor is incompetent, drug-addicted, sexually assaults patients or steals from Medicaid.

Routinely report the board's actions. Your readers may be interested to know that the doctor charged with sexually assaulting 12-year-olds was suspended for only three months.

■ Tell the public how to recognize incompetence and how to report it to the medical board without fear of reprisal. Most people don't know their state licensing boards exist. Most follow the advice of Ann Landers, who has repeatedly told her readers to contact the American Medical Association or their local medical societies. The public needs to know that reporting a doctor to the AMA is akin to reporting an illegal gun owner to the National Rifle Association.

Nursing Homes

An estimated 10 percent of the nation's nursing homes violate federal or state laws. A substandard home could well exist in your circulation area.

The two nursing homes that Gale Scott and Bruce Locklin of The Record (Hackensack, N.J.) investigated had patients dying of starvation and maggots crawling on patients' bodies.

Their story began with a tip. You, too, will probably get tips about nursing homes. The problem is expanding from tips to solid evidence.

Talk to former inspectors who worked for state agencies monitoring nursing homes. Find former employees. When conditions become unbearable, the doctor who oversees a home may quit and be willing to talk.

Many of Scott's and Locklin's sources wanted to talk, but not have their names used. Instead of going off the record, Scott and Locklin asked each source to agree to testify if legal action developed after publication. This agreement was tape recorded at the start of the interview. The source list became the basis for a state investigation.

Scott and Locklin also dealt with the tempting, but ethically troubling, use of undercover sources. As a compromise, nurses were hired to work undercover only after the reporters had more than enough material for a story that could stand on its own without the sources.

Records helped, too. Wrongful-death lawsuits yielded medical files. State inspection reports and investigated complaints were useful. In New Jersey, both valid complaints and those inspectors consider invalid are public. Invalid complaints can show the state did a poor inspection job.

Do the state inspection systems work? Or, do nursing homes know when inspectors are coming?

What happens when a state decides to revoke a nursing home's license? Does the case die during appeals? Are employees who abuse patients ever convicted of a crime?

Look at how many employees work at a home and how much the nursing home spends on food. The San Jose Mercury News convinced the state office of health planning and development to conduct a study of nursing homes. The study found that homes owned by for-profit chains had 20 percent fewer staff than not-for-profit homes and spent 29 percent less on nursing care and 31 percent less on food.

Home Health Care

Home health care workers can be angels of mercy, allowing elderly or chronically ill people to stay in their homes instead of being shipped off to nursing homes. Or they can be ogres, stealing from or abusing their clients.

Home health care is growing in popularity as Medicare and health insurance companies encourage people to leave hospitals sooner and go home. Reporters need to ask whether problems with home health care are growing as well.

Look at who takes care of the old people and how well. Look at how much Medicare, Medicaid and other insurance pays for home care. Look at what happens to people who can't afford home health care.

How are home health care agencies doing financially? If they are running in the red, they may be giving some clients fewer visits than they are paying for. If the agency is part of a corporation, find out about problems with the other branches. In 1986, for instance, the largest for-profit, home health care corporation in the country was charged with defrauding Medicaid of $1.8 million by billing for the services of people not certified to work as home health care aides.

Who licenses these agencies? That question helped Margo Huston of The Milwaukee Journal win the Pulitzer Prize for her series on home health care. She discovered Wisconsin required all profit-making, home health care agencies be licensed, but had ignored the law while unregulated agencies sprang up.

Check the inspection reports of the state office that oversees home health care organizations. You may find horror stories or simple slaps on the hand for not filing a form. Do the inspectors talk to the clients of these agencies or do they just check office records?

Sources include elderly people, senior-citizen groups, advocates for the elderly and managers of senior-citizen housing.

Dentists

One of the few dentists in Columbia, Mo., treating Medicaid patients told an indigent person he was going to pull seven teeth. She got a second opinion—and still has all her teeth.

The woman told her story to Tracy Barnett of the Columbia Daily Tribune. Barnett found a number of people whose teeth, and even their lives, had been damaged in this dentist's chair.

Dentists are one of the least investigated health-care professionals, even though the dental system has problems. Many fall within two types of dental insurance: Medicaid and employee dental benefits.

Medicaid pays the full cost for only certain kinds of dental work, the kinds varying from state to state. In Missouri, Medicaid pays to have teeth pulled, though some poor people are forced to have teeth pulled needlessly. Many dentists won't take Medicaid patients because Medicaid won't pay enough.

Two kinds of employee dental plans have proven problematic. One is dental insurance that pays amounts good dentists say are too low. But some clinics take that insurance as full payment—sometimes making money by doing the least possible.

Look for lawsuits against these clinics. Other dentists may be willing to tell you about clinics' mistakes they patch up. Former receptionists can give you clients' names.

Some companies take another route with dental insurance: deducting money from paychecks for a prepaid dental plan.

WBRZ-TV in Baton Rouge, La., examined the prepaid program for state employees and found insurance fraud, dentists with checkered pasts, poor-quality care and no state controls to ensure financial stability.

Their investigation showed another depository to mine: campaign contributions. Louisiana usually requires insurance companies to put up capital before they are allowed to operate. This protects the clients in case the company runs short of money. However, the insurance commissioner determined the state dental program was exempt from the regulations because it wasn't an insurance company. WBRZ learned the founder had made a $2,000 campaign contribution to the commissioner.

Emergency Medical Care

A Teaneck, N.J., woman lay in her bedroom, about to have a fatal heart attack. Highly trained paramedics from a nearby hospital stood outside her door carrying equipment and drugs that often save heart attack victims, but they never saw the woman. Volunteers from the local ambulance corps turned them away.

This woman's story was uncovered by Elizabeth Auster, John Cichowski and Jim Dwyer at The Record (Hackensack, N.J.). In 1984, two million people in counties near New York City trusted their health to a system staffed largely by volunteers, half of whom didn't have minimum training. In addition, the state did not regulate emergency care.

In recent years, emergency care has become a specialty in its own right. We have come to expect hospitals on wheels—or even hospitals in helicopters. But that isn't always so. Following are some of the ways the system can break down.

Average Ambulance Response Time

Ambulances don't always respond quickly. In one eight-hour shift in New York City, 22 percent of the ambulances sent to critically ill people took seven minutes to leave the station. Experts say people should be picked up in no longer than six minutes.

Response time can be delayed by staff or ambulance shortages. It can also be slowed by territorial stake-outs. Ambulance companies take control of certain parts of a city and won't let others in, even if they can get there faster.

Don't trust the city's figures for average response time. Calculate them yourself, using records of the ambulance company or the times of calls and dispatches recorded by the 911 system.

Financing

See how the cost of an ambulance ride in your city compares to industry averages. Is the city getting its money's worth from contracted ambulance services? Does the ambulance service cut corners by having paramedics on duty only part of the day? Do for-profit ambulance services refuse to pick up indigent patients?

Training and Regulations

Do states or cities regulate emergency care? Is training required for ambulance workers, both volunteer and professional? Is certain equipment required to be on the ambulance? Does it have to be tested regularly?

Helicopters

More hospitals are using helicopters equipped with emergency equipment to transport severely ill people. As the number of helicopters have increased, so have the accidents: nine in 1984, 18 in 1985, 33 in 1986—out of 150 air ambulance services operating in 1986.

You can get accident reports from the National Transportation Safety Board. If the hospital has its own helicopter ambulance, check the backgrounds of the pilots. The Federal Aviation Administration will tell you if their licenses have been suspended.

Trauma Centers

In many cities, hospital emergency centers have been designated for particular kinds of traumas. Some take burn victims; others take cardiac patients. These designations are available from city or state health departments or from the state Peer Review Organization. You can check the performance of trauma centers by getting death rates for their specialties from the PRO and then comparing them to those at other trauma centers. Also, check whether ambulances and helicopters take patients to trauma centers best-suited for their care, or to the hospital that owns the ambulance.

Indigent Care

In Michigan, Medicaid paid $11,058 for drugs and doctors' visits for a 31-year-old woman. The drugs killed her.

In Texas, private hospitals turned away poor people without money or insurance. Some died en route to other hospitals.

Two ways the health care system fails the poor are misuse of government money and no money for those who can't pay.

Both stories need reporting, but Medicaid fraud leaves a clearer paper trail.

Paper records allowed Norman Sinclair and Fred Girard of the Detroit News to find that, in 21 months, 30 Medicaid patients had died at least partly because doctors had given them too many drugs—paid for by Medicaid.

Sinclair and Girard began their investigation at the county morgue. There they got the names and case numbers of all the people who had died of drug overdoses in a 21-month period. Then they got the complete morgue records on these people. Next Sinclair and Girard asked the state Medicaid office to designate which were Medicaid patients. Medicaid said 175 and sent back printouts of services the people had received—but not their names.

A combination of techniques yielded the names: Medicaid forgot to black out some of them. Others were found by comparing information on Medicaid records to morgue files. In other cases, reporters persuaded Medicaid to name the patients.

Their success illustrates the importance of persistence and negotiation. Much of the eight months Sinclair and Girard spent on the story was used persuading Medicaid officials to let them see records they had originally been denied.

Another Michigan reporter revealed a financial fraud of Medicaid. Mark Lagerkvist of WZZM-TV in Grand Rapids discovered a nursing home scam that cost Medicaid between $3 million and $5 million. The corporation that owned the nursing homes set up a dummy corporation to run the homes, then billed Medicaid for rental fees the dummy corporation paid the actual owners.

Lagerkvist found his first clue in the licensing files kept by the Department of Public Health. The owner and leaser of the homes had the same address, and some correspondence from one corporation had been sent on the other's stationery.

Next he asked for the "Statistical and Operating Cost Report," which must be filed by nursing homes receiving Medicaid reimbursements. The report showed the dummy corporation had paid the owner $3.7 million in rent over five years.

For more specific information, Lagerkvist got the audit work papers—after officials were threatened with an FOIA lawsuit.

Lagerkvist proved the relationship between the corporations by using nursing home licensing records, city directories—which showed that two of the dummy corporation's directors were employees of the parent corporation—and a public record listing all shareholders owning more than 5 percent of a nursing home. This document showed that wives of the owners of the parent corporation were large shareholders in the dummy. Such frauds have moved many states to clamp down on Medicaid, resulting in more forms and less money.

As a result, many doctors refuse Medicaid patients, who then must do without health care. Indigent women who forego health care during pregnancy sometimes have babies with health problems that cost hundreds of thousands of dollars to treat.

Not all poor people can get Medicaid. Some make a few dollars more than the qualifying level, but not enough to pay for health insurance. These are the people for-profit hospitals sometimes turn away. Their numbers are growing.

Mental Health

Common wisdom in the 1960s and 1970s was that mental patients should be freed from the snake pits of large mental institutions and placed in community homes. The key that opened the doors was medication for schizophrenia, the disorder of thought and perception causing almost half of all mental hospitalization.

But time has proven the drugs aren't a cure. Many patients spend their lives in a revolving door that sends them into a mental hospital, out to inadequate community placement, onto the street and back into the hospital.

Find out how well the release of mental patients is working in your community. Talk to the outpatient treatment specialists at the state mental hospitals. Do the patients keep their appointments and take their medication, despite its unpleasant and sometimes serious side effects? Or do they end up sleeping in dumpsters or committing crimes?

Are there enough community residences in your area? How good are they? Do the patients get counseling or do they just watch television? Check the credentials of the people who run the programs.

Many of these community programs get government funds, thus their financial records should be public. The records may show how money that could help the mental patients is lining the pockets of directors and directors' friends.

State officials are supposed to keep records of where the mental patients go. Do they?

Problems still plague traditional mental institutions. Some don't have enough beds. In some cities, mentally ill people who are charged with crimes are put in jails because the mental hospital has no room. In other cities, commitment procedures are too stringent. People can be committed without hearings and trapped in institutions indefinitely because the law does not require mandatory review of their cases.

Some have too many employees, some too few. In some hospitals, occupancy has been more than cut in half while staff has increased. Parts of the hospital, such as kitchens, have become patronage centers for local politicians. Records from the state Department of Mental Health will tell the staffing story.

Keep in mind that staffing requirement have increased in hospitals that treat seriously ill patients. So a hospital with fewer patients than it had in the 1950s may still be understaffed, even if staff levels haven't changed.

Many stories have been published about patient abuse in mental hospitals, but the same abuses still exist. Patients are among the best sources, but their credibility can be very low. The Philadelphia Inquirer overcame this hurdle, and won a Pulitzer Prize, by being cautious. If a patient made a charge, it had to be verified by three other people. If a guard or hospital official said it, verification had to come from two others.

Look at the credentials of the psychiatrists who work at the mental hospitals. Joe Stebbins and Diana Dawson of The Kansas City Star found most doctors at Missouri state hospitals had no formal training in psychiatry.

Medicare and Medicaid records are a good place to check, as are state Health Department and accreditation inspections of the facilities.

Medical Equipment

Betty Medsger wanted to know about wheelchairs made by Everest and Jennings, so she filed a Freedom of Information Act request with the Center for Medical

Devices and Radiological Health of the Food and Drug Administration. The documents told of an electric wheelchair that caught fire and killed a quadriplegic.

At that time, no agency regulated wheelchairs. The irony, Medsger noted in her article for The Progressive, was that one bike accident prompted the recall of 33,500 bicycles by the Consumer Product Safety Commission.

Health care is becoming increasingly mechanized. Handicapped people have become dependent on machines to do what they can't do themselves. Hospitals, too, make extensive use of machines. Machines help people breathe, bring them back to life and monitor them to be sure they stay alive.

As amazing as machines are, they can cause problems, too, either through mechanical or human error.

One good place to find out about problems with medical equipment, from ambulances to implants, is the Emergency Care Research Institute (ECRI) in Plymouth Meeting, Pa. ECRI, established in 1955, is one of the leading institutions committed to improving safety and cost effectiveness of technology and health care facilities.

ECRI publishes the weekly Health Devices Alerts, a summary of problems and studies of medical equipment, and the monthly Health Devices, which has longer articles about problems with medical devices. These publications are available at many medical school and hospital libraries.

ECRI also investigates accidents caused by medical devices and has extensive files on litigation involving devices.

Another good source for problems with medical equipment is advocates for the handicapped. If you hear the name of a device or a company mentioned repeatedly, check for lawsuits.

Drugs

For some people, miracle drugs have been a curse, not a cure.

Diethylstilbestrol (DES) was given to pregnant women for decades to prevent miscarriages. Instead, it produced a generation of women at higher risk of vaginal cancer.

You can start your search for these problematic drugs with the FDA, which keeps a variety of public records on drug testing and adverse reactions (see "Drugs" in the "Documenting the Evidence" section for complete list).

Keep in mind that some serious problems with drugs won't show up in the FDA files. Major drug companies have used lobbying, suppression of reports and outright lying to obtain FDA approval for questionable drugs. The Public Citizen Health Research Group in Washington, D.C., watchdogs many problem drugs and frequently petitions the FDA to ban them.

Check for connections between the drug companies and the researchers who did the reports submitted in support of FDA approval. Such connections can be hidden as contributions to the researcher's university. Also check with experts for weaknesses in the study.

State health departments, too, receive reports of adverse reactions. The Centers for Disease Control receives reports of problems with vaccines at public clinics, where one-third to one-half of childhood shots are administered. The National Cancer Institute keeps records on effects of experimental cancer drugs.

Medical Laboratories

Want to know if you've got diabetes, cancer or too much cholesterol in your blood? Clinical laboratories, with their space-age technology, will tell you — maybe.

As Walt Bogdanich discovered while writing an article for the Wall Street Journal, the labs are far from infallible. Mistakes have caused a death from undetected cancer, a divorce from an incorrect syphilis diagnosis and a lost job from a false positive drug test.

Inaccurate and unreliable testing is a health hazard, as well as a waste of millions of dollars. The blame goes to the labs and to the lack of effective regulation.

Only about half the states regulate labs. Federal law covers only interstate specimens and tests on Medicare patients.

Find out whether your state regulates laboratories. If it does, reports should be available on the accuracy of the labs. If your state has no regulations, find out why.

Several studies of labs have been done by private research groups and the federal government. They will give you clues to where problems exist. Check lawsuits as well. Bogdanich found cases he used in his articles by calling national and state lawyers' associations.

Health Maintenance Organizations

The nation's first health maintenance organization (HMO), was started by a Los Angeles surgeon in 1933 as a better way to provide health care. The Nixon Administration embraced and encouraged the concept in 1973 as a cheaper way to provide health care in an effort to rein in the nation's billion-dollar-a-day health care costs. By 1986, almost 24 million Americans were enrolled in HMOs.

Whether, in the long run, HMOs are better and cheaper than traditional fee-for-service has been debated for decades and is not likely to be settled anytime soon.

In the meantime, millions of employees choose among as many as half a dozen HMOs, traditional insurance, and — the newest player in the health delivery game — preferred provider organizations (PPOs).

While reporters are not likely to settle the debate over the absolute worth of these delivery systems, they can help consumers choose among them, and they can alert employees to the ones that should be avoided. The Detroit Free Press has published two comprehensive evaluations of all HMOs in Detroit. Each package included a chart comparing each plan's costs and benefits, an evaluation of each HMO's strengths and weaknesses, a general article on HMOs, PPOs, and the current controversies over them, and a question-and-answer dealing with some of the most common questions, like whether an HMO member is covered for out-of-town emergencies (the answer is yes).

Unlike traditional insurance, which pays for some or all of a person's medical bills, an HMO actually provides medical care for a flat monthly fee, regardless of how much or how little care the subscriber uses. Some HMOs—Kaiser Permanente, headquartered in California, is the classic example—own their own hospitals and hire their own full-time doctors. Others contract with hospitals and doctors.

HMOs save money primarily because their subscribers are hospitalized only about one third to one half as often as patients in the fee-for-service system. This is not, as proponents like to say, because HMOs are somehow able to keep their subscribers healthier. It is because HMO doctors practice a different style of medicine, one that relies much less on hospitals.

The greatest benefit of an HMO from the subscriber's point of view, is that all services—doctor visits, hospital care, prescriptions—are covered or require only minimal copayments of $1 to $2 per office visit or prescription. The major drawback, again from the subscriber's perspective, is that the subscriber is restricted to using the HMO doctors and hospitals.

Those new delivery systems can cheat people in a very old way—by delivering less than they promise. Subscribers, who are generally locked into an HMO for at least a year, may discover that the lure of no out-of-pocket cost has hooked them into long waits for appointments, an inadequate number of doctors and reliance on substandard hospitals and health professionals.

To check the HMO in your area, start with the state agencies that license them. They'll have data on size, premiums, finances and other basic information. They'll also be able to tell you whether the HMO is in obvious trouble, either financially or in terms of the quality of services offered. If the HMO fails, subscribers may find themselves with no health insurance in the middle of illnesses and pregnancies. One of the HMOs the Free Press profiled had three government agencies trying to figure out its tortured finances, which included losses of over $500,000 a year and administrative expenses exceeding 20 percent.

Look at the HMO's hospitalization rate. If it's not substantially lower than the state average, something's probably wrong. Information on enrollment will tell you whether the HMO is growing or stagnating, and whether it has a high dropout rate.

Look at the doctors at hospitals the HMO uses. Have any of them been in trouble with state licensing agencies? If the HMO contracts with individual physicians' offices, visit some of them. Are they solo or group practices? Studies have found that group practices generally provide better medical care. Where are the offices located, and what hours are they open?

The troubled HMO the Free Press investigated claimed to offer subscribers a choice of over 600 doctors, but actually had fewer than 150. Of those, 18 worked at clinics that were forced to return over $700,000 to the state following a Medicaid fraud investigation. Another of the clinics that was supposed to provide "comprehensive care" was staffed by a single doctor who worked only half days. Check the number of specialists on staff. If the HMO is too small to have many full-time specialists, patients may suffer because the HMO will be reluctant to pay for consultations with expensive neurologists, cardiologists and other high-priced specialists.

If the HMO has applied for federal approval, which confers certain marketing benefits and allows the HMO to get a Medicare contract, the federal Office of Prepaid Health Care will have evaluated it. In addition to the HMO's application material, the compliance officer who monitors the HMO can offer valuable insights.

The HMOs themselves can help you. Ask one HMO for the names of subscribers who have transferred from another, then call those subscribers and ask why. One Detroit group, burned by its first choice of HMO, was very careful about its second, and had valuable guidelines to offer others—as well as important information about the HMO it had left. Talk to the major employers in town about their experiences with HMOs. If they're really big, like Chrysler in Detroit, they may have done their own studies on how well the HMOs are serving them. Chrysler discovered that the HMOs were saving the company money on blue-collar employees, but not on white-collar subscribers.

Pay particular attention to Medicare and Medicaid populations, who are extremely vulnerable to shoddy recruiting and marketing practices. Salespeople may tell recipients they can keep their personal physicians. Some imply they're government officials and that the HMO is an added benefit. Many elderly and poor subscribers may not understand they've joined an HMO, and may discover only when they try to visit their own doctors and hospitals that they're no longer covered.

A major reason people have problems with HMOs is that they don't understand how to use them. HMOs are partly to blame; they need to explain themselves better. But journalists can help, too.

Occupational and Environmental Disease

Some people work at jobs and live in homes that make them sick.

In South Memphis, Tenn., employees at a lead smelting plant suffered fatigue, headaches and joint pains. They had, Michael Mansur of The Commercial Appeal discovered, three times the safe level of lead in their blood.

Lake Dalecarlia, Ind., was no suburban paradise, Olga Briseno, Melanie Csepiga and Frederick Ott of the Times found out. The 1,605 people living around the lake had a cancer rate 253 percent higher than the expected—28 times higher than the cancer rate at Love Canal.

An estimated 100,000 American lives are lost to occupational accidents and diseases each year, yet reporters are only beginning to tell the story.

Clues to unhealthy work places include industries that deal with hazardous chemicals, workers' compensation cases, studies that point to chemicals recently found to cause cancer, an abnormally high incidence of cancer in a particular area and regulatory agencies—or lack of them.

Several annual surveys of hazardous industries are conducted. Check Occupational Illnesses and Injuries of the United States, published by the Bureau of Labor Statistics, and reports from the National Safety Council. Several states compile similar lists through their labor bureaus.

Talk to occupational health clinics, labor unions and workers' compensation attorneys. They can tell you about schools of public health and worker extension schools associated with universities in your area. Other helpful sources are the pro-worker, citizen-staffed committees on occupational safety and health (COSH) that have formed in a number of cities.

Employers must file first injury reports with their state workers' compensation office and with the area Occupational Safety and Health Administration (OSHA) office.

However, these records are only the tip of the iceberg. Studies estimate that only 5 percent of occupational illnesses appear in compensation records.

For more clues, look at the kinds of chemicals used at plants in your area. Cyanide, lead, mercury, benzene, silica dust and petroleum distillates are among those that can be dangerous. The National Institute for Occupational Safety and Health (NIOSH) can give you a computerized list of the most recent research on harmful effects of various chemicals. The National Toxicology Program publishes annual reports listing all substances known or suspected to be carcinogenic. Check libraries at schools of medicine and public health for studies on hazardous chemicals. Remember, there are an estimated 575,000 chemical products in the work place. More and more substances are being found to be hazardous.

In 1985, Ralph Nader's Washington, D.C., based Public Citizen Health Research Group released a list of 249 work places where the government identified, but never notified, some 250,000 workers who face an increased risk of cancer, heart disease and other illnesses. Check with the group for newer studies.

OSHA regulations have created several tools for discovering what chemicals are used at plants and what problems they cause. The hazard communications regulation, which went into effect in 1986, requires companies to tell workers what chemicals they use and to label the containers. The law also requires companies to keep safety data sheets on all hazardous chemicals.

Another OSHA regulation requires a company to give workers or their representatives access to medical records. They can also see records of exposure to hazards in the work place and studies done on work places.

OSHA No. 200, the Employer's Log and Summary of Occupational Injuries and Illnesses, is supposed to be posted each January in a conspicuous place in the work place.

Once you have established that dangerous chemicals are used at a plant and workers are getting sick, you still have to prove the chemicals are misused on the job.

One way is to check a firm's latest OSHA inspection. These reports describe general conditions and list citations that have been issued. You can talk to employees, but be sure to get several testimonies about the same hazard. If possible, back up allegations with documents. Concerned middle-management personnel can confirm employee complaints and also have access to company records.

Another system that needs monitoring is workers' compensation. Workers sometimes get large settlements for job injuries. But occupational disease is a different story. The link to the job is hard to prove, and few workers file a claim. Some states set a time limit, say five years, on filing compensation cases. But some work-related cancers can take 15 years or longer to develop.

Environmental diseases are more difficult to investigate. Fewer government documents exist, and victims are even harder to find than those with occupational illnesses. Her are some guides:

- Check studies on environmentally linked diseases. These could tell you that nitrates from nitrogen fertilizers used by farmers get into underground water supplies and can stay there for many years, causing illnesses like stomach cancer. The studies could also tell you that the green-colored lumber used widely for outdoor decks is treated with arsenic and has injured people and animals.

- Another starting point can be an unusually high incidence of disease. A rumor of a large number of cancer cases instigated the Lake Dalecarlia story. However, the paper needed proof. Environmental experts told the newspaper that only a communitywide survey could confirm the problem. The paper hired a professional interviewing firm, which documented the abnormally high number of cancer cases.

- Other reporters have done their own testing or detective work to find an environmental hazard. Bob Scott and Wendy Black of KOY Radio in Phoenix spent nearly two years searching for the source of a suspected carcinogen in municipal water wells. They found it at a Motorola plant.

- Some records do exist on the release of chemicals from a plant to the environment. Ask the Environmental Protection Agency (EPA) for records of "emergency releases" in which higher-than-allowed levels of a substance escape.

- Water discharges of hazardous chemicals must meet certain levels set by state and federal agencies, such as the department of natural resources. Check reports issued by these agencies. You may find large industries that habitually exceed levels.

- Don't overlook problems with agencies that monitor chemicals. A House subcommittee found in 1985 that the Environmental Protection Agency regulated only five of the 204 chemicals considered hazardous. The subcommittee also found most U.S. chemical plants routinely released "disturbing" levels of toxic substances into the air.

Your sleuthing may lessen the chance of environmental disease. It's not enough to report the disasters, Gaylord Shaw of The Los Angeles Times said; reporters should try to prevent hazards before they happen.

Other Health Care Stories

Medical Research

When a government awards a $10 million contract to build a bridge, reporters sometimes check how well the work was done. But if a research team at your medical school wins a $10 million research grant, the quality of the work is seldom evaluated publicly.

If reporters went searching behind the sanctified façades, they might find misdeeds that would shake the faith in the scientific community. The Boston Globe did. The paper's Spotlight team discovered that a prominent cancer researcher, who wanted to win the Nobel Prize, had falsified his research. He had reported treatments that were never done and invented the existence of a tumor that a patient never had.

Health Care Costs

People are shocked when they open the bill for their hospital stay. Then they forget about it. That's because they usually don't pay most of the cost—insurance does.

But we all pay in some way: federal taxes for Medicare, state taxes for Medicaid, higher health insurance rates, higher costs of goods and services because of higher employee health benefits.

Let's find out what health care costs and why.

Forget about the cost-per-day comparisons produced by your hospitals. These are derived by dividing total revenues by the number of admissions and don't mean much. One hospital may treat fewer, but sicker patients, thus leading to a higher cost per patient.

Look at the costs of individual services, such as urinalysis and electrolyte tests. You may find one hospital charges twice as much as another and four times as much as a private laboratory. Check for errors in hospital bills. In 1990, the General Accounting Office found errors in 99 percent of a sample of bills it checked. Hospitals sometimes hire firms to re-audit already paid bills for overlooked charges. The hospitals then try to collect those supposedly missed charges.

To find out costs, try Medicare and Medicaid cost reports, hospital business offices, health insurance companies, health-care research organizations and consumer groups. You'll probably want an expert to help you decipher them.

General Records

An excellent place to begin an investigation is the Office of Technology Assessment (OTA), a congressional agency that analyzes controversial scientific and technological issues. Whatever the issue—the cost-effectiveness of various treatments and devices, the adequacy of the Public Health Service's response to AIDS or the prospects of gene therapy—the OTA probably has already explored it. Titles of recent health-related reports include "The Effectiveness and Costs of Alcoholism Treatment," "The Contact Lens Industry," "Carcinogen Regulatory

Policy," "Diagnosis Related Groups (DRGs) and the Medicare Program," "Reproductive Health Hazards in the Workplace," "Technology and Child Health," "Monitoring AIDS-Related Activities" and "Scientific Validity of Polygraph Testing." For a list of publications, call (202) 224-8996. For more information about OTA and its current projects, contact the Congressional and Public Affairs Office, Office of Technology Assessment, U.S. Congress, Washington, D.C. 20510-8025; (202) 226-2115.

The Department of Health and Human Services, which has jurisdiction over most of the federal government's myriad health-related activities, will send you a directory of public relations contacts to provide you with an entry into the maze of HHS programs and concerns, from Agent Orange through IUDs and infant mortality to work programs for AFDC families. The directory contains the contacts' office and home telephone numbers. Write or call the Office of Assistant Secretary for Public Affairs, Room 647-D, Hubert Humphrey Bldg., 200 Independence Avenue S.W., Washington, D.C. 20201; (202) 245-1850.

Conclusion

The most important health care story a reporter can write is the one that puts medicine in its place.

The public believes that traditional medicine—antibiotics, doctors and hospitals—is responsible for the dramatic decrease in infant mortality and increase in lifespan that has occurred in the last century. They look to more magic bullets to cure cancer and heart disease, the great Western plagues of the 20th Century.

But in fact, hands-on medicine has played a relatively modest role in the Western health revolution. The most important factors have been better living conditions—clean water, pasteurized milk, plumbing, more spacious housing, improved personal hygiene.

The same is true today. Doctors and hospitals, the pillars of our health care system, are not the pillars of the population's health. Utah has the fewest doctors and hospitals in proportion to its population of any state. But Utah residents enjoy one of the lowest infant mortality rates and longest lifespans in the nation. The reason may be the Mormon lifestyle, which eschews cigarettes, alcohol, coffee and stimulants.

Despite billions of dollars invested in cancer research, no major breakthrough has occurred of the kind the medical establishment has promised Americans—a treatment that cures most victims. Yet we could prevent 30 percent of all cancer deaths by eliminating cigarette smoking.

Prevention has been oversold, too. The cancer establishment has enlisted the media's help to promote a massive change in the American diet. Less fat and more fiber, fruit and vegetables will prevent cancer, we tell the public. More cautious scientists point out that the link between cancer and diet remains tenuous. They call for more research before we attempt to change anything as complex as the national diet. These scientists are largely ignored.

With the enthusiastic support of the press, the medical establishment has promoted breast self-examination as a lifesaver. But nobody has yet proved that BSE reduces breast cancer mortality.

Overselling medicine and prevention discredits both in the public eye. Advocacy without proof wastes time, money and, ultimately, lives. The public is best served by reporters who respond to the enthusiasm of researchers and policymakers with caution, skepticism and a demand for proof.

SUGGESTED READINGS

AAMC Directory of American Medical Education. Washington, D.C.: Association of American Medical Colleges. Lists and describes accredited medical schools, their faculties, clinical facilities, enrollment, etc. Revised annually.

AMA Directory of Physicians, 30th ed. Chicago: American Medical Association, 1985. Alphabetic listing of physicians licensed to practice in the United States includes a geographic index.

Fourth Annual Report on Carcinogens. Research Triangle Park, N.C.: National Toxicology Program, 1987. A listing and description of chemicals and substances that have been found to be carcinogenic.

Berkow, Robert, ed. Merck Manual of Diagnosis and Therapy, 14th ed. Rahway, N.J.: Merck, 1984. Frequently revised physician's treatment manual. Describes prognosis and treatment of diseases.

Blakiston's Gould Medical Dictionary, 4th ed. New York: McGraw-Hill, 1979. One of several excellent standard medical dictionaries.

Brown, Michael. "Laying Waste: The Poisoning of America by Toxic Chemicals." New York: Washington Square Press, 1981. A tour, starting with Love Canal, of toxic waste sites, showing the systematic destruction of the environment—and the people who live there.

Clemente, Carmine D., ed. "Gray's Anatomy of the Human Body," American ed. Philadelphia: Lea & Febiger, 1984. Basic anatomy text with excellent illustrations.

Diagnostic and Statistical Manual of Mental Disorders, 3rd ed. Washington, D.C.: American Psychiatric Association, 1980. Describes symptoms, diagnostic criteria and courses of mental disorders.

Directory of Medical Specialists, 22nd ed. Chicago: Marquis, 1985. Geographic listing by specialty of physicians in the United States. Includes alphabetic list of physicians. Also lists officers and addresses of the specialty boards.

Epstein, Samuel, M.D. "The Politics of Cancer." San Francisco: Sierra Club Books, 1978. Tells why cancerous materials aren't removed from our environment.

Fuchs, Victor. "The Health Economy." Cambridge, Mass.: Harvard University Press, 1986. One of the nation's leading health economists looks at why health care has become so expensive and analyzes the implications of DRGs and other efforts to reduce the costs.

Galton, Lawrence. "Med Tech." New York: Harper & Row, 1985. A layperson's guide to medical technology.

Grossman, Karl. "The Poison Conspiracy." Sag Harbor, N.Y.: The Pergament Press, 1983. Using government documents and whistle-blowers, Grossman shows how government agencies fail to protect people from poisons in food and the environment.

Guide to the Health Care Field (annual), rev. ed. Chicago: American Hospital Association. Annual Directory listing hospitals geographically and giving number of beds, ownership information, services offered, occupancy rates, etc.

Handbook of Nonprescription Drugs. Washington: American Pharmaceutical Association, 1986. References to over-the-counter drugs arranged by drug type, e.g., foot-care products, dental products, contraceptives, etc. Includes product index.

Harris, Richard. "A Sacred Trust." New York: New American Library, 1966. A good history of the bitter, but unsuccessful, battle the American Medical Association waged against passage of the Medicare bill in 1965.

Hiatt, Howard H. "America's Health in the Balance: Choice or Chance." New York: Harper & Row, 1987. A respected public health specialist explains medicine's true role in maintaining health, details what he believes is wrong and offers an alternative way to finance and deliver medical care.

Hospital Statistics. Chicago: American Hospital Association. Annual guide to national and state statistics.

Jones, James H. "Bad Blood: The Tuskegee Syphilis Experiment." New York: Free Press, 1981. An investigative book that uses some unusual sources of medical documents.

Kaufman, Joel; Rabinowitz-Dagi, Linda; Levin, Joan; McCarthy, Phyliss; Wolfe, Sidney; Bargmann, Eve; and Public Citizen Health Research Group. "Over the Counter Pills That Don't Work." Washington, D.C.: Public Citizen Health Research Group, 1983. A look at nonprescription drugs with ingredients that lack evidence of safety or effectiveness.

Last, John M. and Rosenau, Maxcy. "Public Health and Preventive Medicine," 11th ed. New York: Appleton-Century-Crofts, 1984. A good guide to occupational illnesses.

Law, Sylvia. "Blue Cross: What Went Wrong." New Haven, CT.: Yale University Press, 1974. An in-depth study of the nation's largest health insurance organization.

Martin, Eric W., ed. "Hazards of Medication," 2nd ed. Philadelphia: J.B. Lippincott, 1978. A manual on drug interactions and adverse reactions.

Medical Device Register. Stamford, Conn.: Directory Systems, 1986. Listing of medical products and companies that supply them. Includes detailed information about the devices and risks they pose to health. Also profiles suppliers.

Mintz, Morton. "At Any Cost—Corporate Greed, Women and the Dalkon Shield." New York: Pantheon Books, 1985. Shows how the complicity of the medical, legal and corporate communities allowed this untested IUD to reach the market, ravaging the lives of many women.

Neustadt, Richard and Feinberg, Harvey. "The Epidemic That Never Was—Policymaking and the Swine Flu Affair." New York: Vintage Books, 1983. The decision behind the decision to immunize the nation against a disease that never materialized and that resulted in an epidemic of vaccine-caused paralysis.

Physician's Desk Reference. Oradell, N.J.: Medical Economics. Annual publication with supplemental updates. Generic and brand name descriptions of current medications with counter-indications, adverse reactions, composition, administration and dosage, side effects, etc.

Sax, N. Irving. "Dangerous Properties of Industrial Materials." New York: Van Nostrand Reinhold, 1984. Lists materials alphabetically and explains which ones impair health.

Scott, Rachel. "Muscle and Blood." New York: E.P. Dutton, 1974. A good example of how to turn what some think is the dry subject of occupational health into a compelling story.

Sittig, Marshall. Handbook of Toxic and Hazardous Chemicals. Park Ridge, N.J.: Noyes Publications, 1981. Explains potential exposures, where chemicals are used, symptoms of exposure and allowable exposure limits.

Socio-Economic Factbook for Surgery. Chicago: American College of Surgeons. Annual pamphlet providing statistical information on surgical manpower, number and types of operations performed, length of hospital stays, etc. Also includes American College of Surgeons position papers on various issues.

Starr, Paul. "The Social Transformation of American Medicine." New York: Basic Books, 1982. An important analysis of American medicine, showing the transformation of doctors from poorly paid tradespeople to wealthy respected professionals, and the growth of health care from a cottage industry to a corporate giant.

Szasz, Thomas. "Insanity: The Idea and Its Consequences." New York: John Wiley & Sons, 1987. Dr. Szasz, a professor of psychiatry, takes the controversial position that the concept of mental illness is a coercive tool for the incarceration of innocent people in mental hospitals, not a way to explain aberrant behavior.

PERIODICALS AND OTHER SOURCES

There are a number of good periodicals on health issues. Here are some of the more useful ones. For others, check Ulrich's International Periodicals Directory.

American Journal of Industrial Medicine. Monthly. Alan R. Liss, Inc. 41 E. 11th St., New York, N.Y.

American Medical News. The weekly journal of the American Medical Association, 535 N. Dearborn St., Chicago, Ill. 60610.

Art Hazards News (10/year). Center for Occupational Hazards, 5 Beekman St., New York, N.Y. 10038.

British Journal of Industrial Medicine. British Medical Association, BMA House, Tavistock Square, London, England.

Envirofiche. Microfiched articles on environmental and occupational health issues. Available at some libraries, such as those associated with graduate schools of public health.

Environmental Health and Safety. Monthly. Available free from the University of Washington, Department of Environmental Health, School of Public Health and Community Medicine, Seattle, Wash. 98195.

Health Care Financing Review; U.S. Health Care Financing Administration, Department of Health and Human Services, East High Rise Building, Room 365, 6401 Security Boulevard, Baltimore, Md. 21207. Each year this quarterly journal contains a breakdown of the nation's annual health-care expenditures. HCFA has other useful publications available.

Health Policy Weekly. United Communication Group, 4550 Montgomery Ave., Suite 700N, Bethesda, Md. 10814.

JAMA. Weekly journal of the American Medical Association. Reporters can get this for free.

Journal of Occupational Medicine, (American Occupational Medical Assoc.) Flournoy Publishers Inc., 1845 W. Morse Ave., Chicago, Ill. 60626.

Medical Benefits. 410 E. Water St., Charlottesville, Va. 22901. Digest of articles from leading periodicals.

Modern Healthcare. Crain Communications Inc., 740 N. Rush St., Chicago, Ill., 60611. This biweekly journal for hospital and nursing home administrators contains many articles on how to run hospitals more profitably and how to cope with Medicare's prospective payment system.

The New England Journal of Medicine. Massachusetts Medical Society, 1440 Main St., Waltham, Mass. 02254. Published weekly, this is often the first place groundbreaking research results are announced. If you ask for a first-class mail subscription, you will receive the magazine before publication. Sometimes has articles and editorials on ethical issues in medicine.

Occupational Safety and Health Reporter (weekly) and Occupational Safety and Health Newsletter (bimonthly). Both published by the Bureau of National Affairs, 1231 25th St. N.W., Washington, D.C. 20037. The Reporter lists all appeals to the State Occupational and Health Review Commission by name of employer, address and some information about the case. Many law offices, especially workers' compensation firms, subscribe. Try business or medical libraries, too.

Science (10/year). American Association for the Advancement of Science, 1333 H St., N.W., Washington, D.C. 20005. Will send advance abstracts and entire articles free to reporters.

GROUPS AND INDIVIDUAL SOURCES

When looking for experts on health issues, check Government Research Directory, Medical and Health Information Directory, Medical Research Centres and Research Centers Directory, all published by Gale Research Company, Book Tower, Detroit, Mich. 48226.

An extensive list of sources on scientific and medical issues is available from the Science Journalism Center at the University of Missouri School of Journalism, Columbia, Mo. 65205. Here are some of the leading groups and individuals to consult on specific issues.

American Association of Retired People, 1909 K. St. N.W., Washington, D.C. 20049. Active in health issues and publishes a magazine.

American Industrial Health Council, 1330 Connecticut Ave. N.W., Washington, D.C. 20036. Gives industry side of worker health issues.

Center for Hospital Finance and Management, Johns Hopkins University, 624 North Broadway, Room 300, Baltimore, Md. 21205. Studies hospital finance, management and cost containment.

Center for Policy Studies, 2221 University Ave. S.E., Suite 134, Minneapolis, Minn. 55414. Independent not-for-profit organization supported by private foundations and speaking and consulting fees. Researches health policy issues, including improved methods for health care delivery and financing, health care system reform and market-oriented approaches to medical cost containment.

Center for Occupational Hazards, 5 Beekman St., New York, N.Y. 10038. Independent nonprofit research and educational organization supported by arts grants and foundations. Studies and serves as national clearinghouse for hazards of arts, crafts and theaters.

Citizen's Clearinghouse for Hazardous Wastes Inc., P.O. Box 926, Arlington, Va. 22216. This group, which grew out of the Love Canal scandal, publishes a newsletter and a number of publications about health effects of hazardous wastes.

Employee Benefit Research Institute, 2121 K St. N.W., Washington, D.C. 20036. Not-for-profit organization supported by industry and labor. Researches employee benefits in public and private sectors. Topics have included financing health care for the elderly and government regulation of employee benefit plans.

The Hastings Center, Hastings-on-Hudson, N.Y. 10706. One of the nation's leading think tanks on ethical issues in medicine. Conducts 10–12 research projects annually. Topics include occupational health and care of the terminally ill.

Health Insurance Association of America, 1001 Pennsylvania Ave. N.W., Washington, D.C. 20004. Public relations and lobby group for private insurance companies, which includes most companies except Blue Cross/Blue Shield. Conducts surveys and does research on current issues in health care and health insurance.

Some labor unions have good health and safety experts, including AFL-CIO, Department of Occupational Safety and Health, 815 16th St. N.W., Washington, D.C. 20006; Oil, Chemical and Atomic Workers' Union, Health and Safety Division, P.O. Box 2812, Denver, Colo. 80201; United Rubber, Cork, Linoleum and Plastic Workers Union, 87 S. High St., Akron, Ohio 44308; United Auto Workers, 8000 E. Jefferson, Detroit, Mich. 48214.

National Safety Council Research Department, 444 North Michigan Ave., Chicago, Ill. 60611. An independent not-for-profit organization supported by U.S. government, industry and membership fees. Studies safety in industry, homes, farms, labor and transportation.

Public Citizen Health Research Group, 2000 P Street N.W., Suite 708, Washington, D.C. 20036. Research arm of Public Citizen, an independent consumer advocacy organization established by Ralph Nader. Studies health care delivery, workplace safety and health, drug regulation, food additives, medical device safety and environmental influences on health. Publishes books, reports and bimonthly Health Letter.

Rand Corporation, 1700 Main St., Santa Monica, Calif. 90406. Does research for the federal government on health care issues and has done a number of studies on Medicare's prospective payment system.

SIPI (Scientist's Institute for Public Information), 355 Lexington Ave., New York, N.Y. 10017; (212) 661-9110. Reporters can call to get the names of experts to answer questions about medical and scientific topics.

Society for Occupational and Environmental Health, 2021 K St. N.W., Suite 305, Washington, D.C. 20006. Seeks to improve the quality of both working and living places by operating as a neutral forum for conferences involving all aspects of occupational health.

U.S. Senate Special Committee on Aging, Hart Building, Room 628, Washington, DC 20510. Does research and issues reports on health issues of importance to the elderly, including Medicare. Some-times has internal government reports not available under the FOIA.

University of California, San Francisco, Institute for Health and Aging, Room N-631y, San Francisco, Ca. 94143. Publishes books and reports on aging and health policy, including home health care and indigent elderly.

Women's Occupational Health Resource Center, Columbia University, School of Public Health, 600 W. 168th St., New York N.Y. 10032. Clearinghouse for women's occupational health and safety issues.

DOCUMENTING THE EVIDENCE

HOSPITALS AND OTHER HEALTH CARE INSTITUTIONS

Accreditation Reports

The Joint Commission on Accreditation of Hospitals, 875 N. Michigan Ave., Chicago, Ill. 60611, is the primary accrediting association. If the hospital you are investigating is publicly owned, the inspection report should be available from the hospital. The commission has been criticized for looking too much at construction and not enough at patient care. In response, it announced recently it would develop measures for looking at quality of care.

Financial Records

Budgets   Hospital budgets detail net profits, what percentage of a hospital's income comes from patient fees, how much is spent on new equipment and how much is spent on different departments.

The budgets of publicly supported hospitals, such as city and county, should be public information. If administrators are uncooperative, consult the local, state or federal agency that contributes the greatest amount of funds to the hospital. Private hospitals probably won't show you their budgets. However, much of the information will be in Medicare cost reports.

When looking at hospital budgets, keep in mind the differences among community, for-profit and teaching hospitals. Community hospitals often don't have a lot of sophisticated equipment, meaning their costs should be lower. However, community hospitals that are often not-for-profit usually have to take a large share of indigent cases. This cuts into these hospitals' profits. Teaching hospitals get more complicated cases, making for higher costs. For-profit hospitals often avoid complicated cases to make more money. They rarely have obstetrics departments.

Medicare and Medicaid Cost Reports   Hospitals that care for Medicare and/or Medicaid patients must file cost reports every year. Medicare reports are available by making a FOIA request to the company that administers the program in your state or area. This company, called the Medicare fiscal intermediary, is usually Blue Cross. The name of the intermediary is available from the Health Care Financing Administration, Freedom of Information Office, Professional Building, Room 100, 6660 Security Blvd., Baltimore, Md. 21207, or your HCFA regional office (see listing at end of this section).

Medicaid reports, which contain similar information, are available from the state Medicaid agency, usually the Department of Social Services.

The reports are long and difficult to understand. Ask a friendly accountant, the area health planning agency or a health statistics expert at a local university to help interpret them.

380

The reports do have a few key pages that summarize a hospital's status and are understandable:

- *The statement of revenues* gives revenues, net profits, long-term debt and cash reserves. Reserves help absorb losses and can convince a bank to lend money for a new wing.
- *Part II—Hospital Statistics* shows occupancy rates, admissions, number of employees and average lengths of stay for all patients and Medicare patients.
- *Calculation of Reimbursement Settlement* shows the total amount a hospital gets from Medicare and whether the hospital made or lost money that year on Medicare patients. To understand the reimbursement settlement, you need to know a little about how it is calculated.

Most hospitals are now or soon will be operating under national diagnosis-related groups (DRG) rates. In general, there is one rate for urban areas and one for rural areas, with some modifications for local conditions and teaching hospitals.

Before 1984, Medicare paid hospitals whatever it cost to deliver the services. From 1984 through 1986, when the government phased in the DRG system, payments to hospitals for the same DRG often varied widely.

The first year, each hospital's payments were based 25 percent on the national rate and 75 percent on the hospital's costs. The next year, the formula was 50–50, and the year after 75–25.

DRG rates should be available from HCFA. If you have trouble, a health statistician can figure them out from the cost reports, or ask one hospital to tell you its competitor's rates.

Audit Work Papers   You can also get the audit work papers for the Medicare cost reports. These are rough drafts and analyses accountants use to formulate the reports. The accountants' comments can be very revealing.

Ownership Documents   If your hospital is owned by a for-profit corporation, such as Humana, check records filed with the Securities and Exchange Commission. Form 10-K, the basic annual report, provides information on corporate structure; property owned; income and expenditures, names, salaries and backgrounds of officers and directors; and recent actions in the stockholders' meetings. This information may apply to the entire corporation, not your hospital specifically. (For more information, see Chapter 11, "Business.")

Internal Revenue Service Form 990   Another avenue for information on a not-for-profit hospital or a for-profit hospital that runs a not-for-profit foundation is the Internal Revenue Service Form 990. This lists gross income and receipts; contributions, gifts and grants; fundraising efforts; assets and investments; compensation of officers and the highest-paid employees; the largest amount of money paid to outside individuals; and organizations that provide services to the hospital. Also ask for independent audits required for preparation of the 990s.

Many hospitals have separate foundations that must file 990PFs (for private foundations). These may provide other types of financial information in such areas as research and lobbying.

Forms 990 and 990PFs can be obtained with a FOIA request to the regional IRS office. (For more information on these forms, see Chapter 11, "Business.")

Federal Grants and Contracts

(See "Medical Research" later in this section.)

Peer Review Organizations

Here is a summary of what the Peer Review Organization (PRO) is required to do and what records are public.

PROs review admissions to hospitals within seven days of discharge, every cardiac pacemaker implant, transfers to another hospital, all DRGs and longer-than-average stays. Recently PRO reviews were extended to outpatient surgery and ambulatory care. PROs also validate 3 percent of DRGs to make sure patients' diagnoses were not miscoded as more lucrative DRGs.

The PRO must release, for each hospital, the number of discharges and deaths for each DRG, length of stay by DRG, age distribution of patients, patient disposition (discharge to home, nursing home, other hospital or died), readmissions within seven days and DRGs that were changed because of miscoding.

Getting DRG records is not a job for the faint-hearted. It costs you much time, money and frustration. PROs can take weeks or months to respond to your request, may withhold information because it could identify a specific doctor and may tell you the information is not available in the form you requested. Some PROs can't easily retrieve public records from their computer and have to write special programs that can cost hundreds or even thousands of dollars. Even after the information is retrieved, the law requires each named hospital be given 30 days to respond before the record is released.

A few PROs, like California's, have been surprisingly forthcoming, and have published extensive reports.

If you despair of getting anything from your PRO, the records may be available from two other sources.

When the Alabama PRO stonewalled Bob Blalock of the Birmingham News, he asked HCFA instead. It took six months, but he got, for free, a computer printout showing patient disposition for several of the most frequent DRGs.

However, HCFA has since changed the way it collects data and has restricted access to its records. Now HCFA says it will provide only data that already have been extracted from the computer for HCFA's own studies (such as the "tracer condition" study that Knight-Ridder obtained and used for its coronary artery bypass story), or a full year's tape containing all 10 million Medicare admissions nationwide. To interpret the tape, you need a mainframe computer and considerable expertise.

HCFA will provide national average mortality rates, lengths of stay and readmission rates for each DRG, which you can use as a yardstick for individual hospitals.

However, it is still worth asking HCFA for all the data, citing Blalock as a precedent. It may also be worthwhile to talk to a HCFA computer expert before filing the FOIA request, so you know exactly what to ask for.

Call the FOIA chief at (301) 966–5352 for referral to a HCFA data specialist. FOIA requests go to Health Care Financing Administration, Freedom of Information Office, Professional Building, Room 100, 6660 Security Blvd., Baltimore, Md. 21207.

For the name and location of your state PRO, call the HCFA regional office.

You may be able to bypass HCFA and the PRO entirely if you live in a state, such as New York, that collects its own DRG data either for Medicaid patients, hospital rate setting or other purposes. About half the states have agencies. Contact the National Association of Health Data Organizations, 229 Pennsylvania Ave. S.E., Washington, D.C. 20003, for the names of these agencies.

If your newspaper's data processing department does computer work for the editorial department, or you have access to a mainframe computer elsewhere, getting the full computer tapes from HCFA or state health data agencies is an attractive option. Tapes usually come faster and cost less. The Center for Medical Consumers in New York City —(212) 674-7105—has used the computer tapes for several years to analyze death rates for several health procedures. The center will provide that information to reporters.

Here is a list of HCFA Regional Offices.

REGION ONE

Maine, Vermont, New Hampshire,
  Massachusetts, Connecticut,
  Rhode Island
HCFA Region One
JFK Federal Building, Room 1309
Boston, Mass. 02203
(617) 565–1188

REGION TWO

New York, New Jersey, Puerto Rico,
  Virgin Islands
HCFA Region Two
26 Federal Plaza, Room 3811
New York, N.Y. 10278
(212) 264–4488

REGION THREE

Pennsylvania, Maryland, Delaware,
  West Virginia, Virginia and D.C.
HCFA Region Three
3535 Market St., Box 7760
Philadelphia, Pa. 19101
(215) 596–0324

REGION FOUR

Georgia, Kentucky, Tennessee,
  Mississippi, North Carolina, South
  Carolina and Florida
HCFA Region Four

101 Marietta Tower, Suite 701
Atlanta, Ga. 30323
(404) 331–2329

REGION FIVE

Minnesota, Wisconsin, Illinois, Indiana,
  Michigan and Ohio
HCFA Region Five
105 W. Adams, 15th Floor
Chicago, Ill. 60603
(312) 886–6432

REGION SIX

Texas, Oklahoma, New Mexico,
  Arkansas and Louisiana
HCFA Region Six
1200 Main Tower Bldg., Room 2000
Dallas, Texas 75202
(214) 767–6427

REGION SEVEN

Nebraska, Kansas, Iowa and Missouri
HCFA Region Seven
New Federal Office Building,
  Room 235
601 E. 12th St.
Kansas City, Mo. 64106
(816) 426–5233

REGION EIGHT
Colorado, Utah, Wyoming, Montana,
 North Dakota and South Dakota
HCFA Region Eight
Federal Building, Room 574
1961 Stout St.
Denver, Colo. 80294
(303) 844–2111

REGION NINE
Nevada, Arizona, California, Hawaii,
 Guam and Samoa

HCFA Region Nine
75 Hawthorne, Fourth Floor
San Francisco, Calif. 94105
(415) 744–3502

REGION TEN
Washington, Oregon, Idaho and Alaska
HCFA Region Ten
Mail Stop RX40
2201 Sixth Ave.
Seattle, Wash. 98121
(206) 442–0425

Patient Fee and Care Records

Fees   A hip-replacement operation could cost from $2,500 to $10,600, depending on the hospital where the surgery is performed, the doctor who does it and who pays: Medicare, Medicaid, a health insurance company or (rarely) the patient.

A comparative list of prices for common procedures at your local hospitals is an eye-opening document for your readers.

You'll need several sources to obtain the information. The hospital may, but probably won't, give it to you. The Medicaid offices in some states are helpful on Medicaid costs.

It is difficult to figure costs of procedures from Medicare cost reports. However, fiscal intermediaries do studies of costs and may have what you are interested in.

It appears that the law requires PROs to release comparative prices. But most refuse. Reporters must consider filing lawsuits to force PROs to release this information.

HCFA and some state health departments can provide computer tapes of hospital costs.

A good source for health costs can be your area business-health coalition. Many of these organizations keep track of hospital charges, almost to the penny.

Talk to area health maintenance and preferred provider organizations. They make money by having the lowest costs for medical care, so they probably have surveyed rates at area hospitals.

Other potential sources include state centers for health statistics, state and county medical societies, Blue Cross/Blue Shield and non-governmental consumer agencies. For public hospitals, this information should be available at the hospital, or through the appropriate government agency, such as the state division of health.

When figuring costs, though, don't accept averages, such as total cost divided by number of patients. Try to get prices of the most frequently performed procedures as well as the components, such as tests.

Try talking to elderly people who have been in the hospital recently. Some are outraged at costs, and will be glad to show you their bills.

Patient Records   Patient records are confidential. However, you may be able to convince patients involved in your story to request their records. Court cases are another source in which at least parts of patient records are revealed.

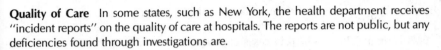

Quality of Care In some states, such as New York, the health department receives "incident reports" on the quality of care at hospitals. The reports are not public, but any deficiencies found through investigations are.

State Fire Marshal Reports The fire inspection report should show whether the hospital is meeting code requirements. This may be especially important in the case of older hospitals: Has the sprinkler system been installed?

You can also investigate how well the fire marshal enforces the code. Are reports of deficiencies followed up?

Inspection reports are available at the office of the state fire marshal or the state hospital regulatory agency.

Statistics General statistics on hospital income and occupancy rates can be obtained from state hospital associations, state health departments and the American Hospital Association.

Other Sources of Information

Legislative committees on the state and federal level can be useful sources in the areas of standards and finances of hospitals.

The state health plan, if one exists, has useful background material on the overall health system in a state. Check with the state health department planning agency.

The Commission on Professional and Hospital Activities (CPHA) collects hospitalization data on a representative sample of two million patients and has statistics on numbers of operations, length of stay, fatality rates by DRG and demographic data. It publishes similar data on outpatient surgery. The not-for-profit CPHA is sponsored by the American College of Physicians, the American College of Surgeons, the American Hospital Association and the Southwestern Michigan Hospital Council. Call (313) 796–6511, or write to the CPHA at 1968 Green Rd., Box 1809, Ann Arbor, Mich. 48106. State pharmacy boards are an often overlooked source of aggressive hospital inspectors.

VETERANS HOSPITALS

Records on DVA hospitals are available from the Department of Veterans Affairs and other agencies that oversee veterans concerns.

Accreditation

All DVA hospitals are surveyed at least once every three years by the Joint Commission on Accreditation of Hospitals. Reports are available from Director Medical Administration Service, Department of Veterans Affairs, Department of Medicine and Surgery, Washington, D.C. 20420.

Patient Injury Control Reports

DVA Form 10–2633 is filed in cases of patient injury or unexpected death. Patient names are confidential. Contact: Medical Inspector, DVA Central Office, Washington, D.C. 20420.

DVA Inspector General Audits

The inspector general reviews about 30 hospitals annually, audits construction grants and reviews policy matters. Contact: Inspector General, DVA Central Office, Department of Veterans Affairs, Washington, D.C. 20420.

Patient Satisfaction Surveys

These DVA records assess whether patients are dissatisfied with conditions at a DVA hospital. Contact: Director, Quality Assurance, Department of Veterans Affairs, Washington, D.C. 20420.

General Accounting Office Surveys

The GAO audits DVA hospitals and medical programs and will search its files for free. Contact: General Accounting Office, Document Handling and Information, Box 6015, Gaithersburg, Md. 20877.

Transcripts of Veterans Affairs Committee Hearings

Veterans affairs committees oversee facets of the DVA system. Contact: Staff Director, Senate Committee on Veterans Affairs, Washington, D.C. 20515, and Staff Director, House Committee on Veterans Affairs, Washington, D.C. 20510.

Veterans' Groups

Several veterans' groups survey DVA hospitals and generally make their reports available. Some groups maintain offices in the hospitals and pick up rumors. Contact: Director, National Veterans Affairs and Rehabilitation Commission, The American Legion, 1608 K Street N.W., Washington, D.C. 20006.

DOCTORS

Public access to disciplinary records varies from state to state. In some, like Michigan, most of the record is public—including the formal charge and supporting documentation, the hearing and hearing record, the deliberations of the medical board and the investigation files on cases that are closed with no action. In other states, notably Wyoming, almost nothing is public—not the formal charge, not the hearing, not even the reason for the board's final action. That in itself is a story.

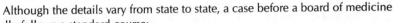

Although the details vary from state to state, a case before a board of medicine generally follows a standard course:

The case begins when a doctor comes to the board's attention, through an allegation filed by a patient, a routine review of malpractice cases, a report filed by a hospital or some other source. A board investigator interviews witnesses, does undercover work and obtains subpoenas for records to support the case. A state attorney then decides whether to file formal charges against the doctor. If no charges are filed, a formal hearing is held at which both sides present evidence and witnesses. Before, during and after the hearing, the doctor and the state engage in informal plea bargaining in an effort to cut short the expensive proceedings.

The conclusions and recommendations of the hearing officer—or a proposed consent order worked out informally—are sent to the board, which decides whether to accept them. The board also determines any penalty, which can range from a reprimand to license revocation. The doctor can appeal any board decision to the courts.

At the end of this section are the names, telephone numbers and addresses of all the state medical licensing boards. (In some states, osteopaths, or D.O.s, are licensed by a separate board.) Other agencies that have information about doctors include:

- *The American Medical Association*, which has a computerized Physician Masterfile that tracks every M.D. in America from entry into medical school through graduation, residency and every change of practice and address until retirement. The AMA, which soon will start charging for information, will provide the doctor's address, date and place of birth, medical school attended and date of graduation, date and place of residency, any board certifications and academic appointments, and what states licensed the doctor and when. However, the AMA will not tell you about any disciplinary actions by a board or any other agency. Dr. Joseph Rucker, whose Michigan license was revoked in 1983, was listed by the AMA as "semiretired" for at least the next four years. Contact the American Medical Association, Department of Data Release Services, 535 N. Dearborn Ave. Chicago 60601. The same information, less up-to-date, is printed in the American Medical Directory, updated about every two years, available in most public and medical libraries.
- *State insurance bureaus and state-funded patient compensation funds*, which keep records on malpractice claims. Rosemary Goudreau and Alex Beasley of The Orlando Sentinel made extensive use of these records in their state to find out, among other things, which doctors were sued the most and for what. They discovered that 3 percent of Florida doctors accounted for nearly half the money paid to malpractice victims in the state. Unfortunately, such information is not public in many other states.
- *Medicare*. The Inspector General's office publishes a list of doctors and other health professionals who have been suspended from the Medicare program. The list, which indicates the length of each suspension and the reason for it, is updated every three months. Information on a particular doctor or a copy of the whole list is available from the public affairs office (202) 472–3142. If you want more details, you must file an FOIA request with the Office of the Inspector General, FOIA Privacy Act Office, North Building, Room 5246, 330 Independence Ave. S.W., Washington, D.C. 20201.

- *The Federation of State Medical Boards,* which collects statistics on disciplinary actions by medical and osteopathic boards and publishes an annual summary. Contact the federation of at 2630 West Freeway, Suite 138, Fort Worth, Texas 76102–7199; (817) 335–1141.
- *Local county medical societies,* which sometimes conduct investigations of doctors. Most of these groups have incomplete records.
- *The Public Citizen Health Research Group,* Washington, D.C., releases names of doctors, dentists, chiropractors and podiatrists disciplined by state and federal medical boards.

Here is a list of physician licensing boards.

ALABAMA
Board of Medical Examiners
Box 946
Montgomery, Ala. 36102
(205) 242–4116

ALASKA
Alaska Medical Board
Department of Commerce and
  Economic Development
Division of Occupational Licensing,
  Box D
Juneau, Alaska 99811
(907) 465–2541

ARIZONA
Board of Medical Examiners
1990 W. Camelback Rd., Suite 401
Phoenix, Ariz. 85015
(602) 255–3751

ARKANSAS
Arkansas State Medical Board
Box 102
Harrisburg, Ark. 72432
(501) 578–2448

CALIFORNIA
California Board of Medical Quality
  Assurance
1430 Howe Ave.
Sacramento, Calif. 95825
(916) 920–6393

COLORADO
Board of Medical Examiners
1525 Sherman St., No. 132
Denver, Colo. 80203
(303) 866–2468

CONNECTICUT
Department of Health Services
Division of Medical Quality
  Assurance, Physician Licensure
150 Washington St.
Hartford, Conn. 06106
(203) 566–7398

DELAWARE
Board of Medical Practice
Margaret O'Neill Bldg., 2nd Floor
Dover, Del. 19903
(302) 736–4522

DISTRICT OF COLUMBIA
Occupational and Professional
  Licensing Administration
Box 37200, Room 904
Washington, D.C. 20013
(202) 727–7480

FLORIDA
Board of Medicine Examiners
130 N. Monroe Ave.
Tallahassee, Fla. 32399–0750
(904) 488–0595

GEORGIA
Composite State Board of Medical
  Examiners
166 Pryor St. S.W.
Atlanta, Ga. 30303
(404) 656–3913

HAWAII
Board of Medical Examiners
Department of Commerce and
  Consumer Affairs
Box 3469

Honolulu, Hawaii 96801
(808) 548–4392

IDAHO
Idaho State Board of Medicine
500 S. 10 St.
Suite 103, Statehouse
Boise, Idaho 83720
(208) 334–2822

ILLINOIS
Department of Professional Regulation
320 W. Washington St.
Springfield, Ill. 62786
(217) 785–0800

INDIANA
Medical Licensing Board
1 American Square, Suite 1020
Box 82067
Indianapolis, Ind. 46282
(317) 232–2960

IOWA
Board of Medical Examiners
State Capitol Complex
Executive Hills West
Des Moines, Iowa 50319
(515) 281–5171

KANSAS
State Board of Healing Arts
503 Kansas Ave., Suite 500
Topeka, Kan. 66612
(913) 296–7413

KENTUCKY
Board of Medical Licensure
400 Sherburn Lane, Suite 222
Louisville, Ky. 40207
(502) 896–1516

LOUISIANA
Board of Medical Examiners
830 Union St., Suite 100
New Orleans, La. 70112
(504) 524–6763

MAINE
Board of Registration in Medicine
2 Bangor St., Statehouse Station 137

Augusta, Me. 04333
(207) 289–3601

MARYLAND
Board of Physician Quality Assurance
201 W. Preston St.
Baltimore, Md. 21201
(301) 225–5900

MASSACHUSETTS
Board of Registration in Medicine
10 West St.
Boston, Mass. 02111
(617) 727–3086

MICHIGAN
Board of Medicine
611 W. Ottawa St.
Box 30018
Lansing, Mich. 48909
(517) 373–6873

MINNESOTA
Board of Medical Examiners
2700 University Ave. W., Suite 106
St. Paul, Minn. 55114
(612) 642–0538

MISSISSIPPI
State Board of Medical Licensure
2688D Insurance Center Dr.
Jackson, Miss. 39216
(601) 354–6645

MISSOURI
Board of Registration for the Healing Arts
Box 4
Jefferson City, Mo. 65102
(314) 751–2334

MONTANA
Board of Medical Examiners
1424 Ninth Ave.
Helena, Mont. 59620
(406) 444–3737

NEBRASKA
Bureau of Examining Boards
Box 95007
Lincoln, Neb. 65809
(402) 471–2215

NEVADA
Board of Medical Examiners
Box 7238
Reno, Nev. 89510
(702) 329–2559

NEW HAMPSHIRE
Board of Registration in Medicine
Health and Welfare Bldg.
6 Hazen Drive
Concord, N.H. 03301
(603) 271-1203

NEW JERSEY
State Board of Medical Examiners
of New Jersey
28 W. State St.
Trenton, N.J. 08608
(609) 292–4843

NEW MEXICO
Board of Medical Examiners
Drawer 1388
Santa Fe, N.M. 87504
(505) 827–9930

NEW YORK
State Board of Medicine
Cultural Education Center
Albany, N.Y. 12230
(518) 474–3841

NORTH CAROLINA
Board of Medical Examiners
1313 Navaho Dr.
Raleigh, N.C. 27609
(919) 876–3885

NORTH DAKOTA
Board of Medical Examiners
418 East Broadway Ave., Suite C-10
Bismarck, N.D. 58501
(701) 223–9485

OHIO
State Medical Board
77 S. High St., 17th Fl.
Columbus, Ohio 43266–0315
(614) 466–3934

OKLAHOMA
Board of Medical Examiners
Box 18256
Oklahoma City, Okla. 73154–0256
(405) 848–6841

OREGON
Board of Medical Examiners
1002 Loyalty Building
317 S.W. Alder St.
Portland, Ore. 97204
(503) 229–5770

PENNSYLVANIA
State Board of Medicine
Box 2649
Harrisburg, Pa. 17105
(717) 787–2381

RHODE ISLAND
Division of Professional
    Regulation
State Department of Health
104 Cannon Building
75 Davis St.
Providence, R.I. 02908–5097
(401) 277–2827

SOUTH CAROLINA
Board of Medical Examiners
1315 Blanding St.
Columbia, S.C. 29201
(803) 734–8901

SOUTH DAKOTA
State Board of Medical and
    Osteopathic Examiners
1323 Minnesota Ave. S.
Sioux Falls, S.D. 57105
(605) 336–1965

TENNESSEE
Board of Medical Examiners
283 Plus Park Boulevard
Nashville, Tenn. 37219
(615) 367–6231

TEXAS
Registration Division
Board of Medical Examiners

Box 13562
Austin, Texas 78711
(512) 452–1078

UTAH
Division of Occupational Professional
  Licensing
Box 45802
Salt Lake City, Utah 84145
(801) 530–6628

VERMONT
Board of Medical Practice
109 State St.
Montpelier, Vt. 05602
(802) 828–2673

VIRGINIA
State Board of Medicine
Surrey Bldg., 2nd Fl.
1601 Rolling Hills Drive
Richmond, Va. 23229
(804) 662–9908

WASHINGTON
Division of Professional Licensing
Box 9649
Olympia, Wash. 98504
(206) 753–3199

WEST VIRGINIA
Board of Medicine
100 Dee Drive, Suite 104
Charleston, W.Va. 25311
(304) 348–2921

WISCONSIN
Medical Examining Board
1400 E. Washington Ave.
Madison, Wis. 53702
(608) 266–2811

WYOMING
Board of Medical Examiners
Hathaway Building, 4th Floor
Cheyenne, Wyo. 82002
(307) 777–6463

HEALTH MAINTENANCE ORGANIZATIONS

State Agencies

In most states, responsibility for HMO licensing is divided between the state health department, which monitors quality of care, and the state insurance department, which has jurisdiction over rates and finances. The kinds of information available will vary from state to state. In Michigan, the state health department requires each HMO to file a quarterly report listing the number of subscribers who received care during the quarter and the kind of care they received; the HMO's hospitalization rate; the number of new subscribers and dropouts; and a breakdown of membership by age, sex and type of contract (Medicare, Medicaid, group and individual). The state insurance department requires monthly, quarterly or annual reports, depending on the HMO's financial condition. The reports detail the HMO's history, names of officers and directors, revenue and expenses, and other financial details. The insurance department also has each HMO's rates, marketing plans and copies of subscriber contracts and the contracts between the HMO and its health care providers.

If the HMO has a Medicaid contract, the state's Medicaid agency will have detailed information about money paid out and services provided to Medicaid subscribers.

Hospitalization Rates

Your state health department's planning agency can give you the state hospitalization rate, measured in number of patient days per thousand population. If your state doesn't have a planning agency, call the Blue Cross-Blue Shield plan in your state or region.

Federal Certification

HMOs that are certified by the federal Office of Prepaid Health Care can get Medicare contracts and certain marketing advantages. The HMO's entire federal application and all subsequent dealings with Medicare are public, except during the application process. If the HMO is refused certification, the application is public, along with the reasons for the denial.

The agency also publishes a variety of reports on HMOs, including 10-year annual reports on the industry. Write to the Office of Prepaid Health Care, Department of Health and Human Services, 200 Independence Ave. S.W., Room 317-H, Washington, D.C. 20201; (202) 245–0197.

Private Organizations

Interstudy, an HMO think tank, publishes a quarterly report that lists all the HMOs in the U.S., their enrollment, federal status, profit or not-for-profit status, age and other data. Interstudy also has a Center for Aging and Long Term Care that explores innovative ways of delivering and financing care for the elderly. Write to Interstudy, Box 458, Excelsior, Minn. 55331; (612) 474–1176.

Group Health Association of America, the HMO trade organization, has the nation's largest library on HMOs and other kinds of prepaid health care. Its legislative department tracks all bills affecting the industry. Write Group Health Association of America, 1129 20th St. N.W., Washington, D.C. 20036; (202) 778–3200.

Preferred Provider Organizations

PPOs are hybrids of fee-for-service HMOs. They were originated by health care providers in response to the HMO threat, and attempt to cater to both ends of the health care market. For a monthly fee, they offer more comprehensive benefits than traditional insurance (but less than HMOs) if the subscriber goes to their doctors or hospitals. Subscribers can go to non-PPO providers, but at the price of large copayments and deductibles.

PPOs are not as closely regulated as HMOs. The state of Michigan requires only that they file rates, standards and a financial report at the end of the year. Not all PPOs are even required to register with the state.

The American Association of Preferred Provider Organizations, a trade group, acts as a clearinghouse for information on PPOs. Write to them at: 1101 Connecticut Ave. N.W., Suite 700, Washington, D.C. 20036; (202) 857–1128.

NURSING HOMES

Accreditation Reports

Currently, no national program exists for accrediting nursing homes. The Joint Commission on Accreditation of Hospitals accredits about 5 percent of the nursing homes. See "Hospitals" earlier in this section. Supporters of accreditation had hoped the American Health Care Association 1200 15th St. N.W., Washington, D.C. 20005, would get involved in certification. However, many member nursing homes objected.

Nursing homes must be certified by states to take Medicare patients. See below for how to obtain these reports.

Financial Records

Nursing homes are required to file financial reports similar to those required for hospitals: Medicare and Medicaid cost reports, contracts and audits of public funds, Securities and Exchange Commission reports and IRS Form 990s.

As with hospitals, the audit papers will flesh out the figures on the Medicaid and Medicare reports.

States pay a large portion of nursing home costs through Medicaid. With more people being sent from hospitals to nursing homes, states are feeling the burden of increased costs. State agencies and legislatures may be studying nursing home costs.

Ownership Records

Nursing homes incorporated as businesses must file yearly incorporation papers listing principal officers with the secretary of state. Some states, however, allow hidden participation by silent partners.

To get around this, obtain from the state agency that regulates nursing homes a copy of Federal Disclosure Ownership Form HCFA-1513, form showing all principal owners, including addresses.

Also check the licensing files of state departments of health. The forms a nursing home submits to get a license will show names and addresses of the home's owners and leasers.

Check whether the owners or leasers are part of a larger corporation that runs other problematic nursing homes. (For more information, see Chapter 11, "Business.")

Health Systems Agency Reviews

Though no longer mandated by the federal government, health systems agencies, or planning councils, still exist in some states. (For more information, see "Hospitals and Other Health Care Institutions" at the beginning of this section.)

State and Medicare Inspection Reports

Nursing homes are licensed by the states where they operate, and nearly all states provide for periodic inspections. These inspection reports can be a starting point for an investigation. Learn the law and the regulations. Then go to the state agency and check the inspection reports.

States conduct a variety of inspections. State laws require a certain number of announced or unannounced visits a year. In addition, the state conducts patient medical reviews and utilization reviews. The reviews are often closed to reporters, but ask to see the "exit report," a summary submitted to the nursing home administrators.

After an inspection, a nursing home with problems is given a list of deficiencies. The home then presents a plan of correction. This is public information.

The state also conducts special inspections upon receipt of complaints. In some states, reporters can see investigation reports on both verified complaints and those the inspectors determined were unsubstantiated. The invalid complaints may show not that the complaint was ungrounded, but that the inspectors didn't do a good job. Ask for the complaint letters, even if the agency blacks out the names of the letter writers.

If conditions are bad enough at a nursing home, the state may hold a hearing. HHS has survey reports for homes with Medicare patients.

In 1989 and 1990, HCFA compiled a series titled "Medicare and Medicaid Nursing Home Information." This contains a four-page profile on each of the approximately 16,000 homes that participate in Medicare or Medicaid. The 1990 series had 93 volumes. Volumes covering particular states can be purchased from the Superintendent of Documents, U.S. Government Printing Office, Washington, D.C. 20402; (202) 783–3238. The reports are also available at state health departments and regional offices of the American Association of Retired Persons.

Local Reports

State regulatory agencies may not be the only groups inspecting a nursing home. The area veterans hospital may have a contract with the home and, therefore, send its own inspectors. The reports can be obtained from the DVA hospital.

The city or county may have its health department or other inspectors checking the homes. Don't forget local fire, building, electrical and food preparation codes.

Litigation

Check court files for wrongful-death lawsuits against nursing homes. Lawyers could have valuable medical records, including records showing when nurses worked. If you compare these to the names of the nurses that signed patients' files, you may find the signers weren't even on duty. This could mean the records were falsified.

Court records may also give you lists of the nursing homes' suppliers, which are important if you suspect Medicaid fraud.

Obituaries

Search the obituaries in your own paper for people who died at nursing homes. Their relatives may be good sources.

Promotional Publications

Most nursing homes will provide reporters with promotional literature that details what services they are supposed to provide. The promises may not be the reality.

Ombudsman

The federal ombudsman program requires each state to have a long-term care ombudsman program. For a list, call your state department of aging, or write to the

Office of State and Tribal Programs, Administration on Aging, Office of Human Development Services, Department of HHS, 330 Independence Ave. S.W., Washington, D.C. 20201.

Lobbyists

The National Citizens Coalition for Nursing Home Reform is a lobbying group and national clearinghouse for information on nursing homes. Their members include advocacy groups and ombudsmen in more than 40 states. Their address is: 1424 16th St. N.W., Suite L-2, Washington, D.C. 20036; (202) 797–0657.

MENTAL HEALTH

The trend in the care of both the mentally disabled and the mentally ill has been to release them from large institutions and place them in group homes. Because of the large amounts of federal and state money poured into these places, records are available on the finances and quality of care at both the institutions and the homes.

Finances

Budgets Budgets for most hospitals and group homes are available from the state division of social services, retardation or mental health. Not-for-profit agencies receiving state money to operate community residences must submit annual, and often quarterly, reports of expenditures and earnings.

Budgets for small, privately owned group homes may be more difficult to get. If they don't receive state funding, they may still get federal money from Medicare or the National Institute of Mental Health. Write to the Health Care Financing Administration, Professional Building, Room 100, 6660 Security Blvd., Baltimore, Md. 21207, to find out who is the fiscal intermediary for these homes. Make your FOIA request to the intermediary for Medicare cost reports.

When looking at budgets, determine what percentage of money goes to treatment. If there has been construction, especially at large institutions, was it done in the most economical way? Or did the contract go to an administrator's friend?

Audits State and federal agencies will periodically audit institutions they fund. Ask the agencies for the audits.

Patient Care

Inspections All hospitals and many homes are licensed by the state department of mental health or department of social services. Ask for inspection reports and lists of deficiencies. Inspections may also be conducted by the National Institute of Mental Health or the Joint Commission on Accreditation of Hospitals. HCFA requires inspections of homes getting Medicare funds, but the state agency often does those inspections.

Some states may not license smaller group homes, or may not inspect them diligently. Check the policies on licensing and inspection in your state.

Staffing   Doctors and counselors caring for the mentally ill and mentally disabled may not be qualified. Check personnel records doctors' and counselors' educational credentials.

Building Safety

Inspections   The buildings housing mentally ill and mentally disabled have to be constructed in accordance with state building and health department codes. Ask for inspection reports. Also get the codes and check to see if your institutions meet the codes in terms of construction material, fire escapes and other safety features.

Other Records   Other records that may prove useful are coroners' reports and police reports of brutality to patients by staff or vice versa.

DRUGS

Food and Drug Administration Records

For the following FDA records, make your FOIA request to the Freedom of Information Staff, Room 12A-30, 5600 Fishers Lane, Rockville, Md. 20857.

Investigational New Drugs   This form must be submitted by a drug producer to the FDA before a new drug may be tested on human subjects in the United States. Because there are many federal regulations concerning new drugs, these products may first appear on the market in other countries.

New Drug Applications   A company planning to market a new drug must give the FDA information on its intended use, chemical composition, interactions with other drugs, dosage, adverse reactions and a general evaluation of safety and efficacy.

Clinical Investigator Files   Clinical investigator files include evaluations of the quality of work performed by doctors testing new drug products. These also may be useful for uncovering unorthodox relationships between physicians and drug companies.

Enforcement Actions   The FDA may recall or limit products that may be ineffective or could cause adverse reactions. Files are usually released only after the investigations are completed. Information may include informal regulatory actions, actual recalls and reports on the safety and efficacy of the drug.

Drug Experience Reports   A manufacturer must submit a drug experience report to the FDA any time it receives a complaint about an adverse drug reaction. Although it is not required, physicians and patients may also submit these reports. Information includes the name of the drug, the reason for its use, dosage and length of time drug was administered, adverse reactions and patient's prior disorders and reports of laboratory studies and autopsies. The report also will state whether the patient is still under treatment or has recovered.

Community Pharmacists' Drug Defect Report Program Pharmacists in the community and hospitals receive complaints from customers about reactions to drugs. Pharmacists report these to the FDA.

Registration of a Drug Establishment Any establishment that sells prescription drugs must submit information to the FDA, including the name(s) of the owner or partners and titles; corporate officers and members of the board of directors; and firm names used by the establishment. Check whether local physicians are either owners or members of the board of directors.

Import Drug List This is a list of drugs that can be exported, even though they haven't been approved for use in this country. It also lists drugs that can be imported into the United States.

Additional Prescription Drug Information Outside the FDA, information on prescription drugs may be available from state health or consumer affairs departments. Data on adverse reactions to prescription drugs is also included in the Physician's Desk Reference.

Drug Misuse Reports Is the abuse of a certain drug, such as cocaine, on the rise in your area? The Drug Abuse Warning Network (DAWN), under the jurisdiction of the National Institute on Drug Abuse, collects reports filed by emergency room staff and medical examiners. Individual reports are compiled into statistical reports on use of certain drugs nationwide and in major metropolitan areas. You can't get reports on an individual hospital, however. Summaries are available from the National Institute on Drug Abuse.

Treatment centers are excellent sources for background information on drug abuse.

Drug Theft or Loss Reports Hospitals are required to report thefts and losses of drugs to the Drug Enforcement Administration (DEA), the top federal agency that enforces narcotics and controlled substances laws. The individual reports may not be public. You will be able to get statistics on the amount of drugs stolen in a state, but you may not be able to find out from the DEA which hospitals in your area are losing drugs. Check reports at your local police department, which may receive reports of drug thefts.

For DEA information, make your FOIA request to the DEA, FOI-PA Section, Room 200, 1405 I St. N.W., Washington, D.C. 20537.

MEDICAL DEVICE APPLICATIONS AND COMPLAINTS

Under FDA regulations, manufacturers of medical devices file applications for any new device they plan to market, including pacemakers, scanners, blood pressure equipment, artificial hearts, wheelchairs, lithotripters and other medical equipment.

Clinical data, test results, labeling requirements, promotional materials, progress reports, adverse reaction data and related correspondence are public. Trade secrets are confidential, but FDA notices of approval and disapproval are public.

Other information available includes lists of registered devices, firms registered to manufacture devices, recalls and regulatory letters issued when an inspector finds something that needs correction.

The FDA also takes complaints about medical devices from consumers. You can ask for the complaints about a device made by a specific manufacturer or complaints about a type of device.

Make your FOIA request to the Center for Devices and Radiological Health, Food and Drug Administration, 5600 Fishers Lane, Rockville, Md. 20857.

Also check Health Devices Alerts—Action Items, Health Devices Alerts—Abstracts and Health Devices, published by the Emergency Care Research Institute, 5200 Butler Pike, Plymouth Meeting, Pa. 19462. Action Items, published weekly, lists problems with devices on which action must be taken immediately. Abstracts summarizes FDA and other studies of devices as well as hazards that have been reported.

Another records source is the Office of Technology Assessment, which evaluates economic, social and practical impacts of new technology and policies. Recent reports have examined lithotripters, hearing aids for the elderly and native American health care. Contact the Congressional and Public Affairs Office, Office of Technology Assessment, U.S. Congress, Washington, D.C. 20510; (202) 226–2115.

MEDICAL RESEARCH

A $10 million grant for medical research is rarely evaluated as closely as a $10 million public contract to build a bridge. Here are some records that may help you discover misdeeds among medical miracles.

Most of the money the federal government allocates for research comes in two forms: contracts and grants. The records differ.

Contracts

Available records on contracts include the proposal (without information that might jeopardize a future patent), the contract (which includes the contract payment) and some evaluations of the work (with many critical comments deleted). Evaluations aren't always done, however.

Grants

A grant is an award of money to a researcher. The guidelines for the work are general. Only approved applications for original grants are public. However, many researchers who have government grants reapply for more money to continue the work. These reapplications are public, whether approved or not. The federal government does little formal assessment of the work performed for this grant money. Research results are usually published in medical journals.

Federal Record Repositories

Most records on research are available from each of the institutes at the National Institutes of Health, 9000 Rockville Pike, Bethesda, Md. 20014. Among the institutes and areas that cover biomedical research are:

- National Institute of Allergy and Infectious Diseases
- National Institute of Arthritis, Musculoskeletal and Skin Diseases
- National Cancer Institute
- National Institute of Child Health and Human Development
- National Institute of Dental Research
- National Eye Institute
- National Institute on Aging
- National Heart, Lung and Blood Institute
- National Institute of Neurological and Communicative Disorders and Stroke
- National Institute of Diabetes and Digestive and Kidney Diseases
- National Institute of General Medicine Sciences (covering areas not supported by other National Institutes of Health, such as genetics and trauma)

Other granting agencies, such as the Alcohol, Drug Abuse and Mental Health Administration and National Science Foundation disburse some health research funds. Check the United States Government Manual for descriptions of programs within agencies related to health care research. (For more information on how to use the manual, see Chapter 3, "Finding a Government Document: An Overall Strategy.")

Audits

The Office of the Inspector General of Health and Human Services audits many of the final reports on research dollars that go to hospitals. These audits are a good place to look for fraud. For example, only a certain amount of the research money can go to salaries. Hospitals can get around that by charging two funding sources for the same employee's salary. Try to get the budgets and final reports from both funding sources. For audits, contact Health and Human Services, Office of the Inspector General, Public Affairs, Room 5246, North Building, 330 Independence Ave. S.W., Washington, D.C. 20201.

The General Accounting Office audits major research programs, such as those of the National Cancer Institute. Contact the GAO, Human Resources Division, 441 G St. N.W., Washington, D.C. 20548.

Private Research Funds

Most private funding of medical research is provided by foundations. You can check two sources to find what private groups fund research.

The Foundation Center, with repositories around the country, can help reporters locate information on a specific foundation. Contact the Foundation Center, 888

Seventh Ave., New York, N.Y. 10019. (For more information, see Chapter 2, "Using Publications.")

The Foundation Directory lists major foundations by state, along with a brief description. Many states publish foundation directories listing officers, assets and disbursements. This could be invaluable for the more obscure foundations.

Almost every foundation issues an annual report that lists the organizations or individuals receiving funds; how much was received; and the purpose of the funds. This report can be obtained from the foundation, the secretary of state or the Foundation Center or its state repositories.

Most foundations are not-for-profit organizations. IRS Form 990, which not-for-profit agencies must file, gives a detailed account of how foundations distribute funds. The IRS or Foundation Center can provide these reports. The foundation itself must make the form available for inspection. (For more information, see Chapter 11, "Business.")

Also check Medical Research Centres, a guide by Gale Research Company, Book Tower, Detroit, Mich. 48226. This detailed guide lists organizations that conduct or finance medical research.

Once you've discovered the foundation or agency that has awarded research money to an individual or institution, contact an officer of the foundation, requesting a copy of the proposal, criteria for use of the money and any evaluation of the research. Most of the people you contact will be willing to help you, as they, too, want to be sure their money is well spent.

MEDICAL EDUCATION

Medical Schools

The health of your local medical school is important because many of the graduates practice in the area.

Accreditation   Medical school accreditation is conducted by the Liaison Committee on Medical Education, sponsored by the American Medical Association and the Association of American Medical Colleges, 535 N. Dearborn St., Chicago, Ill. 60610.

The committee will give you the accreditation status of the medical school. But you should, if possible, get the accreditor's full report. It includes administrative operations and financial stability, faculty credentials, planning, relations between administration and faculty, and other strengths and weaknesses. If you are investigating a school with financial problems, the section on planning and budgets may provide potential investigative areas.

The full accreditor's report should be available for public institutions. If a private institution refuses to provide a copy of the report, the state regulatory agency over higher education may have a copy and may be required by state access laws to divulge the contents.

Catalogs   These publications provide an overview of the medical school. Although primarily geared to attract the student, a catalog gives important background information, including admission requirements; financial aid and eligibility; tuition and fees;

description of facilities; areas of specialization; lists of college officers, trustees and faculty, sometimes with biographical information; course descriptions; and student services. Catalogs are available at your library or from the admissions and public relations offices.

Other Records Medical schools receive some public funds, which must be accounted for. (See "Medical Research.")

The Liaison Committee on Medical Education conducts research and publishes reports. The Council on Medical Education of the American Medical Association participates in accreditation and also publishes reports.

Training Programs Open any magazine with a good-sized classified section and you're bound to find ads selling degrees in the health care professions. Most schools and programs are legitimate, but diploma mills and other frauds are not unusual.

Accreditation Standards Some public and private programs may be accredited by professional organizations or governmental agencies. If so, you can learn the standards for accreditation and whether the program you're investigating meets those standards. The Council on Postsecondary Accreditation, 1 Dupont Circle N.W., Suite 305, Washington, D.C. 20036, has names of accrediting agencies responsible for each health care area.

Other Records Beyond catalogs and the accreditation process, information may be difficult to get. If the program is run by a public institution, most of its financial records should be open. Also check the tax status of the school; if it is not-for-profit, its IRS Form 990 gives detailed financial information. (For more information, see Chapter 11, "Business.") Also check for civil suits against the institution.

OTHER MEDICAL TRAILS

Birth Certificates and Death Certificates

For information on birth and death certificates, see Chapter 5, "Backgrounding Individuals."

Coroner's Reports

Coroners and medical examiners may investigate deaths caused by violence, occupational disease or injury; deaths that happen without medical attendance; deaths that occur to persons while in police custody; and deaths associated with diagnostic or anesthetic procedures, abortion, contagious diseases and other unusual circumstances.

The most valuable part of the coroner's report is the autopsy on the cause of death. You should also ask for the toxicology report, which will provide information on the presence of drugs and other foreign substances in the body. When inquests are done, transcripts may be useful.

Most of this information is open to the public, but availability will vary from state to state. Consult the local medical examiner or coroner and check state statutes.

For more information on coroners, see Chapter 13, "Law Enforcement," which details the harm caused by untrained coroners.

Disease Statistics

Information on disease incidence can be found in local, state and federal records. Doctors are supposed to report infectious and certain other diseases to health officials. The completeness of reporting varies by state and by disease. While most cases of gonorrhea aren't reported, for example, most cases of polio are.

Data on immunization levels also are available from the local health department.

Disease statistics are available on the federal level from the Centers for Disease Control, 1600 Clifton Road, N.E., Atlanta, Ga. 30333; (404) 329–3286. The Centers conduct research on a wide range of diseases, from measles to heart disease, and assist local and state health agencies with outbreaks.

Statistics on births and deaths are kept by the National Center for Health Statistics, 5600 Fishers Lane, Rockville, Md. 20857; (301) 436–8980.

Health Codes

Health codes cover such places as motels, restaurants, public schools and other public accommodations. The codes are enforced by inspections. These records usually are open and virtually ignored by reporters. You may find that some of your finest restaurants are also your dirtiest. These records are available from your local or state health department.

Health Insurance Records

The spiralling costs of health care and an increasing number of malpractice suits, accompanied by increased malpractice insurance costs, make health insurance a complex but important area of investigation.

Watch for cost-shifting, which occurs when hospitals charge more to privately insured patients because they can no longer make money on Medicare patients. A good source is the Health Insurance Association of America.

Some insurance companies (those owned by public stock companies) are regulated by the Securities and Exchange Commission. Others are regulated at the state level by the division of insurance. Information available will vary and may include articles of incorporation and bylaws, policies and rates, financial stability information, consumer complaints, names of officers and directors, securities held, subsidiaries and controlled companies, registered brokers and annual reports.

The annual report is particularly important. Insurance companies publish more information in their reports than any other type of corporation: every real estate holding, every stock and bond, major salaries and legal fees are listed. Unfortunately, an insurance company's annual report can be hard to understand. Consult a friendly accountant, another insurance company or an insurance trade association.

Check who's on the board of directors at an insurance company. The majority may be health care providers.

Medical Laboratory Records

State Inspections   About half the states have laboratory regulations. Some have standards that labs must meet before they can do certain kinds of tests. The state regulatory agency will tell you whether a lab meets these standards.

Federal Regulations   The Clinical Laboratories Improvement Act of 1967 covers labs doing interstate business—a fraction of the total. Under this law, HCFA can prohibit a lab from doing tests it has been found incapable of performing up to standards. However, the lab can only be prohibited from performing tests on interstate specimens. Records on labs not allowed to do certain tests are available from HCFA.

Until 1987, the Centers for Disease Control tested the proficiency of all labs doing interstate tests. However, that procedure has been suspended while the government decides which agency, if any, should do it.

If a lab is endangering lives, HCFA can revoke the lab's Medicare certification. This, however, only halts tests on Medicare patients; it doesn't shut the lab down. Records on decertified labs are available from HCFA.

More than 5,000 laboratories are exempt from Medicare regulation. These are labs in the hospitals accredited by the Joint Commission on Accreditation of Hospitals. However, the Commission's inspections of labs have found fewer violations than those done by state inspectors.

Private Studies   In 1985, the College of American Pathologists asked 5,000 of the nation's top laboratories to run cholesterol tests on identical samples, for which the cholesterol level was already known to be 262.6 milligrams per deciliter. The laboratory reports ranged from 101 to 524. Check the medical literature for other groups doing studies on labs' accuracy.

Social Service Agency Records

The list of health-care-related social service agencies is extensive and includes counseling centers, rape crisis centers, drug abuse agencies, home health care agencies, alcohol abuse centers and many others. Local, state and federal funding may be involved. How do they spend their money and who controls them?

On the federal level, check with the Alcohol, Drug Abuse and Mental Health Administration, 5600 Fishers Lane, Rockville, Md. 20857. At the state level, contact the divisions of social services and mental health. Through the secretary of state, articles of incorporation and a list of the board of directors can usually be obtained. Most of these organizations are not-for-profit. IRS Form 990s are useful in looking at their finances (For more information, see Chapter 11, "Business").

Many communities provide social service funding. Contact the office of community services or other appropriate local agency for financial information and data about the quality of services provided. Other sources include the local United Way and Voluntary Action Center. A community services directory may be available from these agencies or the city.

OCCUPATIONAL DISEASE

Occupational Health and Safety Administration Records

OSHA No. 200/Employer's Log and Summary of Occupational Injuries and Illnesses   This notice is supposed to be posted each January in a conspicuous place in the work place. Visit the plant yourself, or ask an employee to read it for you.

OSHA Inspector's Report on General Plant Conditions   This report gives information on working conditions. The inspection is done either by the state OSHA or the federal OSHA office in your area.

Ask, too, for any citations issued for substandard conditions. These are supposed to be posted conspicuously in the work place. If the company or the government appealed the citation, your state Occupational Safety and Health Review Commission will have files. If it's been appealed beyond that, check the U.S. Occupational Safety and Health Review Commission, 1825 K St. N.W., Washington, D.C. 20006.

Complaints and Imminent Danger Inspection Requests   OSHA Form 7, the Imminent Danger Inspection Request, may have sparked an OSHA inspection and will be on file.

Hazard Communication Act   This "right-to-know" law helps workers understand more about hazardous materials in their work places. The law has created new records available at the work place:

- List of hazardous chemicals in the work place.
- Material safety data sheets that explain the health hazards of chemicals and permissible exposure limits.

Injuries and Illnesses at Federal Agencies   Federal agencies must make regular reports to OSHA on injuries and illnesses. Report on individual agencies are available from OSHA.

Standards for Exposure to Chemicals and Other Materials   Title 29 of the Code of Federal Regulations contains OSHA's standards for exposure to specific chemicals, mists, fumes, dusts, etc., as well as the government's rules for state occupational safety plans, inspections and employers' reporting requirements. Most of the standards are consensus standards developed by the affected industries years ago and adopted wholesale by the government. As more information becomes public, the standards are challenged in court as being too permissive. To determine the background of the standard in which you're interested or to find out what the legal exposure limits are for various chemicals, request standards for specific industries from the Occupational Safety and Health Administration, Department of Labor, 200 Constitution Ave. N.W., Washington, D.C. 20210.

The National Institute of Occupational Safety and Health publishes "A Pocket Guide to Chemical Hazards," available at NIOSH Publications Office, 4676 Columbia Parkway, Cincinnati, Ohio 45226.

NIOSH conducts health hazard evaluations at work sites upon request. Check with one of NIOSH's three regional offices for HHEs that have been done in your

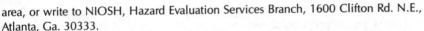

area, or write to NIOSH, Hazard Evaluation Services Branch, 1600 Clifton Rd. N.E., Atlanta, Ga. 30333.

The National Institutes of Health, 9000 Rockville Pike, Bethesda, Md. 20892, can tell you about the most recent research on harmful effects of various chemicals.

Workers' Compensation Reports

First Injury Reports—OSHA No. 101   All states must collect reports, known as first injury reports, from major businesses. These are cross filed with the area OSHA office. The federal form is known as OSHA 101 and contains the worker's name, age, wage, how long employed, how the death or accident occurred and witnesses, if any. In some states, the form is public in the workers' compensation office but private in the OSHA office.

Some states have computerized workers' compensation records and can make quick searches, for instance, of all cancer-related deaths. But remember, studies have shown only a small percentage of occupational illnesses appear in compensation records.

State Labor Departments

Records of Exposure   Some state labor departments keep records on reports of worker exposure to harmful substances.

Art Hazards

Because of ignorance and inadequate labeling, artists and art teachers sometimes don't realize they are using hazardous materials. You need to know what materials are being used and their hazards. If you are looking at art supplies in the classroom, ask the school for the purchase records and inventory lists. These will show what materials are being used.

Center for Occupational Hazards   This New York City group (5 Beekman St., 10038) is considered the leader in art supply safety and will tell you which materials are hazardous. Also check the material safety data sheets required by OSHA, available at the school.

Other Places to Check   Check the classrooms to see which materials are actually used and whether precautions are taken. Ask the students and teachers whether they ever feel sick after using the materials. Check workers' compensation records and talk to teachers' unions.

Other Records

Congressional Reports and Hearings   The federal agencies that oversee worker health and safety, including the Occupational Safety and Health Administration and the Mine Safety and Health Administration, are required to make regular reports to Congress that are publicly available. For example, the "President's Report on Occupational Safety and Health" includes a summary of inspection and enforcement activities and an analysis of major occupational diseases.

To find out what reports are required, check Requirements for Recurring Reports to the Congress, available at government documents libraries.

Also check the documents library for any congressional hearings that have been held on occupational safety and health.

NIOSH Studies   NIOSH has studied occupational disease in various industries. Check with NIOSH in Cincinnati, Ohio.

ENVIRONMENTAL HEALTH

Contaminated water, air and food can make people sick. To investigate environmental hazards, you need to know whether contamination exists and whether it is making people sick. A number of records can be obtained from government agencies that monitor water, air and food and the toxins that can pollute them.

Environmental Protection Agency

Clean Air Act   Under this law, records are kept of emissions of hazardous substances that exceed levels set by the EPA. Records are kept on substances, such as vinyl chloride and radionuclides, as well as specific plants where emissions take place. A few of the records are kept by the EPA in Washington, D.C., but most are kept by state agencies, such as the department of environment or natural resources, or by the regional EPA office.

Clean Water Act   Industries, public sewage treatment plants and other plants that discharge hazardous substances into lakes, rivers and streams must report discharges of substances above the allowable levels. Ask for the following reports and records:

- *National Pollution Discharge Elimination System Permits.* Files on a company contain permits, details of violations, letters and even notes of telephone conversations.
- *Discharge Monitor Report.* Regular reports that companies are required to file on the amounts they discharge.
- *Quarterly Non-Compliance Report.* Lists all companies that have reported non-compliance in certain time periods. You can ask for these by geographic area.
- *Significant Reportable Non-Compliance Reports.* Issued if a company exceeds the acceptable limit by 40 percent or more for two out of six months or by 20 percent for toxic materials.
- *Violation Warnings, Notices and Orders.* If a company violates the limits too many times, warning letters and then notices of violations are issued. If the company continues the violations, a formal administrative order is issued under Section 309 of the law, telling the company what to do to correct the violations. If the violations continue, the EPA institutes a judicial hearing either with the Department of Justice or a state attorney general.

These records are kept by the state EPA equivalent, if the state has the authority to enforce EPA regulations. If your state doesn't, records will be at the regional EPA office.

Toxic Release Inventory (TRI)   Since 1987 the EPA has released annual reports of amounts of toxic materials companies with 10 or more employees release to air or water or cart away. Available from the EPA TRI Reporting Center, 470–490 L'Enfant Plaza, Suite 7103, Washington, D.C., or at regional EPA offices. Available on floppy computer disks from the National Technical Information Service (703) 487–4650.

Federal Insecticide, Fungicide and Rodenticide Act (FIFRA)   This law requires companies to report toxic or adverse effects from pesticides they produce. Reports are also required when the level of pesticides exceed allowable levels in human and animal food and in soil and water.

Ask if a notice of special review has been issued on the pesticide you are investigating. This means the EPA has determined that one or more uses of the pesticide may pose significant risks. After a hearing, the EPA usually cancels or modifies the allowable use of the pesticide.

Before a pesticide is allowed to be used commercially, EPA requires a number of toxicology and other studies, publicly available.

Make your FOIA request to the Office of Pesticides and Toxic Substances, TS76C, EPA, 401 M Street S.W., Washington, D.C. 20460.

Toxic Substances Control Act (TSCA)   The EPA requires firms producing toxic substances to keep records of reports of adverse human reactions and environmental damage. The reports at the company probably won't be public. However, some reports, including those of cases the company does not resolve, must be filed with the EPA and are public.

TSCA requires a number of reports on substances a firm wants to produce, including worker exposure, release to the environment, byproducts resulting from production and disposal, health effects and ecological effects.

Under TSCA, too, firms must report when there has been an accidental release that could cause harm. These reports are public.

TSCA also requires reports to the EPA concerning asbestos and health and safety studies or other potentially toxic substances. Most of these are publicly available.

To file an FOIA request, contact the Office of Pesticides and Toxic Substances, TS76C, 401 M Street S.W., Washington, D.C. 20460.

Agency for Toxic Substances and Disease Registry of the Centers for Disease Control

This agency was established in 1983 to carry out the health-related responsibilities of the Comprehensive Environmental Response Compensation and Liability Act of 1980 and the Resource Conservation and Recovery Act.

The agency collects information about serious diseases and deaths from exposure to toxic substances.

Among the records it keeps are lists of areas closed to the public or otherwise restricted because of toxic contamination.

Contact the agency at 1600 Clifton Road N.E., Atlanta, Ga. 30333.

Other Records

State Environmental and Health Departments   Contact these departments for records on release of hazardous substances to the environment.

Federal and State Departments of Agriculture   These agencies periodically inspect food sold at wholesale and retail markets and produce reports on specific foods and establishments.

Congressional Hearings and Reports   As with occupational health and safety, the federal agencies overseeing environmental health must make regular reports to Congress.

National Institute of Environmental Health Science   Researches behavioral and physical effects of toxic substances, particularly long-term exposure to low levels of a variety of chemical and physical agents. Studies are published in primary scientific journals and the Institute's own journal, Environmental Health Perspectives. Their address is P.O. Box 12233, Research Triangle Park, N.C. 27709.

CHAPTER 16

Education

As any education reporter can tell you, the beat is not just busy, it's sometimes overwhelming. The education reporter is supposed to cover pre-elementary and high schools as well as local colleges and universities. Topics include teacher strikes, school board infighting, pedagogical practices, political battles over intelligence tests and the annual school budget. The subject seems like a bottomless pit because nearly everything connected with schools is lumped under the label "education," making it difficult enough to cover as a beat; for investigative reporters, the complexity of the field may induce numbness.

by NANCY WEAVER and REAGAN WALKER

Public school officials get skittish about reporters sitting in their classrooms. While many are rightly concerned about disrupting the instruction, others may be worried about what reporters might see.

While researching a series about the quality of education in Mississippi, reporters Fred Anklam and Nancy Weaver traveled across the state and spent many afternoons sitting in classrooms. Traveling as a pair helped considerably. They took turns, one being led around by the principal or superintendent who wanted to show off the new library or auditorium and the other roaming freely throughout the classrooms.

Observing classrooms can be tedious and offer little concrete material for a story, but it can be useful. For example, some teachers taught by reading from books in a hot classroom while the students followed along. A boring teacher may not be a banner headline, but the experience can provide insight into problems at that school. Talk to the students and eavesdrop on casual conversations in the hall. Look at the physical surroundings to see if they are conducive to learning. Check the students' books for the date of publication.

The most important investigative story for an education reporter is about the quality of education offered by local schools and colleges. Sitting in the back of the room makes you realize just how difficult it is to measure the quality of education. Reaching a conclusion is difficult.

409

Measuring the Quality

Student Achievement Test Scores

Don't become despondent looking at sheet after sheet of three-digit scores. Elementary and secondary student test scores usually are publicized once a year when the superintendent has a press conference to announce the gains made since last year.

The California Achievement Test measures basic math, reading and language skills. Test scores tell whether students are scoring at their grade level. The scores available at the superintendent or principal's office are listed for each school and include grades in all three subject areas.

What makes the scores understandable is the ranking of the scores on national percentiles. For example, if the students scored in the 60th percentile, that means they achieved scores better than 60 percent of most of the students in this country or that 40 percent earned better scores. If you have reason to doubt your district's interpretation of the scores, talk with the chairman of the education department at a local university. Education reporters should take advantage of the expertise often available from professors.

The scores also should be compared to the scores of students in neighboring school districts and the state in general. Check the scores by subject matter to look for particular problems in the school's math or English programs. Obtain from your superintendent's office a history of the test scores for past years to determine if the scores are better or worse.

Jay P. Goldman, formerly a reporter for the Syracuse Herald-Journal and Herald-American, found that one of every four incoming students at a local community college scored low enough on standard English tests to warrant a semester-long remedial course.

Another comparison that can be made is the test scores and the amount of money spent per student for instruction. If you have the time, compare your district's scores and expenditures against others in the state.

Additional scores worthy of examination include college entrance examination results on the Scholastic Achievement Test or the American College Test. An important factor to consider when interpreting student achievement test scores is the economic background of the students. Unfortunately, some students begin their academic careers a step behind others. Their disadvantaged backgrounds may have deprived these children of access to books or instruction at home. The percentage of students getting free or reduced lunches can be a good indicator. Another factor to consider is whether students score lower on the tests because of cultural or language differences.

Teacher Quality

TEACHER TEST SCORES   States set a minimum score necessary on the National Teacher Examinations, standardized tests prepared by the Educational

Testing Service in Princeton, N.J. A fruitful check might be made of your state's certification standards for teachers and how they compare with other states' requirements. In Mississippi, reporters found that the required score was so low that only 3 percent of those taking the test nationally would have failed.

The quality of instruction being offered by colleges and state universities producing teachers can be measured by the average scores graduating students achieve on the tests. Look at how many graduating students passed the National Teacher Examinations. A look at past years' scores can show if the educational quality is increasing or decreasing.

Many teachers are required to undergo periodic testing and recertification. Find out how many teachers fail to gain recertification. What type of in-service training is offered to teachers? This training can improve the quality of teaching or provide only the short-lived inspiration of a pep rally.

SALARIES   Teacher salaries can be a determining factor in the quality of instruction. The National Education Association can provide rankings for your state's salaries. Many districts already have suffered strikes and more are looming in the future. Most districts are having trouble keeping qualified math and science teachers because of low salaries. Many states have proposed linking teacher pay with a merit scale to keep more qualified teachers in the classroom.

Ron Thibodeaux, a reporter for the New Orleans Times-Picayune and States-Item, compared local teachers' salaries to other schools in the state, to the national average teacher's salary and to other professions.

Goldman found that teachers in the Syracuse area were on the brink of mutiny with 40 percent considering leaving the profession.

DISCIPLINARY ACTION   Public access to records may vary, but statistics should be available about disciplinary actions taken against teachers and how many were fired. In some states, the actual records on disciplinary cases are available.

Does the state adequately investigate teachers for criminal backgrounds? Mark Vogler reported at the Winter Haven (Fla.) News-Chief more than three dozen convicted felons, including child molesters, had lied about their pasts to win certificates to teach in Florida. He gleaned his case studies from teacher discipline files, which are public records in Florida's Department of Education.

Finances

PER-STUDENT EXPENDITURES   How much money does your school district spend to educate each student? A high per-student expenditure doesn't necessarily guarantee that the district is providing a good education. But inadequate financing can be an important factor in a district's failure.

Usually school districts break their per-student expenditures into two categories. The most important figure is how much is spent per student on instruction. The other figure is how much is spent per student on administration. Ask how those expenditures have changed over the years. How does your district's per-student expenditure rank against the national average or the average of the neighboring states?

The Kansas City Times found that the city spent more money than suburban districts on remedial programs, building operations and maintenance, and special education. However, reporters Katherine Foran and Lynn Byczynski reported that more money didn't buy a level of education comparable to that of the suburbs.

Compared with 11 other metropolitan-area districts, Kansas City ranked second. That same year, its schools were last among the 12 districts on Missouri's Basic Essential Skills Test.

FEDERAL FUNDS   State education officials should be able to provide percentages of school operating funds that come from the local board, the state and the federal government. These figures can point to several possible stories.

For example, school districts can be overly dependent on federal funds, making them susceptible to budget cuts. Another school district may fail to take advantage of the federal money available, depriving its students of opportunities.

Major federal assistance includes Chapter 1 of the Education Consolidation and Improvement Act (ECIA), which supports compensatory education for disadvantaged students, education for the handicapped, vocational and adult education, and impact aid for areas with children living on federal installations where their parents don't pay taxes. Chapter 2 of the ECIA assists schools undergoing court-ordered desegregation.

The Urban Institute, a Washington, D.C.-based think tank that has studied the policy changes under the Reagan administration, found that Chapter 1 funding was reduced about 20 percent during the Reagan years. The researchers found most funds were not replaced with local funds, resulting in about 1 million fewer children being served. Federal budget cuts may have forced poor school districts to eliminate programs for disadvantaged or handicapped children.

The Reagan administration changed the formula for distribution of federal funds under Chapter 2. Instead of being based on the needs of the students, the distribution is based only on the number of students. Districts undergoing desegregation or districts with more disadvantaged children get no more Chapter 2 funds than districts without those problems.

Dropout Rates

Break down the statistics provided by the school board into figures easily understood by parents, such as how many of the students entering the first grade this year will graduate. Compare the district's dropout rate with the national average and your state's average. How adequate is your state's compulsory attendance law? How adequately is the law enforced?

The students themselves may say why they've quit school. Many school districts ask students for a reason and may be able to provide statistics about the most common reason for dropping out. The reasons given by students for quitting can themselves generate story ideas. For example, if many female students are quitting because of pregnancy, maybe the district needs a better program to enable these women to finish school.

When the New Orleans Times-Picayune and States-Item checked the national ranking for high school dropout rates, they found Louisiana at the bottom. The articles quoted statistics from the U.S. Department of Education which showed that nationally 26.1 percent of the students who begin the ninth grade drop out of school. In Louisiana, 42.8 percent dropped out.

The New Orleans newspaper also used U.S. census figures to show that Louisiana had more illiterate adults, on a per-capita basis, than any other state.

State Accreditation and Independent Evaluations

Accreditation is a process almost all schools—elementary, secondary and post-secondary—are required to pass. The state usually sets accreditation standards for public elementary and secondary schools. Look at how those standards compare with other states. Do others require more course offerings or more units of credit in English or math? Does your state provide enough financial support to meet its own accreditation standards? How many school districts have been threatened with or actually lost their accreditation? Are the penalties for losing accreditation tough enough?

Public colleges and universities should be willing to provide the full report from the regional accrediting association. The report should include a self-study prepared by college officials offering opinions on their own strengths and weaknesses. The visiting accreditation team also files a report showing areas of "strength" and "concern," ranging from administrative performance to faculty credentials. The schools will submit follow-up reports about problem areas. Junior and community colleges either are accredited by the state or regional associations.

Other schools, which may not seek general accreditation, may be judged eligible for federal funds and student financial aid by a federal agency. The Division of Eligibility and Agency Evaluation of the U.S. Department of Education has records available about those schools.

What other outside groups have looked at your schools and what conclusions did they reach on the quality or the problems limiting the quality? Special committees appointed by the governor, state legislature or local school can provide a starting place for a serious look at how well the schools are doing their jobs.

In Mississippi, we found that several committees appointed by the state had made recommendations on how to improve the quality of education. The reports, stacked a foot high and dating back for decades, often focused on the same problems. The recommendations made by committee after committee had never been acted upon by state officials.

Insight into problems at the state level can be gleaned from the dozens or hundreds of educational proposals made each year to the state legislature. Lobbyists for the district, teachers' association or association of school administrators can explain the problems prompting such legislation.

Such studies can help a reporter focus on the problem, opening the way for a more thorough examination. University graduate students in education may have written theses providing insight into the inner workings of the classrooms. Many of these studies are written in educational jargon, but perseverance will be rewarded.

Textbook Selection

Teachers, parents and school board members may sit privately in a room and with little fanfare pick textbooks to be used. Or, parents may make impassioned speeches at the microphone against or for a particular book at a public hearing. Textbook selection is an important issue.

Find out from the superintendent which books were not chosen and why, who does the selecting and how the library selections are made. One source of controversy can be history books and the portrayal of the Civil Rights Movement or Vietnam War protests. Have certain literature books been thrown out by the selection committee because members felt they were in poor taste?

But don't stop there. Examine the books chosen to see if they're updated and well-written. The Hartford Courant found that some textbooks were illogical. Look at how much the state allocates per student for textbook purchases compared with the actual costs.

Vocational Education Programs

The Reagan administration attempted to make vocational education a sacrificial lamb to the Gramm-Rudman budget cuts. At the same time, national attention had turned to the growing trade deficit and technological advances of other countries. Many believe vocational programs are necessary for a productive society to maintain a competitive edge.

Does your state offer potential new industries cheap labor or the quality of workers they need? State development agency officials may be willing to tell you what industries being courted have to say about vocational education or the overall quality of the schools. Industry leaders should be interviewed about the quality of training they see in potential employees. The officials of industries that decide not to locate in your state should be asked if educational quality was a deciding factor.

Alexander Grant & Co. of Chicago conducts surveys of business climates in states; education has become a more important consideration in that rating.

Coleman Warner, a reporter for the New Orleans Times-Picayune and States-Item, found that the personnel manager for one of the city's largest employers was never called by schools about job openings or advice on what training to offer. His request for a special blueprint reading course was rejected by two vocational-technical schools.

Special Education

In his story for "The Wisconsin Magazine," a program produced by Wisconsin public television, reporter Rick Rodwell found that children with special learning needs were not being educated properly. His research on the Madison school district's programs took time because parents and teachers were reluctant to talk on camera for fear of retribution.

Rockwell used federal and state court records, school records for individual students, complaints filed with the Office of Civil Rights, state and federal regulations covering special education, and articles in academic journals.

To tackle such a story, Rockwell suggests enlisting help from a support group of parents who have learning-disabled children. Those parents can give you access to their children's school records and lead you to sympathetic teachers willing to discuss the problems.

Complaints filed with the state can help build a case of neglect by school districts. But be warned that many documents will have names erased due to privacy restrictions.

Other Measurements

Other ways to determine the quality of education in your community include:

- Look at the percentage of graduating students who go to college, and how prestigious the colleges are. Examine what percentage of minorities go on to college. Keep in mind that family income can be a factor.
- Compare the electives offered by various school districts. Some school districts can afford to offer calculus and others can't. Some schools offer modern dance while others can't even afford physical education classes. How much does the quality of the education received by students depend on the district in which they reside?
- How safe are the hallways? School districts will have information about teacher and student assaults, the number and types of weapons confiscated, and the number of student arrests.
- Ask teachers whether students are being promoted to the next grade without being prepared. Those who are active in the teachers' association may have insight into whether this is a problem throughout the district or at one particular school.
- Look into civil lawsuits filed against school districts or universities as a source of story ideas. Reporters may find that students have claimed injuries resulting from negligence on the part of school officials or that teachers have claimed discrimination. Check the claims for damages made against the district.
- Examine employment applications submitted to local employers. The Times-Picayune and States-Item used a clever way to illustrate the quality of education by reproducing job applications submitted to a local employer. When

asked what city the applicant came from, some wrote "New Orlance" or "New Orlennes." Another wrote the type of work wanted was "aney tihig open."

School Board Spending

Budgets, Contracts and Purchases

Budgets detail revenues and expenditures showing where the money is coming from and how it is spent. The state superintendent's office has an annual budget showing how state funds are allocated to districts. The local superintendent's office has the budget for a local school district. Compare the budgets to previous years to look for unusual expenses or shifts in emphasis.

Most fruitful for investigation are contracts and purchases. Contracts awarded by school boards include those for construction, busing services, in-service training for teachers and supplies. Bid notices are published and posted. Check to see if the bid solicitation is tailored toward one specific vendor by checking with suppliers. See if the district's own bidding procedures were followed. Especially examine contracts or purchases not awarded to the lowest provider because of provisions allowing the best product to be purchased. Always keep an eye open for relationships between the companies getting the contracts and school officials in charge of the hiring, including the department chairmen who may have initiated the request.

Reporters Foran and Bycznyski of The Kansas City Times went over their district's budget line-by-line and found the superintendent had spent $13,352 for new furniture, carpeting and draperies for the executive suite. The money spent for science equipment and supplies that year was $1,400.

A year-long investigation of Rose State College by The Daily Oklahoman revealed that the college president and chief financial officer had embezzled more than $400,000. Reporter Ellie Sutter and Randy Ellis pored through college account ledgers, invoices, teacher retirement files and minutes of the regents meetings to uncover several schemes. They found personal use of college credit cards, funneling money through a dummy corporation, setting up a beneficial retirement fund and billing for undocumented expenditures.

Most districts have provisions for emergency expenditures that bypass routine bidding procedures. Even in emergencies, oral bids usually are solicited, but such contracts or purchases should be closely examined.

Vendor performance should be examined if the story involves a specific provider. You may find out an often-used supplier frequently isn't on time with deliveries, creating hardships for teachers.

All consultant contracts should be studied. Checks should be made to find out if salaried employees could have provided the consulting services or if friends or family of school officials have such contracts. The contracts usually stipulate performance requirements, such as reports to the school board. See if the requirements are being met.

Travel Expenses

A routine check of all expenses submitted by school board members may show unusual or unsubstantiated expenditures. Checks should be made of long-distance telephone calls made from their offices.

Linda Eardley, a reporter for the St. Louis Post-Dispatch, examined hundreds of expense vouchers and receipts to uncover that the superintendent had spent $62,000 in two years on travel expenses, far more than his $15,000 annual limit.

She also determined the superintendent had overcharged the school district by comparing the number of nights in hotel rooms claimed by the superintendent with the hotel records and his itineraries. Eardley also listed meals costing more than $100. The articles resulted in a number of new rules regulating the superintendent's spending.

Audits, Bonds and Grants

Audits provide insight into the school's financial status. The financial statement lists assets, liabilities and the balances of special funds. Management advisory reports will highlight any practices by the school that deviate from standard business practices. Check the accompanying opinion letter from the auditor. An unqualified opinion means that based on the records the auditors could verify the financial picture with reasonable confidence. A qualified opinion means the auditors disclaim responsibility for the accuracy because some funds may have insufficient records. No opinion means the auditors will not vouch for the accuracy of the financial records.

The most complete financial picture can be obtained from records made available because the institution is selling bonds to generate revenue. An offering statement or prospectus discloses the institution's finances to the public considering buying the bonds. The records should detail assessed valuation of property, salaries, construction costs, debts, lawsuits and future borrowing plans. These records can disclose that the institution is in the red or financially well-off. Bond-rating agencies then establish the creditability of the institution influencing how well the bonds will sell. Any drop in the bond rating from a high of AAA to a low of C should warrant a story and further investigation of the cause.

Colleges applying for federal and state grants have to establish need in hopes of getting those dollars. Their applications are public records and may disclose problems to win grants to help solve them.

Land Ownership

A school district or university may own land in addition to school grounds. Find out about other property by checking the name of the institution with records at the county assessor's or recorder's office.

The university may have parcels of land off-campus that were donated. If the property or buildings are leases, check if a fair price is being collected.

Clarion-Ledger reporters Don Hoffman and Kevin Haney found that school districts failed to take advantage of state land set aside to be leased out for their benefit.

Using land records, lease agreements and court records, the reporters showed that thousands of acres were leased for just pennies an acre annually, benefitting the leaseholder more than the school districts. Among those with low-rate leases were school officials, a private golf course and state and local governments.

Private Schools

Private schools are tougher to investigate. Some headmasters welcome reporters while others may force you to observe the "No Trespassing" signs out in front.

Most states can provide information about accredited private schools. You might want to make some comparisons between private and public schools, using such variables as classroom size, test scores, teacher salaries and elective offerings.

Finding out about unaccredited private schools can be more difficult. How many there are in your area and what type of education is provided can be the basis for a story. The State Department of Education may not have exact statistics, but a local private school association may have information. Some private schools also may house students. Check to be sure county health and fire regulations are followed.

Most schools are not-for-profit and tax exempt. They file a Form 990 with the Internal Revenue Service, which includes income, gifts and salaries paid to board members or other officials.

Backgrounding a Student

Because federal and state laws protect the privacy of students, most available information on students may come from high school or college yearbooks. Usually school officials will release only the years of attendance and degree earned. Other sources include student newspaper files, the student's former fraternity or sorority and the local alumni office, which may be able to provide an address.

Social Problems Addressed by Schools

Desegregation

The desegregation of public schools is not a dead issue. Many school districts are asking to be officially declared desegregated, ending decades of supervision by the federal government. The U.S. Department of Justice has shown its desire to end federal intervention in local schools. The loss of federal supervision is sure to allow some school districts to become more segregated.

The Justice Department's Civil Rights Division filed only one desegregation lawsuit under Reagan. Where only a portion of a district has been intentionally segregated, federal officials are not requiring systemwide desegregation, as they have before.

In portions of the South and the Northeast, communities may have two school systems—public schools for minorities and private schools for whites. Some school districts lost much of their white student population with desegregation and haven't yet attracted them back.

The Courier-Journal and The Louisville Times found that the Jefferson County, Ky., school system didn't provide any racial breakdown of student test scores despite being the subject of one of the nation's most comprehensive court-ordered desegregation programs.

Getting access to raw data from the school system's computers, a team of four reporters fed the statistics onto their own computer tapes. They reported that black students scored below average in most grades in reading while white students were above average in all grades. They found the same gaps in math, scores on college entrance tests and first-grade failures.

All school districts getting federal funds file federal forms 101 and 102 to the U.S. Department of Education's Office of Civil Rights. The reports include statistics on the race and sex of students, the number of students in special education programs and faculty and student suspensions.

Sex Education

With the appearance of AIDS, sex education is becoming even more controversial than it had been in years past. Schools across the nation have wrestled with the question of how much information should be provided to students about AIDS. See if your school district provides AIDS information to its students. Also see what their policy is about people with AIDS attending school.

Drugs

Education reporters, just like school officials, can't skirt the issue of alcohol and drug abuse in schools. Police officers in the narcotics division probably are willing to discuss their perceptions of the drug problem on campus. But don't be manipulated by unsubstantiated and exaggerated claims from the police. Verify the problem with arrest reports, records of overdoses and students seeking treatment, and the policies and results of searches of lockers for drugs.

Check with the school system to see what drug-education programs the schools offer and at what grade levels. In the community there are likely to be drug counseling centers or an Alcoholics Anonymous office that can offer insight.

The Syracuse Herald-American surveyed high school seniors to gauge the extent of drug abuse and came up with startling results. The survey showed nearly two-thirds of the seniors said they observed frequent or daily use of drugs in school. Two-thirds said they occasionally or frequently drank alcohol.

Sources

Following is a list of sources that will help you investigate education:

- *U.S. Department of Education's Office of Educational Research and Improvement* offers an information service called the Educational Resources Information Center. ERIC acts as a clearinghouse for educational research on nearly any topic from adult education to student testing. A directory of where the centers are can be obtained through the DERI office, Capitol Place, 555 New Jersey Ave. N.W., Washington, D.C. 20208.
- *The National Schools Public Relations Association* offers "Ed Line," an electronic news service available to reporters at a reduced rate. The service reports on current research and news from Washington, D.C. Check with your local librarian for access information.
- *The Chronicle of Higher Education*, a weekly tabloid, focuses on recent developments, such as court decisions and legislation and trends in postsecondary education. To subscribe, write to 1255 23rd St. N.W., Washington, D.C. 20037.
- *Education Week*, the weekly counterpart to the Chronicle of Higher Education, covers a gamut of issues affecting elementary and secondary education. To subscribe, write to 4301 Connecticut Ave. N.W., Suite 250, Washington, D.C. 20008.
- *Education Daily* is a newsletter reporting about trends, such as the decline in the number of black school officials, that could affect policies. To subscribe, write to 1300 N. 17th St., Arlington, Va. 22209. Higher Education Daily also available.
- *The American Council on Education* publishes Higher Education and National Affairs weekly and the Educational Record on a quarterly basis. To subscribe, write to Dupont Circle N.W., Washington, D.C. 20036.
- *The Center for Educational Policy Studies* publishes special reports. Write to 245 Peil Hall, 159 Pillsbury Dr. S.E., University of Minnesota, Minneapolis, Minn. 55455.
- *Education Writers Association* publishes The Education Reporter and a directory of news sources and reports. Write to 1001 Connecticut Ave. N.W., Suite 310, Washington, D.C. 20036.
- *Education Committee of the States* produces several publications. Write to 300 Lincoln Tower Bldg., 1860 Lincoln St., Denver, Colo. 80259.

DOCUMENTING THE EVIDENCE

ELEMENTARY AND SECONDARY EDUCATION

Benchmark documents for public elementary and secondary schools are state statutes and local school district rules and regulations. They govern everything from curriculum to fiscal operations, from busing to athletic events.

These are big money operations, and they should be evaluated like any other government operations, with the operative rule being "follow the dollar." Begin with the budget, comparing line items and totals with previous years to see what shifts in emphasis have occurred. Be sure to enlist the aid of a qualified budget analyst to help you spot entries that are significant because they are missing or because they have changed from previous budgets.

Budgets at the state level are available from the state superintendent's office, and for local schools at the superintendent's office.

Purchases

All educational institutions purchase goods and services. From test tubes for a chemistry class to a workshop on drug abuse for high school teachers, state and local statutes specify the process by which these acquisitions must be purchased. Look closely at what types of goods or services require bids. Even non-bid items sometimes require that school officials seek informal cost estimates. The bidding procedure usually follows these steps:

- *Bid notices* are published in one form or another, either in the local newspaper or posted on bulletin boards outside the business office. Check state statutes and local ordinances. Be sure to notice if the solicitation has been written in such a way that only one supplier will be qualified to bid. For instance, if the solicitation is for automobiles, are the specifications written in such a way that only the local Chevrolet dealer can get the contract? Examine the list of where the solicitations were sent. Are important suppliers left off? Why?
- *Contract offers* or *bids* on the advertised solicitation are submitted by each potential supplier. Compare the bid with the notice to see which supplier came closest to meeting the advertised specifications. Under certain conditions, specified by law or regulation, school systems may give contracts to vendors who are not the lowest bidders. Know the law and evaluate the reasons when the lowest bidder does not receive the contract. Be sure to talk to the bidders who lost out as well.
- *The written contract* should not vary from the bid specification without good reason. If it does, find out why.
- *Vendor performance files* are another access point in reviewing the purchasing process. When you know the name of the vendor, consult this file for the purchase date, the goods or services and other information.

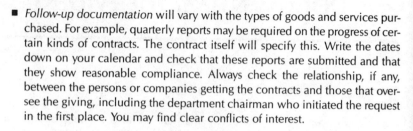

- *Follow-up documentation* will vary with the types of goods and services purchased. For example, quarterly reports may be required on the progress of certain kinds of contracts. The contract itself will specify this. Write the dates down on your calendar and check that these reports are submitted and that they show reasonable compliance. Always check the relationship, if any, between the persons or companies getting the contracts and those that oversee the giving, including the department chairman who initiated the request in the first place. You may find clear conflicts of interest.

These records are available from the business office of the school. (For more information, see Chapter 1, "Following the Paper Trail.")

Audits

Almost every educational institution's financial condition is audited annually, and this applies not only to the school districts, but to the individual schools as well. Among those sections of the audits to be sure to check are the following:

- *Management advisory reports* detail any deviation by the school from standard business practices and should highlight and suggest appropriation changes when school practices are at variance with the law.
- *Financial statements* list assets, liabilities and fund balances. Assets may include the value of investments, other income and accounts receivable. Liabilities include outstanding (unpaid) debts. The fund balance includes unspent revenues, expenditures and encumbrances; changes in fund balances or retained earnings; and changes in financial positions, such as bond ratings.

Often the most important statement in an audit is the accompanying opinion letter, usually taking one of three forms:

- *The unqualified or clean opinion,* which means the institution's records were maintained so that auditors could verify its true financial picture with reasonable confidence.
- *The qualified opinion,* which means that the records for some funds or activities were in such disarray that auditors disclaim responsibility for their accuracy or inaccuracy. The remaining funds or activities, however, had sufficient records.
- *No opinion* which means the auditors will not vouch for the accuracy of the institution's books because the record cannot support the claims.

If federal dollars are involved, audits can be obtained from the General Accounting Office, Distribution Section, Room 1000, 441 G St. N.W., Washington, D.C. 20548. Audits of local public schools can be obtained from the appropriate state education agency. Audits of private schools are not public, and a source will be needed. (For more information, see Chapter 1, "Following the Paper Trail.")

Bonds

School districts often issue bonds in order to generate revenue. The information required in this process provides a pretty complete financial picture of the institutions.

Because financial markets are about as obscure to most reporters as the language the participants use, here's a brief rundown of who's who.

- *The issuer*—in this case the school board—goes to the market through intermediaries known as underwriters.
- *The underwriters*, who are bankers or bond brokers, buy all the bonds from the school board at a bit less than face value, keeping the difference as their profit.
- *The investors*, with whom the underwriters place the bonds, are generally banks, insurance companies and private individuals. Sometimes, the underwriters keep a portion of the bonds for themselves as an investment.
- *An offering statement or prospectus* is prepared by school officials, accountants, attorneys and underwriters before the bond issue goes to the market. The prospectus details the overall financial picture and includes such areas as assessed valuation of property, salaries, construction costs and other information. Comments also may be included on the tax base, debts and future borrowing plans.
- *One or both of the principal independent, bond-rating agencies* in New York, Standard & Poor's Corp. or Moody's Investors Services, receive the prospectus. For a fee, these agencies evaluate the credit-worthiness of the issue and assign a rating from AAA at the top to C at the bottom. The lower the rating, the higher the interest rate. If the rating falls below the BBB or BAA level (each house has a different rating code), it becomes increasingly difficult to sell the securities at any price.

The Securities and Exchange Commission closely monitors the sale of bonds and notes by private corporations, but has looser standards for scrutinizing government issuers. That means the task of the reporter covering the school board is tougher than that of financial reporters covering Exxon and General Motors. Begin with the public school system.

Student Test Scores

In many states, students are regularly given standardized tests in written, verbal and mathematical skills. National, state and local school district averages can be obtained from your state education office or the public school district. Ask for a complete list of all the tests given students. Some tests are not taken by all students, and others provide different types of information beside mathematical, written and verbal skills. For example, Scholastic Aptitude Tests (college entrance exams) are not taken by all students; to use only these test averages in measuring the quality of education in a school district would be incomplete.

But there's another side to this story. In some situations, the validity of the test procedures and scoring have been challenged. A writing skills test in Texas offers a good example. A certain question was posed that some students considered illogical. They gave a well-reasoned argument defending their position. Another group of students answered the question with a sentence or two—but the writing was not nearly as good. The first group received a lower score because they did not answer the question.

Make sure you obtain a copy of the test and find out from the state who prepared it and who scored it.

Additional Sources

Additional information available at state or local levels includes records on salaries; certification records for individual teachers; records of any disciplinary action revoking or suspending a teacher's certification; annual reports on budgets and operations, curricula and class enrollments; adjusted gross income per capita for the school district; financial aid to dependent children in the district; records of state aid payment by the district for operations and construction; accreditation reports by regional associations or state agencies; collective bargaining contracts; payments and investments for teachers' and administrators' retirement systems; and standard textbook prices filed with state agencies and distributed to local districts through state agencies. All of these records are available at the state education office.

Federal records on individual school districts are scanty unless the district is monitored by the Department of Education for civil rights violations or unless it is the recipient of a federal grant or subsidy. Check the federal agency that granted the funds.

HIGHER EDUCATION

Sources of information for state-supported institutions of higher education are virtually identical to their high school counterparts, but there are some additional places to check.

Accreditation

Despite attacks on its credibility, accreditation of colleges and schools by panels of academic peers remains the education consumer's most comprehensive check on the quality of educational institutions. Accreditation historically has been more common among senior four-year colleges than in the community or junior colleges, vocational-technical schools or elementary and secondary schools.

General accreditation is carried out by a network of so-called regional accrediting associations, supported financially by member schools. The name, address and telephone number of the accrediting association that covers an individual reporter's region can be obtained from the Council on Postsecondary Accreditation, 1 Dupont Circle N.W., Washington, D.C. 20036. Contact with the accrediting association, though, may prove disappointing. These agencies typically reveal no more than the current status of the institution. In some cases, when special conditions are tacked onto the accreditation status that information also is made available. The accreditors generally insist that full reports be obtained from the institution concerned.

When dealing with public institutions, obtaining the accreditor's full report—sometimes running to dozens of pages—should pose few problems because of "sunshine" laws. If a private institution refuses to provide a copy of the report, the state regulatory agency for higher education may have been given a copy and might have to divulge the contents under access laws. Another approach: If the college runs a program on a military base, the base commander or educational liaison officer may have a copy that can be obtained under the Freedom of Information Act. (For more information, see Chapter 4, "The Freedom of Information Act.")

These basic documents emerge in the general accreditation process:

- *The self-study.* This report, usually compiled by a faculty-administration committee at the college, provides an internal look at perceived strengths and weaknesses in curricula, faculty credentials, administrative operations, financial stability and the gamut of issues the college may face. Self-studies usually must be obtained from the college.
- *The visiting team report.* A typical report will include a recommendation on accreditation status; a statement on the college's mission and whether it achieves it; an evaluation of the short- and long-range planning mechanisms at the school; an assessment of administrative performance, particularly if the school faces morale or financial problems; an assessment of general education patterns; a judgment on financial stability; an analysis of development activity; an analysis of faculty credentials overall; a comparison of the faculty salary level with that at competing institutions; the role of faculty in governing the college; an analysis of students' academic credentials, geographic spread, educational interests and retention rates; an evaluation of the physical plant; and areas of "strength" and "concern." This report is likely to be more objective and even more hard-hitting than a self-study.
- *The final action.* The accrediting association governing body's final action on granting accreditation may be obtained from the accrediting association or the individual school.
- *Follow-up reports.* Accrediting associations increasingly require that colleges submit follow-up reports on trouble spots—such as a weak core curriculum or financial instability—within a year to three years after accreditation is extended. A college may receive full accreditation for 10 years, but a follow-up report may prompt downgrading to provisional accreditation or withholding of further accreditation. Accreditors, for example, don't want to be accused of not warning the public if a private college goes bankrupt.

Increasingly, professional associations are creating or expanding separate accrediting agencies that only evaluate schools for that particular profession. A longstanding example is the review of law schools conducted by the American Bar Association and the American Association of Law Schools. These accrediting bodies generally follow the same operating rules as the regional organizations. As these specialized accrediting arms have expanded, colleges and universities have pressed the Council of Postsecondary Accreditations and the Department of Education to limit that growth. Consequently, some of the specialized accrediting agencies have no impact except within the profession. Check with the division of eligibility and agency evaluation on whether an accreditor's decisions have impact on federal funding to a school or financial aid to students enrolled there.

Junior or community colleges are often evaluated in the same way as elementary and secondary schools, although more seek regional accreditation. If not, the state's regulatory agency over higher education will usually evaluate non-accredited junior colleges. Often these reviews are required under cooperative arrangements with the Department of Veterans Affairs, which usually designates a state agency as the "approval authority" for schools where students may enroll and receive veteran's benefits.

Those institutions, such as proprietary schools, that do not or cannot seek general accreditation may become eligible for federal funds or student financial aid under a separate review and accreditation by the U.S. Office of Education's Division of Eligibility and Agency Evaluation. Similar general procedures are used by the federal agency in conducting that review. All records are open, and they should contain transcripts of hearings before a citizens' council advisory to the division.

After checking the regular accreditation avenues, pick up the Encyclopedia of Associations. There is always a good chance that some association deals with a particular education area. For instance, the National Home Study Council publishes the Directory of Accredited Private Home Study Schools, and it's free on request. Write to the National Home Study Council, 1601 18th St. N.W., Washington, D.C. 20009.

Catalogs

The most comprehensive, though not necessarily up-to-date, document on a college, university or private elementary or secondary school is its catalog, which amounts to a prospectus for its programs, policies and facilities. It is often stored on library shelves or available from admissions and public relations offices.

A catalog usually contains the accreditation status; a mission statement; admissions procedures, including necessary high school rank and standardized test scores; the college's academic calendar; policies on the release of student information; requirements for majors and graduation; tuition, room, board, book and other fees; available financial aid and eligibility requirements; tuition payment plans; available counseling and advising services; student organizations; residence hall policies; descriptions of the campus physical plant, and sometimes a map of the campus; available health care; names of college officers and trustees; lists of college faculty and their academic background; alumni association information and officers; and descriptions of course requirements for entrance and frequency of offering.

Grants

Universities often stay afloat on grant income. At a state university or college, grant files should be open. They contain proposals for funding; final budgets; approval forms from an evaluating committee, if the research involved human subjects in biomedical tests; settlements, if the grant had reimbursement clauses; a copy of research summaries or reports given to the granting agency; any post-audits of grant activity; and the resolution of any adverse findings in those audits.

Educational institutions receive federal funding from many sources, and those discussed in this section are by no means a complete list. Some of these programs apply to private and post-secondary schools. Contact your school district or the state education agency to find out which federal programs are involved. A complete list of available grants can be obtained from the Office of Elementary and Secondary Education, U.S. Department of Education, Washington, D.C. 20202, or the regional office. Evaluations and audits of the use of these funds can also be obtained from the Department of Education or the General Accounting Office.

The Department of Education has a number of other funding programs. Some of those include cooperative education—integrating academic study with public or private employment, education for public service and the upward bound program— to motivate young people from disadvantaged environments to succeed in post-secondary education.

Along with the grant proposal, evaluations, audits and need assessments can be obtained from the Secretary of the Department of Education. A complete program list can also be obtained from this office.

Among the existing programs:

- *Occupational, adult, vocational and career education programs* offer financial assistance to secondary and post-secondary institutions. Contact the Division of Vocational and Adult Education for grant proposals, evaluations and audits.
- *Programs of education for the handicapped* provide assistance to elementary and secondary institutions. Educational opportunities as well as the eradication of physical barriers are funded in these programs. Contact the Office of Special Education.
- *The Alcohol and Drug Abuse Education Program* provides leadership training to develop prevention programs. Local education agencies may apply. Contact the Office of Elementary and Secondary Education, Division of Special Programs. The Secretary of Education's Handbook "Schools Without Drugs" can be ordered by phone at 1–800–624–0100 or by writing "Schools Without Drugs," Mail Stop 6350, Washington, D.C. 20202.
- *Bilingual education programs* are most prevalent in large urban areas with many children whose primary or only language is not English. These programs are primarily for local and state education agencies. Contact the Office of Bilingual Education and Minority Language Affairs.
- *Desegregation assistance programs* provide aid to school districts to promote integration and educational programs. State and local education institutions and, in some projects, public and private not-for-profit organizations and post-secondary schools may apply. Contact the Office of Elementary and Secondary Education.
- *Education for the Disadvantaged* under Title 1 of the Elementary and Secondary Education Act assists educationally disadvantaged children from low-income areas. Local and state schools may apply. Contact the Office of Elementary and Secondary Education.

In these programs and others, reporters will find an abundance of information from the grant application to "a needs assessment survey" of the particular area of assistance. For example, the desegregation assistance programs require reports on the race and sex of students.

Other areas in which educational institutions may receive funding include international studies, Indian education and libraries and learning resources.

If the granting agency was a federal department, it may provide peer evaluations of grant proposals if the research wasn't classified. For example, peer evaluations of successful grant proposals to the Department of Education may be obtained from the Privacy and Information Rights Office, 400 Maryland Ave. S.W., Rm. 3851, Donohue Bldg., Washington, D.C. 20202.

National Institute of Education—ERIC System

The Educational Resources Information Center (ERIC), a nationwide information system, sponsored and supported by the Office of Educational Research and Improvement, a division of the U.S. Department of Education, is a clearinghouse of reports and research in every education area imaginable, including adult education, the teaching of English, urban/rural education, junior colleges, educational management, tests, measurement and evaluation, reading and educational facilities. Many of these reports include evaluations of specific institutions.

For more information on the ERIC system, contact the regional office of the Department of Education to locate the nearest ERIC clearinghouse.

Student Housing Records

Students at universities and colleges often live in rental housing that is unsafe and unhealthy, with leaky roofs, dangerous electrical systems and poor plumbing facilities, and at inflated prices. A few educational institutions keep approved lists of student housing, but the best records in this area are property ownership and rental housing records.

Many communities have housing codes which require that certain standards be met. Some codes require regular inspections of some rental units. The records of these inspections can be invaluable in looking at the rental housing situation. The city public works department or appropriate local agency is the best source for this information.

Be sure to check land ownership records. The biggest student slumlord may be the university itself. (For more information, see Chapter 9, "Tracing Land Holdings.")

Additional Sources

Higher Education General Information Survey   Standardized data are obtained by the federal government from colleges and universities in the Higher Education General Information Survey (HEGIS). Those forms are sent to the Center for Education Statistics, 555 New Jersey Ave. N.W., Washington, D.C. 20208, where they are tabulated and form the basis for the periodic Education Directory, Colleges and Universities. The forms, however, may also be obtained from the local college or university or a HEGIS depository or coordinator within the state. Usually state boards of higher education have the information on file. Among the forms:

- *Institutional Characteristics of Colleges and Universities* indicates top administrative and academic officers with their religious, military or educational titles; regional and specialized professional accreditations; types of academic programs offered; tuition and fees; controlling body or affiliation, indicating whether the institution is public, private not-for-profit, or proprietary; type of student body; academic calendar; and headquarters address.

- *Degrees and Other Formal Awards Conferred* (year) is a document of up to 50 pages. It shows for each school the number of men and women by degree field, such as M.D., D.O., D.V.M. or L.L.B., or their major, if the degree is a B.A. or B.S.

- *Fall Enrollment and Compliance Report of Institutions of Higher Education* (year) is a summary of undergraduate, unclassified, graduate and first professional students by sex and racial origin and also by full-time or part-time status. The broad grouping of data—such as undergraduate or graduate—subsequently are broken down by disciplinary field.

- *Salaries, Tenure and Fringe Benefits of Full-Time Instructional Faculty* (year). For each topic, a breakdown by academic rank is available by sex, total salary outlay, total number of persons in rank, number with tenure and number who are active members of the military. The faculty is tabulated for both nine-month and 11- or 12-month contracts. The charts also show distribution of all full-time faculty on nine- and 12-month contracts by sex and academic rank for salaries and tenure. The information does not include instructors in clinical or preclinical medicine.

  For faculty members who taught both of the past two years, the HEGIS form also shows salaries by rank, according to number of faculty, and total salary outlay, and by contract length.

  In the area of fringe benefits, the HEGIS form shows the college's expenditures in the current year for retirement benefits; medical and dental plans; guaranteed disability income protection; tuition plans; housing; social security taxes; unemployment compensation; group life insurance; workers' compensation; and other benefits with cash value.

- *Number of Employees in Higher Education Institutions by Manpower Resource Category.* This is a breakdown of employees by executive, administrative or managerial level; whether assigned to instruction or research; number of instruction or research assistants; specialists and support staff; and non-professionals. Salaries of selected administrators from president and deans to head football and basketball coaches are included.

- *Financial Statistics of Institutions of Higher Education* (year). The breakdown of current funds is by revenue source: federal, state and local appropriations, government grants and contracts, private gifts, private grants and contracts, endowment income, sales of educational services (including tuition), auxiliary enterprises and hospital services. The breakdown of current funds expenditures is by instructional purpose: research, public services and academic support, teaching and so on. The form also reports changes in the book value of land, buildings and equipment, indebtedness on the physical plant, value of endowment and fund balances. In a separate section for public colleges, HEGIS asks for information on gifts, earnings on investments, receipts from property taxes and cash and security holdings.

- *Adult and Continuing Education: Non-credit Activities in Institutions of Higher Education.* This sample survey of institutions selected by the National Center of Education Statistics shows types of programs offered by academic unit; administrative structure of extension; financial support of extension; extension expenditures broken down by administrative, instructional and overhead costs; whether extension is self-supporting; percentage of extension instructors from regular faculty; and teaching load in night programs.
- *Department of Education Grant documents and readers' evaluations of original proposals* are available from the Privacy and Information Rights Officer, 400 Maryland Ave. S.W., Rm. 3851, Donohue Bldg., Washington, D.C. 20202.

State Sources of Information   With controls over higher education relatively decentralized, state departments of higher education often obtain detailed information beyond the HEGIS forms. Such information may be available on a college-by-college basis for such statistics as enrollment; credentials of entering students (test scores and high school ranks); retention statistics; general age breakdown of academic and other college staff; student financial aid statistics separated into academic grants and athletic awards; loans; student employment and federal assistance by sex; and detailed internal financial information. This information should be obtained from the state department of higher education.

PRIVATE EDUCATION

The finances of private educational institutions are more difficult to investigate. But in almost all cases, these schools are not-for-profit and tax exempt, and so must file an Internal Revenue Service (IRS) Form 990.

That form includes information on gross income and receipts; contributions; gifts and grants; assets and investments; compensation of officers and the highest paid employees; and the largest amount of money paid to outside individuals and organizations which provide services. Other financial relationships are also detailed in this report.

IRS Form 990 can be obtained by writing to one of seven IRS Regional Service centers under provisions of the Internal Revenue Code Sections 6104(a) and (b). (For more information, see Chapter 11, "Business.")

Also check with your state education office to be sure the school is licensed and with the secretary of state's office for incorporation papers.

Another source is the National Center for Education Statistics, 1001 Presidential Bldg., 400 Maryland Ave. S.W., Washington, D.C. 20202.

BACKGROUNDING A STUDENT

Because of federal and state privacy laws, little information is available about individual students unless they, or in some cases their parents, grant permission.

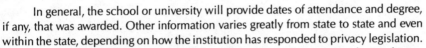

In general, the school or university will provide dates of attendance and degree, if any, that was awarded. Other information varies greatly from state to state and even within the state, depending on how the institution has responded to privacy legislation.

Good places to check when seeking information about a person who is a former student include the alumni office for current address, the student newspaper files and yearbooks, and any fraternities or sororities the student may have joined. If you find out the area in which the student received his degree, check with teachers in that department. Many students stay in touch with their former teachers for long periods of time. (For more information, see Chapter 5, "Backgrounding Individuals.")

Bibliography

by STEVE WEINBERG

This bibliography is selective, consisting of books only. Much of the time, the most useful examples of work on each topic can be found in the files at IRE headquarters, Box 838, Columbia, Mo., 65205; (314) 882–2042. The Paul Williams Memorial Resource Center contains thousands of print and broadcast projects, indexed by subject. The majority of the projects arrive during the annual awards competition. Others come from IRE members, newsroom librarians and the gleanings of the headquarters staff. An up-to-date data base of IRE's holdings is on the headquarters computer. Abstracts of all holdings are published as often as possible in the morgue book. Numerous examples of print and broadcast journalism that might help you are mentioned throughout "The Reporter's Handbook"; most of the projects described can be obtained from IRE.

Additional help can be obtained by consulting the index to The IRE Journal, our magazine. It is indexed back to 1977. Since then, we have published at least one how-to piece on almost every topic imaginable—how to investigate a hospital, a bank, and a variety of other institutions; how to background an individual; and how to delve into any number of issue stories, from toxic waste to child abuse.

This bibliography does not list our morgue projects or articles from the IRE Journal. It also does not list the reference books and other published sources mentioned in the text. Instead, this is a list of selected readings that you can probably find in a nearby newsroom or public library, new or used bookstore, or in the libraries of friends and relatives. Some are a bit dated but are included for the perspective they provide or the new ground they covered. Some are out of print. Some are in paperback only. But none is totally unobtainable. The list is designed to help you think about a topic through reading books, whether you are in a large city or a small town. The books listed here may lead you to other books, government documents and the like.

GENERAL BOOKS ON INVESTIGATIVE TECHNIQUES

Anderson, David, and Peter Benjaminson. "Investigative Reporting." Bloomington: Indiana University Press, 1976.
Bernstein, Carl, and Bob Woodward. "All the President's Men." New York: Warner Books, 1976.
Brady, John. "The Craft of Interviewing." New York: Vintage Books, 1977.

Davidson, James West, and Mark Hamilton Lytle. "After the Fact." 2d ed. 2 vols. New York: Knopf, 1985.

Downie, Leonard, Jr. "The New Muckrakers." New York: New American Library, 1978.

Eakle, Arlene, and Johni Cerny, eds. The Source: A Guidebook of American Geneaology. Salt Lake City: Ancestry Publishing, 1984.

Franklin, Jon. "Writing for Story." New York: Atheneum, 1986.

Fry, Don, ed. "Best Newspaper Writing." St. Petersburg: Poynter Institute, annual.

Fuld, Leonard M. "Competitor Intelligence." New York: John Wiley & Sons, 1985.

Killenberg, George M., and Rob Anderson. "Before the Story." New York: St. Martin's Press, 1989.

Lambeth, Edmund B. "Committed Journalism." Bloomington: Indiana University Press, 1986.

Mann, Thomas. A Guide to Library Research Methods. New York: Oxford University Press, 1987.

Mitford, Jessica. "Poison Penmanship." New York: Vintage Books, 1980.

Morehead, Joe. "Introduction to United States Public Documents." 3d ed. Englewood, Colo.: Libraries Unlimited, 1983.

Prucha, Francis P. Handbook for Research in American History. Lincoln: University of Nebraska Press, 1987.

Rose, Louis J. "How to Investigate Your Friends and Enemies." rev. ed. St. Louis: Albion Press, 1983.

Russell, Robert H., and Margaret J. Patterson, eds. "Behind the Lines." New York: Columbia University Press, 1986.

Sims, Norman, ed. "The Literary Journalists." New York: Ballantine, 1984.

Taibbi, Mike, and Anna Sims-Phillips. "Unholy Alliances." San Diego: Harcourt Brace Jovanovich, 1989.

Thompson, Josiah. "Gumshoe." New York: Fawcett, 1989.

Ward, Jean, and Kathleen A. Hansen. "Search Strategies in Mass Communication." White Plains, N.Y.: Longman, 1986.

Williams, Paul. N. "Investigative Reporting and Editing." Englewood Cliffs, N.J.: Prentice Hall, 1978.

Wills, Kendall, ed. "The Pulitzer Prizes." New York: Simon & Schuster, annual.

Winks, Robin, W., ed. "The Historian as Detective." New York: Harper & Row, 1970.

POLITICS AND GOVERNMENT (FEDERAL, STATE AND LOCAL)

Bamford, James. "The Puzzle Palace." New York: Penguin, 1983.

Barlett, Donald L., and James B. Steele. "Forevermore." New York: Norton, 1986.

Brown, Michael. "Laying Waste: The Poisoning of America by Toxic Chemicals." New York: Washington Square Press, 1981.

Caro, Robert A. "The Power Broker." New York: Vintage, 1975.

Collender, Stanley E. "The Guide to the Federal Budget." Washington, D.C.: Urban Institute Press, annual.

Dahl, Robert A. "Who Governs." New Haven: Yale University Press, 1961.

Fitzgerald, A. Ernest. "The Pentagonists." Boston: Houghton Mifflin, 1989.

Glazer, Myron P., and Penina M. Glazer. "The Whistleblowers." New York: Basic Books, 1989.

Greider, William. "Secrets of the Temple." New York: Simon & Schuster, 1989.
Henriques, Diana D. "The Machinery of Greed." Lexington, Mass.: Lexington Books, 1986.
Hersh, Seymour. "The Price of Power." New York: Summit Books, 1984.
Jackson, Brooks. "Honest Graft." New York: Knopf, 1988.
Kotz, Nick. "Wild Blue Yonder." New York: Pantheon, 1987.
Maas, Peter. "Marie." New York: Pocket Books, 1984.
Mayhew, David R. "Congress: The Electoral Connection." New Haven: Yale University Press, 1974.
Nance, John J. "Blind Trust." New York: Morrow, 1987.
Noonan, John T., Jr. "Bribes." New York: Macmillan, 1984.
Rhodes, Richard. "The Making of the Atomic Bomb." New York: Simon & Schuster, 1987.
Sabato, Larry J. "PAC Power." New York: Norton, 1984.
Sheehan, Neil. "A Bright Shining Lie." New York: Random House, 1988.
Smith, Hedrick. "The Power Game." New York: Random House, 1988.
Stern, Philip. "The Best Congress Money Can Buy." New York: Pantheon, 1988.
Thompson, Dennis F. "Political Ethics and Public Office." Cambridge, Mass.: Harvard University Press, 1987.
Woodward, Bob. "Veil." New York: Simon & Schuster, 1987.

COURTS
Bazelon, David L. "Questioning Authority." New York: Knopf, 1988.
Brill, Steven, and Karen McCoy, eds. "Trial by Jury." New York: Simon & Schuster, 1990.
Denniston, Lyle W. "The Reporter and the Law." New York: Hastings House, 1980.
DiPerna, Paula. "Juries on Trial." New York: Dembner, 1984.
Forer, Lois G. "Criminals and Victims." New York: Norton, 1980.
Gerald, Edward J. "News of Crime." Westport, Conn.: Greenwood, 1983.
Woodward, Bob, and Scott Armstrong. "The Brethren." New York: Avon Books, 1981.

CRIME AND LAW ENFORCEMENT
Anderson, David C. "Crimes of Justice." New York: Times Books, 1988.
Buchanan, Edna. "The Corpse Had a Familiar Face." New York: Random House, 1987.
Crewdson, John. "By Silence Betrayed." New York: Harper & Row, 1989.
Giancana, Antoinette, and Thomas C. Renner. "Mafia Princess." New York: Avon, 1985.
Greene, Robert W. "The Sting Man." New York: Ballantine, 1982.
Gugliotta, Guy, and Jeff Leen. "Kings of Cocaine." New York: Simon & Schuster, 1989.
Kramer, Rita. "At a Tender Age." Fort Worth: Holt, 1988.
Kwitny, Jonathan. "Vicious Circles." New York: Norton, 1981.
Mitford, Jessica. "Kind and Unusual Punishment." New York: Vintage Books, 1974.
Morris, James E. "Victim Aftershock." New York: Watts, Franklin, Inc., 1983.
Noguchi, Thomas T., and Joseph DiMona. "Coroner." New York: Pocket Books, 1984.
Pileggi, Nicholas. "Wiseguy." New York: Pocket Books, 1987.
Silberman, Charles E. "Criminal Violence, Criminal Justice." New York: Random House, 1980.
Stewart, James B. "The Prosecutors." New York: Simon & Schuster, 1987.

Uviller, Richard H. "Tempered Zeal." Chicago: Contemporary Books, 1988.

Wilson, James Q. "Thinking About Crime." rev. ed. New York: Random House, 1985.

HEALTH AND WELFARE

Brown, J. Larry, and H. F. Pizer. "Living Hungry in America." New York: Macmillan, 1987.

Califano, Joseph A., Jr. "America's Health Care Revolution." New York: Random House, 1986.

Hall, John R. "Gone From the Promised Land." New Brunswick, N.J.: Transaction Pubs., 1987.

Kozol, Jonathan. "Rachel and Her Children." New York: Crown, 1988.

Longman, Philip. "Born to Pay." Boston: Houghton Mifflin, 1987.

Nelson, Barbara J. "Making an Issue of Child Abuse." Chicago: University of Chicago Press, 1986.

Page, Benjamin I. "Who Gets What From Government." Berkeley: University of California Press, 1983.

Patterson, James T. "The Dread Disease." Cambridge, Mass.: Harvard University Press, 1987.

Pekkanen, John. "M.D." New York: Delacorte, 1988.

Schorr, Lisbeth, and Daniel Schorr. "Within Our Reach." New York: Doubleday, 1988.

Sheehan, Susan. "Is There No Place on Earth for Me?" Boston: Houghton Mifflin, 1982.

Shilts, Randy. "And the Band Played On." New York: St. Martin's Press, 1987.

Starr, Paul. "The Social Transformation of American Medicine." New York: Basic Books, 1984.

Torrey, E. Fuller. "Nowhere to Go." New York: Harper & Row, 1988.

EDUCATION AND EQUAL OPPORTUNITY

Bledstein, Burton J. "The Culture of Professionalism." New York: Norton, 1978.

Bloom, Allan. "The Closing of the American Mind." New York: Simon & Schuster, 1988.

Bowen, Howard R., and Jack H. Schuster. "American Professors." New York: Oxford University Press, 1986.

Boyer, Ernest L. "High School." New York: Harper & Row, 1983.

Branch, Taylor. "Parting the Waters." New York: Simon & Schuster, 1988.

Kluger, Richard. "Simple Justice." New York: Vintage Books, 1977.

Kozol, Jonathan. "Illiterate America." New York: New American Library, 1986.

Lukas, J. Anthony. "Common Ground." New York: Knopf, 1985.

Owen, David. "None of the Above." Boston: Houghton Mifflin, 1986.

Ravitch, Diane. "The Schools We Deserve." New York: Basic Books, 1985.

BUSINESS, LABOR, WORK PLACES

Barlett, Donald L., and James B. Steele. "Empire." New York: Norton, 1981.

Brill, Steven. "The Teamsters." New York: Pocket Books, 1979.

Brodeur, Paul. "Outrageous Misconduct." New York: Pantheon, 1985.

Commons, Dorman L. "Tender Offer." Berkeley: University of California Press, 1985.

Howard, Robert. "Brave New Workplace." New York: Penguin USA, 1985.

Mintz, Morton. "At Any Cost." New York: Pantheon, 1985.

Mokhiber, Russell. "Corporate Crime and Violence." San Francisco: Sierra Club Books, 1988.

Nader, Ralph, and William Taylor. "The Big Boys." New York: Pantheon, 1987.

Neff, James. "Mobbed Up." New York: Atlantic Monthly Press, 1989.

Pizzo, Stephen, Mary Fricker and Paul Muolo. "Inside Job." New York: McGraw-Hill, 1989.

Stevens, Mark. "The Big Eight." New York: Macmillan, 1984.

Taylor, Peter. "The Smoke Ring." rev. ed. New York: New American Library, 1985.

Tobias, Andrew. "The Invisible Bankers." New York: Linden/Simon & Schuster, 1982.

Trost, Cathy. "Elements of Risk." New York: Times Books, 1984.

LAND

Appalachian Land Ownership Task Force Staff. "Who Owns Appalachia?" University Press of Kentucky, 1983.

Jacobs, Jane. "The Death and Life of Great American Cities." New York: Random House, 1961.

Mayer, Carl, and George Riley. "Public Domain, Private Dominion." Sierra Club Books, 1985.

Opie, John. "Law of the Land." Lincoln: University of Nebraska Press, 1987.

Rhodes, Richard. "Farm." New York: Simon & Schuster, 1989.

White, William. "City." New York: Doubleday, 1989.

CONTRIBUTORS

THE EDITORS

John Ullmann is a consultant, freelance investigative reporter and frequent speaker on investigative reporting topics. From 1984 through 1989, he was assistant managing editor for projects at the Star Tribune in Minneapolis/St. Paul. Projects he supervised during that time won more than four dozen awards and citations, including the 1990 Pulitzer Prize for investigative reporting and the IRE Bronze Medal. The previous five years, Ullmann was executive director of Investigative Reporters and Editors Inc. (IRE) and was responsible for conceiving and implementing many of the organization's programs and projects, including The IRE Journal, the projects data base and this book. Ullmann has taught journalism full time at two universities and worked for a number of newspapers and magazines. He is completing his Ph.D. in journalism and environmental science at the University of Missouri – Columbia.

Jan Colbert is the acting executive director of IRE. She is also assistant professor of journalism at the University of Missouri – Columbia.

THE AUTHORS

FOREWORD / Robert W. Greene

Robert W. Greene is a two-time Pulitzer Prize winner, past president and former board chairman of IRE and the father of team investigative reporting. He is an assistant managing editor at Newsday, and the author of "The Stingman."

INTRODUCTION / John Ullmann

PART 1   Getting Started

1   Following the Paper (or Computer) Trail / Tom Hamburger, Jerry Uhrhammer and Randy McConnell

Tom Hamburger is a Washington correspondent for the Minneapolis Star Tribune. Before moving to Washington in 1988 he spent two years in Minneapolis on projects that uncovered mismanagement or corruption in government and the private sector. His work has received more than a dozen awards and citations.

Jerry Uhrhammer, investigative reporter at The Morning News Tribune in Tacoma, Washington, did his first investigative reporting during the 1960s as a beat reporter at the Eugene (Ore.) Register-Guard. He left Oregon in 1982 and worked at the Riverside (Calif.) Free-Enterprise, Orange County Register and The Pittsburgh (Pa.) Press before returning to the Pacific Northwest in 1989. Uhrhammer has followed paper trails for stories ranging from local corruption and land scams to defense and HUD loan fraud.

Randy McConnell is a former newspaper reporter for several dailies in Missouri and worked three years for the Missouri state auditor's office. He received his master's degree in journalism from the University of Missouri—Columbia.

Using Computers in Reporting

John Bender is assistant professor at the College of Journalism, University of Nebraska—Lincoln. He was a researcher at the Freedom Information Center and instructor at the University of Missouri—Columbia.

2   Using Publications / John Ullmann and Kathleen Hansen

Kathleen Hansen is associate professor and Sevareid Librarian at the University of Minnesota School of Journalism and Mass Communication. She is co-author (with Professor Jean Ward) of "Search Strategies in Mass Communication" and numerous articles about news workers' uses of information sources and new technologies.

3   Finding a Government Document: An Overall Strategy / Gerry Everding

Gerry Everding began working on an update of "The Reporter's Handbook" as a student intern at IRE in 1984. He has a bachelor's degree in business from St. Louis University and a master's degree in journalism from the University of Missouri—Columbia. He has worked on investigative projects at the Minneapolis Star Tribune, St. Louis Post-Dispatch and the Associated Press.

4   Freedom of Information Act / Harry Hammitt

Harry Hammitt is editor and publisher of Access Reports, a biweekly newsletter of the Freedom of Information. A graduate of the University of Michigan, he has a master's degree in journalism from the University of Missouri—Columbia and a law degree from George Washington University. He previously worked as an information specialist at the Consumer Product Safety Commission and at FOI Services. He has edited Access Reports since 1985 and has been both editor and publisher since 1989.

PART 2   Individuals

5   Backgrounding Individuals / Jack Tobin

Jack Tobin, in 50 years of journalism, has covered everything from tree plantings to presidential campaigns. Since the 1950s he has specialized in investigative assignments and has been a contributor-correspondent to Sports Illustrated since its inception. He has written four as-told-to autobiographies, including "They Call Me Coach" with John Wooden, who won 10 NCAA titles at UCLA.

6   Using Tax Records / David B. Offer

David B. Offer is the editor of Newport Daily News in Newport News, Va. He is a former managing editor for the La Crosse Tribune and was a reporter for The Milwaukee Journal. He was a member of IRE's Arizona Project.

7   Finding Out About Licensed Professionals / Myrta Pulliam

Myrta Pulliam is assistant managing editor of The Indianapolis Star. She is a founder and board member of IRE and worked on IRE's Arizona Project. She is a former member of the Star's investigative team.

8   Investigating Politicians / Penny Loeb

Penny Loeb has reported on health care, politics and housing and has been a finalist for the Pulitzer Prize. She is a member of New York Newsday's investigative team and received her master's degree in journalism from the University of Missouri.

9   Tracing Land Holdings / George Kennedy

George Kennedy is an associate professor at the University of Missouri School of Journalism and managing editor of the Columbia Missourian, the daily paper published by the school. He has been a reporter and editor at the Miami Herald and a panelist at regional and national IRE conferences and is co-author of two books on reporting and writing.

10   Putting It All Together / Patrick Riordan

Patrick Riordan was Tallahassee bureau chief for the Miami Herald and spent the 1980 election year cycle in the Washington, D.C., bureau of Knight-Ridder Newspapers covering federal campaign finance. He previously worked for the Better Government Association in Chicago and The Oak Ridger. From 1983 to 1985 he was deputy press secretary and speech writer for Florida Governor Bob Grahm. Since 1985, he has been director of public information at the Florida State University System Board of Regents.

PART 3   Institutions

11   Business

For-Profit Corporations / James K. Gentry

James K. Gentry, associate professor of journalism at the University of Missouri — Columbia, is executive director of the Society of American Business Editors and Writers. Gentry, who recently completed a four-year term as chairman of the School of Journalism's editorial department, has directed the Business Journalism Program for 10 years.

Not-for-Profit Corporations and Organizations / Gerry Everding

Bankruptcies / Elliot Jaspin

Elliot Jaspin has spent a year at the Gannett Center for Media Studies, Columbia University, developing the computer as a tool in reporting. By buying and analyzing government computer tapes while at the Providence Journal-Bulletin, Jaspin produced stories on property taxes and the criminal justice system. He has reported at the Philadelphia Daily News, and won a Pulitzer Prize at the Pottsville (Pa.) Republican. He is on the faculty of the University of Missouri School of Journalism and directs a mid-career program on computers in reporting.

12   The Work Place / Mike McGraw

Mike McGraw, an investigative reporter for the Kansas City Star, has covered labor or labor-related subjects for most of his 16 years as a reporter at the Star, The Des Moines Register and The Hartford Courant.

13   Law Enforcement / J. Harry Jones, Jr.

J. Harry Jones, Jr. was a reporter for The Kansas City Star from 1956 to 1980. He is author of The Minutemen and recipient of the American Bar Association's Silver Gavel award in 1974 and the Madeline Dane Ross award for international reporting from the Overseas Press Club the same year. He was a member of IRE's Arizona Project and a former member of the IRE board of directors.

14   Courts / Fredric N. Tulsky

Fredric N. Tulsky has been a reporter for The Philadelphia Inquirer for 11 years. He is a lawyer and writes stories about problems in the criminal justice system. He was a Nieman Fellow and his national awards include a Pulitzer Prize. He is president of IRE.

15   Health Care / Penny Loeb and Dolly Katz

Dolly Katz was a medical reporter for Detroit Free Press for 17 years. She received her master's degree in public health from the University of Michigan in 1990 and is now working on a doctoral degree in epidemiology.

16   Education / Nancy Weaver and Reagan Walker

Nancy Weaver, a reporter for The Sacramento Bee, was part of a team of reporters whose coverage of problems plaguing public schools in Mississippi earned a Pulitzer Prize for public service for the Clarion-Ledger. The series also won several other national awards. She also worked for The Denver Post.

Reagan Walker graduated with a master's degree in journalism from the University of Missouri in 1987. While at Missouri, she worked at IRE. After graduation she covered the U.S. Congress and several state legislatures for Education Week in Washington, D.C. In 1990 she joined the education team of the Clarion-Ledger in Jackson, Mississippi.

BIBLIOGRAPHY / Steve Weinberg

Steve Weinberg has worked for newspapers and magazines in Washington, D.C., and the Midwest. Currently he is associate professor of journalism at the University of Missouri—Columbia, where he teaches and does investigative reporting. From 1983 to 1990 he was executive director of IRE. He is the author of "Trade Secrets of Washington Journalists" and "Armand Hammer: The Untold Story."

I N D E X

443

U.S. Bureau of the Census, 34
U.S. Code, 39
U.S. Code Congressional and Administrative News, 38
U.S. Department of Commerce, 72
U.S. Department of Defense, 59–70, 78
U.S. Department of Education, 413
U.S. Department of Health and Human Services, 373
U.S. Department of Housing and Urban Development, 183
U.S. Department of Justice, 419
U.S. Department of Labor, 265–267
U.S. Department of Veteran Affairs, 356
U.S. Government Accounting Office, 62, 64–66
U.S. Government Manual, 32, 39, 59, 72
U.S. Supreme Court, 341
U.S. Parole Commission Annual Report, 343
U.S. Senate Special Committee on Aging, 379
U.S. Statutes at Large, 38, 39
U.S. Tax Court, 17, 105, 127, 129–130, 133–134
Utility records, 243–244

Vanderbilt University Television News Archives, 44
Veterans hospitals, 356
  accreditation, 385
  patient injury reports, 386
  DVA Inspector General Audits, 386
  patient satisfaction surveys, 386

General Accounting Office surveys, 386
  transcripts of Veterans Affairs committee hearings, 386
  veterans groups, 386
  records, 385–386
Victims' rights, 327, 332
Vocational education, 412, 414, 427
Voter registration records, 103

Wage and Hour division, 267
Wall Street Journal Index, 41, 44
Washington Information Directory, 43, 63
Washington Post Index, 44
Washington Representatives Book, 163
Weekly Compilation of Presidential Documents, 38–39
Weights and Measures bureaus, 17
WESTLAW, 40
Whistle-blowers, 267, 272, 276
Who's Who publications, 42
Wire taps, 342
Witnesses, 319
Women's Occupational Health Resource Center, 292, 379
Workers' compensation, 269, 289–291, 370–371, 405
Writ, legal, 336

Zoning/rezoning, 173, 175, 177, 186–187, 188–189
  bribes, 174
  records, 16